REASON AND EXPERIENCE
Dialogues in Modern Philosophy

FcᵓᶏFcᵓᶏFcᵓᶏ TITLES IN PHILOSOPHY

Ayer, Sir Alfred J. · Oxford University · *The Origins of Pragmatism*—Studies in the Philosophy of Charles Sanders Peirce and William James

Ayer, Sir Alfred J. · *Metaphysics and Common Sense*

Baum, Robert J. · Rennselaer Polytechnic Institute · *Philosophy of Mathematics*

De Lucca, John · Queen's University · *Reason and Experience*—Dialogues in Modern Philosophy

Hanson, Norwood Russell · *Perception and Discovery*—An Introduction to Scientific Inquiry

Hudson, W. D. · Exeter University · *Reason and Right*—A Critical Examination of Richard Price's Moral Philosophy

Humphreys, Willard C. · Evergreen College · *Anomalies and Scientific Theories*

Ross, Stephen David · State University of New York, Binghamton · *Moral Decision*—An Introduction to Ethics

Ross, Stephen David · *In Pursuit of Value*

REASON AND EXPERIENCE
DIALOGUES IN MODERN PHILOSOPHY

Edited by JOHN DE LUCCA
QUEEN'S UNIVERSITY
ONTARIO

FREEMAN, COOPER & CO.
SAN FRANCISCO · 94133

TO: _____
MARGARET · DANIELLE · DAVID

CONTENTS

A Note re Footnotes and This Book's Usage

Footnotes are a necessity for a scholar, but they also may be a distraction. Both factors combine in a work of this kind to present the problem of satisfying the necessity without distracting one's reading.

We have tried to resolve this matter by adopting the following procedures. The citations of sources and acknowledgments for permission to reprint will be found in the usual place at the foot of a page. Foreign language words or phrases of original editions whose translation may be disputed or whose meanings cannot be conveyed precisely in English have been inserted in the running text immediately following the English, regardless of whether the original writer, translator(s), or present editor deemed it advisable to indicate such non-English words and expressions. Notes of the original authors are numbered and come at the end of the paragraph to which they are pertinent. Notes of the translators and the present editor are also numbered but appear at the foot of a page. Translators' notes are marked by 'Tr.' and those of the present editor by 'Ed.'

Some of the selections are from works now in the public domain and in these a few of the original authors' footnotes have been omitted because in the opinion of the present editor they were either anachronistic, added nothing to the understanding of the authors' points, or might only confuse the contemporary student. No notes of philosophic import or reflecting upon an author's position have been omitted.

PREFACE

It long has seemed to me that the distinction drawn between a 'problems' approach and an 'historical' approach to the teaching of philosophy, at least in the extreme form sometimes put forth, is an untenable one. I see no just opposition between the two. A pedagogically sound historical approach must single out and focus upon those common core issues which have been of central concern to our major philosophers and on which divergent positions have resulted in widely disparate philosophic systems. The manifest differences in the systems of Plato and of Aristotle, for example, can be traced to radically different conceptions of the nature of sense-perception, of the appropriate methods of inquiry, and of the locus of the constitutive principles of nature and of man which ground the possibility of inter-subjective knowledge and of discourse. Thus, the teaching of philosophy from an historical approach requires much more than a mere cataloguing of dates, works, and statements as to what the philosophers have said. A proper historical approach must draw out and make clear to the student the critical issues to which philosophers have applied themselves and the manner in which they have reacted or responded to their predecessors or contemporaries. Hence, even in an 'historical' orientation the 'problem' is the proper unit of study.

Nonetheless, it is a mistake to think that one can isolate precisely demarcated 'problems' and treat these apart from their historical roots, as if the past were full of error and delusion with very little or nothing of import to be gleaned from our acquaintance with it. Every philosopher hopes to reach some seminal insights and seeks a way to creative wisdom. But such reflective undertakings are rarely fruitful if one severs connection with past philosophical thought. As in science it is he who is most fully acquainted with the results, the successes and the failures of his predecessors, who is, except in rare instances, likely to contribute something novel of genuine worth, so too is a philosopher's originality strongly dependent upon his familiarity with the history of thought. Instances of novel insights from those unfamiliar with the fundamentally significant contributions of the past are very few. A problems approach to the teaching of philosophy likely will be more productive of understanding and appreciation of the issues if it strives to make the student constantly aware of their relations to earlier thought. Usually, the neglect or misunderstanding of such historical relations has had serious deleterious effects, *e.g.,* denial of the autonomy of philosophy.

In this collection of readings I have sought to show that a 'problems' approach to the teaching of philosophy can be combined with an 'historical' one; that, in short, the two approaches are not antithetical, but complementary. There is no need to bypass classical selections, as is often done in textbooks, in order to concentrate attention upon some relatively well-defined issues engaging our contemporaries. My hope is that this collection will succeed in arousing in students an awareness of the inter-connectedness of themes and the continuity of philosophic thought as well as providing a deep understanding of some of the persistent and vital questions of philosophy. Since the problems of the theory of knowledge exist in some form for every serious philosopher and are, I believe, the pivotal ones for every systematic philosophy, the readings are directed entirely to such problems. It will be found, however, that these issues will provide central points of departure for numerous other questions. The collection begins with readings on the problem of method primarily because this issue loomed so large during the two centuries of philosophic thought here encompassed.

This volume may be used as the sole textbook for courses in History of Modern Philosophy and in Rationalism and Empiricism or it may be complemented by books as diverse as, for example, Whitehead's *Science and the Modern World*, Lovejoy's *The Great Chain of Being,* and Randall's *The Making of the Modern Mind.* For courses in Epistemology this volume may be aptly conjoined with such anthologies as Hirst's *Perception and the External World*, Swartz's *Perceiving, Sensing, and Knowing,* or one or more of the numerous shorter works generally entitled 'theory of knowledge' in various series of publications in philosophy. As will be apparent, selection of the introduction and of the 'discussion' pieces following the main texts of this volume have been made so as to minimize duplication of selections in such collections as the aforementioned. Obviously, viable combinations will depend upon the level of the course, the specific focus desired, and other factors. I leave to the ingenuity of each instructor of philosophy other possible combinations of the present volume with existing materials for courses other than those here specified.

The discussion pieces added at the close of the main text materials on the principal topics are intended merely to illustrate the continuation of the 'dialogues' beyond the Eighteenth Century and to stimulate the students to examine some of the suggested readings. Source volumes, commentaries, and other materials listed in the Bibliography (Appendix) should not be overlooked.

Two questions which undoubtedly will be raised by some instructors need to be met. First, it may be queried how a volume intended to cover the 17th and 18th centuries can fail to include selections from Francis Bacon. I answer that I have been completely convinced by Morris R. Cohen's deflation of the 'Baconian myth' and refer the interested reader to his *Studies in Philosophy and Science*, pp. 99 *ff.* (New York: Henry Holt and Company, 1949). Second, it may be questioned how students can be expected to gain some comprehension of the total views of the philosophers here encompassed through the consideration of only a few of the issues central to their thought. Classroom experience, however, has revealed that by the time the selections of Part Three have been digested, the majority of students have such a reasonably clear conception of the total position of each of the individual philosophers that they are able not merely to anticipate what the philosophers will say on the issues of Part Four but to have fairly accurate conceptions of their respective positions on issues in moral philosophy and in the philosophy of religion. Confucius is alleged to have said: "I show the student three corners of the subject, and if he cannot find the fourth, I do not repeat the lesson."

It is a commonplace among contemporary philosophers to say that philosophy is primarily a dialogue on fundamental questions of perennial significance. But few textbooks have succeeded either in revealing the dialogistic nature of philosophical writings or in isolating the *fundamentum* of the issues which divide men. It is my hope that, in conjunction, the structure and the contents of this collection will succeed to some extent in satisfying both of these desiderata. It has been part of my aim to exhibit philosophers as men seeking to clarify for each other what they do not understand. Paradoxically, the enterprise rests upon faith in the power of man's reason to understand both man and nature. "Raffiniert ist der Herr Gott," said Einstein, "aber boshaft ist er nicht." Such a conviction, or something akin to it, must underlie all serious philosophizing.

JOHN DE LUCCA

May 5, 1972.

REASON AND EXPERIENCE
Dialogues in Modern Philosophy

INTRODUCTION · JOSIAH ROYCE
The Periods of Modern Philosophy*

It is in vain that one seeks, in the history of thought, to choose any perfectly satisfactory place of beginning for the purpose of a course of lectures like this. Always one must run a risk of producing the illusion in your minds that the point where he chances to begin is somehow peculiarly significant as a beginning. But always, of course, if you should ever hereafter come to look deeper, you would find this point of beginning very arbitrary, and what immediately preceded it vastly important for the true understanding of the whole matter. My beginning, therefore, as I must warn you, will be indeed very arbitrary, just as my methods will have to be very different from those of a textbook.

As to the general scope of our course, modern philosophy, our topic in what follows, is as wealthy and complex an evolution in its way as is the life which it depicts. What we call modern thought, in these matters, is a very recent affair, dating back only to the seventeenth century. Since then, however, philosophy has lived through several great periods, which for our purpose we may reduce to three.

The first period was one of what we may call naturalism, pure and simple. It belongs almost wholly to the seventeenth century. The philosophy of this first age lived in a world where two things seemed clear: first, that nature is full of facts which conform fatally to exact and irreversible law, and second, that man lives best under a strong, a benevolently despotic civil government. The philosophers of this time had left off contemplating the heaven of mediaeval piety, and were disposed to deify nature. They adored the rigidity of geo-

* From *The Spirit of Modern Philosophy*, Lecture II, Houghton. Mifflin Company, Boston and New York, 1892. Reprinted by permission of Houghton Mifflin Company.

Josiah Royce (1855–1916) took his doctorate at The Johns Hopkins University in 1878 and professed philosophy at Harvard University from 1882 until his death. His philosophy was a species of absolute or objective idealism which he preferred to call absolute voluntarism.

metrical methods; they loved the study of the new physical science, which had
begun with Galileo. Man they conceived as a mechanism. Human emotions,
even the loftiest, they delighted in explaining by very simple and fundamental
natural passions. There is often something merciless and cynical about their
analysis of many things sacred in human life. They are cold, formal, systematic, at least as to the outward shape of their doctrines. At heart, however,
they are not without a deep piety of their own. The nature which they deify
has its magnificent dignity. It is no respecter of our sentimentalities; but it
does embody a certain awful justice. You would pray to it in vain; but you
may interrogate it fearlessly, for it hides no charmed and magical secrets in its
breast which an unlucky word might render dangerous to the inquirer. It no-
tices no insult; it blasts no curious questioner for his irreverence. This nature is
a wise nature. Her best children are those who labor most patiently to comprehend her laws. The weak she crushes; but the thoughtful she honors. She
knows no miracles; but her laws are an inexhaustible treasure house of resources to the knowing. In fact, knowledge of such laws is the chief end of
man's life. God isn't any longer what he had often seemed in more clerical
ages,—a God that hides himself from the natural and unassisted intellect of
man. He showed himself of old to the Greek geometers, to Euclid, to Archimedes. In these days of the seventeenth century he unveils new mysteries to the
students of physics. In the world of such a ruler, fear is out of place; you may
even doubt if you will. The incredulous are no longer public enemies; they are
merely the learners. Descartes, a representative thinker of the century, and the
one from whom our period is often dated, begins his reflection by doubting everything. As for the method of escaping from doubt, that consists in the use of
reason and in the study of the facts of experience; nothing else serves. Revelation you treat with such respect as political and social considerations require;
but for philosophy, in this age of the seventeenth century, the supernatural has
only a secondary interest, if it has any interest at all. Religious conformity is a
matter of policy; a noisy atheist would be, of course, a cause of scandal, and
might even bring philosophy into discredit. Besides, almost every serious philosopher of this our first period believes in God as in some sense the source of
nature. It is, however, not well to tell the unlearned too much about what sort
of God you believe in. The unlearned are gross, still dread witches, carry amu-
lets, know nothing of geometry; best be cautious of speech to them. Philosophy
makes no propaganda, appeals to philosophers, lets faith alone. Besides, loyalty to the state counsels some measure of religious conformity. Hobbes, the
great Englishman, himself a speculative materialist, and, as I fancy, the most
well-knit and highly organized thinker in the whole history of English philosophy, was clear that whatever a man's opinion might be, it was his duty to submit all matters of religious conformity to the judgment of the state. "I submit,"
he says in effect somewhere, "to the Church of England, because that is the
church ordained for me by the will of my sovereign, the king of England."
And this confession of Hobbes involves no hypocrisy. It is the frankest confession in the world. His conformity is openly a conformity to civil laws. Philoso-

phy and religion are once for all separated. It is a matter of accident whether
the philosopher has or has not a traditional creed left him by his philosophy.
His thought is no longer the handmaid of his faith, as had generally been the
case with the thinkers of the Middle Ages. But as for his faith itself, social and
political considerations must decide how and in what way he shall give evidence of it to his fellows. His very loyalty, his good citizenship, his frank benevolence, counsel prudence of speech.

And here appears again another side of the philosophy of this first period.
It is a loyal philosophy, a philosophy of good citizenship; it has a great respect
for the highest political interests of man; it studies jurisprudence, statecraft, international law, natural justice; it founds its loyalty, indeed, upon reason,
makes little of the divine right of kings, loves to declare all men equal, despises
tradition in social matters, throws contempt on the mere customs of mankind,
looks for the sanction of law in the eternal and just order of the world, in short
seeks most distinctly not in the clouds, but here upon earth, for an abiding
city. Hence, it generally opposes clerical interference in political matters; it
gives to the kingdom of God a naturalistic interpretation, takes no interest in
the jeweled walls and the pearl gates of a scriptural new Jerusalem, but under-
takes to build a terrestrial one of its own on a geometrical plan of modern devising, a city not without foundations, but very sober as to ornamentation.
Better a rational constitution than golden streets.

Does this first period of modern philosophy, thus very rudely outlined as
to its most general interests, seem to some of you dishearteningly unspiritual?
Then reflect, it surely has not pleased God to save his people by anarchy; and
these who in this recent century, in the age when science first grew lusty in its
young strength, and when the sanctions of mediaevalism were already partly
obsolete, spoke the word for the freedom of human reason, and the reasonableness of good order, served the spiritual necessities of mankind no whit the less
because they told only part of the truth. What they bequeathed to us was a
faith in sober realities, a reverence for the dignity of the world of law, a love of
lucidity, for which we cannot thank them too much. As to their deification of
nature, it was surely the beginning of modern wisdom, an insight that whatever God is, he is not far from every one of us, a turning away from the mere
gazing up into heaven after a distant and ascended divine ruler, a sense that if
the spirit is indeed poured out on earth, you have a right to look upon the simplest facts as containing it. These men may be cold; for my part I find a clearness about the snowy mountain summits amongst which they live, which goes
far to compensate for the hardness of the outlines of their world. That they,
too, have a genuine and lofty piety to proclaim to us, I shall try to exemplify
in the case of Spinoza. For nature, also, has its divine side; the hard, clear outlines of the mountains stand out, after all, against the heavens of God. He who
reflects upon our human love of clear reason and of sound order reflects upon
certain of the deepest, though surely not upon the hottest, passions of man.
And Spinoza, as we shall find, knew how to give to this eternal order of nature
a mystical and almost romantic glamor. Under the gently glowing evening

twilight of his peaceful reflection, these mountain peaks, if we may yet again strain our figure, gleam with an almost ghostly dignity, and seem no longer sharp or cruel. Spinoza, like other mystical souls, knows of a peace which the world of sense can neither give nor take away. This peace he finds in an absorbing contemplation of the divine order as eternal and necessary. It is of the nature of reason, he says, to regard all things under the form of eternity. So regarded, even this passionate, struggling life of ours seems an apparition of the changeless. God is everywhere. The wise man asks no happy fortune; his unalterable fortune it is to love God with the same love wherewith God loves himself.

But the second age of modern philosophy, rejecting this sublime indifference to the concerns of the individual human being, turned curiously back to the study of the wondrous inner world of man's soul. To deify nature is not enough. Man is the most interesting thing in nature, and he is not yet deified; nor can he be until we have won a true knowledge of his wayward heart. He may be a part of nature's mechanism, or he may not; still, if he be a mechanism, he is that most paradoxical of things, a knowing mechanism. His knowledge itself, what it is, how it comes about, whence he gets it, how it grows, what it signifies, how it can be defended against skepticism, what it implies, both as to moral truth and as to theoretical truth,—these problems are foremost in the interests of the second period of modern thought, whose beginnings we can see in Locke, and whose culmination was in the philosophic movement that expressed itself, towards the close of the eighteenth century, in Kant's "Critique of Pure Reason." The early thinkers of this period, Locke, the early English moralists, Leibnitz, belong in part to the first period, as is always likely to be the case in such orderly evolutions. Gradually, attention is turned more and more from the outer world to the mind of man. The first period had been one of naturalism; the second is one of a sort of new humanism. In the first half of the eighteenth century this humanism developed the works of the great classical representatives of English ethics, as well as the idealism of Berkeley. Reflection is now more an inner study, an analysis of the mind, than an examination of the business of physical science. Human reason is still the trusted instrument, but it soon turns its criticism upon itself. It distinguishes prejudices from axioms, fears dogmatism, scrutinizes the evidences of faith, suspects, or at best has consciously to defend, even the apparently irresistible authority of conscience, and so comes at length, in the person of the greatest of the British eighteenth century thinkers, David Hume, to a questioning even of its own capacity to know truth, a doubting attitude which brings philosophy into a sharp and admitted opposition to common sense. At this point, however, a new interest begins in Europe. If the age was already disposed to self-analysis, Rousseau, with his paradoxes and his even pathological love of limitless self-scrutiny, introduced into this man-loving period a sentimental tendency, from which, erelong, came a revival of passion, of poetry, and of enthusiasm, whose influence we shall never outgrow. Contemporaneous with this influence was the appearance of the modern romance in its early forms. Not much later

came the "Storm and Stress" period of German literature, and by the time
this had run its course, the French Revolution, overthrowing all the mechanical restraints of civilization, demonstrated afresh to the world's outer sense the
central importance of passion in the whole life of humanity.

The philosophy of Kant, developing in the quiet solitudes of his professo-
rial studies at Königsberg, in far eastern Prussia, reflected with a most wonderful ingenuity the essential interests of the time when all this transformation
was preparing. In 1781, he published his "Critique of Pure Reason," nearly, if
not quite, the most important philosophical treatise ever written. The essential
doctrine of this book is the thought that man's nature is the real creator of
man's world. It isn't the external world, as such, that is the deepest truth for us
at all; it is the inner structure of the human spirit which merely expresses itself
in the visible nature about us. The interest of Kant's presentation of this paradoxical thought lay not so much in the originality of the conception, for philosophers never invent fundamental beliefs, and this idea of Kant's is as old as
deeper spiritual faith itself; but rather in the cool, reflective, mercilessly critical ingenuity with which he carries it out. Issued several years before the
French Revolution, the book seems a sort of deliberate justification of the
proud consciousness of man's own absolute rights with which, in that mighty
struggle, the human spirit rose against all external restraints, and declared, as
we in America had already showed men how to do, that the true world for humanity is the world which the freeman makes, and that the genuinely natural
order is one which is not external until reason decrees that it shall exist.

And herewith begins what I have ventured to call in its wholeness the
third period of modern philosophy, a period not yet ended. The great thoughts
of Kant ruled the philosophic reflection of the next fifty years after the appearance of the "Critique," with what extravagancies and with what excellen-
cies of result we shall in a measure see hereafter. There is a sense in which this
doctrine of Kant's is the very soul of all our modern life, not, I repeat, as if the
philosopher had invented it, but because once for all this is the essentially hu-
mane view of reality. You can easily make wild and romantic misuse of it. But
when rightly interpreted, Kant's world, where the inner reason is lord over the
outer sense, will prove to be as hard and fast a world of fact, of law, and of
eternal majesty, as ever the seventeenth century had conceived. At all events,
whether we will it or no, in this universe of Kant's philosophy we all still live.[1]

But the outcome of these fifty years of post-Kantian speculation was, after
all, an unfinished organization of philosophic thought. The undertaking was
too vast for one generation. After a period of speculative quiescence, a period
when attention was directed away from philosophy by other human concerns,
this, our third period of modern thought, has come to see a revival of philosophic activity, a revival in the midst of which we now live. To the legacy of

---

[1] [The reader is reminded that Royce wrote these words more than eighty
years ago.—*Ed.*]

Kant has been added the wealth of problems offered to us by recent advances in natural science and in the study of the history of humanity. The doctrine of evolution, itself no novelty in opinion, has received a wholly unlooked-for empirical formulation and confirmation. The sciences have grown until no one can even remotely hope to overlook their whole field. In consequence, however, external nature has once more gained for us an imposing authority which makes us in many ways sympathize afresh with the pure naturalism of the seventeenth century. Man we once more see to be, not merely the sentimental rebel and creative hero of Rousseau and the romanticists, not merely the organ of the world-forming reason of the Kantian schools, but also, and just as truly, the mechanism which the seventeenth century declared him to be. How can he be both these things, that is, both natural and spiritual? How can he have sprung from an animal ancestry, yes, ultimately from dead matter, and yet be the embodiment, the organ of the absolute reason? How can he at once be part of the spirit whose live thinking dreams out this whole frame of things, and yet he himself the slave of the very order of nature which this dream creates? How can he, this mere mechanism, this creature of nerves, this mortal thing whose brain secretes thought, be also, as Kant made him, the very source of the laws of nature themselves? How comprehend this paradox? Well, I answer, after all, it is the ancient paradox of the double nature of man. It would be unpardonably absurd even to mention such a strange problem, were it not so real, so pertinacious, so every day a matter, were it not absolutely forced on us afresh by every new word of modern science, as by every old word of the devotional books. And this problem, I insist, is now in the forefront of speculation as it never was before: in what sense, with what prospect of solution, with what beauty of statement, with what depth of significance, with what manifold illustration in facts, with what passionate longing of inquiry, I should be glad, indeed, if I could hope to express in the subsequent lectures of this course. And so, for the first, our rude sketch is before us.

PRINCIPAL PROTAGONISTS

THOMAS HOBBES (1588–1679) was born at Malmesbury, England, and received his education at Oxford where he studied scholastic logic and physics. Agreeing only with their nominalistic conclusions, he was repelled by the scholastic methods in thought and left the University, taking up a position as tutor to the young Earl of Devonshire. His position occasioned repeated journeys in different countries of Europe and enabled him to devote himself to the study of literature, in particular the classic historians and poets. From 1634–37 he lived in Paris, making the acquaintance of Mersenne, Gassendi, and Descartes. During these years, and the period of his exile in Paris for his political views, 1640–51, he devoted himself to the study of mathematics and optics and was greatly influenced by the doctrines of Galileo. Writing during the period of the Civil Wars, he was led to adopt an absolutist theory of the state, which he sought to justify on the general principles of his materialist system. After the Restoration he returned to England and was subsequently accepted, somewhat reluctantly, by his former pupil in France, Charles II. His chief works are the *Leviathan*, 1651, and his *Elementa Philosophiae*, in three parts (*De Cive*, 1642, enlarged 1647; *De Corpore*, 1655, *De Homine*, 1658). These had been preceded by *On Human Nature* and *De Corpore Politico*, composed in 1640 and printed in 1650 under the title *Elements of Law, Natural and Politic*. In 1668 he prepared a collected edition of his works (in Latin).

RENÉ DESCARTES (1596–1650) was born at La Haye in Touraine and was educated at the new Jesuit school at La Flèche. He studied physics and philosophy according to the scholastic system but only mathematics was able to satisfy his craving for clear and certain knowledge. He spent the years 1613–17 in Paris, then, in 1618, enlisted as an officer in the military service of Holland and, in 1619, joined the army of the Elector of Bavaria. During the campaigns from 1618 to 1621 he devoted every quiet hour to study, particularly mathematics, becoming a famous mathematician and discovering the principles of analytic geometry. After a stay in Paris, where he found the distractions of society irreconcilable with his desire for complete privacy and leisure for scientific work, he went to live in Holland in 1629. There he spent twenty years of quiet productivity although, in order to escape the annoyances of both friends and antagonists, he moved more than a dozen times. He conducted his correspondence with his French friends through Father Mersenne. Due to his growing reputation as the great new philosopher he received pressing invitations from Queen Christina of Sweden to join her court and to personally initiate her into his philosophy. In 1649 he yielded and left Holland for Stockholm, where he died the following year. His chief works include the *Regulae ad directionem ingenii*, probably composed in 1628 but left unfinished, *Le Monde*, begun in 1630 and also left unfinished, the *Discours de la Méthode*, published in 1637 together with three dissertations *(Dioptrique, Méteorés, Géométrie)* under the common title *Essais Philosophiques,* the *Meditationes de Prima Philosophia*, 1641, the *Principia philosophiae*, 1644, and *Les passions de l'âme*, 1649.

BENEDICT SPINOZA (1632–1677) was born in Amsterdam and grew up in the Spanish- and Portuguese-Jewish community of that city, to which his family had fled to take refuge from the Inquisition. He studied at the Hebrew school of the community under Rabbi Morteira and received instruction in Latin from Van den Ende, a physician who had the reputation of being a freethinker. His widening interests in the humanities and natural science together with expressed doubts about the Mosaic theology aroused the suspicion of the Jewish theologians. In July, 1656, he formally was expelled by anathema from the Jewish congregation on account of heretical views. He moved away, studying philosophy, science, and theology while supporting himself by grinding optical lenses. In 1673 he declined the professorship at Heidelberg offered him by Karl Ludwig, the Elector Palatine, in fear of his freedom of thought, notwithstanding the assurances given to him. He died on February 21, 1677, of an inherited disease of the chest. During his life Spinoza published just two works: the *Principia Philosophiae Cartesianae*, with an appendix, *Cogitata Metaphysica*, 1663, and the *Tractatus Theologico-Politicus*, published anonymously in 1670. Soon after his death some friends collected his chief works and published them under the title *Opera Posthuma*, 1677. Besides the aforementioned works the other philosophical writings include the *Tractatus Brevis de Deo et Homine ejusque Felicitate, Tractatus de Intellectus Emendatione*, the *Tractatus Politicus*, and the *Ethica Ordine Geometrico Demonstrata*.

JOHN LOCKE (1632–1704) was born at Wrington, near Bristol, and educated at Westminster and Oxford. His educational experiences were not happy ones, for at Westminster he learnt classics according to the strictly grammatical method while at Oxford he found Puritanism and scholasticism in the ascendency. He studied natural sciences and medicine and owed his philosophical awakening to the study of Descartes' writings. Although trained as a physician he spent most of his life in government service. In 1683 he went into voluntary exile in Holland and remained there until 1689, when the ascension to the throne by William of Orange made it possible for him to return to England.

He was made Commissioner of Appeals and, later, one of the Commissioners of Trade and Plantations (till 1700). His most important works are the *Letters on Toleration* (1689, 1690, 1692, 1704), *Two Treatises on Government*, 1690, *An Essay Concerning Human Understanding*, 1690, *Some Thoughts Concerning Education*, 1693, and *The Reasonableness of Christianity as delivered in the Scriptures*, 1695.

GOTTFRIED WILHELM LEIBNIZ (1646–1716) was born in Leipzig, where his father was a jurist and professor of moral philosophy. He entered the university of his native city in his fifteenth year to study law, later studying philosophy and mathematics at the universities at Jena and Altdorf. In 1666 he received his Doctor of Laws from Altdorf and then declined the professorship extraordinary offered him by that institution. He entered the service of the Elector of Mainz and in 1672 he went to Paris, where he lived for four years and met the leading scientists, mathematicians, and philosophers of the period. He made visits to London, where he was made a member of the Royal Society, and to Holland, where he met with Spinoza. From the end of 1676 until his death in 1716 Leibniz lived in Hanover, where he served as court councillor and librarian. At his suggestion Queen Sophie Charlotte of Prussia, who had shown great kindness to him, founded the Academy of Sciences of Berlin in 1700 and Leibniz became its first president. He was interested in virtually all areas of study and made significant contributions in logic, law, physics, history, linguistics, and, in particular, mathematics, discovering the calculus independently of Newton. Leibniz's works are voluminous, although mostly occasional in nature. The only *book* published in his lifetime is the *Theodicy*, 1710. Publication of his principal philosophical book, *New Essays Concerning Human Understanding*, a detailed criticism of Locke's *Essay*, was deferred on account of the death of Locke in 1704 and was not published until 1765.

GEORGE BERKELEY (1685–1753) was born in Dysert, Ireland, the descendant of an English family which appears to have settled in Ireland immediately after the Restoration. He early displayed brilliance of mind and went to university at Dublin where, at that time, the works of Boyle, Newton, and Locke formed the basis of instruction. He conceived the fundamental notions of his philosophy in early youth and began publication of his major works in his twenties. After publication of a popular exposition of his philosophical ideas in the form of dialogues, 1713, he spent several years travelling in France and Italy. He returned to Ireland to fill a clerical office but was unable to endure it for long. From 1729 to 1731 he was in America attempting to establish a missionary college in the islands of Bermuda. Promises of aid for his plan were not kept and he returned to his home, never getting over the disappointment of his great hope. In 1734 he was made Bishop of Cloyne in the south of Ireland where he served with great zeal and was esteemed by both Protestants and Catholics, the latter constituting nearly five-sixths of the population of his bishopric. He spent his last years in Oxford, where he died in 1753. His most important writings are *An Essay toward a New Theory of Vision*, 1709, *A Treatise Concerning the Principles of Human Knowledge*, 1710, *Three Dialogues between Hylas and Philonous*, 1713, *Alciphron, or the Minute Philosopher*, 1732, and *Siris*, 1744.

DAVID HUME (1711–1776) was born on the estate of Ninewells in the south of Scotland, the son of a landed proprietor. His family wished him to study law but he very early in life was seized by a passion for literature and his main ambition was to gain fame as a writer. For a brief time he became a merchant but then went to live in France where he wrote his *Treatise of Human Nature*. It appeared in 1739–40 in London but, as Hume later wrote, 'It fell dead-born from the press without reaching such distinction as even to excite a murmur among the zealots.' He later revised and rewrote much of the teaching of the *Treatise* and published the three books of that work as separate essays. A post of Keeper to the Advocates' Library, Edinburgh, 1752–57, gave him the opportunity to write his *History of England*, which added to the fame and popularity which his philosophical and other essays had won for him. By the time of his second journey to France, 1763–66, as secretary to Lord Hertford, the English Ambassador to France, Hume already was honored as a philosopher of worldwide renown. After serving for a year as Under-Secretary of State for Scotland he resigned in 1769 to retire to private life in Edinburgh. His principal works are *A Treatise of Human Nature*, 1739–40, *Enquiry concerning Human Understanding*, 1748, *An Enquiry concerning the Principles of Morals*, 1751, *A Dissertation on the Passions*, 1757, *Natural History of Religion*, 1757. Hume's *Autobiography*, 1777, the *Dialogues Concering Natural Religion*, 1779, and the two small essays on *Suicide* and on the *Immortality of the Soul*, 1783, were published posthumously.

THOMAS REID (1710–1796) was the most important thinker of the Scotch Philosophy of Common Sense, sometimes called simply the Scottish School. He was first a minister, then taught philosophy at King's College, Aberdeen, and later was Professor of Moral Philosophy in the University of Glasgow. In his *Inquiry into the Human Mind on the Principles of Common Sense* he tells us that he had been an adherent of the philosophy of Locke and Berkeley until a reading of Hume's *Treatise* showed him that the 'ideal philosophy' led to the subversion of all science, all religion, and all virtue. The argument given in a shorter form in *An Inquiry into the Human Mind on the Principles of Common Sense*, 1764, is greatly elaborated in his larger works, *Essays on the Intellectual Powers of Man*, 1785, and *Essays on the Active Powers of Mind*, 1788.

IMMANUEL KANT (1724–1804) was born in Königsberg, the son of a saddler of Scottish descent. His home and school training were both strict and of a markedly religious type. From his sixteenth to his twenty-second year he studied

Wolff's philosophy and Newton's physics at the university of his native city. For the nine years following, from 1746–54, he was a private tutor in several families belonging to the East Prussian nobility. In 1775, at the age of thirty-one he returned to Königsberg to become a *privat-docent* at the University, a post which he held until his forty-sixth year. In 1770 he was appointed professor of philosophy, a position which he occupied until his retirement in 1797. His principal writings of philosophical importance include *Dreams of a Ghost-seer illustrated by the Dreams of Metaphysics*, 1766, *On the Form and Principles of the Sensible and Intelligible World*, 1770, *Critique of Pure Reason*, 1781 (second, revised edition, 1787), *Prolegomena to every Future Metaphysic which may present itself as Science*, 1783, *What is Enlightenment?*, 1784, *Fundamental Principles of the Metaphysics of Ethics*, 1785, *Critique of Practical Reason*, 1788, *Critique of Judgment*, 1790, *Religion within the Limits of Reason Alone*, 1793, and *On Everlasting Peace*, 1795.

PART ONE   IN SEARCH OF TRUTH:
THE PROBLEM OF METHOD

A·METHODS OF INQUIRY

1 THOMAS HOBBES
Philosophy and Method*

Of Philosophy

1. PHILOSOPHY seems to me to be amongst men now, in the same manner as corn and wine are said to have been in the world in ancient time. For from the beginning there were vines and ears of corn growing here and there in the fields; but no care was taken for the planting and sowing of them. Men lived therefore upon acorns; or if any were so bold as to venture upon the eating of those unknown and doubtful fruits, they did it with danger of their health. In like manner, every man brought Philosophy, that is, Natural Reason, into the world with him; for all men can reason to some degree, and concerning some things: but where there is need of a long series of reasons, there most men wander out of the way, and fall into error for want of method, as it were for want of sowing and planting, that is, of improving their reason. And from hence it comes to pass, that they who content themselves with daily experience, which may be likened to feeding upon acorns, and either reject, or not much regard philosophy, are commonly esteemed, and are, indeed, men of sounder judgment than those who, from opinions, though not vulgar, yet full of uncertainty, and carelessly received, do nothing but dispute and wrangle, like men that are not well in their wits. I confess, indeed, that that part of philosophy by which magnitudes and figures are computed, is highly improved. But because I have not observed the like advancement in the other parts of it, my purpose is, as far forth as I am able, to lay open the few and first Elements of Philosophy in general, as so many seeds from which pure and true Philosophy may hereafter spring up by little and little.

I am not ignorant how hard a thing it is to weed out of men's minds such inveterate opinions as have taken root there, and been confirmed in them by the authority of most eloquent writers; especially seeing true (that is, accurate) Philosophy professedly rejects not only the paint and false colours of language, but even the very ornaments and graces of the same; and the first grounds of all science are not only not beautiful, but poor, arid, and, in appearance, deformed. Nevertheless, there being certainly some men, though but few, who are delighted with truth and strength of reason in all things, I thought I might do well to take this pains for the sake even of those few. I proceed therefore to the matter, and take my beginning from the very definition of philosophy, which is this.

2. PHILOSOPHY *is such knowledge of effects or appearances, as we acquire by true ra-*

---

* From *De Corpore*, Chapters 1 and 6. First published in 1655.

tiocination from the knowledge we have first of their causes or generation: And again, of such causes or generations as may be from knowing first their effects.

For the better understanding of which definition, we must consider, first, that although Sense and Memory of things, which are common to man and all living creatures, be knowledge, yet because they are given us immediately by nature, and not gotten by ratiocination, they are not philosophy.

Secondly, seeing Experience is nothing but memory; and Prudence, or prospect into the future time, nothing but expectation of such things as we have already had experience of, Prudence also is not to be esteemed philosophy.

By RATIOCINATION, I mean *computation*. Now to compute, is either to collect the sum of many things that are added together, or to know what remains when one thing is taken out of another. *Ratiocination*, therefore, is the same with *addition* and *subtraction*[1]; and if any man add *multiplication* and *division*, I will not be against it, seeing multiplication is nothing but addition of equals one to another, and division nothing but a subtraction of equals one from another, as often as is possible. So that all ratiocination is comprehended in these two operations of the mind, addition and subtraction.

3. But how by the *ratiocination* of our mind, we add and subtract in our silent thoughts, without the use of words, it will be necessary for me to make intelligible by an example or two. If therefore a man see something afar off and obscurely, although no appellation had yet been given to anything, he will, notwithstanding, have the same idea of that thing for which now, by imposing a name on it, we call it *body*. Again, when, by coming nearer, he sees the same thing thus and thus, now in one place and now in another, he will have a new idea thereof, namely, that for which we now call such a thing *animated*. Thirdly, when standing nearer, he perceives the figure, hears the voice, and sees other things which are signs of a rational mind, he has a third idea, though it have yet no appellation, namely, that for which we now call anything *rational*. Lastly, when, by looking fully and distinctly upon it, he conceives all that he has seen as one thing, the idea he has now is compounded of his former ideas, which are put together in the mind in the same order in which these three single names, *body, animated, rational,* are in speech compounded into this one name, *body-animated-rational*, or *man*. In like manner, of the several conceptions of *four sides, equality of sides, and right angles,* is compounded the conception of a *square*. For the mind may conceive a figure of four sides without any conception of their equality, and of that equality without conceiving a right angle; and may join together all these single conceptions into one conception or one idea of a square. And thus we see how the conceptions of the mind are compounded. Again, whosoever sees a man standing near him, conceives the whole idea of that man; and if, as he goes away, he

---

[1] [Original text reads *substraction* and *substract* here and throughout the work. —*Ed.*]

follow him with his eyes only, he will lose the idea of those things which were signs of his being rational, whilst, nevertheless, the idea of a body-animated remains still before his eyes, so that the idea of rational is subtracted from the whole idea of man, that is to say, of body-animated-rational, and there remains that of body-animated; and a while after, at a greater distance, the idea of animated will be lost, and that of body only will remain; so that at last, when nothing at all can be seen, the whole idea will vanish out of sight. By which examples, I think, it is manifest enough what is the internal ratiocination of the mind without words.

We must not therefore think that computation, that is, ratiocination, has place only in numbers, as if man were distinguished from other living creatures (which is said to have been the opinion of *Pythagoras*) by nothing but the faculty of numbering; for *magnitude, body, motion, time, degrees of quality, action, conception, proportion, speech and names* (in which all the kinds of philosophy consist) are capable of addition and subtraction. Now such things as we add or subtract that is, which we put into an account, we are said to *consider*, in Greek λογίζεσθαι, in which language also συλλογίεσθαι signifies to *compute, reason*, or *reckon*.

4. But *effects* and the *appearances* of things to sense, are faculties or powers of bodies, which make us distinguish them from one another; that is to say, conceive one body to be equal or unequal, like or unlike to another body; as in the example above, when by coming near enough to any body, we perceive the motion and going of the same, we distinguish it thereby from a tree, a column, and other fixed bodies; and so that motion or going is the *property* thereof, as being proper to living creatures, and a faculty by which they make us distinguish them from other bodies.

5. How the knowledge of any effect may be gotten from the knowledge of the generation thereof, may easily be understood by the example of a circle: for if there be set before us a plain figure, having, as near as may be, the figure of a circle, we cannot possibly perceive by sense whether it be a true circle or no; than which, nevertheless, nothing is more easy to be known to him that knows first the generation of the propounded figure. For let it be known that the figure was made by the circumduction of a body whereof one end remained unmoved, and we may reason thus; a body carried about, retaining always the same length, applies itself first to one *radius*, then to another, to a third, a fourth, and successively to all; and, therefore, the same length, from the same point, toucheth the circumference in every part thereof, which is as much as to say, as all the *radii* are equal. We know, therefore, that from such generation proceeds a figure, from whose one middle point all the extreme points are reached unto by equal *radii*. And in like manner, by knowing first what figure is set before us, we may come by ratiocination to some generation of the same, though perhaps not that by which it was made, yet that by which it might have been made; for he that knows that a circle has the property above declared, will easily know whether a body carried about, as is said, will generate a circle or no.

6. The *end* or *scope* of philosophy is, that we may make use to our benefit of effects formerly seen; or that, by application of bodies to one another, we may produce the like effects of those we conceive in our mind, as far forth as matter, strength, and industry, will permit, for the commodity of human life. For the inward glory and triumph of mind that a man may have for the mastering of some difficult and doubtful matter, or for the discovery of some hidden truth, is not worth so much pains as the study of Philosophy requires; nor need any man care much to teach another what he knows himself, if he think that will be the only benefit of his labour. The end of knowledge is power; and the use of theorems (which, among geometricians, serve for the finding out of properties) is for the construction of problems; and lastly, the scope of all speculation is the performing of some action, or thing to be done.

7. But what the *utility* of philosophy is, especially of natural philosophy and geometry, will be best understood by reckoning up the chief commodities of which mankind is capable, and by comparing the manner of life of such as enjoy them, with that of others which want the same. Now, the greatest commodities of mankind are the arts; namely, of measuring matter and motion; of moving ponderous bodies; of architecture; of navigation; of making instruments for all uses; of calculating the celestial motions, the aspects of the stars, and the parts of time; of geography, &c. By which sciences, how great benefits men receive is more easily understood than expressed. These benefits are enjoyed by almost all the people of Europe, by most of those of Asia, and by some of Africa: but the Americans, and they that live near the Poles, do totally want them. But why? Have they sharper wits than these? Have not all men one kind of soul, and the same faculties of mind? What, then, makes this difference, except philosophy? Philosophy, therefore, is the cause of all these benefits. But the utility of moral and civil philosophy is to be estimated, not so much by the commodities we have by knowing these sciences, as by the calamities we receive from not knowing them. Now, all such calamities as may be avoided by human industry, arise from war, but chiefly from civil war; for from this proceed slaughter, solitude, and the want of all things. But the cause of war is not that men are willing to have it; for the will has nothing for object but good, at least that which seemeth good. Nor is it from this, that men know not that the effects of war are evil; for who is there that thinks not poverty and loss of life to be great evils? The cause, therefore, of civil war is, that men know not the causes neither of war nor peace, there being but few in the world that have learned those duties which unite and keep men in peace, that is to say, that have learned the rules of civil life sufficiently. Now, the knowledge of these rules is moral philosophy. But why have they not learned them, unless for this reason, that none hitherto have taught them in a clear and exact method? For what shall we say? Could the ancient masters of Greece, Egypt, Rome, and others, persuade the unskilful multitude to their innumerable opinions concerning the nature of their gods, which they themselves know not whether they were true or false, and which were indeed manifestly false and absurd; and could they not persuade the same multitude to civil duty, if they

themselves had understood it? Or shall those few writings of geometricians which are extant, be thought sufficient for the taking away of all controversy in the matters they treat of, and shall those innumerable and huge volumes of *ethics* be thought unsufficient, if what they teach had been certain and well demonstrated? What, then, can be imagined to be the cause that the writings of those men have increased science, and the writings of these have increased nothing but words, saving that the former were written by men that knew, and the latter by such as know not, the doctrine they taught only for ostentation of their wit and eloquence? Nevertheless, I deny not but the reading of some such books is very delightful; for they are most eloquently written, and contain many clear, wholesome and choice sentences, which yet are not universally true, though by them universally pronounced. From whence it comes to pass, that the circumstances of times, places, and persons being changed, they are no less frequently made use of to confirm wicked men in their purposes, than to make them understand the precepts of civil duties. Now that which is chiefly wanting in them, is a true and certain rule of our actions, by which we might know whether that we undertake be just or unjust. For it is to no purpose to be bidden in every thing to do right, before there be a certain rule and measure of right established, which no man hitherto hath established. Seeing, therefore, from the not knowing of civil duties, that is, from the want of moral science, proceed civil wars, and the greatest calamities of mankind, we may very well attribute to such science the production of the contrary commodities. And thus much is sufficient, to say nothing of the praises and other contentment proceeding from philosophy, to let you see the utility of the same in every kind thereof.

8. The *subject* of Philosophy, or the matter it treats of, is every body of which we can conceive any generation, and which we may, by any consideration thereof, compare with other bodies, or which is capable of composition and resolution; that is to say, every body of whose generation or properties we can have any knowledge. And this may be deduced from the definition of philosophy, whose profession it is to search out the properties of bodies from their generation, or their generation from their properties; and, therefore, where there is no generation or property, there is no philosophy. Therefore it excludes *Theology,* I mean the doctrine of God, eternal, ingenerable, incomprehensible, and in whom there is nothing neither to divide nor compound, nor any generation to be conceived.

It excludes the doctrine of *angels,* and all such things as are thought to be neither bodies nor properties of bodies; there being in them no place neither for composition nor division, nor any capacity of more and less, that is to say, no place for ratiocination.

It excludes *history,* as well *natural* as *political,* though most useful (nay necessary) to philosophy; because such knowledge is but experience, or authority, and not ratiocination.

It excludes all such knowledge as is acquired by Divine inspiration, or revelation, as not derived to us by reason, but by Divine grace in an instant, and, as it were, by some sense supernatural.

It excludes not only all doctrines which are false, but such also as are not well-grounded; for whatsoever we know by right ratiocination, can neither be false nor doubtful; and, therefore, *astrology*, as it is now held forth, and all such divinations rather than sciences, are excluded.

Lastly, the doctrine of *God's worship* is excluded from philosophy, as being not to be known by natural reason, but by the authority of the Church; and as being the object of faith, and not of knowledge.

9. The principal parts of philosophy are two. For two chief kinds of bodies, and very different from one another, offer themselves to such as search after their generation and properties; one whereof being the work of nature, is called a *natural body,* the other is called a *commonwealth,* and is made by the wills and agreement of men. And from these spring the two parts of philosophy, called *natural* and *civil.* But seeing that, for the knowledge of the properties of a commonwealth, it is necessary first to know the dispositions, affections, and manners of men, civil philosophy is again commonly divided into two parts, whereof one, which treats of men's dispositions and manners, is called *ethics;* and the other, which takes cognizance of their civil duties, is called *politics,* or simply *civil philosophy.* In the first place, therefore (after I have set down such premises as appertain to the nature of philosophy in general), I will discourse of *bodies natural;* in the second, of the *dispositions and manners of men;* and in the third, of the *civil duties of subjects.*

10. To conclude; seeing there may be many who will not like this my definition of philosophy, and will say, that, from the liberty which a man may take of so defining as seems best to himself, he may conclude any thing from any thing (though I think it no hard matter to demonstrate that this definition of mine agrees with the sense of all men); yet, lest in this point there should be any cause of dispute betwixt me and them, I here undertake no more than to deliver the elements of that science by which the effects of anything may be found out from the known generation of the same, or contrarily, the generation from the effects; to the end that they who search after other philosophy, may be admonished to seek it from other principles.

Of Method

1. For the understanding of *method,* it will be necessary for me to repeat the definition of philosophy, delivered above (Chap. I, art. 2) in this manner. *Philosophy is the knowledge we acquire, by true ratiocination, of appearances, or apparent effects, from the knowledge we have of some possible production or generation of the same; and of such production, as has been or may be, from the knowledge we have of the effects.* METHOD, therefore, in the study of philosophy, *is the shortest way of finding out effects by their known causes, or of causes by their known effects.* But we are then said to know any effect, when we know *that there be causes of the same,* and *in what subject*

those causes are, and *in what subject they produce that effect,* and *in what manner they work the same.* And this is the science of causes, or, as they call it, óf the διότι. All other science, which is called the ὅτι, is either perception by sense, or the imagination, or memory remaining after such perception.

The first beginnings, therefore, of knowledge, are the phantasms of sense and imagination; and that there be such phantasms we know well enough by nature; but to know why they be, or from what causes they proceed, is the work of ratiocination; which consists (as is said above, in the 1st Chapter, Art. 2) in *composition,* and *division* or *resolution.* There is therefore no method, by which we find out the causes of things, but is either *compositive* or *resolutive,* or *partly compositive,* and *partly resolutive.* And the resolutive is commonly called *analytical* method, as the compositive is called *synthetical.*

2. It is common to all sorts of method, to proceed from known things to unknown; and this is manifest from the cited definition of philosophy. But in knowledge by sense, the whole object is more known, than any part thereof; as when we see a man, the conception or whole idea of that man is first or more known, than the particular ideas of this being *figurate, animate,* and *rational;* that is, we first see the whole man, and take notice of his being, before we observe in him those other particulars. And therefore in any knowledge of the ὅτι, or that any thing *is,* the beginning of our search is from the whole idea; and contrarily, in our knowledge of the διότι, or of the causes of any thing, that is, in the sciences, we have more knowledge of the causes of the parts than of the whole. For the cause of the whole is compounded of the causes of the parts; but it is necessary that we know the things that are to be compounded, before we can know the whole compound. Now, by parts, I do not here mean parts of the thing itself, but parts of its nature; as, by the parts of man, I do not understand his head, his shoulders, his arms, &c. but his figure, quantity, motion, sense, reason, and the like; which accidents being compounded or put together, constitute the whole nature of man, but not the man himself. And this is the meaning of that common saying, namely, that some things are more known to us, others more known to nature; for I do not think that they, which so distinguish, mean that something is known to nature, which is known to no man; and therefore, by those things, that are more known to us, we are to understand things we take notice of by our senses, and, by more known to nature, those we acquire the knowledge of by reason; for in this sense it is, that the *whole,* that is, those things that have universal names, (which, for brevity's sake, I call *universal)* are more known to us than the *parts,* that is, such things as have names less universal, (which I therefore call *singular*); and the causes of the parts are more known to nature than the cause of the whole; that is, universals than singulars.

3. In the study of philosophy, men search after science either simply or indefinitely; that is, to know as much as they can, without propounding to themselves any limited question; or they enquire into the cause of some determined appearance, or endeavour to find out the certainty of something in question,

as what is the cause of *light,* of *heat,* of *gravity,* of a *figure* propounded, and the like; or in what *subject* any propounded *accident* is inherent; or what may conduce most to the *generation* of some propounded effect from many *accidents;* or in what manner particular causes ought to be compounded for the production of some certain effect. Now, according to this variety of things in question, sometimes the *analytical method* is to be used, and sometimes the *synthetical.*

4. But to those that search after science indefinitely, which consists in the knowledge of the causes of all things, as far forth as it may be attained, (and the causes of singular things are compounded of the causes of universal or simple things) it is necessary that they know the causes of universal things, or of such accidents as are common to all bodies, that is, to all matter, before they can know the causes of singular things, that is, of those accidents by which one thing is distinguished from another. And, again, they must know what those universal things are, before they can know their causes. Moreover, seeing universal things are contained in the nature of singular things, the knowledge of them is to be acquired by reason, that is, by resolution. For example, if there be propounded a conception or *idea* of some singular thing, as of a *square,* this square is to be resolved into a *plain, terminated with a certain number of equal and straight lines and right angles.* For by this resolution we have these things universal or agreeable to all matter, namely, *line, plain,* (which contains *superficies*) *terminated, angle, straightness, rectitude,* and *equality;* and if we can find out the causes of these; we may compound them altogether into the cause of a square. Again, if any man propound to himself the conception of *gold,* he may, by resolving, come to the ideas of *solid, visible, heavy,* (that is, tending to the centre of the earth, or downwards) and many other more universal than gold itself; and these he may resolve again, till he come to such things as are most universal. And in this manner, by resolving continually, we may come to know what those things are, whose causes being first known severally, and afterwards compounded, bring us to the knowledge of singular things. I conclude, therefore, that the method of attaining to the universal knowledge of things, is purely *analytical.*

5. But the causes of universal things (of those, at least, that have any cause) are manifest of themselves, or (as they say commonly) known to nature; so that they need no method at all; for they have all but one universal cause, which is motion. For the variety of all figures arises out of the variety of those motions by which they are made; and motion cannot be understood to have any other cause besides motion; nor has the variety of those things we perceive by sense, as of *colours, sounds, savours,* &c. any other cause than motion, residing partly in the objects that work upon our senses, and partly in ourselves, in such manner, as that it is manifestly some kind of motion, though we cannot, without ratiocination, come to know what kind. For though many cannot understand till it be in some sort demonstrated to them, that all mutation consists in motion; yet this happens not from any obscurity in the thing itself, (for it is not intelligible that anything can depart either from rest, or from the mo-

tion it has, except by motion), but either by having their natural discourse corrupted with former opinions received from their masters, or else for this, that they do not at all bend their mind to the enquiring out of truth.

6. By the knowledge therefore of universals, and of their causes (which are the first principles by which we know the διότι of things) we have in the first place their definitions, (which are nothing but the explication of our simple conceptions.) For example, he that has a true conception of *place,* cannot be ignorant of this definition, *place is that space which is possessed or filled adequately by some body;* and so, he that conceives *motion* aright, cannot but know that *motion is the privation of one place, and the acquisition of another.* In the next place, we have their generations or descriptions; as (for example) that *a line is made by the motion of a point, superficies by the motion of a line,* and *one motion by another motion,* &c. It remains, that we enquire what motion begets such and such effects; as, what motion makes a straight line, and what a circular; what motion thrusts, what draws, and by what way; what makes a thing which is seen or heard, to be seen or heard sometimes in one manner, sometimes in another. Now the method of this kind of enquiry, is *compositive.* For first, we are to observe what effect a body moved produceth, when we consider nothing in it besides its motion; and we see presently that this makes a line, or length; next, what the motion of a long body produces, which we find to be superficies; and so forwards, till we see what the effects of simple motion are; and then, in like manner, we are to observe what proceeds from the addition, multiplication, subtraction, and division, of these motions, and what effects, what figures, and what properties, they produce; from which kind of contemplation sprung that part of philosophy which is called *geometry.*

From this consideration of what is produced by simple motion, we are to pass to the consideration of what effects one body moved worketh upon another; and because there may be motion in all the several parts of a body, yet so as that the whole body remain still in the same place, we must enquire first, what motion causeth such and such motion in the whole, that is, when one body invades another body which is either at rest or in motion, what way, and with what swiftness, the invaded body shall move; and, again, what motion this second body will generate in a third, and so forwards. From which contemplation shall be drawn that part of philosophy which treats of motion.

In the third place we must proceed to the enquiry of such effects as are made by the motion of the parts of any body, as, how it comes to pass, that things when they are the same, yet seem not to be the same, but changed. And here the things we search after are sensible qualities, such as *light, colour, transparency, opacity, sound, odour, savour, heat, cold,* and the like; which because they cannot be known till we know the causes of sense itself, therefore the consideration of the causes of *seeing, hearing, smelling, tasting* and *touching,* belongs to this third place; and all those qualities and changes, above mentioned, are to be referred to the fourth place; which two considerations comprehend that part of philosophy which is called *physics.* And in these four parts is contained whatsoever in natural philosophy may be explicated by demonstration, properly so called. For if a cause were to be rendered of natural appearances in special, as, what are the motions and influences of the heavenly bodies, and of their parts, the reason hereof must either be drawn from the parts of the sciences above mentioned, or no reason at all will be given, but all left to uncertain conjecture.

After *physics* we must come to *moral philosophy;* in which we are to consider the motions of the mind, namely, *appetite, aversion, love, benevolence, hope, fear, anger, emulation, envy,* &c.; what causes they have, and of what they be causes. And the reason why these are to be considered after *physics* is, that they have their causes in sense and imagination, which are the subject of *physical* contemplation. Also the reason, why all these things are to be searched after in the order above-said, is, that physics cannot be understood, except we know first what motions are in the smallest parts of bodies; nor such motion of parts, till we know what it is that makes another body move; nor this, till we know what simple motion will effect. And because all appearance of things to sense is determined, and made to be of such and such quality and quantity by compounded motions, every one of which has a certain degree of velocity, and a certain and determined way; therefore, in the first place, we are to search out the ways of motion simply (in which geometry consists); next the ways of such generated motions as are manifest; and, lastly, the ways of internal and invisible motions (which is the enquiry of natural philosophers). And, therefore, they that study natural philosophy, study in vain, except they begin at geometry; and such writers or disputers thereof, as are ignorant of geometry, do but make their readers and hearers lose their time.

7. *Civil* and *moral philosophy* do not so adhere to one another, but that they may be severed. For the causes of the motions of the mind are known, not only by ratiocination, but also by the experience of every man that takes the pains to observe those motions within himself. And, therefore, not only they that have attained the knowledge of the passions and perturbations of the mind, by the *synthetical method,* and from the very first principles of philosophy, may by proceeding in the same way, come to the causes and necessity of constituting commonwealths, and to get the knowledge of what is natural right, and what are civil duties; and, in every kind of government, what are the rights of the commonwealth, and all other knowledge appertaining to civil philosophy; for this reason, that the principles of the politics consist in the knowledge of the motions of the mind, and the knowledge of these motions from the knowledge of sense and imagination; but even they also that have not learned the first part of philosophy, namely, *geometry* and *physics,* may, notwithstanding, attain the principles of civil philosophy, by the *analytical method.* For if a question be propounded, as, *whether such an action be just or unjust;* if that *unjust* be resolved into *fact against law,* and that notion *law* into the command of him or them that have *coercive power;* and that *power* be derived from the *wills* of men that constitute such power, to the end they may live in peace, they may at last come to this, that the appetites of men and the passions of their minds are such, that, unless they be restrained by some power, they will always be making war

upon one another; which may be known to be so by any man's experience, that will but examine his own mind. And, therefore, from hence he may proceed, by compounding, to the determination of the justice or injustice of any propounded action. So that it is manifest, by what has been said, that the method of philosophy, to such as seek science simply, without propounding to themselves the solution of any particular question, is partly analytical, and partly synthetical; namely, that which proceeds from sense to the invention of principles, analytical; and the rest synthetical.

8. To those that seek the cause of some certain and propounded appearance or effect, it happens, sometimes, that they know not whether the thing, whose cause is sought after, be matter or body, or some accident of a body. For though in geometry, when the cause is sought of magnitude, or proportion, or figure, it be certainly known that these things, namely magnitude, proportion, and figure, are accidents; yet in natural philosophy, where all questions are concerning the causes of the phantasms of sensible things, it is not so easy to discern between the things themselves, from which those phantasms proceed, and the appearances of those things to the sense; which have deceived many, especially when the phantasms have been made by light. For example, a man that looks upon the sun, has a certain shining idea of the magnitude of about a foot over, and this he calls the sun, though he know the sun to be truly a great deal bigger; and, in like manner, the phantasm of the same thing appears sometimes round, by being seen afar off, and sometimes square, by being nearer. Whereupon it may well be doubted, whether that phantasm be matter, or some body natural, or only some accident of a body; in the examination of which doubt we may use this method. The properties of matter and accidents already found out by us, by the synthetical method, from their definitions, are to be compared with the idea we have before us; and if it agree with the properties of matter or body, then it is a body; otherwise it is an accident. Seeing, therefore, matter cannot by any endeavor of ours be either made or destroyed, or increased, or diminished, or moved out of its place, whereas that idea appears, vanishes, is increased and diminished, and moved hither and thither at pleasure; we may certainly conclude that it is not a body, but an accident only. And this method is *synthetical.*

9. But if there be a doubt made concerning the subject of any known accident (for this may be doubted sometimes, as in the precedent example, doubt may be made in what subject that splendour and apparent magnitude of the sun is), then our enquiry must proceed in this manner. First, matter in general must be divided into parts, as, into object, medium, and the sentient itself, or such other parts as seem most conformable to the thing propounded. Next, these parts are severally to be examined how they agree with the definition of the subject; and such of them as are not capable of that accident are to be rejected. For example, if by any true ratiocination the sun be found to be greater than its apparent magnitude, then that magnitude is not in the sun; if the sun be in one determined straight line, and one determined distance, and the magnitude and splendour be seen in more lines and distances than one, as it is

in reflection or refraction, then neither that splendour nor apparent magnitude are in the sun itself, and, therefore, the body of the sun cannot be the subject of that splendour and magnitude. And for the same reasons the air and other parts will be rejected, till at last nothing remain which can be the subject of that splendour and magnitude but the sentient itself. And this method, in regard the subject is divided into parts, is analytical; and in regard the properties, both of the subject and accident, are compared with the accident concerning whose subject the enquiry is made, it is synthetical.

10. But when we seek after the cause of any propounded effect, we must in the first place get into our mind an exact notion or idea of that which we call cause, namely, that *a cause is the sum or aggregate of all such accidents, both in the agents and the patient, as concur to the producing of the effect propounded; all of which existing together, it cannot be understood but that the effect existeth with them; or that it can possibly exist if any one of them be absent.* This being known, in the next place we must examine singly every accident that accompanies or precedes the effect, as far forth as it seems to conduce in any manner to the production of the same, and see whether the propounded effect may be conceived to exist, without the existence of any of those accidents; and by this means separate such accidents, as do not concur, from such as concur to produce the said effect; which being done, we are to put together the concurring accidents, and consider whether we can possibly conceive, that when these are all present, the effect propounded will not follow; and if it be evident that the effect will follow, then that aggregate of accidents is the entire cause, otherwise not; but we must still search out and put together other accidents. For example, if the cause of light be propounded to be sought out; first, we examine things without us, and find that whensoever light appears, there is some principal object, as it were the fountain of light, without which we cannot have any perception of light; and, therefore, the concurrence of that object is necessary to the generation of light. Next we consider the medium, and find, that unless it be disposed in a certain manner, namely, that it be transparent, though the object remain the same, yet the effect will not follow; and, therefore, the concurrence of transparency is also necessary to the generation of light. Thirdly, we observe our own body, and find that by the indisposition of the eyes, the brain, the nerves, and the heart, that is, by obstructions, stupidity, and debility we are deprived of light, so that a fitting disposition of the organs to receive impressions from without is likewise a necessary part of the cause of light. Again, of all the accidents inherent in the object, there is none that can conduce to the effecting of light, but only action (or a certain motion), which cannot be conceived to be wanting, whensoever the effect is present; for, that anything may shine, it is not requisite that it be of such or such magnitude or figure, or that the whole body of it be moved out of the place it is in (unless it may perhaps be said, that in the sun, or other body, that which causes light is the light it hath in itself; which yet is but a trifling exception, seeing nothing is meant thereby but the cause of light; as if any man should say that the cause of light is that in the sun which produceth it); it remains, therefore, that the action, by which light is gener-

ated, is motion only in the parts of the object. Which being understood, we may easily conceive what it is the medium contributes, namely, the continuation of that motion to the eye; and, lastly, what the eye and the rest of the organs of the sentient contribute, namely, the continuation of the same motion to the last organ of sense, the heart. And in this manner the cause of light may be made up of motion continued from the original of the same motion, to the original of vital motion, made by the impression upon it of motion continued from the object. But I give this only for an example, for I shall speak more at large of light, and the generation of it, in its proper place. In the mean time it is manifest, that in the searching out of causes, there is need partly of the analytical, and partly of the synthetical method; of the analytical, to conceive how circumstances conduce severally to the production of effects; and of the synthetical, for the adding together and compounding of what they can effect singly by themselves. And thus much may serve for the method of invention. It remains that I speak of the method of teaching, that is, of demonstration, and of the means by which we demonstrate.

11. In the method of invention, the use of words consists in this, that they may serve for marks, by which, whatsoever we have found out may be recalled to memory; for without this all our inventions perish, nor will it be possible for us to go on from principles beyond a syllogism or two, by reason of the weakness of memory. For example, if any man, by considering a triangle set before him, should find that all its angles together taken are equal to two right angles, and that by thinking of the same tacitly, without any use of words either understood or expressed; and it should happen afterwards that another triangle, unlike the former, or the same in different situation, should be offered to his consideration, he would not know readily whether the same property were in this last or no, but would be forced, as often as a different triangle were brought before him (and the difference of triangles is infinite) to begin his contemplation anew; which he would have no need to do if he had the use of names, for every universal name denotes the conceptions we have of infinite singular things. Nevertheless, as I said above, they serve as *marks* for the help of our memory, whereby we register to ourselves our own inventions; but not as *signs* by which we declare the same to others; so that a man may be a philosopher alone by himself, without any master; Adam had this capacity. But to teach, that is, to demonstrate, supposes two at the least, and syllogistical speech.

12. And seeing teaching is nothing but leading the mind of him we teach, to the knowledge of our inventions, in that track by which we attained the same with our own mind; therefore, the same method that served for our invention, will serve also for demonstration to others, saving that we omit the first part of method which proceeded from the sense of things to universal principles, which, because they are principles, cannot be demonstrated; and seeing they are known by nature, (as was said above in the 5th article) they need no demonstration, though they need explication. The whole method, therefore, of demonstration, is *synthetical,* consisting of that order of speech

which begins from primary or most universal propositions, which are manifest of themselves, and proceeds by a perpetual composition of propositions into syllogisms, till at last the learner understand the truth of the conclusion sought after.

13. Now, such principles are nothing but definitions, whereof there are two sorts; one of names, that signify such things as have some conceivable cause, and another of such names as signify things of which we can conceive no cause at all. Names of the former kind are, *body*, or *matter, quantity*, or *extension, motion*, and whatsoever is common to all matter. Of the second kind, are *such a body, such and so great motion, so great magnitude, such figure*, and whatsoever we can distinguish one body from another by. And names of the former kind are well enough defined, when, by speech as short as may be, we raise in the mind of the hearer perfect and clear ideas or conceptions of the things named, as when we define motion to be *the leaving of one place, and the acquiring of another continually;* for though no thing moved, nor any cause of motion be in that definition, yet, at the hearing of that speech, there will come into the mind of the hearer an *idea* of motion clear enough. But definitions of things, which may be understood to have some cause, must consist of such names as express the cause or manner of their generation, as when we define a circle to be a figure made by the circumduction of a straight line in a plane, &c. Besides definitions, there is no other proposition that ought to be called primary, or (according to severe truth) be received into the number of principles. For those *axioms of Euclid*, seeing they may be demonstrated, are no principles of demonstration, though they have by the consent of all men gotten the authority of principles, because they need not be demonstrated. Also, those *petitions*, or *postulata*, (as they call them) though they be principles, yet they are not principles of demonstration, but of construction only; that is, not of science, but of power; or (which is all one) not of *theorems,* which are speculations, but of *problems*, which belong to practice, or the doing of something. But as for those common received opinions, *Nature abhors vacuity, Nature doth nothing in vain*, and the like, which are neither evident in themselves, nor at all to be demonstrated, and which are oftener false than true, they are much less to be acknowledged for principles.

To return, therefore, to definitions; the reason why I say that the cause and generation of such things, as have any cause or generation, ought to enter into their definitions, is this. The end of science is the demonstration of the causes and generation of things; which if they be not in the definitions, they cannot be found in the conclusion of the first syllogism, that is made from those definitions; and if they be not in the first conclusion, they will not be found in any further conclusion deduced from that; and, therefore, by proceeding in this manner, we shall never come to science; which is against the scope and intention of demonstration.

14. Now, seeing definitions (as I have said) are principles, or primary propositions, they are therefore speeches; and seeing they are used for the raising of an *idea* of some thing in the mind of the learner, whensoever that thing

has a name, the definition of it can be nothing but the explication of that name by speech; and if that name be given it for some compounded conception, the definition is nothing but a resolution of that name into its most universal parts. As when we define man, saying *man is a body animated, sentient, rational,* those names, *body animated,* &c., are parts of that whole name *man;* so that definitions of this kind always consist of *genus* and *difference;* the former names being all, till the last, *general;* and the last of all, *difference.* But if any name be the most universal in its kind, then the definition of it cannot consist of *genus* and *difference,* but is to be made by such circumlocution, as best explicateth the force of that name. Again, it is possible, and happens often, that the *genus* and *difference,* are put together, and yet make no definition; as these words, *a straight line,* contain both the *genus* and *difference;* but are not a definition, unless we should think a straight line may be thus defined, *a straight line is a straight line:* and yet if there were added another name, consisting of different words, but signifying the same thing which these signify, then these might be the definition of that name. From what has been said, it may be understood how a definition ought to be defined, namely, *that it is a proposition, whose predicate resolves the subject, when it may; and when it may not, it exemplifies the same.*

15. The properties of a definition are:

First, that it takes away equivocation, as also all that multitude of distinctions, which are used by such as think they may learn philosophy by disputation. For the nature of a definition is to define, that is, to determine the signification of the defined name, and to pare from it all other signification besides what is contained in the definition itself; and therefore one definition does as much, as all the distinctions (how many soever) that can be used about the name defined.

Secondly, that it gives an universal notion of the thing defined, representing a certain universal picture thereof, not to the eye, but to the mind. For as when one paints a man, he paints the image of some man; so he, that defines the name man, makes a representation of some man to the mind.

Thirdly, that it is not necessary to dispute whether definitions are to be admitted or no. For when a master is instructing his scholar, if the scholar understand all the parts of the thing defined, which are resolved in the definition, and yet will not admit of the definition, there needs no further controversy betwixt them, it being all one as if he refused to be taught. But if he understand nothing, then certainly the definition is faulty; for the nature of a definition consists in this, that it exhibit a clear idea of the thing defined; and principles are either known by themselves, or else they are not principles.

Fourthly, that, in philosophy, definitions are before defined names. For in teaching philosophy, the first beginning is from definitions; and all progression in the same, till we come to the knowledge of the thing compounded, is compositive. Seeing, therefore, definition is the explication of a compounded name by resolution, and the progression is from the parts to the compound, definitions must be understood before compounded names; nay, when the names of the parts of any speech be explicated, it is not necessary that the definition should be a name compounded of them. For example, when these names, *equilateral, quadrilateral, right-angled,* are sufficiently understood, it is not necessary in geometry that there should be at all such a name as *square;* for defined names are received in philosophy for brevity's sake only.

Fifthly, that compounded names, which are defined one way in some one part of philosophy, may in another part of the same be otherwise defined; as a *parabola* and an *hyperbole* have one definition in geometry, and another in rhetoric; for definitions are instituted and serve for the understanding of the doctrine which is treated of. And, therefore, as in one part of philosophy, a definition may have in it some one fit name for the more brief explanation of some proposition in geometry; so it may have the same liberty in other parts of philosophy; for the use of names is particular (even where many agree to the settling of them) and arbitrary.

Sixthly, that no name can be defined by any one word; because no one word is sufficient for the resolving of one or more words.

Seventhly, that a defined name ought not to be repeated in the definition. For a defined name is the whole compound, and a definition is the resolution of that compound into parts; but no total can be part of itself.

16. Any two definitions, that may be compounded into a syllogism, produce a conclusion; which, because it is derived from principles, that is, from definitions, is said to be demonstrated; and the derivation or composition itself is called a demonstration. In like manner, if a syllogism be made of two propositions, whereof one is a definition, the other a demonstrated conclusion, or neither of them is a definition, but both formerly demonstrated, that syllogism is also called a demonstration, and so successively. The definition therefore of a demonstration is this, *a demonstration is a syllogism, or series of syllogisms, derived and continued from the definitions of names, to the last conclusion.* And from hence it may be understood, that all true ratiocination, which taketh its beginning from true principles, produceth science, and is true demonstration. For as for the original of the name, although that, which the Greeks called ἀπόδειξις, and the Latins *demonstratio,* was understood by them for that sort only of ratiocination, in which, by the describing of certain lines and figures, they placed the thing they were to prove, as it were before men's eyes, which is properly ἀποδεικνύειν, or to *shew* by the figure; yet they seem to have done it for this reason, that unless it were in geometry, (in which only there is place for such figures) there was no ratiocination certain, and ending in science, their doctrines concerning all other things being nothing but controversy and clamour; which, nevertheless, happened, not because the truth to which they pretended could not be made evident without figures, but because they wanted true principles, from which they might derive their ratiocination; and, therefore, there is no reason but that if true definitions were premised in all sorts of doctrines, the demonstrations also would be true.

17. It is proper to methodical demonstration,

First, that there be a true succession of one reason to another, according to the rules of syllogizing delivered above.

Secondly, that the premises of all syllogisms be demonstrated from the first definitions.

Thirdly, that after definitions, he that teaches or demonstrates any thing, proceed in the same method by which he found it out; namely, that in the first place those things be demonstrated, which immediately succeed to universal definitions (in which is contained that part of philosophy which is called *philosophia prima*). Next, those things which may be demonstrated by simple motion (in which geometry consists). After geometry, such things as may be taught or shewed by manifest action, that is, by thrusting from, or pulling towards. And after these, the motion or mutation of the invisible parts of things, and the doctrine of sense and imaginations, and of the internal passions, especially those of men, in which are comprehended the grounds of civil duties, or civil philosophy; which takes up the last place. And that this method ought to be kept in all sorts of philosophy, is evident from hence, that such things as I have said are to be taught last, cannot be demonstrated, till such as are propounded to be first treated of, be fully understood. Of which method no other example can be given, but that treatise of the elements of philosophy, which I shall begin in the next chapter, and continue to the end of the work.

18. Besides those *paralogisms,* whose fault lies either in the falsity of the premises, or the want of true composition, of which I have spoken in the precedent chapter, there are two more, which are frequent in demonstration; one whereof is commonly called *petitio principii;* the other is the supposing of a *false cause;* and these do not only deceive unskilful learners, but sometimes masters themselves, by making them take that for well demonstrated, which is not demonstrated at all. *Petitio principii* is, when the conclusion to be proved is disguised in other words, and put for the definition or principle from whence it is to be demonstrated; and thus, by putting for the cause of the thing sought, either the thing itself or some effect of it, they make a circle in their demonstration. As for example, he that would demonstrate that the earth stands still in the centre of the world, and should suppose the earth's gravity to be the cause thereof, and define gravity to be a quality by which every heavy body tends towards the centre of the world, would lose his labour; for the question is, what is the cause of that quality in the earth? and, therefore, he that supposes gravity to be the cause, puts the thing itself for its own cause.

Of a *false cause* I find this example in a certain treatise where the thing to be demonstrated is the motion of the earth. He begins, therefore, with this, that seeing the earth and the sun are not always in the same situation, it must needs be that one of them be locally moved, which is true; next, he affirms that the vapours which the sun raises from the earth and sea, are, by reason of this motion, necessarily moved, which also is true; from whence he infers the winds are made, and this may pass for granted; and by these winds he says, the waters of the sea are moved, and by their motion the bottom of the sea, as if it were beaten forwards, moves round; and let this also be granted; wherefore, he concludes the earth is moved; which is, nevertheless, a paralogism. For, if that wind were the cause why the earth was, from the beginning, moved round, and the motion either of the sun or the earth were the cause of that wind, then the motion of the sun or the earth was before the wind itself; and if the earth were moved, before the wind was made, then the wind would not be the cause of the earth's revolution; but, if the sun were moved, and the earth stand still, then it is manifest the earth might remain unmoved, notwithstanding that wind; and therefore that motion was not made by the cause which he allegeth. But paralogisms of this kind are very frequent among the writers of *physics,* though none can be more elaborate than this in the example given.

19. It may to some men seem pertinent to treat in this place of that art of the geometricians, which they call *logistica,* that is, the art, by which, from supposing the thing in question to be true, they proceed by ratiocination, till either they come to something known, by which they may demonstrate the truth of the thing sought for; or to something which is impossible, from whence they collect that to be false, which they supposed true. But this art cannot be explicated here, for this reason, that the method of it can neither be practised, nor understood, unless by such as are well versed in geometry; and among geometricians themselves, they, that have most theorems in readiness, are the most ready in the use of this *logistica;* so that, indeed, it is not a distinct thing for geometry itself; for there are, in the method of it, three parts; the first whereof consists in the finding out of equality betwixt known and unknown things, which they call equation; and this equation cannot be found out, but by such as know perfectly the nature, properties, and transpositions of proportion, as also the addition, subtraction, multiplication, and division of lines and superficies, and the extraction of roots; which are the parts of no mean geometrician. The second is, when an equation is found, to be able to judge whether the truth or falsity of the question may be deduced from it, or no; which yet requires greater knowledge. And the third is, when such an equation is found, as is fit for the solution of the question, to know how to resolve the same in such manner, that the truth or falsity may thereby manifestly appear; which, in hard questions, cannot be done without the knowledge of the nature of crooked-lined figures; but he that understands readily the nature and properties of these, is a complete geometrician. It happens besides, that for the finding out of equations, there is no certain method, but he is best able to do it, that has the best natural wit.

2 RENÉ DESCARTES
Rules for the Direction of the Mind*

Rule I

   The end of study should be to direct the mind towards the enunciation of sound and correct judgments on all matters that come before it.

   Whenever men notice some similarity between two things, they are wont to ascribe to each, even in those respects in which the two differ, what they have found to be true of the other. Thus they erroneously compare the sciences, which entirely consist in the cognitive exercise of the mind, with the arts, which depend upon an exercise and disposition of the body. They see that not all the arts can be acquired by the same man, but that he who restricts himself to one, most readily becomes the best executant, since it is not so easy for the same hand to adapt itself both to agricultural operations and to harp-playing, or to the performance of several such tasks as to one alone. Hence they have held the same to be true of the sciences also, and distinguishing them from one another according to their subject matter, they have imagined that they ought to be studied separately, each in isolation from all the rest. But this is certainly wrong. For since the sciences taken all together are identical with human wisdom, which always remains one and the same, however applied to different subjects, and suffers no more differentiation proceeding from them than the light of the sun experiences from the variety of the things which it illumines, there is no need for minds to be confined at all within limits; for neither does the knowing of one truth have an effect like that of the acquisition of one art and prevent us from finding out another, it rather aids us to do so. Certainly it appears to me strange that so many people should investigate human customs with such care, the virtues of plants, the motions of the stars, the transmutations of metals, and the objects of similar sciences, while at the same time practically none bethink themselves about good understanding, or universal Wisdom, though nevertheless all other studies are to be esteemed not so much for their own value as because they contribute something to this. Consequently we are justified in bringing forward this as the first rule of all, since there is nothing more prone to turn us aside from the correct way of seeking out truth than this directing of our inquiries, not towards their general end, but towards certain special investigations. I do not here refer to

* From *The Philosophical Works of Descartes*, Vol. I, translated by E. S. Haldane and G. R. T. Ross, Cambridge University Press, London, 1931. Unless otherwise indicated, throughout the present volume notes are given as they appear in the Haldane and Ross translation. The *Regulae ad Directionem Ingenii* probably was composed in its present unfinished form about 1628. First published posthumously in 1701. Reprinted by permission of Cambridge University Press.

perverse and censurable pursuits like empty glory or base gain; obviously counterfeit reasonings and quibbles suited to vulgar understanding open up a much more direct route to such a goal than does a sound apprehension of the truth. But I have in view even honourable and laudable pursuits, because these mislead us in a more subtle fashion. For example take our investigations of those sciences conducive to the conveniences of life or which yield that pleasure which is found in the contemplation of truth, practically the only joy in life that is complete and untroubled with any pain. There we may indeed expect to receive the legitimate fruits of scientific inquiry; but if, in the course of our study, we think of them, they frequently cause us to omit many facts which are necessary to the understanding of other matters, because they seem to be either of slight value or of little interest. Hence we must believe that all the sciences are so inter-connected, that it is much easier to study them all to-gether than to isolate one from all the others. If, therefore, anyone wishes to search out the truth of things in serious earnest, he ought not to select one spe-cial science; for all the sciences are conjoined with each other and interde-pendent: he ought rather to think how to increase the natural light of reason, not for the purpose of resolving this or that difficulty of scholastic type *(scho-lae),* but in order that his understanding may light his will to its proper choice in all the contingencies of life. In a short time he will see with amazement that he has made much more progress than those who are eager about particular ends, and that he has not only obtained all that they desire, but even higher results than fall within his expectation . . .

Rule IV

There is need of a method for finding out the truth.

So blind is the curiosity by which mortals are possessed, that they often conduct their minds along unexplored routes, having no reason to hope for success, but merely being willing to risk the experiment of finding whether the truth they seek lies there. As well might a man burning with an unintelligent desire to find treasure, continuously roam the streets, seeking to find some-thing that a passer by might have chanced to drop. This is the way in which most Chemists, many Geometricians, and Philosophers not a few prosecute their studies. I do not deny that sometimes in these wanderings they are lucky enough to find something true. But I do not allow that this argues greater in-dustry on their part, but only better luck. But however that may be, it were far better never to think of investigating truth at all, than to do so without a method. For it is very certain that unregulated inquiries and confused reflec-tions of this kind only confound the natural light and blind our mental pow-ers. Those who so become accustomed to walk in darkness weaken their eye-sight so much that afterwards they cannot bear the light of day. This is confirmed by experience; for how often do we not see that those who have never taken to letters, give a sounder and clearer decision about obvious mat-ters than those who have spent all their time in the schools? Moreover by a method I mean certain and simple rules, such that, if a man observe them accurately, he shall never assume what is false as true, and will never spend his mental efforts to no purpose, but will always gradually increase his knowledge and so arrive at a true understanding of all that does not surpass his powers.

These two points must be carefully noted, viz. never to assume what is false as true, and to arrive at a knowledge which takes in all things. For, if we are without the knowledge of any of the things which we are capable of understanding, that is only because we have never perceived any way to bring us to this knowledge, or because we have fallen into the contrary error. But if our method rightly explains how our mental vision should be used, so as not to fall into the contrary error, and how deduction should be discovered in order that we may arrive at the knowledge of all things, I do not see what else is needed to make it complete; for I have already said that no science is acquired except by mental intuition or deduction. There is besides no question of extending it further in order to show how these said operations ought to be effected, because they are the most simple and primary of all. Consequently, unless our understanding were already able to employ them, it could comprehend none of the precepts of that very method, not even the simplest. But as for the other mental operations, which Dialectic does its best to direct by making use of these prior ones, they are quite useless here; rather they are to be accounted impediments, because nothing can be added to the pure light of reason which does not in some way obscure it.

Since then the usefulness of this method is so great that without it study seems to be harmful rather than profitable, I am quite ready to believe that the greater minds of former ages had some knowledge of it, nature even conducting them to it. For the human mind has in it something that we may call divine, wherein are scattered the first germs of useful modes of thought. Consequently it often happens that however much neglected and choked by interfering studies they bear fruit of their own accord. Arithmetic and Geometry, the simplest sciences, give us an instance of this; for we have sufficient evidence that the ancient Geometricians made use of a certain analysis which they extended to the resolution of all problems, though they grudged the secret to posterity. At the present day also there flourishes a certain kind of Arithmetic, called Algebra, which designs to effect, when dealing with numbers, what the ancients achieved in the matter of figures. These two methods are nothing else than the spontaneous fruit sprung from the inborn principles of the discipline here in question; and I do not wonder that these sciences with their very simple subject matter (*objecta*) should have yielded results so much more satisfactory than others in which greater obstructions choke all growth. But even in the latter case, if only we take care to cultivate them assiduously, fruits will certainly be able to come to full maturity.

This is the chief result which I have had in view in writing this treatise. For I should not think much of these rules, if they had no utility save for the solution of the empty problems with which Logicians and Geometers have been wont to beguile their leisure; my only achievement thus would have seemed to be an ability to argue about trifles more subtly than others. Further, though much mention is here made of numbers and figures, because no other sciences furnish us with illustrations of such self-evidence and certainty, the reader who follows my drift with sufficient attention will easily see that nothing is less in my mind than ordinary Mathematics, and that I am expounding quite another science, of which these illustrations are rather the outer husk than the constituents. Such a science should contain the primary rudiments of human reason, and its province ought to extend to the eliciting of true results in every subject. To speak freely, I am convinced that it is a more powerful instrument of knowledge than any other that has been bequeathed to us by human agency, as being the source of all others. But as for the outer covering I mentioned, I mean not to employ it to cover up and conceal my method for the purpose of warding off the vulgar; rather I hope so to clothe and embellish it that I may make it more suitable for presentation to the human mind.

When first I applied my mind to Mathematics I read straight away most of what is usually given by the mathematical writers, and I paid special attention to Arithmetic and Geometry, because they were said to be the simplest and so to speak the way to all the rest. But in neither case did I then meet with authors who fully satisfied me. I did indeed learn in their works many propositions about numbers which I found on calculation to be true. As to figures, they in a sense exhibited to my eyes a great number of truths and drew conclusions from certain consequences. But they did not seem to make it sufficiently plain to the mind itself why those things are so, and how they discovered them. Consequently I was not surprised that many people, even of talent and scholarship, should, after glancing at these sciences, have either given them up as being empty and childish or, taking them to be very difficult and intricate, been deterred at the very outset from learning them. For really there is nothing more futile than to busy one's self with bare numbers and imaginary figures in such a way as to appear to rest content with such trifles, and so to resort to those superficial demonstrations, which are discovered more frequently by chance than by skill, and are a matter more of the eyes and the imagination than of the understanding, that in a sense one ceases to make use of one's reason. I might add that there is no more intricate task than that of solving by this method of proof new difficulties that arise, involved as they are with numerical confusions. But when I afterwards bethought myself how it could be that the earliest pioneers of Philosophy in bygone ages refused to admit to the study of wisdom any one who was not versed in Mathematics, evidently believing that this was the easiest and most indispensable mental exercise and preparation for laying hold of other more important sciences, I was confirmed in my suspicion that they had knowledge of a species of Mathematics very different from that which passes current in our time. I do not indeed imagine that they had a perfect knowledge of it, for they plainly show how little advanced they were by the insensate rejoicings they display and the pompous thanksgivings (*sacrificia*) they offer for the most trifling discoveries. I am not shaken in my opinion by the fact that historians make a great deal of certain

machines of theirs. Possibly these machines were quite simple, and yet the ignorant and wonder-loving multitude might easily have lauded them as miraculous. But I am convinced that certain primary germs of truth implanted by
nature in human minds—though in our case the daily reading and hearing of
innumerable diverse errors stifle them—had a very great vitality in that rude
and unsophisticated age of the ancient world. Thus the same mental illumination which let them see that virtue was to be preferred to pleasure, and honour
to utility, although they knew not why this was so, made them recognize true
notions in Philosophy and Mathematics, although they were not yet able thoroughly to grasp these sciences. Indeed I seem to recognize certain traces of this
true Mathematics in Pappus and Diophantus, who though not belonging to
the earliest age, yet lived many centuries before our own times. But my opinion is that these writers then with a sort of low cunning, deplorable indeed,
suppressed this knowledge. Possibly they acted just as many inventors are
known to have done in the case of their discoveries, i.e. they feared that their
method being so easy and simple would become cheapened on being divulged,
and they preferred to exhibit in its place certain barren truths, deductively
demonstrated with show enough of ingenuity, as the results of their art, in
order to win from us our admiration for these achievements, rather than to
disclose to us that method itself which would have wholly annulled the admiration accorded. Finally there have been certain men of talent who in the
present age have tried to revive this same art. For it seems to be precisely that
science known by the barbarous name Algebra, if only we could extricate it
from that vast array of numbers and inexplicable figures by which it is over-
whelmed, so that it might display the clearness and simplicity which, we
imagine, ought to exist in a genuine Mathematics. It was these reflections that
recalled me from the particular studies of Arithmetic and Geometry to a general investigation of Mathematics, and thereupon I sought to determine what
precisely was universally meant by that term, and why not only the above
mentioned sciences, but also Astronomy, Music, Optics, Mechanics and several others are styled parts of Mathematics. Here indeed it is not enough to
look to the origin of the word; for since the name 'Mathematics' means exactly
the same thing as 'scientific study' (disciplina), these other branches could, with
as much right as Geometry itself, be called Mathematics. Yet we see that almost anyone who has had the slightest schooling, can easily distinguish what
relates to Mathematics in any question from that which belongs to the other
sciences. But as I considered the matter carefully it gradually came to light
that all those matters only were referred to Mathematics in which order and
measurement are investigated, and that it makes no difference whether it be
in numbers, figures, stars, sounds or any other object that the question of
measurement arises. I saw consequently that there must be some general science to explain that element as a whole which gives rise to problems about
order and measurement, restricted as these are to no special subject matter.
This, I perceived, was called 'Universal Mathematics', not a far fetched designation, but one of long standing which has passed into current use, because in

this science is contained everything on account of which the others are called parts of Mathematics. We can see how much it excels in utility and simplicity the sciences subordinate to it, by the fact that it can deal with all the objects of which they have cognizance and many more besides, and that any difficulties it contains are found in them as well, added to the fact that in them fresh difficulties arise due to their special subject matter which in it do not exist. But now how comes it that though everyone knows the name of this science and understands what is its province even without studying it attentively, so many people laboriously pursue the other dependent sciences, and no one cares to master this one? I should marvel indeed were I not aware that everyone thinks it to be so very easy, and had I not long since observed that the human mind passes over what it thinks it can easily accomplish, and hastens straight away to new and more imposing occupations.

I, however, conscious as I am of my inadequacy, have resolved that in my investigation into truth I shall follow obstinately such an order as will require me first to start with what is simplest and easiest, and never permit me to proceed farther until in the first sphere there seems to be nothing further to be done. This is why up to the present time to the best of my ability I have made a study of this universal Mathematics; consequently I believe that when I go on to deal in their turn with more profound sciences, as I hope to do soon, my efforts will not be premature. But before I make this transition I shall try to bring together and arrange in an orderly manner, the facts which in my previous studies I have noted as being more worthy of attention. Thus I hope both that at a future date, when through advancing years my memory is enfeebled, I shall, if need be, conveniently be able to recall them by looking in this little book, and that having now disburdened my memory of them I may be free to concentrate my mind on my future studies . . .

Rule V

Method consists entirely in the order and disposition of the objects towards which our mental vision must be directed if we would find out any truth. We shall comply with it exactly if we reduce involved and obscure propositions step by step to those that are simpler, and then starting with the intuitive apprehension of all those that are absolutely simple, attempt to ascend to the knowledge of all others by precisely similar steps.

In this alone lies the sum of all human endeavour, and he who would approach the investigation of truth must hold to this rule as closely as he who enters the labyrinth must follow the thread which guided Theseus. But many people either do not reflect on the precept at all, or ignore it altogether, or presume not to need it. Consequently they often investigate the most difficult questions with so little regard to order, that, to my mind, they act like a man who should attempt to leap with one bound from the base to the summit of a house, either making no account of the ladders provided for his ascent or not noticing them. It is thus that all Astrologers behave, who, though in ignorance of the nature of the heavens, and even without having made proper observations of the movements of the heavenly bodies, expect to be able to indicate their effects. This is also what many do who study Mechanics apart from Physics, and rashly set about devising new instruments for producing motion. Along with them go also those Philosophers who, neglecting experience, imagine that truth will spring from their brain like Pallas *(Minerva)* from the head of Zeus *(Jovis)*.

Now it is obvious that all such people violate the present rule. But since the order here required is often so obscure and intricate that not everyone can make it out, they can scarcely avoid error unless they diligently observe what is laid down in the following proposition.

Rule VI

In order to separate out what is quite simple from what is complex, and to arrange these matters methodically, we ought, in the case of every series in which we have deduced certain facts the one from the other, to notice which fact is simple, and to mark the interval, greater, less, or equal, which separates all the others from this.

Although this proposition seems to teach nothing very new, it contains, nevertheless, the chief secret of method, and none in the whole of this treatise is of greater utility. For it tells us that all facts can be arranged in certain series, not indeed in the sense of being referred to some ontological genus such as the categories employed by Philosophers in their classification, but in so far as certain truths can be known from others; and thus, whenever a difficulty occurs we are able at once to perceive whether it will be profitable to examine certain others first, and which, and in what order.

Further, in order to do that correctly, we must note first that for the purpose of our procedure, which does not regard things as isolated realities *(naturas)*, but compares them with one another in order to discover the dependence in knowledge of one upon the other, all things can be said to be either absolute or relative.

I call that absolute which contains within itself the pure and simple essence of which we are in quest. Thus the term will be applicable to whatever is considered as being independent, or a cause, or simple, universal, one, equal, like, straight, and so forth; and the absolute I call the simplest and the easiest of all, so that we can make use of it in the solution of questions.

But the relative is that which, while participating in the same nature, or at least sharing in it to some degree which enables us to relate it to the absolute and to deduce it from that by a chain of operations, involves in addition something else in its concept which I call relativity *(respectus)*. Examples of this are found in whatever is said to be dependent, or an effect, composite, particular, many, unequal, unlike, oblique, etc. These relatives are the further removed from the absolute, in proportion as they contain more elements of relativity subordinate the one to the other. We state in this rule that these should all be distinguished and their correlative connection and natural order so observed, that we may be able by traversing all the intermediate steps to proceed from the most remote to that which is in the highest degree absolute.

Herein lies the secret of this whole method, that in all things we should diligently mark that which is most absolute. For some things are from one point of view more absolute than others, but from a different standpoint are more relative. Thus though the universal is more absolute than the particular because its essence is simpler, yet it can be held to be more relative than the latter, because it depends upon individuals for its existence, and so on. Certain things likewise are truly more absolute than others, but yet are not the most absolute of all. Thus relatively to individuals, species is something absolute, but contrasted with genus it is relative. So too, among things that can be measured, extension is something absolute, but among the various aspects of extension (*extensiones*) it is length that is absolute, and so on. Finally also, in order to bring out more clearly that we are considering here not the nature of each thing taken in isolation, but the series involved in knowing them, we have purposely enumerated cause and equality among our absolutes, though the nature of these terms is really relative. For though Philosophers make cause and effect correlative, we find that here even, if we ask what the effect is, we must first know the cause and not conversely. Equals too mutually imply one another, but we can know unequals only by comparing them with equals and not *per contra*.

Secondly we must note that there are but few pure and simple essences (*naturas*), which either our experiences or some sort of light innate in us enable us to behold as primary and existing *per se*, not as depending on any others. These we say should be carefully noticed, for they are just those facts which we have called the simplest in any single series. All the others can only be perceived as deductions from these either immediate and proximate, or not to be attained save by two or three or more acts of inference. The number of these acts should be noted in order that we may perceive whether the facts are separated from the primary and simplest proposition by a greater or smaller number of steps. And so pronounced is everywhere the inter-connection of ground and consequence, which gives rise, in the objects to be examined, to those series to which every inquiry must be reduced, that it can be investigated by a sure method. But because it is not easy to make a review of them all, and besides, since they have not so much to be kept in the memory as to be detected by a sort of mental penetration, we must seek for something which will so mould our intelligence as to let it perceive these connected sequences immediately whenever it needs to do so. For this purpose I have found nothing so effectual as to accustom ourselves to turn our attention with a sort of penetrative insight (*cum quadam sagacitate*) on the very minutest of the facts which we have already discovered.

Finally we must in the third place note that our inquiry ought not to start with the investigation of difficult matters. Rather, before setting out to attack any definite problem, it behoves us first, without making any selection, to assemble those truths that are obvious as they present themselves to us, and afterwards, proceeding step by step, to inquire whether any others can be deduced from these, and again any others from these conclusions and so on, in order. This done, we should attentively think over the truths we have discovered and mark with diligence the reasons why we have been able to detect some more easily than others, and which these are. Thus, when we come to attack some definite problem we shall be able to judge what previous questions it were best to settle first. For example, if it comes into my thought that the number 6 is twice 3, I may then ask what is twice 6, viz. 12; again, perhaps I seek for the double of this, viz. 24, and again of this, viz. 48. Thus I may easily deduce that there is the same proportion between 3 and 6, as between 6 and 12, and likewise 12 and 24, and so on, and hence that the numbers 3, 6, 12, 24, 48, etc. are in continued proportion. But though these facts are all so clear as to seem almost childish, I am now able by attentive reflection to understand what is the form involved by all questions that can be propounded about the proportions or relations *(habitudines)* of things, and the order in which they should be investigated; and this discovery embraces the sum of the entire science of Pure Mathematics.

For first I perceive that it was not more difficult to discover the double of six than that of three; and that equally in all cases, when we have found a proportion between any two magnitudes, we can find innumerable others which have the same proportion between them. So too there is no increase of difficulty, if three, or four, or more of such magnitudes are sought for, because each has to be found separately and without any relation to the others. But next I notice that though, when the magnitudes 3 and 6 are given, one can easily find a third in continued proportion, viz. 12, it is yet not equally easy, when the two extremes, 3 and 12, are given, to find the mean proportional, viz. 6. When we look into the reason for this, it is clear that here we have a type of difficulty quite different from the former; for, in order to find the mean proportional, we must at the same time attend to the two extremes and to the proportion which exists between these two in order to discover a new ratio by dividing the previous one; and this is a very different thing from finding a third term in continued proportion with two given numbers. I go forward likewise and examine whether, when the numbers 3 and 24 were given, it would have been equally easy to determine one of the two intermediate proportionals, viz. 6 and 12. But here still another sort of difficulty arises more involved than the previous ones, for on this occasion we have to attend not to one or two things only but to three, in order to discover the fourth. We may go still further and inquire whether if only 3 and 48 had been given it would have been still more difficult to discover one of the three mean proportionals, viz. 6, 12, and 24. At the first blush this indeed appears to be so; but immediately afterwards it comes to mind that this difficulty can be split up and lessened, if first of all we ask only for the mean proportional between 3 and 48, viz. 12, and then seek for the other mean proportional between 3 and 12, viz. 6, and the other between 12 and 48, viz. 24. Thus we have reduced the problem to the difficulty of the second type shown above.

These illustrations further lead me to note that the quest for knowledge about the same thing can traverse different routes, the one much more difficult and obscure than the other. Thus to find these four continued proportionals, 3, 6, 12, and 24, if two consecutive numbers be assumed, e.g. 3 and 6, or 6 and 12, or 12 and 24, in order that we may discover the others, our task will be easy. In this case we shall say that the proposition to be discovered is directly examined. But if the two numbers given are alternates, like 3 and 12, or 6 and 24, which are to lead us to the discovery of the others, then we shall call this an indirect investigation of the first mode. Likewise if we are given two extremes like 3 and 24, in order to find out from these the intermediates 6 and 12, the investigation will be indirect and of the second mode. Thus I should be able to proceed further and deduce many other results from this example; but these will be sufficient, if the reader follows my meaning when I say that a proposition is directly deduced, or indirectly, and will reflect that from a knowledge of each of these matters that are simplest and primary, much may be discovered in other sciences by those who bring to them attentive thought and a power of sagacious analysis.

Rule VII

If we wish our science to be complete, those matters which promote the end we have in view must one and all be scrutinized by a movement of thought which is continuous and nowhere interrupted; they must also be included in an enumeration which is both adequate and methodical.

It is necessary to obey the injunctions of this rule if we hope to gain admission among the certain truths for those which, we have declared above, are not immediate deductions from primary and self-evident principles. For this deduction frequently involves such a long series of transitions from ground to consequent that when we come to the conclusion we have difficulty in recalling the whole of the route by which we have arrived at it. This is why I say that there must be a continuous movement of thought to make good this weakness of the memory. Thus, e.g. if I have first found out by separate mental operations what the relation is between the magnitudes A and B, then what between B and C, between C and D, and finally between D and E, that does not entail my seeing what the relation is between A and E, nor can the truths previously learnt give me a precise knowledge of it unless I recall them all. To remedy this I would run them over from time to time, keeping the imagination moving continuously in such a way that while it is intuitively perceiving each fact it simultaneously passes on to the next; and this I would do until I had learned to pass from the first to the last so quickly, that no stage in the process was left to the care of the memory, but I seemed to have the whole in intuition before me at the same time. This method will both relieve the memory, diminish the sluggishness of our thinking, and definitely enlarge our mental capacity.

But we must add that this movement should nowhere be interrupted. Often people who attempt to deduce a conclusion too quickly and from remote principles do not trace the whole chain of intermediate conclusions with sufficient accuracy to prevent them from passing over many steps without due consideration. But it is certain that wherever the smallest link is left out the chain is broken and the whole of the certainty of the conclusion falls to the ground.

Here we maintain that an enumeration [of the steps in a proof] is required as well, if we wish to make our science complete. For resolving most problems other precepts are profitable, but enumeration alone will secure our always passing a true and certain judgment on whatsoever engages our attention; by means of it nothing at all will escape us, but we shall evidently have some knowledge of every step.

This enumeration or induction is thus a review or inventory of all those matters that have a bearing on the problem raised, which is so thorough and accurate that by its means we can clearly and with confidence conclude that we have omitted nothing by mistake. Consequently as often as we have employed it, if the problem defies us, we shall at least be wiser in this respect, viz. that we are quite certain that we know of no way of resolving it. If it chance, as often it does, that we have been able to scan all the routes leading to it which lie open to the human intelligence, we shall be entitled boldly to assert that the solution of the problem lies outside the reach of human knowledge.

Furthermore we must note that by adequate enumeration or induction is only meant that method by which we may attain surer conclusions than by any other type of proof, with the exception of simple intuition. But when the knowledge of some matter cannot be reduced to this, we must cast aside all syllogistic fetters and employ induction, the only method left us, but one in which all confidence should be reposed. For whenever single facts have been immediately deduced the one from the other, they have been already reduced, if the inference was evident, to a true intuition. But if we infer any single thing from various and disconnected facts, often our intellectual capacity is not so great as to be able to embrace them all in a single intuition; in which case our mind should be content with the certitude attaching to this operation. It is in precisely similar fashion that though we cannot with one single gaze distinguish all the links of a lengthy chain, yet if we have seen the connection of each with its neighbour, we shall be entitled to say that we have seen how the first is connected with the last.

I have declared that this operation ought to be adequate, because it is often in danger of being defective and consequently exposed to error. For sometimes, even though in our enumeration we scrutinize many facts which are highly evident, yet if we omit the smallest step the chain is broken and the whole of the certitude of the conclusion falls to the ground. Sometimes also, even though all the facts are included in an accurate enumeration, the single steps are not distinguished from one another, and our knowledge of them all is thus only confused.

Further, while now the enumeration ought to be complete, now distinct, there are times when it need have neither of these characters; it was for this reason that I said only that it should be adequate. For if I want to prove by enumeration how many genera there are of corporeal things, or of those that in any way fall under the senses, I shall not assert that they are just so many and no more, unless I previously have become aware that I have included them all in my enumeration, and have distinguished them each separately from all the others. But if in the same way I wish to prove that the rational soul is not corporeal, I do not need a complete enumeration; it will be sufficient to include all bodies in certain collections in such a way as to be able to demonstrate that the rational soul has nothing to do with any of these. If, finally, I wish to show by enumeration that the area of a circle is greater than the area of all other figures whose perimeter is equal, there is no need for me to call in review all other figures; it is enough to demonstrate this of certain others in particular, in order to get thence by induction[1] the same conclusion about all the others.

I added also that the enumeration ought to be methodical. This is both because we have no more serviceable remedy for the defects already instanced, than to scan all things in an orderly manner; and also because it often happens that if each single matter which concerns the quest in hand were to be investigated separately, no man's life would be long enough for the purpose, whether because they are far too many, or because it would chance that the same things had to be repeated too often. But if all these facts are arranged in the best order, they will for the most part be reduced to determinate classes, out of which it will be sufficient to take one example for exact inspection, or some one feature in a single case, or certain things rather than others, or at least we shall never have to waste our time in traversing the same ground twice. The advantage of this course is so great that often many particulars can, owing to a well devised arrangement, be gone over in a short space of time and with little trouble, though at first view the matter looked immense.

But this order which we employ in our enumerations can for the most part be varied and depends upon each man's judgment. For this reason, if we would elaborate it in our thought with greater penetration, we must remember what was said in our fifth proposition.[2] There are also many of the trivial things of man's devising, in the discovery of which the whole method lies in the disposal of this order. Thus if you wish to construct a perfect anagram by the transposition of the letters of a name, there is no need to pass from the easy to the difficult, nor to distinguish absolute from relative. Here there is no place for these operations; it will be sufficient to adopt an order to be followed in the

---

[1] This seems to be a different sense of the word 'inductio' from that above.—
    Tr.

[2] [*Cf.* p. 39.—*Ed.*]

transpositions of the letters which we are to examine, such that the same ar-
rangements are never handled twice over. The total number of transpositions
should, e.g. be split up into definite classes, so that it may immediately appear
in which there is the best hope of finding what is sought. In this way the task is
often not tedious but merely child's play.

However, these three propositions[1] should not be separated, because for
the most part we have to think of them together, and all equally tend towards
the perfecting of our method. There was no great reason for treating one before the other, and we have expounded them but briefly here. The reason for
this is that in the rest of the treatise we have practically nothing else left for
consideration. Therefore we shall then exhibit in detail what here we have
brought together in a general way.

Rule VIII

*If in the matters to be examined we come to a step in the series of which our under-
standing is not sufficiently well able to have an intuitive cognition, we must stop short there.
We must make no attempt to examine what follows; thus we shall spare ourselves superfluous labour.*

The three preceding rules prescribe and explain the order to be followed.
The present rule, on the other hand, shows when it is wholly necessary and
when it is merely useful. Thus it is necessary to examine whatever constitutes a
single step in that series, by which we pass from relative to absolute, or conversely, before discussing what follows from it. But if, as often happens, many
things pertain to the same step, though it is indeed always profitable to review
them in order, in this case we are not forced to apply our method of observation so strictly and rigidly. Frequently it is permissible to proceed farther, even
though we have not clear knowledge of all the facts it involves, but know only
a few or a single one of them.

This rule is a necessary consequence of the reasons brought forward in
support of the second.[2] But it must not be thought that the present rule contributes nothing fresh towards the advancement of learning, though it seems
only to bid us refrain from further discussion, and apparently does not unfold
any truth. For beginners, indeed, it has no further value than to teach them
how not to waste time, and it employs nearly the same arguments in doing so
as Rule II. But it shows those who have perfectly mastered the seven preceding maxims, how in the pursuit of any science so to satisfy themselves as not to
desire anything further. For the man who faithfully complies with the former
rules in the solution of any difficulty, and yet by the present rule is bidden de-
sist at a certain point, will then know for certainty that no amount of applica-

---

[1] [*i.e.,* Rules V, VI, and VII. — *Ed.*]

[2] [Omitted from this collection. Rule II reads: "Only those objects should en-
    gage our attention, to the sure and indubitable knowledge of which our
    mental powers seem to be adequate."—*Ed.*]

tion will enable him to attain to the knowledge desired, and that not owing to a defect in his intelligence, but because the nature of the problem itself, or the fact that he is human, prevents him. But this knowledge is not the less science than that which reveals the nature of the thing itself; in fact he would seem to have some mental defect who should extend his curiosity farther.

But what we have been saying must be illustrated by one or two examples. If, for example, one who studies only Mathematics were to seek to find that curve which in dioptrics is called the anaclastic, that from which parallel rays are so refracted that after the refraction they all meet in one point,—it will be easy to see, by applying Rules V and VI, that the determination of this line depends upon the relation which the angles of refraction bear to the angles of incidence. But because he is unable to discover this, since it is a matter not of Mathematics but of Physics, he is here forced to pause at the threshold. Nor will it avail him to try and learn this from the Philosophers or to gather it from experience; for this would be to break Rule III.[1] Furthermore this proposition is both composite and relative; but in the proper place we shall show that experience is unambiguous only when dealing with the wholly simple and absolute. Again, it will be vain for him to assume some relation or other as being that which prevails between such angles, and conjecture that this is the truest to fact; for in that case he would be on the track not of the anaclastic, but merely of that curve which could be deduced from his assumption.

If however, a man who does not confine his studies to Mathematics, but, in accordance with the first rule, tries to discover the truth on all points, meets with the same difficulty, he will find in addition that this ratio between the angles of incidence and of refraction depends upon changes in their relation produced by varying the medium. Again these changes depend upon the manner in which the ray of light traverses the whole transparent body; while the knowledge of the way in which the light thus passes through presupposes a knowledge of the nature of the action of light, to understand which finally we must know what a natural potency is in general, this last being the most absolute term in the whole series in question. When, therefore, by a mental intuition he has clearly comprehended the nature of this, he will, in compliance with Rule V, proceed backwards by the same steps. And if when he comes to the second step he is unable straightway to determine the nature of light, he will, in accordance with the seventh rule, enumerate all the other natural potencies, in order that the knowledge of some other of them may help him, at least by analogy (of which more anon), to understand this. This done, he will ask how the ray traverses the whole of the transparent body, and will so follow out the other points methodically, that at last he will arrive at the anaclastic itself. Though this has long defied the efforts of many inquirers, I see no reason why a man who fully carried out our method should fail to arrive at a convincing knowledge of the matter.

But let us give the most splendid example of all. If a man proposes to

---

[1] [Omitted here—included in Selection 15, *q.v.—Ed.*]

himself the problem of examining all the truths for the knowledge of which
human reason suffices—and I think that this is a task which should be undertaken once at least in his life by every person who seriously endeavours to attain equilibrium *(bonam mentem)* of thought—, he will, by the rules given
above, certainly discover that nothing can be known prior to the understanding, since the knowledge of all things else depends upon this and not conversely. Then, when he has clearly grasped all those things which follow proxi-
mately on the knowledge of the naked understanding, he will enumerate
among other things whatever instruments of thought we have other than the
understanding; and these are only two, viz. imagination and sense. He will
therefore devote all his energies to the distinguishing and examining of these
three modes of cognition, and seeing that in the strict sense truth and falsity
can be a matter of the understanding alone, though often it derives its origin
from the other two faculties, he will attend carefully to every source of deception in order that he may be on his guard. He will also enumerate exactly all
the ways leading to truth which lie open to us, in order that he may follow the
right way. They are not so many that they cannot all be easily discovered and
embraced in an adequate enumeration. And though this will seem marvellous
and incredible to the inexpert, as soon as in each matter he has distinguished
those cognitions which only fill and embellish the memory, from those which
cause one to be deemed really more instructed, which it will be easy for him to
do. . . .[1]; he will feel assured that any absence of further knowledge is not due
to lack of intelligence or of skill, and that nothing at all can be known by anyone else which he is not capable of knowing, provided only that he gives to it
his utmost mental application. And though many problems may present
themselves, from the solution of which this rule prohibits him, yet because he
will clearly perceive that they pass the limits of human intelligence, he will
deem that he is not the more ignorant on that account; rather, if he is reasonable, this very knowledge, that the solution can be discovered by no one, will
abundantly satisfy his curiosity.

But lest we should always be uncertain as to the powers of the mind, and
in order that we may not labour wrongly and at random before we set ourselves to think out things in detail, we ought once in our life to inquire diligently what the thoughts are of which the human mind is capable. In order
the better to attain this end we ought, when two sets of inquiries are equally
simple, to choose the more useful.

This method of ours resembles indeed those devices employed by the mechanical crafts, which do not need the aid of anything outside of them, but
themselves supply the directions for making their own instruments. Thus if a
man wished to practise any one of them, e.g. the craft of a smith, and were
destitute of all instruments, he would be forced to use at first a hard stone or a
rough lump of iron as an anvil, take a piece of rock in place of a hammer,

---

[1] The Amsterdam ed. of 1701 indicates an omission here.—*Tr.*

make pieces of wood serve as tongs, and provide himself with other such tools as necessity required. Thus equipped, he would not then at once attempt to forge swords or helmets or any manufactured articles of iron for others to use. He would first of all fashion hammer, anvil, tongs, and the other tools useful for himself. This example teaches us that, since thus at the outset we have been able to discover only some rough precepts, apparently the innate possession of our mind, rather than the product of technical skill, we should not forthwith attempt to settle the controversies of Philosophers, or solve the puzzles of the Mathematicians, by their help. We must first employ them for searching out with our utmost attention all the other things that are more urgently required in the investigation of truth. And this since there is no reason why it should appear more difficult to discover these than any of the answers which the problems propounded by Geometry or Physics or the other sciences are wont to demand.

Now no more useful inquiry can be proposed than that which seeks to determine the nature and the scope of human knowledge. This is why we state this very problem succinctly in the single question, which we deem should be answered at the very outset with the aid of the rules which we have already laid down. This investigation should be undertaken once at least in his life by anyone who has the slightest regard for truth, since in pursuing it the true instruments of knowledge and the whole method of inquiry come to light. But nothing seems to me more futile than the conduct of those who boldly dispute about the secrets of nature, the influence of the heavens on these lower regions, the predicting of future events and similar matters, as many do, without yet having ever asked even whether human reason is adequate to the solution of these problems. Neither ought it to seem such a toilsome and difficult matter to define the limits of that understanding (ingenii) of which we are directly aware (sentimus) as being within us, when we often have no hesitation in passing judgment even on things that are without us and quite foreign to us. Neither is it such an immense task to attempt to grasp in thought all the objects comprised within this whole of things in order to discover how they singly fall under our mental scrutiny. For nothing can prove to be so complex or so vague as to defeat the efforts of the method of enumeration above described, directed towards restraining it within certain limits or arranging it under certain categories (capita). But to put this to the test in the matter of the question above propounded, we first of all divide the whole problem relative to it into two parts; for it ought either to relate to us who are capable of knowledge, or to the things themselves which can be known: and these two factors we discuss separately.

In ourselves we notice that while it is the understanding alone which is capable of knowing, it yet is either helped or hindered by three other faculties, namely imagination, sense, and memory. We must therefore examine these faculties in order, with a view to finding out where each may prove to be an impediment, so that we may be on our guard; or where it may profit us, so that we may use to the full the resources of these powers. This first part of our problem will accordingly be discussed with the aid of a sufficient enumeration, as will be shown in the succeeding proposition.

We come secondly to the things themselves which must be considered only in so far as they are the objects of the understanding. From this point of view we divide them into the class (1) of those whose nature is of the extremest simplicity and (2) of the complex and composite. Simple natures must be either spiritual or corporeal or at once spiritual and corporeal. Finally among the composites there are some which the understanding realises to be complex before it judges that it can determine anything about them; but there are also others which it itself puts together. All these matters will be expounded at greater length in the twelfth proposition, where it will be shown that there can be no falsity save in the last class—that of the compounds made by the understanding itself. This is why we further subdivide these into the class of those which are deducible from natures which are of the maximum simplicity and are known *per se,* of which we shall treat in the whole of the succeeding book[1]; and into those which presuppose the existence of others which the facts themselves show us to be composite. To the exposition of these we destine the whole of the third[2] book.

But we shall indeed attempt in the whole of this treatise to follow so accurately the paths which conduct men to the knowledge of the truth and to make them so easy, that anyone who has perfectly learned the whole of this method, however moderate may be his talent, may see that no avenue to the truth is closed to him from which everyone else is not also excluded, and that his ignorance is due neither to a deficiency in his capacity nor to his method of procedure. But as often as he applies his mind to the understanding of some matter, he will either be entirely successful, or he will realise that success depends upon a certain experiment which he is unable to perform, and in that case he will not blame his mental capacity although he is compelled to stop short there. Or finally he may show that the knowledge desired wholly exceeds the limits of the human intelligence; and consequently he will believe that he is none the more ignorant on that account. For to have discovered this is knowledge in no less degree than the knowledge of anything else. . . .

Rule XI

If, after we have recognized intuitively a number of simple truths, we wish to draw any inference from them, it is useful to run them over in a continuous and uninterrupted act of thought, to reflect upon their relations to one another, and to grasp together distinctly a number of these propositions so far as is possible at the same time. For this is a way of making our knowledge much more certain, and of greatly increasing the power of the mind.

---

[1] This begins at Prop. XIII. Of the later propositions we have the titles only in the case of XIX–XXI, while the last three are entirely lacking.—*Tr.*

[2] Apparently not even begun.—*Tr.*

Here we have an opportunity of expounding more clearly what has been already said of mental intuition in the third and seventh rules.[1] In one passage we opposed it to deduction, while in the other we distinguished it from enumeration only, which we defined as an inference drawn from many and diverse things.[2] But the simple deduction of one thing from another, we said in the same passage, was effected by intuition.

It was necessary to do this, because two things are requisite for mental intuition. Firstly the proposition intuited must be clear and distinct; secondly it must be grasped in its totality at the same time and not successively. As for deduction, if we are thinking of how the process works, as we were in Rule III, it appears not to occur all at the same time, but involves a sort of movement on the part of our mind when it infers one thing from another. We were justified therefore in distinguishing deduction in that rule from intuition. But if we wish to consider deduction as an accomplished fact, as we did in what we said relatively to the seventh rule, then it no longer designates a movement, but rather the completion of a movement, and therefore we suppose that it is presented to us by intuition when it is simple and clear, but not when it is complex and involved. When this is the case we give it the name of enumeration or induction, because it cannot then be grasped as a whole at the same time by the mind, and its certainty depends to some extent on the memory in which our judgments about the various matters enumerated must be retained, if from their assemblage a single fact is to be inferred.

All these distinctions had to be made if we were to elucidate this rule. We treated of mental intuition solely in Rule IX;[3] the tenth dealt with enumeration alone; but now the present rule explains how these two operations aid and complete each other. In doing so they seem to grow into a single process by virtue of a sort of motion of thought which has an attentive and vision-like knowledge of one fact and yet can pass at the very same moment to another.

Now to this co-operation we assign a two-fold advantage. Firstly it promotes a more certain knowledge of the conclusion with which we are concerned, and secondly it makes the mind readier to discover fresh truths. In fact the memory, on which we have said depends the certainty of the conclusions which embrace more than we can grasp in a single act of intuition, though weak and liable to fail us, can be renewed and made stronger by this continuous and constantly repeated process of thought. Thus if diverse mental acts have led me to know what is the relation between a first and a second magnitude, next between the second and a third, then between the third and a fourth, and finally the fourth and a fifth, that need not lead me to see what is the relation between the first and the fifth, nor can I deduce it from what I already know, unless I remember all the other relations. Hence what I have to do is to run over them all repeatedly in my mind, until I pass so quickly from

---

[1] [Rule III is included in Selection 15. *Cf.* also Rule VII above.—*Ed.*]
[2] [*Cf.* p. 44.—*Ed.*]
[3] [Rules IX and X are omitted from this collection.—*Ed.*]

the first to the last that practically no step is left to the memory, and I seem to view the whole all at the same time.

Everyone must see that this plan does much to counteract the slowness of the mind and to enlarge its capacity. But in addition we must note that the greatest advantage of this rule consists in the fact that, by reflecting on the mutual dependence of two propositions, we acquire the habit of distinguishing at a glance what is more or less relative, and what the steps are by which a relative fact is related to something absolute. For example, if I run over a number of magnitudes that are in continued proportion, I shall reflect upon all the following facts: viz. that the mental act is entirely similar—and not easier in the one case, more difficult in another—by which I grasp the relation between the first and the second, the second and third, third and fourth, and so on; while yet it is more difficult for me to conceive what the relation of the second is to the first and to the third at the same time, and much more difficult still to tell its relation to the first and fourth, and so on. These considerations then lead me to see why, if the first and second alone are given, I can easily find the third and fourth, and all the others; the reason being that this process requires only single and distinct acts of thought. But if only the first and the third are given, it is not so easy to recognize the mean, because this can only be accomplished by means of a mental operation in which two of the previous acts are involved. If the first and the fourth magnitudes alone are given, it is still more difficult to present to ourselves the two means, because here three acts of thought come in simultaneously. It would seem likely as a consequence that it would be even more difficult to discover the three means between the first and the fifth. The reason why this is not so is due to a fresh fact; viz. even though here four mental acts come together they can yet be disjoined, since four can be divided by another number. Thus I can discover the third by itself from the first and fifth, then the second from the first and third, and so on. If one accustoms one's self to reflect on these and similar problems, as often as a new question arises, at once one recognizes what produces its special difficulty, and what is the simplest method of dealing with all cases; and to be able to do so is a valuable aid to the discovery of the truth.

Rule XII

Finally we ought to employ all the aids of understanding, imagination, sense and memory, first for the purpose of having a distinct intuition of simple propositions; partly also in order to compare the propositions to be proved with those we know already, so that we may be able to recognize their truth; partly also in order to discover the truths, which should be compared with each other so that nothing may be left lacking on which human industry may exercise itself.

This rule states the conclusion of all that we said before, and shows in general outline what had to be explained in detail, in this wise.

In the matter of the cognition of facts two things alone have to be considered, ourselves who know and the objects themselves which are to be known.

Within us there are four faculties only which we can use for this purpose, viz. understanding, imagination, sense and memory. The understanding is indeed alone capable of perceiving the truth, but yet it ought to be aided by imagination, sense and memory, lest perchance we omit any expedient that lies within our power. On the side of the facts to be known it is enough to examine three things; first that which presents itself spontaneously, secondly how we learn one thing by means of another, and thirdly what (truths) are deduced from what. This enumeration appears to me to be complete, and to omit nothing to which our human powers can apply.

I should have liked therefore to have turned to the first point and to have explained in this passage, what the human mind is, what body, and how it is 'informed' by mind; what the faculties in the complex whole are which serve the attainment of knowledge, and what the agency of each is. But this place[1] seems hardly to give me sufficient room to take in all the matters which must be premised before the truth in this subject can become clear to all. For my desire is in all that I write to assert nothing controversial unless I have already stated the very reasons which have brought me to that conclusion, and by which I think that others also may be convinced.

But because at present I am prevented from doing this, it will suffice me to explain as briefly as possible that mode of viewing everything within us which is directed towards the discovery of truth, which most promotes my purpose. You need not believe that the facts are so unless you like. But what prevents us following these suppositions, if it appears that they do no harm to the truth, but only render it all much clearer? In Geometry you do precisely the same thing when you make certain assumptions about a quantity which do not in any way weaken the force of your arguments, though often our experience of its nature in Physics makes us judge of it quite otherwise.

Let us then conceive of the matter as follows: all our external senses, in so far as they are part of the body, and despite the fact that we direct them towards objects, so manifesting activity, viz. a movement in space, nevertheless properly speaking perceive in virtue of passivity alone, just in the way that wax receives an impression (*figuram*) from a seal. And it should not be thought that all we mean to assert is an analogy between the two. We ought to believe that the way is entirely the same in which the exterior figure of the sentient body is really modified by the object, as that in which the shape of the surface of the wax is altered by the seal. This has to be admitted not only in the case of the figure, hardness, roughness, etc. of a body which we perceive by touch, but even when we are aware of heat, cold, and the like qualities. It is likewise with the other senses. The first opaque structure in the eye receives the figure impressed upon it by the light with its various colours; and the first membrane (*cutem*) in the ears, the nose, and the tongue that resists the further passage of the object, thus also acquires a new figure from the sound, the odour, and the savour, as the case may be.

---

[1] <locus> is added in another hand in the Hanover MS.—*Tr.*

It is exceedingly helpful to conceive all those matters thus, for nothing falls more readily under sense than figure, which can be touched and seen. Moreover that nothing false issues from this supposition more than from any other, is proved by the fact that the concept of figure is so common and simple that it is involved in every object of sense. Thus whatever you suppose colour to be, you cannot deny that it is extended and in consequence possessed of figure. Is there then any disadvantage, if, while taking care not to admit any new entity uselessly, or rashly to imagine that it exists, and not denying indeed the beliefs of others concerning colour, but merely abstracting from every other feature except that it possesses the nature of figure, we conceive the diversity existing between white, blue, and red, etc., as being like the differences between the following similar figures? The same argument applies to all cases;

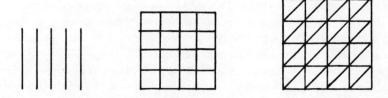

for it is certain that the infinitude of figures suffices to express all the differences in sensible things.

Secondly we must believe that while the external sense is stimulated *(movetur)* by the object, the figure which is conveyed to it is carried off to some other part of the body, that part called the common sense *(sensus communis)*[1], in the very same instant and without the passage of any real entity from one to the other. It is in exactly the same manner that now when I write I recognize that at the very moment when the separate characters are being written down on the paper, not only is the lower end of the pen moved, but every motion in that part is simultaneously shared by the whole pen. All these diverse motions are traced by the upper end of the pen likewise in the air, although I do not conceive of anything real passing from the one extremity to the other. Now who imagines that the connection between the different parts of the human body is slighter than that between the ends of a pen, and what simpler way of expressing this could be found?

Thirdly we must believe that the common sense has a function like that of a seal, and impresses on the fancy or imagination, as though on wax, those very figures and ideas which come uncontaminated and without bodily admixture from the external senses. But this fancy is a genuine part of the body, of sufficient size to allow its different parts to assume various figures in dis-

---

[1] This theory is indistinguishable from one interpretation of the Aristotelian doctrine of a central sense with a central organ in the body.—*Tr.*

tinctness from each other and to let those parts acquire the practice of retaining the impressions for some time. In the latter case we give the faculty the
name of memory.

In the fourth place we must conceive that the motor force or the nerves
themselves derive their origin from the brain, in which the fancy is located,
and that the fancy moves them in various ways, just as the external senses act
on the common sense, or the lower extremity of the pen moves the whole pen.
This example also shows how the fancy can be the cause of many motions in
the nerves, motions of which, however, it does not have the images stamped
upon it, possessing only certain other images from which these latter follow.
Just so the whole pen does not move exactly in the way in which its lower end
does; nay the greater part seems to have a motion that is quite different from
and contrary to that of the other. This lets us understand how all the motions
of the other animals can come about, though we can ascribe to them no
knowledge at all, but only fancy of a purely corporeal kind. We can explain
also how in ourselves all those operations occur which we perform without any
aid from the reason.

Finally and in the fifth place, we must think that that power by which we
are properly said to know things, is purely spiritual, and not less distinct from
every part of the body than blood from bone, or hand from eye. It is a single
agency, whether it receives impressions from the common sense simultaneously with the fancy, or applies itself to those that are preserved in the memory, or forms new ones. Often the imagination is so beset by these impressions
that it is unable at the same time to receive ideas from the common sense, or
to transfer them to the motor mechanism in the way befitting its purely corporeal character. In all these operations this cognitive power is at one time passive, at another active, and resembles now the seal and now the wax. But the
resemblance on this occasion is only one of analogy, for among corporeal
things there is nothing wholly similar to this faculty. It is one and the same
agency which, when applying itself along with the imagination to the common
sense, is said to see, touch, etc.; if applying itself to the imagination alone in so
far as that is endowed with diverse impressions, it is said to remember; if it
turn to the imagination in order to create fresh impressions, it is said to imagine or conceive; finally if it act alone it is said to understand. How this latter
function takes place I shall explain at greater length in the proper place. Now
it is the same faculty that in correspondence with those various functions is
called either pure understanding, or imagination, or memory, or sense. It is
properly called mind *(ingenium)* when it either forms new ideas in the fancy, or
attends to those already formed. We consider it as capable of the above various operations, and this distinction between those terms must in the sequel be
borne in mind. But after having grasped these facts the attentive reader will
gather what help is to be expected from each particular faculty, and discover
how far human effort can avail to supplement the deficiencies of our mental
powers.

For, since the understanding can be stimulated by the imagination, or on the contrary act on it; and seeing that the imagination can act on the senses by means of the motor power applying them to objects, while they on the contrary can act on it, depicting on it the images of bodies; considering on the other hand that the memory, at least that which is corporeal and similar to that of the brutes, is in no respect distinct from the imagination; we come to the sure conclusion that, if the understanding deal with matters in which there is nothing corporeal or similar to the corporeal, it cannot be helped by those faculties, but that, on the contrary, to prevent their hampering it, the senses must be banished and the imagination as far as possible divested of every distinct impression. But if the understanding proposes to examine something that can be referred to the body, we must form the idea of that thing as distinctly as possible in the imagination; and in order to effect this with greater ease, the thing itself which this idea is to represent must be exhibited to the external senses. Now when the understanding wishes to have a distinct intuition of particular facts a multitude of objects is of no use to it. But if it wishes to deduce one thing from a number of objects, as often has to be done, we must banish from the ideas of the objects presented whatsoever does not require present attention, in order that the remainder may be the more readily retained in memory. In the same way it is not on those occasions that the objects themselves ought to be presented to the external senses, but rather certain compendious abbreviations which, provided they guard the memory against lapse, are the handier the shorter they are. Whosoever observes all these recommendations, will, in my opinion, omit nothing that relates to the first part of our rule.

Now we must approach the second part of our task. That was to distinguish accurately the notions of simple things from those which are built up out of them; to see in both cases where falsity might come in, so that we might be on our guard and give our attention to those matters only in which certainty was possible. But here, as before, we must make certain assumptions which probably are not agreed on by all. It matters little, however, though they are not believed to be more real than those imaginary circles by means of which Astronomers describe their phenomena, provided that you employ them to aid you in discerning in each particular case what sort of knowledge is true and what false.

Finally, then, we assert that relatively to our knowledge single things should be taken in an order different from that in which we should regard them when considered in their more real nature. Thus, for example, if we consider a body as having extension and figure, we shall indeed admit that from the point of view of the thing itself it is one and simple. For we cannot from that point of view regard it as compounded of corporeal nature, extension and figure, since these elements have never existed in isolation from each other. But relatively to our understanding we call it a compound constructed out of these three natures, because we have thought of them separately before we were able to judge that all three were found in one and the same subject. Hence here we shall treat of things only in relation to our understanding's

awareness of them, and shall call those only simple, the cognition of which is
so clear and so distinct that they cannot be analysed by the mind into others
more distinctly known. Such are figure, extension, motion, etc.; all others we
conceive to be in some way compounded out of these. This principle must be
taken so universally as not even to leave out those objects which we sometimes
obtain by abstraction from the simple natures themselves. This we do, for example, when we say that figure is the limit of an extended thing, conceiving by
the term limit something more universal than by the term figure, since we can
talk of a limit of duration, a limit of motion, and so on. But our contention is
right, for then, even though we find the meaning of limit by abstracting it
from figure, nevertheless it should not for that reason seem simpler than figure.
Rather, since it is predicated of other things, as for example of the extreme
bounds of a space of time or of a motion, etc., things which are wholly different from figure, it must be abstracted from those natures also; consequently
it is something compounded out of a number of natures wholly diverse, of
which it can be only ambiguously predicated.

Our second assertion is that those things which relatively to our understanding *(intellectus)* are called simple, are either purely intellectual *(intellectu-
ales)* or purely material, or else common both to intellect and to matter. Those
are purely intellectual which our understanding *(intellectus)* apprehends by
means of a certain inborn light, and without the aid of any corporeal image.
That a number of such things exist is certain; and it is impossible to construct
any corporeal idea which shall represent to us what the act of knowing is,
what doubt is, what ignorance, and likewise what the action of the will is
which it is possible to term volition, and so with other things. Yet we have a
genuine knowledge of all these things, and know them so easily that in order
to recognize them it is enough to be endowed with reason. Those things are
purely material which we discern only in bodies; e.g. figure, extension, motion, etc. Finally those must be styled common which are ascribed now to corporeal things, now to spirits, without distinction. Such are existence, unity, duration and the like. To this group also we must ascribe those common notions
which are, as it were, bonds for connecting together the other simple natures,
and on whose evidence all the inferences which we obtain by reasoning depend. The following are examples:—things that are the same as a third thing
are the same as one another. So too:—things which do not bear the same relation to a third thing, have some diversity from each other, etc. As a matter of
fact these common notions can be discerned by the understanding either
unaided *(puro)* or when it is aware of the images of material things.

But among these simple natures we must rank the privative and negative
terms corresponding to them in so far as our intelligence grasps them. For it is
quite as genuinely an act of knowledge by which I am intuitively aware of
what nothing is, or an instant, or rest, as that by which I know what existence
is, or lapse of time, or motion. This way of viewing the matter will be helpful
in enabling us henceforth to say that all the rest of what we know is formed by

composition out of these simple natures. Thus, for example, if I pronounce the judgment that some figure is not moving, I shall say that in a certain sense my idea *(cogitatio)* is a complex of figure and rest; and so in other cases.

Thirdly we assert that all these simple natures are known *per se* and are wholly free from falsity. It will be easy to show this, provided we distinguish that faculty of our understanding by which it has intuitive awareness of things and knows them, from that by which it judges, making use of affirmation and denial. For we may imagine ourselves to be ignorant of things which we really know, for example on such occasions as when we believe that in such things, over and above what we have present to us or attain to by thinking, there is something else hidden from us, and when this belief of ours is false. Whence it is evident that we are in error if we judge that any one of these simple natures is not completely known by us. For if our mind attains to the least acquaintance with it, as must be the case, since we are assumed to pass some judgment on it, this fact alone makes us infer that we know it completely. For otherwise it could not be said to be simple, but must be complex—a compound of that which is present in our perception of it, and that of which we think we are ignorant.

In the fourth place we point out that the union of these things one with another is either necessary or contingent. It is necessary when one is so implied in the concept of another in a confused sort of way that we cannot conceive either distinctly, if our thought assigns to them separateness from each other. Thus figure is conjoined with extension, motion with duration or time, and so on, because it is impossible to conceive of a figure that has no extension, nor of a motion that has no duration. Thus likewise if I say 'four and three are seven,' this union is necessary. For we do not conceive the number seven distinctly unless we include in it the numbers three and four in some confused way. In the same way whatever is demonstrated of figures or numbers is necessarily united with that of which it is affirmed. Further, this necessity is not restricted to the field of sensible matters alone. The conclusion is necessary also in such a case— If Socrates says he doubts everything, it follows necessarily that he knows this at least—that he doubts. Likewise he knows that something can be either true or false, and so on, for all those consequences necessarily attach to the nature of doubt. The union, however, is contingent in those cases where the things are conjoined by no inseparable bond. Thus when we say a body is animate, a man is clothed, etc. Likewise many things are often necessarily united with one another, though most people, not noticing what their true relation is, reckons them among those that are contingently connected. As example, I give the following proposition:—'I exist, therefore God exists': also 'I know, therefore I have a mind distinct from my body', etc. Finally we must note that very many necessary propositions become contingent when converted. Thus though from the fact that I exist I may infallibly conclude that God exists, it is not for that reason allowable to affirm that because God exists I also exist.

Fifthly we remark that no knowledge is at any time possible of anything beyond those simple natures and what may be called their intermixture or combination with each other. Indeed it is often easier to be aware of several of them in union with each other, than to separate one of them from the others. For, to illustrate, I am able to know what a triangle is, though I have never thought that in that knowledge was contained the knowledge of an angle, a line, the number three, figure, extension, etc. But that does not prevent me from saying that the nature of the triangle is composed of all these natures, and that they are better known than the triangle since they are the elements which we comprehend in it. It is possible also that in the triangle many other features are involved which escape our notice, such as the magnitude of the angles, which are equal to two right angles, and the innumerable relations which exist between the sides and the angles, or the size of the area, etc.

Sixthly, we say that those natures which we call composite are known by us, either because experience shows us what they are, or because we ourselves are responsible for their composition. Matter of experience consists of what we perceive by sense, what we hear from the lips of others, and generally whatever reaches our understanding either from external sources or from that contemplation which our mind directs backwards on itself. Here it must be noted that no direct experience can ever deceive the understanding if it restrict its attention accurately to the object presented to it, just as it is given to it either at firsthand *(prout illam habet vel in se ipso)* or by means of an image; and if it moreover refrain from judging that the imagination faithfully reports the objects of the senses, or that the senses take on the true forms of things, or in fine that external things always are as they appear to be; for in all these judgments we are exposed to error. This happens, for example, when we believe as fact what is merely a story that someone has told us; or when one who is ill with jaundice judges everything to be yellow because his eye is tinged with yellow. So finally, too, when the imagination is diseased, as in cases of melancholia, and a man thinks that his own disorderly fancies represent real things. But the understanding of a wise man will not be deceived by these fancies, since he will judge that whatever comes to him from his imagination is really depicted in it, but yet will never assert that the object has passed complete and without any alteration from the external world to his senses, and from his senses to his imagination, unless he has some previous ground for believing this. Moreover we ourselves are responsible for the composition of the things present to our understanding when we believe that there is something in them which our mind never experiences when exercising direct perception.[1] Thus if a man suffering from jaundice persuades himself that the things he sees are yellow, this thought of his will be composite, consisting partly of what his imagination represents to him, and partly of what he assumes on his own account, namely that the colour looks yellow not owing to the defect in his eye, but because the things he sees really are yellow. Whence the conclusion comes that we can go

---

[1] This translation is doubtful. The Latin might at least equally well mean 'which our mind perceives immediately without any experience.'—*Tr.*

wrong only when the things we believe are in some way compounded by ourselves.

Seventhly, this compounding can come about in other ways, namely by impulse, by conjecture, or by deduction. Impulse sways the formation of judgments about things on the part of those whom their own initiative constrains to believe something, though they can assign no reason for their belief, but are merely determined either by some higher Power, or by their own free will, or by their fanciful disposition. The first cause is never a source of error, the second rarely, the third almost always. But a consideration of the first does not concern us here because it does not fall within the province of human skill (*artem*). The working of conjecture is shown, for example, in this: water which is at a greater distance from the centre of the globe than earth, is likewise less dense substance, and likewise the air which is above the water, is still rarer; hence we hazard the guess that above the air nothing exists but a very pure aether, which is much rarer than air itself. Moreover nothing that we construct in this way really deceives us, if we merely judge it to be probable and never affirm it to be true; in fact it makes us better instructed.

Deduction is thus left to us as the only means of putting things together so as to be sure of their truth. Yet in it too there may be many defects. Thus, if, in this space which is full of air, there is nothing to be perceived either by sight, touch, or any other sense, we conclude that the space is empty, we are in error, and our synthesis of the nature of a vacuum with that of this space is wrong. This is the result as often as we judge that we can deduce anything universal and necessary from a particular or contingent fact. But it is within our power to avoid this error, if, for example, we never interconnect any objects unless we are directly aware that the conjunction of the one with the other is wholly necessary. Thus we are justified if we deduce that nothing can have figure which has not extension, from the fact that figure and extension are necessarily conjoined.

From all these considerations we conclude firstly—that we have shown distinctly and, as we judge, by an adequate enumeration, what we were originally able to express only confusedly and in a rough and ready way. This was that mankind has no road towards certain knowledge open to it, save those of self-evident intuition and necessary deduction; further, that we have shown what those simple natures are of which we spoke in the eighth proposition. It is also quite clear that this mental vision extends both to all those simple natures, and to the knowledge of the necessary connections between them, and finally to everything else which the understanding accurately experiences either at first hand (*in se ipso*) or in the imagination. Deduction, however, will be further treated in what follows.

Our second conclusion is that in order to know these simple natures no pains need to be taken, because they are of themselves sufficiently well known. Application comes in only in isolating them from each other and scrutinizing them separately with steadfast mental gaze. There is no one whose intelligence is so dull as not to perceive that when he is seated he in some way differs from

what he is when standing. But not everyone separates with equal distinctness
the nature of position *(situs)* from the other elements contained in the cognition in question, or is able to assert that in this case nothing alters save the position. Now it is not without reason that we call attention to the above doctrine; for the learned have a way of being so clever as to contrive to render
themselves blind to things that are in their own nature evident, and known by
the simplest peasant. This happens when they try to explain by something
more evident those things that are self-evident. For what they do is either to
explain something else, or nothing at all. Who, for instance, does not perfectly
see what that is, whatsoever it may be, in respect of which alteration occurs
when we change position *(locum)?* But is there anyone who would grasp that
very thing when he was told that *place* (locum) *is the surface of the body surrounding
us?* [1] This would be strange seeing that that surface can change though I stay
still and do not change my place, or that, on the contrary, it can so move
along with me that, although it continues to surround me, I am nevertheless
no longer in the same place. Do not these people really seem to use magic
words which have a hidden force that eludes the grasp of human apprehension? They define *motion,* a fact with which everyone is quite familiar, as *the
actualisation of what exists in potentiality, in so far as it is potential!* Now who understands these words? And who at the same time does not know what motion is?
Will not everyone admit that those philosophers have been trying to find a
knot in a bulrush? We must therefore maintain that no definitions are to be
used in explaining things of this kind lest we should take what is complex in
place of what is simple. We must be content to isolate them from each other,
and to give them, each of us, our individual attention, studying them with that
degree of mental illumination which each of us possesses.

Our third conclusion is that the whole of human knowledge consists in a
distinct perception of the way in which those simple natures combine in order
to build up other objects. It is important to note this; because whenever some
difficulty is brought forward for examination, almost everyone is brought to a
standstill at the very outset, being in doubt as to the nature of the notions he
ought to call to mind, and believing that he has to search for some new kind of
fact previously unknown to him. Thus, if the question is, 'what is the nature of
the magnet?' people like that at once prognosticate difficulty and toil in the
inquiry, and dismissing from mind every well-known fact, fasten on whatsoever is most difficult, vaguely hoping that by ranging over the fruitless field
where multifarious causes lie, they will find something fresh. But he who
reflects that there can be nothing to know in the magnet which does not consist of certain simple natures evident in themselves, will have no doubt how to
proceed. He will first collect all the observations with which experience can
supply him about this stone, and from these he will next try to deduce the
character of that inter-mixture of simple natures which is necessary to produce
all those effects which he has seen to take place in connection with the mag-

---

[1] *Cf.* reply to VI. Obj. (7).—*Tr.* [Not included in this collection.—*Ed.*]

net. This achieved, he can boldly assert that he has discovered the real nature of the magnet in so far as human intelligence and the given experimental observations can supply him with this knowledge.

Finally, it follows fourthly from what has been said that we must not fancy that one kind of knowledge is more obscure than another, since all knowledge is of the same nature throughout, and consists solely in combining what is self-evident. This is a fact recognized by very few. People have their minds already occupied by the contrary opinion, and the more bold among them, indeed, allow themselves to uphold their private conjectures as though they were sound demonstrations, and in matters of which they are wholly ignorant feel premonitions of the vision of truths which seem to present themselves through a cloud. These they have no hesitation in propounding, attaching to their concepts certain words by means of which they are wont to carry on long and reasoned out discussions, but which in reality neither they nor their audience understand. On the other hand more diffident people often refrain from many investigations that are quite easy and are in the first degree necessary to life, merely because they think themselves unequal to the task. They believe that these matters can be discovered by others who are endowed with better mental faculties, and embrace the opinion of those in whose authority they have most confidence.

We assert fifthly[1] that by deduction we can get only things from words, cause from effect, or effect from cause, like from like, or parts or the whole itself from the parts. . . .[2]

For the rest, in order that there may be no want of coherence in our series of precepts, we divide the whole matter of knowledge into simple propositions and 'questions'[3] (*quaestiones*). In connection with simple propositions the only precepts we give are those which prepare our cognitive faculties for fixing distinctly before them any objects, whatsoever they are, and scrutinizing them with keen intelligence, since propositions of this type do not arise as the result of inquiry, but present themselves to us spontaneously. This part of our task we have undertaken in the first twelve rules, in which, we believe, we have displayed everything which, in our opinion, can facilitate the exercise of our reason. But as to 'questions' some of them can be perfectly well comprehended, even though we are ignorant of their solution; these we shall treat by themselves in the next twelve rules. Finally there are others, whose meaning is not quite clear, and those we reserve for the last twelve. This division has been made advisedly, both in order to avoid mentioning anything which presupposes an acquaintance with what follows, and also for the purpose of unfolding

---

[1] So Leibniz's MS. The Amsterdam edition has *eighthly* which carries on the previous list of assertions.—*Tr.*

[2] There seems to be a break here.—*Tr.* [For a continuation of the doctrine refer to Rule XIII, par. 4; not included in this collection.— *Ed.*]

[3] Inverted commas have been employed wherever it is important to remember Descartes' special technical of this term.—*Tr.*

first what we feel to be most important first to inculcate in cultivating the mental powers. Among the 'questions' whose meaning is quite plain, we must to begin with note that we place those only in which we perceive three things distinctly; to wit, the marks by which we can identify what we are looking for when it occurs; what precisely the fact is from which our answer ought to be deduced; and how it is to be proved that these (the ground and its consequence) so depend one on another that it is impossible for either to change while the other remains unchanged. In this way we shall have all the premises we require, and the only thing remaining to be shown will be how to discover the conclusion. This will not be a matter of deducing some one fact from a single simple matter (we have already said that we can do this without the help of rules), but of disentangling so skilfully some one fact that is conditioned by a number of others which all involve one another, that in recognizing it there shall be no need to call upon a higher degree of mental power than in making the simplest inference. 'Questions' of this kind, being highly abstract and occurring almost exclusively in Arithmetic and Geometry, seem to the inexperienced of little value. But I warn them that people ought to busy and exercise themselves a long time in learning this art, who desire to master the subsequent portions of this method, in which all the other types of 'question' are treated.

3 BENEDICT SPINOZA
On the Improvement of the Understanding *

. . . I will here only briefly state what I mean by true good, and also what is the nature of the highest good. In order that this may be rightly understood, we must bear in mind that the terms good and evil are only applied relatively, so that the same thing may be called both good and bad, according to the relations in view, in the same way as it may be called perfect or imperfect. Nothing regarded in its own nature can be called perfect or imperfect; especially when we are aware that all things which come to pass, come to pass according to the eternal order and fixed laws of nature. However, human weakness cannot attain to this order in its own thoughts, but meanwhile man conceives a human character much more stable than his own, and sees that there is no reason why he should not himself acquire such a character. Thus he is led to seek for means which will bring him to this pitch of perfection, and calls everything which will serve as such means a true good. The chief good is

* From the *Tractatus de Intellectus Emendatione*, which probably was composed in its present unfinished form in 1661. First published posthumously in 1677. This translation is by R. H. M. Elwes (1884).

that he should arrive, together with other individuals if possible, at the possession of the aforesaid character. What that character is we shall show in due time, namely, that it is the knowledge of the union existing between the mind and the whole of nature.[1] This, then, is the end for which I strive, to attain to such a character myself, and to endeavour that many should attain to it with me. In other words, it is part of my happiness to lend a helping hand, that many others may understand even as I do, so that their understanding and desire may entirely agree with my own. In order to bring this about, it is necessary to understand as much of nature as will enable us to attain to the aforesaid character, and also to form a social order such as is most conducive to the attainment of this character by the greatest number with the least difficulty and danger. We must seek the assistance of Moral Philosophy[2] and the Theory of Education; further, as health is no insignificant means for attaining our end, we must also include the whole science of Medicine, and, as many difficult things are by contrivance rendered easy, and we can in this way gain much time and convenience, the science of Mechanics must be devised for improving the understanding and purifying it, as far as may be at the outset, so that it may apprehend things without error, and in the best possible way.

---

[1] These matters are explained more at length elsewhere. [Not in this Treatise as we have it, but see pp. 66–8.—*Ed.*]

[2] N. B. I do no more here than enumerate the sciences necessary for our purpose; I lay no stress on their order.

Thus it is apparent to everyone that I wish to direct all sciences to one end and aim,[3] so that we may attain to the supreme human perfection which we have named; and, therefore, whatsoever in the sciences does not serve to promote our object will have to be rejected as useless. To sum up the matter in a word, all our actions and thoughts must be directed to this one end. Yet, as it is necessary that while we are endeavouring to attain our purpose, and bring the understanding into the right path, we should carry on our life, we are compelled first of all to lay down certain rules of life as provisionally good, to wit the following:

---

[3] There is for the sciences but one end, to which they should all be directed.

I. To speak in a manner intelligible to the multitude, and to comply with every general custom that does not hinder the attainment of our purpose. For we can gain from the multitude no small advantages, provided that we strive to accommodate ourselves to its understanding as far as possible: moreover, we shall in this way gain a friendly audience for the reception of the truth.

II. To indulge ourselves with pleasures only in so far as they are necessary for preserving health.

III. Lastly, to endeavour to obtain only sufficient money or other commodities to enable us to preserve our life and health, and to follow such general customs as are consistent with our purpose.[1]

Having laid down these preliminary rules, I will betake myself to the first and most important task, namely, the amendment of the understanding, and the rendering it capable of understanding things in the manner necessary for attaining our end.

In order to bring this about, the natural order demands that I should here recapitulate all the modes of perception, which I have hitherto employed for affirming or denying anything with certainty, so that I may choose the best, and at the same time begin to know my own powers and the nature which I wish to perfect.

Reflection shows that all modes of perception or knowledge may be reduced to four:

I. Perception arising from hearsay or from some sign which everyone may name as he pleases.

II. Perception arising from mere experience—that is, from experience not yet classified by the intellect, and only so called because the given event has happened to take place, and we have no contradictory fact to set against it, so that it therefore remains unassailed in our mind.

III. Perception arising when the essence of one thing is inferred from another thing, but not adequately; this comes when from some effect we gather its cause,[2] or when it is inferred from some general proposition that some property is always present.

---

[2] In this case we do not understand anything of the cause from the consideration of it in the effect. This is sufficiently evident from the fact that the cause is only spoken of in very general terms, such as— there exists then something; there exists then some power, &c.; or from the fact that we only express it in a negative manner—it is not this or that, &c. In the second case something is ascribed to the cause because of the effect, as we shall show in an example, but only a property, never the essence.

IV. Lastly, there is the perception arising when a thing is perceived solely through its essence, or through the knowledge of its proximate cause.[3]

---

[1] [Descartes also had a provisory code of conduct. For a noteworthy contrast between the two see Descartes' *Discourse on Method*, Part III—not included in this collection.—*Ed.*]

[3] [The four modes of knowledge are arranged differently in the *Ethics*. See Note 2, Prop. 40, Pt. II, in Selection 16. The definition of the fourth mode as there given is that which 'proceeds from an adequate idea of the absolute essence of certain attributes of God to the adequate knowledge of the essence of things.'—*Ed.*]

All these kinds of perception I will illustrate by examples. By hearsay I know the day of my birth, my parentage, and other matters about which I have never felt any doubt. By mere experience I know that I shall die, for this I can affirm from having seen that others like myself have died, though all did not live for the same period, or die by the same disease. I know by mere experience that oil has the property of feeding fire, and water of extinguishing it. In the same way I know that a dog is a barking animal, man a rational animal, and in fact nearly all the practical knowledge of life.

We deduce one thing from another as follows: when we clearly perceive that we feel a certain body and no other, we thence clearly infer that the mind is united to the body,[1] and that their union is the cause of the given sensation; but we cannot thence absolutely understand the nature of the sensation and the union.[2] Or, after I have become acquainted with the nature of vision, and know that it has the property of making one and the same thing appear smaller when far off than when near, I can infer that the sun is larger than it appears, and can draw other conclusions of the same kind.

---

[1] From this example may be clearly seen what I have just drawn attention to. For through this union we understand nothing beyond the sensation, the effect, to wit, from which we inferred the cause, of which we understand nothing.

[2] A conclusion of this sort, though it be certain, is yet not to be relied on without great caution; for unless we are exceedingly careful we shall forthwith fall into error. When things are conceived thus abstractedly, and not through their true essence, they are apt to be confused by the imagination. For that which is in itself one, men imagine to be multiplex. To those things which are conceived abstractedly, apart, and confusedly, terms are applied which are apt to become wrested from their strict meaning, and bestowed on things more familiar; whence it results that these latter are imagined in the same way as the former to which the terms were originally given.

Lastly, a thing may be perceived solely through its essence; when, from the fact of knowing something, I know what it is to know that thing, or when, from knowing the essence of the mind, I know that it is united to the body. By the same kind of knowledge we know that two and three make five, or that two lines each parallel to a third, are parallel to one another, &c. The things which I have been able to know by this kind of knowledge are as yet very few . . .[3]

. . . In order that from these modes of perception the best may be se-

---

[3] [*Cf.* what Spinoza says in the *Ethics*, Part II, Prop. 40–42, in Selection 16.— *Ed.*]

lected, it is well that we should briefly enumerate the means necessary for attaining our end.

I. To have an exact knowledge of our nature which we desire to perfect, and to know as much as is needful of nature in general.

II. To collect in this way the differences, the agreements, and the oppositions of things.

III. To learn thus exactly how far they can or cannot be modified.

IV. To compare this result with the nature and power of man. We shall thus discern the highest degree of perfection to which man is capable of attaining. We shall then be in a position to see which mode of perception we ought to choose.

As to the first mode, it is evident that from hearsay our knowledge must always be uncertain, and, moreover, can give us no insight into the essence of a thing, as is manifest in our illustration; now one can only arrive at knowledge of a thing through knowledge of its essence, as will hereafter appear. We may, therefore, clearly conclude that the certainty arising from hearsay cannot be scientific in its character. For simple hearsay cannot affect anyone whose understanding does not, so to speak, meet it half way.

The second mode of perception[1] cannot be said to give us the idea of the proportion of which we are in search. Moreover its results are very uncertain and indefinite, for we shall never discover anything in natural phenomena by its means, except accidental properties, which are never clearly understood, unless the essence of the things in question be known first. Wherefore this mode also must be rejected.

[1] I shall here treat a little more in detail of experience, and shall examine the method adopted by the Empirics, and by recent philosophers.

Of the third mode of perception we may say in a manner that it gives us the idea of the thing sought, and that it enables us to draw conclusions without risk of error; yet it is not by itself sufficient to put us in possession of the perfection we aim at.

The fourth mode alone apprehends the adequate essence of a thing without danger of error. This mode, therefore, must be the one which we chiefly employ. How, then, should we avail ourselves of it so as to gain the fourth kind of knowledge with the least delay concerning things previously unknown? I will proceed to explain.

Now that we know what kind of knowledge is necessary for us, we must indicate the way and the method whereby we may gain the said knowledge concerning the things needful to be known. In order to accomplish this, we must first take care not to commit ourselves to a search, going back to infinity —that is, in order to discover the best method for finding out the truth, there is no need of another method to discover such method; nor of a third method for

discovering the second, and so on to infinity. By such proceedings, we should
never arrive at the knowledge of the truth, or, indeed, at any knowledge at all.
The matter stands on the same footing as the making of material tools, which
might be argued about in a similar way. For, in order to work iron, a hammer
is needed, and the hammer cannot be forthcoming unless it has been made;
but, in order to make it, there was need of another hammer and other tools,
and so on to infinity. We might thus vainly endeavour to prove that men have
no power of working iron. But as men at first made use of the instruments supplied by nature to accomplish very easy pieces of workmanship, laboriously
and imperfectly, and then, when these were finished, wrought other things
more difficult with less labour and greater perfection; and so gradually
mounted from the simplest operations to the making of tools, and from the
making of tools to the making of more complex tools, and fresh feats of workmanship, till they arrived at making, with small expenditure of labour, the
vast number of complicated mechanisms which they now possess. So, in like
manner, the intellect, by its native strength,[1] makes for itself intellectual instruments, whereby it acquires strength for performing other intellectual operations,[2] and from these operations gets again fresh instruments, or the power of
pushing its investigations further, and thus gradually proceeds till it reaches
the summit of wisdom.

---

[1] By native strength, I mean that not bestowed on us by external
   causes, as I shall afterwards explain in my philosophy.
[2] I here term them operations: I shall explain their nature in my philosophy.

That this is the path pursued by the understanding may be readily seen,
when we understand the nature of the method for finding out the truth, and of
the natural instruments so necessary for the construction of more complex instruments, and for the progress of investigation. I thus proceed with my demonstration.

A true idea[1] (for we possess a true idea) is something different from its
correlate *(ideatum);* thus a circle is different from the idea of a circle. The idea
of a circle is not something having a circumference and a centre, as a circle
has; nor is the idea of a body that body itself. Now, as it is something different
from its correlate, it is capable of being understood through itself; in other
words, the idea, in so far as its actual essence *(essentia formalis)* is concerned,
may be the subject of another subjective essence *(essentia objectiva)*. And, again,
this second subjective essence will, regarded in itself, be something real, and
capable of being understood; and so on, indefinitely. For instance, the man
Peter is something real; the true idea of Peter is the reality of Peter represented subjectively, and is in itself something real, and quite distinct from the
actual Peter. Now, as this true idea of Peter is in itself something real, and has
its own individual existence, it will also be capable of being understood—that
is, of being the subject of another idea, which will contain by representation

(objective) all that the idea of Peter contains actually *(formaliter)*. And, again, this idea of the idea of Peter has its own individuality, which may become the subject of yet another idea; and so on, indefinitely. This everyone may make trial of for himself, by reflecting that he knows what Peter is, and also knows that he knows, and further knows that he knows that he knows, &c. Hence it is plain that, in order to understand the actual Peter, it is not necessary first to understand the idea of Peter, and still less the idea of the idea of Peter. This is the same as saying that, in order to know, there is no need to know that we know, much less to know that we know that we know. This is no more necessary than to know the nature of a circle before knowing the nature of a triangle.[2] But, with these ideas, the contrary is the case: for, in order to know that I know, I must first know. Hence it is clear that certainty is nothing else than the subjective essence of a thing: in other words, the mode in which we perceive an actual reality is certainty. Further, it is also evident that, for the certitude of truth, no further sign is necessary beyond the possession of a true idea: for, as I have shown, it is not necessary to know that we know that we know. Hence, again, it is clear that no one can know the nature of the highest certainty, unless he possesses an adequate idea, or the subjective essence of a thing: for certainty is identical with such subjective essence. Thus, as the truth needs no sign—it being sufficient to possess the subjective essence of things, or, in other words, the ideas of them, in order that all doubts may be removed—it follows that the true method does not consist in seeking for the signs of truth after the acquisition of the idea, but that the true method teaches us the order in which we should seek for truth itself [3], or the subjective essences of things, or ideas, for all these expressions are synonymous. Again, method must necessarily be concerned with reasoning or understanding—I mean, method is not identical with reasoning in the search for causes, still less is it the comprehension of the causes of things: it is the discernment of a true idea, by distinguishing it from other perceptions, and by investigating its nature, in order that we may thus know our power of understanding, and may so train our mind that it may, by a given standard, comprehend whatsoever is intelligible, by laying down certain rules as aids, and by avoiding useless mental exertion.

---

[1] I shall take care not only to demonstrate what I have just advanced, but also that we have hitherto proceeded rightly, and other things needful to be known.

[2] Observe that we are not here inquiring how this first subjective essence is innate in us. This belongs to an investigation into nature, where all these matters are amply explained, and it is shown that without ideas neither affirmation, nor negation, nor volition are possible.

[3] The nature of mental search is explained in my philosophy.

Whence we may gather that method is nothing else than reflective knowledge, or the idea of an idea; and that as there can be no idea of an idea—unless an idea exists previously,—there can be no method without a pre-existent idea. Therefore, that will be a good method which shows us how the mind should be directed, according to the standard of the given true idea.

Again, seeing that the ratio existing between two ideas is the same as the ratio between the actual realities corresponding to those ideas, it follows that the reflective knowledge which has for its object the most perfect being is more excellent than reflective knowledge concerning other objects—in other words, that method will be most perfect which affords the standard of the given idea of the most perfect being whereby we may direct our mind. We thus easily understand how, in proportion as it acquires new ideas, the mind simultaneously acquires fresh instruments for pursuing its inquiries further. For we may gather from what has been said, that a true idea must necessarily first of all exist in us as a natural instrument; and that when this idea is apprehended by the mind, it enables us to understand the difference existing between itself and all other perceptions. In this, one part of the method consists.

Now it is clear that the mind apprehends itself better in proportion as it understands a greater number of natural objects; it follows, therefore, that this portion of the method will be more perfect in proportion as the mind attains to the comprehension of a greater number of objects, and that it will be absolutely perfect when the mind gains a knowledge of the absolutely perfect being, or becomes conscious thereof. Again, the more things the mind knows, the better does it understand its own strength and the order of nature; by increased self-knowledge, it can direct itself more easily, and lay down rules for its own guidance; and, by increased knowledge of nature, it can more easily avoid what is useless.

And this is the sum total of method, as we have already stated. We may add that the idea in the world of thought is in the same case as its correlate in the world of reality. If, therefore, there be anything in nature which is without connection[1] with any other thing, and if we assign to it a subjective essence, which would in every way correspond to the objective reality, the subjective essence would have no connection with any other ideas—in other words, we could not draw any conclusion with regard to it. On the other hand, those things which are connected with others—as all things that exist in nature— will be understood by the mind, and their subjective essences will maintain the same mutual relations as their objective realities—that is to say, we shall infer from these ideas other ideas, which will in turn be connected with others, and thus our instruments for proceeding with our investigation will increase. This is what we were endeavouring to prove. Further, from what has just been said —namely, that an idea must, in all respects, correspond to its correlate in the world of reality,—it is evident that, in order to reproduce in every respect the faithful image of nature, our mind must deduce all its ideas from the idea which represents the origin and source of the whole of nature, so that it may itself become the source of other ideas.

---

[1] To be connected with other things is to be produced by them, or to produce them.

It may, perhaps, provoke astonishment that, after having said that the good method is that which teaches us to direct our mind according to the standard of the given true idea, we should prove our point by reasoning, which would seem to indicate that it is not self-evident. We may, therefore, be questioned as to the validity of our reasoning. If our reasoning be sound, we must take as a starting-point a true idea. Now, to be certain that our starting-point is really a true idea, we need a proof. This first course of reasoning must be supported by a second, the second by a third, and so on to infinity. To this I make answer that, if by some happy chance anyone had adopted this method in his investigations of nature—that is, if he had acquired new ideas in the proper order, according to the standard of the original true idea, he would never have doubted of the truth of his knowledge,[1] inasmuch as truth, as we have shown, makes itself manifest, and all things would flow, as it were, spontaneously towards him. But as this never, or rarely happens, I have been forced so to arrange my proceedings, that we may acquire by reflection and forethought what we cannot acquire by chance, and that it may at the same time appear that, for proving the truth, and for valid reasoning, we need no other means than the truth and valid reasoning themselves: for by valid reasoning I have established valid reasoning, and, in like measure, I seek still to establish it. Moreover, this is the order of thinking adopted by men in their inward meditations. The reasons for its rare employment in investigations of nature are to be found in current misconceptions, whereof we shall examine the causes hereafter in our philosophy. Moreover, it demands, as we shall show, a keen and accurate discernment. Lastly, it is hindered by the conditions of human life, which are, as we have already pointed out, extremely changeable. There are also other obstacles, which we will not here inquire into.

---

[1] In the same way as we have here no doubt of the truth of our knowledge.

If anyone asks why I have not at the starting-point set forth all the truths of nature in their due order, inasmuch as truth is self-evident, I reply by warning him not to reject as false any paradoxes he may find here, but to take the trouble to reflect on the chain of reasoning by which they are supported; he will then be no longer in doubt that we have attained to the truth. This is why I have begun as above.

If there yet remains some sceptic, who doubts of our primary truth, and of all deductions we make, taking such truth as our standard, he must either be arguing in bad faith, or we must confess that there are men in complete mental blindness, either innate or due to misconceptions—that is, to some external influence.

Such persons are not conscious of themselves. If they affirm or doubt anything, they know not that they affirm or doubt: they say that they know nothing, and they say that they are ignorant of the very fact of their knowing nothing. Even this they do not affirm absolutely, they are afraid of confessing that they exist, so long as they know nothing; in fact, they ought to remain dumb, for fear of haply supposing something which should smack of truth. Lastly, with such persons, one should not speak of sciences; for, in what relates to life and conduct, they are compelled by necessity to suppose that they exist, and seek their own advantage, and often affirm and deny, even with an oath. If they deny, grant, or gainsay, they know not that they deny, grant, or gainsay, so that they ought to be regarded as automata, utterly devoid of intelligence . . .

4 GOTTFRIED WILHELM LEIBNIZ
On Method

I.*

*On Universal Synthesis and Analysis, or the
Art of Discovery and Judgment*
1679(?)

As a boy I learned logic, and having already developed the habit of digging more deeply into the reasons for what I was taught, I raised the following question with my teachers. Seeing that there are categories for the simple terms by which concepts are ordered, why should there not also be categories for complex terms, by which truths may be ordered? I was then unaware that geometricians do this very thing when they demonstrate and order propositions according to their dependence upon each other. It seemed to me, however, that this could be achieved universally if we first had the true categories for simple terms and if, to obtain these, we set up something new in the nature of an alphabet of thoughts, or a catalogue of the highest genera or of those we assume to be highest, such as *a, b, c, d, e, f,* out of whose combination inferior concepts may be formed. For we must note that genera may serve as differentiae to each other, so that every difference can be conceived of as a genus, and every genus as a difference. It is as right to say 'rational animal' as 'animal rational being', if such a concept can be formed. But since our common genera do not reveal the species in their combination, I concluded that they were not correctly formed and that the genera next below the highest should be binions, such as *ab, ac, bd, cf;* the genera on the third level would be ternions, such as

---

* From *G. W. Leibniz: Philosophical Papers and Letters,* translated and edited by Leroy E. Loemker, Second Edition, D. Reidel Publishing Company, Dordrecht, Holland, 1970 (pp. 229–233). Reprinted by permission of D. Reidel Publishing Company.

abc, bdf, and so on. But if the highest genera, or those assumed to be highest, should happen to be infinite, as is the case with numbers, we should only have to establish the order of these highest genera, and some order would then become apparent in the lower genera. For in the case of numbers, the prime numbers can be taken as the highest genera, since all even numbers can be called binaries, all divisible by three, ternaries, and so forth. Then every derivative number can be expressed through prime ones as genera. Thus every multiple of six [senary] is a binary ternary. So if some particular species is proposed, the propositions which are demonstrable about it could be enumerated in order, or all its predicates could be listed, whether broader than it or convertible with it, and the more meaningful could then be selected from these. Thus assume that there is a species *y*, whose concept is *abcd;* and for *ab* substitute *l;* for *ac, m;* for *ad, n;* for *bc, p;* for *bd, q;* for *cd, r,* which are binions. Then come ternions; for *abc* substitute *s;* for *abd, v;* for *acd, w;* for *bcd, x.* These would all be predicates of *y,* but only the following would be convertible with *y: ax, bw, cv, ds, lr, mq, np.* I have said more about this in my little treatise on the *Art of Combinations* which I brought out soon after my adolescence, before the long-promised work of the same title by Kircher had appeared. I hoped to find similar matters discussed in it, but when it did appear later, I found that it had merely revived the Lullian art or something similar to it but that the author had not even dreamed of the true analysis of human thoughts any more than had the others who have tried to reform philosophy.

The primary concepts from whose combination the rest are made are either distinct or confused. Those are distinct which are understood through themselves, such as 'being'. Those are confused though clear, which are perceived through themselves, such as color, because we can only explain them to someone else by showing them to him. For though the nature of color is analyzable since it has a cause, we cannot sufficiently describe or recognize it by any concepts that are separately explained; it is known only confusedly and hence cannot be given a *nominal definition.* A nominal definition consists in the enumeration of signs or elements sufficient to distinguish the thing defined from everything else. If we proceed to seek the elements of the elements, we shall come at last to primitive concepts which have no elements at all, or none which we can explain to a sufficient degree. This is the art of dealing with distinct concepts. The art of dealing with confused concepts, however, must discover the distinct concepts which accompany the confused ones, whether these distinct concepts can be understood through themselves or can at least be resolved into such as are understood, for with their help we can sometimes arrive at some cause or resolution of the confused notion.

All derivative concepts, moreover, arise from a combination of primitive ones, and the more composite concepts from the combination of less composite ones. But one must take care that the combinations do not become useless through the joining-together of incompatible concepts. This can be avoided only by experience or by resolving them into distinct single concepts. One must be especially careful, in setting up real definitions, to establish their possibility, that is, to show that the concepts from which they are formed are compatible with each other. So while every reciprocal property of a thing can serve as its nominal definition, since all the other attributes of the thing can always be demonstrated from it, not every such property suffices for a real definition. For as I have pointed out, there are certain properties which I call paradoxical, whose possibility can be doubted. For example, it can be doubted whether there is a curve for which it is true that given any segment and any point on the curve, the lines connecting this point with the ends of the segment will always form the same angle. For assuming that we have so adjusted the points of the curve to one segment, we still cannot foresee that what may seem to have succeeded by chance in one case will succeed in others, namely that the same points on the curve will satisfy this condition with respect to another segment as well, since all of the points are now determined and no further ones can be assumed. Yet we know that this is the nature of a circle. So, although someone might give a name to the curve having this property, it would not yet be certain that such a curve is possible, and hence that its definition is real. But the concept of the circle set up by Euclid, that of a figure described by the motion of a straight line in a plane about a fixed end, affords a real definition, for such a figure is evidently possible. Hence it is useful to have definitions involving the generation of a thing, or if this is impossible, at least its constitution, that is, a method by which the thing appears to be producible or at least possible. I have already used this observation in the past to examine the imperfect demonstration which Descartes proposed of the existence of God, about which I have often argued in writing with the most learned Cartesians. Descartes argues as follows. Whatever can be demonstrated from the definition of a thing can be predicated of that thing. Now from the definition of God—that he is the most perfect being, or as certain Scholastics said, a being than whom no greater can be thought—there follows his existence, for existence is a perfection, and whatever possesses existence will therefore be greater or more perfect than it would be without it. Therefore existence can be predicated of God, or God exists. This argument, revived by Descartes, was defended by one of the old Scholastics in a special book called *Contra insipientem*. But following some others, Thomas replied to it that this presupposes that God is, or as I interpret this, that he has an essence, at least in the sense that the rose has an essence in winter, or that such a concept is possible. This therefore is the privilege of the most perfect being, that, given its possibility, it at once exists or that its existence follows from its essence or its possible concept. But to make this demonstration rigorous, the possibility must first be proved. Obviously we cannot build a secure demonstration on any concept unless we know that this concept is possible, for from impossibles or concepts involving contradictions contradictory propositions can be demonstrated. This is an a priori reason why possibility is a requisite in a real definition. A difficulty raised by Hobbes can also be answered on this basis. For Hobbes saw that all truths can be demonstrated from definitions but held that all definitions are arbitrary and nominal, since we impose arbitrary names upon things. He therefore concluded that truths also consist merely in names and are arbitrary. But we must recognize that if we are to have a real definition, we cannot combine notions arbitrarily, but the concept we form out of them must be possible. Hence every real definition must contain at least the affirmation of some possibility. Furthermore, although names are arbitrary, once they are adopted, their consequences are necessary, and certain truths arise which are real even though they depend on the characters which have been imposed. For example, the rule of nines depends on characters imposed by the decimal system, yet it contains real truth. Moreover, to set up a hypothesis or to explain the method of production is merely to demonstrate the possibility of a thing, and this is useful even though the thing in question often has not been generated in that way. Thus the same ellipse can be thought of either as described in a plane with the aid of two foci and the motion of a thread about them or as a conic or a cylindrical section. Once a hypothesis or a manner of generation is found, one has a real definition from which others can also be derived, and from them those can be selected which best satisfy the other conditions, when a method of actually producing the thing is sought. Those real definitions are most perfect, furthermore, which are common to all the hypotheses or methods of generation and which involve the proximate cause of a thing, and from which the possibility of the thing is immediately apparent without presupposing any experiment or the demonstration of any further possibilities. In other words, those real definitions are most perfect which resolve the thing into simple primitive notions understood in themselves. Such knowledge I usually call adequate or intuitive, for, if there were any inconsistency, it would appear here at once, since no further resolution can take place.

From such ideas or definitions, then, there can be demonstrated all truths with the exception of identical propositions, which by their very nature are evidently indemonstrable and can truly be called axioms. What are popularly called axioms, however, can be reduced to identities by analyzing either the subject or the predicate or both, and so demonstrated; for by assuming the contrary, we can show that the same thing would at the same time be and not be. Hence it is evident that in the last analysis the direct and indirect methods of demonstration coincide and that the Scholastics were right in observing that every axiom, once its terms are understood, may be reduced to the principle of contradiction. Thus any truth whatever can be justified, for the connection of the predicate with the subject is either evident in itself as in identities, or can be explained by an analysis of the terms. This is the only, and the highest, criterion of truth in abstract things, that is, things which do not depend on experience—that it must either be an identity or be reducible to identities.

From this can be derived the elements of eternal truth in all things insofar as we understand them, as well as a method for proceeding demonstratively, as in geometry. In this way God understands everything a priori and through eternal truth, since he does not need experience and knows all things adequately, whereas we know hardly anything adequately, few things a priori, and most things through experience. In this last case other principles and other criteria must be applied. In factual or contingent matters, therefore, which do not depend on reason but on observation and experiment, primary truths (for us) are those that are perceived immediately within us or those of which we are conscious within ourselves. For it is impossible to prove these to ourselves through other experiences nearer or more intrinsic to us. But within myself I perceive not only myself who thinks but also many differences in my thoughts, from which I conclude that there are other things outside of me and gradually gain faith in my senses in opposition to the skeptics. For in matters which do not possess metaphysical necessity, we must regard the agreement of phenomena as truth, since such agreement does not occur by chance but has a cause. Certainly it is only through this agreement among phenomena that we distinguish dreams from waking, and we predict that the sun will rise tomorrow only because it has fulfilled our faith so often. To this is added the great power of authority and of public testimony, since it is not likely that so many should conspire to deceive us. To these factors can be added what Saint Augustine has said on the utility of faith. The authority of the senses and of other witnesses once established, we may prepare a record of phenomena from which a mixed knowledge can be formed by combining with them truths abstracted from experience. But we need a particular art for arranging as well as for ordering and combining our experiments, so that useful inductions can be made from them, causes discovered, and general truths and postulates *[aphorismi et praenotiones]* set up. The carelessness of men is amazing, wasting their time in trifles and neglecting the matters by which they could take care of health and well-being. For perhaps they would have within their power the remedies for a great part of their ills if only they would make right use of the great wealth of observations already available to our century and of the true analysis. Our human knowledge of nature seems to me at present like a shop well provided with all kinds of wares but without any order or inventory.

The distinction between synthesis and analysis also becomes apparent from these considerations. Synthesis is achieved when we begin from principles and run through truths in good order, thus discovering certain progressions and setting up tables, or sometimes general formulas, in which the answers to emerging questions can later be discovered. Analysis goes back to the principles in order to solve the given problems only, just as if neither we nor others had discovered anything before. It is more important to establish syntheses, because this work is of permanent value, while we often do work that has already been done in beginning the analysis of a particular problem. But it is a lesser art to use syntheses already set up by others and theorems already discovered, than to achieve everything through one's own work, by carrying out analyses, especially since we do not always remember or have at hand the truths which we ourselves or others have already discovered. Analysis is of two kinds. The common type advances by leaps and is used in algebra. The other is special and far more elegant but less well known; I call it 'reductive' analysis. Analysis is more necessary in practice, in order to solve problems that are given to us. But whoever is capable of more theoretical pursuits will be content to practice analysis only far enough to master the art but will then prefer to synthesize and will willingly tackle only such questions to which he is led by the order of research itself. In this way he will always progress pleasantly and easily and will not feel any difficulties or be disappointed in the outcome, for in a short time he will achieve much more than he could ever have hoped at the start. But ordinarily people destroy the fruits of their thinking through undue haste and attack too difficult problems at a leap, thus achieving nothing despite great effort. It must be realized that our method of inquiry is at last perfected when we can foresee whether it will lead us to a solution. Those who think that the analytic presentation consists in revealing the origin of a discovery, the synthetic in keeping it concealed, are in error. I have often observed that of the great geniuses of discovery, some are more inclined to analysis, others to the art of combinations. Combination or synthesis is the better means for discovering the use or application of something, as for example, given the magnetic needle, to think of its application in the compass. Analysis, on the contrary, is best suited for discovering the means when the thing to be discovered or the proposed end is given. Analysis is rarely pure, however, for usually, when we search for the means, we come upon contrivances which have already been discovered by others or by ourselves either accidentally or by reason, and which we find stored up as in a table or inventory, either in our own memory or in the accounts of others, and which we now apply for our purpose. But this is synthesis. For the rest, the art of combinations in particular, as I take it (it can also be called a general characteristic or algebra), is that science in which are treated the forms or formulas of things in general, that is, *quality* in general or similarity and dissimilarity; in the same way that ever new formulas arise from the elements, *a, b, c* themselves when combined with each other, whether these elements represent quantities or something else. This art is distinct from common algebra, which deals with formulas applied to *quantity* only or to equality and inequality. This algebra is thus subordinate to the art of combinations and constantly uses its rules. But these rules of combination are far more general and find application not only in algebra but in the art of deciphering, in various games, in geometry itself when it is treated linearly in the manner of the ancients, and finally, in all matters involving relations of similarity.

II.*

*On Wisdom—The Art of Reasoning Well, the Art
of Discovery, the Art of Remembering*
1693(?)

Wisdom is a perfect knowledge of the principles of all the sciences and of the art of applying them. I call *principles* all the fundamental truths which

---

* From *The Philosophical Works of Leibnitz*, translated and edited by George Martin Duncan; Tuttle, Morehouse & Taylor, New Haven, 1890.

suffice for drawing thence all conclusions in case of need, after some exercise and with some little application. In a word, that which serves to lead the mind to regulate the manners, to subsist honestly, and everywhere, even if one were amid barbarians, to preserve the health, to perfect one's self in every kind of thing of which one may have need, and to provide, finally, the conveniences of life. The art of applying these principles to exigencies, embraces the art of judging well or reasoning, the art of discovering unknown truths, and finally, of remembering what one knows, in the nick of time and when one has need of it.

THE ART OF REASONING WELL consists in the following maxims:

1. Nothing is ever to be recognized as true but what is so manifest that no ground for doubt can be found. This is why it will be well, in beginning one's investigations, to imagine one's self interested in sustaining the contrary, in order to see if this incitement could not arouse one to find that the matter has something solid to be said in its favor. For prejudices must be avoided and nothing be ascribed to things but what they include. But also one must never be opinionated.

2. When there appears to be no means of attaining this assurance, we must, in waiting for greater light, content ourselves with probability. But we must distinguish the degrees of probability and we must remember that all that we infer from a principle which is but probable must bear the marks of the imperfection of its source, especially when several probabilities must be supposed in order to reach this conclusion, for it thereby becomes still less certain than was each probability which serves it as basis.

3. To infer one truth from another, a certain connection, which shall be without interruption, must be observed. For as one may feel sure that a chain will hold when he is assured that each separate link is of good material and that it clasps the two neighboring links, viz: the one preceding and the one following it, so we may be sure of the accuracy of the reasoning when the matter is good, that is to say, when nothing doubtful enters into it, and when the form consists in a perpetual concatenation of truths which allows of no gap. For example, A is B and B is C and C is D, hence A is D. This concatenation will always teach us never to put in the conclusion more than there was in the premises.

THE ART OF DISCOVERY consists in the following maxims:

1. In order to know a thing we must consider all the requisites of that thing, that is to say, all that which suffices to distinguish it from every other thing. This is what is called definition, nature, reciprocal property.

2. Having once found a means of distinguishing it from every other thing, this same first rule must be applied to the consideration of each condition or requisite which enters into this means, and all the requisites of each requisite must be considered. And this is what I call true *analysis* or distribution of the difficulty into several parts.

3. When we have pushed the analysis to the end, that is to say, when we have considered the requisites which enter into the consideration of the thing

proposed and even the requisites of the requisites, and when we have finally come to the consideration of some natures which are understood only through themselves, which are without requisites and which need nothing outside of themselves in order to be conceived, we have reached a perfect knowledge of the thing proposed.

4. When the thing deserves it, we must try to have this perfect knowledge present in the mind all at once, and this is done by repeating the analysis several times until it seems to us that we see the whole of it at a single glance of the mind. And for this result a certain gradation in repetition must be observed.

5. The mark of perfect knowledge is when nothing presents itself in the thing in question for which we cannot account and when there is no conjuncture the outcome of which we cannot predict beforehand. It is very difficult to carry through an analysis of things, but it is not so difficult to complete the analysis of truths of which we have need. Because the analysis of a truth is completed when its demonstration has been found, and it is not always necessary to complete the analysis of the subject or predicate in order to find the demonstration of a proposition. Most often the beginning of the analysis of a thing suffices for the analysis or perfect knowledge of the truth which we know of the thing.

6. We must always begin our investigations with the easiest thing, such as the most general and the simplest, likewise those on which it is easy to make experiments and to find their reason, such as numbers, lines, motions.

7. We must proceed in order, and from easy things to those which are difficult, and we must try to discover some progression in the order of our meditations, so that we may have nature itself as our guide and voucher.

8. We must try to omit nothing in all our distributions or enumerations. For this, dichotomies by opposite members are very useful.

9. The first of several analyses of different particular matters will be the catalogue of simple thoughts, or those which are not far removed from simple.

10. Having the catalogue of simple thoughts we shall be in position to recommence *a priori* and to explain the origin of things, beginning at their source, in a perfect order and in a combination or synthesis absolutely complete. And this is all that our mind can do in the state in which it is at present.

THE ART OF REMEMBERING in the nick of time and when it is needed what one knows, consists in the following observations:

1. We must accustom ourselves to be present-minded, that is to say, to be able to meditate just as well in a tumult, on occasion, and in danger, as in our cabinet. This is why we must test ourselves on occasions and even seek them; with this precaution, however, that we do not expose ourselves without good reason to irreparable evil. In the meanwhile it is good to exercise ourselves on occasions when the danger is imaginary or small, as in our sport, conversations, conferences, exercises, and comedies.

2. We must accustom ourselves to enumerations. This is why it is well to exercise ourselves in collecting all possible cases of the matter in question, all

the species of a genus, all the conveniences or inconveniences of a means, all possible ways of aiming at some end.

3. We must accustom ourselves to distinctions; namely, two or more very similar things being given, to find on the spot all their differences.

4. We must accustom ourselves to analogies; namely, two or more very different things being given to find their resemblances.

5. We must be able to adduce on the spot things which closely resemble the given thing or which are very different from it. For example, when one denies some general maxim, it is well if I can adduce on the spot some examples. And when another quotes some maxim against me, it is well if I can forthwith oppose an instance to him. When one tells me a story, it is well if I can adduce then and there a similar one.

6. When there are truths or knowledges in which the natural connection of the subject with its predicate is not known to us, as happens in matters of fact and in truths of experience, in order to retain them we must make use of certain artifices, as for example, for the specific properties of simple, natural, civil and ecclesiastical history, geography, customs, laws, canons, languages. I see nothing so fitted to make us retain these things as burlesque verses and sometimes certain figures; also hypotheses invented to explain them in imitation of natural things (as an appropriate etymology, true or false, for languages—Regula mundi, in imagining certain orders of providence for history).

7. Finally, it is well to make an *inventory* in writing of the knowledges which are the most useful, with a register or alphabetical table. And finally a portable *manual* must be drawn therefrom of what is most necessary and most ordinary.

5 JOHN LOCKE
Human Understanding and the
Improvement of Knowledge*

Introduction

1. Since it is the *understanding* that sets man above the rest of sensible beings, and gives him all the advantage and dominion which he has over them; it is certainly a subject, even for its nobleness, worth our labour to inquire into. The understanding, like the eye, whilst it makes us see and perceive all other things, takes no notice of itself; and it requires art and pains to set it at a distance and make it its own subject. But whatever be the difficulties that lie in the way of this inquiry; whatever it be that keeps us so much in the dark to

---

* From *An Essay Concerning Human Understanding*. First published in 1690.

ourselves; sure I am that all the light we can let in upon our minds, all the acquaintance we can make with our own understandings, will not only be very pleasant, but bring us great advantage, in directing our thoughts in the search of other things.

2. This, therefore, being my purpose—to inquire into the original, certainty, and extent of *human knowledge,* together with the grounds and degrees of *belief, opinion,* and *assent;*—I shall not at present meddle with the physical consideration of the mind; or trouble myself to examine wherein its essence consists; or by what motions of our spirits or alterations of our bodies we come to have any *sensation* by our organs, or any *ideas* in our understandings; and whether those ideas do in their formation, any or all of them, depend on matter or not. These are speculations which, however curious and entertaining, I shall decline, as lying out of my way in the design I am now upon. It shall suffice to my present purpose, to consider the discerning faculties of a man, as they are employed about the objects which they have to do with. And I shall imagine I have not wholly misemployed myself in the thoughts I shall have on this occasion, if, in this historical, plain method, I can give any account of the ways whereby our understandings come to attain those notions of things we have; and can set down any measures of the certainty of our knowledge; or the grounds of those persuasions which are to be found amongst men, so various, different, and wholly contradictory; and yet asserted somewhere or other with such assurance and confidence, that he that shall take a view of the opinions of mankind, observe their opposition, and at the same time consider the fondness and devotion wherewith they are embraced, the resolution and eagerness wherewith they are maintained, may perhaps have reason to suspect, that either there is no such thing as truth at all, or that mankind hath no sufficient means to attain a certain knowledge of it.

3. It is therefore worth while to search out the bound between opinion and knowledge; and examine by what measures, in things whereof we have no certain knowledge, we ought to regulate our assent and moderate our persuasion. In order whereunto I shall pursue this following method:—

First, I shall inquire into the original of those *ideas,* notions, or whatever else you please to call them, which a man observes, and is conscious to himself he has in his mind; and the ways whereby the understanding comes to be furnished with them.

Secondly, I shall endeavour to show what *knowledge* the understanding hath by those ideas; and the certainty, evidence, and extent of it.

Thirdly, I shall make some inquiry into the nature and grounds of *faith* or *opinion:* whereby I mean that assent which we give to any proposition as true, of whose truth yet we have no certain knowledge. And here we shall have occasion to examine the reasons and degrees of *assent.*

4. If by this inquiry into the nature of the understanding, I can discover the powers thereof; how far they reach; to what things they are in any degree proportionate; and where they fail us, I suppose it may be of use to prevail with the busy mind of man to be more cautious in meddling with things exceeding

its comprehension; to stop when it is at the utmost extent of its tether; and to sit down in a quiet ignorance of those things which, upon examination, are found to be beyond the reach of our capacities. We should not then perhaps be so forward, out of an affectation of an universal knowledge, to raise questions, and perplex ourselves and others with disputes about things to which our understandings are not suited; and of which we cannot frame in our minds any clear or distinct perceptions, or whereof (as it has perhaps too often happened) we have not any notions at all. If we can find out how far the understanding can extend its view; how far it has faculties to attain certainty; and in what cases it can only judge and guess, we may learn to content ourselves with what is attainable by us in this state.

5. For though the comprehension of our understandings comes exceeding short of the vast extent of things, yet we shall have cause enough to magnify the bountiful Author of our being, for that proportion and degree of knowledge he has bestowed on us, so far above all the rest of the inhabitants of this our mansion. Men have reason to be well satisfied with what God hath thought fit for them, since he hath given them (as St. Peter says) πάντα πρὸς ζωὴν καὶ εὐσέβειαν whatsoever is necessary for the conveniences of life and information of virtue; and has put within the reach of their discovery, the comfortable provision for this life, and the way that leads to a better. How short soever their knowledge may come of an universal or perfect comprehension of whatsoever is, it yet secures their great concernments, that they have light enough to lead them to the knowledge of their Maker, and the sight of their own duties. Men may find matter sufficient to busy their heads, and employ their hands with variety, delight, and satisfaction, if they will not boldly quarrel with their own constitution, and throw away the blessings their hands are filled with, because they are not big enough to grasp everything. We shall not have much reason to complain of the narrowness of our minds, if we will but employ them about what may be of use to us; for of that they are very capable. And it will be an unpardonable, as well as childish peevishness, if we undervalue the advantages of our knowledge, and neglect to improve it to the ends for which it was given us, because there are some things that are set out of the reach of it. It will be no excuse to an idle and untoward servant, who would not attend his business by candle light, to plead that he had not broad sunshine. The Candle that is set up in us shines bright enough for all our purposes. The discoveries we can make with this ought to satisfy us; and we shall then use our understandings right, when we entertain all objects in that way and proportion that they are suited to our faculties, and upon those grounds they are capable of being proposed to us; and not peremptorily or intemperately require demonstration, and demand certainty, where probability only is to be had, and which is sufficient to govern all our concernments. If we will disbelieve everything, because we cannot certainly know all things, we shall do muchwhat as wisely as he who would not use his legs, but sit still and perish, because he had no wings to fly.

6. When we know our own strength, we shall the better know what to under-

take with hopes of success; and when we have well surveyed the *powers* of our own minds, and made some estimate what we may expect from them, we shall not be inclined either to sit still, and not set our thoughts on work at all, in despair of knowing anything; nor on the other side, question everything, and disclaim all knowledge, because some things are not to be understood. It is of great use to the sailor to know the length of his line, though he cannot with it fathom all the depths of the ocean. It is well he knows that it is long enough to reach the bottom, at such places as are necessary to direct his voyage, and caution him against running upon shoals that may ruin him. Our business here is not to know all things, but those which concern our conduct. If we can find out those measures, whereby a rational creature, put in that state in which man is in this world, may and ought to govern his opinions, and actions depending thereon, we need not to be troubled that some other things escape our knowledge . . .

Book IV—Chap. XII. Of the Improvement of Our Knowledge

1. It having been the common received opinion amongst men of letters, that *maxims* were the foundation of all knowledge; and that the sciences were each of them built upon certain *praecognita,* from whence the understanding was to take its rise, and by which it was to conduct itself in its inquiries into the matters belonging to that science, the beaten road of the Schools has been, to lay down in the beginning one or more *general propositions,* as foundations whereon to build the knowledge that was to be had of that subject. These doctrines, thus laid down for foundations of any science, were called *principles,* as the beginnings from which we must set out, and look no further backwards in our inquiries, as we have already observed.

2. One thing which might probably give an occasion to this way of proceeding in other sciences, was (as I suppose) the good success it seemed to have in *mathematics,* wherein men, being observed to attain a great certainty of knowledge, these sciences came by pre-eminence to be called Μαθήματα, and Μάθησις, learning, or things learned, thoroughly learned, as having of all others the greatest certainty, clearness, and evidence in them.

3. But if any one will consider, he will (I guess) find, that the great advancement and certainty of real knowledge which men arrived to in these sciences, was not owing to the influence of these principles, nor derived from any peculiar advantage they received from two or three general maxims, laid down in the beginning; but from the clear, distinct, complete ideas their thoughts were employed about, and the relation of equality and excess so clear between some of them, that they had an intuitive knowledge, and by *that* a way to discover it in others; and this without the help of those maxims. For I ask, Is it not possible for a young lad to know that his whole body is bigger than his little finger, but by virtue of this axiom, that *the whole is bigger than a part;* nor be assured of it, till he has learned that maxim? Or cannot a country wench know that, having received a shilling from one that owes her three, and a shilling also

from another that owes her three, the remaining debts in each of their hands are equal? Cannot she know this, I say, unless she fetch the certainty of it from this maxim, that *if you take equals from equals, the remainder will be equals,* a maxim which possibly she never heard or thought of? I desire any one to consider, from what has been elsewhere said, which is known first and clearest by most people, the particular instance, or the general rule; and which it is that gives life and birth to the other. These general rules are but the comparing our more general and abstract ideas, which are the workmanship of the mind, made, and names given to them for the easier dispatch in its reasonings, and drawing into comprehensive terms and short rules its various and multiplied observations. But knowledge began in the mind, and was founded on particulars; though afterwards, perhaps, no notice was taken thereof: it being natural for the mind (forward still to enlarge its knowledge) most attentively to lay up those general notions, and make the proper use of them, which is to disburden the memory of the cumbersome load of particulars. For I desire it may be considered, what more certainty there is to a child, or any one, that his body, little finger, and all, is bigger than his little finger alone, after you have given to his body the name *whole*, and to his little finger the name *part*, than he could have had before; or what new knowledge concerning his body can these two relative terms give him, which he could not have without them? Could he not know that his body was bigger than his little finger, if his language were yet so imperfect that he had no such relative terms as whole and part? I ask, further, when he has got these names, how is he more certain that his body is a whole, and his little finger a part, than he was or might be certain before he learnt those terms, that his body was bigger than his little finger? Any one may as reasonably doubt or deny that his little finger is a part of his body, as that it is less than his body. And he that can doubt whether it be less, will as certainly doubt whether it be a part. So that the maxim, the whole is bigger than a part, can never be made use of to prove the little finger less than the body, but when it is useless, by being brought to convince one of a truth which he knows already. For he that does not certainly know that any parcel of matter, with another parcel of matter joined to it, is bigger than either of them alone, will never be able to know it by the help of these two relative terms, whole and part, make of them what maxim you please.

4. But be it in the mathematics as it will, whether it be clearer, that, taking an inch from a black line of two inches, and an inch from a red line of two inches, the remaining parts of the two lines will be equal, or that *if you take equals from equals, the remainder will be equals*: which, I say, of these two is the clearer and first known, I leave to any one to determine, it not being material to my present occasion. That which I have here to do, is to inquire, whether, if it be the readiest way to knowledge to begin with general maxims, and build upon them, it be yet a safe way to take the *principles* which are laid down in any other science as unquestionable truths; and so receive them without examination, and adhere to them, without suffering them to be doubted of, because mathematicians have been so happy, or so fair, to use none but self-evident

and undeniable. If this be so, I know not what may not pass for truth in morality, what may not be introduced and proved in natural philosophy.

Let that principle of some of the old philosophers, That all is Matter, and that there is nothing else, be received for certain and indubitable, and it will be easy to be seen by the writings of some that have revived it again in our days, what consequences it will lead us into. Let any one, with Polemo, take the world; or with the Stoics, the aether, or the sun; or with Anaximenes, the air, to be God; and what a divinity, religion, and worship must we needs have! Nothing can be so dangerous as *principles* thus *taken up without questioning or examination;* especially if they be such as concern morality, which influence men's lives, and give a bias to all their actions. Who might not justly expect another kind of life in Aristippus, who placed happiness in bodily pleasure; and in Antisthenes, who made virtue sufficient to felicity? And he who, with Plato, shall place beatitude in the knowledge of God, will have his thoughts raised to other contemplations than those who look not beyond this spot of earth, and those perishing things which are to be had in it. He that, with Archelaus, shall lay it down as a principle, that right and wrong, honest and dishonest, are defined only by laws, and not by nature, will have other measures of moral rectitude and pravity, than those who take it for granted that we are under obligations antecedent to all human constitutions.

5. If, therefore, those that pass for *principles* are *not certain,* (which we must have some way to know, that we may be able to distinguish them from those that are doubtful,) but are only made so to us by our blind assent, we are liable to be misled by them; and instead of being guided into truth, we shall, by principles, be only confirmed in mistake and error.

6. But since the knowledge of the certainty of principles, as well as of all other truths, depends only upon the perception we have of the agreement or disagreement of our ideas, the way to improve our knowledge is not, I am sure, blindly, and with an implicit faith, to receive and swallow principles; but is, I think, to get and fix in our minds clear, distinct, and complete ideas, as far as they are to be had, and annex to them proper and constant names. And thus, perhaps, without any other principles, but *barely considering those* perfect ideas, and by *comparing them one with another,* finding their agreement and disagreement, and their several relations and habitudes; we shall get more true and clear knowledge by the conduct of this one rule, than by taking up principles, and thereby putting our minds into the disposal of others.

7. We must, therefore, if we will proceed as reason advises, adapt our methods of inquiry to *the nature of the ideas we examine,* and the truth we search after. General and certain truths are only founded in the habitudes and relations of *abstract ideas.* A sagacious and methodical application of our thoughts, for the finding out these relations, is the only way to discover all that can be put with truth and certainty concerning them into general propositions. By what steps we are to proceed in these, is to be learned in the schools of the mathematicians, who, from very plain and easy beginnings, by gentle degrees, and a continued chain of reasonings, proceed to the discovery and demonstration of

truths that appear at first sight beyond human capacity. The art of finding proofs, and the admirable methods they have invented for the singling out and laying in order those intermediate ideas that demonstratively show the equality or inequality of unapplicable quantities, is that which has carried them so far, and produced such wonderful and unexpected discoveries: but whether something like this, in respect of other ideas, as well as those of magnitude, may not in time be found out, I will not determine. This, I think, I may say, that if other ideas that are the real as well as nominal essences of their species, were pursued in the way familiar to mathematicians, they would carry our thoughts further, and with greater evidence and clearness than possibly we are apt to imagine. . . .

14. But whether natural philosophy be capable of certainty or no, the ways to enlarge our knowledge, as far as we are capable, seems to me, in short, to be these two:—

First, The first is to get and settle in our minds determined ideas of those things whereof we have general or specific names; as least, so many of them as we would consider and improve our knowledge in, or reason about. And if they be specific ideas of substances, we should endeavour also to make them as complete as we can, whereby I mean, that we should put together as many simple ideas as, being constantly observed to co-exist, may perfectly determine the species; and each of those simple ideas which are the ingredients of our complex ones, should be clear and distinct in our minds. For it being evident that our knowledge cannot exceed our ideas; as far as they are either imperfect, confused, or obscure, we cannot expect to have certain, perfect, or clear knowledge.

Secondly, The other is the art of finding out those intermediate ideas, which may show us the agreement or repugnancy of other ideas, which cannot be immediately compared. . . .

6 DAVID HUME
The Need for a Science of Man*

. . . 'Tis evident, that all the sciences have a relation, greater or less, to human nature; and that however wide any of them may seem to run from it, they still return back by one passage or another. Even *Mathematics, Natural Philosophy, and Natural Religion,* are in some measure dependent on the science of MAN; since they lie under the cognizance of men, and are judged by their powers and faculties. 'Tis impossible to tell what changes and improvements we might make in these sciences were we thoroughly acquainted with the extent

---

* From the Introduction to *A Treatise of Human Nature.* First published in 1739.

and force of human understanding, and cou'd explain the nature of the ideas we employ, and of the operations we perform in our reasonings. And these improvements are the more to be hoped for in natural religion, as it is not content with instructing us in the nature of superior powers, but carries its views farther, to their disposition towards us, and our duties towards them; and consequently we ourselves are not only the beings, that reason, but also one of the objects, concerning which we reason.

If therefore the sciences of Mathematics, Natural Philosophy, and Natural Religion, have such a dependence on the knowledge of man, what may be expected in the other sciences, whose connexion with human nature is more close and intimate? The sole end of logic is to explain the principles and operations of our reasoning faculty and the nature of our ideas: morals and criticism regard our tastes and sentiments: and politics consider men as united in society, and dependent on each other. In these four sciences of *Logic, Morals, Criticism, and Politics,* is comprehended almost every thing, which it can any way import us to be acquainted with, or which can tend either to the improvement or ornament of the human mind.

Here then is the only expedient, from which we can hope for success in our philosophical researches, to leave the tedious lingring method, which we have hitherto followed, and instead of taking now and then a castle or village on the frontier, to march up directly to the capital or center of these sciences, to human nature itself; which being once masters of, we may every where else hope for an easy victory. From this station we may extend our conquests over all those sciences, which more intimately concern human life, and may afterwards proceed at leisure to discover more fully those, which are the objects of pure curiosity. There is no question of importance, whose decision is not compriz'd in the science of man; and there is none, which can be decided with any certainty, before we become acquainted with that science. In pretending therefore to explain the principles of human nature, we in effect propose a compleat system of the sciences, built on a foundation almost entirely new, and the only one upon which they can stand with any security.

And as the science of man is the only solid foundation for the other sciences, so the only solid foundations we can give to this science itself must be laid on experience and observation. 'Tis no astonishing reflection to consider, that the application of experimental philosophy to moral subjects should come after that to natural at the distance of above a whole century; since we find that in fact, there was about the same interval betwixt the origins of these sciences; and that reckoning from THALES to SOCRATES, the space of time is nearly equal to that betwixt my Lord BACON[1] and some late philosophers in *England,* who have begun to put the science of man on a new footing, and have engaged the attention, and excited the curiosity of the public. So true it is, that however other nations may rival us in poetry, and excel us in some other agreeable arts, the improvements in reason and philosophy can only be owing to a land of toleration and of liberty.

¹ Mr. *Locke,* my Lord *Shaftsbury,* Dr. *Mandeville,* Mr. *Hutchinson.* Dr. *Butler,* &c.

Nor ought we to think, that this latter improvement in the science of man will do less honour to our native country than the former in natural philosophy, but ought rather to esteem it a greater glory, upon account of the greater importance of that science, as well as the necessity it lay under of such a reformation. For to me it seems evident, that the essence of the mind being equally unknown to us with that of external bodies, it must be equally impossible to form any notion of its powers and qualities otherwise than from careful and exact experiments, and the observation of those particular effects, which result from its different circumstances and situations. And tho' we must endeavour to render all our principles as universal as possible, by tracing up our experiments to the utmost, and explaining all effects from the simplest and fewest causes, 'tis still certain we cannot go beyond experience; and any hypothesis, that pretends to discover the ultimate original qualities of human nature, ought at first to be rejected as presumptuous and chimerical.

I do not think a philosopher, who would apply himself so earnestly to the explaining the ultimate principles of the soul, would show himself a great master in that very science of human nature, which he pretends to explain, or very knowing in what is naturally satisfactory to the mind of man. For nothing is more certain, than that despair has almost the same effect upon us with enjoyment, and that we are no sooner acquainted with the impossibility of satisfying any desire, than the desire itself vanishes. When we see, that we have arrived at the utmost extent of human reason, we sit down contented; tho' we be perfectly satisfied in the main of our ignorance, and perceive that we can give no reason for our most general and most refined principles, beside our experience of their reality; which is the reason of the mere vulgar, and what it required no study at first to have discovered for the most particular and most extraordinary phaenomenon. And as this impossibility of making any farther progress is enough to satisfy the reader, so the writer may derive a more delicate satisfaction from the free confession of his ignorance, and from his prudence in avoiding that error, into which so many have fallen, of imposing their conjectures and hypotheses on the world for the most certain principles. When this mutual contentment and satisfaction can be obtained betwixt the master and scholar, I know not what more we can require of our philosophy.

But if this impossibility of explaining ultimate principles should be esteemed a defect in the science of man, I will venture to affirm, that 'tis a defect common to it with all the sciences, and all the arts, in which we can employ ourselves, whether they be such as are cultivated in the schools of the philosophers, or practised in the shops of the meanest artizans. None of them can go beyond experience, or establish any principles which are not founded on that authority. Moral philosophy has, indeed, this peculiar disadvantage, which is not found in natural, that in collecting its experiments, it cannot make them purposely, with premeditation, and after such a manner as to satisfy itself concerning every particular difficulty which may arise. When I am at a loss to know the effects of one body upon another in any situation, I need only put them in that situation, and observe what results from it. But should I endeavour to clear up after the same manner any doubt in moral philosophy, by placing myself in the same case with that which I consider, 'tis evident this reflection and premeditation would so disturb the operation of my natural principles, as must render it impossible to form any just conclusion from the phaenomenon. We must therefore glean up our experiments in this science from a cautious observation of human life, and take them as they appear in the common course of the world, by men's behaviour in company, in affairs, and in their pleasures. Where experiments of this kind are judiciously collected and compared, we may hope to establish on them a science, which will not be inferior in certainty, and will be much superior in utility to any other of human comprehension.

7 IMMANUEL KANT
Reconstruction in Metaphysics*

Whether the treatment of that class of knowledge with which reason is occupied follows the secure method of a science or not, can easily be determined by the result. If, after repeated preparations, it comes to a standstill, as soon as its real goal is approached, or is obliged, in order to reach it, to retrace its steps again and again, and strike into fresh paths; again, if it is impossible to produce unanimity among those who are engaged in the same work, as to the manner in which their common object should be obtained, we may be convinced that such a study is far from having attained to the secure method of a science, but is groping only in the dark. In that case we are conferring a great benefit on reason, if we only find out the right method, though many things should have to be surrendered as useless, which were comprehended in the original aim that had been chosen without sufficient reflection.

That *Logic,* from the earliest times, has followed that secure method, may be seen from the fact that since *Aristotle* it has not had to retrace a single step, unless we choose to consider as improvements the removal of some unnecessary subtleties, or the clearer definition of its matter, both of which refer to the

---

* From Preface to the Second Edition, *Critique of Pure Reason* (1781; Second Edition, 1787), pp. B vii–xviii. Throughout the present volume pagination of the First Edition will be prefixed by 'A' and that of the Second Edition by 'B'. The translation used is that by Max Müller (Macmillan, New York, 1896). Several emendations, made solely for the sake of greater clarity, and omission of some of the original footnotes are due to this editor.

elegance rather than to the solidity of the science. It is remarkable also, that to the present day, it has not been able to make one step in advance, so that, to all appearance, it may be considered as completed and perfect. If some modern philosophers thought to enlarge it, by introducing *psychological* chapters on the different faculties of knowledge (faculty of imagination, wit, etc.), or *metaphysical* chapters on the origin of knowledge, or the different degrees of certainty according to the difference of objects (idealism, scepticism, etc.), or lastly, *anthropological* chapters on prejudices, their causes and remedies, this could only arise from their ignorance of the peculiar nature of logical science. We do not enlarge, but we only disfigure the sciences, if we allow their respective limits to be confounded: and the limits of logic are definitely fixed by the fact, that it is a science which has nothing to do but fully to exhibit and strictly to prove all formal rules of thought (whether it be *a priori* or empirical, whatever be its origin or its object, and whatever be the impediments, accidental or natural, which it has to encounter in the human mind).

That logic should in this respect have been so successful, is due entirely to its limitation, whereby it has not only the right, but the duty, to make abstraction of all the objects of knowledge and their differences, so that the understanding has to deal with nothing beyond itself and its own forms. It was, of course, far more difficult for reason to enter on the secure method of science, when it has to deal not with itself only, but also with objects. Logic, therefore, as a kind of preparation *(propaedeutic)* forms, as it were, the vestibule of the sciences only, and where real knowledge is concerned, is presupposed for critical purposes only, while the acquisition of knowledge must be sought for in the sciences themselves, properly and objectively so called.

If there is to be in those sciences an element of reason, something in them must be known *a priori,* and knowledge may stand in a twofold relation to its object, by either simply *determining* it and its concept (which must be supplied from elsewhere), or by making it *real* also. The former is *theoretical,* the latter *practical knowledge* of reason. In both the *pure* part, namely, that in which reason determines its object entirely *a priori* (whether it contain much or little), must be treated first, without mixing up with it what comes from other sources; for it is bad economy to spend blindly whatever comes in, and not to be able to determine, when there is a stoppage, which part of the income can bear the expenditure, and where reductions must be made.

Mathematics and *physics* are the two theoretical sciences of reason, which have to determine their *objects a priori;* the former quite purely, the latter partially so, and partially from other sources of knowledge besides reason.

Mathematics, from the earliest times to which the history of human reason can reach, has followed, among that wonderful people, the Greeks, the safe way of a science. But it must not be supposed that it was as easy for mathematics as for logic, in which reason is concerned with itself alone, to find, or rather to make for itself that royal road. I believe, on the contrary, that there was a long period of tentative work (chiefly still among the Egyptians), and that the change is to be ascribed to a *revolution,* produced by the happy thought of a single man, whose experiment pointed unmistakably to the path that had to be followed, and opened and traced out for the most distant times the safe way of a science. The history of that intellectual revolution, which was far more important than the discovery of the passage round the celebrated Cape of Good Hope, and the name of its fortunate author, have not been preserved to us. But the story preserved by Diogenes Laertius, who names the reputed author of the smallest elements of ordinary geometrical demonstration, even of such as, according to general opinion, do not require to be proved, shows, at all events, that the memory of the revolution, produced by the very first traces of the discovery of a new method, appeared extremely important to the mathematicians, and thus remained unforgotten. A new light flashed on the first man who demonstrated the properties of the isosceles triangle (whether his name was *Thales* or any other name), for he found that he had not to investigate what he saw in the figure, or the mere concept of that figure, and thus to learn its properties; but that he had to produce (by construction) what he had himself, according to concepts *a priori,* placed into that figure and represented in it, so that, in order to know anything with certainty *a priori,* he must not attribute to that figure anything beyond what necessarily follows from what he has himself placed into it, in accordance with the concept.

It took a much longer time before physics entered on the high way of science: for no more than a century and a half has elapsed, since Bacon's ingenious proposal partly initiated that discovery, partly, as others were already on the right track, gave a new impetus to it,—a discovery which, like the former, can only be explained by a rapid intellectual revolution. In what I have to say, I shall confine myself to natural science, so far as it is founded on *empirical* principles.

When Galilei let balls of a particular weight, which he had himself previously determined, roll down an inclined plane, or when Torricelli made the air carry a weight, which he had previously determined to be equal to that of a definite volume of water; or when, in later times, Stahl changed metal into lime, and lime again into metals, by withdrawing and restoring something,[1] a new light flashed on all students of nature. They comprehended that reason has insight only into that which she herself produces on her own plan, and that she must move forward with the principles of her judgments, according to fixed law, and compel nature to answer her questions, but not let herself be led by nature, as it were in leading strings, because otherwise accidental observations, made on no previously fixed plan, will never converge towards a necessary law, which is the only thing that reason seeks and requires. Reason, holding in one hand its principles, according to which concordant phenomena alone can be admitted as laws of nature, and in the other hand the experiment, which it has devised according to those principles, must approach nature, in order to be taught by it: but not in the character of a pupil, who agrees to everything the master likes, but as the appointed judge, who compels the witnesses to answer the questions which he himself proposes. Therefore even the science of physics entirely owes the beneficial revolution in its character to the happy thought, that we ought to seek in nature (and not import into it by means of fiction) whatever reason must learn from nature, and could not know by itself, and that we must do this in accordance with what reason itself has originally placed into nature. Thus only has the study of nature entered on the secure method of a science, after having for many centuries done nothing but grope in the dark.

---

¹ I am not closely following here the course of the history of the experimental method, nor are the first beginnings of it very well known.

Metaphysic, a completely isolated and speculative science of reason, which declines all teaching of experience, and rests on concepts alone (not on their application to intuition, as mathematics), in which reason therefore is meant to be her own pupil, has hitherto not been so fortunate as to enter upon the secure path of a science, although it is older than all other sciences, and would remain, even if all the rest were swallowed up in the abyss of an all-destroying barbarism. In metaphysic, reason, even if it tries only to understand *a priori* (as it pretends to do) those laws which are confirmed by the commonest experience, is constantly brought to a standstill, and we are obliged again and again to retrace our steps, because they do not lead us where we want to go; while as to any unanimity among those who are engaged in the same work, there is so little of it in metaphysic, that it has rather become an arena, specially destined, it would seem, for those who wish to exercise themselves in mock fights, and where no combatant has, as yet, succeeded in gaining an inch of ground that he could call permanently his own. It cannot be denied, therefore, that the method of metaphysic has hitherto consisted in groping only, and, what is the worst, in groping among mere concepts.

What then can be the cause that hitherto no secure method of science has been discovered? Shall we say that it is impossible? Then why should nature have visited our reason with restless aspirations to look for it, as if it were its most important concern? Nay, more, how little should we be justified in trusting our reason if, with regard to one of the most important objects we wish to know, it not only abandons us, but lures us on by vain hopes, and in the end betrays us! Or, if hitherto we have only failed to meet with the right path, what indications are there to make us hope that, if we renew our researches, we shall be more successful than others before us?

The examples of mathematics and natural science, which by a single revolution have become what they are now, seem to me sufficiently remarkable to induce us to consider, what may have been the essential element in that intellectual revolution which has proved so beneficial to them, and to make the experiment of imitating them, at least, so far as the analogy between them, as sciences of reason, they bear to metaphysic. Hitherto it has been supposed that all our knowledge must conform to the objects: but, under that supposition, all attempts to establish anything about them *a priori,* by means of concepts, and thus to enlarge our knowledge, have come to nothing. The experiment therefore ought to be made, whether we may not succeed better with the problems of metaphysic, by assuming that the objects must conform to our mode of cognition, for this would better agree with the demanded possibility of an *a priori* knowledge of them, which is to settle something about objects, before they are given us. We have here the same case as with the first thought of Copernicus, who, not being able to get on in the explanation of the movements of the heavenly bodies, as long as he assumed that all the stars turned round the spectator, tried whether he could not succeed better by assuming the spectator to be turning round, and the stars to be at rest. A similar experiment may be tried in metaphysic, so far as the *intuition* of objects is concerned. If the intuition had to conform to the constitution of objects, I do not see how we could know anything of it *a priori;* but if the object (as an object of the senses) conforms to the constitution of our faculty of intuition, I can very well conceive such a possibility. As, however, I cannot rest in these intuitions, if they are to become knowledge, but have to refer them, as representations, to something as their object, and must determine that object by them, I have the choice of admitting, either that the *concepts,* by which I carry out that determination, conform to the object, being then again in the same perplexity on account of the manner how I can know anything about it *a priori;* or that the objects, or what is the same, the experience in which alone they are known (as given objects), must conform to those concepts. In the latter case, the solution becomes more easy, because experience, as a kind of knowledge, requires understanding, and I must therefore, even before objects are given to me, presuppose the rules of the understanding as existing within me *a priori,* these rules being expressed in concepts *a priori,* to which all objects of experience must necessarily conform, and with which they must agree. With regard to objects, so far as they are conceived solely by reason, and conceived as necessary, and which can never be given in experience, at least in that form in which they are conceived by reason, we shall find that the attempts at conceiving them (for they must admit of being conceived) will furnish afterwards an excellent test of our new method of thought, according to which we do not know of things anything *a priori* except what we ourselves put into them.[1]

---

[1] This method, borrowed from the student of nature, consists in our looking for the elements of pure reason in that *which can be confirmed or refuted by experiment.* Now it is impossible, in order to test the propositions of pure reason, particularly if they venture beyond all the limits of possible experience, to make any experiment with their *objects* (as in natural science); we can therefore only try with *concepts* and *propositions* which we admit *a priori,* by so contriving that the same objects may be considered on one side as objects of the senses and of the understanding in experience, and, on the *other,* as objects which are only thought, intended, it may be, for the isolated reason which strives to go beyond all the limits of experience. This gives us two different sides to be looked at; and if we find that, by looking on

things from that twofold point of view, there is an agreement with the principle of pure reason, while by admitting one point of view only, there arises an inevitable conflict with reason, then the experiment decides in favour of the correctness of that distinction.

DISCUSSION · RICHARD MCKEON
Philosophy and Method*

The purpose of philosophy in its final discursive form is the discovery, demonstration, or organization of truths and probabilities. Philosophers have devised a variety of ways to accomplish that purpose by the elaboration of dialectics, by the construction of systems, and by the formulation and resolution of problems. Some modesty has been induced in the statement of philosophic purposes and in the claims of philosophic accomplishments by the inconclusiveness of the disputations of any period and by the cycle of refutations which form the sequence of the history of philosophy. Yet the distrust of certainties and dogmatisms does not weaken the confidence of philosophers that the respective ways they follow would, if pushed far enough, resolve all or most or at least the most fundamental problems. However tentative the enunciation of the principles of a philosophy, however hesitant its assertion of truths and probabilities, and however pluralistic its tolerance of other doctrines, the statement of a philosophy is an expression of the unique contribution of this way of philosophizing and of the expectation that it may succeed where so many others have failed. The defects of philosophy are not found in the adequacies of the basic principles and methods of any particular philosophy, or even in the misuses to which principles and methods are put or the errors to which they are subject. The implausibilities of philosophies arise in the plurality of principles and methods which makes the refutation of philosophies a simple exercise of exposing absurd meanings which statements have when interpreted from other points of view than they were intended to express. This play of refuta-

* From "Philosophy and Method," *The Journal of Philosophy*, Vol. XLVIII, No. 22 (1951), pp. 653–682. Reprinted by permission of the editors of The Journal of Philosophy and the author.

Richard McKeon (1900–   ), educated at the University of Paris and Columbia University, has taught at Columbia University and the University of Chicago, and has authored or co-authored several books and numerous articles. He is past-president of the American Philosophical Association and the International Institute of Philosophy.

tion may also borrow the authority of history and science, for the framework of any philosophy will supply arguments to show, at the present stage of history and in the light of available knowledge, that any other doctrine is no longer a promising or defensible philosophic enterprise—because it requires the development of a dialectic, or the systematization and formalization of sciences, or the transformation of the immediate data of experience in the formulation of the problems of man, the world, and God.

The program and pretensions of a philosophy are determined not only in a context of problems and subjects to which it is thought to be adequate and useful but also in a context of other philosophies to which it is opposed on questions of truth and falsity, of adequacy and inadequacy, of clarity, distinctness, and precision, and of relevance, importance, and inclusiveness. Moreover, the history of philosophy is likewise affected by this difference between philosophies viewed in their plurality and philosophies viewed in the systematization imposed by one philosophy. Since conclusions lose their meaning and importance apart from their principles, and since principles cease to be principles in the context of unresolved oppositions, the history of philosophy viewed simply as a juxtaposition and series of philosophies becomes a succession of doctrines and statements, frequently trivial and seldom true, concerning a variety of subjects, frequently bizarre and seldom adequately presented. On the other hand, a philosopher can easily find in his doctrines and methods the means by which to assimilate the doctrines of all other philosophies to the principles and methods of his own philosophy and, in so doing, find inspiration in any tangent to what philosophers have said: he may discover a *philosophia perennis* which persists despite the apparent differences of philosophers but which needs the explicit development of his statement of it; or he may construct a dialectic of history in which the contradictions of earlier philosophies are absorbed in later syntheses and all previous philosophies reach their culmination in the philosophy which expounds this process; or he may trace a progressive resolution of problems by which philosophy has been transformed into sciences and is still, at its present stage, in process of scientific reformulation. . . .

The methods of philosophy are methods of statement and of action. They have been modeled, in different philosophies, on every possible form of statement and action, and every science, belief, and art has suggested doctrines and procedures by which to explain, guide, or control statement and action. Philosophic methods have been formulated as rules of logic, of dialectic, of sophistic, of rhetoric, of grammar, and of algebra, and the foundations of language and communication have been sought in psychology, in physiology, in sociology, in scientific method, in philology, and in the "language of nature," frequently as a first step to explaining knowledge, art, and action by means of language so conceived. Philosophic methods have been modeled on the techniques of mathematical demonstration, physical experimentation, and political debate; on conversation, oratory, and inquiry; on the relations of parts in an organic whole; on the motions of discrete things; and on the creative acts of intelligent production or intervention. Since the problems of philosophy are not determined by, or limited to, a single subject-matter but include, by some device and in some form, things, actions, and statements as well as the sciences by which they are explained and the arts by which they are developed and used, philosophies have not employed a single method or even methods comparable on a single scheme. . . .

The relations among philosophies are not simple differences concerning the same or comparable problems, nor can they be reduced to a translation formula which will transform a philosophic doctrine into the equivalent statement proper to another philosophy. Problems and doctrines move from subject-matter to subject-matter; even within a single subject-matter they take on different meanings and purposes from different principles; and subject-matters and principles are transformed by alterations of method. The subject-matter of philosophy is universal, and there is no reason *a priori* why any starting-point should provide better principles than any other or why any method adapted to the scope and intricacies of a universal subject should be preferable to any other. The sciences, the arts, the moral virtues, and the forms of polity afford neither analogies nor guidance for the resolution of this ultimate problem, since they are conceived and enter discussion in forms determined by philosophical principles and methods. There is no unique determination even of methods and principles which might permit a formal comparison of the structures of philosophic systems or analyses; but instead, the patterns are multidimensional and can be made to coincide only for limited areas. What emerges from such formal comparisons of philosophies is only the constant grounds of opposition and the ready refutations which are available even when all other content is dropped from discussion.

The massive preoccupations and irreducible oppositions of philosophers at the present time—as at all other times—can be stated formally in terms of philosophic principles. The preoccupations of symbolic logicians to extend the precisions of analysis are unaffected by the enthusiasms of dialecticians who find no significant truths except those yielded by synthesis, and neither is affected by the arguments of phenomenologists, pragmatists, and operationalists that the formation of symbolic systems and the reconciliation of contraries must depend on the prior resolution of problems by intelligent inquiry. . . .

Differences of methods, principles, purposes, and subject-matters account at once for the richness of philosophic discussion and the impossibility of bringing it to an unambiguous termination. The natural tendency to think in some one form or derivative of dialectic, logistic, or inquiry is strengthened by the facility of interpreting anything that is said in accordance with other methods in meanings, sometimes fantastic and often false, determined by one's own mode of thought. The fact that what seem common principles are applied by different methods to different subjects for different purposes easily escapes attention, since philosophers assume that the statements which result from their methods and purposes are as universal as their subject-matter. Efforts to resolve philosophic differences and to establish the claims of any one form of philosophy seek their grounds usually, as a consequence, in the relations which philosophy is conceived to have in its various forms with the methods and truths of science or in the practical consequences it might have in action.

For Further Reading

Note. Since the following materials, as well as suggestions in the listings throughout this volume, vary considerably in difficulty and the prerequisite degree of philosophical maturity, students are advised to consult with their instructors concerning which items are most suitable to their purposes and for still further suggestions. Also see the bibliography of sources and works of reference on the principal authors in the Appendix.

Ayer, A. J. (ed.), *Logical Positivism.* The Free Press, Glencoe, Ill., 1959.

Ayer, A. J., *et. al., The Revolution in Philosophy.* Macmillan, London, 1956.

Bergson, H., *An Introduction to Metaphysics.* The Liberal Arts Press, New York, 1949.

Broad, C. D., "Critical and Speculative Philosophy," in J. H. Muirhead (ed.), *Contemporary British Philosophy.* The Macmillan Company, New York, 1924.

Carnap, R., *Philosophy and Logical Syntax.* Kegan Paul, Trench, Trubner & Co., London, 1935.

Danto, A. C., *What Philosophy Is.* Part One. Harper & Row, New York, 1968.

Heidegger, M., *What is Philosophy?* Twayne Publishers, Inc., New York, 1958.

Husserl, E., *The Idea of Phenomenology.* Martinus Nijhoff, The Hague, 1964.

Johnstone, H. W., Jr., *What is Philosophy?* The Macmillan Company, New York, 1965.

Nelson, L., *Socratic Method and Critical Philosophy.* Yale University Press, New Haven, 1949.

Neurath, O., *et. al., Encyclopedia and Unified Science.* (International Encyclopedia of Unified Science, Vol. 1, No. 1) The University of Chicago Press, Chicago, 1938.

Ortega y Gasset, J., *What is Philosophy?* Norton, New York, 1960.

Passmore, J., *Philosophical Reasoning.* Scribner's, New York, 1961.

Pears, D. F. (ed.), *The Nature of Metaphysics.* Macmillan, London, 1957.

Peirce, C. S., "How to Make our Ideas Clear," *Popular Science Monthly,* 12 (1878). Reprinted in numerous anthologies and included in *Collected Papers of Charles Sanders Peirce,* 8 vols., 1931–58.

Plato, *Theaetetus.* 148E–151D. Translation and commentary by F. M. Cornford. Bobbs-Merrill, Indianapolis, n.d.

Urmson, J. O., *Philosophical Analysis.* Clarendon Press, Oxford, 1956.

Waismann, F., "How I See Philosophy," in H. D. Lewis (ed.), *Contemporary British Philosophy, Third Series.* Allen & Unwin, London, 1956.

Wheatley, J., *Prolegomena to Philosophy.* Part One. Wadsworth, Belmont, Calif., 1970.

Whitehead, A. N., *Process and Reality.* Chapter 1. The Macmillan Company, New York, 1929.

PART ONE

B·CONCEPTIONS AND CRITERIA OF TRUTH

8 THOMAS HOBBES
The Locus of Truth

I.*

5. There are many distinctions of propositions, whereof the first is, that some are *universal*, others *particular*, others *indefinite*, and others *singular;* and this is commonly called the distinction of *quantity*. An *universal* proposition is that whose subject is affected with the sign of an universal name, as *every man is a living creature*. *Particular*, that whose subject is affected with the sign of a particular name, as *some man is learned*. An *indefinite* proposition has for its subject a common name, and put without any sign, as *man is a living creature, man is learned*. And a *singular* proposition is that whose subject is a singular name, as *Socrates is a philosopher, this man is black*.

6. The second distinction is into *affirmative* and *negative*, and is called the distinction of *quality*. An *affirmative* proposition is that whose predicate is a positive name, as *man is a living creature*. *Negative*, that whose predicate is a negative name, as *man is not a stone*.

7. The third distinction is, that one is *true*, another *false*. A *true* proposition is that, whose predicate contains, or comprehends its subject, or whose predicate is the name of every thing, of which the subject is the name; as *man is a living creature* is therefore a true proposition, because whatsoever is called *man*, the same is also called *living creature;* and *some man is sick*, is true, because *sick* is the name of *some man*. That which is not true, or that whose predicate does not contain its subject, is called a false proposition, as *man is a stone*.

Now these words *true, truth*, and *true proposition*, are equivalent to one another; for truth consists in speech, and not in the things spoken of; and though *true* be sometimes opposed to *apparent* or *feigned*, yet it is always to be referred to the truth of proposition; for the image of a man in a glass, or a ghost, is therefore denied to be a very man, because this proposition, *a ghost is a man*, is not true; for it cannot be denied but that ghost is a very ghost. And therefore truth or verity is not any affection of the thing, but of the proposition concerning it. As for that which the writers of metaphysics say, that *a thing, one thing*, and *a very thing*, are equivalent to one another, it is but trifling and childish; for who does not know, that *a man, one man*, and *a very man*, signify the same.

8. And from hence it is evident, that truth and falsity have no place but amongst such living creatures as use speech. For though some brute creatures, looking upon the image of a man in a glass, may be affected with it, as if it were the man himself, and for this reason fear it or fawn upon it in vain; yet they do not apprehend it as true or false, but only as like; and in this they are not deceived. Wherefore, as men owe all their true ratiocination to the right

---

* From *De Corpore*, Chapter III.

understanding of speech; so also they owe their errors to the misunderstanding of the same; and as all the ornaments of philosophy proceed only from man, so from man also is derived the ugly absurdity of false opinions. For speech has something in it like to a spider's web, (as it was said of old of *Solon's* laws) for by contexture of words tender and delicate wits are ensnared and stopped; but strong wits break easily through them.

From hence also this may be deduced, that the first truths were arbitrarily made by those that first of all imposed names upon things, or received them from the imposition of others. For it is true (for example) that *man is a living creature,* but it is for this reason, that it pleased men to impose both those names on the same thing. . . .

II.*

. . . The general use of speech, is to transfer our mental discourse, into verbal; or the train of our thoughts, into a train of words; and that for two commodities, whereof one is the registering of the consequences of our thoughts; which being apt to slip out of our memory, and put us to a new labour, may again be recalled, by such words as they were marked by. So that the first use of names is to serve for *marks,* or *notes* of remembrance. Another is, when many use the same words, to signify, by their connexion and order, one to another, what they conceive, or think of each matter; and also what they desire, fear, or have any other passion for. And for this use they are called *signs.* Special uses of speech are these; first, to register, what by cogitation, we find to be the cause of any thing, present or past; and what we find things present or past may produce, or effect; which in sum, is acquiring of arts. Secondly, to show to others that knowledge which we have attained, which is, to counsel and teach one another. Thirdly, to make known to others our wills and purposes, that we may have the mutual help of one another. Fourthly, to please and delight ourselves and others, by playing with our words, for pleasure or ornament, innocently.

To these uses, there are also four correspondent abuses. First, when men register their thoughts wrong, by the inconstancy of the signification of their words; by which they register for their conception, that which they never conceived, and so deceive themselves. Secondly, when they use words metaphorically; that is, in other sense than that they are ordained for; and thereby deceive others. Thirdly, by words, when they declare that to be their will, which is not. Fourthly, when they use them to grieve one another; for seeing nature hath armed living creatures, some with teeth, some with horns, and some with hands, to grieve an enemy, it is but an abuse of speech, to grieve him with the tongue, unless it be one whom we are obliged to govern; and then it is not to grieve, but to correct and amend.

The manner how speech serveth to the remembrance of the consequence

---

* From *Leviathan,* Chapter 4. First published in 1651.

of causes and effects, consisteth in the imposing of names, and the *connexion* of them.

Of names, some are *proper,* and singular to one only thing, as *Peter, John, this man, this tree;* and some are *common* to many things, *man, horse, tree:* every of which, though but one name, is nevertheless the name of divers particular things in respect of all which together, it is called an *universal;* there being nothing in the world universal but names; for the things named are every one of them individual and singular.

One universal name is imposed on many things, for their similitude in some quality, or other accident; and whereas a proper name bringeth to mind one thing only, universals recall any one of those many.

And of names universal, some are of more, and some of less extent; the larger comprehending the less large; and some again of equal extent, comprehending each other reciprocally. As for example: the name *body* is of larger signification than the word *man,* and comprehendeth it; and the names *man* and *rational,* are of equal extent, comprehending mutually one another. But here we must take notice, that by a name is not always understood, as in grammar, one only word; but sometimes, by circumlocution, many words together. For all these words *he that in his actions observeth the laws of his country,* make but one name, equivalent to this one word, *just.*

By this imposition of names, some of larger, some of stricter signification, we turn the reckoning of the consequences of things imagined in the mind, into a reckoning of the consequences of appellations. For example: a man that hath no use of speech at all, such as is born and remains perfectly deaf and dumb, if he set before his eyes a triangle, and by it two right angles, such as are the corners of a square figure, he may, by meditation, compare and find, that the three angles of that triangle, are equal to those two right angles that stand by it. But if another triangle be shown him, different in shape from the former, he cannot know, without a new labour, whether the three angles of that also be equal to the same. But he that hath the use of words, when he observes, that such equality was consequent, not to the length of the sides, nor to any other particular thing in his triangle; but only to this, that the sides were straight, and the angles three; and that that was all, for which he named it a triangle; will boldly conclude universally, that such equality of angles is in all triangles whatsoever; and register his invention in these general terms, *every triangle hath its three angles equal to two right angles.* And thus the consequence found in one particular, comes to be registered and remembered, as a universal rule, and discharges our mental reckoning, of time and place, and delivers us from all labour of the mind, saving the first, and makes that which was found true *here,* and *now,* to be true in *all times* and *places.*

But the use of words in registering our thoughts is in nothing so evident as in numbering. A natural fool that could never learn by heart the order of numeral words, as *one, two,* and *three,* may observe every stroke of the clock, and nod to it, or say *one, one, one,* but can never know what hour it strikes. And it seems, there was a time when those names of number were not in use; and men were fain to apply their fingers of one or both hands, to those things they desired to keep account of; and that thence it proceeded, that now our numeral words are but ten, in any nation, and in some but five; and then they begin again. And he that can tell ten, if he recite them out of order, will lose himself, and not know when he has done. Much less will he be able to add, and subtract, and perform all other operations of arithmetic. So that without words there is no possibility of reckoning of numbers; much less of magnitudes, of swiftness, of force, and other things, the reckonings whereof are necessary to the being, or well-being of mankind.

When two names are joined together into a consequence, or affirmation, as thus, *a man is a living creature;* or thus, *if he be a man, he is a living creature;* if the latter name, *living creature,* signify all that the former name *man* signifieth, then the affirmation, or consequence, is *true;* otherwise *false.* For *true* and *false* are attributes of speech, not of things. And where speech is not, there is neither *truth* nor *falsehood; error* there may be, as when we expect that which shall not be, or suspect what has not been; but in neither case can a man be charged with untruth.

Seeing then that truth consisteth in the right ordering of names in our affirmations, a man that seeketh precise truth had need to remember what every name he uses stands for, and to place it accordingly, or else he will find himself entangled in words, as a bird in lime twigs, the more he struggles the more belimed. And therefore in geometry, which is the only science that it hath pleased God hitherto to bestow on mankind, men begin at settling the significations of their words; which settling of significations they call *definitions,* and place them in the beginning of their reckoning.

By this it appears how necessary it is for any man that aspires to true knowledge, to examine the definitions of former authors; and either to correct them, where they are negligently set down, or to make them himself. For the errors of definitions multiply themselves according as the reckoning proceeds, and lead men into absurdities, which at last they see, but cannot avoid, without reckoning anew from the beginning, in which lies the foundation of their errors. From whence it happens, that they which trust to books do as they that cast up many little sums into a greater, without considering whether those little sums were rightly cast up or not; and at last finding the error visible, and not mistrusting their first grounds, know not which way to clear themselves, but spend time in fluttering over their books; as birds that entering by the chimney, and finding themselves enclosed in a chamber, flutter at the false light of a glass window, for want of wit to consider which way they came in. So that in the right definition of names lies the first use of speech; which is the acquisition of science: and in wrong, or no definitions, lies the first abuse; from which proceed all false and senseless tenets; which make those men that take their instruction from the authority of books, and not from their own meditation, to be as much below the condition of ignorant men, as men endued with true science are above it. For between true science and erroneous doctrines, ignorance is in the middle. Natural sense and imagination are not subject to absurdity. Nature itself cannot err; and as men abound in copiousness of language, so they become more wise, or more mad than ordinary. Nor is it possible without letters for any man to become either excellently wise, or, unless his memory be hurt by disease or ill constitution of organs, excellently foolish. For words are wise men's counters, they do but reckon by them; but they are the money of fools, that value them by the authority of an Aristotle, a Cicero, or a Thomas, or any other doctor whatsoever, if but a man. . . .

9 RENÉ DESCARTES
The Criterion of Truth

I.*

Meditations on the First Philosophy

Synopsis

In the first Meditation I set forth the reasons for which we may, generally speaking, doubt about all things and especially about material things, at least so long as we have no other foundations for the sciences than those which we have hitherto possessed. But although the utility of a Doubt which is so general does not at first appear, it is at the same time very great, inasmuch as it delivers us from every kind of prejudice, and sets out for us a very simple way by which the mind may detach itself from the senses; and finally it makes it impossible for us ever to doubt those things which we have once discovered to be true.

In the second Meditation, mind, which making use of the liberty which pertains to it, takes for granted that all those things of whose existence it has the least doubt, are non-existent, recognises that it is however absolutely impossible that it does not itself exist. This point is likewise of the greatest moment, inasmuch as by this means a distinction is easily drawn between the things which pertain to mind—that is to say to the intellectual nature—and those which pertain to body.

But because it may be that some expect from me in this place a statement of the reasons establishing the immortality of the soul, I feel that I should here make known to them that having aimed at writing nothing in all this Treatise of which I do not possess very exact demonstrations, I am obliged to follow a similar order to that made use of by the geometers, which is to begin by

* From *The Philosophical Works of Descartes*, Vol. 1, translated by E. S. Haldane and G. R. T. Ross, Cambridge University Press, London, 1931. First published in 1641. Reprinted by permission of Cambridge University Press.

putting forward as premises all those things upon which the proposition that we seek depends, before coming to any conclusion regarding it. Now the first and principal matter which is requisite for thoroughly understanding the immortality of the soul is to form the clearest possible conception of it, and one which will be entirely distinct from all the conceptions which we may have of body; and in this Meditation this has been done. In addition to this it is requisite that we may be assured that all the things which we conceive clearly and distinctly are true in the very way in which we think them; and this could not be proved previously to the Fourth Meditation. Further we must have a distinct conception of corporeal nature, which is given partly in this Second, and partly in the Fifth and Sixth Meditations. And finally we should conclude from all this, that those things which we conceive clearly and distinctly as being diverse substances, as we regard mind and body to be, are really substances essentially distinct one from the other; and this is the conclusion of the Sixth Meditation. This is further confirmed in this same Meditation by the fact that we cannot conceive of body excepting in so far as it is divisible, while the mind cannot be conceived of excepting as indivisible. For we are not able to conceive of the half of a mind as we can do of the smallest of all bodies; so that we see that not only are their natures different but even in some respects contrary to one another. I have not however dealt further with this matter in this treatise, both because what I have said is sufficient to show clearly enough that the extinction of the mind does not follow from the corruption of the body, and also to give men the hope of another life after death, as also because the premises from which the immortality of the soul may be deduced depend on an elucidation of a complete system of Physics. This would mean to establish in the first place that all substances generally—that is to say all things which cannot exist without being created by God—are in their nature incorruptible, and that they can never cease to exist unless God, in denying to them his concurrence, reduce them to nought; and secondly that body, regarded generally, is a substance, which is the reason why it also cannot perish, but that the human body, inasmuch as it differs from other bodies, is composed only of a certain configuration of members and of other similar accidents, while the human mind is not similarly composed of any accidents, but is a pure substance. For although all the accidents of mind be changed, although, for instance, it think certain things, will others, perceive others, etc., despite all this it does not emerge from these changes another mind: the human body on the other hand becomes a different thing from the sole fact that the figure or form of any of its portions is found to be changed. From this it follows that the human body may indeed easily enough perish but the mind [or soul of man (I make no distinction between them)] [1] is owing to its nature immortal.

   In the third Meditation it seems to me that I have explained at sufficient

---

[1] [This translation is from the Latin version of the *Meditations*. Additional readings from the French version are indicated by the use of square brackets.—*Ed.*]

length the principal argument of which I make use in order to prove the existence of God. But none the less, because I did not wish in that place to make use of any comparisons derived from corporeal things, so as to withdraw as much as I could the minds of readers from the senses, there may perhaps have remained many obscurities which, however, will, I hope, be entirely removed by the Replies which I have made to the Objections which have been set before me. Amongst others there is, for example, this one, 'How the idea in us of a being supremely perfect possesses so much objective reality [that is to say participates by representation in so many degrees of being and perfection] that it necessarily proceeds from a cause which is absolutely perfect.' This is illustrated in these Replies by the comparison of a very perfect machine, the idea of which is found in the mind of some workman. For as the objective contrivance of this idea must have some cause, i.e. either the science of the workman or that of some other from whom he has received the idea, it is similarly impossible that the idea of God which is in us should not have God himself as its cause.

In the fourth Meditation it is shown that all these things which we very clearly and distinctly perceive are true, and at the same time it is explained in what the nature of error or falsity consists. This must of necessity be known both for the confirmation of the preceding truths and for the better comprehension of those that follow. (But it must meanwhile be remarked that I do not in any way there treat of sin—that is to say of the error which is committed in the pursuit of good and evil, but only of that which arises in the deciding between the true and the false. And I do not intend to speak of matters pertaining to the Faith or the conduct of life, but only of those which concern speculative truths, and which may be known by the sole aid of the light of nature.)

In the fifth Meditation corporeal nature generally is explained, and in addition to this the existence of God is demonstrated by a new proof in which there may possibly be certain difficulties also, but the solution of these will be seen in the Replies to the Objections. And further I show in what sense it is true to say that the certainty of geometrical demonstrations is itself dependent on the knowledge of God.

Finally in the Sixth I distinguish the action of the understanding *(intellectio)* from that of the imagination *(imaginatio)*; the marks by which this distinction is made are described. I here show that the mind of man is really distinct from the body, and at the same time that the two are so closely joined together that they form, so to speak, a single thing. All the errors which proceed from the senses are then surveyed, while the means of avoiding them are demonstrated, and finally all the reasons from which we may deduce the existence of material things are set forth. Not that I judge them to be very useful in establishing that which they prove, to wit, that there is in truth a world, that men possess bodies, and other such things which never have been doubted by anyone of sense; but because in considering these closely we come to see that they are neither so strong nor so evident as those arguments which lead us to the knowledge of our mind and of God; so that these last must be the most certain and most evident facts which can fall within the cognizance of the human mind. And this is the whole matter that I have tried to prove in these Meditations, for which reason I here omit to speak of many other questions with which I dealt incidentally in this discussion.

Meditation II

Of the Nature of the Human Mind: and that it is more easily known than the Body.

The Meditation of yesterday filled my mind with so many doubts that it is no longer in my power to forget them. And yet I do not see in what manner I can resolve them; and, just as if I had all of a sudden fallen into very deep water, I am so disconcerted that I can neither make certain of setting my feet on the bottom, nor can I swim and so support myself on the surface. I shall nevertheless make an effort and follow anew the same path as that on which I yesterday entered, i.e. I shall proceed by setting aside all that in which the least doubt could be supposed to exist, just as if I had discovered that it was absolutely false; and I shall ever follow in this road until I have met with something which is certain, or at least, if I can do nothing else, until I have learned for certain that there is nothing in the world that is certain. Archimedes, in order that he might draw the terrestrial globe out of its place, and transport it elsewhere, demanded only that one point should be fixed and immoveable; in the same way I shall have the right to conceive high hopes if I am happy enough to discover one thing only which is certain and indubitable.

I suppose, then, that all the things that I see are false; I persuade myself that nothing has ever existed of all that my fallacious memory represents to me. I consider that I possess no senses; I imagine that body, figure, extension, movement and place are but the fictions of my mind. What, then, can be esteemed as true? Perhaps nothing at all, unless that there is nothing in the world that is certain.

But how can I know there is not something different from those things that I have just considered, of which one cannot have the slightest doubt? Is there not some God, or some other being by whatever name we call it, who puts these reflections into my mind? That is not necessary, for is it not possible that I am capable of producing them myself? I myself, am I not at least something? But I have already denied that I had senses and body. Yet I hesitate, for what follows from that? Am I so dependent on body and senses that I cannot exist without these? But I was persuaded that there was nothing in all the world, that there was no heaven, no earth, that there were no minds, nor any bodies: was I not then likewise persuaded that I did not exist? Not at all; of a surety I myself did exist since I persuaded myself of something [or merely because I thought of something]. But there is some deceiver or other, very powerful and very cunning, who ever employs his ingenuity in deceiving me. Then without doubt I exist also if he deceives me, and let him deceive me as much as he will, he can never cause me to be nothing so long as I think that I am something. So that after having reflected well and carefully examined all things, we must come to the definite conclusion that this proposition: I am, I exist, is necessarily true each time that I pronounce it, or that I mentally conceive it. . . .

Meditation III

Of God: that He exists

I shall now close my eyes, I shall stop my ears, I shall call away all my senses, I shall efface even from my thoughts all the images of corporeal things, or at least (for that is hardly possible) I shall esteem them as vain and false; and thus holding converse only with myself and considering my own nature, I shall try little by little to reach a better knowledge of and a more familiar acquaintanceship with myself. I am a thing that thinks, that is to say, that doubts, affirms, denies, that knows a few things, that is ignorant of many [that loves, that hates], that wills, that desires, that also imagines and perceives; for as I remarked before, although the things which I perceive and imagine are perhaps nothing at all apart from me and in themselves, I am nevertheless assured that these modes of thought that I call perceptions and imaginations, inasmuch only as they are modes of thought, certainly reside [and are met with] in me.

And in the little that I have just said, I think I have summed up all that I really know, or at least all that hitherto I was aware that I knew. In order to try to extend my knowledge further, I shall now look around more carefully and see whether I cannot still discover in myself some other things which I have not hitherto perceived. I am certain that I am a thing which thinks; but do I not then likewise know what is requisite to render me certain of a truth? Certainly in this first knowledge there is nothing that assures me of its truth, excepting the clear and distinct perception of that which I state, which would not indeed suffice to assure me that what I say is true, if it could ever happen that a thing which I conceived so clearly and distinctly could be false; and accordingly it seems to me that already I can establish as a general rule that all things which I perceive (L. *percipio*, F. *nous concevons*) very clearly and very distinctly are true.

At the same time I have before received and admitted many things to be very certain and manifest, which yet I afterwards recognised as being dubious. What then were these things? They were the earth, sky, stars and all other objects which I apprehended by means of the senses. But what did I clearly [and distinctly] perceive in them? Nothing more than that the ideas or thoughts of these things were presented to my mind. And not even now do I deny that these ideas are met with in me. But there was yet another thing which I affirmed, and which, owing to the habit which I had formed of believing it, I thought I perceived very clearly, although in truth I did not perceive it at all, to wit, that there were objects outside of me from which these ideas proceeded, and to which they were entirely similar. And it was in this that I erred, or, if perchance my judgment was correct, this was not due to any knowledge arising from my perception.

But when I took anything very simple and easy in the sphere of arithmetic or geometry into consideration, e.g. that two and three together made five, and other things of the sort, were not these present to my mind so clearly as to enable me to affirm that they were true? Certainly if I judged that since such matters could be doubted, this would not have been so for any other reason than that it came into my mind that perhaps a God might have endowed me with such a nature that I may have been deceived even concerning things which seemed to me most manifest. But every time that this preconceived opinion of the sovereign power of a God presents itself to my thought, I am constrained to confess that it is easy to Him, if He wishes it, to cause me to err, even in matters in which I believe myself to have the best evidence. And, on the other hand, always when I direct my attention to things which I believe myself to perceive very clearly, I am so persuaded of their truth that I let myself break out into words such as these: Let who will deceive me, He can never cause me to be nothing while I think that I am, or some day cause it to be true to say that I have never been, it being true now to say that I am, or that two and three make more or less than five, or any such thing in which I see a manifest contradiction. And, certainly, since I have no reason to believe that there is a God who is a deceiver, and as I have not yet satisfied myself that there is a God at all, the reason for doubt which depends on this opinion alone is very slight, and so to speak metaphysical. But in order to be able altogether to remove it, I must inquire whether there is a God as soon as the occasion presents itself; and if I find that there is a God, I must also inquire whether He may be a deceiver; for without a knowledge of these two truths I do not see that I can ever be certain of anything. . . .

Meditation IV

Of the True and the False

I have been well accustomed these past days to detach my mind from my senses, and I have accurately observed that there are very few things that one knows with certainty respecting corporeal objects, that there are many more which are known to us respecting the human mind, and yet more still regarding God himself; so that I shall now without any difficulty abstract my thoughts from the consideration of [sensible or] imaginable objects, and carry them to those which, being withdrawn from all contact with matter, are purely intelligible. And certainly the idea which I possess of the human mind inasmuch as it is a thinking thing, and not extended in length, width and depth, nor participating in anything pertaining to body, is incomparably more distinct than is the idea of any corporeal thing. And when I consider that I doubt, that is to say, that I am an incomplete and dependent being, the idea of a being that is complete and independent, that is of God, presents itself to my mind with so much distinctness and clearness—and from the fact alone that this idea is found in me, or that I who possess this idea exist, I conclude so certainly that God exists, and that my existence depends entirely on Him in every moment of my life—that I do not think that the human mind is capable of knowing anything with more evidence and certitude. And it seems to me that I now have before me a road which will lead us from the contemplation of the true God (in whom all the treasures of science and wisdom are contained) to the knowledge of the other objects of the universe.

For, first of all, I recognise it to be impossible that He should ever deceive me; for in all fraud and deception some imperfection is to be found, and although it may appear that the power of deception is a mark of subtilty or power, yet the desire to deceive without doubt testifies to malice or feebleness, and accordingly cannot be found in God.

In the next place I experienced in myself a certain capacity for judging which I have doubtless received from God, like all the other things that I possess; and as He could not desire to deceive me, it is clear that He has not given me a faculty that will lead me to err if I use it aright. . . .

. . . Whereupon, regarding myself more closely, and considering what are my errors (for they alone testify to there being any imperfection in me), I answer that they depend on a combination of two causes, to wit, on the faculty of knowledge that rests in me, and on the power of choice or of free will—that is to say, of the understanding and at the same time of the will. For by the understanding alone I [neither assert nor deny anything, but] apprehend (L. *percipio*) the ideas of things as to which I can form a judgment. But no error is properly speaking found in it, provided the word error is taken in its proper signification; and though there is possibly an infinitude of things in the world of which I have no idea in my understanding, we cannot for all that say that it is deprived of these ideas [as we might say of something which is required by its nature], but simply it does not possess these; because in truth there is no reason to prove that God should have given me a greater faculty of knowledge than He has given me; and however skilful a workman I represent Him to be, I should not for all that consider that He was bound to have placed in each of His works all the perfections which He may have been able to place in some. I likewise cannot complain that God has not given me a free choice or a will which is sufficient, ample and perfect, since as a matter of fact I am conscious of a will so extended as to be subject to no limits. And what seems to me very remarkable in this regard is that of all the qualities which I possess there is no one so perfect and so comprehensive that I do not very clearly recognise that it might be yet greater and more perfect. For, to take an example, if I consider the faculty of comprehension which I possess, I find that it is of very small extent and extremely limited, and at the same time I find the idea of another faculty much more ample and even infinite, and seeing that I can form the idea of it, I recognise from this very fact that it pertains to the nature of God. If in the same way I examine the memory, the imagination, or some other faculty, I do not find any which is not small and circumscribed, while in God it is immense [or infinite]. It is free-will alone or liberty of choice which I find to be so great in me that I can conceive no other idea to be more great; it is indeed the case that it is for the most part this will that causes me to know that in some manner I bear the image and similitude of God. For although the power of will is incomparably greater in God than in me, both by reason of the knowledge and the power which, conjoined with it, render it stronger and more efficacious, and by reason of its object, inasmuch as in God it extends to a great many things; it nevertheless does not seem to me greater if I consider it formally and precisely in itself: for the faculty of will consists alone in our having the power of choosing to do a thing or choosing not to do it (that is, to affirm or deny, to pursue or to shun it), or rather it consists alone in the fact that in order to affirm or deny, pursue or shun those things placed before us by the understanding, we act so that we are unconscious that any outside force constrains us in doing so. For in order that I should be free it is not necessary that I should be indifferent as to the choice of one or the other of two contraries; but contrariwise the more I lean to the one—whether I recognise clearly that the reasons of the good and true are to be found in it, or whether God so disposes my inward thought—the more freely do I choose and embrace it. And undoubtedly both divine grace and natural knowledge, far from diminishing my liberty, rather increase it and strengthen it. Hence this indifference which I feel, when I am not swayed to one side rather than to the other by lack of reason, is the lowest grade of liberty, and rather evinces a lack or negation in knowledge than a perfection of will: for if I always recognised clearly what was true and good, I should never have trouble in deliberating as to what judgment or choice I should make, and then I should be entirely free without ever being indifferent.

From all this I recognise that the power of will which I have received from God is not of itself the source of my errors—for it is very ample and very perfect of its kind—and more than is the power of understanding; for since I understand nothing but by the power which God has given me for understanding, there is no doubt that all that I understand, I understand as I ought, and it is not possible that I err in this. Whence then come my errors? They come from the sole fact that since the will is much wider in its range and compass than the understanding, I do not restrain it within the same bounds, but extend it also to things which I do not understand: and as the will is of itself indifferent to these, it easily falls into error and sin, and chooses the evil for the good, or the false for the true. . . .

II.*

The Principles of Philosophy. First Part

Principle XLIII.
    That we cannot err if we give our assent only to things that we know clearly and distinctly.

---

* *op. cit.* The *Principia Philosophiae* was first published in 1644.

But it is certain that we shall never take the false as the true if we only give our assent to things that we perceive clearly and distinctly. Because since God is no deceiver, the faculty of knowledge that He has given us cannot be fallacious, nor can the faculty of will, so long at least as we do not extend it beyond those things that we clearly perceive. And even if this truth could not be rationally demonstrated, we are by nature so disposed to give our assent to things that we clearly perceive, that we cannot possibly doubt of their truth.

Principle XLIV.

That we shall always judge ill when we assent to what we do not clearly perceive, although our judgment may be true; and that it frequently is our memory that deceives us by leading us to believe that certain things had been satisfactorily established by us.

It is also quite certain that whenever we give our assent to some reason which we do not exactly understand, we either deceive ourselves, or, if we arrive at the truth, it is only by chance, and thus we cannot be certain that we are not in error. It is true that it happens but rarely that we judge of a matter at the same time as we observe that we do not apprehend it, because the light of nature teaches us that we must not judge of anything that we do not understand. But we frequently err when we presume we have known certain things as being stored up in our memory, to which on recollection we give our assent, and of which we have never possessed any knowledge at all.

Principle XLV.

What a clear and distinct perception is.

There are even a number of people who throughout all their lives perceive nothing so correctly as to be capable of judging of it properly. For the knowledge upon which a certain and incontrovertible judgment can be formed, should not alone be clear but also distinct. I term that clear which is present and apparent to an attentive mind, in the same way as we assert that we see objects clearly when, being present to the regarding eye, they operate upon it with sufficient strength. But the distinct is that which is so precise and different from all other objects that it contains within itself nothing but what is clear.

Principle XLVI.

It is shown from the example of pain that a perception may be clear without being distinct, but it cannot be distinct unless it is clear.

When, for instance, a severe pain is felt, the perception of this pain may be very clear, and yet for all that not distinct because it is usually confused by the sufferers with the obscure[1] judgment that they form upon its nature, assuming as they do that something exists in the part affected, similar to the sensation of pain of which they are alone clearly conscious. In this way perception

---

[1] 'false,' French version.—*Tr.*

may be clear without being distinct, and cannot be distinct without being also clear.

III.*

Letter to ·Mersenne (October 16, 1639)

. . . Moreover, since my last ones [letters], I took time out to read the book which you sent to me as a favor.[1] Since you have asked for my opinion and because it deals with a subject on which I have worked all my life, I think that I owe it to you to say something. I find in it many things which are quite good, *sed non publici saporis,* because there are few persons who are capable of understanding Metaphysics. As to the book in general, it holds to a road quite different from that which I have followed. It examines what Truth is; as for me, there was never any doubt, for I believe it to be a notion so transcendentally clear that it is impossible to ignore it. Indeed, one has as many means of examining a balance as there are ways of using it, but we should have no means of learning what truth is, if one did not know it by nature. What reason would we have of consenting to that which would manifest it to us, if we didn't know it to be true, that is to say, if we didn't know what truth is? Thus, one may well explain *quid nominis* to those who do not understand the language, and tell them that this word *truth,* in its proper signification, denotes the conformity of thought with the object, and that, when one attributes it to things which are outside thought, it means only that these things can serve as objects of true thoughts, either of our thoughts or God's. But one cannot give any definition of Logic which helps to know its nature. I believe the same for many other things which are quite simple and are naturally known, as are figure, size, motion, place, time, etc., so much so that when one wants to define these things one only obscures matters and gets entangled. Thus, for example, he who walks through a hall is in a much better position to show what motion is than he who says: *est actus entis in potentia prout in potentia,* and similarly for the others.

The author's criterion of truth is universal consent. As for me, my only criterion is the natural light *[lumière naturelle],* which is well fitted for such things, for all men having a similar natural light, it seems that they should all have the same notions. But this is not the case, because there are very few who make good use of this light, whence many persons (for example, all those we know) may consent to the same error. Furthermore, there are a number of things which can be known by the natural light but upon which no one has yet reflected.

---

* From *Oeuvres de Descartes,* Vol. II, ed. by C. Adam and P. Tannery, L. Cerf, Paris, 1897–1910; pp. 596–99. This translation is by the present editor.
[1] [*De veritate prout distinguitura revelatione, a verisimili, a possibili et a falso* by Herbert of Cherbury, Paris, 1624.—*Ed.*]

He [Herbert of Cherbury] maintains that there are in us as many faculties as there is a diversity of things to be known. I cannot understand this in any other way than if he were to say that, because wax can receive an infinity of shapes, we would say that it has in itself an infinity of faculties to receive them. This is true in a certain sense. But I do not see that one can draw any profit out of talking in this way: on the contrary, it seems to me that it can only be harmful in leading the ignorant to imagine a diversity of little entities in our soul. That is why I prefer to think that the wax, by its flexibility alone, receives all sorts of shapes, and that the soul acquires its knowledge by the reflection it does, either on itself in respect of intellectual things, or on the various dispositions of the brain to which it is joined in respect of corporeal things, whether these dispositions depend on the senses or on some other causes. But it is most practical not to accept anything on faith without considering the justification or the cause for receiving it, which brings us to what he says, that one must always consider the faculty one makes use of, etc.

Undoubtedly one also, as he says, must be careful that nothing is missing on the part of the object, or of the setting, or of the organ, etc., in order not to be misled by the senses.

He wishes that one would especially follow the natural instinct, from which he draws all his common notions. For myself, I distinguish two sorts of instincts: one is in us qua man and is purely intellectual. It is the natural light or *intuitus mentis,* in which alone, I hold, one must have confidence. The other is in us qua animals, and is a certain natural impulse to conserve our body, to enjoy corporeal delights, etc., which should not always be followed. . . .

10 BENEDICT SPINOZA
The Nature of Truth *

[*Cf.* Selection 3, in particular, pp. 68–72.]

Pt. II, Prop. XLIII, Note.

. . . No one, who has a true idea, is ignorant that a true idea involves the highest certainty. For to have a true idea is only another expression for knowing a thing perfectly, or as well as possible. No one, indeed, can doubt of this, unless he thinks that an idea is something lifeless, like a picture on a panel, and not a mode of thinking—namely, the very act of understanding. And who, I ask, can know that he understands anything, unless he do first understand it? In other words, who can know that he is sure of a thing, unless he be first sure of that thing? Further, what can there be more clear, and more cer-

---

* From *Ethica Ordine Geometrico Demonstrata*. First published posthumously in 1677. This translation is by R. H. M. Elwes (1884).

tain, than a true idea as a standard of truth? Even as light displays both itself and darkness, so is truth a standard both of itself and falsity.

I think I have thus sufficiently answered these questions—namely, if a true idea is distinguished from a false idea, only in so far as it is said to agree with its object, a true idea has no more reality or perfection than a false idea (since the two are only distinguished by an extrinsic mark); consequently, neither will a man who has true ideas have any advantage over him who has only false ideas. Further, how comes it that men have false ideas? Lastly, how can anyone be sure, that he has ideas which agree with their objects? These questions, I repeat, I have, in my opinion, sufficiently answered. The difference between a true idea and a false idea is plain: from what was said in II. xxxv., the former is related to the latter as being is to not-being. The causes of falsity I have set forth very clearly in II. xix. and II. xxxv. with the note. From what is there stated, the difference between a man who has true ideas, and a man who has only false ideas, is made apparent. As for the last question—as to how a man can be sure that he has ideas that agree with their objects, I have just pointed out, with abundant clearness, that his knowledge arises from the simple fact, that he has an idea which corresponds with its object—in other words, that truth is its own standard. . . .

Pt. II, Prop. XLIX.

There is in the mind no volition or affirmation and negation, save that which an idea, inasmuch as it is an idea, involves.

Proof.—There is in the mind no absolute faculty of positive or negative volition, but only particular volitions, namely, this or that affirmation, and this or that negation. Now let us conceive a particular volition, namely, the mode of thinking whereby the mind affirms, that the three interior angles of a triangle are equal to two right angles. This affirmation involves the conception or idea of a triangle, that is, without the idea of a triangle it cannot be conceived. It is the same thing to say, that the concept A must involve the concept B, as it is to say, that A cannot be conceived without B. Further, this affirmation cannot be made (II. Ax.iii) without the idea of a triangle. Therefore, this affirmation can neither be nor be conceived, without the idea of a triangle. Again, this idea of a triangle must involve this same affirmation, namely, that its three interior angles are equal to two right angles. Wherefore, and *vice versa*, this idea of a triangle can neither be nor be conceived without this affirmation, therefore, this affirmation belongs to the essence of the idea of a triangle, and is nothing besides. What we have said of this volition (inasmuch as we have selected it at random) may be said of any other volition, namely, that it is nothing but an idea. Q. E. D.

Corollary.—Will and understanding are one and the same.[1]

---

[1] [*Cf.* Descartes' account of the cause of error in the preceding Selection.— *Ed.*]

Proof.—Will and understanding are nothing beyond the individual volitions and ideas (II. xlviii. and note). But a particular volition and a particular idea are one and the same (by the foregoing Prop.); therefore, will and understanding are one and the same. Q. E. D.

Note.—We have thus removed the cause which is commonly assigned for error. For we have shown above, that falsity consists solely in the privation of knowledge involved in ideas which are fragmentary and confused. Wherefore, a false idea, inasmuch as it is false, does not involve certainty. When we say, then, that a man acquiesces in what is false, and that he has no doubts on the subject, we do not say that he is certain, but only that he does not doubt, or that he acquiesces in what is false, inasmuch as there are no reasons, which should cause his imagination to waver (see II. xliv. note). Thus, although the man be assumed to acquiesce in what is false, we shall never say that he is certain. For by certainty we mean something positive (II. xliii. and note), not merely the absence of doubt.[1]

. . . .

11 GOTTFRIED WILHELM LEIBNIZ
Knowledge and Truth

I.*

Dialogue (1677)

A. If you were given a thread and told to bend it in such a way that it shall form a closed line and shall include the greatest possible inclosed space, how would you bend it?

B. In a circle, for the geometricians show that a circle is the most spacious of figures of the same circumference. If there are two islands, one circular and the other square, around which one can walk in the same time, the circular one contains more land.

A. Do you consider that this is true even if you were never to think of it?

---

* From *G. W. Leibniz: Philosophical Papers and Letters*, translated and edited by Leroy E. Loemker, Second Edition, D. Reidel Publishing Company, Dordrecht, Holland, 1970 (pp. 182–185). Reprinted by permission of D. Reidel Publishing Company.

[1] [In the rest of this celebrated lengthy note Spinoza defends his doctrine that there is no possibility of any exercise of the will beyond the intellect by replying to possible objections to it and by citing various advantages of the doctrine.—*Ed.*]

B. Certainly, and even before the geometricians had proved it or men observed it.

A. So you think that truth and falsehood are in things, and not in thoughts.

B. By all means.

A. But can any *thing* be false?

B. I do not think that things are false, but thoughts or propositions about things.

A. Then falsehood is a property of thoughts and not of things.

B. I am forced to agree.

A. Why not truth also, then?

B. So it seems, but I am inclined to doubt whether this conclusion is valid.

A. When a question is proposed, do you not doubt whether or not some answer is true or false until you are certain of your opinion?

B. Of course.

A. You admit, therefore, that it is the same subject which is capable of truth or falsehood, until one or the other is established by the particular nature of the question.

B. I admit it and acknowledge that if falsehood is a property of thoughts, then truth is also and not of things.

A. But this contradicts what you said before, that there is also truth which no one has thought.

B. You have confused me.

A. Yet we must attempt to reconcile the two views. Do you think that all the thoughts that can be made are actually formed? Or, to put it more clearly, do you think that all propositions are thought?

B. I do not.

A. It seems then that truth is a quality of propositions or thoughts, but of possible thoughts, so that what is certain is only that if anyone should think in this way or in the opposite way, his thought would be true or false.

B. You seem to have succeeded in getting us over a slippery place.

A. But since there has to be a cause for the truth or falsity of any thought, I ask you where we shall seek this cause?

B. In the nature of things, I think.

A. But what if it arises from your own nature?

B. Certainly not from my nature alone. For my own nature and the nature of the things of which I think must be such that when I proceed by a valid method I shall necessarily infer the proposition concerned or find it true.

A. Your reply is excellent, but there are still difficulties.

B. Of what kind, I beg of you?

A. Certain men of learning believe that truth arises from the human will and from names or characters.[1]

---

[1] [*Cf.* Hobbes, *De Corpore*, Chap. III, pp. 102–3 above.—*Ed.*]

B. Such an opinion is certainly most paradoxical.

A. But they prove it in this way. Isn't definition the principle of demonstration?

B. I admit this, for certain propositions can be demonstrated solely by joining definitions together.

A. Hence the truth of such propositions depends upon definitions.

B. Granted!

A. But definitions depend upon our will.

B. How so?

A. Don't you see that it is within the choice of mathematicians to use the word 'ellipse' to signify a certain figure? And that it was within the choice of the Latins to ascribe that meaning to the word 'circle' which its definition expresses?

B. What of it? Thoughts can occur without words.

A. But not without some other signs. Try, I pray, whether you can begin any arithmetical calculation without numerical signs.

B. You disturb me very much, for I did not think that characters or signs are so necessary for ratiocination.

A. You grant then that arithmetical truths presuppose some signs or characters?

B. That can't be denied.

A. Therefore such truths depend on the human will?

B. You seem to be getting me tied up by a kind of sleight of hand.

A. These are not my ideas, but those of a very gifted writer.

B. But can anyone depart so far from a sound mind as to persuade himself that truth is arbitrary and depends on names, though he knows that the geometry of the Greeks, Latins, and Germans is the same?

A. You are right; yet the difficulty needs to be resolved.

B. There is just this one thing that makes me pause. I notice that no truth is ever known, discovered, or proved by me except by the use of words and other signs presented to the mind.

A. In fact, if there were no characters, we could neither think of anything distinctly nor reason about it.

B. Yet when we examine the figures of geometry, we sometimes establish truths merely by contemplating them accurately.

A. True, but we must recognize that these figures must also be regarded as characters, for the circle described on paper is not a true circle and need not be; it is enough that we take it for a circle.

B. Nevertheless, it has a certain similarity to the circle, and this is surely not arbitrary.

A. Granted; therefore, figures are the most useful of characters. But what similarity do you think there is between ten and the character 10?

B. There is some relation or order in the characters which is also in things, especially if the characters are well invented.

A. That may be, but what similarity do the first elements themselves have with things; for example, O with nothing, or *a* with a line? You will have to admit, therefore, that in these elements at least, there is no need of similarity to things. This is true, for example, in the words *lux* and *ferens;* even though their compound *lucifer* has a relation to these two words, *light* and *bearing,* which corresponds to that which the thing signified by *lucifer* has to the things signified by *lux* and *ferens.*

B. But the Greek φώσφορος has the same relation to φῶς and φέρω.

A. The Greeks might have used another word than this, however.

B. True. Yet I notice that, if characters can be used for ratiocination, there is in them a kind of complex mutual relation *[situs]* or order which fits the things; if not in the single words at least in their combination and inflection, although it is even better if found in the single words themselves. Though it varies, this order somehow corresponds in all languages. This fact gives me hope of escaping the difficulty. For although characters are arbitrary, their use and connection have something which is not arbitrary, namely a definite analogy between characters and things, and the relations which different characters expressing the same thing have to each other. This analogy or relation is the basis of truth. For the result is that whether we apply one set of characters or another, the products will be the same or equivalent or correspond analogously. But perhaps certain characters are always necessary for thinking.

A. Excellent! You have extricated yourself clearly and fully. And the analytic or arithmetical calculus confirms this view. For in numbers the problem always works out in the same way whether you use the decimal system or as some mathematician did, the duodecimal. Afterward, if you apply the solution you have reached by calculation in several different ways, by arranging kernels or some other countable objects, the answer always comes out the same. In analysis as well, even though different properties of the subject are more easily apparent when different characters are used, the basis of truth is always found in the connection and coordination of these characters. So calling the square of a, a^2, and substituting $b + c$ for a, we have $b^2 + c^2 + 2bc$ as the square. But if we substitute $d - e$ for a, we will have $d^2 + e^2 - 2de$ as the square. In the former case we express the relation of the whole, a, to its parts b and c; in the latter the relation of the part, a, to the whole, d, and the excess, e, of the whole over the part, a. Yet by substitution it becomes apparent that the calculation always leads to the same result. For if we substitute in the formula $d^2 + e^2 - 2de$ (which equals a^2), its equivalent $a + e$ for d, we shall have $a^2 + e^2 + 2ae$ for d^2, and $- 2ae - 2e^2$ for $- 2de$. So, adding these together,

$$+d^2 = a^2 + e^2 + 2ae$$
$$+e^2 = e^2$$
$$-2de = -2e^2 - 2ae$$

the sum produced is. . . . $= a^2$.

You see then that however arbitrarily the characters may be chosen, if you observe a certain order and rule in their use, they always agree. Therefore though truths necessarily presuppose some characters, and are indeed sometimes asserted about these characters themselves (as in the theorem about casting off nines), yet they consist not in the arbitrary element in their characters but in the permanent element in them, namely, in their relation to things. It is always true, without any arbitrary choice of ours, that if certain characters are adopted, some definite argument must proceed, and if others are adopted whose relation to the things signified is known but different, the resulting relation of the new characters will again correspond to the relation of the first characters, as appears by a substitution or comparison.

II.*

Meditations on Knowledge, Truth, and Ideas (1684)

Since distinguished men are today engaged in controversies about true and false ideas, a matter of great importance for understanding the truth and one to which even Descartes did not entirely do justice, I should like briefly to explain what I think may be established about the different kinds and the criteria of ideas and of knowledge. Knowledge is either obscure or *clear;* clear knowledge is either confused or *distinct;* distinct knowledge is either inadequate or *adequate,* and also either symbolic or *intuitive.* The most perfect knowledge is that which is both adequate and intuitive.

A concept is obscure which does not suffice for recognizing the thing represented, as when I merely remember some flower or animal which I have once seen but not well enough to recognize it when it is placed before me and to distinguish it from similar ones; or when I consider some term which the Scholastics had defined poorly, such as Aristotle's entelechy, or cause as a common term for material, formal, efficient, and final cause, or other such terms of which we have no sure definition. A proposition also becomes obscure when it contains such a concept.

Knowledge is *clear,* therefore, when it makes it possible for me to recognize the thing represented. Clear knowledge, in turn, is either confused or distinct. It is *confused* when I cannot enumerate one by one the marks which are sufficient to distinguish the thing from others, even though the thing may in truth have such marks and constituents into which its concept can be resolved. Thus we know colors, odors, flavors, and other particular objects of the senses clearly enough and discern them from each other but only by the simple evidence of the senses and not by marks that can be expressed. So we cannot explain to a blind man what red is, nor can we explain such a quality to others except by bringing them into the presence of the thing and making them see, smell, or taste it, or at least by reminding them of some similar perception they have had in the past. Yet it is certain that the concepts of these qualities are

---

* From *op. cit.,* pp. 291–294.

composite and can be resolved, for they certainly have their causes. Likewise we sometimes see painters and other artists correctly judge what has been done well or done badly; yet they are often unable to give a reason for their judgment but tell the inquirer that the work which displeases them lacks 'something, I know not what.'

A *distinct* concept, however, is the kind of notion which assayers have of gold; one, namely, which enables them to distinguish gold from all other bodies by sufficient marks and observations. We usually have such concepts about objects common to many senses, such as number, magnitude, and figure, and also about many affections of the mind such as hope and fear; in a word, about all concepts of which we have a *nominal definition,* which is nothing but the enumeration of sufficient marks. We may also have distinct knowledge of an indefinable concept, however, when this concept is *primitive* or is the mark of itself, that is, when it is irreducible and to be understood only through itself and therefore lacks requisite marks. But in composite concepts the single component marks are indeed sometimes known clearly but nevertheless confusedly, such as heaviness, color, aqua fortis, and others which are some of the marks of gold. Such knowledge of gold may therefore be distinct, but it is nonetheless *inadequate.* But when every ingredient that enters into a distinct concept is itself known distinctly, or when analysis is carried through to the end, knowledge is adequate. I am not sure that a perfect example of this can be given by man, but our concept of numbers approaches it closely. Yet for the most part, especially in a longer analysis, we do not intuit the entire nature of the subject matter at once but make use of signs instead of things, though we usually omit the explanation of these signs in any actually present thought for the sake of brevity, knowing or believing that we have the power to do it. Thus when I think of a chiliogon, or a polygon of a thousand equal sides, I do not always consider the nature of a side and of equality and of a thousand (or the cube of ten), but I use these words, whose meaning appears obscurely and imperfectly to the mind, in place of the ideas which I have of them, because I remember that I know the meaning of the words but that their interpretation is not necessary for the present judgment. Such thinking I usually call *blind* or *symbolic;* we use it in algebra and in arithmetic, and indeed almost everywhere. When a concept is very complex, we certainly cannot think simultaneously of all the concepts which compose it. But when this is possible, or at least insofar as it is possible, I call the knowledge *intuitive.* There is no other knowledge than intuitive of a distinct primitive concept, while for the most part we have only symbolic thought of composites.

This already shows that we do not perceive the ideas even of those things which we know distinctly, except insofar as we use intuitive thought. It often happens that we falsely believe ourselves to have ideas of things in our mind, when we assume wrongly that we have already explained certain terms which we are using. It is not true, or at least it is ambiguous, to say, as some do, that we cannot speak of anything and understand what we say without having an idea of it. For often we understand after a fashion each single word or remember to have understood it earlier; yet because we are content with this blind thinking and do not sufficiently press the analysis of the concepts, we overlook a contradiction which the composite concept may involve. I was led to examine this point more distinctly by an argument which was famous among the Scholastics long ago and was revived by Descartes. It is an argument for the existence of God and is stated as follows. Whatever follows from the idea or definition of a thing can be predicated of the thing itself. Existence follows from the idea of God, or the most perfect being, or that than which no greater can be thought. For a most perfect being involves all perfections, among which existence is one. Therefore existence can be predicated of God.

It should be noticed however, that the most you can draw out of this argument is that if God is possible, it follows that he exists; for we cannot safely infer from definitions until we know that they are real or that they involve no contradiction. The reason for this is that from concepts which involve a contradiction, contradictory conclusions can be drawn simultaneously, and this is absurd. To explain this I usually make use of the example of the most rapid motion, which involves an absurdity. Suppose that a wheel turns at a most rapid rate. Then anyone can see that if a spoke of the wheel is extended beyond its rim, its extremity will move more rapidly than will a nail in the rim itself. The motion of the nail is therefore not the most rapid, contrary to hypothesis. Yet at first glance we may seem to have an idea of the most rapid motion, for we understand perfectly what we are saying. But we cannot have any idea of the impossible. Likewise it is not enough to think of a most perfect being in order to assert that we have an idea of it, and in the demonstration which I referred to above we must either prove or assume the possibility of a most perfect being in order to reason rightly. However, there is nothing truer than that we have an idea of God and that the most perfect being is possible and indeed necessary. But the above argument is not conclusive and has already been rejected by Thomas Aquinas.

This gives us, too, a means of distinguishing between *nominal definitions,* which contain only marks for discerning one thing from others, and *real definitions,* through which the possibility of the thing is ascertained. In this way we can meet the view of Hobbes, who held truths to be arbitrary because they depend on nominal definitions, not considering that the reality of the definition does not depend upon our free choice and that not all concepts can be combined with each other. *Nominal definitions* do not suffice for perfect knowledge unless it has been established by other means that the defined thing is possible.

Thus the difference between a *true* and a *false idea* also becomes clear. An idea is true when the concept is possible; it is false when it implies a contradiction. Now we know the *possibility* of a thing either a priori or a posteriori. We know it a priori when we resolve the concept into its necessary elements or into other concepts whose possibility is known, and we know that there is nothing incompatible in them. This happens, for instance, when we understand the method by which the thing can be produced; hence *causal definitions* are more useful than others. We know an idea a posteriori when we experience the actual existence of the thing, for what actually exists or has existed is in any case possible. Whenever our knowledge is adequate, we have a priori knowledge of a possibility, for if we have carried out the analysis to the end and no contradiction has appeared, the concept is obviously possible. Whether men will ever be able to carry out a perfect analysis of concepts, that is, to reduce their thoughts to the *first possibles* or to irreducible concepts, or (what is the same thing) to the absolute attributes of God themselves or the first causes and the final end of things, I shall not now venture to decide. For the most part we are content to learn the reality of certain concepts by experience and then to compose other concepts from them after the pattern of nature.

From this therefore I believe we can understand that it is not always safe to appeal to ideas and that many thinkers have abused this deceptive word to establish some of their own fancies. That we do not always at once have an idea of a thing of which we are conscious of thinking, the example of most rapid motion has shown. Nor is it less deceptive, I think, when men today advance the famous principle that *whatever I perceive clearly and distinctly in some thing is true, or may be predicated of it.* For what seems clear and distinct to men when they judge rashly is frequently obscure and confused. This axiom is thus useless unless the criteria of clearness and distinctness which we have proposed are applied and unless the truth of the ideas is established. For the rest, the *rules of common logic,* of which also the geometricians make use, are not to be despised as criteria of the truth of judgments; so, for example, the rule that nothing is to be admitted for certain unless it has been proved by careful experience or by sound demonstration. A demonstration is sound when it observes the form prescribed in logic, although it need not always follow the form of syllogisms arranged in the Scholastic manner (such as Christian Herlinus and Conrad Dasypodius applied to the first six books of Euclid); it is merely necessary that the argument be conclusive by virtue of its form. As an example of such argumentation carried through in proper form one could also quote any valid calculation. Thus no necessary premise is to be omitted, and all premises must be proved in advance, or at least admitted to be hypotheses, in which case the conclusion, too, is hypothetical. Whoever obeys these rules carefully will easily protect himself against deceptive ideas. That brilliant genius Pascal agrees entirely with these principles when he says, in his famous dissertation on the geometrical spirit, a fragment of which is preserved in the outstanding book of the celebrated Antoine Arnauld on the *Art of Thinking*, that it is the task of the geometrician to define all terms though ever so little obscure and to prove all truths though little doubtful. I only wish that he had defined the limits beyond which any concept or judgment is no longer even a little obscure or doubtful. But the necessary conditions for this can be learned from a careful study of what we have just said; we must now strive to be brief.

As to the controversy whether we see all things in God (an old opinion which, properly understood, is not entirely to be rejected) or whether we have some ideas of our own, it must be understood that even if we saw all things in

God, it would still be necessary to have our own ideas also, not in the sense of some kind of little copies, but as affections or modifications of our mind corresponding to the very object we perceive in God. For whenever thoughts succeed each other, some change occurs in our mind. There are also ideas in our mind of things of which we are not actually thinking, as the figure of Hercules is in the rough marble. But in God there must actually be the ideas not only of absolute and infinite extension but also of every figure, since figure is nothing but a modification of absolute extension. Moreover, when we perceive colors or odors, we are having nothing but a perception of figures and motions, but of figures and motions so complex and minute that our mind in its present state is incapable of observing each distinctly and therefore fails to notice that its perception is compounded of single perceptions of exceedingly small figures and motions. So when we mix yellow and blue powders and perceive a green color, we are in fact sensing nothing but yellow and blue thoroughly mixed; but we do not notice this and so assume some new nature instead.

III.*

On the Method of Distinguishing Real from Imaginary Phenomena

A *being* is that whose concept involves something positive or that which can be conceived by us provided what we conceive is possible and involves no contradiction. We know this, first, if the concept is explained perfectly and involves nothing confused, but then in a shorter way, if the thing actually exists, since what exists must certainly be a being or be possible.

Just as being is revealed through a distinct concept, however, so existence is revealed through a distinct perception. To understand this better, we must see by what means existence may be proved. In the first place, I judge without proof, from a simple perception or experience, that those things exist of which I am conscious within me. These are, first, *myself* who am thinking of a variety of things and then, the varied *phenomena* or appearances which exist in my mind. Since both of these namely are perceived immediately by the mind without the intervention of anything else, they can be accepted without question, and it is exactly as certain that there exists in my mind the appearance of a golden mountain or of a centaur when I dream of these, as it is that I who am dreaming exist, for both are included in the one fact that it is certain that a centaur appears to me.

Let us now see by what criteria we may know which phenomena are real. We may judge this both from the phenomenon itself and from the phenomena which are antecedent and consequent to it as well. We conclude it from the phenomenon itself if it is vivid, complex, and internally coherent *[congruum]*. It will be vivid if its qualities, such as light, color, and warmth, appear intense enough. It will be complex if these qualities are varied and support us in un-

---

* From *op. cit.*, pp. 363–365.

dertaking many experiments and new observations; for example, if we experience in a phenomenon not merely colors but also sound, odors, and qualities of taste and touch, and this both in the phenomenon as a whole and in its various parts which we can further treat according to causes. Such a long chain of observations is usually begun by design and selectively and usually occurs neither in dreams nor in those imaginings which memory or fantasy present, in which the image is mostly vague and disappears while we are examining it. A phenomenon will be coherent when it consists of many phenomena, for which a reason can be given either within themselves or by some sufficiently simple hypothesis common to them; next, it is coherent if it conforms to the customary nature of other phenomena which have repeatedly occurred to us, so that its parts have the same position, order, and outcome in relation to the phenomenon which similar phenomena have had. Otherwise phenomena will be suspect, for if we were to see men moving through the air astride the hippogryphs of Ariostus, it would, I believe, make us uncertain whether we were dreaming or awake.

But this criterion can be referred back to another general class of tests drawn from preceding phenomena. The present phenomenon must be coherent with these if, namely, it preserves the same consistency or if a reason can be supplied for it from preceding phenomena or if all together are coherent with the same hypothesis, as if with a common cause. But certainly a most valid criterion is a consensus with the whole sequence of life, especially if many others affirm the same thing to be coherent with their phenomena also, for it is not only probable but certain, as I will show directly, that other substances exist which are similar to us. Yet the most powerful criterion of the reality of phenomena, sufficient even by itself, is success in predicting future phenomena from past and present ones, whether that prediction is based upon a reason, upon a hypothesis that was previously successful, or upon the customary consistency of things as observed previously. Indeed, even if this whole life were said to be only a dream, and the visible world only a phantasm, I should call this dream or this phantasm real enough if we were never deceived by it when we make good use of reason. But just as we know from these marks which phenomena should be seen as real, so we also conclude, on the contrary, that any phenomena which conflict with those that we judge to be real, and likewise those whose fallacy we can understand from their causes, are merely apparent.

We must admit it to be true that the criteria for real phenomena thus far offered, even when taken together, are not demonstrative, even though they have the greatest probability; or to speak popularly, that they provide a moral certainty but do not establish a metaphysical certainty, so that to affirm the contrary would involve a contradiction. Thus by no argument can it be demonstrated absolutely that bodies exist, nor is there anything to prevent certain well-ordered dreams from being the objects of our mind, which we judge to be true and which, because of their accord with each other, are equivalent to truth so far as practice is concerned. Nor is the argument which is popularly offered, that this makes God a deceiver, of great importance. At least no one will fail to see how far it is from a demonstration having metaphysical certainty, for we are deceived not by God but by our judgment, asserting something without accurate proof. And though a great probability may be involved, nevertheless God, in offering us this probability, is not therefore a deceiver. For what if our nature happened to be incapable of real phenomena? Then indeed God ought not so much to be blamed as to be thanked, for since these phenomena could not be real, God would, by causing them at least to be in agreement, be providing us with something equally as valuable in all the practice of life as would be real phenomena. What if this whole short life, indeed, were only some long dream and we should awake at death, as the Platonists seem to think? Since we are destined for eternity, and this whole life, even if it were to contain many thousands of years, would be like a point with respect to eternity, how trifling a thing is this small dream, to be interposed upon such fulness of truth, to which its relation is less than that of a dream to a lifetime. Yet no reasonable person calls God a deceiver if some short dream which is completely distinct and coherent is experienced in the mind.

So far I have spoken of appearances; now we must examine those things which do not appear but which nevertheless can be inferred from appearances. It is indeed certain that every phenomenon has some cause. But if anyone says that the cause of phenomena is in the nature of our mind which contains the phenomena, he will affirm nothing false, but nevertheless he will not be telling the whole truth. For in the first place, there must necessarily be a reason why we ourselves exist rather than not. And even if we are assumed to have existed from eternity, we should still have to find a reason for eternal existence, and this reason must be sought either within the essence of our mind or outside of it. And certainly there is nothing to prevent innumerable other minds from existing as well as ours, although not all possible minds exist. This I demonstrate from the fact that all existing things are interrelated (inter se habent commercium). However, minds of another nature than ours can be conceived which also are interrelated with ours here. That all existing things have this intercourse with each other can be proved, moreover, both from the fact that otherwise no one could say whether anything is taking place in existence now or not, so that there would be no truth or falsehood for such a proposition, which is absurd; but also because there are no extrinsic denominations, and no one becomes a widower in India by the death of his wife in Europe unless a real change occurs in him. For every predicate is in fact contained in the nature of a subject. Now, if some possible minds exist, the question is: Why not all? Furthermore, since all existents must be interrelated, there must be a cause of their interrelations; indeed, everything must necessarily express the same nature but in a different way. But the cause which leads all minds to have intercourse with each other or to express the same nature, and therefore to exist, is that cause which perfectly expresses the universe, namely God. This cause does not have a cause and is unique. Hence it is at once clear that there exist many minds besides ours, and, since it is easy to think that men who converse with us can have exactly the same reason to doubt our existence as we have to doubt theirs; and since no reason operates more strongly for us than for them, they will also exist and have minds. Thus both sacred and profane history, and indeed whatever pertains to the status of minds or rational substances, may be considered confirmed.

Concerning bodies I can demonstrate that not merely light, heat, color, and similar qualities are apparent but also motion, figure, and extension. And that if anything is real, it is solely the force of acting and suffering, and hence that the substance of a body consists in this (as if in matter and form). Those bodies, however, which have no substantial form, are merely phenomena or at least only aggregates of the true ones.

Substances have metaphysical matters or passive power insofar as they express something confusedly; active, insofar as they express it distinctly.

IV.*

The Monadology (1714)

31. Our reasoning is based upon two great principles; first, that of Contradiction, by means of which we decide that to be false which involves contradiction and that to be true which contradicts or is opposed to the false.

32. And second, the principle of Sufficient Reason, in virtue of which we believe that no fact can be real or existing and no statement true unless it has a sufficient reason why it should be thus and not otherwise. Most frequently, however, these reasons cannot be known by us.

33. There are also two kinds of Truths; those of Reasoning and those of Fact. The Truths of Reasoning are necessary, and their opposite is impossible. Those of Fact, however, are contingent, and their opposite is possible. When a truth is necessary, the reason can be found by analysis in resolving it into simpler ideas and into simpler truths until we reach those which are primary.

34. It is thus that with mathematicians the Speculative Theorems and the practical Canons are reduced by analysis to Definitions, Axioms, and Postulates.

35. There are finally simple ideas of which no definition can be given. There are also the Axioms and Postulates or, in a word, the primary principles which cannot be proved and, indeed, have no need of proof. These are identical propositions whose opposites involve express contradictions.

36. But there must be also a sufficient reason for contingent truths or truths of fact; that is to say, for the sequence of the things which extend throughout the universe of created beings, where the analysis into more partic-

---

* From Leibniz: Discourse on Metaphysics, Correspondence with Arnauld, and Monadology, translated by G. R. Montgomery, The Open Court Publishing Company, La Salle, Ill., Reprint Edition, 1962. Reprinted by permission of The Open Court Publishing Company.

ular reasons can be continued into greater detail without limit because of the immense variety of the things in nature and because of the infinite division of bodies. There is an infinity of figures and of movements, present and past, which enter into the efficient cause of my present writing, and in its final cause there are an infinity of slight tendencies and dispositions of my soul, present and past.

37. And as all this detail again involves other and more detailed contingencies, each of which again has need of a similar analysis in order to find its explanation, no real advance has been made. Therefore, the sufficient or ultimate reason must needs be outside of the sequence or series of these details of contingencies, however infinite they may be.

38. It is thus that the ultimate reason for things must be a necessary substance, in which the detail of the changes shall be present merely potentially, as in the fountain-head, and this substance we call God.

12 JOHN LOCKE · GOTTFRIED WILHELM LEIBNIZ
Of True Ideas and Truth in General*

1. *Of True and False Ideas*

Locke, Bk. II, Ch. XXXII of the *Essay*:

1. Though truth and falsehood belong, in propriety of speech, only to *propositions*: yet *ideas* are oftentimes termed true or false (as what words are there that are not used with great latitude, and with some deviation from their strict and proper significations?) Though I think that when ideas themselves are termed true or false, there is still some secret or tacit proposition, which is the foundation of that denomination: as we shall see, if we examine the particular occasions wherein they come to be called true or false. In all which we shall find some kind of affirmation or negation, which is the reason of that denomination. For our ideas, being nothing but bare *appearances*, or perceptions in our minds, cannot properly and simply in themselves be said to be true or false, no more than a single name of anything can be said to be true or false.

2. Indeed both ideas and words may be said to be true, in a metaphysical sense of the word truth; as all other things that any way exist are said to be true, i.e. really to be such as they exist. Though in things called true, even in

---

* From Locke, *An Essay Concerning Human Understanding* and Leibniz, *New Essays Concerning Human Understanding*, translated by A. G. Langley, The Open Court Publishing Company, La Salle, Ill., 3rd Edition, 1949. All passages from the latter work are reprinted by permission of The Open Court Publishing Company. The *New Essays* was first published posthumously in 1765.

that sense, there is perhaps a secret reference to our ideas, looked upon as the standards of that truth; which amount to a mental proposition, though it be usually not taken notice of.

3. But it is not in that metaphysical sense of truth which we inquire here, when we examine, whether our ideas are capable of being true or false, but in the more ordinary acceptation of those words: and so I say that the ideas in our minds, being only so many perceptions or appearances there, none of them are false; the idea of a centaur having no more falsehood in it when it appears in our minds, than the name centaur has falsehood in it, when it is pronounced by our mouths, or written on paper. For truth or falsehood lying always in some affirmation or negation, mental or verbal, our ideas are not capable, any of them, of being false, till the mind passes some judgment on them; that is, affirms or denies something of them.

4. Whenever the mind refers any of its ideas to anything extraneous to them, they are then capable to be called true or false. Because the mind, in such a reference, makes a tacit supposition of their conformity to that thing; which supposition, as it happens to be true or false, so the ideas themselves come to be denominated. The most usual cases wherein this happens, are these following:

5. First, when the mind supposes any idea it has *conformable* to that in *other men's minds,* called by the same common name; v.g. when the mind intends or judges its ideas of justice, temperance, religion, to be the same with what other men give those names to.

Secondly, when the mind supposes any idea it has in itself to be *conformable* to some *real existence.* Thus the two ideas of a man and a centaur, supposed to be the ideas of real substances, are the one true and the other false; the one having a conformity to what has really existed, the other not.

Thirdly, when the mind *refers* any of its ideas to that *real* constitution and *essence* of anything, whereon all its properties depend: and thus the greatest part, if not all our ideas, of substances, are false. . . .

26. Upon the whole matter, I think that our ideas, as they are considered by the mind,—either in reference to the proper signification of their names; or in reference to the reality of things,—may very fitly be called *right* or *wrong* ideas, according as they agree or disagree to those patterns to which they are referred. But if any one had rather call them true or false, it is fit he use a liberty, which every one has, to call things by those names he thinks best; though, in propriety of speech, *truth* or *falsehood* will, I think, scarce agree to them, but as they, some way or other, virtually contain in them some mental proposition. The ideas that are in a man's mind, simply considered, cannot be wrong; unless complex ones, wherein inconsistent parts are jumbled together. All other ideas are in themselves right, and the knowledge about them right and true knowledge; but when we come to refer them to anything, as to their patterns and archetypes, then they are capable of being wrong, as far as they disagree with such archetypes.

Leibniz:

> . . . I believe that true or false ideas might be so understood, but as these different senses do not agree between themselves and cannot be conveniently ranked under a common notion, I prefer to call the *ideas true* or *false* in relation to another tacit *affirmation* which they all include, which is that of possibility. Thus possible ideas are *true,* impossible *false.*

2. *Of Truth in General*

Locke, Bk. IV, Ch. V of the *Essay:*

1. What is truth? was an inquiry many ages since; and it being that which all mankind either do, or pretend to search after, it cannot but be worth our while carefully to examine wherein it consists; and so acquaint ourselves with the nature of it, as to observe how the mind distinguishes it from falsehood.

2. Truth, then, seems to me, in the proper import of the word, to signify nothing but *the joining or separating of Signs, as the Things signified by them do agree or disagree one with another.* The joining or separating of signs here meant, is what by another name we call proposition. So that truth properly belongs only to propositions: whereof there are two sorts, viz. mental and verbal; as there are two sorts of signs commonly made use of, viz. ideas and words.

3. To form a clear notion of truth, it is very necessary to consider truth of thought, and truth of words, distinctly one from another: but yet it is very difficult to treat of them asunder. Because it is unavoidable, in treating of mental propositions, to make use of words: and then the instances given of mental propositions cease immediately to be barely mental, and become verbal. For a *mental proposition* being nothing but a bare consideration of the ideas, as they are in our minds, stripped of names, they lose the nature of purely mental propositions as soon as they are put into words.

4. And that which makes it yet harder to treat of mental and verbal propositions separately is, that most men, if not all, in their thinking and reasonings within themselves, make use of words instead of ideas; at least when the subject of their meditation contains in it complex ideas. Which is a great evidence of the imperfection and uncertainty of our ideas of that kind, and may, if attentively made use of, serve for a mark to show us what are those things we have clear and perfect established ideas of, and what not. For if we will curiously observe the way our mind takes in thinking and reasoning, we shall find, I suppose, that when we make any propositions within our own thoughts about *white* or *black, sweet* or *bitter,* a *triangle* or a *circle,* we can and often do frame in our minds the ideas themselves, without reflecting on the names. But when we would consider, or make propositions about the more complex ideas, as of a *man, vitriol, fortitude, glory,* we usually put the name for the idea: because the ideas these names stand for, being for the most part imperfect, confused, and undetermined, we reflect on the names themselves, because they are more clear, certain, and distinct, and readier occur to our thoughts

than the pure ideas: and so we make use of these words instead of the ideas themselves, even when we would meditate and reason within ourselves, and make tacit mental propositions. In substances, as has been already noticed, this is occasioned by the imperfections of our ideas: we making the name stand for the real essence, of which we have no idea at all. In modes, it is occasioned by the great number of simple ideas that go to the making them up. For many of them being compounded, the name occurs much easier than the complex idea itself, which requires time and attention to be recollected, and exactly represented to the mind, even in those men who have formerly been at the pains to do it; and is utterly impossible to be done by those who, though they have ready in their memory the greatest part of the common words of that language, yet perhaps never troubled themselves in all their lives to consider what precise ideas the most of them stood for. Some confused or obscure notions have served their turns; and many who talk very much of *religion* and *conscience,* of *church* and *faith,* of *power* and *right,* of *obstructions* and *humours, melancholy* and *choler,* would perhaps have little left in their thoughts and meditations, if one should desire them to think only of the things themselves, and lay by those words with which they so often confound others, and not seldom themselves also.

5. But to return to the consideration of truth: we must, I say, observe two sorts of propositions that we are capable of making:—

First, *mental,* wherein the ideas in our understandings are without the use of words put together, or separated, by the mind perceiving or judging of their agreement or disagreement.

Secondly, *Verbal* propositions, which are words, the signs of our ideas, put together or separated in affirmative or negative sentences. By which way of affirming or denying, these signs, made by sounds, are, as it were, put together or separated one from another. So that proposition consists in joining or separating signs; and truth consists in the putting together or separating those signs, according as the things which they stand for agree or disagree.

6. Every one's experience will satisfy him, that the mind, either by perceiving, or supposing, the agreement or disagreement of any of its ideas, does tacitly within itself put them into a kind of proposition affirmative or negative; which I have endeavoured to express by the terms putting together and separating. But this action of the mind, which is so familiar to every thinking and reasoning man, is easier to be conceived by reflecting on what passes in us when we affirm or deny, than to be explained by words. When a man has in his head the idea of two lines, viz. the side and diagonal of a square, whereof the diagonal is an inch long, he may have the idea also of the division of that line into a certain number of equal parts; v.g. into five, ten, a hundred, a thousand, or any other number, and may have the idea of that inch line being divisible, or not divisible, into such equal parts, as a certain number of them will be equal to the sideline. Now, whenever he perceives, believes, or supposes such a kind of divisibility to agree or disagree to his idea of that line, he, as it were, joins or separates those two ideas, viz. the idea of that line, and the idea

of that kind of divisibility; and so makes a mental proposition, which is true or false, according as such a kind of divisibility, a divisibility into such *aliquot* parts, does really agree to that line or no. When ideas are so put together, or separated in the mind, as they or the things they stand for do agree or not, that is, as I may call it, *mental truth*. But *truth of words* is something more; and that is the affirming or denying of words one of another, as the ideas they stand for agree or disagree: and this again is twofold; either purely verbal and trifling, which I shall speak of, (chap. viii.,) or real and instructive; which is the object of that real knowledge which we have spoken of already.

7. But here again will be apt to occur the same doubt about truth, that did about knowledge: and it will be objected, that if truth be nothing but the joining and separating of words in propositions, as the ideas they stand for agree or disagree in men's minds, the knowledge of truth is not so valuable a thing as it is taken to be, nor worth the pains and time men employ in the search of it: since by this account it amounts to no more than the conformity of words to the chimeras of men's brains. Who knows not what odd notions many men's heads are filled with, and what strange ideas all men's brains are capable of? But if we rest here, we know the truth of nothing by this rule, but of the visionary words in our own imaginations; nor have other truth, but what as much concerns harpies and centaurs, as men and horses. For those, and the like, may be ideas in our heads, and have their agreement or disagreement there, as well as the ideas of real beings, and so have as true propositions made about them. And it will be altogether as true a proposition to say *all centaurs are animals,* as that *all men are animals;* and the certainty of one as great as the other. For in both the propositions, the words are put together according to the agreement of the ideas in our minds: and the agreement of the idea of animal with that of centaur is as clear and visible to the mind, as the agreement of the idea of animal with that of man; and so these two propositions are equally true, equally certain. But of what use is all such truth to us?

8. Though what has been said in the foregoing chapter to distinguish real from imaginary knowledge might suffice here, in answer to this doubt, to distinguish real truth from chimerical, or (if you please) barely nominal, they depending both on the same foundation; yet it may not be amiss here again to consider, that though our words signify nothing but our ideas, yet being designed by them to signify things, the truth they contain when put into propositions will be only verbal, when they stand for ideas in the mind that have not an agreement with the reality of things. And therefore truth as well as knowledge may well come under the distinction of verbal and real; that being only verbal truth, wherein terms are joined according to the agreement or disagreement of the ideas they stand for; without regarding whether our ideas are such as really have, or capable of having, an existence in nature. But then it is they contain *real truth,* when these signs are joined, as our ideas agree; and when our ideas are such as we know are capable of having an existence in nature: which in substances we cannot know, but by knowing that such have existed.

9. Truth is the marking down in words the agreement or disagreement of

ideas as it is. Falsehood is the marking down in words the agreement or disagreement of ideas otherwise than it is. And so far as these ideas, thus marked
by sounds, agree to their archetypes, so far only is the truth real. The knowledge of this truth consists in knowing what ideas the words stand for, and the
perception of the agreement or disagreement of those ideas, according as it is
marked by those words.

10. But because words are looked on as the great conduits of truth and
knowledge, and that in conveying and receiving of truth, and commonly in
reasoning about it, we make use of words and propositions, I shall more at
large inquire wherein the certainty of real truths contained in propositions
consists, and where it is to be had; and endeavour to show in what sort of universal propositions we are capable of being certain of their real truth or falsehood.

I shall begin with *general* propositions, as those which most employ our
thoughts, and exercise our contemplation. General truths are most looked
after by the mind as those that most enlarge our knowledge; and by their com-
prehensiveness satisfying us at once of many particulars, enlarge our view, and
shorten our way to knowledge.

11. Besides truth taken in the strict sense before mentioned, there are
other sorts of truths: As, 1. Moral truth, which is speaking of things according
to the persuasion of our own minds, though the proposition we speak agree not
to the reality of things; 2. Metaphysical truth, which is nothing but the real
existence of things, conformable to the ideas to which we have annexed their
names. This, though it seems to consist in the very beings of things, yet, when
considered a little nearly, will appear to include a tacit proposition, whereby
the mind joins that particular thing to the idea it had before settled with the
name to it. But these considerations of truth, either having been before taken
notice of, or not being much to our present purpose, it may suffice here only to
have mentioned them.

Leibniz:

. . . But what I find least to my taste in your definition of truth is that
you seek truth in words. Thus the same sense expressed in Latin, German, English, French, will not be the same truth, and it will be necessary
to say with Hobbes, that truth depends on the good pleasure of men;
which is to speak in a very strange manner. You attribute, indeed, truth
to God, who, you will agree with me (I think), has no need of signs. Finally, I have been astonished already more than once at the disposition of
your friends who are pleased to make essences, species, and truths *nominal*. . . .

. . . We shall then have also *literal* truths, which may be distinguished as
truths upon paper or parchment, of ordinary black ink or of printer's ink,
if truths must be distinguished by signs. It were then better to place truths
in the relation between the objects of ideas which causes the one to be or
not to be included in the other. That does not depend upon languages,

and is common to us with God and the angels; and when God manifests a truth to us we shall acquire that which is in his understanding, for although there is an infinite difference between his ideas and ours, as regards perfection and extent, it is always true that they agree in the same relation. It is, then, in this relation that truth must be placed, and we can distinguish between the *truths* which are independent of our good pleasure, and between the *expressions* which we invent as seems good to us. . . .

. . . Moral truth is by some called *veracity,* and *metaphysical truth* is commonly taken by the metaphysicians as an attribute of being, but it is an attribute very useless and almost void of meaning. Let us content ourselves with seeking truth in the correspondence of the propositions in the mind with the things in question. It is true that I have also attributed truth to ideas in saying that ideas are true or false; but then I mean, in reality, the truth of propositions affirming the possibility of the object of the idea. In the same sense we can say also that a *being is true*, that is to say, the proposition affirming its actual, or at least, possible existence.

13 IMMANUEL KANT
Of Truth, Belief, and Knowledge

I. *

What is truth? is an old and famous question by which people thought they could drive logicians into a corner, and either make them take refuge in a mere circle, or make them confess their ignorance and consequently the vanity of their whole art. The nominal definition of truth, that it is the agreement of the cognition with its object, is granted. What is wanted is to know a general and safe criterion of the truth of any and every kind of knowledge.

It is a great and necessary proof of wisdom and sagacity to know what questions may be reasonably asked. For if a question is absurd in itself and calls for an answer where there is no answer, it does not only throw disgrace on the questioner, but often tempts an uncautious listener into absurd answers, thus presenting, as the ancients said, the spectacle of one person milking a he-goat, and of another holding the sieve.

If truth consists in the agreement of knowledge with its object, that object must thereby be distinguished from other objects; for knowledge is untrue if it does not agree with its object, though it contains something which may be affirmed of other objects. A general criterium of truth ought really to be valid with regard to every kind of knowledge, whatever the objects may be. But it is clear, as no account is thus taken of the contents of knowledge (relation to its

---

* From *Critique of Pure Reason*, A 58–60, B 82–84.

object), while truth concerns these very contents, that it is impossible and absurd to ask for a sign of the truth of the contents of that knowledge, and that therefore a sufficient and at the same time general mark of truth cannot possibly be found. As we have before called the contents of knowledge its material, it will be right to say that of the truth of the knowledge, so far as its material is concerned, no general mark can be demanded, because it would be self-contradictory.

But, when we speak of knowledge with reference to its form only, without taking account of its contents, it is equally clear that logic, as it propounds the general and necessary rules of the understanding, must furnish in these rules criteria of truth. For whatever contradicts those rules is false, because the understanding would thus contradict the general rules of thought, that is, itself. These criteria, however, refer only to the form of truth or of thought in general. They are quite correct so far, but they are not sufficient. For although our knowledge may be in accordance with logical rule, that is, may not contradict itself, it is quite possible that it may be in contradiction with its object. Therefore the purely logical criterium of truth, namely, the agreement of knowledge with the general and formal laws of the understanding and reason, is no doubt a *conditio sine qua non,* or a negative condition of all truth. But logic can go no further, and it has no test for discovering error with regard to the contents, and not the form, of a proposition.

II. *

The holding a thing to be true is an event in our understanding which, though it may rest on objective grounds, requires also subjective causes in the mind of the person who is to judge. If the judgment is valid for everybody, if only he is possessed of reason, then the ground of it is objectively sufficient, and the holding it to be true is called *conviction.* If, on the contrary, it has its ground in the peculiar character of the subject only, it is called *persuasion.*

Persuasion is a mere illusion, the ground of the judgment, though it lies solely in the subject, being regarded as objective. Such a judgment has, therefore, private validity only, and the holding it to be true cannot be communicated to others. Truth, however, depends on agreement with the object, and, with regard to it, the judgments of every understanding must agree with each other *(consentientia uni tertio consentiunt inter se).* An external criterion, therefore, as to whether our holding a thing to be true be conviction or only persuasion, consists in the possibility of communicating it, and finding its truth to be valid for the reason of every man. For, in that case, there is at least a presumption that the ground of the agreement of all judgments, in spite of the diversity of the subjects, rests upon the common ground, namely, on the object with which they all agree, and thus prove the truth of the judgment.

Persuasion, therefore, cannot be distinguished from conviction, subjectively, so long as the subject views its judgment as a phenomenon of his own

---

* From *Critique of Pure Reason,* A 820–3, B 848–51.

mind only; the experiment, however, which we make with the grounds that seem valid to us, by trying to find out whether they will produce the same effect on the reason of others, is a means, though only a subjective means, not indeed of producing conviction, but of detecting the merely private validity of the judgment, that is, of discovering in it what is merely persuasion.

If we are able besides to analyse the subjective *causes* of our judgment, which we have taken for its objective *grounds,* and thus explain the deceptive judgment as a phenomenon in our mind, without having recourse to the object itself, we expose the illusion and are no longer deceived by it, although we may continue to be tempted by it, in a certain degree, if, namely, the subjective cause of the illusion is inherent in our nature.

I cannot *maintain* anything, that is, affirm it as a judgment necessarily valid for everybody, unless it produces conviction. Persuasion I may keep for myself, if it is agreeable to me, but I cannot, and ought not to attempt to make it binding on any but myself.

The holding anything to be true, or the subjective validity of a judgment admits, with reference to the conviction which is at the same time valid objectively, of the three following degrees, *supposing* (Meinen), *believing* (Glauben), *knowing* (Wissen). *Supposing* is to hold true, with the consciousness that it is insufficient *both* subjectively and objectively. If the holding true is sufficient subjectively, but is held to be insufficient objectively, it is called *believing;* while, if it is sufficient both subjectively and objectively, it is called *knowing.* Subjective sufficiency is called *conviction* (for myself), objective sufficiency is called *certainty* (for everybody). I shall not dwell any longer on the explanation of such easy concepts.

I must never venture to *suppose,* or to be of opinion, without *knowing* at least something by means of which a judgment, problematical by itself, is connected with truth, which connection, though it involves not a complete truth, is yet attended with more than arbitrary fiction. Moreover, the law of such a connection must be certain. For if, even with regard to this law, I should have nothing but an opinion, all would become a mere play of the imagination, without the least relation to truth.

In the judgments of pure reason *opinion* is not permitted. For, as they are not based on empirical grounds, but everything has to be known *a priori,* and everything therefore must be necessary, the principle of connection in them requires universality and necessity, and consequently perfect certainty, without which there would be nothing to lead us on to truth. Hence it is absurd to have an opinion in pure mathematics; here one must either know, or abstain from pronouncing any judgment. . . .

DISCUSSION · WILLIAM JAMES
Pragmatism's Conception of Truth*

Truth, as any dictionary will tell you, is a property of certain of our ideas. It means their 'agreement,' as falsity means their disagreement, with 'reality.' Pragmatists and intellectualists both accept this definition as a matter of course. They begin to quarrel only after the question is raised as to what may precisely be meant by the term 'agreement,' and what by the term 'reality,' when reality is taken as something for our ideas to agree with.

In answering these questions the pragmatists are more analytic and painstaking, the intellectualists more offhand and irreflective. The popular notion is that a true idea must copy its reality. Like other popular views, this one follows the analogy of the most usual experience. Our true ideas of sensible things do indeed copy them. Shut your eyes and think of yonder clock on the wall, and you get just such a true picture or copy of its dial. But your idea of its 'works' (unless you are a clockmaker) is much less of a copy, yet it passes muster, for it in no way clashes with reality. Even though it should shrink to the mere word 'works,' that word still serves you truly; and when you speak of the 'time-keeping function' of the clock, or of its spring's 'elasticity,' it is hard to see exactly what your ideas can copy.

You perceive that there is a problem here. Where our ideas cannot copy definitely their object, what does agreement with that object mean? Some idealists seem to say that they are true whenever they are what God means that we ought to think about that object. Others hold the copy-view all through, and speak as if our ideas possessed truth just in proportion as they approach to being copies of the Absolute's eternal way of thinking.

---

* From *Pragmatism*, Lecture VI. First published in 1907. Reprinted by permission of Mr. Alexander R. James, Literary Executor.

William James (1842–1910) taught at Harvard University from 1872 until his death, first in the field of physiology, then psychology, and finally philosophy. He had achieved an international reputation in psychology before turning his full attention to philosophy and developing his distinctive form of pragmatism.

These views, you see, invite pragmatistic discussion. But the great assumption of the intellectualists is that truth means essentially an inert static relation. When you've got your true idea of anything, there's an end of the matter. You're in possession; you *know;* you have fulfilled your thinking destiny. You are where you ought to be mentally; you have obeyed your categorical imperative; and nothing more need follow on that climax of your rational destiny. Epistemologically you are in stable equilibrium.

Pragmatism, on the other hand, asks its usual question. "Grant an idea or belief to be true," it says, "what concrete difference will its being true make in any one's actual life? How will the truth be realized? What experiences will be different from those which would obtain if the belief were false? What, in short, is the truth's cash-value in experiential terms?"

The moment pragmatism asks this question, it sees the answer: *True ideas are those that we can assimilate, validate, corroborate and verify. False ideas are those that we can not.* That is the practical difference it makes to us to have true ideas; that, therefore, is the meaning of truth, for it is all that truth is known-as.

This thesis is what I have to defend. The truth of an idea is not a stagnant property inherent in it. Truth *happens* to an idea. It *becomes* true, is *made* true by events. Its verity *is* in fact an event, a process: the process namely of its verifying itself, its veri-*fication.* Its validity is the process of its valid-*ation.*

But what do the words verification and validation themselves pragmatically mean? They again signify certain practical consequences of the verified and validated idea. It is hard to find any one phrase that characterizes these consequences better than the ordinary agreement-formula—just such consequences being what we have in mind whenever we say that our ideas 'agree' with reality. They lead us, namely, through the acts and other ideas which they instigate, into or up to, or towards, other parts of experience with which we feel all the while—such feeling being among our potentialities—that the original ideas remain in agreement. The connexions and transitions come to us from point to point as being progressive, harmonious, satisfactory. This function of agreeable leading is what we mean by an idea's verification. Such an account is vague and it sounds at first quite trivial, but it has results which it will take the rest of my hour to explain.

Let me begin by reminding you of the fact that the possession of true thoughts means everywhere the possession of invaluable instruments of action; and that our duty to gain truth, so far from being a blank command from out of the blue, or a 'stunt' self-imposed by our intellect, can account for itself by excellent practical reasons.

The importance to human life of having true beliefs about matters of fact is a thing too notorious. We live in a world of realities that can be infinitely useful or infinitely harmful. Ideas that tell us which of them to expect count as the true ideas in all this primary sphere of verification, and the pursuit of such ideas is a primary human duty. The possession of truth, so far from being here an end in itself, is only a preliminary means towards other vital satisfactions. If I am lost in the woods and starved, and find what looks like a cow-path, it is of the utmost importance that I should think of a human habitation at the end of it, for if I do so and follow it, I save myself. The true thought is useful here because the house which is its object is useful. The practical value of true ideas is thus primarily derived from the practical importance of their objects to us. Their objects are, indeed, not important at all times. I may on another occasion have no use for the house; and then my idea of it, however verifiable, will be practically irrelevant, and had better remain latent. Yet since almost any object may some day become temporarily important, the advantage of having a general stock of *extra* truths, of ideas that shall be true of merely possible situations, is obvious. We store such extra truths away in our memories, and with the overflow we fill our books of reference. Whenever such an extra truth becomes practically relevant to one of our emergencies, it passes from cold-storage to do work in the world and our belief in it grows active. You can say of it then either that 'it is useful because it is true' or that 'it is true because it is useful.' Both these phrases mean exactly the same thing, namely that here is an idea that gets fulfilled and can be verified. True is the name for whatever idea starts the verification-process, useful is the name for its completed function in experience. True ideas would never have been singled out as such, would never have acquired a class-name, least of all a name suggesting value, unless they had been useful from the outset in this way.

From this simple cue pragmatism gets her general notion of truth as something essentially bound up with the way in which one moment in our experience may lead us towards other moments which it will be worth while to have been led to. Primarily, and on the common-sense level, the truth of a state of mind means this function of *a leading that is worth while*. When a moment in our experience, of any kind whatever, inspires us with a thought that is true, that means that sooner or later we dip by that thought's guidance into the particulars of experience again and make advantageous connexion with them. This is a vague enough statement, but I beg you to retain it, for it is essential.

Our experience meanwhile is all shot through with regularities. One bit of it can warn us to get ready for another bit, can 'intend' or be 'significant of' that remoter object. The object's advent is the significance's verification. Truth, in these cases, meaning nothing but eventual verification, is manifestly incompatible with waywardness on our part. Woe to him whose beliefs play fast and loose with the order which realities follow in his experience; they will lead him nowhere or else make false connexions.

By 'realities' or 'objects' here, we mean either things of common sense, sensibly present, or else common-sense relations, such as dates, places, distances, kinds, activities. Following our mental image of a house along the cowpath, we actually come to see the house; we get the image's full verification. *Such simply and fully verified leadings are certainly the originals and prototypes of the truth-process.* Experience offers indeed other forms of truth-process, but they are all conceivable as being primary verifications arrested, multiplied or substituted one for another.

Take, for instance, yonder object on the wall. You and I consider it to be a 'clock,' altho no one of us has seen the hidden works that make it one. We let our notion pass for true without attempting to verify. If truths mean verification-process essentially, ought we then to call such unverified truths as this abortive? No, for they form the overwhelmingly large number of the truths we live by. Indirect as well as direct verifications pass muster. Where circumstantial evidence is sufficient, we can go without eye-witnessing. Just as we here assume Japan to exist without ever having been there, because it *works* to do so, everything we know conspiring with the belief, and nothing interfering, so we assume that thing to be a clock. We *use* it as a clock, regulating the length of our lecture by it. The verification of the assumption here means its leading to no frustration or contradiction. Verifi*ability* of wheels and weights and pendulum is as good as verification. For one truth-process completed there are a million in our lives that function in this state of nascency. They turn us *towards* direct verification; lead us into the *surroundings* of the objects they envisage; and then, if everything runs on harmoniously, we are so sure that verification is possible that we omit it, and are usually justified by all that happens.

Truth lives, in fact, for the most part on a credit system. Our thoughts and beliefs 'pass,' so long as nothing challenges them, just as bank-notes pass so long as nobody refuses them. But this all points to direct face-to-face verifications somewhere, without which the fabric of truth collapses like a financial system with no cash-basis whatever. You accept my verification of one thing, I yours of another. We trade on each other's truth. But beliefs verified concretely by *somebody* are the posts of the whole superstructure.

Another great reason—beside economy of time—for waiving complete verification in the usual business of life is that all things exist in kinds and not singly. Our world is found once for all to have that peculiarity. So that when we have once directly verified our ideas about one specimen of a kind, we consider ourselves free to apply them to other specimens without verification. A mind that habitually discerns the kind of thing before it, and acts by the law of the kind immediately, without pausing to verify, will be a 'true' mind in ninety-nine out of a hundred emergencies, proved so by its conduct fitting everything it meets, and getting no refutation.

Indirectly or only potentially verifying processes may thus be true as well as full verification-processes. They work as true processes would work, give us the same advantages, and claim our recognition for the same reasons. All this on the common-sense level of matters of fact, which we are alone considering.

But matters of fact are not our only stock in trade. *Relations among purely mental ideas* form another sphere where true and false beliefs obtain, and here the beliefs are absolute, or unconditional. When they are true they bear the name either of definitions or of principles. It is either a principle or a definition that 1 and 1 make 2, that 2 and 1 make 3, and so on; that white differs less from gray than it does from black; that when the cause begins to act the effect also commences. Such propositions hold of all possible 'ones,' of all conceivable 'whites' and 'grays' and 'causes.' The objects here are mental objects.

Their relations are perceptually obvious at a glance, and no sense-verification is necessary. Moreover, once true, always true, of those same mental objects. Truth here has an 'eternal' character. If you can find a concrete thing anywhere that is 'one' or 'white' or 'gray' or an 'effect,' then your principles will everlastingly apply to it. It is but a case of ascertaining the kind, and then applying the law of its kind to the particular object. You are sure to get truth if you can but name the kind rightly, for your mental relations hold good of everything of that kind without exception. If you then, nevertheless, failed to get truth concretely, you would say that you had classed your real objects wrongly.

In this realm of mental relations, truth again is an affair of leading. We relate one abstract idea with another, framing in the end great systems of logical and mathematical truth, under the respective terms of which the sensible facts of experience eventually arrange themselves, so that our eternal truths hold good of realities also. This marriage of fact and theory is endlessly fertile. What we say is here already true in advance of special verification, *if we have subsumed our objects rightly.* Our ready-made ideal framework for all sorts of possible objects follows from the very structure of our thinking. We can no more play fast and loose with these abstract relations than we can do so with our sense-experiences. They coerce us; we must treat them consistently, whether or not we like the results. The rules of addition apply to our debts as rigorously as to our assets. The hundredth decimal of π, the ratio of the circumference to its diameter, is predetermined ideally now, tho no one may have computed it. If we should ever need the figure in our dealings with an actual circle we should need to have it given rightly, calculated by the usual rules; for it is the same kind of truth that those rules elsewhere calculate.

Between the coercions of the sensible order and those of the ideal order, our mind is thus wedged tightly. Our ideas must agree with realities, be such realities concrete or abstract, be they facts or be they principles, under penalty of endless inconsistency and frustration.

So far, intellectualists can raise no protest. They can only say that we have barely touched the skin of the matter.

Realities mean, then, either concrete facts, or abstract kinds of things and relations perceived intuitively between them. They furthermore and thirdly mean, as things that new ideas of ours must no less take account of, the whole body of other truths already in our possession. But what now does 'agreement' with such threefold realities mean?—to use again the definition that is current.

Here it is that pragmatism and intellectualism begin to part company. Primarily, no doubt, to agree means to copy, but we saw that the mere word 'clock' would do instead of a mental picture of its works, and that of many realities our ideas can only be symbols and not copies. 'Past time,' 'power,' 'spontaneity,'—how can our mind copy such realities?

To 'agree' in the widest sense with a reality *can only mean to be guided either straight up to it or into its surroundings, or to be put into such working touch with it as to handle either it or something connected with it better than if we disagreed.* Better either intellectually or practically! And often agreement will only mean the negative fact that nothing contradictory from the quarter of that reality comes to interfere with the way in which our ideas guide us elsewhere. To copy a reality is, indeed, one very important way of agreeing with it, but it is far from being essential. The essential thing is the process of being guided. Any idea that helps us to *deal,* whether practically or intellectually, with either the reality or its belongings, that doesn't entangle our progress in frustrations, that *fits,* in fact, and adapts our life to the reality's whole setting, will agree sufficiently to meet the requirement. It will hold true of that reality.

Thus, *names* are just as 'true' or 'false' as definite mental pictures are. They set up similar verification-processes, and lead to fully equivalent practical results.

All human thinking gets discursified; we exchange ideas; we lend and borrow verifications, get them from one another by means of social intercourse. All truth thus gets verbally built out, stored up, and made available for every one. Hence, we must *talk* consistently just as we must *think* consistently: for both in talk and thought we deal with kinds. Names are arbitrary, but once understood they must be kept to. We mustn't now call Abel 'Cain' or Cain 'Abel.' If we do, we ungear ourselves from the whole book of Genesis, and from all its connexions with the universe of speech and fact down to the present time. We throw ourselves out of whatever truth that entire system of speech and fact may embody.

The overwhelming majority of our true ideas admit of no direct or face-to-face verification—those of past history, for example, as of Cain and Abel. The stream of time can be remounted only verbally, or verified indirectly by the present prolongations or effects of what the past harbored. Yet if they agree with these verbalities and effects, we can know that our ideas of the past are true. *As true as past time itself was,* so true was Julius Caesar, so true were antediluvian monsters, all in their proper dates and settings. That past time itself was, is guaranteed by its coherence with everything that's present. True as the present *is,* the past *was* also.

Agreement thus turns out to be essentially an affair of leading—leading that is useful because it is into quarters that contain objects that are important. True ideas lead us into useful verbal and conceptual quarters as well as directly up to useful sensible termini. They lead to consistency, stability and flowing human intercourse. They lead away from excentricity and isolation, from foiled and barren thinking. The untrammelled flowing of the leading-process, its general freedom from clash and contradiction, passes for its indirect verification; but all roads lead to Rome, and in the end and eventually, all true processes must lead to the face of directly verifying sensible experiences *somewhere,* which somebody's ideas have copied.

Such is the large loose way in which the pragmatist interprets the word agreement. He treats it altogether practically. He lets it cover any process of conduction from a present idea to a future terminus, provided only it run prosperously. It is only thus that 'scientific' ideas, flying as they do beyond common sense, can be said to agree with their realities. It is, as I have already said, *as if* reality were made of ether, atoms or electrons, but we mustn't think so literally. The term 'energy' doesn't even pretend to stand for anything 'objective.' It is only a way of measuring the surface of phenomena so as to string their changes on a simple formula.

Yet in the choice of these man-made formulas we can not be capricious with impunity any more than we can be capricious on the common-sense practical level. We must find a theory that will *work;* and that means something extremely difficult; for our theory must mediate between all previous truths and certain new experiences. It must derange common sense and previous belief as little as possible, and it must lead to some sensible terminus or other that can be verified exactly. To 'work' means both these things; and the squeeze is so tight that there is little loose play for any hypothesis. Our theories are wedged and controlled as nothing else is. Yet sometimes alternative theoretic formulas are equally compatible with all the truths we know, and then we choose between them for subjective reasons. We choose the kind of theory to which we are already partial; we follow 'elegance' or 'economy.' Clerk-Maxwell somewhere says it would be 'poor scientific taste' to choose the more complicated of two equally well-evidenced conceptions; and you will all agree with him. Truth in science is what gives us the maximum possible sum of satisfactions, taste included, but consistency both with previous truth and with novel fact is always the most imperious claimant.

For Further Reading

Acton, H. B., "The Correspondence Theory of Truth," *Proceedings of the Aristotelian Society,* 35 (1934–35).

Austin, J. L., P. F. Strawson, and D. R. Cousin, "Truth" (Symposium), *Proceedings of the Aristotelian Society,* Supplementary Volume 24 (1950).

Ayer, A. J., *Language, Truth and Logic.* Second Edition, Chap. 5. Victor Gollancz, Ltd., London, 1946.

Blanshard, B., *The Nature of Thought.* Volume 2, Chaps. 25–27. Allen & Unwin, London, 1940.

Bradley, F. H., *Appearance and Reality.* Second Edition, Chaps. 15 & 24. Clarendon Press, Oxford, 1897.

Bradley, F. H., *Essays on Truth and Reality.* Chaps. 5, 7, & 8. Clarendon Press, Oxford, 1914.

Brentano, F., "On the Concept of Truth," in J. V. Canfield and F. H. Donnell (eds.), *Readings in the Theory of Knowledge.* Appleton-Century-Crofts, New York, 1964.

Dewey, J., "Propositions, Warranted Assertibility, and Truth," *The Journal of Philosophy,* 38 (1941).

Dummet, M., "Truth," *Proceedings of the Aristotelian Society,* 59 (1958–59).

Ewing, A. C., *The Fundamental Questions of Philosophy,* Chap. 3. Routledge & Kegan Paul, London, 1951.

Ezorsky, G., "Truth in Context," *The Journal of Philosophy,* 60 (1963).

Heinemann, F. H., "Are There Only Two Kinds of Truth?," *Philosophy and Phenomenological Research,* 16 (1956).

James. W., *The Meaning of Truth.* Preface & Chap. VI. Longman's, Green, New York, 1909.

James, W., *Pragmatism.* Lecture II. David McKay Co., New York, 1907.

Joachim, H. H., *The Nature of Truth.* Clarendon Press, Oxford, 1906.

Kaufmann, F., "Three Meanings of 'Truth'," *The Journal of Philosophy,* 45 (1948).

Montague, W. P., *The Ways of Knowing.* Part One. The Macmillan Company, New York, 1925.

Moore, G. E., *Some Main Problems of Philosophy.* Chaps. 3, 14–15, & 17. Allen & Unwin, London, 1953.

Pitcher, G. (ed.), *Truth.* Prentice-Hall, Englewood Cliffs, N.J., 1964.

Royce, J., "The Nature of Truth," in A. C. Ewing (ed.), *The Idealist Tradition from Berkeley to Blanshard.* Free Press, New York, 1957.

Russell, B., *An Inquiry into Meaning and Truth.* Chaps. 10, 16, 17, 21, & 23. Allen & Unwin, London, 1940.

Russell, B., *Philosophical Essays.* Chaps. 5–7. Longman's, Green, London, 1910.

Russell, B., *The Problems of Philosophy.* Chaps. 12 & 13. Oxford University Press, London, 1912.

Tarski, A., "The Semantic Conception of Truth," *Philosophy and Phenomenological Research,* 4 (1944).

Woozley, A. D., *Theory of Knowledge: An Introduction.* Chaps. 6 & 7. Hutchinson, London, 1949.

PART TWO

14 THOMAS HOBBES
Sense, Imagination, Reason*

Of Sense

Concerning the thoughts of man, I will consider them first singly and afterwards in train or dependence upon one another. Singly, they are every one a *representation* or *appearance* of some quality or other accident of a body without us which is commonly called an *object*. Which object works on the eyes, ears, and other parts of a man's body, and by diversity of working produces diversity of appearances.

The original of them all is that which we call SENSE, for there is no conception in a man's mind which has not at first, totally or by parts, been begotten upon the organs of sense. The rest are derived from that original.

To know the natural cause of sense is not very necessary to the business now in hand, and I have elsewhere written of the same at large.[1] Nevertheless, to fill each part of my present method, I will briefly deliver the same in this place.

The cause of sense is the external body or object which presses the organ proper to each sense, either immediately as in the taste and touch, or mediately as in seeing, hearing, and smelling; which pressure, by the mediation of the nerves and other strings and membranes of the body continued inward to the brain and heart, causes there a resistance or counter-pressure or endeavor of the heart to deliver itself, which endeavor, because *outward*, seems to be some matter without. And this *seeming* or *fancy* is that which men call *sense*, and consists, as to the eye, in a *light* or *color figured;* to the ear, in a *sound;* to the nostril, in an *odor;* to the tongue and palate, in a *savor;* and to the rest of the body, in *heat, cold, hardness, softness,* and such other qualities as we discern by *feeling.* All which qualities, called *sensible,* are in the object that causes them but so many several motions of the matter by which it presses our organs diversely. Neither in us that are pressed are they anything else but divers motions, for motion produces nothing but motion. But their appearance to us is fancy, the same waking that dreaming. And as pressing, rubbing, or striking the eye makes us fancy a light, and pressing the ear produces a din, so do the bodies also we see or hear produce the same by their strong, though unobserved, action. For if those colors and sounds were in the bodies or objects that cause them, they could not be severed from them as by glasses, and in echoes by reflection, we

---

* From *Leviathan,* Chaps. I, II, III, & V.

[1] [In *Human Nature* written in 1640 which, combined with *De Corpore Politico,* was published under the title *The Elements of Law* in 1650. Excerpts from *Human Nature* are included in Selection 22.—*Ed.*]

see they are, where we know the thing we see is in one place, the appearance in another. And though at some certain distance the real and very object seem invested with the fancy it begets in us, yet still the object is one thing, the image or fancy is another. So that sense, in all cases, is nothing else but original fancy, caused, as I have said, by the pressure—that is, by the motion—of external things upon our eyes, ears, and other organs thereunto ordained. . . .

Of Imagination

That when a thing lies still, unless somewhat else stir it, it will lie still forever is a truth that no man doubts of. But that when a thing is in motion it will eternally be in motion unless somewhat else stay it, though the reason be the same—namely, that nothing can change itself—is not so easily assented to. For men measure not only other men but all other things by themselves, and, because they find themselves subject after motion to pain and lassitude, think everything else grows weary of motion and seeks repose of its own accord, little considering whether it be not some other motion, wherein that desire of rest they find in themselves, consists. From hence it is that the schools say heavy bodies fall downward out of an appetite to rest and to conserve their nature in that place which is most proper for them, ascribing appetite and knowledge of what is good for their conservation, which is more than man has, to things inanimate, absurdly.

When a body is once in motion, it moves, unless something else hinder it, eternally; and whatsoever hinders it cannot in an instant, but in time and by degrees, quite extinguish it; and as we see in the water, though the wind cease, the waves give not over rolling for a long time after, so also it happens in that motion which is made in the internal parts of a man then when he sees, dreams, etc. For after the object is removed or the eye shut, we still retain an image of the thing seen, though more obscure than when we see it. And this is it the Latins call *imagination* from the image made in seeing, and apply the same, though improperly, to all the other senses. But the Greeks call it *fancy,* which signifies *appearance* and is as proper to one sense as to another. IMAGINATION, therefore, is nothing but *decaying sense* and is found in men and many other living creatures as well sleeping as waking.

The decay of sense in men waking is not the decay of the motion made in sense but an obscuring of it in such manner as the light of the sun obscures the light of the stars, which stars do no less exercise their virtue by which they are visible in the day than in the night. But because among many strokes which our eyes, ears, and other organs receive from external bodies the predominant only is sensible, therefore, the light of the sun being predominant, we are not affected with the action of the stars. And any object being removed from our eyes, though the impression it made in us remain, yet other objects more present succeeding and working on us, the imagination of the past is obscured and made weak, as the voice of a man is in the noise of the day. From whence it follows that the longer the time is after the sight or sense of any object, the weaker is the imagination. For the continual change of man's body destroys in time the parts which in sense were moved, so that distance of time and of place has one and the same effect in us. For as at a great distance of place that which we look at appears dim and without distinction of the smaller parts, and as voices grow weak and inarticulate, so also, after great distance of time, our imagination of the past is weak and we lose, for example, of cities we have seen many particular streets, and of actions many particular circumstances. This *decaying sense,* when we would express the thing itself—I mean *fancy* itself —we call *imagination,* as I said before; but when we would express the decay and signify that the sense is fading, old, and past, it is called *memory.* So that imagination and memory are but one thing, which for divers considerations has divers names.

Much memory, or memory of many things, is called *experience.* Again, imagination being only of those things which have been formerly perceived by sense, either all at once or by parts at several times, the former, which is the imagining the whole object as it was presented to the sense, is *simple* imagination, as when one imagines a man or horse which he has seen before. The other is *compounded,* as when, from the sight of a man at one time and of a horse at another, we conceive in our mind a centaur. So when a man compounds the image of his own person with the image of the actions of another man, as when a man imagines himself a Hercules or an Alexander—which happens often to them that are much taken with reading of romances—it is a compound imagination and properly but a fiction of the mind. There be also other imaginations that rise in men, though waking, from the great impression made in sense: as from gazing upon the sun, the impression leaves an image of the sun before our eyes a long time after; and from being long and vehemently attent upon geometrical figures, a man shall in the dark, though awake, have the images of lines and angles before his eyes; which kind of fancy has no particular name, as being a thing that does not commonly fall into men's discourse.

The imaginations of them that sleep are those we call *dreams.* And these also, as all other imaginations, have been before, either totally or by parcels, in the sense. And because in sense the brain and nerves, which are the necessary organs of sense, are so benumbed in sleep as not easily to be moved by the action of external objects, there can happen in sleep no imagination and therefore no dream but what proceeds from the agitation of the inward parts of man's body; which inward parts, for the connection they have with the brain and other organs, when they be distempered do keep the same in motion; whereby the imaginations there formerly made appear as if a man were waking, saving that the organs of sense being now benumbed so as there is no new object which can master and obscure them with a more vigorous impression, a dream must needs be more clear, in this silence of sense, than our waking thoughts. And hence it comes to pass that it is a hard matter, and by many thought impossible, to distinguish exactly between sense and dreaming. For my part, when I consider that in dreams, I do not often nor constantly think of the same persons, places, objects, and actions that I do waking, nor remember so long a train of coherent thoughts dreaming as at other times; and because waking I often observe the absurdity of dreams, but never dream of the absurdities of my waking thoughts—I am well satisfied that, being awake, I know I dream not, though when I dream I think myself awake. . . .

The imagination that is raised in man, or any other creature endowed with the faculty of imagining, by words or other voluntary signs is that we generally call *understanding* and is common to man and beast. For a dog by custom will understand the call or the rating of his master, and so will many other beasts. That understanding which is peculiar to man is the understanding not only his will but his conceptions and thoughts by the sequel and contexture of the names of things into affirmations, negations, and other forms of speech; and of this kind of understanding I shall speak hereafter.

Of the Consequence or Train of Imaginations

By *consequence* or TRAIN of thoughts, I understand that succession of one thought to another which is called, to distinguish it from discourse in words, *mental discourse.*

When a man thinks on anything whatsoever, his next thought after is not altogether so casual as it seems to be. Not every thought to every thought succeeds indifferently. But as we have no imagination whereof we have not formerly had sense, in whole or in parts, so we have no transition from one imagination to another whereof we never had the like before in our senses. The reason whereof is this. All fancies are motions within us, relics of those made in the sense; and those motions that immediately succeeded one another in the sense continue also together after sense; insomuch as the former coming again to take place and be predominant, the latter follows by coherence of the matter moved, in such manner as water upon a plane table is drawn which way any one part of it is guided by the finger. But because in sense to one and the same thing perceived sometimes one thing, sometimes another succeeds, it comes to pass in time that in the imagining of anything there is no certainty what we shall imagine next; only this is certain: it shall be something that succeeded the same before at one time or another.

This train of thoughts, or mental discourse, is of two sorts. The first is *unguided,* without design and inconstant, wherein there is no passionate thought to govern and direct those that follow to itself as the end and scope of some desire or other passion—in which case the thoughts are said to wander, and seem impertinent one to another as in a dream. Such are commonly the thoughts of men that are not only without company but also without care of anything, though even then their thoughts are as busy as at other times but without harmony—as the sound which a lute out of tune would yield to any man, or in tune to one that could not play. And yet in this wild ranging of the mind, a man may ofttimes perceive the way of it and the dependence of one thought upon another. For in a discourse of our present civil war, what could seem more impertinent than to ask, as one did, what was the value of a Roman penny? Yet the coherence to me was manifest enough. For the thought of the war introduced the thought of the delivering up the king to his enemies; the thought of that brought in the thought of the delivering up of Christ; and that again the thought of the thirty pence, which was the price of that treason; and thence easily followed that malicious question—and all this in a moment of time, for thought is quick.

The second is more constant, as being *regulated* by some desire and design. For the impression made by such things as we desire or fear is strong and permanent, or, if it cease for a time, of quick return; so strong it is sometimes as to hinder and break our sleep. From desire arises the thought of some means we have seen produce the like of that which we aim at; and from the thought of that, the thought of means to that mean; and so continually till we come to some beginning within our own power. And because the end, by the greatness of the impression, comes often to mind, in case our thoughts begin to wander they are quickly again reduced into the way; which, observed by one of the seven wise men, made him give men this precept, which is now worn out: *Respice finem*—that is to say, in all your actions look often upon what you would have as the thing that directs all your thoughts in the way to attain it.

The train of regulated thoughts is of two kinds: one, when of an effect imagined we seek the causes or means that produce it, and this is common to man and beast. The other is when, imagining anything whatsoever, we seek all the possible effects that can by it be produced—that is to say, we imagine what we can do with it when we have it. Of which I have not at any time seen any sign but in man only, for this is a curiosity hardly incident to the nature of any living creature that has no other passion but sensual, such as are hunger, thirst, lust, and anger. In sum, the discourse of the mind, when it is governed by design, is nothing but *seeking* or the faculty of invention—which the Latins called *sagacitas* and *solertia,* a hunting out of the causes of some effect, present or past, or of the effects of some present or past cause. Sometimes a man seeks what he has lost; and from that place and time wherein he misses it his mind runs back, from place to place and time to time, to find where and when he had it—that is to say, to find some certain and limited time and place in which to begin a method of seeking. Again, from thence his thoughts run over the same places and times to find what action or other occasion might make him lose it. This we call *remembrance* or calling to mind; the Latins call it *reminiscentia,* as it were a *reconning* of our former actions.

Sometimes a man knows a place determinate, within the compass whereof he is to seek; and then his thoughts run over all the parts thereof, in the same manner as one would sweep a room to find a jewel, or as a spaniel ranges the field till he find a scent, or as a man should run over the alphabet to start a rhyme.

Sometimes a man desires to know the event of an action; and then he thinks of some like action past and the events thereof one after another, supposing like events will follow like actions. As he that foresees what will become of a criminal re-cons what he has seen follow on the like crime before, having this order of thoughts: the crime, the officer, the prison, the judge, and the gallows. Which kind of thoughts is called *foresight,* and *prudence* or *providence,* and sometimes *wisdom,* though such conjecture, through the difficulty of observing all circumstances, be very fallacious. But this is certain: by how much one man has more experience of things past than another, by so much also he is more prudent, and his expectations the seldomer fail him. The *present* only has a being in nature; things *past* have a being in the memory only; but things *to come* have no being at all, the *future* being but a fiction of the mind applying the sequels of actions past to the actions that are present, which with most certainty is done by him that has most experience, but not with certainty enough. And though it be called prudence when the event answers our expectation, yet in its own nature it is but presumption. For the foresight of things to come, which is providence, belongs only to him by whose will they are to come. From him only and supernaturally, proceeds prophecy. The best prophet naturally is the best guesser, and the best guesser he that is most versed and studied in the matters he guesses at, for he has most *signs* to guess by.

A *sign* is the evident antecedent of the consequent, and, contrarily, the consequent of the antecedent when the like consequences have been observed before; and the oftener they have been observed, the less uncertain is the sign. And therefore he that has most experience in any kind of business has most signs whereby to guess at the future time and consequently is the most prudent; and so much more prudent than he that is new in that kind of business as not to be equaled by any advantage of natural and extemporary wit— though perhaps many young men think the contrary.

Nevertheless it is not prudence that distinguishes man from beast. There be beasts that at a year old observe more, and pursue that which is for their good more prudently, than a child can do at ten.

As prudence is a *presumption* of the *future,* contracted from the *experience* of time *past,* so there is a presumption of things past taken from other things, not future but past also. For he that has seen by what courses and degrees a flourishing state has first come into civil war and then to ruin, upon the sight of the ruins of any other state will guess the like war and the like courses have been there also. But this conjecture has the same uncertainty almost with the conjecture of the future, both being grounded only upon experience.

There is no other act of man's mind that I can remember, naturally planted in him, so as to need no other thing to the exercise of it but to be born a man and live with the use of his five senses. Those other faculties of which I shall speak by and by, and which seem proper to man only, are acquired and increased by study and industry, and of most men learned by instruction and discipline, and proceed all from the invention of words and speech. For besides sense and thoughts and the train of thoughts, the mind of man has no other motion; though by the help of speech and method the same faculties may be improved to such a height as to distinguish men from all other living creatures. . . .

Of Reason and Science

When a man *reasons,* he does nothing else but conceive a sum total from *addition* of parcels, or conceive a remainder from *subtraction* of one sum from another; which if it be done by words; is conceiving of the consequence of the names of all the parts to the name of the whole and one part to the name of the other part. And though in some things, as in numbers, besides adding and subtracting men name other operations, as *multiplying* and *dividing,* yet they are the same; for multiplication is but adding together of things equal, and division but subtracting of one thing as often as we can. These operations are not incident to numbers only, but to all manner of things that can be added together and taken one out of another. For as arithmeticians teach to add and subtract in *numbers,* so the geometricians teach the same in *lines, figures* solid and superficial, *angles, proportions, times,* degrees of *swiftness, force, power,* and the like; the logicians teach the same in *consequences of words,* adding together two *names* to make an *affirmation,* and two *affirmations* to make a *syllogism,* and *many syllogisms* to make a *demonstration;* and from the *sum* or *conclusion* of a *syllogism* they subtract one *proposition* to find the other. Writers of politics add together *pactions* to find man's *duties,* and lawyers *laws* and *facts* to find what is *right* and *wrong* in the actions of private men. In sum, in what matter soever there is place for *addition* and *subtraction,* there also is place for *reason;* and where these have no place, there *reason* has nothing at all to do.

Out of all which we may define—that is to say, determine—what that is which is meant by this word *reason* when we reckon it among the faculties of the mind. For REASON, in this sense, is nothing but *reckoning*—that is, adding and subtracting—of the consequences of general names agreed upon for the *marking* and *signifying* of our thoughts; I say marking them when we reckon by ourselves, and *signifying* when we demonstrate or approve our reckonings to other men.

And as in arithmetic unpracticed men must, and professors themselves may often, err and cast up false, so also in any other subject of reasoning the ablest, most attentive, and most practiced men may deceive themselves and infer false conclusions; not but that reason itself is always right reason, as well as arithmetic is a certain and infallible art, but no one man's reason, nor the reason of any one number of men, makes the certainty, no more than an account is therefore well cast up because a great many men have unanimously approved it. And therefore as when there is a controversy in an account the parties must by their own accord set up, for right reason, the reason of some arbitrator or judge, to whose sentence they will both stand, or their controversy must either come to blows or be undecided for want of a right reason constituted by nature, so is it also in all debates of what kind soever. And when men that think themselves wiser than all other clamor and demand right reason for judge, yet seek no more but that things should be determined by no other men's reason but their own, it is as tolerable in the society of men as it is in play after trump is turned to use for trump on every occasion that suit whereof they have most in their hand. For they do nothing else that will have every of their passions, as it comes to bear sway in them, to be taken for right reason, and that in their own controversies, betraying their want of right reason by the claim they lay to it.

The use and end of reason is not the finding of the sum and truth of one or a few consequences remote from the first definitions and settled significations of names, but to begin at these and proceed from one consequence to another. For there can be no certainty of the last conclusion without a certainty of all those affirmations and negations on which it was grounded and inferred. As when a master of a family, in taking an account, casts up the sums of all the bills of expense into one sum, and not regarding how each bill is summed up by those that give them in account nor what it is he pays for, he advantages himself no more than if he allowed the account in gross, trusting to every of the accountants' skill and honesty; so also in reasoning of all other things he that takes up conclusions on the trust of authors, and does not fetch them from the first items in every reckoning, which are the significations of names settled by definitions, loses his labor; and does not know anything, but only believes.

When a man reckons without the use of words, which may be done in particular things, as when upon the sight of any one thing we conjecture what was likely to have preceded or is likely to follow upon it, if that which he thought likely to have preceded it has not preceded it, this is called *error,* to which even the most prudent men are subject. But when we reason in words of general signification and fall upon a general inference which is false, though it be commonly called *error,* it is indeed an *absurdity* or senseless speech. For error is but a deception in presuming that somewhat is past or to come of which, though it were not past, or not to come, yet there was no impossibility discoverable. But when we make a general assertion, unless it be a true one, the possibility of it is inconceivable. And words whereby we conceive nothing but the sound are those we call *absurd, insignificant,* and *nonsense.* And therefore if a man should talk to me of a *round quadrangle,* or *accidents of bread in cheese,* or *immaterial substances,* or of *a free subject, a free-will,* or any *free* but free from being hindered by opposition, I should not say he were in an error but that his words were without meaning—that is to say, absurd.

I have said before, in the second chapter, that a man did excel all other animals in this faculty: that when he conceived anything whatsoever, he was apt to inquire the consequences of it and what effects he could do with it. And now I add this other degree of the same excellence: that he can by words reduce the consequences he finds to general rules, called *theorems* or *aphorisms*— that is, he can reason or reckon not only in number but in all other things whereof one may be added unto or subtracted from another.

But this privilege is allayed by another, and that is, by the privilege of absurdity, to which no living creature is subject but man only. And of men, those are of all most subject to it that profess philosophy. For it is most true that Cicero says of them somewhere that there can be nothing so absurd but may be found in the books of philosophers. And the reason is manifest. For there is not one of them that begins his ratiocination from the definitions or explications of the names they are to use, which is a method that has been used only in geometry, whose conclusions have thereby been made indisputable.

1. The first cause of absurd conclusions I ascribe to the want of method in that they begin not their ratiocination from definitions—that is, from settled significations of their words—as if they could cast account without knowing the value of the numeral words *one, two,* and *three.*

And whereas all bodies enter into account upon divers considerations, which I have mentioned in the precedent chapter, these considerations being diversely named, divers absurdities proceed from the confusion and unfit connection of their names into assertions. And therefore,

2. The second cause of absurd assertions I ascribe to the giving of names of *bodies* to *accidents,* or of *accidents* to *bodies:* as they do that say *faith is infused* or *inspired* when nothing can be *poured* or *breathed* into anything but body; and that *extension* is *body;* that *phantasms* are *spirits,* etc.

3. The third I ascribe to the giving of the names of the *accidents* of *bodies without us* to the *accidents* of our *own bodies:* as they do that say the *color is in the body, the sound is in the air,* etc.

4. The fourth, to the giving of the names of *bodies* to *names* or *speeches:* as they do that say that *there be things universal,* that a *living creature is genus* or *a general thing,* etc.

5. The fifth, to the giving of the names of *accidents* to *names* and *speeches:* as they do that say *the nature of a thing is its definition, a man's command is his will,* and the like.

6. The sixth, to the use of metaphors, tropes, and other rhetorical figures instead of words proper. For though it be lawful to say, for example, in common speech *the way goes or leads hither or thither, the proverb says this or that,* whereas ways cannot go nor proverbs speak, yet in reckoning and seeking of truth such speeches are not to be admitted.

7. The seventh, to names that signify nothing but are taken up and learned by rote from the schools: as *hypostatical, transubstantiate, consubstantiate, eternal-now,* and the like canting of Schoolmen.

To him that can avoid these things it is not easy to fall into any absurdity, unless it be by the length of an account, wherein he may perhaps forget what went before. For all men by nature reason alike and well when they have good principles. For who is so stupid as both to mistake in geometry and also to persist in it when another detects his error to him?

By this it appears that reason is not, as sense and memory, born with us, nor gotten by experience only, as prudence is, but attained by industry: first in apt imposing of names, and secondly by getting a good and orderly method in proceeding from the elements, which are names, to assertions made by connection of one of them to another, and so to syllogisms, which are the connections of one assertion to another, till we come to a knowledge of all the consequences of names appertaining to the subject in hand; and that is it men call SCIENCE. And whereas sense and memory are but knowledge of fact, which is a thing past and irrevocable, *science* is the knowledge of consequences and dependence of one fact upon another, by which out of that we can presently do we know how to do something else when we will, or the like another time; because when we see how anything comes about, upon what causes and by what manner when the like causes come into our power we see how to make it produce the like effects.

Children, therefore, are not endowed with reason at all till they have attained the use of speech, but are called reasonable creatures for the possibility apparent of having the use of reason in time to come. And the most part of men, though they have the use of reasoning a little way, as in numbering to some degree, yet it serves them to little use in common life, in which they govern themselves, some better, some worse, according to their differences of experience, quickness of memory, and inclinations to several ends, but specially according to good or evil fortune and the errors of one another. For as for *science* or certain rules of their actions, they are so far from it that they know not what it is. Geometry they have thought conjuring; but for other sciences, they who have not been taught the beginnings and some progress in them, that they may see how they be acquired and generated, are in this point like children that, having no thought of generation, are made believe by the women that their brothers and sisters are not born but found in the garden.

But yet they that have no *science* are in better and nobler condition with their natural prudence than men that, by misreasoning or by trusting them that reason wrong, fall upon false and absurd general rules. For ignorance of causes and of rules does not set men so far out of their way as relying on false rules and taking for causes of what they aspire to those that are not so, but rather causes of the contrary.

To conclude, the light of human minds is perspicuous words, but by exact definitions first snuffed and purged from ambiguity; *reason* is the *pace;* increase of *science,* the *way;* and the benefit of mankind, the *end.* And, on the contrary, metaphors and senseless and ambiguous words are like *ignes fatui;* and reasoning upon them is wandering among innumerable absurdities; and their end, contention and sedition, or contempt.

As much experience is *prudence,* so is much science *sapience.* For though we usually have one name of wisdom for them both, yet the Latins did always distinguish between *prudentia* and *sapientia,* ascribing the former to experience, the latter to science. But to make their difference appear more clearly, let us suppose one man endowed with an excellent natural use and dexterity in handling his arms, and another to have added to that dexterity an acquired science of where he can offend or be offended by his adversary in every possible posture or guard; the ability of the former would be to the ability of the latter as prudence to sapience: both useful, but the latter infallible. But they that, trusting only to the authority of books, follow the blind blindly are like him that, trusting to the false rules of a master of fence, ventures presumptuously upon an adversary that either kills or disgraces him.

The signs of science are some certain and infallible, some uncertain. Certain, when he that pretends the science of anything can teach the same—that is to say, demonstrate the truth thereof perspicuously to another; uncertain, when only some particular events answer to his pretense, and upon many occasions prove so as he says they must. Signs of prudence are all uncertain, because to observe by experience and remember all circumstances that may alter the success is impossible. But in any business whereof a man has not infallible science to proceed by, to forsake his own natural judgment and be guided by general sentences read in authors and subject to many exceptions is a sign of folly and generally scorned by the name of pedantry. And even of those men themselves that in councils of the commonwealth love to show their reading of politics and history, very few do it in their domestic affairs where their particular interest is concerned, having prudence enough for their private affairs; but in public they study more the reputation of their own wit than the success of another's business.

15 RENÉ DESCARTES
Conscious Experience and Its Objects *

I.

Rules for the Direction of the Mind

[*Cf.* Rule VII, pp. 43–46, and Rule XII, pp. 53–56.]

Rule III

In the subjects we propose to investigate, our inquiries should be directed, not to what others have thought (senserint), *nor to what we ourselves conjecture, but to what we can clearly and perspicuously behold and with certainty deduce; for knowledge is not won in any other way.*

To study the writings of the ancients is right, because it is a great boon for us to be able to make use of the labours of so many men; and we should do so, both in order to discover what they have correctly made out in previous ages, and also that we may inform ourselves as to what in the various sciences is still left for investigation. But yet there is a great danger lest in a too absorbed

* From *The Philosophical Works of Descartes*, Vols. I & II, translated by E. S. Haldane and G. R. T. Ross, Cambridge University Press, London, 1931. Reprinted by permission of Cambridge University Press.

study of these works we should become infected with their errors, guard against them as we may. For it is the way of writers, whenever they have allowed themselves rashly and credulously to take up a position in any controverted matter, to try with the subtlest of arguments to compel us to go along with them. But when, on the contrary, they have happily come upon something certain and evident, in displaying it they never fail to surround it with ambiguities, fearing, it would seem, lest the simplicity of their explanation should make us respect their discovery less, or because they grudge us an open vision of the truth.

Further, supposing now that all were wholly open and candid, and never thrust upon us doubtful opinions as true, but expounded every matter in good faith, yet since scarce anything has been asserted by any one man the contrary of which has not been alleged by another, we should be eternally uncertain which of the two to believe. It would be no use to total up the testimonies in favour of each, meaning to follow that opinion which was supported by the greater number of authors; for if it is a question of difficulty that is in dispute, it is more likely that the truth would have been discovered by few than by many. But even though all these men agreed among themselves, what they teach us would not suffice for us. For we shall not, e.g. all turn out to be mathematicians though we know by heart all the proofs that others have elaborated, unless we have an intellectual talent that fits us to resolve difficulties of any kind. Neither, though we have mastered all the arguments of Plato and Aristotle, if yet we have not the capacity for passing a solid judgment on these matters, shall we become Philosophers; we should have acquired the knowledge not of a science, but of history.

I lay down the rule also, that we must wholly refrain from ever mixing up conjectures with our pronouncements on the truth of things. This warning is of no little importance. There is no stronger reason for our finding nothing in the current *(vulgari)* Philosophy which is so evident and certain as not to be capable of being controverted, than the fact that the learned, not content with the recognition of what is clear and certain, in the first instance hazard the assertion of obscure and ill-comprehended theories, at which they have arrived merely by probable conjecture. Then afterwards they gradually attach complete credence to them, and mingling them promiscuously with what is true and evident, they finish by being unable to deduce any conclusion which does not appear to depend upon some proposition of the doubtful sort, and hence is not uncertain.

But lest we in turn should slip into the same error, we shall here take note of all those mental operations by which we are able, wholly without fear of illusion, to arrive at the knowledge of things. Now I admit only two, viz. intuition and induction.[1]

---

[1] [*sic.—Ed.*]

By *intuition* I understand, not the fluctuating testimony of the senses, nor the misleading judgment that proceeds from the blundering constructions of imagination, but the conception which an unclouded and attentive mind gives us so readily and distinctly that we are wholly freed from doubt about that which we understand. Or, what comes to the same thing, *intuition* is the undoubting conception of an unclouded *(purae)* and attentive mind, and springs from the light of reason alone; it is more certain than deduction itself, in that it is simpler, though deduction, as we have noted above, cannot by us be erroneously conducted. Thus each individual can mentally have intuition of the fact that he exists, and that he thinks; that the triangle is bounded by three lines only, the sphere by a single superficies, and so on. Facts of such a kind are far more numerous than many people think, disdaining as they do to direct their attention upon such simple matters.

But in case anyone may be put out by this new use of the term intuition[1] and of other terms which in the following pages I am similarly compelled to dissever from their current meaning, I here make the general announcement that I pay no attention to the way in which particular terms have of late been employed in the schools, because it would have been difficult to employ the same terminology while my theory was wholly different. All that I take note of is the meaning of the Latin of each word, when, in cases where an appropriate term is lacking, I wish to transfer to the vocabulary that expresses my own meaning those that I deem most suitable.

This evidence and certitude, however, which belongs to intuition, is required not only in the enunciation of propositions, but also in discursive reasoning of whatever sort. For example consider this consequence: 2 and 2 amount to the same as 3 and 1. Now we need to see intuitively not only that 2 and 2 make 4, and that likewise 3 and 1 make 4, but further that the third of the above statements is a necessary conclusion from these two.

Hence now we are in a position to raise the question as to why we have, besides intuition, given this supplementary method of knowing, viz. knowing by *deduction,* by which we understand all necessary inference from other facts that are known with certainty. This, however, we could not avoid, because many things are known with certainty, though not by themselves evident, but only deduced from true and known principles by the continuous and uninterrupted action of a mind *(cogitationis)* that has a clear vision of each step in the process. It is in a similar way that we know that the last link in a long chain is connected with the first, even though we do not take in by means of one and the same act of vision all the intermediate links on which that connection depends, but only remember that we have taken them successively under review and that each single one is united to its neighbour, from the first even to the last. Hence we distinguish this mental intuition from deduction by the fact that into the conception of the latter there enters a certain movement or succession, into that of the former there does not. Further deduction does not re-

---

[1] 'Intuitus' is but sparingly used in Descartes' later writings.—*Tr.*

quire an immediately presented evidence such as intuition possesses; its certitude is rather conferred upon it in some way by memory. The upshot of the matter is that it is possible to say that those propositions indeed which are immediately deduced from first principles are known now by intuition, now by deduction, i.e. in a way that differs according to our point of view. But the first principles themselves are given by intuition alone, while, on the contrary, the remote conclusions are furnished only by deduction.

These two methods are the most certain routes to knowledge, and the mind should admit no others. All the rest should be rejected as suspect of error and dangerous. But this does not prevent us from believing matters that have been divinely revealed as being more certain than our surest knowledge, since belief in these things,[1] as all faith in obscure matters *(<ut> quaecunque est de obscuris),* is an action not of our intelligence *(ingenii),* but of our will. They should be heeded also since, if they have any basis in our understanding, they can and ought to be, more than all things else, discovered by one or other of the ways above-mentioned, as we hope perhaps to show at greater length on some future opportunity.

II.

Meditations on First Philosophy—Meditation III

. . . In order that I may have an opportunity of inquiring into this in an orderly way [without interrupting the order of meditation which I have proposed to myself, and which is little by little to pass from the notions which I find first of all in my mind to those which I shall later on discover in it] it is requisite that I should here divide my thoughts into certain kinds, and that I should consider in which of these kinds there is, properly speaking, truth or error to be found. Of my thoughts some are, so to speak images of the things, and to these alone is the title 'idea' properly applied; examples are my thought of a man or of a chimera, of heaven, of an angel, or [even] of God. But other thoughts possess other forms as well. For example in willing, fearing, approving, denying, though I always perceive something as the subject of the action of my mind,[2] yet by this action I always add something else to the idea[3] which I have of that thing; and of the thoughts of this kind some are called volitions or affections, and others judgments.

Now as to what concerns ideas, if we consider them only in themselves and do not relate them to anything else beyond themselves, they cannot prop-

---

[1]   'that faith of ours,' Leibniz's MS.—*Tr.*

[2]   The French version is followed here as being more explicit. In it 'action de mon esprit' replaces 'mea cogitatio'.—*Tr.*

[3]   In the Latin version 'similitudinem.'—*Tr.*

erly speaking be false; for whether I imagine a goat or a chimera, it is not less true that I imagine the one than the other. We must not fear likewise that falsity can enter into will and into affections, for although I may desire evil things, or even things that never existed, it is not the less true that I desire them. Thus there remains no more than the judgments which we make, in which I must take the greatest care not to deceive myself. But the principal error and the commonest which we may meet with in them, consists in my judging that the ideas which are in me are similar or conformable to the things which are outside me; for without doubt if I considered the ideas only as certain modes of my thoughts, without trying to relate them to anything beyond, they could scarcely give me material for error.

But among these ideas, some appear to me to be innate, some adventitious, and others to be formed [or invented] by myself; for, as I have the power of understanding what is called a thing, or a truth, or a thought, it appears to me that I hold this power from no other source than my own nature. But if I now hear some sound, if I see the sun, or feel heat, I have hitherto judged that these sensations proceeded from certain things that exist outside of me; and finally it appears to me that sirens, hippogryphs, and the like, are formed out of my own mind. But again I may possibly persuade myself that all these ideas are of the nature of those which I term adventitious, or else that they are all innate, or all fictitious: for I have not yet clearly discovered their true origin.

And my principal task in this place is to consider, in respect to those ideas which appear to me to proceed from certain objects that are outside me, what are the reasons which cause me to think them similar to these objects. It seems indeed in the first place that I am taught this lesson by nature; and, secondly, I experience in myself that these ideas do not depend on my will nor therefore on myself—for they often present themselves to my mind in spite of my will. Just now, for instance, whether I will or whether I do not will, I feel heat, and thus I persuade myself that this feeling, or at least this idea of heat, is produced in me by something which is different from me, i.e. by the heat of the fire near which I sit. And nothing seems to me more obvious than to judge that this object imprints its likeness rather than anything else upon me.

Now I must discover whether these proofs are sufficiently strong and convincing. When I say that I am so instructed by nature, I merely mean a certain spontaneous inclination which impels me to believe in this connection and not a natural light which makes me recognise that it is true. But these two things are very different; for I cannot doubt that which the natural light causes me to believe to be true, as, for example, it has shown me that I am from the fact that I doubt, or other facts of the same kind. And I possess no other faculty whereby to distinguish truth from falsehood, which can teach me that what this light shows me to be true is not really true, and no other faculty that is equally trustworthy. But as far as [apparently] natural impulses are concerned, I have frequently remarked, when I had to make active choice between virtue and vice, that they often enough led me to the part that was worse; and this is why I do not see any reason for following them in what regards truth and error.

And as to the other reason, which is that these ideas must proceed from objects outside me, since they do not depend on my will, I do not find it any the more convincing. For just as these impulses of which I have spoken are found in me, notwithstanding that they do not always concur with my will, so perhaps there is in me some faculty fitted to produce these ideas without the assistance of any external things, even though it is not yet known by me; just as, apparently, they have hitherto always been found in me during sleep without the aid of any external objects.

And finally, though they did proceed from objects different from myself, it is not a necessary consequence that they should resemble these. On the contrary, I have noticed that in many cases there was a great difference between the object and its idea. I find, for example, two completely diverse ideas of the sun in my mind; the one derives its origin from the senses, and should be placed in the category of adventitious ideas; according to this idea the sun seems to be extremely small; but the other is derived from astronomical reasonings, i.e. is elicited from certain notions that are innate in me, or else it is formed by me in some other manner; in accordance with it the sun appears to be several times greater than the earth. These two ideas cannot, indeed, both resemble the same sun, and reason makes me believe that the one which seems to have originated directly from the sun itself, is the one which is most dissimilar to it.

All this causes me to believe that until the present time it has not been by a judgment that was certain [or premeditated], but only by a sort of blind impulse that I believed that things existed outside of, and different from me, which, by the organs of my senses, or by some other method whatever it might be, conveyed these ideas or images to me [and imprinted on me their similitudes].

But there is yet another method of inquiring whether any of the objects of which I have ideas within me exist outside of me. If ideas are only taken as certain modes of thought, I recognise amongst them no difference or inequality, and all appear to proceed from me in the same manner; but when we consider them as images, one representing one thing and the other another, it is clear that they are very different one from the other. There is no doubt that those which represent to me substances are something more, and contain so to speak more objective reality within them [that is to say, by representation participate in a higher degree of being or perfection] than those that simply represent modes or accidents; and that idea again by which I understand a supreme God, eternal, infinite, [immutable], omniscient, omnipotent, and Creator of all things which are outside of Himself, has certainly more objective reality in itself than those ideas by which finite substances are represented.

Now it is manifest by the natural light that there must at least be as much reality in the efficient and total cause as in its effect. For, pray, whence can the effect derive its reality, if not from its cause? And in what way can this cause communicate this reality to it, unless it possessed it in itself? And from this it follows, not only that something cannot proceed from nothing, but likewise that what is more perfect—that is to say, which has more reality within itself —cannot proceed from the less perfect. And this is not only evidently true of those effects which possess actual or formal reality, but also of the ideas in which we consider merely what is termed objective reality. To take an example, the stone which has not yet existed not only cannot now commence to be unless it has been produced by something which possesses within itself, either formally or eminently, all that enters into the composition of the stone [i.e. it must possess the same things or other more excellent things than those which exist in the stone] and heat can only be produced in a subject in which it did not previously exist by a cause that is of an order [degree or kind] at least as perfect as heat, and so in all other cases. But further, the idea of heat, or of a stone, cannot exist in me unless it has been placed within me by some cause which possesses within it at least as much reality as that which I conceive to exist in the heat or the stone. For although this cause does not transmit anything of its actual or formal reality to my idea, we must not for that reason imagine that it is necessarily a less real cause; we must remember that [since every idea is a work of the mind] its nature is such that it demands of itself no other formal reality than that which it borrows from my thought, of which it is only a mode [i.e. a manner or way of thinking]. But in order that an idea should contain some one certain objective reality rather than another, it must without doubt derive it from some cause in which there is at least as much formal reality as this idea contains of objective reality. For if we imagine that something is found in an idea which is not found in the cause, it must then have been derived from nought; but however imperfect may be this mode of being by which a thing is objectively [or by representation] in the understanding by its idea, we cannot certainly say that this mode of being is nothing, nor, consequently, that the idea derives its origin from nothing.

Nor must I imagine that, since the reality that I consider in these ideas is only objective, it is not essential that this reality should be formally in the causes of my ideas, but that it is sufficient that it should be found objectively. For just as this mode of objective existence pertains to ideas by their proper nature, so does the mode of formal existence pertain to the causes of those ideas (this is at least true of the first and principal) by the nature peculiar to them. And although it may be the case that one idea gives birth to another idea, that cannot continue to be so indefinitely; for in the end we must reach an idea whose cause shall be so to speak an archetype, in which the whole reality [or perfection] which is so to speak objectively [or by representation] in these ideas is contained formally [and really]. Thus the light of nature causes me to know clearly that the ideas in me are like [pictures or] images which can, in truth, easily fall short of the perfection of the objects from which they have been derived, but which can never contain anything greater or more perfect . . .

III.

Reply to Third Set of Objections[1]

Objection X: . . . I should like to know whether the minds of those who are in a profound and dreamless sleep yet think. If not, they have at that time no ideas. Whence no idea is innate, for what is innate is always present.

Reply: . . . when I say that an idea is innate in us [or imprinted in our souls by nature], I do not mean that it is always present to us. This would make no idea innate. I mean merely that we possess the faculty of summoning up this idea.

IV.

Notes Directed against a Certain Programme [2]

Art. XII. The mind has no need of innate ideas, or notions, or axioms, but of itself the faculty of thinking suffices for the accomplishment of its processes *(actiones)*.

Art. XIII. Therefore all common notions engraven on the mind, owe their origin to the observation of things or to tradition.

Descartes' Rejoinder:

In article twelve he appears to dissent from me only in words, for when he says that *the mind has no need of innate ideas, or notions, or axioms,* and at the same time allows it the faculty of thinking (to be considered natural or innate), he makes an affirmation in effect identical with mine, but denies it in words. For I never wrote or concluded that the mind required innate ideas which were in some sort different from its faculty of thinking; but when I observed the existence in me of certain thoughts which proceeded, not from extraneous objects nor from the determination of my will, but solely from the faculty of thinking which is within me, then, that I might distinguish the ideas or notions (which are the forms of these thoughts) from other thoughts *adventitious* or *factitious,* I termed the former '*innate.*' In the same sense we say that in some families generosity is innate, in others certain diseases like gout or gravel, not that on this account the babes of these families suffer from these diseases in their mother's womb, but because they are born with a certain disposition or propensity for contracting them.

---

[1] [Generally attributed to Hobbes.—*Ed.*]

[2] The former follower and now opponent of Descartes, Henricus Regius (Henri de Roy), had issued from Utrecht in anonymous form a sort of poster or manifesto on the nature of the human mind. Descartes undertook a refutation written in Latin which was printed, apparently without his knowledge, in December 1647. [From Prefatory Note to the *Notae* by E. S. Haldane.—*Ed.*]

The conclusion which he deduces in *article XIII* from the preceding article is indeed wonderful. *'For this reason,'* he says (i.e. because the mind has no need of innate ideas, but the faculty of thinking of itself is sufficient), *'all common notions, engraven on the mind, owe their origin to the observation of things or to tradition'*—as though the faculty of thinking could of itself execute nothing, nor perceive nor think anything save what it received from observation or tradition, that is, from the senses. So far is this from being true, that, on the contrary, any man who rightly observes the limitations of the senses, and what precisely it is that can penetrate through this medium to our faculty of thinking must needs admit that no ideas of things, in the shape in which we envisage them by thought, are presented to us by the senses. So much so that in our ideas there is nothing which was not innate in the mind, or faculty of thinking, except only these circumstances which point to experience—the fact, for instance, that we judge that this or that idea, which we now have present to our thought, is to be referred to a certain extraneous thing, not that these extraneous things transmitted the ideas themselves to our minds through the organs of sense, but because they transmitted something which gave the mind occasion to form these ideas, by means of an innate faculty, at this time rather than at another. For nothing reaches our mind from external objects through the organs of sense beyond certain corporeal movements, as *our author* himself affirms, in *article XIX*, taking the doctrine from my *Principles;* but even these movements and the figures which arise from them, are not conceived by us in the shape they assume in the organs of sense, as I have explained at great length in my *Dioptrics*. Hence it follows that the ideas of the movements and figures are themselves innate in us. So much the more must the ideas of pain, colour, sound and the like be innate, that our mind may, on occasion of certain corporeal movements, envisage these ideas, for they have no likeness to the corporeal movements. Could anything be imagined more preposterous than that all common notions which are inherent in our mind should arise from these movements, and should be incapable of existing without them? I should like *our friend* to instruct me as to what corporeal movement it is which can form in our mind any common notion, e.g. the notion that *'things which are equal to the same thing are equal to one another,'* or any other he pleases; for all these movements are particular, but notions are universal having no affinity with movements and no relation to them.

V.

The Principles of Philosophy. First Part

[*Cf.* Selection 9, in particular, pp. 111–113.]

PRINCIPLE IX.

> *What thought (cogitatio) is.*
> By the word thought I understand all that of which we are conscious as

operating in us. And that is why not alone understanding, willing, imagining, but also feeling, are here the same thing as thought. For if I say I see, or I walk, I therefore am, and if by seeing and walking I mean the action of my eyes or my legs, which is the work of my body, my conclusion is not absolutely certain; because it may be that, as often happens in sleep, I think I see or I walk, although I never open my eyes or move from my place, and the same thing perhaps might occur if I had not a body at all. But if I mean only to talk of my sensation *(sensu)*, or my consciously seeming to see or to walk, it becomes quite true because my assertion now refers only to my mind, which alone is concerned with my feeling or thinking that I see and I walk. . . .

PRINCIPLE XIII.

In what sense the knowledge of all other things depends on the knowledge of God.
But when the mind which thus knows itself but still doubts all other things, looks around in order to try to extend its knowledge further, it first of all finds in itself the ideas of a multitude of things, and while it contemplates these simply and neither affirms nor denies that there is anything outside itself which corresponds to these ideas, it is beyond any danger of falling into error. The mind likewise discovers certain common ideas out of which it frames various demonstrations which absolutely convince us of their truth if we give attention to them. For example the mind has within itself the ideas of number and figure; it has also, amongst its ordinary conceptions this, that *'if equals are added to equals, the result is equal,'* and so on. From this it is easy to demonstrate that the three angles of a triangle are equal to two right angles, etc. Now mind perceives these and other facts to be true so long as the premises from which they are derived *(praemissas ex quibus)* are attended to. But since it cannot always devote this attention to them [when it remembers the conclusion and yet cannot recollect the order of its deduction], and conceives that it may have been created of such a nature that it has been deceived even in what is most evident, it sees clearly that it has great cause to doubt the truth of such conclusions, and to realise that it can have no certain knowledge until it is acquainted with its creator. . . .

PRINCIPLE XXXII.

That in us there are but two modes of thought, the perception of the understanding and the action of the will.
For all the modes of thinking that we observed in ourselves may be related to two general modes, the one of which consists in perception, or in the operation of the understanding, and the other in volition, or the operation of the will. Thus sense-perception *(sentire)*, imagining, and conceiving things that are purely intelligible, are just different methods of perceiving *(percipiendi)*; but desiring, holding in aversion, affirming, denying, doubting, all these are the different modes of willing.

PRINCIPLE XXXIII.

That we deceive ourselves only when we form judgments about anything insufficiently known to us.

When we perceive anything, we are in no danger of misapprehending it, if we do not judge of it one way or the other; and even when we judge of it we should not fall into error, provided that we do not give our assent to what we do not know clearly and distinctly; but what usually misleads us is that we very frequently form a judgment although we have no very exact knowledge regarding that of which we judge.

PRINCIPLE XXXIV.

That the will is requisite for judgment as well as the understanding.

I admit that we can judge of nothing unless our understanding is made use of, because there is no reason to suppose we can judge of what we in no wise apprehend; but the will is absolutely essential for our giving our assent to what we have in some manner perceived. Nor, in order to form any judgment whatever, is it necessary that we should have a perfect and entire knowledge of a thing; for we often give our assent to things of which we have never had any but a very obscure and confused knowledge.

PRINCIPLE XXXV.

That the will is more extended than the understanding, and that our errors proceed from this cause.

Further, the perception of the understanding only extends to the few objects which present themselves to it, and is always very limited. The will, on the other hand, may in some measure be said to be the infinite, because we perceive nothing which may be the object of some other will, even of the immensity of the will that is in God, to which our will cannot also extend, so that we easily extend it beyond that which we apprehend clearly. And when we do this there is no wonder if it happens that we are deceived. . . .

PRINCIPLE XLIX.

That eternal truths cannot be enumerated thus, and that this is not requisite.

What I have hitherto enumerated are regarded either as the qualities of things or their modes.

[We must now talk of what we know as eternal truths.]

When we apprehend that it is impossible that anything can be formed of nothing, the proposition *ex nihilo nihil fit* is not to be considered as an existing thing, or the mode of a thing, but as a certain eternal truth which has its seat in our mind, and is a common notion or axiom. Of the same nature are the following: 'It is impossible that the same thing can be and not be at the same time,' and that 'what has been done cannot be undone,' 'that he who thinks must exist while he thinks,' and very many other propositions the whole of which it would not be easy to enumerate. But [this is not necessary since] we cannot fail to recognise them when the occasion presents itself for us to do so, and if we have no prejudices to blind us.

PRINCIPLE L.

That these eternal truths are clearly perceived, but not by all, by reason of prejudice.

As regards the common notions, indeed, there is no doubt that they may be clearly and distinctly perceived, for otherwise they would not deserve to bear this name; but it is also true that there are some that do not in regard to all men deserve the name equally with others, because they are not equally perceived by all. Not, however, that I believe the faculty of knowledge to extend further with some men than with others; it is rather that these common opinions are opposed to the prejudices of some who are thereby prevented from easily perceiving them, although they are perfectly manifest to those who are free from these prejudices. . . .

PRINCIPLE LXXIII.

The third cause [of our errors] *is that our mind fatigues itself when it applies its attention to the objects which are not present to the senses; and that we are therefore in the habit of judging of these not from present perceptions, but from preconceived opinions.*

Further, since our mind cannot pause to consider any one thing with attention without difficulty and fatigue, and since of all objects it applies itself with the greatest difficulty to those which are present neither to the senses nor to the imagination, whether because it derives this nature from its union with the body, or because in the first years of our life we are so much occupied with feeling and imagining that we have acquired a greater facility for thinking in this way than in any other, besides acquiring the habit of so-doing, it comes about that many men are unable to believe that there is any substance unless it is imaginable and corporeal and even sensible. For they are ignorant that the only things that are imaginable are those that exist in extension, motion and figure, while there are many others that are intelligible; and they persuade themselves that there is nothing that can subsist but body, and finally, that there is no body which is not sensible. And since in truth we do not perceive any object as it is in itself by sense alone, as will be clearly shown later on, it comes to pass that most men in life perceive nothing but in a confused way.

16 BENEDICT SPINOZA
Three Kinds of Knowledge*

[*Cf.* Selection 3, in particular, pp. 65–68.]

Pt. II, Prop. XL. Whatsoever ideas in the mind follow from ideas which are therein adequate, are also themselves adequate.

Proof.—This proposition is self-evident. For when we say that an idea in the human mind follows from ideas which are therein adequate, we say, in other words (II. xi. Coroll.), that an idea is in the divine intellect, whereof God is the cause, not in so far as he is infinite, nor in so far as he is affected by the ideas of very many particular things, but only in so far as he constitutes the essence of the human mind.

Note I.—I have thus set forth the cause of those notions, which are common to all men, and which form the basis of our ratiocination. But there are other causes of certain axioms or notions, which it would be to the purpose to set forth by this method of ours; for it would thus appear what notions are more useful than others, and what notions have scarcely any use at all. Furthermore, we should see what notions are common to all men, and what notions are only clear and distinct to those who are unshackled by prejudice, and we should detect those which are ill-founded. Again we should discern whence the notions called *secondary* derived their origin, and consequently the axioms on which they are founded, and other points of interest connected with these questions. But I have decided to pass over the subject here, partly because I have set it aside for another treatise, partly because I am afraid of wearying the reader by too great prolixity. Nevertheless, in order not to omit anything necessary to be known, I will briefly set down the causes, whence are derived the terms styled *transcendental,* such as Being, Thing, Something. These terms arose from the fact, that the human body, being limited, is only capable of distinctly forming a certain number of images (what an image is I explained in II. xvii. note) within itself at the same time; if this number be exceeded, the images will begin to be confused; if this number of images, which the body is capable of forming distinctly within itself, be largely exceeded, all will become entirely confused one with another. This being so, it is evident (from II. Prop. xvii. Coroll. and xviii.) that the human mind can distinctly imagine as many things simultaneously, as its body can form images simultaneously. When the images become quite confused in the body, the mind also imagines all bodies confusedly without any distinction, and will comprehend them, as it were, under one attribute, namely, under the attribute of Being, Thing, &c. The same conclusion can be drawn from the fact that images are not always equally vivid, and from other analogous causes, which there is no need to explain here; for the purpose which we have in view it is sufficient for us to con-

* From the *Ethics.*

sider one only. All may be reduced to this, that these terms represent ideas in the highest degree confused. From similar causes arise those notions, which we call *general,* such as man, horse, dog, &c. They arise, to wit, from the fact that so many images, for instance, of men, are formed simultaneously in the human mind, that the powers of imagination break down, not indeed utterly, but to the extent of the mind losing count of small differences between individuals (*e.g.* colour, size, &c.) and their definite number, and only distinctly imagining that, in which all the individuals, in so far as the body is affected by them, agree; for that is the point, in which each of the said individuals chiefly affected the body; this the mind expresses by the name man, and this it predicates of an infinite number of particular individuals. For, as we have said, it is unable to imagine the definite number of individuals. We must, however, bear in mind, that these general notions are not formed by all men in the same way, but vary in each individual according as the point varies, whereby the body has been most often affected and which the mind most easily imagines or remembers. For instance, those who have most often regarded with admiration the stature of man, will by the name of man understand an animal of erect stature; those who have been accustomed to regard some other attribute, will form a different general image of man, for instance, that man is a laughing animal, a two-footed animal without feathers, a rational animal, and thus, in other cases, everyone will form general images of things according to the habit of his body.

It is thus not to be wondered at, that among philosophers, who seek to explain things in nature merely by the images formed of them, so many controversies should have arisen.

Note II.—From all that has been said above it is clear, that we, in many cases, perceive and form our general notions:—(1.) From particular things represented to our intellect fragmentarily, confusedly, and without order through our senses (II. xxix. Coroll.); I have settled to call such perceptions by the name of knowledge from the mere suggestions of experience. (2.) From symbols, *e.g.,* from the fact of having read or heard certain words we remember things and form certain ideas concerning them, similar to those through which we imagine things (II. xviii. note). I shall call both these ways of regarding things *knowledge of the first kind, opinion,* or *imagination.* (3.) From the fact that we have notions common to all men, and adequate ideas of the properties of things (II. xxxviii. Coroll., xxxix, and Coroll. and xl.); this I call *reason* and *knowledge of the second kind.* Besides these two kinds of knowledge, there is, as I will hereafter show, a third kind of knowledge, which we will call intuition. This kind of knowledge proceeds from an adequate idea of the absolute essence of certain attributes of God to the adequate knowledge of the essence of things. I will illustrate all three kinds of knowledge by a single example. Three numbers are given for finding a fourth, which shall be to the third as the second is to the first. Tradesmen without hesitation multiply the second by the third, and divide the product by the first; either because they have not forgotten the rule which they received from a master without any proof, or because they have often made trial of it with simple numbers, or by virtue of the proof of the nineteenth proposition of the seventh book of Euclid, namely, in virtue of the general property of proportionals.

But with very simple numbers there is no need of this. For instance, one, two, three, being given, everyone can see that the fourth proportional is six; and this is much clearer, because we infer the fourth number from an intuitive grasping of the ratio, which the first bears to the second.

Pt. II, Prop. XLI. Knowledge of the first kind is the only source of falsity, knowledge of the second and third kinds is necessarily true.

Proof.—To knowledge of the first kind we have (in the foregoing note) assigned all those ideas, which are inadequate and confused; therefore this kind of knowledge is the only source of falsity (II. xxxv.). Furthermore, we assigned to the second and third kinds of knowledge those ideas which are adequate; therefore these kinds are necessarily true (II. xxxiv.). Q.E.D.

Pt. II, Prop. XLII. Knowledge of the second and third kinds, not knowledge of the first kind, teaches us to distinguish the true from the false.

Proof.—This proposition is self-evident. He, who knows how to distinguish between true and false, must have an adequate idea of true and false. That is (II. xl., note ii.), he must know the true and the false by the second or third kind of knowledge.

17 JOHN LOCKE · GOTTFRIED WILHELM LEIBNIZ
Of the Nature of the Mind and
the Origins of Knowledge *

Leibniz, Preface to the *New Essays:*

The Essay on the Understanding, by a distinguished Englishman, being one of the most beautiful and esteemed works of this period, I have resolved to make some remarks upon it, because having sufficiently meditated for a long time upon the same subject and upon the greater part of the matters therein touched upon, I have thought that it would be a favorable opportunity to publish something under the title of "New Essays on the Understanding," and to procure a favorable reception to my

* From Locke, *An Essay Concerning Human Understanding* and Leibniz, *New Essays Concerning Human Understanding,* translated by A. G. Langley, The Open Court Publishing Company, La Salle, Ill., 3rd Edition, 1949. All passages from the latter work are reprinted by permission of The Open Court Publishing Company.

thoughts, by putting them in so good company. I have thought also that I could profit from the labor of another not only to lessen my own (since in fact it is less difficult to follow the thread of a good author than to work wholly independently), but further to add something to what he has given us, which is always easier than to start from the beginning; for I think I have cleared up some difficulties which he had left in their entirety. Thus his reputation is an advantage to me; having for the rest a disposition to render justice, and very far from wishing to diminish the esteem in which this work is held, I would increase it, if my approval carried any weight. It is true I often differ in my views (from him), but very far from denying the merit of celebrated writers, we bear witness to it, by making known in what and why we differ from their views, when we judge it necessary to prevent their authority from prevailing over reason on some important points; besides, by satisfying such excellent men, we render the truth more acceptable, and it must be supposed that it is principally for truth that they labor. . . .

Our differences are upon subjects of some importance. The question is to know whether the soul in itself is entirely empty as the tablets upon which as yet nothing has been written *(tabula rasa)* according to Aristotle, and the author of the Essay, and whether all that is traced thereon comes solely from the senses and from experience; or whether the soul contains originally the principles of many ideas and doctrines which external objects merely call up on occasion, as I believe with Plato, and even with the schoolmen, and with all those who interpret in this way the passage of St. Paul (Rom. 2:15) where he states that the law of God is written in the heart. The Stoics call these principles *prolepses, i.e.* fundamental assumptions, or what is taken for granted in advance. The Mathematicians call them *general notions* (κοιναὶ ἔννοιαι). Modern philosophers give them other beautiful names, and Julius Scaliger in particular named them *semina aeternitatis,* also *zopyra, i.e.* living fires, luminous flashes, concealed within us, but which the encounter of the senses makes appear like the sparks which the blow makes spring from the steel. And the belief is not without reason, that these glitterings indicate something divine and eternal which appears especially in the necessary truths. Whence another question arises, whether all truths depend upon experience, *i.e.* upon induction and examples, or whether there are some which have still another foundation. For if some events can be foreseen prior to any proof which may have been made of them, it is manifest that we ourselves contribute something thereto. The senses, although necessary for all our actual knowledge, are not sufficient to give it all to us, since the senses never give us anything but examples, *i.e.* particular or individual truths. Now all the examples which confirm a general truth, whatever their number, do not suffice to establish the universal necessity of that same truth, for it does not follow that what has happened will happen in the same way. For example, the Greeks and the Romans, and all the other peoples of the earth known to the ancients, have always observed that before the lapse of twenty-four hours day changes into night, and night into day. But we would be deceived, if we believed that the same law holds good everywhere else; for since then, the contrary has been experienced in the region of Nova Zembla. And he would still be in error who believed that, in our climates at least, this is a necessary and eternal truth, which will always endure, since we must think that the earth, and the sun even, do not necessarily exist, and that there will perhaps be a time when this beautiful star, together with its whole system, will not longer exist, at least in its present form. Whence it appears that necessary truths such as are found in pure mathematics, and particularly in arithmetic and in geometry, must have principles whose proof does not depend upon examples, nor consequently upon the testimony of the senses, although without the senses it would never have occurred to us to think of them. This distinction must be carefully made, and was so well understood by Euclid, that he often proved by the reason, what is sufficiently seen through experience and by sensible images. Logic also, together with metaphysics and ethics, one of which shapes theology and the other jurisprudence, both natural (sciences), are full of such truths, and consequently their proof can come only from internal principles which are called innate. It is true that we must not imagine that these eternal laws of the reason can be read in the soul as in an open book, as the praetor's edict is read upon his *album* without difficulty and research; but it is sufficient that they can be discovered in us by dint of attention, for which the senses furnish occasions, and successful experience serves to confirm reason, in much the same way as proofs in arithmetic serve for the better avoidance of error in calculating when the reasoning is long. Herein, also, human knowledge differs from that of the brutes: the brutes are purely empirics and only guide themselves by examples; for, so far as we can judge of them, they never attain to the formation of necessary propositions; while men are capable of demonstrative sciences. It is also for this reason that the faculty the brutes have for making *consecutions* is something inferior to the reason of man. . . . The consecutions of the brutes are only a shadow of reasoning, *i.e.* are only connections of the imagination and passages from one image to another, because in a new juncture which appears similar to the preceding they expect anew that connection which they formerly met with, as if things were united in fact because their images are united in the memory. It is true that reason also counsels us to expect ordinarily to see that happen in the future which is conformed to a long past experience, but it is not on this account a necessary and infallible truth, and success may cease when least expected, when the reasons change which have sustained it. Therefore the wisest men do not so commit themselves to it as not to try to discover, if possible, something of the reason of this fact in order to judge when it is necessary to make exceptions. For reason is alone capable of establishing sure rules, and supplying what is wanting to those which were not such by inserting their exceptions; and of finding at length certain connections in the force of necessary consequences, which often furnish the means of foreseeing the result without the necessity of experiencing the sense-connections of images, to which the brutes are reduced, so that that which justifies the internal principles of necessary truths also distinguishes man from the brutes.

Perhaps our clever author will not wholly differ from my view. For after having employed the whole of his first book in rejecting innate intelligence, taken in a certain sense, he nevertheless, at the beginning of the second and in the sequel, admits that ideas, which do not originate in sensation, come from reflection. Now reflection is nothing else than attention to what is in us, and the senses do not give us what we already carry with us. That being so, can it be denied that there is much that is innate in our mind, since we are innate, so to speak, in ourselves? and that there is in us: being, unity, substance, duration, change, action, perception, pleasure, and a thousand other objects of our intellectual ideas? And these objects being immediate to our understanding and always present (although they cannot always be perceived by reason of our distractions and needs), what wonder that we say that these ideas with all depending upon them are innate in us? I have made use also of the comparison of a block of marble which has veins, rather than of a block of marble wholly even, or of blank tablets, *i.e.* of what is called among philosophers a *tabula rasa*. For if the soul resembled these blank tablets, truths would be in us as the figure of Hercules is in the marble, when the marble is wholly indifferent to the reception of this figure or some other. But if there were veins in the block which should indicate the figure of Hercules rather than other figures, this block would be more determined thereto, and Hercules would be in it as in some sense innate, although it would be needful to labor to discover these veins, to clear them by polishing, and by cutting away what prevents them from appearing. Thus it is that ideas and truths are for us innate, as inclinations, dispositions, habits, or natural potentialities, and not as actions; although these potentialities are always accompanied by some actions, often insensible, which correspond to them.

It seems that our clever author claims that there is nothing *virtual* in us, and indeed nothing of which we are not always actually conscious; but he cannot take this rigorously, otherwise his opinion would be too paradoxical; since, moreover, acquired habits and the stores of our memory are not always perceived and do not even always come to our aid at need, although we often easily recall them to the mind upon some slight occasion which makes us remember them, just as we need only the beginning of a song to remember it. He limits his thesis also in other places, by saying that there is nothing in us of which we have not at least formerly been conscious. But besides the fact that no one can be assured by reason alone how far our past *apperceptions*, which we may have forgotten, may have gone, especially according to the Platonic doctrine of reminiscence which, wholly fabulous as it is, is in no respect incompatible at least in part with reason wholly pure: besides this, I say, why must we acquire all through the perception of external things, and nothing be unearthed in ourselves? Is our soul then by itself such a blank that besides the images borrowed from without, it is nothing? This is not an opinion (I am sure) that our judicious author could approve. And where do we find tablets that have no variety in themselves? For we never see a plane perfectly even and uniform. Why, then, could we not furnish also ourselves with something of thought from our own depths if we should dig therein? Thus I am led to believe that at bottom his opinion upon this point is not different from mine, or rather from the common view, inasmuch as he recognizes two sources of our knowledge, the Senses and Reflection.

I do not know whether it will be so easy to harmonize him with us and with the Cartesians, when he maintains that the mind does not always think, and particularly that it is without perception when we sleep without dreaming; and he objects that since bodies can exist without motion, souls can also exist without thought. But here I make a somewhat different reply than is customary, for I hold that naturally a substance cannot exist without action, and that there is indeed never a body without movement. Experience already favors me, and you have only to consult the book of the distinguished Mr. Boyle against absolute rest, to be convinced of it; but I believe reason favors it also, and this is one of the proofs I have for doing away with atoms.

Moreover, there are a thousand indications which make us think that there are at every moment an infinite number of *perceptions* in us, but without apperception and reflection, *i.e.* changes in the soul itself of which we are not conscious, because the impressions are either too slight and too great in number, or too even, so that they have nothing sufficiently distinguishing them from each other; but joined to others, felt at least confusedly in the mass. Thus it is that habit makes us take no notice of the motion of a mill or a waterfall when we have lived quite near it for some time. It is not that the motion does not always strike our organs, and that something no longer enters into the soul corresponding thereto, in virtue of the harmony of the soul and the body, but these impressions which are in the soul and the body, being destitute of the attractions of novelty, are not strong enough to attract our attention and our memory, attached to objects more engrossing. For all attention requires memory, and often when we are not admonished, so to speak, and warned to take note of some of our own present perceptions, we allow them to pass without reflection, and even without being noticed; but if any one directs our attention to them immediately after, and makes us notice, for example, some noise which was just heard, we remember it, and are conscious of having had at the time some feeling of it. Thus there were perceptions of which we were not conscious at once, consciousness arising in this case only from the warning after some interval, however small it may be. And to judge still better of the minute perceptions which we cannot distinguish in the crowd, I am wont to make use of the example of the roar or noise of the sea which strikes one when on its shore. To understand this noise as it is made, it would be necessary to hear the parts which compose this whole, *i.e.* the noise of each wave, although each of these little noises makes itself known only in the confused collection of all the others, *i.e.* in the roar itself, and would not be noticed if the wave which makes it were alone. For it must be that we are affected a little by the motion of this wave, and that we have some perception of each one of these noises, small as they are; otherwise we would not have that of a hundred thousand waves, since a hundred thousand nothings cannot make something. One never sleeps so soundly as not to have some feeble and confused sensation, and one would never be awakened by the greatest noise in the world if he did not have some perception of its small beginning; just as one would never break a rope by the greatest effort in the world if it were not stretched and lengthened a little by smaller efforts, although the slight extension they produce is not apparent.

These minute perceptions are, then, of greater efficacy in their results than one supposes. They form I know not what, these tastes, these images of the sense-qualities, clear in the mass, but confused in the parts, these impressions which surrounding bodies make upon us, which involve the infinite, this connection which each being has with all the rest of the universe. We may even say that in consequence of these minute perceptions, the present is big with the future and laden with the past, that all things conspire ($\sigma\acute{v}\mu\pi\nu o\iota\alpha$ $\pi\acute{\alpha}\nu\tau\alpha$, as Hippocrates said), and that in the least of substances eyes as penetrating as those of God could read the whole course of the things in the universe. . . .

Locke, Bk. I, Ch. I of the *Essay:*

1. It is an established opinion amongst some men, that there are in the understanding certain *innate principles;* some primary notions, κοιναὶ ἔννοιαι, characters, as it were stamped upon the mind of man; which the soul receives in its very first being, and brings into the world with it. It would be sufficient to convince unprejudiced readers of the falseness of this supposition, if I should only show (as I hope I shall in the following parts of this Discourse) how men, barely by the use of their natural faculties, may attain to all the knowledge they have, without the help of any innate impressions; and may arrive at certainty, without any such original notions or principles. For I imagine any one will easily grant that it would be impertinent to suppose the ideas of colours innate in a creature to whom God hath given sight, and a power to receive them by the eyes from external objects: and no less unreasonable would it be to attribute several truths to the impressions of nature, and innate characters, when we may observe in ourselves faculties fit to attain as easy and certain knowledge of them as if they were originally imprinted on the mind.

But because a man is not permitted without censure to follow his own thoughts in the search of truth, when they lead him ever so little out of the common road, I shall set down the reasons that made me doubt of the truth of that opinion, as an excuse for my mistake, if I be in one; which I leave to be considered by those who, with me, dispose themselves to embrace truth wherever they find it.

Leibniz:

> . . . I have always held, as I still hold, to the innate idea of God, which Descartes maintained, and as a consequence to the other innate ideas, which cannot come to us from the senses. Now, I go still farther in conformity to the new system, and I believe even that all the thoughts and acts of our soul come from its own depths, with no possibility of their being given to it by the senses, as you shall see in the sequel. But at present I will put this investigation aside, and, accommodating myself to the received expressions, since in fact they are good and tenable, and one can say in a certain sense that the external senses are in part causes of our thoughts, I shall consider how in my opinion one must say even in the common system (speaking of the action of bodies upon the soul, as the Copernicans speak with other men of the movement of the sun, and with cause), that there are some ideas and some principles which do not come to us from the senses, and which we find in ourselves without forming them, although the senses give us occasion to perceive them. I imagine that your clever author has remarked that under the name of innate principles one often maintains his prejudices, and wishes to free himself from the trouble of discussion, and that this abuse doubtless has stirred up his zeal against this supposition. He desired, no doubt, to combat the indolence and the superficial manner of thinking of those who, under the specious pretext of innate ideas and of truths naturally engraved upon the mind, to which we readily give our consent, care nothing about investigating or considering the sources, the relations, and the certainty of this knowledge. In that I am entirely agreed with him, and I go even farther. I would that our analysis should not be limited, that definitions should be given of all the terms which are capable of definition, and that one should demonstrate, or give the means of demonstrating, all the axioms which are not primitive, without distinguishing the opinions which men have of them, and without caring whether they give their consent or not. There would be more profit in this than one thinks. But it seems that the author has been carried too far on the other side by his zeal, otherwise very praiseworthy. He has not sufficiently distinguished, in my opinion, the origin of the necessary truths, whose source is in the understanding, from that of the truths of fact drawn from the experience of the senses, and even from those confused perceptions which are in us. You see, then, that I do not agree with what you lay down as fact—that we can acquire all our knowledge without the need of innate impressions. . . .

2. There is nothing more commonly taken for granted than that there are certain *principles,* both *speculative* and *practical* (for they speak of both), universally agreed upon by all mankind: which therefore, they argue, must needs be the constant impressions which the souls of men receive in their first beings, and which they bring into the world with them, as necessarily and really as they do any of their inherent faculties.

3. This argument, drawn from universal consent, has this misfortune in it, that if it were true in matter of fact, that there were certain truths wherein all mankind agreed, it would not prove them innate, if there can be any other way shown how men may come to that universal agreement, in the things they do consent in, which I presume may be done.

4. But, which is worse, this argument of universal consent, which is made use of to prove innate principles, seems to me a demonstration that there are none such: because there are none to which all mankind give an universal assent. I shall begin with the speculative, and instance in those magnified principles of demonstration, 'Whatsoever is, is,' and 'It is impossible for the same thing to be and not to be'; which of all others, I think have the most allowed title to innate. These have so settled a reputation of maxims universally received, that it will no doubt be thought strange if any one should seem to question it. But yet I take liberty to say, that these propositions are far from having an universal assent, that there are a great part of mankind to whom they are not so much as known.

Leibniz:

I do not ground the certainty of innate principles upon universal consent, for I have already told you that my opinion is that we ought to labor to be able to demonstrate all the axioms which are not primitive. I grant you also that a consent very general, but which is not universal, may come from a tradition diffused throughout the human race, . . . I conclude that a consent sufficiently general amongst men is an indication, and not a demonstration, of an innate principle; but that the exact and decisive proof of these principles consists in showing that their certitude comes only from what is in us. To reply further to what you say against the general approbation which is given to the two great speculative principles, which are, nevertheless, the best established, I may say to you that even if they were not known they would not cease to be innate, because they are recognized as soon as heard; but I will add further that at bottom everybody knows them, and makes use at every moment of the principle of contradiction (for example) without considering it distinctly; and there is no barbarian who, in an affair of any moment, is not offended by the conduct of a liar who contradicts himself. Thus, these maxims are employed without an express consideration of them. And in nearly the same way we have virtually in the mind the propositions suppressed in enthymemes, which are set aside not only externally, but further in our thought.

5. For, first, it is evident, that all children and idiots have not the least apprehension or thought of them. And the want of that is enough to destroy that universal assent which must needs be the necessary concomitant of all innate truths: it seeming to me near a contradiction to say, that there are truths imprinted on the soul, which it perceives or understands not: imprinting, if it signify anything, being nothing else but the making certain truths to be perceived. For to imprint anything on the mind without the mind's perceiving it, seems to me hardly intelligible. If therefore children and idiots have souls, have minds, with those impressions upon them, *they* must unavoidably perceive them, and necessarily know and assent to these truths; which since they do not, it is evident that there are no such impressions. For if they are not notions naturally imprinted, how can they be innate? and if they are notions imprinted, how can they be unknown? To say a notion is imprinted on the mind, and yet at the same time to say, that the mind is ignorant of it, and never yet took notice of it, is to make this impression nothing. No proposition can be said to be in the mind which it never yet knew, which it was never yet conscious of. For if any one may, then, by the same reason, all propositions that are true, and the mind is capable ever of assenting to, may be said to be in the mind, and to be imprinted: since, if any one can be said to be in the mind, which it never yet knew, it must be only because it is capable of knowing it; and so the mind is of all truths it ever shall know. Nay, thus truths may be imprinted on the mind which it never did, nor ever shall know; for a man may live long, and die at last in ignorance of many truths which his mind was capable of knowing, and that with certainty. So that if the capacity of knowing be the natural impression contended for, all the truths a man ever comes to know will, by this account, be every one of them innate; and this great point will amount to no more, but only to a very improper way of speaking; which, whilst it pretends to assert the contrary, says nothing different from those who deny innate principles. For nobody, I think, ever denied that the mind was capable of knowing several truths. The capacity, they say, is innate; the knowledge acquired. But then to what end such contest for certain innate maxims? If truths can be imprinted on the understanding without being perceived, I can see no difference there can be between any truths the mind is *capable* of knowing in respect of their original: they must all be innate or all adventitious: in vain shall a man go about to distinguish them. He therefore that talks of innate notions in the understanding, cannot (if he intend thereby any distinct sort of truths) mean such truths to be in the understanding as it never perceived, and is yet wholly ignorant of. For if these words 'to be in the understanding' have any propriety, they signify to be understood. So that to be in the understanding, and not to be understood; to be in the mind and never to be perceived, is all one as to say anything is and is not in the mind or understanding. If therefore these two propositions, 'Whatsoever is, is,' and 'It is impossible for the same thing to be and not to be,' are by nature imprinted, children cannot be ignorant of them: infants, and all that have souls, must

necessarily have them in their understandings, know the truth of them, and assent to it.

6. To avoid this, it is usually answered, that all men know and assent to them, *when they come to the use of reason;* and this is enough to prove them innate. I answer:

7. Doubtful expressions, that have scarce any signification, go for clear reasons to those who, being prepossessed, take not the pains to examine even what they themselves say. For, to apply this answer with any tolerable sense to our present purpose, it must signify one of these two things: either that as soon as men come to the use of reason these supposed native inscriptions come to be known and observed by them; or else, that the use and exercise of men's reason, assists them in the discovery of these principles, and certainly makes them known to them. . . .

11. Those who will take the pains to reflect with a little attention on the operations of the understanding, will find that this ready assent of the mind to some truths, depends not, either on native inscription, or the use of reason, but on a faculty of the mind quite distinct from both of them, as we shall see hereafter. Reason, therefore, having nothing to do in procuring our assent to these maxims, if by saying, that 'men know and assent to them, when they come to the use of reason,' be meant, that the use of reason assists us in the knowledge of these maxims, it is utterly false; and were it true, would prove them not to be innate. . . .

Leibniz:

If you are thus prejudiced, I am not astonished that you reject innate knowledge. But I am astonished that the thought has not occurred to you that we have an infinite amount of knowledge of which we are not always conscious, not even when we need it. It is for the memory to preserve this, and for the reminiscence to represent it to us, as it often, but not always, does at need. That is very well called remembrance *(subvenire),* for reminiscence needs some aid. And it must certainly be that in this multiplicity of our knowledge we are determined by something to renew one part rather than another, since it is impossible to think distinctly and at once of everything we know.

. . . In this sense it must be said that all arithmetic and all geometry are innate, and are in us virtually, so that we can find them there if we consider attentively and set in order what we already have in the mind, without making use of any truth learned through experience or through the tradition of another, as Plato has shown in a dialogue in which he introduces Socrates leading a child to abstract truths by questions alone without giving him any information. We can then make for ourselves these sciences in our study, and even with closed eyes, without learning through sight or even through touch the truths which we need; although it is true that we would not consider the ideas in question if we had never seen or touched anything. . . .

. . . Since an acquired knowledge can be concealed therein by the memory, as you admit, why could not nature have also concealed therein some original knowledge? Must everything that is natural to a substance which knows itself be known by it actually at once? Cannot and must not this substance (such as our soul) have many properties and affections which it is impossible to consider all at once and all together? It was the opinion of the Platonists that all our knowledge was reminiscence, and that thus the truths which the soul has brought with the birth of the man, and which are called innate, must be the remains of an express anterior knowledge. But this opinion has no foundation; and it is easy to believe that the soul must already have innate knowledge in the precedent state (if there were any pre-existence), however remote it might be, entirely as here: it would then have to come also from another precedent state, or it would be finally innate, or at least concrete, or else it would be needful to go to infinity and to make souls eternal, in which case this knowledge would be innate in fact, because it would never have commenced in the soul; and if any one claimed that each anterior state has had something from another more anterior, which it has not left to the succeeding, the reply will be made that it is manifest that certain evident truths must have been in all these states; and in whatever manner it may be taken, it is always clear in all states of the soul that necessary truths are innate, and are proved by what is within, it not being possible to establish them through experience, as we establish truths of fact. Why should it be necessary also that we could have no possession in the soul of which we had never made use? And is it the same thing to have a thing without using it as to have only the faculty of acquiring it? If that were so, we should never possess anything but the things which we enjoy; instead of which, we know that, besides the faculty and the object, some disposition in the faculty or in the object, or in both, is often necessary, that the faculty may exercise itself upon the object.

. . . The mind is not only capable of knowing them [necessary truths], but further of finding them in itself; and, if it had only the simple capacity of receiving knowledge, or the passive power therefor, as indeterminate as that which the wax has for receiving figures and the blank tablet for receiving letters, it would not be the source of necessary truths, as I have just shown that it is; for it is incontestable that the senses do not suffice to show their necessity, and that thus the mind has a disposition (active as well as passive) to draw them from itself from its own depths; although the senses are necessary to give it the occasion and attention for this, and to carry it to some rather than to others. You see, then, that these elsewhere very clever persons who are of another opinion appear not to have thought enough upon the consequences of the difference which there is between necessary or eternal truths and the truths of experience, as I have already observed, and as all our discussion shows. The original proof of the necessary truths comes from the understanding alone, and the other truths come from experience or from the observation of the senses. Our mind is capable of knowing both; but it is the source of the former, and, whatever number of particular experiences we may have of a universal truth, we could not be assured of it forever by induction without knowing its necessity through the reason.

. . . It is this particular relation of the human mind to these truths which renders the exercise of the faculty easy and natural in respect to them, and which causes them to be called innate. It is not, then, a naked faculty which consists in the mere possibility of understanding them; it is a disposition, an aptitude, a preformation, which determines our soul and which makes it possible for them to be derived from it. Just as there is the difference between the figures which are given to the stone or the marble indifferently, and between those which its veins already indicate, or are disposed to indicate, if the workman profits by them.

The intellectual ideas, which are the source of necessary truths, do not come from the senses; and you admit that there are some ideas which are due to the reflection of the mind upon itself. For the rest, it is true that the express knowledge of truths is subsequent *(tempore vel natura)* to the express knowledge of ideas; as the nature of truths depends upon the nature of ideas, before we expressly form one or the other, and the truths, into which enter ideas which come from the senses, depend upon the senses, at least in part. But the ideas which come from the senses are confused, and the truths which depend upon them are likewise confused, at least in part; while the intellectual ideas, and the truths dependent upon them, are distinct, and neither the one nor the other have their origin in the senses, although it may be true that we would never think of them without the senses.

Locke, Bk. II, Ch. I of the *Essay:*

1. Every man being conscious to himself that he thinks; and that which his mind is applied about whilst thinking being the *ideas* that are there, it is past doubt that men have in their minds several ideas,—such as are those expressed by the words *whiteness, hardness, sweetness, thinking, motion, man, elephant, army, drunkenness,* and others: it is in the first place then to be inquired, *How he comes by them?*

I know it is a received doctrine, that men have native ideas, and original characters, stamped upon their minds in their very first being. This opinion I have at large examined already; and, I suppose what I have said in the foregoing Book will be much more easily admitted, when I have shown whence the understanding may get all the ideas it has; and by what ways and degrees they may come into the mind;—for which I shall appeal to every one's own observation and experience.

2. Let us then suppose the mind to be, as we say, white paper, void of all characters, without any ideas:—How comes it to be furnished? Whence comes it by that vast store which the busy and boundless fancy of man has painted on

it with an almost endless variety? Whence has it all the *materials* of reason and knowledge? To this I answer, in one word, from EXPERIENCE. In that all our knowledge is founded; and from that it ultimately derives itself. Our observation employed either, about external sensible objects, or about the internal operations of our minds perceived and reflected on by ourselves, is that which supplies our understandings with all the *materials* of thinking. These two are the fountains of knowledge, from whence all the ideas we have, or can naturally have, do spring.

Leibniz:

> This *tabula rasa*, of which so much is said, is in my opinion only a fiction which nature does not admit, and which is based only upon the imperfect notions of philosophers, like the vacuum, atoms, and rest, absolute or relative, of two parts of a whole, or like the primary matter which is conceived as without form. Uniform things and those which contain no variety are never anything but abstractions, like time, space, and the other entities of pure mathematics. There is no body whatever whose parts are at rest, and there is no substance whatever that has nothing by which to distinguish it from every other. Human souls differ, not only from other souls, but also among themselves, although the difference is not at all of the kind called specific. And, according to the proofs which I believe we have, every substantial thing, be it soul or body, has its own characteristic relation to every other; and the one must always differ from the other by *intrinsic connotations.* Not to mention the fact that those who speak so frequently of this *tabula rasa* after having taken away the ideas cannot say what remains, like the scholastic philosophers, who leave nothing in their primary matter. You may perhaps reply that this *tabula rasa* of the philosophers means that the soul has by nature and originally only bare faculties. But faculties without some act, in a word the pure powers of the school, are also only fictions, which nature knows not, and which are obtained only by the process of abstraction. For where in the world will you ever find a faculty which shuts itself up in the power alone without performing any act? There is always a particular disposition to action, and to one action rather than to another. And besides the disposition there is a tendency to action, of which tendencies there is always an infinity in each subject at once; and these tendencies are never without some effect. Experience is necessary, I admit, in order that the soul be determined to such or such thoughts, and in order that it take notice of the ideas which are in us; but by what means can experience and the senses give ideas? Has the soul windows, does it resemble tablets, is it like wax? It is plain that all who so regard the soul, represent it as at bottom corporeal. You oppose to me this axiom received by the philosophers, *that there is nothing in the soul which does not come from the senses.* But you must except the soul itself and its affections. *Nihil est in intellectu, quod non fuerit in sensu,*

excipe: *nisi ipse intellectus.* Now the soul comprises being, substance, unity, identity, cause, perception, reason, and many other notions which the senses cannot give. . . .

In order to avoid a discussion upon what has delayed us too long, I declare to you in advance, sir, that when you say that ideas come to us from one or the other of these causes [sensation or reflection], I understand the statement to mean their actual perception, for I think I have shown that they are in us before they are perceived so far as they have any distinct character.

3. First, our Senses, conversant about particular sensible objects, do convey into the mind several distinct perceptions of things, according to those various ways wherein those objects do affect them. And thus we come by those *ideas* we have of *yellow, white, heat, cold, soft, hard, bitter, sweet,* and all those which we call sensible qualities; which when I say the senses convey into the mind, I mean, they from external objects convey into the mind what produces there those perceptions. This great source of most of the ideas we have, depending wholly upon our senses, and derived by them to the understanding, I call SENSATION.

4. Secondly, the other fountain from which experience furnisheth the understanding with ideas is,—the perception of the operations of our own mind within us, as it is employed about the ideas it has got;—which operations, when the soul comes to reflect on and consider, do furnish the understanding with another set of ideas, which could not be had from things without. And such are *perception, thinking, doubting, believing, reasoning, knowing, willing,* and all the different actings of our own minds;—which we being conscious of, and observing in ourselves, do from these receive into our understandings as distinct ideas as we do from bodies affecting our senses. This source of ideas every man has wholly in himself; and though it be not sense, as having nothing to do with external objects, yet it is very like it, and might properly enough be called *internal sense.* But as I call the other Sensation, so I call this REFLECTION, the ideas it affords being such only as the mind gets by reflecting on its own operations within itself. By reflection then, in the following part of this discourse, I would be understood to mean, that notice which the mind takes of its own operations, and the manner of them, by reason whereof there come to be ideas of these operations in the understanding. These two, I say, viz. external material things, as the objects of SENSATION, and the operations of our own minds within, as the objects of REFLECTION, are to me the only originals from whence all our ideas take their beginnings. The term *operations* here I use in a large sense, as comprehending not barely the actions of the mind about its ideas, but some sort of passions arising sometimes from them, such as is the satisfaction or uneasiness arising from any thought.

5. The understanding seems to me not to have the least glimmering of any ideas which it doth not receive from one of these two. *External objects* fur-

nish the mind with the ideas of sensible qualities, which are all those different perceptions they produce in us; and *the mind* furnishes the understanding with ideas of its own operations.

These, when we have taken a full survey of them, and their several modes, combinations, and relations, we shall find to contain all our whole stock of ideas; and that we have nothing in our minds which did not come in one of these two ways. Let any one examine his own thoughts, and thoroughly search into his understanding; and then let him tell me, whether all the original ideas he has there, are any other than of the objects of his senses, or of the operations of his mind, considered as objects of his reflection. And how great a mass of knowledge soever he imagines to be lodged there, he will, upon taking a strict view, see that he has not any idea in his mind but what one of these two have imprinted;—though perhaps, with infinite variety compounded and enlarged by the understanding, as we shall see hereafter. . . .

22. Follow a child from its birth, and observe the alterations that time makes, and you shall find, as the mind by the senses comes more and more to be furnished with ideas, it comes to be more and more awake; thinks more, the more it has matter to think on. After some time it begins to know the objects which, being most familiar with it, have made lasting impressions. Thus it comes by degrees to know the persons it daily converses with, and distinguishes them from strangers; which are instances and effects of its coming to retain and distinguish the ideas the senses conveyed to it. And so we may observe how the mind, *by degrees,* improves in these; and *advances* to the exercise of those other faculties of enlarging, compounding, and abstracting its ideas, and of reasoning about them, and reflecting upon all these; of which I shall have occasion to speak more hereafter.

23. If it shall be demanded then, *when* a man *begins* to have any ideas, I think the true answer is,—*when he first has any sensation.* For, since there appear not to be any ideas in the mind before the senses have conveyed any in, I conceive that ideas in the understanding are coeval with *sensation; which is such an impression or motion made in some part of the body, as produces some perception in the understanding.* It is about these impressions made on our senses by outward objects that the mind seems *first* to employ itself, in such operations as we call perception, remembering, consideration, reasoning, &c.

Leibniz:

> I am of the same opinion; but it is by a principle a little peculiar, for I believe that we are never without thoughts, and also never without sensation. I distinguish only between ideas and thoughts; for we always have all pure or distinct ideas independently of the senses; but thoughts always correspond to some sensation.

24. In time the mind comes to reflect on its own operations about the ideas got by sensation, and thereby stores itself with a new set of ideas, which I call ideas of reflection. These are the impressions that are made on our senses

by outward objects that are extrinsical to the mind; and its own operations, proceeding from powers intrinsical and proper to itself, which, when reflected on by itself, become also objects of its contemplation—are, as I have said, the original of all knowledge. Thus the first capacity of human intellect is,—that the mind is fitted to receive the impressions made on it; either through the senses by outward objects, or by its own operations when it reflects on them. This is the first step a man makes towards the discovery of anything, and the groundwork whereon to build all those notions which ever he shall have naturally in this world. All those sublime thoughts which tower above the clouds, and reach as high as heaven itself, take their rise and footing here: in all that great extent wherein the mind wanders, in those remote speculations it may seem to be elevated with, it stirs not one jot beyond those ideas which *sense* or *reflection* have offered for its contemplation.

25. In this part the understanding is merely passive; and whether or no it will have these beginnings, and as it were materials of knowledge, is not in its own power. For the objects of our senses do, many of them, obtrude their particular ideas upon our minds whether we will or not; and the operations of our minds will not let us be without, at least, some obscure notions of them. No man can be wholly ignorant of what he does when he thinks. These simple ideas, when offered to the mind, the understanding can no more refuse to have, nor alter when they are imprinted, nor blot them out and make new ones itself, than a mirror can refuse, alter, or obliterate the images or ideas which the objects set before it do therein produce. As the bodies that surround us do diversely affect our organs, the mind is forced to receive the impressions; and cannot avoid the perception of those ideas that are annexed to them.

Leibniz:

How can it be that the mind is passive merely with regard to the perception of all simple ideas, since, according to your own admission, there are simple ideas whose perception comes from reflection, and since the mind gives itself thoughts from reflection, for it is itself which reflects? Whether it can refuse them is another question, and doubtless it cannot (refuse them) without some reason, which turns it aside from them, when there is some occasion for it.

Locke, Bk. II, Ch. II of the *Essay:*

1. The better to understand the nature, manner, and extent of our knowledge, one thing is carefully to be observed concerning the ideas we have; and that is, that some of them are *simple* and some *complex*.

Though the qualities that affect our senses are, in the things themselves, so united and blended, that there is no separation, no distance between them; yet it is plain, the ideas they produce in the mind enter by the senses simple and unmixed. For, though the sight and touch often take in from the same object, at the same time, different ideas;—as a man sees at once motion and colour; the hand feels softness and warmth in the same piece of wax: yet the simple ideas thus united in the same subject, are as perfectly distinct as those that come in by different senses. The coldness and hardness which a man feels in a piece of ice being as distinct ideas in the mind as the smell and whiteness of a lily; or as the taste of sugar, and smell of a rose. And there is nothing can be plainer to a man than the clear and distinct perception he has of those simple ideas; which, being each in itself uncompounded, contains in it nothing but *one uniform appearance, or conception in the mind,* and is not distinguishable into different ideas.

2. These simple ideas, the materials of all our knowledge, are suggested and furnished to the mind only by those two ways above mentioned, viz. sensation and reflection. When the understanding is once stored with these simple ideas, it has the power to repeat, compare, and unite them, even to an almost infinite variety, and so can make at pleasure new complex ideas. But it is not in the power of the most exalted wit, or enlarged understanding, by any quickness or variety of thought, to *invent* or *frame* one new simple idea in the mind, not taken in by the ways before mentioned: nor can any force of the understanding *destroy* those that are there. The dominion of man, in this little world of his own understanding being muchwhat the same as it is in the great world of visible things; wherein his power, however managed by art and skill, reaches no farther than to compound and divide the materials that are made to his hand; but can do nothing towards the making the least particle of new matter, or destroying one atom of what is already in being. The same inability will every one find in himself, who shall go about to fashion in his understanding one simple idea, not received in by his senses from external objects, or by reflection from the operations of his own mind about them. I would have any one try to fancy any taste which had never affected his palate; or frame the idea of a scent he had never smelt: and when he can do this, I will also conclude that a blind man hath ideas of colours, and a deaf man true distinct notions of sounds. . . .

Leibniz:

I believe that we can affirm that these sense-ideas are simple in appearance, because, being confused, they do not give the mind the means of distinguishing their contents. In like manner distant things appear round, because their angles cannot be discerned, although some confused impression of them is received. It is manifest, for example, that green arises from a mixture of blue and yellow; thus it is possible to believe that the idea of green is also composed of these two ideas. And yet the idea of green appears to us as simple as that of blue or that of warmth. So we are to believe that the ideas of blue and warmth are not as simple as they appear. I readily consent, however, to treat these ideas as simple ideas, because at least our apperception does not divide them, but it is necessary to proceed to their analysis by means of other experiences and by reason, in proportion as they can be rendered more intelligible. And it is also seen thereby that there are perceptions of which we are not conscious. For the perceptions of ideas simple in appearance are composed of perceptions of the parts of which these ideas are composed, without the mind's being conscious of them, for these confused ideas appear simple to it.

Locke, Bk. II, Ch. III of the *Essay:*

1. The better to conceive the ideas we receive from sensation, it may not be amiss for us to consider them, in reference to the different ways whereby they make their approaches to our minds, and make themselves perceivable by us.

First, then, There are some which come into our minds *by one sense only.*

Secondly, There are others that convey themselves into the mind *by more senses than one.*

Thirdly, Others that are had from *reflection only.*

Fourthly, There are some that make themselves way, and are suggested to the mind *by all the ways of sensation and reflection.*

We shall consider them apart under these several heads.

There are some ideas which have admittance only through one sense, which is peculiarly adapted to receive them. Thus light and colours, as white, red, yellow, blue; with their several degrees or shades and mixtures, as green, scarlet, purple, sea-green, and the rest, come in only by the eyes. All kinds of noises, sounds, and tones, only by the ears. The several tastes and smells, by the nose and palate. And if these organs, or the nerves which are the conduits to convey them from without to their audience in the brain,—the mind's presence-room (as I may so call it)—are any of them so disordered as not to perform their functions, they have no postern to be admitted by; no other way to bring themselves into view, and be perceived by the understanding.

The most considerable of those belonging to the touch, are heat and cold, and solidity: all the rest, consisting almost wholly in the sensible configuration, as smooth and rough; or else, more or less firm adhesion of the parts, as hard and soft, tough and brittle, are obvious enough.

2. I think it will be needless to enumerate all the particular simple ideas belonging to each sense. Nor indeed is it possible if we would; there being a great many more of them belonging to most of the senses than we have names for. The variety of smells, which are as many almost, if not more, than species of bodies in the world, do most of them want names. Sweet and stinking commonly serve our turn for these ideas, which in effect is little more than to call them pleasing or displeasing; though the smell of a rose and violet, both sweet, are certainly very distinct ideas. Nor are the different tastes, that by our palates we receive ideas of, much better provided with names. Sweet, bitter, sour, harsh, and salt are almost all the epithets we have to denominate that numberless variety of relishes, which are to be found distinct, not only in almost every sort of creatures, but in the different parts of the same plant, fruit, or animal. The same may be said of colours and sounds. I shall, therefore, in the account of simple ideas I am here giving, content myself to set down only such as are most material to our present purpose, or are in themselves less apt to be

taken notice of though they are very frequently the ingredients of our complex ideas; amongst which, I think, I may well account solidity, which therefore I shall treat of in the next chapter.[1]

Locke, Bk. II, Ch. V of the *Essay:*

The ideas we get by more than one sense are, of *space* or *extension, figure, rest,* and *motion.* For these make perceivable impressions, both on the eyes and touch; and we can receive and convey into our minds the ideas of the extension, figure, motion, and rest of bodies, both by seeing and feeling. But having occasion to speak more at large of these in another place,[2] I here only enumerate them.

Leibniz:

The ideas which are said to come from more than one sense, like those of space, figure, motion, rest, are rather from common-sense, that is to say, from the mind itself, for they are ideas of the pure understanding, but related to externality, and which the senses make us perceive; they are also capable of definition and demonstration.

Locke, Bk. II, Ch. VI of the *Essay:*

The mind receiving the ideas mentioned in the foregoing chapters from without, when it turns its view inward upon itself, and observes its own actions about those ideas it has, takes from thence other ideas, which are as capable to be the objects of its contemplation as any of those it received from foreign things.

The two great and principal actions of the mind, which are most frequently considered, and which are so frequent that every one that pleases may take notice of them in himself, are these two:—

Perception, or *Thinking;* and *Volition,* or *Willing.*

The power of thinking is called the *Understanding,* and the power of volition is called the *Will;* and these two powers or abilities in the mind are denominated faculties. . . . .

Leibniz:

It is doubtful if all these ideas are simple, for it is clear, for example, that the idea of the will includes that of the understanding, and that the idea of motion contains that of figure.

Locke, Bk. II, Ch. VII of the *Essay:*

1. There be other simple ideas which convey themselves into the mind by all the ways of sensation and reflection, viz. *pleasure* or *delight,* and its opposite, *pain* or *uneasiness; power; existence; unity.*

---

[1] [Ch. IV, omitted here.—*Ed.*]
[2] [Bk. II, Chaps. XIII & XV—not included in this volume.—*Ed.*]

Leibniz:

> It seems that the senses cannot convince us of *the existence* of sensible things without the aid of the reason. Thus I should think that the idea of existence comes from reflection. That of power also and of unity comes from the same source, and are of a wholly different nature from the perceptions of pleasure and pain.

2. Delight or uneasiness, one or other of them, join themselves to almost all our ideas both of sensation and reflection: and there is scarce any affection of our senses from without, any retired thought of our mind within, which is not able to produce in us pleasure or pain. By pleasure and pain, I would be understood to signify, whatsoever delights or molests us; whether it arises from the thoughts of our minds, or anything operating on our bodies. For, whether we call it satisfaction, delight, pleasure, happiness, &c., on the one side, or uneasiness, trouble, pain, torment, anguish, misery, &c., on the other, they are still but different degrees of the same thing, and belong to the ideas of pleasure and pain, delight or uneasiness; which are the names I shall most commonly use for those two sorts of ideas. . . .

7. *Existence* and *Unity* are two other ideas that are suggested to the understanding by every object without, and every idea within. When ideas are in our minds, we consider them as being actually there, as well as we consider things to be actually without us;—which is, that they exist, or have existence. And whatever we can consider as one thing, whether a real being or idea, suggests to the understanding the idea of unity.

8. *Power* also is another of those simple ideas which we receive from sensation and reflection. For, observing in ourselves that we do and can think, and that we can at pleasure move several parts of our bodies which were at rest; the effects, also, that natural bodies are able to produce in one another, occurring every moment to our senses,—we both these ways get the idea of power.

9. Besides these there is another idea, which, though suggested by our senses, yet is more constantly offered to us by what passes in our minds; and that is the idea of *succession.* For if we look immediately into ourselves, and reflect on what is observable there, we shall find our ideas always, whilst we are awake, or have any thought, passing in train, one going and another coming, without intermission.

10. These, if they are not all, are at least (as I think) the most considerable of those simple ideas which the mind has, and out of which is made all its other knowledge; all which it receives only by the two forementioned ways of sensation and reflection.

Nor let anyone think these too narrow bounds for the capacious mind of man to expatiate in, which takes its flight further than the stars, and cannot be confined by the limits of the world; that extends its thoughts often even beyond the utmost expansion of Matter, and makes excursions into that incomprehensible Inane. I grant all this, but desire any one to assign any *simple idea* which is not received from one of those inlets before mentioned, or any *complex idea* not made out of those simple ones. Nor will it be so strange to think these few simple ideas sufficient to employ the quickest thought, or the largest capacity; and to furnish the materials of all that various knowledge, and more various fancies and opinions of all mankind, if we consider how many words may be made out of the various composition of twenty-four letters; or if, going one step further, we will but reflect on the variety of combinations that may be made with barely one of the above-mentioned ideas, viz. number, whose stock is inexhaustible and truly infinite: and what a large and immense field doth extension alone afford the mathematicians?

Locke, Bk. II, Ch. IX of the *Essay:*

1. PERCEPTION, as it is the first faculty of the mind exercised about our ideas; so it is the first and simplest idea we have from reflection, and is by some called thinking in general. Though thinking, in the propriety of the English tongue, signifies that sort of operation in the mind about its ideas, wherein the mind is active; where it, with some degree of voluntary attention, considers anything. For in bare naked perception, the mind is, for the most part, only passive; and what it perceives, it cannot avoid perceiving.

2. What perception is, every one will know better by reflecting on what he does himself, when he sees, hears, feels, &c., or thinks, than by any discourse of mine. Whoever reflects on what passes in his own mind cannot miss it. And if he does not reflect, all the words in the world cannot make him have any notion of it.

3. This is certain, that whatever alterations are made in the body, if they reach not the mind; whatever impressions are made on the outward parts, if they are not taken notice of within, there is no perception. Fire may burn our bodies with no other effect than it does a billet, unless the motion be continued to the brain, and there the sense of heat, or idea of pain, be produced in the mind; wherein consists actual perception.

4. How often may a man observe in himself, that whilst his mind is intently employed in the contemplation of some objects, and curiously surveying some ideas that are there, it takes no notice of impressions of sounding bodies made upon the organ of hearing, with the same alteration that uses to be for the producing the idea of sound? A sufficient impulse there may be on the organ; but it not reaching the observation of the mind, there follows no perception: and though the motion that uses to produce the idea of sound be made in the ear, yet no sound is heard. Want of sensation, in this case, is not through any defect in the organ, or that the man's ears are less affected than at other times when he does hear: but that which uses to produce the idea, though conveyed in by the usual organ, not being taken notice of in the understanding, and so imprinting no idea in the mind, there follows no sensation. So that wherever there is sense or perception, there some idea is actually produced, and present in the understanding. . . .

Leibniz:

      I should prefer to distinguish between *perception* and *consciousness* (s'appercevoir). The perception of light and color, for example, of which we are conscious, is composed of many minute perceptions, of which we are not conscious; and a noise which we perceive, but of which we take no notice, becomes *apperceptible* by a little addition or increase; for if what precedes make no impression upon the soul, this little addition would also make none, and the whole would make no more. . . .

Locke, Bk. II, Ch. XI of the *Essay:*

      17. I pretend not to teach, but to inquire; and therefore cannot but confess here again,—that external and internal sensations are the only passages I can find of knowledge to the understanding. These alone, as far as I can discover, are the windows by which light is let into this *dark room.* For, methinks, the understanding is not much unlike a closet wholly shut from light, with only some little openings left, to let in external visible resemblances, or ideas of things without: would the pictures coming into such a dark room but stay there, and lie so orderly as to be found upon occasion, it would very much resemble the understanding of a man, in reference to all objects of sight, and the ideas of them. . . .

Leibniz:

      To make the resemblance greater, you should suppose that in this room there was a canvas to receive the images, not even, but diversified by folds, representing the (kinds of) innate knowledge; further, that this canvas or membrane being stretched would have a kind of elasticity or power of action, and also an action and reaction accommodated as much to the past folds as to the newly arrived kinds of impressions. And this action would consist in certain vibrations or oscillations, such as are seen in a stretched string so touched that it gives forth a kind of musical sound. For not only do we receive images or outlines in the brain; but we form besides new ones, when we look at *complex ideas.* Thus the canvas that represents our brain is necessarily active and elastic. This comparison would explain tolerably well what passes in the brain; but as for the soul, which is a simple substance or *monad,* it represents without extension these same varieties of extended masses and perceives them.

Locke, Bk. II, Ch. XII of the *Essay:*

      1. We have hitherto considered those ideas, in the reception whereof the mind is only passive, which are those simple ones received from sensation and reflection before mentioned, whereof the mind cannot make one to itself, nor have any idea which does not wholly consist of them. But as the mind is wholly passive in the reception of all its simple ideas, so it exerts several acts of its own, whereby out of its simple ideas, as the materials and foundations of the rest, the others are framed. The acts of the mind, wherein it exerts its

power over its simple ideas, are chiefly these three: (1) Combining several simple ideas into one compound one; and thus all *complex ideas* are made. (2) The second is bringing two ideas, whether simple or complex, together, and setting them by one another, so as to take a view of them at once, without uniting them into one; by which way it gets all its *ideas of relations*. (3) The third is separating them from all other ideas that accompany them in their real existence: this is called abstraction: and thus all its *general ideas* are made. This shows man's power, and its ways of operation, to be much the same in the material and intellectual world. For the materials in both being such as he has no power over, either to make or destroy, all that man can do is either to unite them together, or to set them by one another, or wholly separate them. I shall here begin with the first of these in the consideration of complex ideas, and come to the other two in their due places. As simple ideas are observed to exist in several combinations united together, so the mind has a power to consider several of them united together as one idea; and that not only as they are united in external objects, but as itself has joined them together. Ideas thus made up of several simple ones put together, I call *complex;*—such as are beauty, gratitude, a man, an army, the universe; which, though complicated of various simple ideas, or complex ideas made up of simple ones, yet are, when the mind pleases, considered each by itself, as one entire thing, and signified by one name. . . .

3. *Complex ideas,* however compounded and decompounded, though their number be infinite, and the variety endless, wherewith they fill and entertain the thoughts of men; yet I think they may be all reduced under these three heads:—

1. MODES.
2. SUBSTANCES.
3. RELATIONS.

4. First, *Modes* I call such complex ideas which, however compounded, contain not in them the supposition of subsisting by themselves, but are considered as dependences on, or affections of substances;—such as are the ideas signified by the words triangle, gratitude, murder, &c. And if in this I use the word mode in somewhat a different sense from its ordinary signification, I beg pardon; it being unavoidable in discourses, differing from the ordinary received notions, either to make new words, or to use old words in somewhat a new signification; the later whereof, in our present case, is perhaps the more tolerable of the two. . . .

6. Secondly, the ideas of *substances* are such combinations of simple ideas as are taken to represent distinct *particular* things subsisting by themselves; in which the supposed or confused idea of substance, such as it is, is always the first and chief. Thus if to substance be joined the simple idea of a certain dull whitish colour, with certain degrees of weight, hardness, ductility, and fusibility, we have the idea of lead; and a combination of the ideas of a certain sort of figure, with the powers of motion, thought and reasoning, joined to substance, make the ordinary idea of a man. Now of substance also, there are two

sorts of ideas:—one of *single* substances, as they exist separately, as of a man or a sheep; the other of several of those put together, as an army of men, or flock of sheep—which *collective* ideas of several substances thus put together are as much each of them one single idea as that of a man or an unit.

7. Thirdly, the last sort of complex ideas is that we call *relation,* which consists in the consideration and comparing one idea with another. . . .

Locke, Bk. IV, Ch. I of the *Essay:*

1. Since the mind, in all its thoughts and reasonings, hath no other immediate object but its own ideas, which it alone does or can contemplate, it is evident that our knowledge is only conversant about them.

2. *Knowledge* then seems to me to be nothing but *the perception of the connexion of and agreement, or disagreement and repugnancy of any of our ideas.* In this alone it consists. Where this perception is, there is knowledge, and where it is not, there, though we may fancy, guess, or believe, yet we always come short of knowledge. For when we know that white is not black, what do we else but perceive, that these two ideas do not agree? When we possess ourselves with the utmost security of the demonstration, that the three angles of a triangle are equal to two right ones, what do we more but perceive, that equality to two right ones does necessarily agree to, and is inseparable from, the three angles of a triangle?

Leibniz:

Knowledge has a still more general signification, so that we find it also in ideas or terms, before we reach propositions or truths. And it may be said that he who has attentively looked at more pictures of plants and animals, more diagrams of machines, more descriptions or representations of houses or fortresses, who has read more ingenious romances, heard more curious narratives, this one, I say, will have more knowledge than another, even though there should not be a word of truth in all that which was portrayed or related to him; for the custom he has of representing in his mind many express and actual conceptions or ideas, renders him more fit to conceive what is placed before him; and it is certain that he will be better instructed and more capable than another who has neither seen nor read nor heard anything, provided that in these stories and representations he takes nothing as true which is not so and that these impressions do not prevent him elsewhere from distinguishing the real from the imaginary, or the existent from the possible. . . . But taking *knowledge* in a narrower sense, *i.e.* as knowledge of truth, as you, sir, do here, I say it is quite true that truth is always grounded in the agreement or disagreement of ideas, but it is not true in general that our knowledge of truth is a perception of this agreement or disagreement. For when we know truth only empirically, from having experienced it, without knowing the connection of things and the reason there is in what we have experienced, we have no perception of this agreement or disagreement, unless we mean that we feel it in a confused way without being conscious of it. But your examples, it seems, show that you always demand a knowledge in which one is conscious of connection or opposition, and this is what cannot be granted you.

3. But to understand a little more distinctly wherein this agreement or disagreement consists, I think we may reduce it all to these four sorts:

     I. *Identity*, or *diversity*.

     II. *Relation*.

     III. *Co-existence*, or *necessary connexion*.

     IV. *Real existence*.

4. *First,* As to the first sort of agreement or disagreement, viz. *identity* or *diversity.* It is the first act of the mind, when it has any sentiments or ideas at all, to perceive its ideas; and so far as it perceives them, to know each what it is, and thereby also to perceive their difference, and that one is not another. This is so absolutely necessary, that without it there could be no knowledge, no reasoning, no imagination, no distinct thoughts at all. By this the mind clearly and infallibly perceives each idea to agree with itself, and to be what it is; and all distinct ideas to disagree, i.e. the one not to be the other: and this it does without pains, labour, or deduction; but at first view, by its natural power of perception and distinction. And though men of art have reduced this into those general rules, *What is, is,* and *It is impossible for the same thing to be and not to be,* for ready application in all cases, wherein there may be occasion to reflect on it: yet it is certain that the first exercise of this faculty is about particular ideas. A man infallibly knows, as soon as ever he has them in his mind, that the ideas he calls *white* and *round* are the very ideas they are; and that they are not other ideas which he calls *red* or *square.* Nor can any maxim or proposition in the world make him know it clearer or surer than he did before, and without any such general rule. This then is the first agreement or disagreement which the mind perceives in its ideas; which it always perceives at first sight: and if there ever happen any doubt about it, it will always be found to be about the names, and not the ideas themselves, whose identity and diversity will always be perceived, as soon and clearly as the ideas themselves are; nor can it possibly be otherwise.

5. *Secondly,* The next sort of agreement or disagreement the mind perceives in any of its ideas may, I think, be called *relative,* and is nothing but the perception of the *relation* between any two ideas, of what kind soever, whether substances, modes, or any other. For, since all distinct ideas must eternally be known not to be the same, and so be universally and constantly denied one of another, there could be no room for any positive knowledge at all, if we could not perceive any relation between our ideas, and find out the agreement or disagreement they have one with another, in several ways the mind takes of comparing them.

6. *Thirdly,* The third sort of agreement or disagreement to be found in our ideas, which the perceptions of the mind is employed about, is *co-existence* or

non-co-existence in the *same subject;* and this belongs particularly to substances. Thus when we pronounce concerning gold, that it is fixed, our knowledge of this truth amounts to no more but this, that fixedness, or a power to remain in the fire unconsumed, is an idea that always accompanies and is joined with that particular sort of yellowness, weight, fusibility, malleableness, and solubility in *aqua regia,* which make our complex idea signified by the word gold.

7. *Fourthly,* The fourth and last sort is that of *actual real existence* agreeing to any idea.

Within these four sorts of agreement or disagreement is, I suppose, contained all the knowledge we have, or are capable of. For all the inquiries we can make concerning any of our ideas, all that we know or can affirm concerning any of them is, That it is, or is not, the same with some other; that it does or does not always co-exist with some other idea in the same subject; that it has this or that relation with some other idea; or that it has a real existence without the mind. Thus, 'blue is not yellow,' is of identity. 'Two triangles upon equal bases between two parallels are equal,' is of relation. 'Iron is susceptible of magnetical impressions,' is of co-existence. 'God is,' is of real existence. Though identity and co-existence are truly nothing but relations, yet they are such peculiar ways of agreement or disagreement of our ideas, that they deserve well to be considered as distinct heads, and not under relation in general; since they are so different grounds of affirmation and negation, as will easily appear to any one, who will but reflect on what is said in several places of this *Essay.* . . .

Leibniz:

I believe it may be said that the connection is nothing else than the *agreement* or the relation taken generally. And I have remarked above that every relation is either of *comparison* or *concurrence.* That of *comparison* gives diversity and identity, either complete or partial; whereby are constituted the concepts of the same or the diverse, the like or unlike. *Concurrence* contains what you call co-existence, *i.e.* connection of existence. But when we say that a thing exists or that it has real existence, this existence itself is the predicate, *i.e.* it has a notion joined with the idea in question, and there is connection between these two notions. The *existence* of the object of an idea may also be conceived, as the concurrence of this object with the Ego. Thus I believe it may be said that there is only comparison or concurrence; but that the comparison which marks identity or diversity, and the concurrence of the thing with the Ego, are the relations which deserve to be distinguished among others. More exact and more profound researches might perhaps be made; but I content myself here with making remarks.

Locke, Bk. IV, Ch. II of the *Essay:*

1. All our knowledge consisting, as I have said, in the view the mind has of its own ideas, which is the utmost light and greatest certainty we, with our

faculties, and in our way of knowledge, are capable of, it may not be amiss to consider a little the degrees of its evidence. The different clearness of our knowledge seems to me to lie in the different way of perception the mind has of the agreement or disagreement of any of its ideas. For if we will reflect on our own ways of thinking, we will find, that sometimes the mind perceives the agreement or disagreement of two ideas *immediately by themselves*, without the intervention of any other: and this I think we may call *intuitive knowledge*. For in this the mind is at no pains of proving or examining, but perceives the truth as the eye doth light, only by being directed towards it. Thus the mind perceives that *white* is not *black*, that a *circle* is not a *triangle*, that *three* are more than *two* and equal to *one and two*. Such kinds of truths the mind perceives at the first sight of the ideas together, by bare intuition; without the intervention of any other idea: and this kind of knowledge is the clearest and most certain that human frailty is capable of. This part of knowledge is irresistible, and, like bright sunshine, forces itself immediately to be perceived, as soon as ever the mind turns its view that way; and leaves no room for hesitation, doubt, or examination, but the mind is presently filled with the clear light of it. *It is on this intuition that depends all the certainty and evidence of all our knowledge;* which certainty every one finds to be so great, that he cannot imagine, and therefore not require a greater: for a man cannot conceive himself capable of a greater certainty than to know that any idea in his mind is such as he perceives it to be; and that two ideas, wherein he perceives a difference, are different and not precisely the same. He that demands a greater certainty than this, demands he knows not what, and shows only that he has a mind to be a sceptic, without being able to be so. Certainty depends so wholly on this intuition, that, in the next degree of knowledge which I call demonstrative, this intuition is necessary in all the connexions of the intermediate ideas, without which we cannot attain knowledge and certainty.

Leibniz:

Primitive truths, which are known by *intuition*, are of two kinds, like the *derivative*. They are truths of *reason* or truths of *fact*. Truths of reason are necessary, and those of fact are contingent. The primitive truths of reason are those which I call by the general name of *identical*, because they seem only to repeat the same thing without giving us any information. They are affirmative or negative. . . .

As for the *primitive truths of fact*, they are the immediate internal experiences of an *immediateness of feeling*. And here it is that the first truth of the Cartesians or of St. Augustine: *I think, therefore I am*, i.e. *I am a thing which thinks*, holds good. But we must know, that as the identicals are general or particular, and as one is as clear as the other (since the statement that A *is* A is as clear as the statement that *a thing is what it is*), so is it also with the first truths of fact. For not only is it immediately clear to me that *I think*, but it is wholly as clear to me that *I have different thoughts*, that sometimes *I think* of A, and sometimes of B, etc. Thus the Cartesian principle is valid, but it is not the only one of its kind. You see by this that all *primitive truths* of reason or of fact have this in common, that they cannot be proved by anything more certain.

2. The next degree of knowledge is, where the mind perceives agreement or disagreement of any ideas, but not immediately. Though wherever the mind perceives the agreement or disagreement of any of its ideas, there be certain knowledge; yet it does not always happen, that the mind sees that agreement or disagreement, which there is between them, even where it is discoverable; and in that case remains in ignorance, and at most gets no further than a probable conjecture. The reason why the mind cannot always perceive presently the agreement or disagreement of two ideas, is, because those ideas, concerning whose agreement or disagreement the inquiry is made, cannot by the mind be so put together as to show it. In this case then, when the mind cannot so bring its ideas together as by their immediate comparison, and as it were juxta-position or application one to another, to perceive their agreement or disagreement, it is fain, *by the intervention of other ideas* (one or more, as it happens) to discover the agreement or disagreement which it searches; and this is what we call *reasoning*. Thus, the mind being willing to know the agreement or disagreement in bigness between the three angles of a triangle and two right ones, cannot by an immediate view and comparing them do it: because the three angles of a triangle cannot be brought at once, and be compared with any other one, or two, angles; and so of this the mind has no immediate, no intuitive knowledge. In this case the mind is fain to find out some other angles, to which the three angles of a triangle have an equality; and, finding those equal to two right ones, comes to know their equality to two right ones. . . .

14. These two, viz. intuition and demonstration, are the degrees of our *knowledge;* whatever comes short of one of these, with what assurance soever embraced, is but *faith* or *opinion,* but not knowledge, at least in all general truths. There is, indeed, another perception of the mind, employed about *the particular existence of finite beings without us,* which, going beyond bare probability, and yet not reaching perfectly to either of the foregoing degrees of certainty, passes under the name of *knowledge.* There can be nothing more certain than that the idea we receive from an external object is in our minds: this is intuitive knowledge. But whether there be anything more than barely that idea in our minds; whether we can thence certainly infer the existence of anything without us, which corresponds to that idea, is that whereof some men think there may be a question made; because men may have such ideas in their minds, when no such thing exists, no such object affects their senses. But yet here I think we are provided with an evidence that puts us past doubting, For I ask any one, Whether he be not invincibly conscious to himself of a different perception, when he looks on the sun by day, and thinks on it by night; when he actually tastes wormwood, or smells a rose, or only thinks on that savour or odour? We as plainly find the difference there is between any idea revived in our minds by our own memory, and actually coming into our minds by our

senses, as we do between any two distinct ideas. If any one say, a dream may do the same thing, and all these ideas may be produced in us without any external objects; he may please to dream that I make him this answer:— 1. That it is no great matter, whether I remove his scruple or no: where all is but dream, reasoning and arguments are of no use, truth and knowledge nothing. 2. That I believe he will allow a very manifest difference between dreaming of being in the fire, and being actually in it. But yet if he be resolved to appear so sceptical as to maintain, that what I call being actually in the fire is nothing but a dream; and that we cannot thereby certainly know, that any such thing as fire actually exists without us: I answer, That we certainly finding that pleasure or pain follows upon the application of certain objects to us, whose existence we perceive, by our senses; this certainty is as great as our happiness or misery, beyond which we have no concernment to know or to be. So that, I think, we may add to the two former sorts of knowledge this also, of the existence of particular external objects, by that perception and consciousness we have of the actual entrance of ideas from them, and allow these three degrees of knowledge, viz. *intuitive, demonstrative,* and *sensitive:* in each of which there are different degrees and ways of evidence and certainty. . . .

Leibniz:

   . . . But let us come to this dispute of the Sceptics and the Dogmatists upon the existence of things without us. We have already touched upon it, but we must return to it here. I formerly discussed the subject a great deal *viva voce* and in writing with the late Abbé Foucher, Canon of Dijon, a learned and subtle man. . . . Now I showed him that the truth of sensible things consisted only in the connection of phenomena, which must have its reason and is that which distinguishes them from dreams; but that the truth of our existence and the cause of phenomena is of a different nature, because it establishes substances, and that the Sceptics spoiled what they rightly say by carrying it too far, and by wishing indeed to extend their doubts even to immediate experience, and to the geometrical truths, a thing which Foucher did not do however, and to the other truths of reason, which he did a little too much. But to return to you, sir, you are right in saying that there is ordinarily some difference between feelings and imaginations; but the Sceptics will say that the more or less does not alter the species. Besides, although feelings are wont to be more vivid than imaginations, it is nevertheless a fact that there are cases where imaginative persons are impressed as much or perhaps more by their imaginations than another is by the truth of things; so that I think the true *criterion* concerning the objects of the senses is the connection of the phenomena, *i.e.* the connection of that which takes place in different places and times, and in the experience of different men who are themselves, each to the others, very important phenomena in this respect. And the connection of the phenomena which guarantees the *truths of fact* in respect to sensible things outside of us, is verified by means of the *truths of reason;* as the phenomena of optics are explained by geometry. It must, however, be admitted that none of this certitude is of the highest degree, as you have well recognized. For it is not impossible, metaphysically speaking, that there may be a dream continuous and lasting like the life of a man; but it is a thing as contrary to reason as would be the fiction of a book which should be formed by chance by throwing together the type pell-mell. For the rest, it is also true that, provided the phenomena are connected, it does not matter whether they are called dreams or not, since experience shows that we are not deceived in the measures we take concerning phenomena when they are understood according to the truths of reason.

18 GEORGE BERKELEY
The Principles of Human Knowledge*

1. It is evident to anyone who takes a survey of the *objects* of human knowledge that they are either ideas actually imprinted on the senses, or else such as are perceived by attending to the passions and operations of the mind, or lastly, ideas formed by help of memory and imagination—either compounding, dividing, or barely representing those originally perceived in the aforesaid ways. By sight I have the ideas of light and colors, with their several degrees and variations. By touch I perceive, for example, hard and soft, heat and cold, motion and resistance, and of all these more and less either as to quantity or degree. Smelling furnishes me with odors, the palate with tastes, and hearing conveys sounds to the mind in all their variety of tone and composition. And as several of these are observed to accompany each other, they come to be marked by one name, and so to be reputed as one thing. Thus, for example, a certain color, taste, smell, figure, and consistence having been observed to go together, are accounted one distinct thing signified by the name *"apple";* other collections of ideas constitute a stone, a tree, a book, and the like sensible things—which as they are pleasing or disagreeable excite the passions of love, hatred, joy, grief, and so forth.

2. But, besides all that endless variety of ideas or objects of knowledge, there is likewise something which knows or perceives them and exercises divers operations, as willing, imagining, remembering, about them. This perceiving, active being is what I call *mind, spirit, soul,* or *myself.* By which words I do not

---

* From *A Treatise Concerning the Principles of Human Knowledge.* First published in 1710.

denote any one of my ideas, but a thing entirely distinct from them, wherein they exist or, which is the same thing, whereby they are perceived—for the existence of an idea consists in being perceived.

3. That neither our thoughts, nor passions, nor ideas formed by the imagination exist without the mind is what everybody will allow. And it seems no less evident that the various sensations or ideas imprinted on the sense, however blended or combined together (that is, whatever objects they compose), cannot exist otherwise than in a mind perceiving them.—I think an intuitive knowledge may be obtained of this by anyone that shall attend to what is meant by the term *exist* when applied to sensible things. The table I write on I say exists, that is, I see and feel it; and if I were out of my study I should say it existed—meaning thereby that if I was in my study I might perceive it, or that some other spirit actually does perceive it. There was an odor, that is, it was smelled, there was a sound, that is to say, it was heard; a color or figure, and it was perceived by sight or touch. This is all that I can understand by these and the like expressions. For as to what is said of the absolute existence of unthinking things without any relation to their being perceived, that seems perfectly unintelligible. Their *esse* is *percipi,* nor is it possible they should have any existence out of the minds or thinking things which perceive them. . . .

25. All our ideas, sensations, or the things which we perceive, by whatsoever names they may be distinguished, are visibly inactive—there is nothing of power or agency included in them. So that one idea or object of thought cannot produce or make any alteration in another. To be satisfied of the truth of this, there is nothing else requisite but a bare observation of our ideas. For since they and every part of them exist only in the mind, it follows that there is nothing in them but what is perceived; but whoever shall attend to his ideas, whether of sense or reflection, will not perceive in them any power or activity; there is, therefore, no such thing contained in them. A little attention will discover to us that the very being of an idea implies passiveness and inertness in it, insomuch that it is impossible for any idea to do anything or, strictly speaking, to be the cause of anything; neither can it be the resemblance or pattern of any active being, as is evident from sect. 8. Whence it plainly follows that extension, figure, and motion cannot be the cause of our sensations. To say, therefore, that these are the effects of powers resulting from the configuration, number, motion, and size of corpuscles must certainly be false.

26. We perceive a continual succession of ideas, some are anew excited, others are changed or totally disappear. There is, therefore, some cause of these ideas, whereon they depend and which produces and changes them. That this cause cannot be any quality or idea or combination of ideas is clear from the preceding section. It must therefore be a substance; but it has been shown that there is no corporeal or material substance: it remains, therefore, that the cause of ideas is an incorporeal, active substance or spirit.

27. A spirit is one simple, undivided, active being—as it perceives ideas it is called the *understanding,* and as it produces or otherwise operates about them it is called the *will.* Hence there can be no *idea* formed of a soul or spirit; for all

ideas whatever, being passive and inert (*vide* sect. 25), they cannot represent unto us, by way of image or likeness, that which acts. A little attention will make it plain to anyone that to have an idea which shall be like that active principle of motion and change of ideas is absolutely impossible. Such is the nature of *spirit,* or that which acts, that it cannot be of itself perceived, but only by the effects which it produces. If any man shall doubt of the truth of what is here delivered, let him but reflect and try if he can frame the idea of any power or active being, and whether he has ideas of two principal powers marked by the names *will* and *understanding,* distinct from each other as well as from a third idea of substance or being in general, with a relative notion of its supporting or being the subject of the aforesaid powers—which is signified by the name *soul* or *spirit.* This is what some hold; but, so far as I can see, the words *will, soul, spirit* do not stand for different ideas or, in truth, for any idea at all, but for something which is very different from ideas, and which, being an agent, cannot be like unto, or represented by, any idea whatsoever. Though it must be owned at the same time that we have some notion of soul, spirit, and the operations of the mind, such as willing, loving, hating—in as much as we know or understand the meaning of those words.

28. I find I can excite ideas in my mind at pleasure, and vary and shift the scene as oft as I think fit. It is no more than willing, and straightway this or that idea arises in my fancy; and by the same power it is obliterated and makes way for another. This making and unmaking of ideas does very properly denominate the mind active. Thus much is certain and grounded on experience; but when we talk of unthinking agents or of exciting ideas exclusive of volition, we only amuse ourselves with words. . . .

89. Nothing seems of more importance toward erecting a firm system of sound and real knowledge, which may be proof against the assaults of skepticism, than to lay the beginning in a distinct explication of what is meant by *thing, reality, existence;* for in vain shall we dispute concerning the real existence of things or pretend to any knowledge thereof, so long as we have not fixed the meaning of those words. *Thing* or *being* is the most general name of all; it comprehends under it two kinds entirely distinct and heterogeneous, and which have nothing common but the name, to wit, *spirits* and *ideas.* The former are active, indivisible substances; the latter are inert, fleeting, dependent beings which subsist not by themselves, but are supported by or exist in minds or spiritual substances. We comprehend our own existence by inward feeling or reflection, and that of other spirits by reason. We may be said to have some knowledge or notion of our own minds, of spirits and active beings, whereof in a strict sense we have not ideas. In like manner, we know and have a notion of relations between things or ideas—which relations are distinct from the ideas or things related, in as much as the latter may be perceived by us without our perceiving the former. To me it seems that *ideas, spirits,* and *relations* are all in their respective kinds the object of human knowledge and subject of discourse, and that the term *idea* would be improperly extended to signify everything we know or have any notion of. . . .

19 DAVID HUME
The Limits of the Understanding*

Section II.—*Of the Origin of Ideas*

Every one will readily allow, that there is a considerable difference between the perceptions of the mind, when a man feels the pain of excessive heat, or the pleasure of moderate warmth, and when he afterwards recalls to his memory this sensation, or anticipates it by his imagination. These faculties may mimic or copy the perceptions of the senses; but they never can entirely reach the force and vivacity of the original sentiment. The utmost we say of them, even when they operate with greatest vigour, is, that they represent their object in so lively a manner, that we could *almost* say we feel or see it: But, except the mind be disordered by disease or madness, they never can arrive at such a pitch of vivacity, as to render these perceptions altogether undistinguishable. All the colours of poetry, however splendid, can never paint natural objects in such a manner as to make the description be taken for a real landskip. The most lively thought is still inferior to the dullest sensation.

We may observe a like distinction to run through all the other perceptions of the mind. A man in a fit of anger, is actuated in a very different manner from one who only thinks of that emotion. If you tell me, that any person is in love, I easily understand your meaning, and form a just conception of his situation; but never can mistake that conception for the real disorders and agitations of the passion. When we reflect on our past sentiments and affections, our thought is a faithful mirror, and copies its objects truly; but the colours which it employs are faint and dull, in comparison of those in which our original perceptions were clothed. It requires no nice discernment or metaphysical head to mark the distinction between them.

Here therefore we may divide all the perceptions of the mind into two classes or species, which are distinguished by their different degrees of force and vivacity. The less forcible and lively are commonly denominated *Thoughts* or *Ideas*. The other species want a name in our language, and in most others; I suppose, because it was not requisite for any, but philosophical purposes, to rank them under a general term or appellation. Let us, therefore, use a little freedom, and call them *Impressions;* employing that word in a sense somewhat different from the usual. By the term *impression,* then, I mean all our more lively perceptions, when we hear, or see, or feel, or love, or hate, or desire, or will. And impressions are distinguished from ideas, which are the less lively perceptions, of which we are conscious, when we reflect on any of those sensations or movements above mentioned.

Nothing, at first view, may seem more unbounded than the thought of

---

* From *An Enquiry concerning the Human Understanding*. First published in 1748.

man, which not only escapes all human power and authority, but is not even restrained within the limits of nature and reality. To form monsters, and join incongruous shapes and appearances, costs the imagination no more trouble than to conceive the most natural and familiar objects. And while the body is confined to one planet, along which it creeps with pain and difficulty; the thought can in an instant transport us into the most distant regions of the universe; or even beyond the universe, into the unbounded chaos, where nature is supposed to lie in total confusion. What never was seen, or heard of, may yet be conceived; nor is any thing beyond the power of thought, except what implies an absolute contradiction.

But though our thought seems to possess this unbounded liberty, we shall find, upon a nearer examination, that it is really confined within very narrow limits, and that all this creative power of the mind amounts to no more than the faculty of compounding, transposing, augmenting, or diminishing the materials afforded us by the senses and experience. When we think of a golden mountain, we only join two consistent ideas, *gold,* and *mountain,* with which we were formerly acquainted. A virtuous horse we can conceive; because, from our own feeling, we can conceive virtue; and this we may unite to the figure and shape of a horse, which is an animal familiar to us. In short, all the materials of thinking are derived either from our outward or inward sentiment: the mixture and composition of these belongs alone to the mind and will. Or, to express myself in philosophical language, all our ideas or more feeble perceptions are copies of our impressions or more lively ones.

To prove this, the two following arguments will, I hope, be sufficient. First, when we analyze our thoughts or ideas, however compounded or sublime, we always find that they resolve themselves into such simple ideas as were copied from a precedent feeling or sentiment. Even those ideas, which, at first view, seem the most wide of this origin, are found, upon a nearer scrutiny, to be derived from it. The idea of God, as meaning an infinitely intelligent, wise, and good Being, arises from reflecting on the operations of our own mind, and augmenting, without limit, those qualities of goodness and wisdom. We may prosecute this enquiry to what length we please; where we shall always find, that every idea which we examine is copied from a similar impression. Those who would assert that this position is not universally true nor without exception, have only one, and that an easy method of refuting it; by producing that idea, which, in their opinion, is not derived from this source. It will then be incumbent on us, if we would maintain our doctrine, to produce the impression, or lively perception, which corresponds to it.

Secondly. If it happen, from a defect of the organ, that a man is not susceptible of any species of sensation, we always find that he is as little susceptible of the correspondent ideas. A blind man can form no notion of colours; a deaf man of sounds. Restore either of them that sense in which he is deficient; by opening this new inlet for his sensations, you also open an inlet for the ideas; and he finds no difficulty in conceiving these objects. The case is the same, if the object, proper for exciting any sensation, has never been applied to the organ. A Laplander or Negro has no notion of the relish of wine. And though there are few or no instances of a like deficiency in the mind, where a person has never felt or is wholly incapable of a sentiment or passion that belongs to his species; yet we find the same observation to take place in a less degree. A man of mild manners can form no idea of inveterate revenge or cruelty; nor can a selfish heart easily conceive the heights of friendship and generosity. It is readily allowed, that other beings may possess many senses of which we can have no conception; because the ideas of them have never been introduced to us in the only manner by which an idea can have access to the mind, to wit, by the actual feeling and sensation.

There is, however, one contradictory phenomenon, which may prove that it is not absolutely impossible for ideas to arise, independent of their correspondent impressions. I believe it will readily be allowed, that the several distinct ideas of colour, which enter by the eye, or those of sound, which are conveyed by the ear, are really different from each other; though, at the same time, resembling. Now if this be true of different colours, it must be no less so of the different shades of the same colour; and each shade produces a distinct idea, independent of the rest. For if this should be denied, it is possible, by the continual gradation of shades, to run a colour insensibly into what is most remote from it; and if you will not allow any of the means to be different, you cannot, without absurdity, deny the extremes to be the same. Suppose, therefore, a person to have enjoyed his sight for thirty years, and to have become perfectly acquainted with colours of all kinds except one particular shade of blue, for instance, which it never has been his fortune to meet with. Let all the different shades of that colour, except that single one, be placed before him, descending gradually from the deepest to the lightest; it is plain that he will perceive a blank, where that shade is wanting, and will be sensible that there is a greater distance in that place between the contiguous colours than in any other. Now I ask, whether it is possible for him, from his own imagination, to supply this deficiency, and raise up to himself the idea of that particular shade, though it had never been conveyed to him by his senses? I believe there are few but will be of opinion that he can: and this may serve as a proof that the simple ideas are not always, in every instance, derived from the correspondent impressions; though this instance is so singular, that it is scarcely worth our observing, and does not merit that for it alone we should alter our general maxim.

Here, therefore, is a proposition, which not only seems, in itself, simple and intelligible; but, if a proper use were made of it, might render every dispute equally intelligible, and banish all that jargon, which has so long taken possession of metaphysical reasonings, and drawn disgrace upon them. All ideas, especially abstract ones, are naturally faint and obscure: the mind has but a slender hold of them: they are apt to be confounded with other resembling ideas; and when we have often employed any term, though without a distinct meaning, we are apt to imagine it has a determinate idea annexed to it. On the contrary, all impressions, that is, all sensations, either outward or

inward, are strong and vivid: the limits between them are more exactly determined: nor is it easy to fall into any error or mistake with regard to them.
When we entertain, therefore, any suspicion that a philosophical term is employed without any meaning or idea (as is but too frequent), we need but enquire, *from what impression is that supposed idea derived?* And if it be impossible to
assign any, this will serve to confirm our suspicion. By bringing ideas into so
clear a light we may reasonably hope to remove all dispute, which may arise,
concerning their nature and reality.[1]

---

[1] It is probable that no more was meant by those, who denied innate
ideas, than that all ideas were copies of our impressions; though it
must be confessed, that the terms, which they employed, were not
chosen with such caution, nor so exactly defined, as to prevent all
mistakes about their doctrine. For what is meant by *innate?* If innate
be equivalent to natural, then all the perceptions and ideas of the
mind must be allowed to be innate or natural, in whatever sense we
take the latter word, whether in opposition to what is uncommon,
artificial, or miraculous. If by innate be meant, contemporary to our
birth, the dispute seems to be frivolous; nor is it worth while to enquire at what time thinking begins; whether before, at, or after our
birth. Again, the word *idea,* seems to be commonly taken in a very
loose sense, by Locke and others; as standing for any of our perceptions, our sensations and passions, as well as thoughts. Now in this
sense, I should desire to know, what can be meant by asserting, that
self-love, or resentment of injuries, or the passion between the sexes is
not innate?

But admitting these terms, *impressions* and *ideas,* in the sense
above explained, and understanding by *innate,* what is original or
copied from no precedent perception, then may we assert that all our
impressions are innate, and our ideas not innate.

To be ingenuous, I must own it to be my opinion, that Locke
was betrayed into this question by the schoolmen, who, making use
of undefined terms, draw out their disputes to a tedious length, without ever touching the point in question. A like ambiguity and circumlocution seem to run through that philosopher's reasonings on
this as well as most other subjects.

Section III.—*Of the Association of Ideas*

It is evident that there is a principle of connexion between the different
thoughts or ideas of the mind, and that, in their appearance to the memory or
imagination, they introduce each other with a certain degree of method and
regularity. In our more serious thinking or discourse this is so observable that
any particular thought, which breaks in upon the regular tract or chain of

ideas, is immediately remarked and rejected. And even in our wildest and most wandering reveries, nay in our very dreams, we shall find, if we reflect, that the imagination ran not altogether at adventures, but that there was still a connexion upheld among the different ideas, which succeeded each other. Were the loosest and freest conversation to be transcribed, there would immediately be observed something which connected it in all its transitions. Or where this is wanting, the person who broke the thread of discourse might still inform you, that there had secretly revolved in his mind a succession of thought, which had gradually led him from the subject of conversation. Among different languages, even where we cannot suspect the least connexion or communication, it is found, that the words, expressive of ideas, the most compounded, do yet nearly correspond to each other: a certain proof that the simple ideas, comprehended in the compound ones, were bound together by some universal principle, which had an equal influence on all mankind.

Though it be too obvious to escape observation, that different ideas are connected together; I do not find that any philosopher has attempted to enumerate or class all the principles of association; a subject, however, that seems worthy of curiosity. To me, there appear to be only three principles of connexion among ideas, namely, *Resemblance, Contiguity* in time or place, and *Cause or Effect.*

That these principles serve to connect ideas will not, I believe, be much doubted. A picture naturally leads our thoughts to the original [1]: the mention of one apartment in a building naturally introduces an enquiry or discourse concerning the others[2]: and if we think of a wound, we can scarcely forbear reflecting on the pain which follows it[3]. But that this enumeration is complete, and that there are no other principles of association except these, may be difficult to prove to the satisfaction of the reader, or even to a man's own satisfaction. All we can do, in such cases is to run over several instances, and examine carefully the principle which binds the different thoughts to each other, never stopping till we render the principle as general as possible[4]. The more instances we examine, and the more care we employ, the more assurance shall we acquire, that the enumeration, which we form from the whole, is complete and entire.

---

[1] Resemblance. [2] Contiguity. [3] Cause and effect.

[4] For instance, Contrast or Contrariety is also a connexion among Ideas: but it may, perhaps, be considered as a mixture of *Causation* and *Resemblance*. Where two objects are contrary, the one destroys the other; that is, the cause of its annihilation, and the idea of the annihilation of an object, implies the idea of its former existence.

Section IV.—*Sceptical Doubts Concerning the Operations of the Understanding.*

Part I.

All the objects of human reason or enquiry may naturally be divided into two kinds, to wit, *Relations of Ideas,* and *Matters of Fact.* Of the first kind are the sciences of Geometry, Algebra, and Arithmetic; and in short, every affirmation which is either intuitively or demonstratively certain. *That the square of the hypothenuse is equal to the square of the two sides*, is a proposition which expresses a relation between these figures. *That three times five is equal to the half of thirty,* expresses a relation between these numbers. Propositions of this kind are discoverable by the mere operation of thought, without dependence on what is anywhere existent in the universe. Though there never were a circle or triangle in nature, the truths demonstrated by Euclid would for ever retain their certainty and evidence.

Matters of fact, which are the second objects of human reason, are not ascertained in the same manner; nor is our evidence of their truth, however great, of a like nature with the foregoing. The contrary of every matter of fact is still possible; because it can never imply a contradiction, and is conceived by the mind with the same facility and distinctness, as if ever so conformable to reality. *That the sun will not rise to-morrow* is no less intelligible a proposition, and implies no more contradiction than the affirmation, *that it will rise*. We should in vain, therefore, attempt to demonstrate its falsehood. Were it demonstratively false, it would imply a contradiction, and could never be distinctly conceived by the mind.

It may, therefore, be a subject worthy of curiosity, to enquire what is the nature of that evidence which assures us of any real existence and matter of fact, beyond the present testimony of our senses, or the records of our memory. This part of philosophy, it is observable, has been little cultivated, either by the ancients or moderns; and therefore our doubts and errors, in the prosecution of so important an enquiry, may be the more excusable; while we march through such difficult paths without any guide or direction. They may even prove useful, by exciting curiosity, and destroying the implicit faith and security, which is the bane of all reasoning and free enquiry. The discovery of defects in the common philosophy, if any such there be, will not, I presume, be a discouragement, but rather an incitement, as is usual, to attempt something more full and satisfactory than has yet been proposed to the public.

All reasonings concerning matter of fact seem to be founded on the relation of *Cause and Effect*. By means of that relation alone we can go beyond the evidence of our memory and senses. If you were to ask a man, why he believes any matter of fact, which is absent; for instance, that his friend is in the country, or in France; he would give you a reason; and this reason would be some other fact; as a letter received from him, or the knowledge of his former resolutions and promises. A man finding a watch or any other machine in a desert island, would conclude that there had once been men in that island. All our reasonings concerning fact are of the same nature. And here it is constantly supposed that there is a connexion between the present fact and that which is inferred from it. Were there nothing to bind them together, the inference would be entirely precarious. The hearing of an articulate voice and rational discourse in the dark assures us of the presence of some person: Why? because these are the effects of the human make and fabric, and closely connected with it. If we anatomize all the other reasonings of this nature, we shall find that they are founded on the relation of cause and effect, and that this relation is either near or remote, direct or collateral. Heat and light are collateral effects of fire, and the one effect may justly be inferred from the other.

If we would satisfy ourselves, therefore, concerning the nature of that evidence, which assures us of matters of fact, we must enquire how we arrive at the knowledge of cause and effect.

I shall venture to affirm, as a general proposition, which admits of no exception, that the knowledge of this relation is not, in any instance, attained by reasonings *a priori;* but arises entirely from experience, when we find that any particular objects are constantly conjoined with each other. Let an object be presented to a man of ever so strong natural reason and abilities; if that object be entirely new to him, he will not be able, by the most accurate examination of its sensible qualities, to discover any of its causes or effects. Adam, though his rational faculties be supposed, at the very first, entirely perfect, could not have inferred from the fluidity and transparency of water that it would suffocate him, or from the light and warmth of fire that it would consume him. No object ever discovers, by the qualities which appear to the senses, either the causes which produced it, or the effects which will arise from it; nor can our reason, unassisted by experience, ever draw any inference concerning real existence and matter of fact.

This proposition, *that causes and effects are discoverable, not by reason but by experience,* will readily be admitted with regard to such objects, as we remember to have once been altogether unknown to us; since we must be conscious of the utter inability, which we then lay under, of foretelling what would arise from them. Present two smooth pieces of marble to a man who has no tincture of natural philosophy; he will never discover that they will adhere together in such a manner as to require great force to separate them in a direct line, while they make so small a resistance to a lateral pressure. Such events, as bear little analogy to the common course of nature, are also readily confessed to be known only by experience; nor does any man imagine that the explosion of gunpowder, or the attraction of a loadstone, could ever be discovered by arguments *a priori.* In like manner, when an effect is supposed to depend upon an intricate machinery or secret structure of parts, we make no difficulty in attributing all our knowledge of it to experience. Who will assert that he can give the ultimate reason, why milk or bread is proper nourishment for a man, not for a lion or a tiger? . . .

Part II.

But we have not yet attained any tolerable satisfaction with regard to the question first proposed. Each solution still gives rise to a new question as difficult as the foregoing, and leads us on to farther enquiries. When it is asked, *What is the nature of all our reasonings concerning matter of fact?* the proper answer seems to be, that they are founded on the relation of cause and effect. When again it is asked, *What is the foundation of all our reasonings and conclusions concerning that relation?* it may be replied in one word, Experience. But if we still carry on our sifting humour, and ask, *What is the foundation of all conclusions from experience?* this implies a new question, which may be of more difficult solution and explication. Philosophers, that give themselves airs of superior wisdom and sufficiency, have a hard task when they encounter persons of inquisitive dispositions, who push them from every corner to which they retreat, and who are sure at last to bring them to some dangerous dilemma. The best expedient to prevent this confusion, is to be modest in our pretensions; and even to discover the difficulty ourselves before it is objected to us. By this means, we may make a kind of merit of our very ignorance.

I shall content myself, in this section, with an easy task, and shall pretend only to give a negative answer to the question here proposed. I say then, that, even after we have experience of the operations of cause and effect, our conclusions from that experience are *not* founded on reasoning, or any process of the understanding. This answer we must endeavour both to explain and to defend.

It must certainly be allowed, that nature has kept us at a great distance from all her secrets, and has afforded us only the knowledge of a few superficial qualities of objects; while she conceals from us those powers and principles on which the influence of those objects entirely depends. Our senses inform us of the colour, weight, and consistence of bread; but neither sense nor reason can ever inform us of those qualities which fit it for the nourishment and support of a human body. Sight or feeling conveys an idea of the actual motion of bodies; but as to that wonderful force or power, which would carry on a moving body for ever in a continued change of place, and which bodies never lose but by communicating it to others; of this we cannot form the most distant conception. But notwithstanding this ignorance of natural powers[1] and principles, we always presume, when we see like sensible qualities, that they have like secret powers, and expect that effects, similar to those which we have experienced, will follow from them. If a body of like colour and consistence with that bread, which we have formerly eat, be presented to us, we make no scruple of repeating the experiment, and foresee, with certainty, like nourishment and support. Now this is a process of the mind or thought, of which I would willingly know the foundation. It is allowed on all hands that there is no known connexion between the sensible qualities and the secret powers; and consequently, that the mind is not led to form such a conclusion concerning their constant and regular conjunction, by anything which it knows of their nature. As to past *Experience,* it can be allowed to give *direct* and certain information of those precise objects only, and that precise period of time, which fell under its cognizance: but why this experience should be extended to future times, and to other objects, which for aught we know, may be only in appearance similar; this is the main question on which I would insist. The bread, which I formerly eat, nourished me; that is, a body of such sensible qualities was, at that time, endued with such secret powers: but does it follow, that other bread must also nourish me at another time, and that like sensible qualities must always be attended with like secret powers? The consequence seems nowise necessary. At least, it must be acknowledged that there is here a consequence drawn by the mind; that there is a certain step taken; a process of thought, and an inference, which wants to be explained. These two propositions are far from being the same, *I have found that such an object has always been attended with such an effect*, and *I foresee, that other objects, which are, in appearance, similar, will be attended with similar effects*. I shall allow, if you please, that the one proposition may justly be inferred from the other: I know, in fact, that it always is inferred. But if you insist that the inference is made by a chain of reasoning, I desire you to produce that reasoning. The connexion between these propositions is not intuitive. There is required a medium, which may enable the mind to draw such an inference, if indeed it be drawn by reasoning and argument. What that medium is, I must confess, passes my comprehension; and it is incumbent on those to produce it, who assert that it really exists, and is the origin of all our conclusions concerning matter of fact.

---

¹ The word, Power, is here used in a loose and popular sense. The more accurate explication of it would give additional evidence to this argument. See Sect. 7. [Omitted from this collection.—*Ed.*]

This negative argument must certainly, in process of time, become altogether convincing, if many penetrating and able philosophers shall turn their enquiries this way and no one be ever able to discover any connecting proposition or intermediate step, which supports the understanding in this conclusion. But as the question is yet new, every reader may not trust so far to his own penetration, as to conclude, because an argument escapes his enquiry, that therefore it does not really exist. For this reason it may be requisite to venture upon a more difficult task; and enumerating all the branches of human knowledge, endeavour to show that none of them can afford such an argument.

All reasonings may be divided into two kinds, namely, demonstrative reasoning, or that concerning relations of ideas, and moral reasoning, or that concerning matter of fact and existence. That there are no demonstrative arguments in the case seems evident; since it implies no contradiction that the course of nature may change, and that an object, seemingly like those which we have experienced, may be attended with different or contrary effects. May I not clearly and distinctly conceive that a body, falling from the clouds, and which, in all other respects, resembles snow, has yet the taste of salt or feeling of fire? Is there any more intelligible proposition than to affirm, that all the trees will flourish in December and January, and decay in May and June? Now whatever is intelligible, and can be distinctly conceived, implies no contradiction, and can never be proved false by any demonstrative argument or abstract reasoning *a priori*.

If we be, therefore, engaged by arguments to put trust in past experience, and make it the standard of our future judgement, these arguments must be probable only, or such as regard matter of fact and real existence, according to the division above mentioned. But that there is no argument of this kind, must appear, if our explication of that species of reasoning be admitted as solid and satisfactory. We have said that all arguments concerning existence are founded on the relation of cause and effect; that our knowledge of that relation is derived entirely from experience; and that all our experimental conclusions proceed upon the supposition that the future will be conformable to the past. To endeavour, therefore, the proof of this last supposition by probable arguments, or arguments regarding existence, must be evidently going in a circle, and taking that for granted, which is the very point in question.

In reality, all arguments from experience are founded on the similarity which we discover among natural objects, and by which we are induced to expect effects similar to those which we have found to follow from such objects. And though none but a fool or madman will ever pretend to dispute the authority of experience, or to reject that great guide of human life, it may surely be allowed a philosopher to have so much curiosity at least as to examine the principle of human nature, which gives this mighty authority to experience, and makes us draw advantage from that similarity which nature has placed among different objects. From causes which appear *similar* we expect similar effects. This is the sum of all our experimental conclusions. Now it seems evident that, if this conclusion were formed by reason, it would be as perfect at first, and upon one instance, as after ever so long a course of experience. But the case is far otherwise. Nothing so like as eggs; yet no one, on account of this appearing similarity, expects the same taste and relish in all of them. It is only after a long course of uniform experiments in any kind, that we attain a firm reliance and security with regard to a particular event. Now where is that process of reasoning which, from one instance, draws a conclusion, so different from that which it infers from a hundred instances that are nowise different from that single one? This question I propose as much for the sake of information, as with an intention of raising difficulties. I cannot find, I cannot imagine any such reasoning. But I keep my mind still open to instruction, if any one will vouchsafe to bestow it on me.

Should it be said that, from a number of uniform experiments, we *infer* a connexion between the sensible qualities and the secret powers; this, I must confess, seems the same difficulty, couched in different terms. The question still recurs, on what process of argument this *inference* is founded? Where is the medium, the interposing ideas, which join propositions so very wide of each other? It is confessed that the colour, consistence, and other sensible qualities of bread appear not, of themselves, to have any connexion with the secret powers of nourishment and support. For otherwise we could infer these secret powers from the first appearance of these sensible qualities, without the aid of experience; contrary to the sentiment of all philosophers, and contrary to plain matter of fact. Here, then, is our natural state of ignorance with regard to the powers and influence of all objects. How is this remedied by experience? It only shows us a number of uniform effects, resulting from certain objects, and teaches us that those particular objects, at that particular time, were endowed with such powers and forces. When a new object, endowed with similar sensible qualities, is produced, we expect similar powers and forces, and look for a like effect. From a body of like colour and consistence with bread we expect like nourishment and support. But this surely is a step or progress of the mind, which wants to be explained. When a man says, *I have found, in all past instances, such sensible qualities conjoined with such secret powers:* And when he says, *Similar sensible qualities will always be conjoined with similar secret powers,* he is not guilty of a tautology, nor are these propositions in any respect the same. You say that the one proposition is an inference from the other. But you must confess that the inference is not intuitive; neither is it demonstrative: Of what nature is it, then? To say it is experimental, is begging the question. For all inferences from experience suppose, as their foundation, that the future will resemble the past, and that similar powers will be conjoined with similar sensible qualities. If there be any suspicion that the course of nature may change, and that the past may be no rule for the future, all experience becomes useless, and can give rise to no inference or conclusion. It is impossible, therefore, that any arguments from experience can prove this resemblance of the past to the future; since all these arguments are founded on the supposition of that resemblance. Let the course of things be allowed hitherto ever so regular; that alone, without some new argument or inference, proves not that, for the future, it will continue so. In vain do you pretend to have learned the nature of bodies from your past experience. Their secret nature, and consequently all their effects and influence, may change, without any change in their sensible qualities. This happens sometimes, and with regard to some objects: Why may it not happen always, and with regard to all objects? What logic, what process of argument secures you against this supposition? My practice, you say, refutes my doubts. But you mistake the purport of my question. As an agent, I am quite satisfied in the point; but as a philosopher, who has some share of curiosity, I will not say scepticism, I want to learn the foundation of this inference. No reading, no enquiry has yet been able to remove my difficulty, or give me satisfaction in a matter of such importance. Can I do better than propose the difficulty to the public, even though, perhaps, I have small hopes of obtaining a solution? We shall at least, by this means, be sensible of our ignorance, if we do not augment our knowledge. . . .

Section V.—*Sceptical Solution of These Doubts.*

Part I.

The passion for philosophy, like that for religion, seems liable to this inconvenience, that, though it aims at the correction of our manners, and extirpation of our vices, it may only serve, by imprudent management, to foster a predominant inclination, and push the mind, with more determined resolution, towards that side which already *draws* too much, by the bias and propensity of the natural temper. It is certain that, while we aspire to the magnanimous firmness of the philosophic sage, and endeavour to confine our pleasures altogether within our own minds, we may, at last, render our philosophy like that of Epictetus, and other *Stoics,* only a more refined system of selfishness, and reason ourselves out of all virtue as well as social enjoyment. While we study with attention the vanity of human life, and turn all our thoughts towards the empty and transitory nature of riches and honours, we are, perhaps, all the while flattering our natural indolence, which, hating the bustle of the world, and drudgery of business, seeks a pretence of reason to give itself a full and uncontrolled indulgence. There is, however, one species of philosophy which seems little liable to this inconvenience, and that because it strikes in with no disorderly passion of the human mind, nor can mingle itself with any natural affection or propensity; and that is the Academic or Sceptical philosophy. The academics always talk of doubt and suspense of judgement, of danger in hasty determinations, of confining to very narrow bounds the enquiries of the understanding, and of renouncing all speculations which lie not within the limits of common life and practice. Nothing, therefore, can be more contrary than such a philosophy to the supine indolence of the mind, its rash arrogance, its lofty pretensions, and its superstitious credulity. Every passion is mortified by it, except the love of truth; and that passion never is, nor can be, carried to too high a degree. It is surprising, therefore, that this philosophy, which, in almost every instance, must be harmless and innocent, should be the subject of so much groundless reproach and obloquy. But, perhaps, the very circumstance which renders it so innocent is what chiefly exposes it to the public hatred and resentment. By flattering no irregular passion, it gains few partizans: By opposing so many vices and follies, it raises to itself abundance of enemies, who stigmatize it as libertine, profane, and irreligious.

Nor need we fear that this philosophy, while it endeavours to limit our enquiries to common life, should ever undermine the reasonings of common life, and carry its doubts so far as to destroy all action, as well as speculation. Nature will always maintain her rights, and prevail in the end over any abstract reasoning whatsoever. Though we should conclude, for instance, as in the foregoing section, that, in all reasonings from experience, there is a step taken by the mind which is not supported by any argument or process of the understanding; there is no danger that these reasonings, on which almost all knowledge depends, will ever be affected by such a discovery. If the mind be not engaged by argument to make this step, it must be induced by some other principle of equal weight and authority; and that principle will preserve its influence as long as human nature remains the same. What that principle is may well be worth the pains of enquiry.

Suppose a person, though endowed with the strongest faculties of reason and reflection, to be brought on a sudden into this world; he would, indeed, immediately observe a continual succession of objects, and one event following another; but he would not be able to discover anything farther. He would not, at first, by any reasoning, be able to reach the idea of cause and effect; since the particular powers, by which all natural operations are performed, never appear to the senses; nor is it reasonable to conclude, merely because one event, in one instance, precedes another, that therefore the one is the cause, the other the effect. Their conjunction may be arbitrary and casual. There may be no reason to infer the existence of one from the appearance of the other. And in a word, such a person, without more experience, could never employ his conjecture or reasoning concerning any matter of fact, or be assured of anything beyond what was immediately present to his memory and senses.

Suppose, again, that he has acquired more experience, and has lived so long in the world as to have observed familiar objects or events to be constantly conjoined together; what is the consequence of this experience? He immediately infers the existence of one object from the appearance of the other. Yet he has not, by all his experience, acquired any idea or knowledge of the secret power by which the one object produces the other; nor is it, by any process of reasoning, he is engaged to draw this inference. But still he finds himself determined to draw it: And though he should be convinced that his understanding has no part in the operation, he would nevertheless continue in the same course of thinking. There is some other principle which determines him to form such a conclusion.

This principle is Custom or Habit. For wherever the repetition of any particular act or operation produces a propensity to renew the same act or operation, without being impelled by any reasoning or process of the understanding, we always say, that this propensity is the effect of *Custom*. By employing that word, we pretend not to have given the ultimate reason of such a propensity. We only point out a principle of human nature, which is universally acknowledged, and which is well known by its effects. Perhaps we can push our enquiries no farther, or pretend to give the cause of this cause; but must rest contented with it as the ultimate principle, which we can assign, of all our conclusions from experience. It is sufficient satisfaction, that we can go so far, without repining at the narrowness of our faculties because they will carry us no farther. And it is certain we here advance a very intelligible proposition at least, if not a true one, when we assert that, after the constant conjunction of two objects—heat and flame, for instance, weight and solidity—we are determined by custom alone to expect the one from the appearance of the other. This hypothesis seems even the only one which explains the difficulty, why we draw, from a thousand instances, an inference which we are not able to draw from one instance, that is, in no respect, different from them. Reason is incapable of any such variation. The conclusions which it draws from considering one circle are the same which it would form upon surveying all the circles in the universe. But no man, having seen only one body move after being impelled by another, could infer that every other body will move after a like impulse. All inferences from experience, therefore, are effects of custom, not of reasoning.[1]

---

[1] [A lengthy footnote appearing in the original is omitted here.—*Ed.*]

Custom, then, is the great guide of human life. It is that principle alone which renders our experience useful to us, and makes us expect, for the future, a similar train of events with those which have appeared in the past. Without the influence of custom, we should be entirely ignorant of every matter of fact beyond what is immediately present to the memory and senses. We should never know how to adjust means to ends, or to employ our natural powers in the production of any effect. There would be an end at once of all action, as well as of the chief part of speculation.

But here it may be proper to remark, that though our conclusions from experience carry us beyond our memory and senses, and assure us of matters of fact which happened in the most distant places and most remote ages, yet some fact must always be present to the senses or memory, from which we may first proceed in drawing these conclusions. A man, who should find in a desert country the remains of pompous buildings, would conclude that the country had, in ancient times, been cultivated by civilized inhabitants; but did nothing of this nature occur to him, he could never form such an inference. We learn the events of former ages from history; but then we must peruse the volumes in which this instruction is contained, and thence carry up our inferences from one testimony to another, till we arrive at the eyewitnesses and spectators of these distant events. In a word, if we proceed not upon some fact, present to the memory or senses, our reasonings would be merely hypothetical; and however the particular links might be connected with each other, the whole chain of inferences would have nothing to support it, nor could we ever, by its means, arrive at the knowledge of any real existence. If I ask why you believe any particular matter of fact, which you relate, you must tell me some reason; and this reason will be some other fact, connected with it. But as you cannot proceed after this manner, *in infinitum*, you must at last terminate in some fact, which is present to your memory or senses; or must allow that your belief is entirely without foundation.

What, then, is the conclusion of the whole matter? A simple one; though, it must be confessed, pretty remote from the common theories of philosophy. All belief of matter of fact or real existence is derived merely from some object, present to the memory or senses, and a customary conjunction between that and some other object. Or in other words; having found, in many instances, that any two kinds of objects—flame and heat, snow and cold—have always been conjoined together; if flame or snow be presented anew to the senses, the mind is carried by custom to expect heat or cold, and to *believe* that such a quality does exist, and will discover itself upon a nearer approach. This belief is the necessary result of placing the mind in such circumstances. It is an operation of the soul, when we are so situated, as unavoidable as to feel the passion of love, when we receive benefits; or hatred, when we meet with injuries. All these operations are a species of natural instincts, which no reasoning or process of the thought and understanding is able either to produce or to prevent. . . .

20

THOMAS REID
Natural Principles of Belief

I.*

Principles Taken for Granted

As there are words common to philosophers and to the vulgar, which need no explication, so there are principles common to both, which need no proof, and which do not admit of direct proof.

One who applies to any branch of science, must be come to years of understanding, and, consequently, must have exercised his reason, and the other powers of his mind, in various ways. He must have formed various opinions and principles, by which he conducts himself in the affairs of life. Of those principles, some are common to all men, being evident in themselves, and so necessary in the conduct of life that a man cannot live and act according to the rules of common prudence without them. . . .

There are, therefore, common principles, which are the foundation of all reasoning and of all science. Such common principles seldom admit of direct proof, nor do they need it. Men need not to be taught them; for they are such as all men of common understanding know; or such, at least, as they give a ready assent to, as soon as they are proposed and understood.

Such principles, when we have occasion to use them in science, are called *axioms*. . . .

It may, however be observed, that the first principles of natural philosophy are of a quite different nature from mathematical axioms: they have not the same kind of evidence, nor are they necessary truths, as mathematical axioms are. They are such as these: That similar effects proceed from the same or similar causes; That we ought to admit of no other causes of natural effects, but such as are true, and sufficient to account for the effects. These are principles which, though they have not the same kind of evidence that mathematical axioms have; yet have such evidence that every man of common understanding readily assents to them, and finds it absolutely necessary to conduct his actions and opinions by them, in the ordinary affairs of life. . . .

Their evidence is not demonstrative, but intuitive. They require not proof, but to be placed in a proper point of view. . . .

1. *First,* then, I shall take it for granted, that I *think,* that I *remember,* that I *reason,* and, in general, that I really perform all those operations of mind of which I am conscious.

The operations of our minds are attended with consciousness; and this consciousness is the evidence, the only evidence, which we have or can have of

* From Essay I, Chapter II, *Essays on the Intellectual Powers of Man.* First published in 1785.

their existence. If a man should take it into his head to think or to say that his consciousness may deceive him, and to require proof that it cannot, I know of no proof that can be given him; he must be left to himself, as a man that denies first principles, without which there can be no reasoning. Every man finds himself under a necessity of believing what consciousness testifies, and everything that hath this testimony is to be taken as a first principle.

2. As by consciousness we know certainly the existence of our present thoughts and passions; so we know the past by remembrance. And, when they are recent, and the remembrance of them fresh, the knowledge of them, from such distinct remembrance, is, in its certainty and evidence, next to that of consciousness. . . .

6. I take it for granted that, in most operations of the mind, there must be an object distinct from the operation itself. I cannot see, without seeing something. To see without having any object of sight is absurd. I cannot remember, without remembering something. The thing remembered is past, while the remembrance of it is present; and, therefore, the operation and the object of it must be distinct things. The operations of our mind are denoted, in all languages, by active transitive verbs, which, from their construction in grammar, require not only a person or agent, but likewise an object of the operation. Thus, the verb know, denotes an operation of mind. From the general structure of language, this verb requires a person—I know, you know, or he knows; but it requires no less a noun in the accusative case, denoting the thing known; for he that knows must know something; and, to know, without having any object of knowledge, is an absurdity too gross to admit of reasoning.

7. We ought likewise to take for granted, as first principles, things wherein we find an universal agreement, among the learned and unlearned, in the different nations and ages of the world. A consent of ages and nations, of the learned and vulgar, ought, at least, to have great authority, unless we can shew some prejudice as universal as that consent is, which might be the cause of it. Truth is one, but error is infinite. There are many truths so obvious to the human faculties, that it may be expected that men should universally agree in them. And this is actually found to be the case with regard to many truths, against which we find no dissent, unless perhaps that of a few sceptical philosophers, who may justly be suspected, in such cases, to differ from the rest of mankind, through pride, obstinacy, or some favourite passion. . . .

Perhaps it may be thought that it is impossible to collect the opinions of all men upon any point whatsoever; and, therefore, that this maxim can be of no use. But there are many cases wherein it is otherwise. Who can doubt, for instance, whether mankind have, in all ages, believed the existence of a material world, and that those things which they see and handle are real, and not mere illusions and apparitions? Who can doubt whether mankind have universally believed that everything that begins to exist, and every change that happens in nature, must have a cause? . . .

8. I need hardly say that I shall also take for granted such facts as are attested to the conviction of all sober and reasonable men, either by our senses, by

memory, or by human testimony. Although some writers on this subject have disputed the authority of the senses, of memory, and of every human faculty, yet we find that such persons, in the conduct of life, in pursuing their ends, or in avoiding dangers, pay the same regard to the authority of their senses and other faculties, as the rest of mankind. By this they give us just ground to doubt of their candour in their professions of scepticism.

This, indeed, has always been the fate of the few that have professed scepticism, that, when they have done what they can to discredit their senses, they find themselves, after all, under a necessity of trusting to them. Mr. Hume has been so candid as to acknowledge this; and it is no less true of those who have not shewn the same candour; for I never heard that any sceptic run his head against a post, or stepped into a kennel, because he did not believe his eyes.

Upon the whole, I acknowledge that we ought to be cautious that we do not adopt opinions as first principles which are not entitled to that character. But there is surely the least danger of men's being imposed upon in this way, when such principles openly lay claim to the character, and are thereby fairly exposed to the examination of those who may dispute their authority. We do not pretend that those things that are laid down as first principles may not be examined, and that we ought not to have our ears open to what may be pleaded against their being admitted as such. Let us deal with them as an upright judge does with a witness who has a fair character. He pays a regard to the testimony of such a witness while his character is unimpeached; but, if it can be shewn that he is suborned, or that he is influenced by malice or partial favour, his testimony loses all its credit, and is justly rejected.

II.*

Sensation, Memory, and the Nature of Belief

I can think of the smell of a rose when I do not smell it; and it is possible that when I think of it, there is neither rose nor smell anywhere existing. But when I smell it, I am necessarily determined to believe that the sensation really exists. This is common to all sensations, that, as they cannot exist but in being perceived, so they cannot be perceived but they must exist. I could as easily doubt of my own existence, as of the existence of my sensations. Even those profound philosophers who have endeavoured to disprove their own existence, have yet left their sensations to stand upon their own bottom, stript of a subject, rather than call in question the reality of their existence.

Here, then, a sensation, a smell for instance, may be presented to the mind three different ways: it may be smelled, it may be remembered, it may be imagined or thought of. In the first case, it is necessarily accompanied with a belief of its present existence; in the second, it is necessarily accompanied

---

* From Chapter II, Secs. III & V, *An Inquiry into the Human Mind on the Principles of Common Sense.* First published in 1764.

with a belief of its past existence; and in the last, it is not accompanied with belief at all, but is what the logicians call *a simple apprehension.*

Why sensation should compel our belief of the present existence of the thing, memory a belief of its past existence, and imagination no belief at all, I believe no philosopher can give a shadow of reason, but that such is the nature of these operations; they are all simple and original, and therefore inexplicable acts of the mind.

Suppose that once, and only once, I smelled a tuberose in a certain room, where it grew in a pot, and gave a very grateful perfume. Next day I relate what I saw and smelled. When I attend as carefully as I can to what passes in my mind in this case, it appears evident that the very thing I saw yesterday, and the fragrance I smelled, are now the immediate objects of my mind, when I remember it. Further, I can imagine this pot and flower transported to the room where I now sit, and yielding the same perfume. Here likewise it appears, that the individual thing which I saw and smelled, is the object of my imagination.

Philosophers indeed tell me that the immediate object of my memory and imagination in this case, is not the past sensation, but an idea of it, an image, phantasm, or species, of the odour I smelled: that this idea now exists in my mind, or in my sensorium; and the mind, contemplating this present idea, finds it a representation of what is past, or of what may exist; and accordingly calls it memory, or imagination. This is the doctrine of the ideal philosophy; which we shall not now examine, that we may not interrupt the thread of the present investigation. Upon the strictest attention, memory appears to me to have things that are past, and not present ideas, for its object. We shall afterwards examine this system of ideas, and endeavour to make it appear, that no solid proof has ever been advanced of the existence of ideas; that they are a mere fiction and hypothesis, contrived to solve the phaenomena of the human understanding; that they do not at all answer this end; and that this hypothesis of ideas or images of things in the mind, or in the sensorium, is the parent of those many paradoxes so shocking to common sense, and of that scepticism which disgrace our philosophy of the mind, and have brought upon it the ridicule and contempt of sensible men.

In the meantime, I beg leave to think, with the vulgar, that, when I remember the smell of the tuberose, that very sensation which I had yesterday, and which has now no more any existence, is the immediate object of my memory; and when I imagine it present, the sensation itself, and not any idea of it, is the object of my imagination. But, though the object of my sensation, memory, and imagination, be in this case the same, yet these acts or operations of the mind are as different, and as easily distinguishable, as smell, taste, and sound. I am conscious of a difference in kind between sensation and memory and between both and imagination. I find this also, that the sensation compels my belief of the present existence of the smell, and memory my belief of its past existence. There is a smell, is the immediate testimony of sense; there was a smell, is the immediate testimony of memory. If you ask me, why I

believe that the smell exists, I can give no other reason, nor shall ever be able
to give any other, than that I smell it. If you ask, why I believe that it existed
yesterday, I can give no other reason but that I remember it.

Sensation and memory, therefore, are simple, original, and perfectly distinct operations of the mind, and both of them are original principles of belief.
Imagination is distinct from both, but is no principle of belief. Sensation implies the present existence of its object, memory its past experience, but imagination views its object naked, and without any belief of its existence or non-existence, and is therefore what the schools call *Simple Apprehension*.

But what is this belief or knowledge which accompanies sensation and
memory? Every man knows what it is, but no man can define it. Does any
man pretend to define sensation, or to define consciousness? It is happy, indeed, that no man does. And if no philosopher had endeavoured to define and
explain belief, some paradoxes in philosophy, more incredible than ever were
brought forth by the most abject superstition or the most frantic enthusiasm,
had never seen the light. Of this kind surely is that modern discovery of the
ideal philosophy, that sensation, memory, belief, and imagination, when they
have the same object, are only different degrees of strength and vivacity in the
idea. Suppose the idea to be that of a future state after death: one man believes it firmly—this means no more than that he hath a strong and lively idea
of it; another neither believes nor disbelieves—that is, he has a weak and faint
idea. Suppose, now, a third person believes firmly that there is no such thing, I
am at a loss to know whether his idea be faint or lively: if it is faint, then there
may be a firm belief where the idea is faint; if the idea is lively, then the belief
of a future state and the belief of no future state must be one and the same.
The same arguments that are used to prove that belief implies only a stronger
idea of the object than simple apprehension, might as well be used to prove
that love implies only a stronger idea of the object than indifference. And then
what shall we say of hatred, which must upon this hypothesis be a degree of
love, or a degree of indifference? If it should be said, that in love there is something more than an idea—to wit, an affection of the mind—may it not be said
with equal reason, that in belief there is something more than an idea—to wit,
an assent or persuasion of the mind?

I mentioned before Locke's notion of belief or knowledge; he holds that it
consists in a perception of the agreement or disagreement of ideas; and this he
values himself upon as a very important discovery.

We shall have occasion afterwards to examine more particularly this
grand principle of Locke's philosophy, and to shew that it is one of the main
pillars of modern scepticism, although he had no intention to make that use of
it. At present let us only consider how it agrees with the instances of belief now
under consideration; and whether it gives any light to them. I believe that the
sensation I have exists; and that the sensation I remember does not now exist,
but did exist yesterday. Here, according to Locke's system, I compare the idea
of a sensation with the ideas of past and present existence: at one time I perceive that this idea agrees with that of present existence, but disagrees with

that of past existence; but, at another time, it agrees with the idea of past existence, and disagrees with that of present existence. Truly these ideas seem to be very capricious in their agreements and disagreements. Besides, I cannot, for my heart, conceive what is meant by either. I say a sensation exists, and I think I understand clearly what I mean. But you want to make the thing clearer, and for that end tell me, that there is an agreement between the idea of that sensation and the idea of existence. To speak freely, this conveys to me no light, but darkness; I can conceive no otherwise of it, than as an odd and obscure circumlocution. I conclude, then, that the belief which accompanies sensation and memory, is a simple act of the mind, which cannot be defined. It is, in this respect, like seeing and hearing, which can never be so defined as to be understood by those who have not these faculties; and to such as have them, no definition can make these operations more clear than they are already. In like manner, every man that has any belief—and he must be a curiosity that has none—knows perfectly what belief is, but can never define or explain it. I conclude, also, that sensation, memory, and imagination, even where they have the same object, are operations of a quite different nature, and perfectly distinguishable by those who are sound and sober. A man that is in danger of confounding them, is indeed to be pitied; but whatever relief he may find from another art, he can find none from logic or metaphysic. I conclude further, that it is no less a part of the human constitution, to believe the present existence of our sensations, and to believe the past existence of what we remember, than it is to believe that twice two make four. The evidence of sense, the evidence of memory, and the evidence of the necessary relations of things, are all distinct and original kinds of evidence, equally grounded on our constitution: none of them depends upon, or can be resolved into another. To reason against any of these kinds of evidence, is absurd; nay, to reason for them is absurd. They are first principles; and such fall not within the province of reason, but of common sense.

21 IMMANUEL KANT
Sensibility and Understanding

I.*

Since the Essays of Locke and Leibnitz, or rather since the origin of metaphysics so far as we know its history, nothing has ever happened which was more decisive to its fate than the attack made upon it by David Hume. He threw no light on this species of knowledge, but he certainly struck a spark from which light might have been obtained, had it caught some inflammable substance and had its smouldering fire been carefully nursed and developed.

Hume started from a single but important concept in Metaphysics, viz., that of Cause and Effect (including its derivatives force and action, etc.). He challenges reason, which pretends to have given birth to this idea from herself, to answer him by what right she thinks anything to be so constituted, that if that thing be posited, something else also must necessarily be posited; for this is the meaning of the concept of cause. He demonstrated irrefutably that it was perfectly impossible for reason to think *a priori* and by means of concepts a combination involving necessity. We cannot at all see why, in consequence of the existence of one thing, another must necessarily exist, or how the concept of such a combination can arise *a priori*. Hence he inferred, that reason was altogether deluded with reference to this concept, which she erroneously considered as one of her children, whereas in reality it was nothing but a bastard of imagination, impregnated by experience, which subsumed certain representations under the Law of Association, and mistook the subjective necessity of habit for an objective necessity arising from insight. Hence he inferred that reason had no power to think such combinations, even generally, because her concepts would then be purely fictitious, and all her pretended *a priori* cognitions nothing but common experiences marked with a false stamp. In plain language there is not, and cannot be, any such thing as metaphysics at all.

However hasty and mistaken Hume's conclusion may appear, it was at least founded upon investigation, and this investigation deserved the concentrated attention of the brighter spirits of his day as well as determined efforts on their part to discover, if possible, a happier solution of the problem in the sense proposed by him, all of which would have speedily resulted in a complete reform of the science.

But Hume suffered the usual misfortune of metaphysicians, of not being understood. It is positively painful to see how utterly his opponents, Reid, Oswald, Beattie, and lastly Priestley, missed the point of the problem; for while they were ever taking for granted that which he doubted, and demonstrating

---

* From *Prolegomena to Any Future Metaphysics*, translated and edited by Paul Carus, The Open Court Publishing Co., La Salle, Ill., 1947. Reprinted by permission of The Open Court Publishing Co.

with zeal and often with impudence that which he never thought of doubting, they so misconstrued his valuable suggestion that everything remained in its old condition, as if nothing had happened.

The question was not whether the concept of cause was right, useful, and even indispensable for our knowledge of nature, for this Hume had never doubted; but whether that concept could be thought by reason *a priori*, and consequently whether it possessed an inner truth, independent of all experience, implying a wider application than merely to the objects of experience. This was Hume's problem. It was a question concerning the *origin*, not concerning the *indispensable need* of the concept. Were the former decided, the conditions of the use and the sphere of its valid application would have been determined as a matter of course.

But to satisfy the conditions of the problem, the opponents of the great thinker should have penetrated very deeply into the nature of reason, so far as it is concerned with pure thinking,—a task which did not suit them. They found a more convenient method of being defiant without any insight, viz., the appeal to *common sense*. It is indeed a great gift of God, to possess right, or (as they now call it) plain common sense. But this common sense must be shown practically, by well-considered and reasonable thoughts and words, not by appealing to it as an oracle, when no rational justification can be advanced. To appeal to common sense, when insight and science fail, and no sooner—this is one of the subtile discoveries of modern times, by means of which the most superficial ranter can safely enter the lists with the most thorough thinker, and hold his own. But as long as a particle of insight remains, no one would think of having recourse to this subterfuge. For what is it but an appeal to the opinion of the multitude, of whose applause the philosopher is ashamed, while the popular charlatan glories and confides in it? I should think that Hume might fairly have laid as much claim to common sense as Beattie, and in addition to a critical reason (such as the latter did not possess), which keeps common sense in check and prevents it from speculating, or, if speculations are under discussion, restrains the desire to decide because it cannot satisfy itself concerning its own arguments. By this means alone can common sense remain sound. Chisels and hammers may suffice to work a piece of wood, but for steel-engraving we require an engraver's needle. Thus common sense and speculative understanding are each serviceable in their own way, the former in judgments which apply immediately to experience, the latter when we judge universally from mere concepts, as in metaphysics, where sound common sense, so called in spite of the inapplicability of the word, has no right to judge at all.

I openly confess, the suggestion of David Hume was the very thing, which many years ago first interrupted my dogmatic slumber, and gave my investigations in the field of speculative philosophy quite a new direction. I was far from following him in the conclusions at which he arrived by regarding, not the whole of his problem, but a part, which by itself can give us no information. If we start from a well-founded, but undeveloped, thought, which another has bequeathed to us, we may well hope by continued reflection to advance farther than the acute man, to whom we owe the first spark of light.

I therefore first tried whether Hume's objection could not be put into a general form, and soon found that the concept of the connexion of cause and effect was by no means the only idea by which the understanding thinks the connexion of things *a priori,* but rather that metaphysics consists altogether of such connexions. I sought to ascertain their number, and when I had satisfactorily succeeded in this by starting from a single principle, I proceeded to the deduction of these concepts, which I was now certain were not deduced from experience, as Hume had apprehended, but sprang from the pure understanding. This deduction (which seemed impossible to my acute predecessor, which had never even occurred to any one else, though no one had hesitated to use the concepts without investigating the basis of their objective validity) was the most difficult task ever undertaken in the service of metaphysics; and the worst was that metaphysics, such as it then existed, could not assist me in the least, because this deduction alone can render metaphysics possible. But as soon as I had succeeded in solving Hume's problem not merely in a particular case, but with respect to the whole faculty of pure reason, I could proceed safely, though slowly, to determine the whole sphere of pure reason completely and from general principles, in its circumference as well as in its contents. This was required for metaphysics in order to construct its system according to a reliable method.

But I fear that the execution of Hume's problem in its widest extent (viz., my Critique of the Pure Reason) will fare as the problem itself fared, when first proposed. It will be misjudged because it is misunderstood, and misunderstood because men choose to skim through the book, and not to think through it—a disagreeable task, because the work is dry, obscure, opposed to all ordinary notions, and moreover long-winded. I confess, however, I did not expect to hear from philosophers complaints of want of popularity, entertainment, and facility, when the existence of a highly prized and indispensable cognition is at stake, which cannot be established otherwise, than by the strictest rules of methodic precision. . . .

II.*

INTRODUCTION

Of the Difference between Pure and Empirical Knowledge

That all our knowledge begins with experience there can be no doubt. For how should the faculty of knowledge be called into activity, if not by objects which affect our senses, and which either produce representations by themselves, or rouse the activity of our understanding to compare, to connect,

---

* From *Critique of Pure Reason*, B 1–6; A 6–10, B 10–14; B 14–24; A 11–16, B 24–30.

or to separate them; and thus to convert the raw material of our sensuous impressions into a knowledge of objects, which we call experience? In respect of time, therefore, no knowledge within us is antecedent to experience, but all knowledge begins with it.

But although all our knowledge begins with experience, it does not follow that it arises from experience. For it is quite possible that even our empirical experience is a compound of that which we receive through impressions, and of that which our own faculty of knowledge (incited only by sensuous impressions), supplies from itself, a supplement which we do not distinguish from that raw material, until long practice has roused our attention and rendered us capable of separating one from the other.

It is therefore a question which deserves at least closer investigation, and cannot be disposed of at first sight, whether there exists a knowledge independent of experience, and even of all impressions of the senses? Such *knowledge* is called *a priori*, and distinguished from *empirical* knowledge, which has its sources *a posteriori*, that is, in experience.

This term *a priori*, however, is not yet definite enough to indicate the full meaning of our question. For people are wont to say, even with regard to knowledge derived from experience, that we have it, or might have it, *a priori*, because we derive it from experience, not *immediately*, but from a general rule, which, however, has itself been derived from experience. Thus one would say of a person who undermines the foundations of his house, that he might have known *a priori* that it would tumble down, that is, that he need not wait for the experience of its really tumbling down. But still he could not know this entirely *a priori*, because he had first to learn from experience that bodies are heavy, and will fall when their supports are taken away.

We shall therefore, in what follows, understand by knowledge *a priori* knowledge which is *absolutely* independent of all experience, and not of this or that experience only. Opposed to this is empirical knowledge, or such as is possible *a posteriori* only, that is, by experience. Knowledge *a priori*, if mixed up with nothing empirical, is called *pure*. Thus the proposition, for example, that every change has its cause, is a proposition *a priori*, but not pure: because change is a concept which can only be derived from experience.

We are in Possession of Certain Cognitions a priori, *and even the Ordinary Understanding is never without them*

All depends here on a criterion, by which we may safely distinguish between pure and empirical knowledge. Now experience teaches us, no doubt, that something is so or so, but not that it cannot be different. *First*, then, if we have a proposition, which is thought, together with its necessity, we have a judgment *a priori;* and if, besides, it is not derived from any proposition, except such as is itself again considered as necessary, we have an absolutely *a priori* judgment. *Secondly,* experience never imparts to its judgments true or strict, but only assumed or relative universality (by means of induction), so that we ought always to say, so far as we have observed hitherto, there is no exception to this or that rule. If, therefore, a judgment is thought with strict universality, so that no exception is admitted as possible, it is not derived from experience, but is valid absolutely *a priori*. Empirical universality, therefore, is only an arbitrary extension of a validity which applies to most cases, to one that applies to all: as for instance, in the proposition, all bodies are heavy. If, on the contrary, strict universality is essential to a judgment, this always points to a special source of knowledge, namely, a faculty of knowledge *a priori*. Necessity, therefore, and strict universality are safe criteria of knowledge *a priori*, and are inseparable one from the other. As, however, in the use of these criteria, it is sometimes easier to show the contingency than the empirical limitation of judgments, and as it is sometimes more convincing to prove the unlimited universality which we attribute to a judgment than its necessity, it is advisable to use both criteria separately, each being by itself infallible.

That there really exist in our knowledge such necessary, and in the strictest sense universal, and therefore pure judgments *a priori*, is easy to show. If we want a scientific example, we have only to look to any of the propositions of mathematics; if we want one from the sphere of the ordinary understanding, such a proposition as that each change must have a cause, will answer the purpose; nay, in the latter case, even the concept of cause contains so clearly the concept of the necessity of its connection with an effect, and of the strict universality of the rule, that it would be destroyed altogether if we attempted to derive it, as Hume does, from the frequent concomitancy of that which happens with that which precedes, and from a habit arising thence (therefore from a purely subjective necessity), of connecting representations. It is possible even, without having recourse to such examples in proof of the reality of pure propositions *a priori* within our knowledge, to prove their indispensability for the possibility of experience itself, thus proving it *a priori*. For whence should experience take its certainty, if all the rules which it follows were always again and again empirical, and therefore contingent and hardly fit to serve as first principles? For the present, however, we may be satisfied for having shown the pure employment of the faculty of our knowledge as a matter of fact, with the criteria of it.

Not only in judgments, however, but even in certain concepts, can we show their origin *a priori*. Take away, for example, from the concept of a body, as supplied by experience, everything that is empirical, one by one; such as colour, hardness or softness, weight, and even impenetrability, and there still remains the space which the body (now entirely vanished) occupied: that you cannot take away. And in the same manner, if you remove from your empirical concept of any object, corporeal or incorporeal, all properties which experience has taught you, you cannot take away from it that property by which you conceive it as a substance, or inherent in a substance (although such a concept contains more determinations than that of an object in general). Convinced, therefore, by the necessity with which that concept forces itself upon you, you will have to admit that it has its seat in your faculty of knowledge *a priori*.

Of the Distinction between Analytical and Synthetical Judgments

In all judgments in which there is a relation between subject and predicate (I speak of affirmative judgments only, the application to negative ones being easy), that relation can be of two kinds. Either the predicate B belongs to the subject A as something contained (though covertly) in the concept A; or B lies outside the sphere of the concept A, though somehow connected with it. In the former case I call the judgment analytical, in the latter synthetical. Analytical judgments (affirmative) are therefore those in which the connection of the predicate with the subject is conceived through identity, while others in which that connection is conceived without identity, may be called synthetical. The former might be called illustrating, the latter expanding judgments, because in the former nothing is added by the predicate to the concept of the subject, but the concept is only divided into its constituent concepts which were always conceived as existing within it, though confusedly; while the latter add to the concept of the subject a predicate not conceived as existing within it, and not to be extracted from it by any process of mere analysis. If I say, for instance, All bodies are extended, this is an analytical judgment. I need not go beyond the concept connected with the name of body, in order to find that extension is connected with it. I have only to analyse that concept and become conscious of the manifold elements always contained in it, in order to find that predicate. This is therefore an analytical judgment. But if I say, All bodies are heavy, the predicate is something quite different from what I think as the mere concept of body. The addition of such a predicate gives us a synthetical judgment.

[It becomes clear from this,

[1. That our knowledge is in no way extended by analytical judgments, but that all they effect is to put the concepts which we possess into better order and render them more intelligible.

2. That in synthetical judgments I must have besides the concept of the subject something else *(x)* on which the understanding relies in order to know that a predicate, not contained in the concept, nevertheless belongs to it.

In empirical judgments this causes no difficulty, because this *x* is here simply the complete experience of an object which I conceive by the concept A, that concept forming one part only of my experience. For though I do not include the predicate of gravity in the general concept of body, that concept nevertheless indicates the complete experience through one of its parts, so that I may add other parts also of the same experience, all belonging to that concept. I may first, by an analytical process, realise the concept of body through the predicates of extension, impermeability, form, etc., all of which are contained in it. Afterwards I expand my knowledge, and looking back to the experience from which my concept of body was abstracted, I find gravity always connected with the before-mentioned predicates. Experience therefore is the *x* which lies beyond the concept A, and on which rests the possibility of a synthesis of the predicate of gravity B with the concept A.] [1]

---

[1] The bracketed paragraphs, from 'It becomes clear from this,' are left out in the Second Edition, and replaced by the following paragraph:

Empirical judgments, as such, are all synthetical; for it would be absurd to found an analytical judgment on experience, because, in order to form such a judgment, I need not at all step out of my concept, or appeal to the testimony of experience. That a body is extended, is a proposition perfectly certain *a priori*, and not an empirical judgment. For, before I call in experience, I am already in possession of all the conditions of my judgment in the concept of body itself. I have only to draw out from it, according to the principle of contradiction, the required predicate, and I thus become conscious, at the same time, of the necessity of the judgment, which experience could never teach me. But, though I do not include the predicate of gravity in the general concept of body, that concept, nevertheless, indicates an object of experience through one of its parts: so that I may add other parts also of the same experience, besides those which belonged to the former concept. I may, first, by an analytical process, realise the concept of body, through the predicates of extension, impermeability, form, etc., all of which are contained in it. Afterwards I expand my knowledge, and looking back to the experience from which my concept of body was abstracted, I find gravity always connected with the before-mentioned predicates, and therefore I add it synthetically to that concept as a predicate. It is, therefore, experience on which the possibility of the synthesis of the predicate of gravity with the concept of body is founded: because both concepts, though neither of them is contained in the other, belong to each other, though accidentally only, as parts of a whole, namely, of experience, which is itself a synthetical connection of intuitions.

In synthetical judgments *a priori*, however, that help is entirely wanting. If I want to go beyond the concept A in order to find another concept B connected with it, where is there anything on which I may rest and through which a synthesis might become possible, considering that I cannot have the advantage of looking about in the field of experience? Take the proposition that all which happens has its cause. In the concept of something that happens I no doubt conceive of something existing preceded by time, and from this certain analytical judgments may be deduced. But the concept of cause is entirely outside that concept, and indicates something different from that which happens, and is by no means contained in that representation. How can I venture then to predicate of that which happens something totally different from it, and to represent the concept of cause, though not contained in it, as belonging to it, and belonging to it by necessity? What is here the unknown *x*, on which the understanding may rest in order to find beyond the concept A a foreign predicate B, which nevertheless is believed to be connected with it? It cannot be experience, because the proposition that all which happens has its cause represents this second predicate as added to the subject not only with greater generality than experience can ever supply, but also with a character of necessity, and therefore purely *a priori*, and based on concepts. All our speculative knowledge *a priori* aims at and rests on such synthetical, i.e. expanding propositions, for the analytical are no doubt very important and necessary, yet only in order to arrive at that clearness of concepts which is requisite for a safe and wide synthesis, serving as a really new addition to what we possess already. . . .

In all Theoretical Sciences of Reason Synthetical Judgments a priori *are contained as Principles*

1. All mathematical judgments are synthetical. This proposition, though incontestably certain, and very important to us for the future, seems to have hitherto escaped the observation of those who are engaged in the anatomy of human reason: nay, to be directly opposed to all their conjectures. For as it was found that all mathematical conclusions proceed according to the principle of contradiction (which is required by the nature of all apodictic certainty), it was supposed that the fundamental principles of mathematics also rested on the authority of the same principle of contradiction. This, however, was a mistake: for though a synthetical proposition may be understood according to the principle of contradiction, this can only be if another synthetical proposition is presupposed, from which the latter is deduced, but never by itself. First of all, we ought to observe, that mathematical propositions, properly so called, are always judgments *a priori*, and not empirical, because they carry along with them necessity, which can never be deduced from experience. If people should object to this, I am quite willing to confine my statement to pure mathematics, the very concept of which implies that it does not contain empirical, but only pure knowledge *a priori*.

At first sight one might suppose indeed that the proposition $7 + 5 = 12$ is merely analytical, following, according to the principle of contradiction, from the concept of a sum of 7 and 5. But, if we look more closely, we shall find that the concept of the sum of 7 and 5 contains nothing beyond the union of both sums into one, whereby nothing is told us as to what this single number may be which combines both. We by no means arrive at a concept of Twelve, by thinking that union of Seven and Five; and we may analyse our concept of such a possible sum as long as we will, still we shall never discover in it the concept of Twelve. We must go beyond these concepts, and call in the assistance of the intuition corresponding to one of the two, for instance, our five fingers, or, as Segner does in his arithmetic, five points, and so by degrees add the units of the Five, given in intuition, to the concept of the Seven. For I first take the number 7, and taking the intuition of the fingers of my hand, in order to form with it the concept of the 5, I gradually add the units, which I before took together, to make up the number 5, by means of the image of my hand, to the number 7, and I thus see the number 12 arising before me. That 5 should be added to 7 was no doubt implied in my concept of a sum $7 + 5$, but not that that sum should be equal to 12. An arithmetical proposition is, therefore, always synthetical, which is seen more easily still by taking larger numbers, where we clearly perceive that, turn and twist our conceptions as we may, we could never, by means of the mere analysis of our concepts and without the help of intuition, arrive at the sum that is wanted.

Nor is any proposition of pure geometry analytical. That the straight line between two points is the shortest, is a synthetical proposition. For my concept of *straight* contains nothing of magnitude (quantity), but a quality only. The concept of the *shortest* is, therefore, purely adventitious, and cannot be deduced from the concept of the straight line by any analysis whatsoever. The aid of intuition, therefore, must be called in, by which alone the synthesis is possible.

It is true that some few propositions, presupposed by the geometrician, are really analytical, and depend on the principle of contradiction: but then they serve only, like identical propositions, to form the chain of the method, and not as principles. Such are the propositions, $a = a$, the whole is equal to itself, or $(a + b) > a$, that the whole is greater than its part. And even these, though they are valid according to mere concepts, are only admitted in mathematics, because they can be represented in intuition. What often makes us believe that the predicate of such apodictic judgments is contained in our concept, and the judgment therefore analytical, is merely the ambiguous character of the expression. We are told that we *ought* to join in thought a certain predicate to a given concept, and this necessity is inherent in the concepts themselves. But the question is not what we *ought* to join to the given concept, but what we *really think* in it, though confusedly only, and then it becomes clear that the predicate is no doubt inherent in those concepts by necessity, not, however, as thought in the concept itself, but by means of an intuition, which must be added to the concept.

2. *Natural science (physica) contains synthetical judgments* a priori *as principles.* I shall adduce, as examples, a few propositions only, such as, that in all changes of the material world the quantity of matter always remains unchanged: or that in all communication of motion, action and reaction must always equal each other. It is clear not only that both convey necessity, and that, therefore, their origin is *a priori,* but also that they are synthetical propositions. For in the concept of matter I do not conceive its permanency, but only its presence in the space which it fills. I therefore go beyond the concept of matter in order to join something to it *a priori,* which I did not before conceive *in it.* The proposi-

tion is, therefore, not analytical, but synthetical, and yet *a priori,* and the same applies to the other propositions of the pure part of natural science.

3. *Metaphysic,* even if we look upon it as hitherto a tentative science only, which, however, is indispensable to us, owing to the very nature of human reason, is meant to *contain synthetical knowledge a priori.* Its object is not at all merely to analyse such concepts as we make to ourselves of things *a priori,* and thus to explain them analytically, but to expand our knowledge *a priori.* This we can only do by means of concepts which add something to a given concept that was not contained in it; nay, we even attempt, by means of synthetical judgments *a priori,* to go so far beyond a given concept that experience itself cannot follow us: as, for instance, in the proposition that the world must have a first beginning. Thus, according at least to its intentions, metaphysics consists merely of synthetical propositions *a priori.*

The General Problem of Pure Reason

Much is gained if we are able to bring a number of investigations under the formula of one single problem. For we thus not only facilitate our own work by defining it accurately, but enable also everybody else who likes to examine it to form a judgment, whether we have really done justice to our purpose or not. Now the real problem of pure reason is contained in the question, *How are synthetical judgments* a priori *possible?*

That metaphysic has hitherto remained in so vacillating a state of ignorance and contradiction is entirely due to people not having thought sooner of this problem, or perhaps even of a distinction between *analytical* and *synthetical* judgments. The solution of this problem, or a sufficient proof that a possibility which is to be explained does in reality not exist at all, is the question of life or death to metaphysic. *David Hume,* who among all philosophers approached nearest to that problem, though he was far from conceiving it with sufficient definiteness and universality, confining his attention only to the synthetical proposition of the connection of an effect with its causes *(principium causalitatis),* arrived at the conclusion that such a proposition *a priori* is entirely impossible. According to his conclusions, everything which we call metaphysic would turn out to be a mere delusion of reason, fancying that it knows by itself what in reality is only borrowed from experience, and has assumed by mere habit the appearance of necessity. If he had grasped our problem in all its universality, he would never have thought of an assertion which destroys all pure philosophy, because he would have perceived that, according to his argument, no pure mathematical science was possible either, on account of its certainly containing synthetical propositions *a priori;* and from such an assertion his good sense would probably have saved him.

On the solution of our problem depends, at the same time, the possibility of the pure employment of reason, in establishing and carrying out all sciences which contain a theoretical knowledge *a priori* of objects, i.e. the answer to the questions

How is pure mathematical science possible?

How is pure natural science possible?

As these sciences really exist, it is quite proper to ask, *How* they are possible? for *that* they must be possible, is proved by their reality.

But as to *metaphysic,* the bad progress which it has hitherto made, and the impossibility of asserting of any of the metaphysical systems yet brought forward that it really exists, so far as its essential aim is concerned, must fill every one with doubts as to its possibility.

Yet, in a certain sense, this *kind of knowledge* also must be looked upon as given, and though not as a science, yet as a natural disposition *(metaphysica naturalis)* metaphysic is real. For human reason, without being moved merely by the conceit of omniscience, advances irresistibly, and urged on by its own need, to questions such as cannot be answered by any empirical employment of reason, or by principles thence derived, so that we may really say, that all men, as soon as their reason became ripe for speculation, have at all times possessed some kind of metaphysic, and will always continue to possess it. And now it will also have to answer the question

How is metaphysic possible, as a natural disposition? that is, how does the nature of universal human reason give rise to questions which pure reason proposes to itself, and which it is urged on by its own need to answer as well as it can?

As, however, all attempts which have hitherto been made at answering these natural questions (for instance, whether the world has a beginning, or exists from all eternity) have always led to inevitable contradictions, we cannot rest satisfied with the mere natural disposition to metaphysic, that is, with the pure faculty of reason itself, from which some kind of metaphysic (whatever it may be) always arises; but it must be possible to arrive with it at some certainty as to our either knowing or not knowing its objects; that is, we must either decide that we can judge of the objects of these questions, or of the power or want of power of reason, in deciding anything upon them,—therefore that we can either enlarge our pure reason with certainty, or that we have to impose on it fixed and firm limits. This last question, which arises out of the former more general problem, would properly assume this form,

How is metaphysic possible, as a science?

The critique of reason leads, therefore, necessarily, to true science, while its dogmatical use, without criticism, lands us in groundless assertions, to which others, equally specious, can always be opposed, that is, in *scepticism.*

Nor need this science be very formidable by its great prolixity, for it has not to deal with the objects of reason, the variety of which is infinite, but with reason only, and with problems, suggested by reason and placed before it, not by the nature of things, which are different from it, but by its own nature; so that, if reason has only first completely understood its own power, with reference to objects given to it in experience, it will have no difficulty in determining completely and safely the extent and limits of its attempted application beyond the limits of all experience.

We may and must therefore regard all attempts which have hitherto been made at building up a metaphysic dogmatically, as *non-avenu*. For the mere analysis of the concepts that dwell in our reason *a priori*, which has been attempted in one or other of those metaphysical systems, is by no means the aim, but only a preparation for true metaphysic, namely, the answer to the question, how we can enlarge our knowledge *a priori* synthetically; nay, it is utterly useless for that purpose, because it only shows what is contained in those concepts, but not by what process *a priori* we arrive at them, in order thus to determine the validity of their employment with reference to all objects of knowledge in general. Nor does it require much self-denial to give up these pretensions considering that the undeniable and, in the dogmatic procedure, inevitable contradictions of reason with itself, have long deprived every system of metaphysic of all authority. More firmness will be required in order not to be deterred by difficulties from within and resistance from without, from trying to advance a science, indispensable to human reason (a science of which we may lop off every branch, but will never be able to destroy the root), by a treatment entirely opposed to all former treatments, which promises, at last, to ensure the successful and fruitful growth of metaphysical science.

Idea and Division of an Independent Science under the Name of Critique of Pure Reason

It will now be seen how there can be a special science serving as a critique of pure reason. [Every kind of knowledge is called pure, if not mixed with anything heterogeneous. But more particularly is that knowledge called absolutely pure, which is not mixed up with any experience or sensation, and is therefore possible entirely *a priori*.] [1] Reason is the faculty which supplies the principles of knowledge *a priori*. Pure reason therefore is that faculty which supplies the principles of knowing anything entirely *a priori*. . . .

I call all knowledge *transcendental* which is occupied not so much with objects, as with our *a priori* concepts of objects.[2] A system of such concepts might be called Transcendental Philosophy. But for the present this is again too great an undertaking. We should have to treat therein completely both of analytical knowledge, and of synthetical knowledge *a priori*, which is more than we intend to do, being satisfied to carry on the analysis so far only as is indispensably necessary in order to recognise in their whole extent the principles of synthesis *a priori* which alone concern us. This investigation which should be called a transcendental critique, but not a systematic doctrine, is all we are occupied with at present. It is not meant to extend our knowledge, but only to rectify it, and to become the test of the value of all *a priori* knowledge. . . .

If we wish to carry out a proper division of our science systematically, it must contain first *a doctrine of the elements*, secondly, *a doctrine of the method* of pure

---

[1] [The two preceding sentences are omitted in B.—*Ed.*]

[2] ['. . . as with our manner of knowing objects, so far as this is meant to be possible *a priori*' in B.—*Ed.*]

reason. Each of these principal divisions will have its subdivisions, the grounds of which cannot however be explained here. So much only seems necessary for previous information, that there are two stems of human knowledge, which perhaps may spring from a common root, unknown to us, viz. *sensibility* and the *understanding*, objects being given by the former and thought by the latter. If our sensibility should contain *a priori* representations, constituting conditions under which alone objects can be given, it would belong to transcendental philosophy, and the doctrine of this transcendental sense-perception would necessarily form the first part of the doctrine of elements, because the conditions under which alone objects of human knowledge can be given must precede those under which they are thought.

III.*

TRANSCENDENTAL AESTHETIC

Whatever the process and the means may be by which knowledge reaches its objects, there is one that reaches them directly, and forms the ultimate material of all thought, viz. intuition (Anschauung). This is possible only when the object is given, and the object can be given only (to human beings at least) through a certain affection of the mind (Gemüth).

This faculty (receptivity) of receiving representations (Vorstellungen), according to the manner in which we are affected by objects, is called sensibility (Sinnlichkeit).

Objects therefore are given to us through our sensibility. Sensibility alone supplies us with intuitions (Anschauungen). These intuitions become thought through the understanding (Verstand), and hence arise conceptions (Begriffe). All thought therefore must, directly or indirectly, go back to intuitions (Anschauungen), i.e. to our sensibility, because in no other way can objects be given to us.

The effect produced by an object upon the faculty of representation (Vorstellungsfähigkeit), so far as we are affected by it, is called sensation (Empfindung). An intuition (Anschauung) of an object, by means of sensation, is called empirical. The undefined object of such an empirical intuition is called phenomenon (Erscheinung).

In a phenomenon I call that which corresponds to the sensation its *matter;* but that which causes the manifold matter of the phenomenon to be perceived as arranged in a certain order, I call its *form.*

Now it is clear that it cannot be sensation again through which sensations are arranged and placed in certain forms. The matter only of all phenomena is given us *a posteriori;* but their form must be ready for them in the mind

---

* From *Critique of Pure Reason*, A 19–23, B 33–38; A 26–28, B 42–44; A 32–36, B 49–53.

(Gemüth) *a priori,* and must therefore be capable of being considered as separate from all sensations.

I call all representations in which there is nothing that belongs to sensation, *pure* (in a transcendental sense). The pure form therefore of all sensuous intuitions, that form in which the manifold elements of the phenomena are seen in a certain order, must be found in the mind *a priori.* And this pure form of sensibility may be called the pure intuition (Anschauung).

Thus, if we deduct from the representation (Vorstellung) of a body what belongs to the thinking of the understanding, viz. substance, force, divisibility, etc., and likewise what belongs to sensation, viz. impermeability, hardness, colour, etc., there still remains something of that empirical intuition (Anschauung), viz. extension and form. These belong to pure intuition, which *a priori,* and even without a real object of the senses or of sensation, exists in the mind as a mere form of sensibility.

The science of all the principles of sensibility *a priori* I call *Transcendental Æsthetic.* There must be such a science, forming the first part of the Elements of Transcendentalism, as opposed to that which treats of the principles of pure thought, and which should be called *Transcendental Logic.*

In Transcendental Æsthetic therefore we shall first isolate sensibility, by separating everything which the understanding adds by means of its concepts, so that nothing remains but empirical intuition (Anschauung).

Secondly, we shall separate from this all that belongs to sensation (Empfindung), so that nothing remains but pure intuition (reine Anschauung) or the mere form of the phenomena, which is the only thing which sensibility *a priori* can supply. In the course of this investigation it will appear that there are, as principles of *a priori* knowledge, two pure forms of sensuous intuition (Anschauung), namely, *Space* and *Time.* We now proceed to consider these more in detail.

Of Space

By means of our external sense, a property of our mind (Gemüth), we represent to ourselves objects as external or outside ourselves, and all of these in space. It is within space that their form, size, and relative position are fixed or can be fixed. The internal sense by means of which the mind perceives itself or its internal state, does not give an intuition (Anschauung) of the soul (Seele) itself, as an object, but it is nevertheless a fixed form under which alone an intuition of its internal state is possible, so that whatever belongs to its internal determinations (Bestimmungen) must be represented in relations of time. Time cannot be perceived (angeschaut) externally, as little as space can be perceived as something within us.

What then are space and time? Are they real beings? Or, if not that, are they determinations of relations of things, but such as would belong to them even if they were not perceived? Or lastly, are they determinations and relations which are inherent in the form of intuition only, and therefore in the subjective nature of our mind, without which such predicates as space and time would never be ascribed to anything?. . . .

a. Space does not represent any quality of objects by themselves, or objects in their relation to one another; i.e. space does not represent any determination which is inherent in the objects themselves, and would remain, even if all subjective conditions of intuition were removed. For no determinations of objects, whether belonging to them absolutely or in relation to others, can enter into our intuition before the actual existence of the objects themselves, that is to say, they can never be intuitions *a priori.*

b. Space is nothing but the form of all phenomena of the external senses; it is the subjective condition of our sensibility, without which no external intuition is possible for us. If then we consider that the receptivity of the subject, its capacity of being affected by objects, must necessarily precede all intuition of objects, we shall understand how the form of all phenomena may be given before all real perceptions, may be, in fact, *a priori* in the soul, and may, as a pure intuition, by which all objects must be determined, contain, prior to all experience, principles regulating their relations.

It is therefore from the human standpoint only that we can speak of space, extended objects, etc. If we drop the subjective condition under which alone we can gain external intuition, that is, so far as we ourselves may be affected by objects, the representation of space means nothing. For this predicate is applied to objects only in so far as they appear to us, and are objects of our senses. The constant form of this receptivity, which we call sensibility, is a necessary condition of all relations in which objects, as without us, can be perceived; and, when abstraction is made of these objects, what remains is that pure intuition which we call space. As the peculiar conditions of our sensibility cannot be looked upon as conditions of the possibility of the objects themselves, but only of their appearance as phenomena to us, we may say indeed that space comprehends all things which may appear to us externally, but not all things by themselves, whether perceived by us or not, or by any subject whatsoever. We cannot judge whether the intuitions of other thinking beings are subject to the same conditions which determine our intuition, and which for us are generally binding. If we add the limitation of a judgment to a subjective concept, the judgment gains absolute validity. The proposition 'all things are beside each other in space,' is valid only under the limitation that things are taken as objects of our sensuous intuition (Anschauung). If I add that limitation to the concept and say 'all things, as external phenomena, are beside each other in space,' the rule obtains universal and unlimited validity. Our discussions teach therefore the reality, i.e. the objective validity, of space with regard to all that can come to us externally as an object, but likewise the *ideality* of space with regard to things, when they are considered in themselves by our reason, and independent of the nature of our senses. We maintain the empirical reality of space, so far as every possible external experience is concerned, but at the same time its transcendental ideality; that is to say, we maintain that space is nothing, if we leave out of consideration the condition of a possible experience, and accept it as something on which things by themselves are in any way dependent. . . .

Of Time

a. Time is not something existing by itself, or inherent in things as an objective determination of them, something therefore that might remain when abstraction is made of all subjective conditions of intuition. For in the former case it would be something real, without being a real object. In the latter it could not, as a determination or order inherent in things themselves, be antecedent to things as their condition, and be known and perceived by means of synthetical propositions *a priori.* All this is perfectly possible if time is nothing but a subjective condition under which alone intuitions take place within us. For in that case this form of internal intuition can be represented prior to the objects themselves, that is, *a priori.*

b. Time is nothing but the form of the internal sense, that is, of our intuition of ourselves, and of our internal state. Time cannot be a determination peculiar to external phenomena. It refers neither to their shape, nor their position, etc., it only determines the relation of representations in our internal state. And exactly because this internal intuition supplies no shape, we try to make good this deficiency by means of analogies, and represent to ourselves the succession of time by a line progressing to infinity, in which the manifold constitutes a series of one dimension only; and we conclude from the properties of this line as to all the properties of time, with one exception, i.e. that the parts of the former are simultaneous, those of the latter successive. From this it becomes clear also, that the representation of time is itself an intuition, because all its relations can be expressed by means of an external intuition.

c. Time is the formal condition, *a priori,* of all phenomena whatsoever. Space, as the pure form of all external intuition, is a condition, *a priori,* of external phenomena only. But, as all representations, whether they have for their objects external things or not, belong by themselves, as determinations of the mind, to our inner state, and as this inner state falls under the formal conditions of internal intuition, and therefore of time, time is a condition, *a priori,* of all phenomena whatsoever, and is so directly as a condition of internal phenomena (of our mind) and thereby indirectly of external phenomena also. If I am able to say, *a priori,* that all external phenomena are in space, and are determined, *a priori,* according to the relations of space, I can, according to the principle of the internal sense, make the general assertion that all phenomena, that is, all objects of the senses, are in time, and stand necessarily in relations of time.

If we drop our manner of looking at ourselves internally, and of comprehending by means of that intuition all external intuitions also within our power of representation, and thus take objects as they may be by themselves, then time is nothing. Time has objective validity with reference to phenomena only, because these are themselves things which we accept as objects of our senses; but time is no longer objective, if we remove the sensuous character of our intuitions, that is to say, that mode of representation which is peculiar to ourselves, and speak of things in general. Time is therefore simply a subjective condition of our (human) intuition (which is always sensuous, that is so far as we are affected by objects), but by itself, apart from the subject, nothing. Nevertheless, with respect to all phenomena, that is, all things which can come within our experience, time is necessarily objective. We cannot say that all things are in time, because, if we speak of things in general, nothing is said about the manner of intuition, which is the real condition under which time enters into our representation of things. If therefore this condition is added to the concept, and if we say that all things as phenomena (as objects of sensuous intuition) are in time, then such a proposition has its full objective validity and *a priori* universality.

What we insist on therefore is the empirical reality of time, that is, its objective validity, with reference to all objects which can ever come before our senses. And as our intuition must at all times be sensuous, no object can ever fall under our experience that does not come under the conditions of time. What we deny is, that time has any claim on absolute reality, so that, without taking into account the form of our sensuous condition, it should by itself be a condition or quality inherent in things; for such qualities which belong to things by themselves can never be given to us through the senses. This is what constitutes the transcendental ideality of time, so that, if we take no account of the subjective conditions of our sensuous intuitions, time is nothing, and cannot be added to the objects by themselves (without their relation to our intuition) whether as subsisting or inherent. This ideality of time, however, as well as that of space, should not be confounded with the deceptions of our sensations, because in their case we always suppose that the phenomenon to which such predicates belong has objective reality, which is not at all the case here, except so far as this objective reality is purely empirical, that is, so far as the object itself is looked upon as a mere phenomenon.

IV.*

TRANSCENDENTAL LOGIC

Of Logic in General

Our knowledge springs from two fundamental sources of our soul; the first receives representations (receptivity of impressions), the second is the power of knowing an object by these representations (spontaneity of concepts). By the first an object is *given* us, by the second the object is *thought*, in relation

---

* From *Critique of Pure Reason*, A 50–52; B 74–76.

to that representation which is a mere determination of the soul. Intuition therefore and concepts constitute the elements of all our knowledge, so that neither concepts without an intuition corresponding to them, nor intuition without concepts can yield any real knowledge.

Both are either pure or empirical. They are empirical when sensation, presupposing the actual presence of the object, is contained in it. They are pure when no sensation is mixed up with the representation. The latter may be called the material of sensuous knowledge. Pure intuition therefore contains the form only by which something is seen, and pure conception the form only by which an object is thought. Pure intuitions and pure concepts only are possible *a priori,* empirical intuitions and empirical concepts *a posteriori.*

We call *sensibility* the *receptivity* of our soul, or its power of receiving representations whenever it is in any wise affected, while the *understanding,* on the contrary, is with us the power of producing representations, or the *spontaneity* of knowledge. We are so constituted that our intuition must always be sensuous, and consist of the mode in which we are affected by objects. What enables us to think the objects of our sensuous intuition is the understanding. Neither of these qualities or faculties is preferable to the other. Without sensibility objects would not be given to us, without understanding they would not be thought by us. *Thoughts without contents are empty, intuitions without concepts are blind.* Therefore it is equally necessary to make our concepts sensuous, i.e. to add to them their object in intuition, as to make our intuitions intelligible, i.e. to bring them under concepts. These two powers or faculties cannot exchange their functions. The understanding cannot see, the senses cannot think. By their union only can knowledge be produced. But this is no reason for confounding the share which belongs to each in the production of knowledge. On the contrary, they should always be carefully separated and distinguished, and we have therefore divided the science of the rules of sensibility in general, i.e. aesthetic, from the science of the rules of the understanding in general, i.e. logic. . . .

V.*

TRANSCENDENTAL ANALYTIC

Metaphysical Deduction of the Categories

General logic, as we have often said, takes no account of the contents of our knowledge, but expects that representations will come from elsewhere in order to be turned into concepts by an analytical process. Transcendental logic, on the contrary, has before it the manifold contents of sensibility *a priori,* supplied by transcendental aesthetic as the material for the concepts of the

---

* From *Critique of Pure Reason,* A 76–80, B 102–106; A 92–94, B 124–127; A 110–114.

pure understanding, without which those concepts would be without any contents, therefore entirely empty. It is true that space and time contain what is manifold in the pure intuition *a priori,* but they belong also to the conditions of the receptivity of our mind under which alone it can receive representations of objects, and which therefore must affect the concepts of them also. The spontaneity of our thought requires that what is manifold in the pure intuition should first be in a certain way examined, received, and connected, in order to produce a knowledge of it. This act I call *synthesis.*

In its general sense, I understand by synthesis the act of arranging different representations together, and of comprehending what is manifold in them under one form of knowledge. Such a synthesis is pure, if the manifold is not given empirically, but *a priori* (as in time and space). Before we can proceed to an analysis of our representations, these must first be given, and, as far as their contents are concerned, no concepts can arise analytically. Knowledge is first produced by the synthesis of what is manifold (whether given empirically or *a priori*). That knowledge may at first be crude and confused and in need of analysis, but it is synthesis which really collects the elements of knowledge, and unites them to a certain extent. It is therefore the first thing which we have to consider, if we want to form an opinion on the first origin of our knowledge.

We shall see hereafter that synthesis in general is the mere result of what I call the faculty of imagination, a blind but indispensable function of the soul, without which we should have no knowledge whatsoever, but of the existence of which we are scarcely conscious. But to reduce this synthesis to concepts is a function that belongs to the understanding, and by which the understanding supplies us for the first time with knowledge properly so called.

Pure synthesis in its most general meaning gives us the pure concept of the understanding. By this pure synthesis I mean that which rests on the foundation of what I call synthetical unity *a priori.* Thus our counting (as we best perceive when dealing with higher numbers) is a synthesis according to concepts, because resting on a common ground of unity, as for instance, the decade. The unity of the synthesis of the manifold becomes necessary under this concept.

By means of analysis different representations are brought under one concept, a task treated of in general logic; but how to bring, not the representations, but the pure synthesis of representations, under concepts, that is what transcendental logic means to teach. The *first* that must be given us *a priori* for the sake of knowledge of all objects, is the manifold in pure intuition. The *second* is, the synthesis of the manifold by means of imagination. But this does not yet produce true knowledge. The concepts which impart unity to this pure synthesis and consist entirely in the representation of this necessary synthetical unity, add the *third* contribution towards the knowledge of an object, and rest on the understanding.

The same function which imparts unity to various representations in one judgment imparts unity likewise to the mere synthesis of various representations in one intuition, which in a general way may be called the pure concept of the understanding. The same understanding, and by the same operations by which in concepts it achieves through analytical unity the logical form of a judgment, introduces also, through the synthetical unity of the manifold in intuition, a transcendental element into its representations. They are therefore called pure concepts of the understanding, and they refer *a priori* to objects, which would be quite impossible in general logic.

In this manner there arise exactly so many pure concepts of the understanding which refer *a priori* to objects of intuition in general, as there were in our table logical functions in all possible judgments, because those functions completely exhaust the understanding, and comprehend every one of its faculties. Borrowing a term of Aristotle, we shall call these concepts *categories,* our intention being originally the same as his, though widely diverging from it in its practical application.

TABLE OF CATEGORIES

I

Of Quantity
Unity
Plurality
Totality

II

Of Quality
Reality
Negation
Limitation

III

Of Relation
Of Inherence and Subsistence
(*substantia et accidens*)
Of Causality and Dependence
(cause and effect)
Of Community (reciprocity
between agent and patient)

IV

Of Modality
Possibility—Impossibility
Existence—Non-existence
Necessity—Contingency

. This then is a list of all original pure concepts of synthesis, which belong to the understanding *a priori,* and for which alone it is called pure understanding; for it is by them alone that it can understand something in the manifold of intuition, that is, think an object in it. . . .

Transcendental Deduction of the Categories[1]

Two ways only are possible in which synthetical representations and their objects can agree, can refer to each other with necessity, and so to say meet each other. Either it is the object alone that makes the representation possible, or it is the representation alone that makes the object possible. In the former case their relation is empirical only, and the representation therefore never possible *a priori.* This applies to phenomena with reference to whatever in them belongs to sensation. In the latter case, though representation by itself (for we do not speak here of its causality by means of the will) cannot produce its object so far as its existence is concerned, nevertheless the representation determines the object *a priori,* if through it alone it is possible to know anything as an object. To know a thing as an object is possible only under two conditions. First, there must be intuition by which the object is given us, though as a phenomenon only, secondly, there must be a concept by which an object is thought as corresponding to that intuition. From what we have said before it is clear that the first condition, namely, that under which alone objects can be seen, exists, so far as the form of intuition is concerned, in the soul *a priori.* All phenomena therefore must conform to that formal condition of sensibility, because it is through it alone that they appear, that is, that they are given and empirically seen.

Now the question arises whether there are not also antecedent concepts *a priori,* forming conditions under which alone something can be, if not seen, yet thought as an object in general; for in that case all empirical knowledge of objects would necessarily conform to such concepts, it being impossible that anything should become an object of experience without them. All experience contains, besides the intuition of the senses by which something is given, a concept also of the object, which is given in intuition as a phenomenon. Such concepts of objects in general therefore must form conditions *a priori* of all knowledge produced by experience, and the objective validity of the categories, as being such concepts *a priori,* rests on this very fact that by them alone, so far as the form of thought is concerned, experience becomes possible. If by them only it is possible to think any object of experience, it follows that they refer by necessity and *a priori* to all objects of experience.

There is therefore a principle for the transcendental deduction of all concepts *a priori* which must guide the whole of our investigation, namely, that all must be recognized as conditions *a priori* of the possibility of experience, whether of intuition, which is found in it, or of thought. Concepts which supply the objective ground of the possibility of experience are for that very reason necessary. An analysis of the experience in which they are found would not be a deduction, but a mere illustration, because they would there have an accidental character only. Nay, without their original relation to all possible

---

[1] [The first three paragraphs appear in both A and B; the remainder was omitted from the Second Edition.—*Ed.*]

experience in which objects of knowledge occur, their relation to any single object would be quite incomprehensible. . . .

There is but one experience in which all perceptions are represented as in permanent and regular connection, as there is but one space and one time in which all forms of phenomena and all relations of being or not being take place. If we speak of different experiences, we only mean different perceptions so far as they belong to one and the same general experience. It is the permanent and synthetical unity of perceptions that constitutes the form of experience, and experience is nothing but the synthetical unity of phenomena according to concepts.

Unity of synthesis, according to empirical concepts, would be purely accidental, nay, unless these were founded on a transcendental ground of unity, a whole crowd of phenomena might rush into our soul, without ever forming real experience. All relation between our knowledge and its objects would be lost at the same time, because that knowledge would no longer be held together by general and necessary laws; it would therefore become thoughtless intuition, never knowledge, and would be to us the same as nothing.

The conditions *a priori* of any possible experience in general are at the same time conditions of the possibility of any objects of our experience. Now I maintain that the categories of which we are speaking are nothing but the conditions of thought which make experience possible, as much as space and time contain the conditions of that intuition which forms experience. These categories therefore are also fundamental concepts by which we think objects in general for the phenomena, and have therefore *a priori* objective validity. This is exactly what we wish to prove.

The possibility, nay the necessity of these categories rests on the relation between our whole sensibility, and therefore all possible phenomena, and that original apperception in which everything must be necessarily subject to the conditions of the permanent unity of self-consciousness, that is, must submit to the general functions of that synthesis which we call synthesis according to concepts, by which alone our apperception can prove its permanent and necessary identity *a priori*. Thus the concept of cause is nothing but a synthesis of that which follows in temporal succession, with other phenomena, but a synthesis according to concepts: and without such a unity which rests on a rule *a priori*, and subjects all phenomena to itself, no permanent and general, and therefore necessary unity of consciousness would be formed in the manifold of our perceptions. Such perceptions would then belong to no experience at all, they would be without an object, a blind play of representations,—less even than a dream.

All attempts therefore at deriving those pure concepts of the understanding from experience, and ascribing to them a purely empirical origin, are perfectly vain and useless. I shall not dwell here on the fact that a concept of cause, for instance, contains an element of necessity, which no experience can ever supply, because experience, though it teaches us that after one phenomenon something else follows habitually, can never teach us that it follows necessarily, nor that we could *a priori,* and without any limitation, derive from it, as a condition, any conclusion as to what must follow. And thus I ask with reference to that empirical rule of association, which must always be admitted if we say that everything in the succession of events is so entirely subject to rules that nothing ever happens without something preceding it on which it always follows,—What does it rest on, if it is a law of nature, nay, how is that very association possible? You call the ground for the possibility of the association of the manifold, so far as it is contained in the objects themselves, the *affinity* of the manifold. I ask, therefore, how do you make that permanent affinity by which phenomena stand, nay, must stand, under permanent laws, conceivable to yourselves?

According to my principles it is easily conceivable. All possible phenomena belong, as representations, to the whole of our possible self-consciousness. From this, as a transcendental representation, numerical identity is inseparable and *a priori* certain, because nothing can become knowledge except by means of that original apperception. As this identity must necessarily enter into the synthesis of the whole of the manifold of phenomena, if that synthesis is to become empirical knowledge, it follows that the phenomena are subject to conditions *a priori* to which their synthesis (in apprehension) must always conform. The representation of a general condition according to which something manifold *can* be arranged (with uniformity) is called *a rule,* if it *must* be so arranged, *a law.* All phenomena therefore stand in a permanent connection according to necessary laws, and thus possess that transcendental affinity of which the empirical is a mere consequence.

It sounds no doubt very strange and absurd that nature should have to conform to our subjective ground of apperception, nay, be dependent on it, with respect to her laws. But if we consider that what we call nature is nothing but a whole of phenomena, not a thing by itself, but a number of representations in our soul, we shall no longer be surprised that we only see her through the fundamental faculty of all our knowledge, namely, the transcendental apperception, and in that unity without which it could not be called the object (or the whole) of all possible experience, that is, nature. We shall thus also understand why we can recognise this unity *a priori,* and therefore as necessary, which would be perfectly impossible if it were given by itself and independent of the first sources of our own thinking. In that case I could not tell whence we should take the synthetical propositions of such general unity of nature. They would have to be taken from the objects of nature themselves, and as this could be done empirically only, we could derive from it none but an accidental unity, which is very different from that necessary connection which we mean when speaking of nature.

VI.*

ANALYTIC OF PRINCIPLES

Of the Highest Principle of All Synthetical Judgments

The explanation of the possibility of synthetical judgments is a subject of which general logic knows nothing, not even its name, while in a transcendental logic it is the most important task of all, nay, even the only one, when we have to consider the possibility of synthetical judgments *a priori,* their conditions, and the extent of their validity. For when that task is accomplished, the object of transcendental logic, namely, to determine the extent and limits of the pure understanding, will have been fully attained.

In forming an analytical judgment I remain within a given concept, while predicating something of it. If what I predicate is affirmative, I only predicate of that concept what is already contained in it; if it is negative, I only exclude from it the opposite of it. In forming synthetical judgments, on the contrary, I have to go beyond a given concept, in order to bring something together with it, which is totally different from what is contained in it. Here we have neither the relation of identity nor of contradiction, and nothing in the judgment itself by which we can discover its truth or its falsehood.

Granted, therefore, that we must go beyond a given concept in order to compare it synthetically with another, something else is necessary in which, as in a third, the synthesis of two concepts becomes possible. What, then, is that third? What is the medium of all synthetical judgments? It can only be that in which all our concepts are contained, namely, the internal sense and its *a priori* form, time. The synthesis of representations depends on imagination, but their synthetical unity, which is necessary for forming a judgment, depends on the unity of apperception. It is here therefore that the possibility of synthetical judgments, and (as all the three contain the sources of representations *a priori*) the possibility of pure synthetical judgments also, will have to be discovered; nay, they will on these grounds be necessary, if any knowledge of objects is to be obtained that rests entirely on a synthesis of representations.

If knowledge is to have any objective reality, that is to say, if it is to refer to an object, and receive by means of it any sense and meaning, the object must necessarily be given in some way or other. Without that all concepts are empty. We have thought in them, but we have not, by thus thinking, arrived at any knowledge. We have only played with representations. To give an object, if this is not meant again as mediate only, but if it means to represent something immediately in intuition, is nothing else but to refer the representation of the object to experience (real or possible). Even space and time, however pure these concepts may be of all that is empirical, and however certain it is that they are represented in the mind entirely *a priori,* would lack nevertheless all objective validity, all sense and meaning, if we could not show the ne-

---

* From *Critique of Pure Reason,* A 154–158, B 193–197.

cessity of their use with reference to all objects of experience. Nay, their representation is a pure schema, always referring to that reproductive imagination which calls up the objects of experience, without which objects would be meaningless. The same applies to all concepts without any distinction.

It is therefore the *possibility of experience* which alone gives objective reality to all our knowledge *a priori*. Experience, however, depends on the synthetical unity of phenomena, that is, on a synthesis according to concepts of the object of phenomena in general. Without it, it would not even be knowledge, but only a rhapsody of perceptions, which would never grow into a connected text according to the rules of an altogether coherent (possible) consciousness, nor into a transcendental and necessary unity of apperception. Experience depends therefore on *a priori* principles of its form, that is, on general rules of unity in the synthesis of phenomena, and the objective reality of these (rules) can always be shown by their being the necessary conditions in all experience; nay, even in the possibility of all experience. Without such a relation synthetical propositions *a priori* would be quite impossible, because they have no third medium, that is, no object in which the synthetical unity of their concepts could prove their objective reality.

Although we know therefore a great deal *a priori* in synthetical judgments with reference to space in general, or to the figures which productive imagination traces in it, without requiring for it any experience, this our knowledge would nevertheless be nothing but a playing with the cobwebs of our brain, if space were not to be considered as the condition of phenomena which supply the material for external experience. Those pure synthetical judgments, therefore refer always, though mediately only, to possible experience, or rather to the possibility of experience, on which alone the objective validity of their synthesis is founded.

As therefore experience, being an empirical synthesis, is in its possibility the only kind of knowledge that imparts reality to every other synthesis, this other synthesis, as knowledge *a priori*, possesses truth (agreement with its object) on this condition only, that it contains nothing beyond what is necessary for the synthetical unity of experience in general.

The highest principle of all synthetical judgments is therefore this, that every object is subject to the necessary conditions of a synthetical unity of the manifold of intuition in a possible experience.

Thus synthetical judgments *a priori* are possible, if we refer the formal conditions of intuition *a priori*, the synthesis of imagination, and the necessary unity of it in a transcendental apperception, to a possible knowledge in general, given in experience, and if we say that the conditions of the possibility of experience in general are at the same time conditions of the possibility of the objects of experience themselves, and thus possess objective validity in a synthetical judgment *a priori*.

Of the Ground of Induction and of the Law of Universal Causation *

Of the Ground of Induction

§1. Induction, properly so called, as distinguished from those mental operations, sometimes though improperly designated by the name, which I have attempted in the preceding chapter to characterise, may, then, be summarily defined as Generalisation from Experience. It consists in inferring from some individual instances in which a phenomenon is observed to occur, that it occurs in all instances of a certain class; namely, in all which *resemble* the former, in what are regarded as the material circumstances.

In what way the material circumstances are to be distinguished from those which are immaterial, or why some of the circumstances are material and others not so, we are not yet ready to point out. We must first observe that there is a principle implied in the very statement of what Induction is; an assumption with regard to the course of nature and the order of the universe; namely, that there are such things in nature as parallel cases; that what happens once will, under a sufficient degree of similarity of circumstances, happen again, and not only again, but as often as the same circumstances recur. This, I say, is an assumption involved in every case of induction. And if we consult the actual course of nature, we find that the assumption is warranted. The universe, so far as known to us, is so constituted, that whatever is true in any one case, is true in all cases of a certain description; the only difficulty is, to find what description.

This universal fact, which is our warrant for all inferences from experience, has been described by different philosophers in different forms of lan-

* From *A System of Logic*, Book III, Chapters III and XXI. First published in 1843.

John Stuart Mill (1806–1873) was a secretary in the East India Company for thirty-five years and later elected to Parliament for three years as a Liberal member. His *System of Logic* attempts a systematic account of the principles of scientific inquiry on empiricist grounds.

guage; that the course of nature is uniform; that the universe is governed by general laws; and the like. One of the most usual of those modes of expression but also one of the most inadequate, is that which has been brought into familiar use by the metaphysicians of the school of Reid and Stewart. The disposition of the human mind to generalise from experience,—a propensity considered by these philosophers as an instinct of our nature,—they usually describe under some such name as "our intuitive conviction that the future will resemble the past." Now it has been well pointed out by Mr. Bailey,[1] that (whether the tendency be or not an original and ultimate element of our nature) Time, in its modifications of past, present, and future, has no concern either with the belief itself, or with the grounds of it. We believe that fire will burn to-morrow, because it burned to-day and yesterday; but we believe, on precisely the same grounds, that it burned before we were born, and that it burns this very day in Cochin-China. It is not from the past to the future, as past and future, that we infer, but from the known to the unknown; from facts observed to facts unobserved; from what we have perceived, or been directly conscious of, to what has not come within our experience. In this last predicament is the whole region of the future; but also the vastly greater portion of the present and of the past.

---

[1] *Essays on the Pursuit of Truth.*

Whatever be the most proper mode of expressing it, the proposition that the course of nature is uniform is the fundamental principle, or general axiom, of Induction. It would yet be a great error to offer this large generalisation as any explanation of the inductive process. On the contrary, I hold it to be itself an instance of induction, and induction by no means of the most obvious kind. Far from being the first induction we make, it is one of the last, or at all events one of those which are latest in attaining strict philosophical accuracy. As a general maxim, indeed, it has scarcely entered into the minds of any but philosophers; nor even by them, as we shall have many opportunities of remarking, have its extent and limits been always very justly conceived. The truth is, that this great generalisation is itself founded on prior generalisations. The obscurer laws of nature were discovered by means of it, but the more obvious ones must have been understood and assented to as general truths before it was ever heard of. We should never have thought of affirming that all phenomena take place according to general laws, if we had not first arrived, in the case of a great multitude of phenomena, at some knowledge of the laws themselves; which could be done no otherwise than by induction. In what sense, then, can a principle, which is so far from being our earliest induction, be regarded as our warrant for all the others? In the only sense in which (as we have already seen) the general propositions which we place at the head of our reasonings when we throw them into syllogisms ever really contribute to their validity. As Archbishop Whately remarks, every induction is a syllogism with the major premise suppressed; or (as I prefer expressing it) every induction may be thrown into the form of a syllogism by supplying a major premise. If this be actually done, the principle which we are now considering, that of the uniformity of the course of nature, will appear as the ultimate major premise of all inductions, and will, therefore, stand to all inductions in the relation in which, as has been shown at so much length, the major proposition of a syllogism always stands to the conclusion; not contributing at all to prove it, but being a necessary condition of its being proved; since no conclusion is proved for which there cannot be found a true major premise.

The statement that the uniformity of the course of nature is the ultimate major premise in all cases of induction may be thought to require some explanation. The immediate major premise in every inductive argument it certainly is not. Of that Archbishop Whately's must be held to be the correct account. The induction, "John, Peter, &c., are mortal, therefore all mankind are mortal," may, as he justly says, be thrown into a syllogism by prefixing as a major premise, (what is at any rate a necessary condition of the validity of the argument,) namely, that what is true of John, Peter, &c., is true of all mankind. But how came we by this major premise? It is not self-evident; nay, in all cases of unwarranted generalisation it is not true. How, then, is it arrived at? Necessarily either by induction or ratiocination; and if by induction, the process, like all other inductive arguments, may be thrown into the form of a syllogism. This previous syllogism it is, therefore, necessary to construct. There is, in the long-run, only one possible construction. The real proof that what is true of John, Peter, &c., is true of all mankind, can only be, that a different supposition would be inconsistent with the uniformity which we know to exist in the course of nature. Whether there would be this inconsistency or not, may be a matter of long and delicate inquiry; but unless there would, we have no sufficient ground for the major of the inductive syllogism. It hence appears, that if we throw the whole course of any inductive argument into a series of syllogisms, we shall arrive by more or fewer steps at an ultimate syllogism, which will have for its major premise the principle or axiom of the uniformity of the course of nature. . . .[1]

----

[1] But though it is a condition of the validity of every induction that there be uniformity in the course of nature, it is not a necessary condition that the uniformity should pervade all nature. It is enough that it pervades the particular class of phenomena to which the induction relates. An induction concerning the motions of the planets, or the properties of the magnet, would not be vitiated though we were to suppose that wind and weather are the sport of chance, provided it be assumed that astronomical and magnetic phenomena are under the dominion of general laws. Otherwise the early experience of mankind would have rested on a very weak foundation; for in the infancy of science it could not be known that *all* phenomena are regular in their course.

Neither would it be correct to say that every induction by which we infer any truth implies the general fact of uniformity *as foreknown*, even in reference to the kind of phenomena concerned. It implies, *either* that this general fact is already known, *or* that we may now know it: as the conclusion, the Duke of Wellington is mortal, drawn from the instances A, B, and C, implies either that we have already concluded all men to be mortal, or that we are now entitled to do so from the same evidence. A vast amount of confusion and paralogism respecting the grounds of Induction would be dispelled by keeping in view these simple considerations.

§3. In order to a better understanding of the problem which the logician must solve if he would establish a scientific theory of Induction, let us compare a few cases of incorrect inductions with others which are acknowledged to be legitimate. Some, we know, which were believed for centuries to be correct, were nevertheless incorrect. That all swans are white, cannot have been a good induction, since the conclusion has turned out erroneous. The experience, however, on which the conclusion rested was genuine. From the earliest records, the testimony of the inhabitants of the known world was unanimous on the point. The uniform experience, therefore, of the inhabitants of the known world, agreeing in a common result, without one known instance of deviation from that result, is not always sufficient to establish a general conclusion.

But let us now turn to an instance apparently not very dissimilar to this. Mankind were wrong, it seems, in concluding that all swans were white; are we also wrong when we conclude that all men's heads grow above their shoulders, and never below, in spite of the conflicting testimony of the naturalist Pliny? As there were black swans, though civilised people had existed for three thousand years on the earth without meeting with them, may there not also be "men whose heads do grow beneath their shoulders," notwithstanding a rather less perfect unanimity of negative testimony from observers? Most persons would answer No; it was more credible that a bird should vary in its colour than that men should vary in the relative position of their principal organs. And there is no doubt that in so saying they would be right; but to say why they are right would be impossible, without entering more deeply than is usually done into the true theory of Induction.

Again, there are cases in which we reckon with the most unfailing confidence upon uniformity, and other cases in which we do not count upon it at all. In some we feel complete assurance that the future will resemble the past, the unknown be precisely similar to the known. In others, however invariable may be the result obtained from the instances which have been observed, we draw from them no more than a very feeble presumption that the like result will hold in all other cases. That a straight line is the shortest distance between two points, we do not doubt to be true even in the region of the fixed stars.[1] When a chemist announces the existence and properties of a newly discovered substance, if we confide in his accuracy, we feel assured that the conclusions he has arrived at will hold universally, though the induction be founded but on a single instance. We do not withhold our assent, waiting for a repetition of the experiment; or if we do, it is from a doubt whether the one experiment was properly made, not whether, if properly made, it would be conclusive. Here, then, is a general law of nature, inferred without hesitation from a single instance; an universal proposition from a singular one. Now mark another case, and contrast it with this. Not all the instances which have been observed since the beginning of the world in support of the general proposition that all crows are black would be deemed a sufficient presumption of the truth of the proposition, to outweigh the testimony of one unexceptionable witness who should affirm that in some region of the earth not fully explored he had caught and examined a crow, and had found it to be grey.

---

[1] In strictness, wherever the present constitution of space exists; which we have ample reason to believe that it does in the region of the fixed stars.

Why is a single instance, in some cases, sufficient for a complete induction, while in others myriads of concurring instances, without a single exception known or presumed, go such a very little way towards establishing an universal proposition? Whoever can answer this question knows more of the philosophy of logic than the wisest of the ancients, and has solved the problem of Induction.

Of the Evidence of the Law of Universal Causation

§1. We have now completed our review of the logical processes by which the laws, or uniformities, of the sequence of phenomena, and those uniformities in their co-existence which depend on the laws of their sequence, are ascertained or tested. As we recognised in the commencement, and have been enabled to see more clearly in the progress of the investigation, the basis of all these logical operations is the law of causation. The validity of all the Inductive Methods depends on the assumption that every event, or the beginning of every phenomenon, must have some cause, some antecedent, on the existence of which it is invariably and unconditionally consequent. In the Method of Agreement this is obvious; that method avowedly proceeding on the supposition that we have found the true cause as soon as we have negatived every other. The assertion is equally true of the Method of Difference. That method authorises us to infer a general law from two instances; one, in which A exists together with a multitude of other circumstances, and B follows; another, in which A being removed, and all other circumstances remaining the same, B is prevented. What, however, does this prove? It proves that B, in the particular instance, cannot have had any other cause than A; but to conclude from this that A was the cause, or that A will on other occasions be followed by B, is only allowable on the assumption that B must have some cause; that among its antecedents in any single instance in which it occurs, there must be one which has the capacity of producing it at other times. This being admitted, it is seen that in the case in question that antecedent can be no other than A; but, that if it be no other than A it must be A, is not proved, by these instances at least, but taken for granted. There is no need to spend time in proving that the same thing is true of the other Inductive Methods. The universality of the law of causation is assumed in them all.

But is this assumption warranted? Doubtless (it may be said) *most* phenomena are connected as effects with some antecedent or cause, that is, are never produced unless some assignable fact has preceded them; but the very circumstance that complicated processes of induction are sometimes necessary, shows that cases exist in which this regular order of succession is not apparent to our unaided apprehension. If, then, the processes which bring these cases within the same category with the rest require that we should assume the universality of the very law which they do not at first sight appear to exemplify, is not this a *petitio principii*? Can we prove a proposition by an argument which takes it for granted? And if not so proved, on what evidence does it rest?

For this difficulty, which I have purposely stated in the strongest terms it will admit of, the school of metaphysicians who have long predominated in this country find a ready salvo. They affirm that the universality of causation is a truth which we cannot help believing; that the belief in it is an instinct, one of the laws of our believing faculty. As the proof of this, they say, and they have nothing else to say, that everybody does believe it; and they number it among the propositions, rather numerous in their catalogue, which may be logically argued against, and perhaps cannot be logically proved, but which are of higher authority than logic, and so essentially inherent in the human mind, that even he who denies them in speculation shows by his habitual practice that his arguments make no impression upon himself.

Into the merits of this question, considered as one of psychology, it would be foreign to my purpose to enter here; but I must protest against adducing, as evidence of the truth of a fact in external nature, the disposition, however strong or however general, of the human mind to believe it. Belief is not proof, and does not dispense with the necessity of proof. . . .

Were we to suppose (what it is perfectly possible to imagine) that the present order of the universe were brought to an end, and that a chaos succeeded in which there was no fixed succession of events, and the past gave no assurance of the future; if a human being were miraculously kept alive to witness this change, he surely would soon cease to believe in any uniformity, the uniformity itself no longer existing. If this be admitted, the belief in uniformity either is not an instinct, or it is an instinct conquerable, like all other instincts, by acquired knowledge. . . .

§2. As was observed in a former place, the belief we entertain in the universality, throughout nature, of the law of cause and effect, is itself an instance of induction, and by no means one of the earliest which any of us, or which mankind in general, can have made. We arrive at this universal law by generalisation from many laws of inferior generality. We should never have had the notion of causation (in the philosophical meaning of the term) as a condition of all phenomena, unless many cases of causation, or, in other words, many partial uniformities of sequence, had previously become familiar. The more obvious of the particular uniformities suggest, and give evidence of, the general uniformity, and the general uniformity, once established, enables us to prove the remainder of the particular uniformities of which it is made up. As, however, all rigorous processes of induction presuppose the general uniformity, our knowledge of the particular uniformities from which it was first inferred was not, of course, derived from rigorous induction, but from the loose and uncertain mode of induction *per enumerationem simplicem;* and the law of universal causation, being collected from results so obtained, cannot itself rest on any better foundation.

It would seem, therefore, that induction *per enumerationem simplicem* not only is not necessarily an illicit logical process, but is in reality the only kind of induction possible; since the more elaborate process depends for its validity on a law, itself obtained in that inartificial mode. Is there not then an inconsistency in contrasting the looseness of one method with the rigidity of another, when that other is indebted to the looser method for its own foundation?

The inconsistency, however, is only apparent. Assuredly, if induction by simple enumeration were an invalid process, no process grounded on it could be valid; just as no reliance could be placed on telescopes if we could not trust our eyes. But though a valid process, it is a fallible one, and fallible in very different degrees: if therefore we can substitute for the more fallible forms of the process an operation grounded on the same process in a less fallible form, we shall have affected a very material improvement. And this is what scientific induction does. . . .

§3. Now the precariousness of the method of simple enumeration is in an inverse ratio to the largeness of the generalisation. The process is delusive and insufficient, exactly in proportion as the subject-matter of the observation is special and limited in extent. As the sphere widens, this unscientific method becomes less and less liable to mislead; and the most universal class of truths, the law of causation for instance, and the principles of number and of geometry, are duly and satisfactorily proved by that method alone, nor are they susceptible of any other proof.

With respect to the whole class of generalisations of which we have recently treated, the uniformities which depend on causation, the truth of the remark just made follows by obvious inference from the principles laid down in the preceding chapters. When a fact has been observed a certain number of times to be true, and is not in any instance known to be false; if we at once affirm that fact as an universal truth or law of nature, without either testing it by any of the four methods of induction, or deducing it from other known laws, we shall in general err grossly; but we are perfectly justified in affirming it as an empirical law, true within certain limits of time, place, and circumstance, provided the number of coincidences be greater than can with any probability be ascribed to chance. The reason for not extending it beyond those limits is, that the fact of its holding true within them may be a consequence of collocations, which cannot be concluded to exist in one place because they exist in another; or may be dependent on the accidental absence of counteracting agencies, which any variation of time, or the smallest change of circumstances, may possibly bring into play. If we suppose, then, the subject-matter of any generalisation to be so widely diffused that there is no time, no place, and no combination of circumstances, but must afford an example either of its truth or of its falsity, and if it be never found otherwise than true, its truth cannot be contingent on any collocations, unless such as exist at all times and places; nor can it be frustrated by any counteracting agencies, unless by such as never actually occur. It is, therefore, an empirical law co-extensive with all human experience, at which point the distinction between empirical laws and laws of nature vanishes, and the proposition takes its place among the most firmly established as well as largest truths accessible to science. . . .

For Further Reading

Austin, J. L., *Philosophical Papers*. Chap. 1. Clarendon Press, Oxford, 1961.

Ayer, A. J., *Language, Truth and Logic*. Second Edition. Chap. 4. Dover Publications, New York, 1950.

Barker, S. F., *Induction and Hypothesis*. Chaps. 8 & 9. Cornell University Press, Ithaca, N.Y., 1957.

Blanshard, B., *Reason and Analysis*. Chap. 10. Allen & Unwin, London, 1962.

Cohen, M. R., *Reason and Nature*. Second Edition. Chap. 3, Sects. III–V. Free Press, New York, 1964.

Dewey, J., *Logic: The Theory of Inquiry*. Chaps. 14 & 20. Henry Holt & Co., New York, 1938.

Ewing, A. C., *The Fundamental Questions of Philosophy*. Chap. 2. Routledge & Kegan Paul, London, 1951.

Grice, H. P., and P. F. Strawson, "In Defence of a Dogma," *The Philosophical Review*, 65 (1956).

Heinemann, F. H., "Truths of Reason and Truths of Fact," *The Philosophical Review*, 17 (1948).

Kneale, W., *Probability and Induction*. Part IV. Clarendon Press, Oxford, 1949.

Langford, C. H., "A Proof that Synthetic A Priori Propositions Exist," *The Journal of Philosophy*, 46 (1949).

Lewis, C. I., *Mind and the World Order*. Chaps. 7–9. Scribner's, New York, 1929.

Lewis, C. I., "A Pragmatic Conception of the *A Priori*," *The Journal of Philosophy*, 20 (1923).

Parkinson, G. H. R., "Necessary Propositions and 'A Priori' Knowledge in Kant," *Mind*, 69 (1960).

Pears, D. F., "Synthetic Necessary Truth," *Mind*, 59 (1950).

Peirce, C. S., *Philosophical Writings of Peirce* (ed. by J. Buchler). Selections 11–13. Dover Publications, New York, 1956.

Plato, *Meno* (numerous translations and editions available).

Quine, W. V., "Necessary Truth" and "Truth by Convention," in *The Ways of Paradox*. Random House, New York, 1966.

Quine, W. V., "Two Dogmas of Empiricism," in *From a Logical Point of View*. Harvard University Press, Cambridge, 1953.

Russell, B., *The Problems of Philosophy*. Chaps. 6–8. Oxford University Press, London, 1912.

Salmon, W. C., "Should We Attempt to Justify Induction?," *Philosophical Studies*, 8 (1957).

Schlick, M., "Is There a Factual a Priori?," in *Readings in Philosophical Analysis* (ed. by H. Feigl and W. Sellars). Appleton-Century-Crofts, New York, 1949.

Sellars, W., *Science, Perception, and Reality*. Chap. 10. Routledge & Kegan Paul, London, 1963.

Toulmin, S., "A Defence of 'Synthetic Necessary Truth'," *Mind*, 58 (1949).

von Wright, G. H., *The Logical Problem of Induction*. Second Edition. Chaps. 5 & 7. Blackwell, Oxford, 1957.

Will, F. L., "Justification and Induction," *The Philosophical Review*, 68 (1959).

Williams, D. C., *The Ground of Induction*. Chaps. 4 & 6. Harvard University Press, Cambridge, 1947.

PART THREE

THE IMMEDIATELY KNOWN:
THE NATURE OF SENSE-PERCEPTION

22 Thomas Hobbes
The Causes and Objects of Sense

[*Cf.* Selection 14, pp. 148–9.]

I.*

The Cause of Sense

1. I have, in the first chapter, defined philosophy to be *knowledge of effects acquired by true ratiocination, from knowledge first had of their causes and generation; and of such causes or generations as may be, from former knowledge of their effects or appearances.* There are, therefore, two methods of philosophy; one, from the generation of things to their possible effects; and the other, from their effects or appearances to some possible generation of the same. In the former of these the truth of the first principles of our ratiocination, namely definitions, is made and constituted by ourselves, whilst we consent and agree about the appellations of things. And this part I have finished in the foregoing chapters; in which, if I am not deceived, I have affirmed nothing, saving the definitions themselves, which hath not good coherence with the definitions I have given; that is to say, which is not sufficiently demonstrated to all those, that agree with me in the use of words and appellations; for whose sake only I have written the same. I now enter upon the other part; which is the finding out by the appearances or effects of nature, which we know by sense, some ways and means by which they may be, I do not say they are, generated. The principles, therefore, upon which the following discourse depends, are not such as we ourselves make and pronounce in general terms, as definitions; but such, as being placed in the things themselves by the Author of Nature, are by us observed in them; and we make use of them in single and particular, not universal propositions. Nor do they impose upon us any necessity of constituting theorems; their use being only, though not without such general propositions as have been already demonstrated, to show us the possibility of some production or generation. Seeing, therefore, the science, which is here taught, hath its principles in the appearances of nature, and endeth in the attaining of some knowledge of natural causes, I have given to this part the title of PHYSICS, or the *Phenomena of Nature*. Now such things as appear, or are shown to us by nature, we call phenomena or appearances.

Of all the phenomena or appearances which are near us, the most admi-

---

* From *De Corpore*, Chap. XXV.

rable is apparition itself, τὸ φαίνεσθαι; namely, that some natural bodies have in themselves the patterns almost of all things, and others of none at all. So that if the appearances be the principles by which we know all other things, we must needs acknowledge sense to be the principle by which we know those principles, and that all the knowledge we have is derived from it. And as for the causes of sense, we cannot begin our search of them from any other phenomenon than that of sense itself. But you will say, by what sense shall we take notice of sense? I answer, by sense itself, namely, by the memory which for some time remains in us of things sensible, though they themselves pass away. For he that perceives that he hath perceived, remembers.

In the first place, therefore, the causes of our perception, that is, the causes of those ideas and phantasms which are perpetually generated within us whilst we make use of our senses, are to be enquired into; and in what manner their generation proceeds. To help which inquisition, we may observe first of all, that our phantasms or ideas are not always the same; but that new ones appear to us, and old ones vanish, according as we apply our organs of sense, now to one object, now to another. Wherefore they are generated, and perish. And from hence it is manifest, that they are some change or mutation in the sentient.

2. Now that all mutation or alteration is motion or endeavour (and endeavour also is motion) in the internal parts of the thing that is altered, hath been proved (in art. 9, chap. VIII) from this, that whilst even the least parts of any body remain in the same situation in respect of one another, it cannot be said that any alteration, unless perhaps that the whole body together hath been moved, hath happened to it; but that it both appeareth and is the same it appeared and was before. Sense, therefore, in the sentient, can be nothing else but motion in some of the internal parts of the organs of sense. For the parts of our body, by which we perceive any thing, are those we commonly call the organs of sense. And so we find what is the subject of our sense, namely, that it is some internal motion in the sentient.

I have shown besides (in chap. IX, art. 7) that no motion is generated but by a body contiguous and moved: from whence it is manifest, that the immediate cause of sense or perception consists in this, that the first organ of sense is touched and pressed. For when the uttermost part of the organ is pressed, it no sooner yields, but the part next within it is pressed also; and, in this manner, the pressure or motion is propagated through all the parts of the organ to the innermost. And thus also the pressure of the uttermost part proceeds from the pressure of some more remote body, and so continually, till we come to that from which, as from its fountain, we derive the phantasm or idea that is made in us by our sense. And this, whatsoever it be, is that we commonly call the object. Sense, therefore, is some internal motion in the sentient, generated by some internal motion of the parts of the object, and propagated through all the media to the innermost part of the organ. By which words I have almost defined what sense is.

Moreover, I have shown (art. 2, chap. XV) that all resistance is endeavour opposite to another endeavour, that is to say, reaction. Seeing, therefore, there is in the whole organ, by reason of its own internal natural motion, some resistance or reaction against the motion which is propagated from the object to the innermost part of the organ, there is also in the same organ an endeavour opposite to the endeavour which proceeds from the object; so that when that endeavour inwards is the last action in the act of sense, then from the reaction, how little soever the duration of it be, a phantasm or idea hath its being; which, by reason that the endeavour is now outwards, doth always appear as something situate without the organ. So that now I shall give you the whole definition of sense, as it is drawn from the explication of the causes thereof and the other of its generation, thus: SENSE *is a phantasm, made by the reaction and endeavour outwards in the organ of sense, caused by an endeavour inwards from the object, remaining for some time more or less.*

3. The *subject* of sense is the *sentient* itself, namely, some living creature; and we speak more correctly, when we say a living creature seeth, than when we say the eye seeth. The object is the thing received; and it is more accurately said, that we see the sun, than that we see the light. For light and colour, and heat and sound, and other qualities which are commonly called sensible, are not objects, but phantasms in the sentients. For a phantasm is the act of sense, and differs no otherwise from sense than *fieri*, that is, being a doing, differs from *factum esse*, that is, being done; which difference, in things that are done in an instant, is none at all; and a phantasm is made in an instant. For in all motion which proceeds by perpetual propagation, the first part being moved moves the second, the second the third, and so on to the last, and that to any distance, how great soever. And in what point of time the first or foremost part proceeded to the place of the second, which is thrust on, in the same point of time the last save one proceeded into the place of the last yielding part; which by reaction, in the same instant, if the reaction be strong enough, makes a phantasm; and a phantasm being made, perception is made together with it.

4. The *organs* of sense, which are in the sentient, are such parts thereof, that if they be hurt, the very generation of phantasms is thereby destroyed, though all the rest of the parts remain entire. Now these parts in the most of living creatures are found to be certain spirits and membranes, which, proceeding from the *pia mater*, involve the brain and all the nerves; also the brain itself, and the arteries which are in the brain; and such other parts, as being stirred, the heart also, which is the fountain of all sense, is stirred together with them. For whensoever the action of the object reacheth the body of the sentient, that action is by some nerve propagated to the brain; and if the nerve leading thither be so hurt or obstructed, that the motion can be propagated no further, no sense follows. Also if the motion be intercepted between the brain and the heart by the defect of the organ by which the action is propagated, there will be no perception of the object.

5. But though all sense, as I have said, be made by reaction, nevertheless it is not necessary that every thing that reacteth should have sense. I know

there have been philosophers, and those learned men, who have maintained that all bodies are endued with sense. Nor do I see how they can be refuted, if the nature of sense be placed in reaction only. And, though by the reaction of bodies inanimate a phantasm might be made, it would nevertheless cease, as soon as ever the object were removed. For unless those bodies had organs, as living creatures have, fit for the retaining of such motion as is made in them, their sense would be such, as that they should never remember the same. And therefore this hath nothing to do with that sense which is the subject of my discourse. For by sense, we commonly understand the judgment we make of objects by their phantasms; namely, by comparing and distinguishing those phantasms; which we could never do, if that motion in the organ, by which the phantasm is made, did not remain there for some time, and make the same phantasm return. Wherefore sense, as I here understand it, and which is commonly so called, hath necessarily some memory adhering to it, by which former and later phantasms may be compared together, and distinguished from one another.

Sense, therefore, properly so called, must necessarily have in it a perpetual variety of phantasms, that they may be discerned one from another. For if we should suppose a man to be made with clear eyes, and all the rest of his organs of sight well disposed, but endued with no other sense; and that he should look only upon one thing, which is always of the same colour and figure, without the least appearance of variety, he would seem to me, whatsoever others may say, to see, no more than I seem to myself to feel the bones of my own limbs by my organs of feeling; and yet those bones are always and on all sides touched by a most sensible membrane. I might perhaps say he were astonished, and looked upon it; but I should not say he saw it; it being almost all one for a man to be always sensible of one and the same thing, and not to be sensible at all of any thing.

6. And yet such is the nature of sense, that it does not permit a man to discern many things at once. For seeing the nature of sense consists in motion; as long as the organs are employed about one object, they cannot be so moved by another at the same time, as to make by both their motions one sincere phantasm of each of them at once. And therefore two several phantasms will not be made by two objects working together, but only one phantasm compounded from the action of both.

Besides, as when we divide a body, we divide its place; and when we reckon many bodies, we must necessarily reckon as many places; and contrarily, as I have shown in the seventh chapter; so what number soever we say there be of times, we must understand the same number of motions also; and as oft as we count many motions, so oft we reckon many times. For though the object we look upon be of divers colours, yet with those divers colours it is but one varied object, and not variety of objects.

Moreover, whilst those organs which are common to all the senses, such as are those parts of every organ which proceed in men from the root of the nerves to the heart, are vehemently stirred by a strong action from some one object, they are, by reason of the contumacy which the motion, they have already, gives them against the reception of all other motion, made the less fit to receive any other impression from whatsoever other objects, to what sense soever those objects belong. And hence it is, that an earnest studying of one object, takes away the sense of all other objects for the present. For *study* is nothing else but a possession of the mind, that is to say, a vehement motion made by some one object in the organs of sense, which are stupid to all other motions as long as this lasteth; according to what was said by Terence, *"Populus studio stupidus in funambulo animum occuparat."* For what is *stupor* but that which the Greeks call ἀναισθησία, that is, a cessation from the sense of other things? Wherefore at one and the same time, we cannot by sense perceive more than one single object; as in reading, we see the letters successively one by one, and not all together, though the whole page be presented to our eye; and though every several letter be distinctly written there, yet when we look upon the whole page at once, we read nothing.

From hence it is manifest, that every endeavour of the organ outwards, is not to be called sense, but that only, which at several times is by vehemence made stronger and more predominant than the rest; which deprives us of the sense of other phantasms, no otherwise than the sun deprives the rest of the stars of light, not by hindering their action, but by obscuring and hiding them with his excess of brightness.

7. But the motion of the organ, by which a phantasm is made, is not commonly called sense, except the object be present. And the phantasm remaining after the object is removed or past by, is called *fancy*, and in Latin *imaginatio*; which word, because all phantasms are not images, doth not fully answer the signification of the word *fancy* in its general acceptation. Nevertheless I may use it safely enough, by understanding it for the Greek Φαντασία.

IMAGINATION therefore is nothing else but *sense decaying*, or *weakened*, by the absence of the object. But what may be the cause of this decay or weakening? Is the motion the weaker, because the object is taken away? If it were, then phantasms would always and necessarily be less clear in the imagination, than they are in sense; which is not true. For in dreams, which are the imaginations of those that sleep, they are no less clear than in sense itself. But the reason why in men waking the phantasms of things past are more obscure than those of things present, is this, that their organs being at the same time moved by other present objects, those phantasms are the less predominant. Whereas in sleep, the passages being shut up, external action doth not at all disturb or hinder internal motion.

If this be true, the next thing to be considered, will be, whether any cause may be found out, from the supposition whereof it will follow, that the passage is shut up from the external objects of sense to the internal organ. I suppose, therefore, that by the continual action of objects, to which a reaction of the organ, and more especially of the spirits, is necessarily consequent, the organ is wearied, that is, its parts are no longer moved by the spirits without some pain; and consequently the nerves being abandoned and grown slack, they retire to their fountain, which is the cavity either of the brain or of the heart; by which means the action which proceeded by the nerves is necessarily intercepted. For action upon a patient, that retires from it, makes but little impression at the first; and at last, when the nerves are by little and little slackened, none at all. And therefore there is no more reaction, that is, no more sense, till the organ being refreshed by rest, and by a supply of new spirits recovering strength and motion, the sentient awaketh. And thus it seems to be always, unless some other preternatural cause intervene; as heat in the internal parts from lassitude, or from some disease stirring the spirits and other parts of the organ in some extra-ordinary manner.

8. Now it is not without cause, nor so casual a thing as many perhaps think it, that phantasms in this their great variety proceed from one another; and that the same phantasms sometimes bring into the mind other phantasms like themselves, and at other times extremely unlike. For in the motion of any continued body, one part follows another by cohesion; and therefore, whilst we turn our eyes and other organs successively to many objects, the motion which was made by every one of them remaining, the phantasms are renewed as often as any one of those motions comes to be predominant above the rest; and they become predominant in the same order in which at any time formerly they were generated by sense. So that when by length of time very many phantasms have been generated within us by sense, then almost any thought may arise from any other thought; insomuch that it may seem to be a thing indifferent and casual, which thought shall follow which. But for the most part this is not so uncertain a thing to waking as to sleeping men. For the thought or phantasm of the desired end brings in all the phantasms, that are means conducing to that end, and that in order backwards from the last to the first, and again forwards from the beginning to the end. But this supposes both appetite, and judgment to discern what means conduce to the end, which is gotten by experience; and experience is store of phantasms, arising from the sense of very many things. For φαντάζεσθαι and *meminisse, fancy,* and *memory,* differ only in this, that memory supposeth the time past, which fancy doth not. In memory, the phantasms we consider are as if they were worn out with time; but in our fancy we consider them as they are; which distinction is not of the things themselves, but of the considerations of the sentient. For there is in memory something like that which happens in looking upon things at a great distance; in which as the small parts of the object are not discerned, by reason of their remoteness; so in memory many accidents and places and parts of things, which were formerly perceived by sense, are by length of time decayed and lost.

The perpetual arising of phantasms, both in sense and imagination, is that which we commonly call discourse of the mind, and is common to men with other living creatures. For he that thinketh, compareth the phantasms that pass, that is, taketh notice of their likeness or unlikeness to one another. And as he that observes readily the likenesses of things of different natures, or that are very remote from one another, is said to have a good fancy; so he is said to have a good judgment, that finds out the unlikenesses or differences of things that are like one another. Now this observation of differences is not perception made by a common organ of sense, distinct from sense or perception properly so called, but is memory of the differences of particular phantasms remaining for some time; as the distinction between hot and lucid, is nothing else but the memory both of a heating, and of an enlightening object. . . .

II.*

Sense and Its Objects

Chapter I.
 . . . 7. Of the powers of the *mind* there be two sorts, *cognitive, imaginative,* or *conceptive* and *motive*; and first of *cognitive.*

For the understanding of what I mean by the power *cognitive,* we must remember and acknowledge that there be in our minds continually certain *images* or conceptions of the things without us, insomuch that if a man could be alive, and all the rest of the world annihilated, he should nevertheless retain the *image* thereof, and all those things which he had before seen or perceived in it; every one by his own experience knowing, that the *absence* or *destruction* of things once imagined doth not cause the *absence* or *destruction* of the *imagination* itself. This *imagery* and *representations* of the qualities of the thing without, is that we call our *conception, imagination, ideas, notice* or *knowledge* of them; and the faculty or power by which we are capable of such knowledge, is that I here call *cognitive power,* or *conceptive,* the power of knowing or conceiving.

Chapter II.
 1. Having declared what I mean by the word *conception,* and other words equivalent thereunto, I come to the *conceptions* themselves, to shew their *differences,* their *causes,* and the *manner of the production,* so far as is necessary for this place.

2. Originally all *conceptions* proceed from the *action* of the thing itself, whereof it is the conception: now when the action is *present,* the conception it produceth is also called *sense*; and the thing by whose action the same is produced, is called the *object of the sense.*

3. By our several *organs* we have several *conceptions* of several qualities in the objects; for by *sight* we have a conception or image composed of *colour* and *figure,* which is all the notice and knowledge the object imparteth to us of its nature by the eye. By *hearing* we have a conception called *sound,* which is all the knowledge we have of the quality of the object from the ear. And so the rest of the senses are also conceptions of several qualities, or natures of their objects.

---

* From *Human Nature,* Chaps. I & II. Completed in 1640 and first published in 1650.

4. Because the *image* in vision consisting of *colour* and *shape* is the knowledge we have of the qualities of the object of that sense; it is no hard matter for a man to fall into this opinion, that the same *colour* and *shape* are the *very qualities themselves*; and for the same cause, that *sound* and *noise* are the *qualities of the bell*, or of the air. And this opinion hath been so long received, that the *contrary* must needs appear a great paradox; and yet the introduction of *species visible* and *intelligible* (which is necessary for the maintenance of that opinion) passing to and fro from the *object,* is *worse* than any paradox, as being a plain *impossibility.* I shall therefore endeavour to make plain these points:

That the subject wherein colour and image are inherent, is *not* the *object* or thing seen.

That there is nothing *without us* (really) which we call an *image* or colour.

That the said image or colour is but an *apparition* unto us of the *motion,* agitation, or alteration, which the *object* worketh in the *brain,* or spirits, or some internal substance of the head.

That as in *vision,* so also in conceptions that arise from the *other senses,* the subject of their *inherence* is not the *object,* but the *sentient.*

5. Every man hath so much experience as to have seen the *sun* and the other visible objects by reflection in the *water* and *glasses*; and this alone is sufficient for this conclusion, that *colour* and *image* may be there where the *thing seen* is *not.* But because it may be said that notwithstanding the *image* in the water be not in the object, but a thing merely *phantastical,* yet there may be *colour* really in the thing itself: I will urge further this experience, that divers times men see directly the *same* object *double,* as *two candles* for *one,* which may happen from distemper, or otherwise without distemper if a man will, the organs being either in their right temper, or equally distempered; the *colours* and *figures* in two such images of the same thing *cannot be inherent* therein, because the thing seen cannot be in *two places.*

One of these images therefore is *not inherent* in the object: but seeing the organs of the sight are then in equal temper or distemper, the *one* of them is no more inherent than the *other*; and consequently *neither* of them both are in the object; which is the first proposition, mentioned in the precedent number.

6. Secondly, that the image of any thing by *reflection* in a *glass* or *water* or the like, is *not* anything *in* or *behind* the glass, or *in* or *under* the water, every man may grant to himself; which is the second proposition.

7. For the third, we are to consider, first that upon every *great agitation* or *concussion* of the *brain* (as it happeneth from a stroke, especially if the stroke be upon the eye) whereby the optic nerve suffereth any great violence, there *appeareth* before the *eyes* a certain light, which light is *nothing without,* but an apparition only, all that is real being the concussion or motion of the parts of that nerve; from which experience we may conclude, that *apparition of light is really nothing but motion* within. If therefore from *lucid bodies* there can be derived *motion,* so as to affect the optic nerve in such manner as is proper thereunto, there will follow an *image* of light somewhere in that line by which the motion was last derived to the eye; that is to say, in the object, if we look directly on it, and

in the glass or water, when we look upon it in the line of reflection, which in effect is the third proposition; namely, that image and colour is but an apparition to us of that motion, agitation, or alteration which the object worketh in the brain or spirits or some *internal* substance in the head.

8. But that *from all lucid*, shining and illuminate bodies, there is a *motion produced* to the eye, and, through the eye, to the *optic* nerve, and so into the *brain*, by which that apparition of *light* or *colour* is affected, is not hard to prove. And first, it is evident that the *fire*, the only lucid body here upon earth, worketh by *motion* equally every way; insomuch as the motion thereof *stopped* or inclosed, it is presently *extinguished*, and no more fire. And further, that that motion, whereby the fire worketh, is *dilation*, and *contraction* of itself *alternately*, commonly called *scintillation* or glowing, is manifest also by experience. From such *motion* in the fire must needs arise a *rejection* or casting from itself of that part of the *medium* which is *contiguous* to it, whereby that part also rejecteth the *next*, and so successively one part beateth back another to the very *eye*; and in the same manner the *exterior* part of the eye presseth the *interior*, (the laws of refraction still observed). Now the interior coat of the eye is nothing else but a piece of the *optic* nerve; and therefore the motion is still continued thereby into the *brain*, and by *resistance* or reaction of the brain, is also a *rebound* into the optic nerve again; which we *not conceiving* as motion or rebound from *within*, do think it is *without*, and call it *light*; as hath been already shewed by the experience of a stroke. We have no reason to doubt, that the fountain of light, the *sun*, worketh by any other ways than the *fire*, at least in this matter. And thus all *vision* hath its original from such *motion* as is here described: for where there is no light, there is no sight; and therefore *colour* also must be the same thing with *light*, as being the effect of the lucid bodies: their *difference* being only this, that when the light cometh *directly* from the fountain to the eye, or *indirectly* by reflection from *clean* and *polite* bodies, and such as have *not* any particular motion internal to alter it, we call it *light*; but when it cometh to the eye by reflection from *uneven*, *rough*, and coarse bodies, or such as are affected with internal motion of their own that may alter it, then we call it *colour*; colour and light differing only in this, that the one is *pure*, and the other *perturbed* light. By that which hath been said, not only the truth of the third proposition, but also the whole manner of producing light and colour, is apparent.

9. As colour is not inherent in the object, but an effect thereof upon us, caused by such motion in the object, as hath been described: so neither is *sound* in the thing we hear, but in ourselves. One manifest sign thereof is, that as a man may *see*, so also he may *hear double* or *treble*, by multiplication of *echoes*, which echoes are sounds as well as the original; and *not* being in one and the *same place*, cannot be *inherent* in the body that maketh them. Nothing can make any thing which is not in itself: the *clapper* hath no *sound* in it, but *motion*, and maketh motion in the internal parts of the bell; so the *bell* hath motion, and not sound, that imparteth *motion* to the *air*; and the *air* hath motion; but not sound; the *air* imparteth motion by the *ear* and *nerve* unto the *brain*; and the brain hath motion but not sound; from the *brain*, it reboundeth back into the

nerves *outward*, and thence it becometh an *apparition without*, which we call *sound*. And to proceed to the *rest* of the *senses*, it is apparent enough, that the *smell* and *taste* of the *same thing*, are *not* the *same* to *every man*; and therefore are not in the thing *smelt* or *tasted*, but in the men. So likewise the *heat* we feel from the fire is manifestly in *us*, and is quite *different* from the heat which is in the *fire*: for *our* heat is *pleasure* or *pain*, according as it is *great* or *moderate*; but in the *coal* there is no such thing. By this the fourth and last proposition is proved, *viz.* that as in vision, so also in conceptions that arise from *other* senses, the subject of their inherence is not in the object, but in the sentient.

10. And from hence also it followeth, that *whatsoever accidents* or qualities, our senses make us think there be in the *world*, they be *not* there, but are *seeming* and *apparitions* only: the things that really *are* in the world without us, are those *motions* by which these seemings are caused. And this is the *great deception of sense*, which also is to be by sense *corrected*: for as sense telleth me, when I see *directly*, that the colour seemeth to *be* in the object; so also sense telleth me, when I see by *reflection*, that colour is not in the object.

23 RENÉ DESCARTES
The Perceptions of the Senses*

[*Cf.* Selections 2, pp. 53–56, and 15, pp. 161–64.]

I.

The Principles of Philosophy. First Part.

PRINCIPLE XLVIII.

That all the objects of our perceptions are to be considered either as things or the affections of things, or else as eternal truths; and the enumeration of things.

I distinguish all the objects of our knowledge either into things or the affections of things[1], or as eternal truths having no existence outside our thought. Of the things we consider as real, the most general are *substance, dura-*

---

* From *The Philosophical Works of Descartes*, Vol. I, trans. by E. S. Haldane and G. R. T. Ross, Cambridge University Press, London, 1931. Reprinted by permission of Cambridge University Press.

[1] 'le premier continent toutes les choses qui ont quelque existence; et l'autre, toutes les veritez qui ne sont rien hors de notre pensée,'—French version. 'I distinguish all the objects of our knowledge into two species; the first contains all things which have an existence; the second all the truths which have no existence outside our thought.' *Tr.*

tion, order, number, and possibly such other similar matters as range through all the classes of real things. I do not however observe more than two ultimate classes of real things—the one is intellectual things, or those of the intelligence, that is, pertaining to the mind, or to thinking substance, the other is material things, or that pertaining to extended substance, i.e. to body. Perception, volition, and every mode of knowing and willing, pertain to thinking substance; while to extended substance pertain magnitude or extension in length, breadth and depth, figure, movement, situation, divisibility into parts themselves divisible, and such like. Besides these, there are, however, certain things which we experience in ourselves and which should be attributed neither to mind nor body alone, but to the close and intimate union that exists between the body and mind as I shall later on explain in the proper place.[1] Such are the appetites of hunger, thirst, etc., and also the emotions or passions of the mind which do not subsist in mind or thought alone, as the emotions of anger, joy, sadness, love, etc.; and, finally all the sensations such as pain, pleasure, light and colour, sounds, odours, tastes, heat, hardness, and all other tactile qualities. . . .

Principle LXVI.

That we also have a clear knowledge of our sensations, affections, and appetites, although we frequently err in the judgments we form of them.

There remain our sensations, affections and appetites, as to which we may likewise have a clear knowledge, if we take care to include in the judgments we form of them that only which we know to be precisely contained in our perception of them, and of which we are intimately conscious. It is, however, most difficult to observe this condition, in regard to our senses at least, because we, everyone of us, have judged from our youth up that all things of which we have been accustomed to have sensation have had an existence outside our thoughts, and that they have been entirely similar to the sensation, that is the idea which we have formed of them. Thus, when, for example, we perceived a certain colour, we thought that we saw something which existed outside of us and which clearly resembled the idea of colour which we then experienced in ourselves, and from the habit of judging in this way we seemed to see this so clearly and distinctly as to be convinced that it is certain and indubitable.

Principle LXVII

That we frequently deceive ourselves in judging of pain itself.

The same is true in regard to all our other sensations, even those which have to do with agreeable sensation and pain. For although we do not believe

---

[1] Part IV. Princ. 189, 190 and 191.—*Tr.* [See below, pp. 275–7.—*Ed.*]

that these feelings exist outside of us, we are not wont to regard them as existing merely in our mind or our perception, but as being in our hands, feet, or some other part of our body. But there is no reason that we should be obliged to believe that the pain, for example, which we feel in our foot, is anything beyond our mind which exists in our foot, nor that the light which we imagine ourselves to see in the sun really is in the sun [as it is in us]; for both these are prejudices of our youth, as will clearly appear in what follows.

Principle LXVIII

How we may distinguish in such matters that which we know clearly from that in which we may err.

But in order that we may here distinguish that which is clear from that which is obscure we ought to observe that we have a clear or distinct knowledge of pain, colour, and other things of the sort when we consider them simply as sensations or thoughts. But when we desire to judge of such matters as existing outside of our mind, we can in no wise conceive what sort of things they are. And when anyone says that he sees colour in a body or feels pain in one of his limbs, it is the same as if he told us that he there saw or felt something but was absolutely ignorant of its nature, or else that he did not know what he saw or felt. For although when he examines his thoughts with less attention he perhaps easily persuades himself that he has some knowledge of it, because he supposes that there is something resembling the sensation of colour or pain which he experiences, yet if he investigates what is represented to him by this sensation of colour or pain appearing as they do to exist in a coloured body or suffering part, he will find that he is really ignorant of it.

Principle LXIX

That we know magnitude, figure, etc. quite differently from colour and pain, etc.

This will be more especially evident if we consider that size in the body which is seen, or figure or movement (local movement at least, for philosophers by imagining other sorts of motion than this, have rendered its nature less intelligible to themselves), or situation, or duration, or number, and the like, which we clearly perceive in all bodies, as has been already described, are known by us in a quite different way from that in which colour is known in the same body, or pain, odour, taste, or any of the properties which, as hitherto mentioned, should be attributed to the senses. For although in observing a body we are not less assured of its existence from the colour which we perceive in its regard than from the figure which bounds it, we yet know this property in it which causes us to call it figured, with much greater clearness than what causes us to say that it is coloured.

Principle LXX

That we may judge in two ways of sensible things, by one of which we shall avoid error, while by the other we shall fall into error.

It is thus evident when we say that we perceive colours in objects, that it is the same as though we said that we perceive something in the objects of whose nature we were ignorant, but which yet caused a very clear and vivid sensation in us, and which is termed the sensation of colours. But there is a great deal of difference in our manner of judging, for, so long as we believe that there is something in objects of which we have no knowledge (that is in things, such as they are, from which sensation comes to us), so far are we from falling into error that, on the contrary, we rather provide against it, for we are less likely to judge rashly of a thing which we have been forewarned we do not know. But when we think we perceive a certain colour in objects although we have no real knowledge of what the name colour signifies, and we can find no intelligible resemblance between the colour which we suppose to exist in objects and what we are conscious of in our senses, yet, because we do not observe this, or remark in these objects certain other qualities like magnitude, figure, number, etc., which we clearly know are or may be in objects, as our senses or understanding show us, it is easy to allow ourselves to fall into the error of holding that what we call colour in objects is something entirely resembling the colour we perceive, and then supposing that we have a clear perception of what we do not perceive at all.

PRINCIPLE LXXI

That the principal cause of error is found in the prejudices of childhood.

It is here that the first and principal of our errors is to be found. For in the first years of life the mind was so closely allied to body that it applied itself to nothing but those thoughts alone by which it was aware of the things which affected the body; nor were these as yet referred to anything existing outside itself, but the fact was merely that pain was felt when the body was hurt, or pleasure experienced when the body received some good, or else if the body was so [slightly] affected that no great good nor evil was experienced, such sensations were encountered as we call tastes, smells, sound, heat, cold, light, colours, etc., which in truth represent nothing to us outside of our mind, but which vary in accordance with the diversities of the parts and modes in which the body is affected.[1] The mind at the same time also perceived magnitudes, figures, movements and the like, which were exhibited to it not as sensations but as things or the modes of things existing, or at least capable of existing, outside thought, although it did not yet observe this distinction between the two. And afterwards when the machine of the body which has been so constituted by nature that it can of its own inherent power turn here and there, by turning fortuitously this way and the other, followed after what was harmful, the mind which was closely allied to it, reflecting on the things which it fol-

---

[1] 'which vary according to the movements which pass from all parts of our body to the part of the brain to which it is closely united.' French version.— *Tr.*

lowed after or avoided, remarked first of all that they existed outside itself, and attributed to them not alone magnitudes, figures, movements, and other such properties which it apprehended as things or modes of things, but also tastes, smells, and the like, the sensations of which it perceived that these things caused in it. And as all other things were only considered in as far as they served for the use of the body in which it was immersed, mind judged that there was more or less reality in each body, according as the impressions made on body were more or less strong. Hence came the belief that there was much more substance or corporeal reality in rocks or metals than in air or water, because the sensations of hardness and weight were much more strongly felt. And thus it was that air was only regarded as anything when it was agitated by some wind, and we experienced it to be either hot or cold. And because the stars did not give more light than tiny lighted candles, it did not hold them to be larger than such flames. Moreover because it did not as yet remark that the earth turned on its own axis, and that the superficies was curved like a sphere, it was more ready to apprehend that it was immovable and that the surface was flat. And we have in this way been imbued with a thousand other such prejudices from infancy, which in later youth we quite forgot we had accepted without sufficient examination, admitting them as though they were of perfect truth and certainty, and as if they had been known by means of our senses or implanted in us by nature.

II.

The Principles of Philosophy. Second Part.

PRINCIPLE I.

What are the reasons for our having a certain knowledge of material things?

Although we are all persuaded that material things exist, yet because we have doubted this before and have placed it in the rank of the prejudices of our childhood, it is now requisite that we should inquire into the reasons through which we may accept this truth with certainty. To begin with we feel that without doubt all our perceptions proceed from some thing which is different from our mind. For it is not in our power to have one perception rather than another, since each one is clearly dependent on the object which affects our senses. It is true that we may inquire whether that object is God, or some other different from God. But inasmuch as we perceive, or rather are stimulated by sense to apprehend clearly and distinctly a matter which is extended in length, breadth, and depth, the various parts of which have various figures and motions, and give rise to the sensations we have of colours, smells, pains, etc., if God immediately and of Himself presented to our mind the idea of this extended matter, or merely permitted it to be caused in us by some other object which possessed no extension, figure, or motion, there would be nothing to prevent Him from being regarded as a deceiver. For we clearly apprehend this matter as different from God, or ourselves, or our mind, and ap-

pear to discern very plainly that the idea of it is due to objects outside of ourselves to which it is absolutely similar. But God cannot deceive us, because
deception is repugnant to His nature, as has been explained. And hence we
must conclude that there is an object extended in length, breadth, and depth,
and possessing all those properties which we clearly perceive to pertain to extended objects. And this extended object is called by us either body or matter.

Principle II.

How we likewise know that the body of man is closely united to the mind.

It may be concluded also that a certain body is more closely united to our
mind than any other, from the fact that pain and other of our sensations occur
without our foreseeing them; and that mind is conscious that these do not arise
from itself alone, nor pertain to it in so far as it is a thinking thing, but only in
so far as it is united to another thing, extended and mobile, which is called the
human body. But this is not the place to explain the matter further.

Principle III.

*That the perceptions of the senses do not teach us what is really in things, but merely
that whereby they are useful or hurtful to man's composite nature.*

It will be sufficient for us to observe that the perceptions of the senses are
related simply to the intimate union which exists between body and mind, and
that while by their means we are made aware of what in external bodies can
profit or hurt this union, they do not present them to us as they are in themselves unless occasionally and accidentally. For [after this observation] we
shall without difficulty set aside all the prejudices of the senses and in this regard rely upon our understanding alone, by reflecting carefully on the ideas
implanted therein by nature.

Principle IV.

*That the nature of body consists not in weight, nor in hardness, nor colour and so on,
but in extension alone.*

In this way we shall ascertain that the nature of matter or of body in its
universal aspect, does not consist in its being hard, or heavy, or coloured, or
one that affects our senses in some other way, but solely in the fact that it is a
substance extended in length, breadth and depth. For as regards hardness we
do not know anything of it by sense, excepting that the portions of the hard
bodies resist the motion of our hands when they come in contact with them;
but if, whenever we moved our hands in some direction, all the bodies in that
part retreated with the same velocity as our hands approached them, we
should never feel hardness; and yet we have no reason to believe that the bodies which recede in this way would on this account lose what makes them bodies. It follows from this that the nature of body does not consist in hardness.
The same reason shows us that weight, colour, and all the other qualities of

the kind that is perceived in corporeal matter, may be taken from it, it remaining meanwhile entire: it thus follows that the nature of body depends on none of these. . . .

III.

The Principles of Philosophy. Fourth Part.

PRINCIPLE CLXXXIX.

What sensation (sensus) is, and how it operates.

We must know, therefore, that although the mind of man informs[1] the whole body, it yet has its principal seat in the brain, and it is there that it not only understands and imagines, but also perceives; and this by means of the nerves which are extended like filaments from the brain to all the other members, with which they are so connected that we can hardly touch any part of the human body without causing the extremities of some of the nerves spread over it to be moved; and this motion passes to the other extremities of those nerves which are collected in the brain round the seat of the soul, as I have just explained quite fully enough in the fourth chapter of the Dioptrics. But the movements which are thus excited in the brain by the nerves, affect in diverse ways the soul or mind, which is intimately connected with the brain, according to the diversity of the motions themselves. And the diverse affections of our mind, or thoughts that immediately arise from these motions, are called perceptions of the senses *(sensuum perceptiones)*, or, in common language, sensations *(sensus)*.

PRINCIPLE CXC

The different kinds of sensation; and firstly of the internal, that is, of the passions or affections (affectibus) of the mind and of the natural appetites.

The diversities of these sensations depend firstly on the diversity in the nerves themselves, and then on the diversities of the motions which occur in the individual nerves. We have not, however, so many individual senses as individual nerves; it is enough merely to distinguish seven chief different kinds, two of which belong to internal senses, and five to the external. The nerves which extend to the stomach, oesophagus, the fauces, and the other interior parts that serve for the satisfaction of our natural wants, constitute one of our internal senses, which is called the natural appetite *(appetitus naturalis)*. The minute nerves, which extend to the heart and the neighbourhood of the heart, operate in the other internal sense which embraces all the emotions *(commotiones)* of the mind or passions, and affections such as joy, sadness, love, hate and the like. For, to take an example, when the blood is pure and well-tempered, so that it dilates in the heart more readily and strongly than usual, this

---

[1] 'is united with,' French version.—*Tr.*

so enlarges and moves the little nerves scattered around the orifices, that there is thence a corresponding movement in the brain which affects the mind with a certain natural sense of cheerfulness; and as often as these same nerves are moved in the same way, even although it be from other causes, they excite in us this same feeling (L. *sensus*, F. *sentiment de joye*). Thus the imagination of the fruition of some good does not contain in itself the sensation of joy, but it causes the animal spirits to pass from the brain to the muscles in which these nerves are inserted; and thus dilating the orifices of the heart, it causes these small nerves to move in the manner which necessarily produces the sensation of joy. Thus, when we are given news the mind first judges of it, and if it is good it rejoices with that intellectual joy which is independent of any emotion *(commotio)* of the body, and which the Stoics did not deny to their wise man [although they wished to regard him as free from all passion]. But as soon as this spiritual joy proceeds [from the understanding] to the imagination, the spirits flow from the brain to the muscles about the heart and these excite a movement in the small nerves by which another motion is excited in the brain which gives the soul the sensation of animal joy *(laetitia animalis)*. In the same way when the blood is so thick that it flows badly into the ventricles of the heart, and is not there sufficiently dilated, it excites in the same nerves a movement quite different from the preceding, which, communicated to the brain, gives a sensation of sadness to the mind, although it is itself perhaps ignorant of the cause of the sadness. And the other causes [which move these little nerves in the same way] may likewise give the same sensation to the soul. But the other movements of the same small nerves produce other affections, such as those of love, hate, fear, anger, &c. in as far as they are merely affections or passions of the mind, that is, in as far as they are confused thoughts which the mind does not have from itself alone, but because it is intimately united to the body, receiving its impressions therefrom. For there is the greatest difference between these passions and the distinct thoughts which we have of what ought to be loved, chosen, or shunned [although they are often found together.] The natural appetites such as hunger, thirst, &c., are likewise sensations excited in the mind by means of the nerves of the stomach, fauces, &c. and are entirely different from the will which we have to eat, drink, &c. [and to do all that we think proper for the conservation of the body]; but because this will or appetition nearly always accompanies them, they are called appetites.

PRINCIPLE CXCI

Of the external senses and first of all of the sense of touch.

As regards the external senses, everyone acknowledges five, because there are five different kinds of objects that stimulate the nerves which are their organs, and because there is the same number of kinds of confused thoughts excited in the soul by these motions in the nerves. In the first place there are nerves terminating in the skin all over the body. The skin serves as a medium by which the nerves can come in contact with any material body whatever, and be moved by these wholes, in one way by their hardness, in another by their gravity, in another by their heat, in another by their humidity &c.; and these nerves excite as many different sensations in the mind as there are different modes by which they are moved, or their ordinary motion is prevented, and from this a corresponding number of tactile qualities derive their names. Besides this, when these nerves are moved a little more vehemently than usual, and yet in such a way that our body is in nowise injured, this causes a sense of gratification which is naturally agreeable to the mind, inasmuch as it gives evidence of the powers of the body to which it is closely joined. But if this action [be strong enough to] cause our body to be in some way hurt, that gives us the sensation of pain. And in this way we see why corporeal pleasure and pain, though absolutely contrary sensations, are almost similar in the objects causing them.

Principle CXCII.

Of Taste.

In the next place the other nerves spread over the tongue and the neighbouring parts, are diversely moved by the particles of the bodies which are separated from one another and float in the saliva in the mouth, and thus cause the diverse tastes to be felt according to the diversity of their own figures.

Principle CXCIII.

Of Smell.

In the third place two nerves or appendages to the brain, for they do not go beyond the skull, are moved by the corporeal particles separated and flying in the air—not indeed by any particles whatsoever, but only by those which, when drawn into the nostrils, are subtle and lively enough to enter the pores of the bones we call the spongy, and thus to reach the nerves. And from the diverse motions of these particles, the diverse sensations of smell arise.

Principle CXCIV.

Of Hearing.

Fourthly, two other nerves hidden in the inward cavities of the ears receive the tremors and vibrations of the whole circumjacent air, for the air agitating the small membranes of the tympanum at the same time disturbs a chain of little bones which are attached, and to which these nerves adhere, and from the diversity of these movements the sensations of different sounds arise.

Principle CXCV.

Of Sight.

Finally the extremities of the optic nerves, composing the covering of the eyes called the retina, are not moved by the air, nor by any other material object, but only by the globules of the second element, from which we derive the sense of light and colours, as I have already sufficiently explained in the Dioptrics and Meteors.

PRINCIPLE CXCVI.

That the soul does not perceive excepting in as far as it is in the brain.

It is however easily proved that the soul feels those things that affect the body not in so far as it is in each member of the body, but only in so far as it is in the brain, where the nerves by their movements convey to it the diverse actions of the external objects which touch the parts of the body [in which they are inserted]. For, in the first place, there are many maladies which, though they affect the brain alone, yet either disorder or altogether take away from us the use of our senses; just like sleep itself which affects the brain alone, and yet every day takes from us during a great part of our time the faculty of perception, which is afterwards restored to us on awakening. Secondly, from the fact that though the brain be healthy [as well as the members in which the organs of the external senses are to be found], if the paths by which the nerves pass from the external parts to the brain are obstructed, that sensation is lost in these external parts of the body. And finally we sometimes feel pain as though it were in certain of our members, and yet its cause is not in these members where it is felt, but in others through which the nerves pass that extend to the brain from the parts where the pain is felt. And this I could prove by innumerable experiments; here, however, one will suffice. When a girl suffering from a serious affection of the hand was visited by the surgeon, her eyes were usually bandaged lest seeing the dressing should have a bad effect upon her. After some 'days, as gangrene set in, her arm had to be cut off from the elbow and several linen cloths tied together were substituted in place of the amputated limb, in such a way that she was quite ignorant of what had been done; meanwhile, however, she had various pains, sometimes in one of the fingers of the hand which was cut off, and sometimes in another. This could clearly only happen because the nerves which previously had been carried all the way from the brain to the hand, and afterwards terminated in the arm near the elbow, were there affected in the same way as it was their function to be stimulated for the purpose of impressing on the mind residing in the brain the sensation of pain in this and that finger. [And this shows clearly that pain in the hand is not felt by the mind inasmuch as it is in the hand, but as it is in the brain.]

PRINCIPLE CXCVII.

That mind is of such a nature that from the motion of the body alone the various sensations can be excited in it.

It may, in the next place, be [easily] proved that our mind is of such a nature that the motions which are in the body are alone sufficient to cause it to have all sorts of thoughts, which do not give us any image of any of the motions which give rise to them; and specially that there may be excited in it those confused thoughts called feelings or sensations *(sensus, sive sensationes)*. For [first of all] we observe that words, whether uttered by the voice or merely written, excite in our minds all sorts of thoughts and emotions. On the same paper, with the same pen and ink, by moving the point of the pen ever so little over the paper in a certain way, we can trace letters which bring to the minds of our readers thoughts of battles, tempests or furies, and the emotions of indignation and sadness; while if the pen be moved in another way, hardly different, thoughts may be given of quite a different kind, viz. those of quietude, peace, pleasantness, and the quite opposite passions of love and joy. Someone will perhaps reply that writing and speech do not immediately excite any passions in the mind, or imaginations of things different from the letters and sounds, but simply so to speak various acts of the understanding; and from these the mind, making them the occasion,[1] then forms for itself the imaginations of a variety of things. But what shall we say of the sensations of what is painful and pleasurable? If a sword moved towards our body cuts it, from this alone pain results which is certainly not less different from the local movement of the sword or of the part of the body which is cut, than are colour or sound or smell or taste. And therefore, as we see clearly that the sensation of pain is easily excited in us from the fact alone that certain parts of our body are locally disturbed by the contact with certain other bodies, we may conclude that our mind is of such a nature that certain local motions can excite in it all the affections belonging to all the other senses.

Principle CXCVIII.

That there is nothing known of external objects by the senses but their figure, magnitude or motion.

Besides this, we observe in the nerves no difference which may cause us to judge that some convey to the brain from the organs of the external sense any one thing rather than another, nor again that anything is conveyed there excepting the local motion of the nerves themselves. And we see that this local motion excites in us not alone the sensations of pleasure or pain, but also the sensations of sound and light. For if we receive a blow in the eye hard enough to cause the vibration to reach the retina, we see myriads of sparks which are yet not outside our eye; and when we place our finger on our ear to stop it, we hear a murmuring sound whose cause cannot be attributed to anything but the agitation of the air which is shut up within it.

Finally we can likewise frequently observe that heat and the other sensible qualities, inasmuch as they are in objects, and also the forms of these bodies which are purely material, such as e.g. the forms of fire, are produced in them by the motions of certain other bodies, and that these again also produce

---

[1] 'understanding the meaning of these words,' French version.—*Tr.*

other motions in other bodies. And we can very well conceive how the movement of one body can be caused by that of another, and diversified by the size,
figure, and situation of its parts, but we can in nowise understand how these
same things (viz. size, figure and motion) can produce something entirely
different in nature from themselves, such as are those substantial forms and
real qualities which many suppose to exist in bodies; nor likewise can we understand how these forms or qualities possess the force adequate to cause motion in other bodies. But since we know that our mind is of such a nature that
the diverse motions of body suffice to produce in it all the diverse sensations
that it has, and as we see by experience that some of the sensations are really
caused by such motions, though we do not find anything but these movements
to pass through the organs of the external senses to the brain, we may conclude that we in no way likewise apprehend that in external objects like light,
colour, smell, taste, sound, heat, cold, and the other tactile qualities, or what
we call their substantial forms, there is anything but the various dispositions of
these objects which have the power of moving our nerves in various ways. . . .

24 BENEDICT SPINOZA
Bodies and Sensations*

*Pt. II, Prop. XIV. The human mind is capable of perceiving a great number of things, and
is so in proportion as its body is capable of receiving a great number of impressions.*

Proof.—The human body (by Post. iii. and vi.) is affected in very many
ways by external bodies, and is capable in very many ways of affecting external bodies. But (II. xii.) the human mind must perceive all that takes place in
the human body; the human mind is, therefore, capable of perceiving a great
number of things, and is so in proportion, &c. Q.E.D.

*Pt. II, Prop. XV. The idea, which constitutes the actual being of the human mind, is not
simple, but compounded of a great number of ideas.*

Proof.—The idea constituting the actual being of the human mind is the
idea of the body (II. xii.), which (Post. i.) is composed of a great number of
complex individual parts. But there is necessarily in God the idea of each individual part whereof the body is composed (II. vii. Coroll.); therefore (II. vii.),
the idea of the human body is composed of these numerous ideas of its component parts. Q.E.D.

*Pt. II, Prop. XVI. The idea of every mode, in which the human body is affected by external
bodies, must involve the nature of the human body, and also the nature of the external body.*

---

* From the *Ethics.*

Proof.—All the modes, in which any given body is affected, follow from the nature of the body affected, and also from the nature of the affecting body (by Ax. i., after the Coroll. of Lemma iii.), wherefore their idea also necessarily (by I. Ax. iv.) involves the nature of both bodies; therefore, the idea of every mode, in which the human body is affected by external bodies, involves the nature of the human body and of the external body. Q.E.D.

Corollary I.—Hence it follows, first, that the human mind perceives the nature of a variety of bodies, together with the nature of its own.

Corollary II.—It follows, secondly, that the ideas, which we have of external bodies, indicate rather the constitution of our own body than the nature of external bodies. I have amply illustrated this in the Appendix to Part I.

Pt. II, Prop. XVII. If the human body is affected in a manner which involves the nature of any external body, the human mind will regard the said external body as actually existing, or as present to itself, until the human body be affected in such a way, as to exclude the existence or the presence of the said external body.

Proof.—This proposition is self-evident, for so long as the human body continues to be thus affected, so long will the human mind (II. xii.) regard this modification of the body—that is (by the last Prop.), it will have the idea of the mode as actually existing, and this idea involves the nature of the external body. In other words, it will have the idea which does not exclude, but postulates the existence or presence of the nature of the external body; therefore the mind (by II. xvi., Coroll. i.) will regard the external body as actually existing, until it is affected, &c. Q.E.D.

Corollary.—The mind is able to regard as present external bodies, by which the human body has once been affected, even though they be no longer in existence or present.

Proof.—When external bodies determine the fluid parts of the human body, so that they often impinge on the softer parts, they change the surface of the last named (Post. v.) hence (Ax. ii., after Coroll. of Lemma iii.) they are refracted therefrom in a different manner from that which they followed before such change; and, further, when afterwards they impinge on the new surfaces by their own spontaneous movement, they will be refracted in the same manner, as though they had been impelled towards those surfaces by external bodies; consequently, they will, while they continue to be thus refracted, affect the human body in the same manner, whereof the mind (II. xii.) will again take cognizance—that is (II. xvii.), the mind will again regard the external body as present, and will do so, as often as the fluid parts of the human body impinge on the aforesaid surfaces by their own spontaneous motion. Wherefore, although the external bodies, by which the human body has once been affected, be no longer in existence, the mind will nevertheless regard them as present, as often as this action of the body is repeated. Q.E.D.

Note.—We thus see how it comes about, as is often the case, that we regard as present things which are not. It is possible that the same result may be brought about by other causes; but I think it suffices for me here to have indicated one possible explanation, just as well as if I had pointed out the true cause. Indeed, I do not think I am very far from the truth, for all my assumptions are based on postulates, which rest, almost without exception, on experience, that cannot be controverted by those who have shown, as we have, that the human body, as we feel it, exists (Coroll. after II. xiii.). Furthermore (II. vii. Coroll., II. xvi. Coroll. ii.), we clearly understand what is the difference between the idea, say, of Peter, which constitutes the essence of Peter's mind, and the idea of the said Peter, which is in another man, say, Paul. The former directly answers to the essence of Peter's own body, and only implies existence so long as Peter exists; the latter indicates rather the disposition of Paul's body than the nature of Peter, and, therefore, while this disposition of Paul's body lasts, Paul's mind will regard Peter as present to itself, even though he no longer exists. Further, to retain the usual phraseology, the modifications of the human body, of which the ideas represent external bodies as present to us, we will call the images of things, though they do not recall the figure of things. When the mind regards bodies in this fashion, we say that it imagines. I will here draw attention to the fact, in order to indicate where error lies, that the imaginations of the mind, looked at in themselves, do not contain error. The mind does not err in the mere act of imagining, but only in so far as it is regarded as being without the idea, which excluded the existence of such things as it imagines to be present to it. If the mind, while imagining non-existent things as present to it, is at the same time conscious that they do not really exist, this power of imagination must be set down to the efficacy of its nature, and not to a fault, especially if this faculty of imagination depend solely on its own nature—that is (I. Def. vii.), if this faculty of imagination be free.

25 GOTTFRIED WILHELM LEIBNIZ
Perceptions as Expressions of the Universe

[*Cf.* Selection 17, in partiçular, pp. 176–7.]

I.*

The Principles of Nature and of Grace (1714)

1. *Substance* is being, capable of action. It is simple or compound. *Simple substance* is that which has no parts. *Compound* substance is a collection of simple substances or *monads*. *Monas* is a Greek word which signifies unity, or that which is one.

---

* From *The Philosophical Works of Leibnitz*, translated and edited by George Martin Duncan; Tuttle, Morehouse & Taylor, New Haven, 1890.

2. Monads, having no parts, cannot be formed or decomposed. They cannot begin or end naturally; and consequently last as long as the universe, which will indeed be changed but will not be destroyed. They cannot have shapes; otherwise they would have parts. And consequently a monad, in itself and at a given moment, could not be distinguished from another except by its internal qualities and actions, which can be nothing else than its *perceptions* (that is, representations of the compound, or of what is external, in the simple), and its *appetitions* (that is, its tendencies from one perception to another), which are the principles of change. For the simplicity of substance does not prevent multiplicity of modifications, which must be found together in this same simple substance, and must consist in the variety of relations to things which are external. Just as in a centre or point, altogether simple as it is, there is found an infinity of angles formed by lines which there meet.

3. Everything in nature is full. There are everywhere simple substances, separated in reality from each other by activities of their own which continually change their relations; and each simple substance, or monad, which forms the centre of a compound substance (as, for example, of an animal) and the principle of its unity, is surrounded by a mass composed of an infinity of other monads, which constitute the body proper of this central monad; and in accordance with the affections of this it represents, as a *centre,* the things which are outside of itself. And this *body* is *organic,* when it forms a sort of automaton or natural machine; which is a machine not only in its entirety, but also in its smallest perceptible parts. And as, because of the plentitude of the world, everything is connected and each body acts upon every other body, more or less according to the distance, and by reaction is itself affected thereby; it follows that each monad is a mirror, living or endowed with internal activity, representative according to its point of view of the universe, and as regulated as the universe itself. And perceptions in the monad spring one from the other, by the law of appetites or by the *final causes of good and evil,* which consist in visible, regulated or unregulated perceptions; just as the changes of bodies and external phenomena spring one from another, by the laws of *efficient causes,* that is, of movements. Thus there is perfect *harmony* between the perceptions of the monad and the movement of bodies, established at the beginning between the system of efficient causes and that of final causes. And in this consists the accord and physical union of the soul and body, although neither one can change the laws of the other.

4. Each monad, with a particular body, makes a living substance. Thus there is not only life everywhere, provided with members or organs, but also there is an infinity of degrees in monads, some dominating more or less over the others. But when the monad has organs so adjusted that by means of them there is clearness and distinctness in the impressions which it receives and consequently in the perceptions which represent them (as, for example, when by means of the shape of the humors of the eyes, the rays of light are concentrated and act with more force); this can extend even to *feeling [sentiment],* that is, even to a perception accompanied by *memory,* that is, one a certain echo of which re-

mains a long time to make itself heard upon occasion; and such a living being is called an *animal*, as its monad is called a soul. And when this soul is elevated to *reason* it is something more sublime and is reckoned among spirits, as will soon be explained.

It is true that animals are sometimes in the condition of simple living beings, and their souls in the condition of simple monads, namely, when their perceptions are not sufficiently distinct to be remembered, as happens in a profound, dreamless sleep, or in a swoon. But perceptions which have become entirely confused must be re-developed in animals, for reasons which I shall shortly (§12) enumerate. Therefore it is well to make a distinction between the *perception*, which is the internal condition of the monad representing external things, and *apperception*, which is *consciousness* or the reflective knowledge of this internal state; the latter not being given to all souls, nor at all times to the same soul. And it is for want of this distinction that the Cartesians have failed, taking no account of the perceptions of which we are not conscious as people take no account of imperceptible bodies. It is this also which made the same Cartesians believe that only spirits are monads, that there is no soul of brutes, and still less other *principles of life*.

And as they shocked too much the common opinion of men by refusing feeling to brutes, they have, on the other hand, accommodated themselves too much to the prejudices of the multitude, by confounding a *long swoon*, caused by a great confusion of perceptions, with *death strictly speaking*, where all perception would cease. This confirmed the ill-founded belief in the destruction of some souls, and the bad opinion of some so-called strong minds, who have contended against the immortality of our soul. . . .

II.*

The Monadology (1714)

14. The passing condition which involves and represents a multiplicity in the unity, or in the simple substance, is nothing else than what is called Perception. This should be carefully distinguished from Apperception or Consciousness, as will appear in what follows. In this matter the Cartesians have fallen into a serious error, in that they treat as non-existent those perceptions of which we are not conscious. It is this also which has led them to believe that spirits alone are Monads and that there are no souls of animals or other Entelechies, and it has led them to make the common confusion between a protracted period of unconsciousness and actual death. They have thus adopted the Scholastic error that souls can exist entirely separated from bodies, and

---

* From *Leibniz: Discourse on Metaphysics, Correspondence with Arnauld and Monadology*, translated by G. R. Montgomery, La Salle, Ill., The Open Court Publishing Company, Reprint Edition, 1962. Reprinted by permission of The Open Court Publishing Company.

have even confirmed ill-balanced minds in the belief that souls are mortal.

15. The action of the internal principle which brings about the change or the passing from one perception to another may be called Appetition. It is true that the desire *(l'appetit)* is not always able to attain to the whole of the perception which it strives for, but it always attains a portion of it and reaches new perceptions.

16. We, ourselves, experience a multiplicity in a simple substance, when we find that the most trifling thought of which we are conscious involves a variety in the object. Therefore all those who acknowledge that the soul is a simple substance ought to grant this multiplicity in the Monad, and Monsieur Bayle should have found no difficulty in it, as he has done in his *Dictionary*, article "Rorarius."

17. It must be confessed, however, that Perception, and that which depends upon it, are inexplicable by mechanical causes, that is to say, by figures and motions. Supposing that there were a machine whose structure produced thought, sensation, and perception, we could conceive of it as increased in size with the same proportions until one was able to enter into its interior, as he would into a mill. Now, on going into it he would find only pieces working upon one another, but never would he find anything to explain Perception. It is accordingly in the simple substance, and not in the composite nor in a machine that the Perception is to be sought. Furthermore, there is nothing besides perceptions and their changes to be found in the simple substance. And it is in these alone that all the internal activities of the simple substance can consist. . . .

III.*

Discourse on Metaphysics (1686)

XXVI. Ideas are all stored up within us. Plato's doctrine of reminiscence.

In order to see clearly what an idea is, we must guard ourselves against a misunderstanding. Many regard the idea as the form or the differentiation of our thinking, and according to this opinion we have the idea in our mind, in so far as we are thinking of it, and each separate time that we think of it anew we have another idea although similar to the preceding one. Some, however, take the idea as the immediate object of thought, or as a permanent form which remains even when we are no longer contemplating it. As a matter of fact our soul has the power of representing to itself any form or nature whenever the occasion comes for thinking about it, and I think that this activity of our soul is, so far as it expresses some nature, form or essence, properly the idea of the thing. This is in us, and is always in us, whether we are thinking of it or no. (Our soul expresses God and the universe and all essences as well as all ex-

* From *op. cit.*

istences.) This position is in accord with my principles that naturally nothing enters into our minds from outside.

It is a bad habit we have of thinking as though our minds receive certain messengers, as it were, or as if they had doors or windows. We have in our minds all those forms for all periods of time because the mind at every moment expresses all its future thoughts and already thinks confusedly of all that of which it will ever think distinctly. Nothing can be taught us of which we have not already in our minds the idea. This idea is as it were the material out of which the thought will form itself. This is what Plato has excellently brought out in his doctrine of reminiscence, a doctrine which contains a great deal of truth, provided that it is properly understood and purged of the error of pre-existence, and provided that one does not conceive of the soul as having already known and thought at some other time what it learns and thinks now. Plato has also confirmed his position by a beautiful experiment.[1] He introduces a small boy, whom he leads by short steps, to extremely difficult truths of geometry bearing on incommensurables, all this without teaching the boy anything, merely drawing out replies by a well arranged series of questions. This shows that the soul virtually knows those things, and needs only to be reminded (animadverted) to recognize the truths. Consequently it possesses at least the idea upon which those truths depend. We may say even that it already possesses those truths, if we consider them as the relations of the ideas.

XXVII. In what respect our souls can be compared to blank tablets and how conceptions are derived from the senses.

Aristotle preferred to compare our souls to blank tablets prepared for writing, and he maintained that nothing is in the understanding which does not come through the senses. This position is in accord with the popular conceptions as Aristotle's positions usually are. Plato thinks more profoundly. Such tenets or practicologies are nevertheless allowable in ordinary use somewhat in the same way as those who accept the Copernican theory still continue to speak of the rising and setting of the sun. I find indeed that these usages can be given a real meaning containing no error, quite in the same way as I have already pointed out that we may truly say particular substances act upon one another. In this same sense we may say that knowledge is received from without through the medium of the senses because certain exterior things contain or express more particularly the causes which determine us to certain thoughts. Because in the ordinary uses of life we attribute to the soul only that which belongs to it most manifestly and particularly, and there is no advantage in going further. When, however, we are dealing with the exactness of metaphysical truths, it is important to recognize the powers and independence of the soul which extend infinitely further than is commonly supposed. In order, therefore, to avoid misunderstandings it would be well to choose separate terms for the two. These expressions which are in the soul whether one is

---

[1] [See Plato's *Meno*, 82a–86c.—*Ed.*]

conceiving of them or not may be called ideas, while those which one conceives of or constructs may be called conceptions, *conceptus*. But whatever terms are used, it is always false to say that all our conceptions come from the so-called external senses, because those conceptions which I have of myself and of my thoughts, and consequently of being, of substance, of action, of identity, and of many others came from an inner experience.

XXVIII. The only immediate object of our perceptions which exists outside of us is God, and in him alone is our light.

In the strictly metaphysical sense no external cause acts upon us excepting God alone, and he is in immediate relation with us only by virtue of our continual dependence upon him. Whence it follows that there is absolutely no other external object which comes into contact with our souls and directly excites perceptions in us. We have in our souls ideas of everything, only because of the continual action of God upon us, that is to say, because every effect expresses its cause and therefore the essences of our souls are certain expressions, imitations or images of the divine essence, divine thought and divine will, including all the ideas which are there contained. We may say, therefore, that God is for us the only immediate external object, and that we see things through him. For example, when we see the sun or the stars, it is God who gives to us and preserves in us the ideas and whenever our senses are affected according to his own laws in a certain manner, it is he, who by his continual concurrence, determines our thinking. God is the sun and the light of souls, *lumen illuminans omnem hominem venientem in hunc mundum*, although this is not the current conception. I think I have already remarked that during the scholastic period many believed God to be the light of the soul, *intellectus agens animae rationalis*, following in this the Holy Scriptures and the fathers who were always more Platonic than Aristotelian in their mode of thinking. The Averroists misused this conception, but others, among whom were several mystic theologians, and William of Saint Amour, also I think, understood this conception in a manner which assured the dignity of God and was able to raise the soul to a knowledge of its welfare.

XXIX. Yet we think directly by means of our own ideas and not through God's.

Nevertheless I cannot approve of the position of certain able philosophers who seem to hold that our ideas themselves are in God and not at all in us. I think that in taking this position they have neither sufficiently considered the nature of substance, which we have just explained, nor the entire extension and independence of the soul which includes all that happens to it, and expresses God, and with him all possible and actual beings in the same way that an effect expresses its cause. It is indeed inconceivable that the soul should think using the ideas of something else. The soul when it thinks of anything must be affected effectively in a certain manner, and it must needs have in itself in advance not only the passive capacity of being thus affected, a capacity already wholly determined, but it must have besides an active power by virtue of which it has always had in its nature the marks of the future production of this thought, and the disposition to produce it at its proper time. All of this shows that the soul already includes the idea which is comprised in any particular thought. . . .

IV.*

Letter to Antoine Arnauld (October 6, 1687)

. . . One thing expresses another, in my use of the term, when there is a constant and regulated relation between what can be said of the one and of the other. It is thus that a projection in perspective expresses a structure. Expression is common to all forms, and is a class of which ordinary perception, animal feeling and intellectual knowledge are species. In ordinary perception and in feeling it is enough that what is divisible and material and what is found common to several beings should be expressed or represented in a single indivisible being, or in the substance which is endowed with a true unity. We cannot at all doubt the possibility of such a representation of several things in a single one, since our own souls furnish us examples; this representation, however, is accompanied by consciousness in a rational soul and becomes then what is called thought.

Now, such expression is found everywhere, because all substances sympathize with one another and receive some proportional change corresponding to the slightest motion which occurs in the whole universe. These changes, however, may be more or less noticeable, as other bodies have more or less relation with ours. I think that M. Descartes would have agreed with this himself, for he would doubtless grant that because of the continuity and divisibility of all matter the slightest movement would have its effect upon neighboring bodies and consequently from body to body to infinity, but in diminishing proportion. Thus, our bodies ought to be affected in some sort by the changes of all others. Now, to all the movements of our bodies certain perceptions or thoughts of our soul, more or less confused, correspond; therefore, the soul also will have some thought of all the movements of the universe, and in my opinion every other soul or substance will have some perception or expression of them. It is true that we do not distinctly perceive all the movements in our body, as for example the movement of the lymph, but to use an example which I have already employed, it is somewhat in the same way that I must have some perception of the motion of every wave upon the shore so that I may perceive what results from the whole; that is to say, that great sound which is heard near the sea. In the same way we feel also some indistinct result from all the movements which go on within us, but, being accustomed to this internal motion, we perceive it clearly and noticeably only when there is a considerable change, as at the beginning of an illness. . . .

---

* From *op. cit.*

26 JOHN LOCKE
The Causes of Ideas of Sensation*

[Also see above, pp. 185–6; 192–3.]

Introduction

6. . . . I must here in the entrance beg pardon of my reader for the frequent use of the word *idea,* which he will find in the following treatise. It being that term which, I think, serves best to stand for whatsoever is the *object* of the understanding when a man thinks, I have used it to express whatever is meant by *phantasm, notion, species,* or *whatever it is which the mind can be employed about in thinking;* and I could not avoid frequently using it.

I presume it will be easily granted me, that there are such *ideas* in men's minds: every one is conscious of them in himself; and men's words and actions will satisfy him that they are in others. . . .

Book II—Chap. VIII. Some Further Considerations Concerning Our Simple Ideas of Sensation

7. To discover the nature of our *ideas* the better, and to discourse of them intelligibly, it will be convenient to distinguish them *as they are ideas or perceptions in our minds; and as they are modifications of matter in the bodies that cause such perceptions in us:* that so we may not think (as perhaps usually is done) that they are exactly the images and resemblances of something inherent in the subject; most of those of sensation being in the mind no more the likeness of something existing without us, than the names that stand for them are the likeness of our ideas, which yet upon hearing they are apt to excite in us.

8. Whatsoever the mind perceives *in itself,* or is the immediate object of perception, thought, or understanding, that I call *idea;* and the power to produce any idea in our mind, I call *quality* of the subject wherein that power is. Thus a snowball having the power to produce in us the ideas of white, cold, and round,—the power to produce those ideas in us, as they are in the snowball, I call qualities; and as they are sensations or perceptions in our understandings, I call them ideas; which *ideas,* if I speak of sometimes as in the things themselves, I would be understood to mean those qualities in the objects which produce them in us.

9. [Qualities thus considered in bodies are,

First, such as are utterly inseparable from the body, in what state soever it be;] and such as in all the alterations and changes it suffers, all the force can be used upon it, it constantly keeps; and such as sense constantly finds in every particle of matter which has bulk enough to be perceived; and the mind finds inseparable from every particle of matter, though less than to make itself singly be perceived by our senses: v.g. Take a grain of wheat, divide it into two

---

* From *An Essay Concerning Human Understanding.*

parts; each part has still solidity, extension, figure, and mobility: divide it again, and it retains still the same qualities; and so divide it on, till the parts become insensible; they must retain still each of them all those qualities. For division (which is all that a mill, or pestle, or any other body, does upon another, in reducing it to insensible parts) can never take away either solidity, extension, figure, or mobility from any body, but only makes two or more distinct separate masses of matter, of that which was but one before; all which distinct masses, reckoned as so many distinct bodies, after division, make a certain number. [These I call *original* or *primary qualities* of body, which I think we may observe to produce simple ideas in us, viz. solidity, extension, figure, motion or rest, and number.

10. *Secondly,* such qualities which in truth are nothing in the objects themselves but powers to produce various sensations in us by their primary qualities, i.e. by the bulk, figure, texture, and motion of their insensible parts, as colours, sounds, tastes, &c. These I call *secondary qualities.* To these might be added a *third* sort, which are allowed to be barely powers; though they are as much real qualities in the subject as those which I, to comply with the common way of speaking, call qualities, but for distinction, secondary qualities. For the power in fire to produce a new colour, or consistency, in *wax* or *clay,*—by its primary qualities, is as much a quality in fire, as the power it has to produce in *me* a new idea or sensation of warmth or burning, which I felt not before,—by the same primary qualities, viz. the bulk, texture, and motion of its insensible parts.]

11. [The next thing to be considered is, how bodies produce ideas in us; and that is manifestly by impulse, the only way which we can conceive bodies to operate in.]

12. If then external objects be not united to our minds when they produce ideas therein; and yet we perceive these *original* qualities in such of them as singly fall under our senses, it is evident that some motion must be thence continued by our nerves, or animal spirits, by some parts of our bodies, to the brains or the seat of sensation, there to produce in our minds the particular ideas we have of them. And since the extension, figure, number, and motion of bodies of an observable bigness, may be perceived at a distance by the sight, it is evident some singly imperceptible bodies must come from them to the eyes, and thereby convey to the brain some motion; which produces these ideas which we have of them in us.

13. After the same manner that the ideas of these original qualities are produced in us, we may conceive that the ideas of *secondary* qualities are also produced, viz. by the operation of insensible particles on our senses. For, it being manifest that there are bodies and good store of bodies, each whereof are so small, that we cannot by any of our senses discover either their bulk, figure, or motion,—as is evident in the particles of the air and water, and others extremely smaller than those; perhaps as much smaller than the particles of air and water, as the particles of air and water are smaller than peas or hailstones;—let us suppose at present that the different motions and figures, bulk

and number, of such particles, affecting the several organs of our senses, produce in us those different sensations which we have from the colours and
smells of bodies; v.g. that a violet, by the impulse of such insensible particles of
matter, of peculiar figures and bulks, and in different degrees and modifications of their motions, causes the ideas of the blue colour, and sweet scent of
that flower to be produced in our minds. It being no more impossible to conceive that God should annex such ideas to such motions, with which they have
no similitude, than that he should annex the idea of pain to the motion of a
piece of steel dividing our flesh, with which that idea hath no resemblance.
14. What I have said concerning colours and smells may be understood also of
tastes and sounds, and other the like sensible qualities; which, whatever reality we by mistake attribute to them, are in truth nothing in the objects themselves, but powers to produce various sensations in us; and depend on those
primary qualities, viz. bulk, figure, texture, and motion of parts [as I have
said].
15. From whence I think it easy to draw this observation,—that the ideas of
primary qualities of bodies are resemblances of them, and their patterns do really exist in the bodies themselves, but the ideas produced in us by these secondary qualities have no resemblance of them at all. There is nothing like our
ideas, existing in the bodies themselves. They are, in the bodies we denominate from them, only a power to produce those sensations in us: and what is
sweet, blue, or warm in idea, is but the certain bulk, figure, and motion of the
insensible parts, in the bodies themselves, which we call so.
16. Flame is denominated hot and light; snow, white and cold; and manna,
white and sweet, from the ideas they produce in us. Which qualities are commonly thought to be the same in those bodies that those ideas are in us, the
one the perfect resemblance of the other, as they are in a mirror, and it would
by most men be judged very extravagant if one should say otherwise. And yet
he that will consider that the same fire that, at one distance produces in us the
sensation of warmth, does, at a nearer approach, produce in us the far different sensation of pain, ought to bethink himself what reason he has to say—
that this idea of warmth, which was produced in him by the fire, is *actually in
the fire;* and his idea of pain, which the same fire produced in him the same
way, is *not* in the fire. Why are whiteness and coldness in snow, and pain not,
when it produces the one and the other idea in us; and can do neither, but by
the bulk, figure, number, and motion of its solid parts?
17. The particular bulk, number, figure, and motion of the parts of fire or
snow are really in them,—whether any one's senses perceive them or no: and
therefore they may be called *real* qualities, because they really exist in those
bodies. But light, heat, whiteness, or coldness, are no more really in them than
sickness or pain is in manna. Take away the sensation of them; let not the eyes
see light or colours, nor the ears hear sounds; let the palate not taste, nor the
nose smell, and all colours, tastes, odours, and sounds, *as they are such particular
ideas,* vanish and cease, and are reduced to their causes, i.e. bulk, figure, and
motion of parts. . . .

22. I have in what just goes before then engaged in physical inquiries a little further than perhaps I intended. But, it being necessary to make the nature of sensation a little understood; and to make the difference between the *qualities* in bodies, and the *ideas* produced by them in the mind, to be distinctly conceived, without which it were impossible to discourse intelligibly of them;—I hope I shall be pardoned this little excursion into natural philosophy; it being necessary in our present inquiry to distinguish the *primary* and *real* qualities of bodies, which are always in them (viz. solidity, extension, figure, number, and motion, or rest, and are sometimes perceived by us, viz. when the bodies they are in are big enough singly to be discerned), from those *secondary* and *imputed* qualities, which are but the powers of several combinations of those primary ones, when they operate without being distinctly discerned;—whereby we may also come to know what ideas are, and what are not, resemblances of something really existing in the bodies we denominate from them.

23. The qualities, then, that are in bodies, rightly considered, are of three sorts:—

First, The bulk, figure, number, situation, and motion or rest of their solid parts. Those are in them, whether we perceive them or not; and when they are of that size that we can discover them, we have by these an idea of the thing as it is in itself; as is plain in artificial things. These I call *primary qualities.*

Secondly, The power that is in any body, by reason of its insensible primary qualities, to operate after a peculiar manner on any of our senses, and thereby produce in *us* the different ideas of several colours, sounds, smells, tastes, &c. These are usually called *sensible qualities.*

Thirdly, The power that is in any body, by reason of the particular constitution of its primary qualities, to make such a change in the bulk, figure, texture, and motion of *another body,* as to make it operate on our senses differently from what it did before. Thus the sun has a power to make wax white, and fire to make lead fluid. [These are usually called *powers.*]

The first of these, as has been said, I think may be properly called real, original, or primary qualities; because they are in the things themselves, whether they are perceived or not: and upon their different modifications it is that the secondary qualities depend.

The other two are only powers to act differently upon other things: which powers result from the different modifications of those primary qualities.

24. But, though the two latter sorts of qualities are powers barely, and nothing but powers, relating to several other bodies, and resulting from the different modifications of the original qualities, yet they are generally otherwise thought of. For the *second* sort, viz. the powers to produce several ideas in us, by our senses, are looked upon as real qualities in the things thus affecting us: but the *third* sort are called and esteemed barely powers. v.g. The idea of heat or light, which we receive by our eyes, or touch, from the sun, are commonly thought real qualities existing in the sun, and something more than mere powers in it. But when we consider the sun in reference to wax, which it melts or blanches, we look on the whiteness and softness produced in the wax, not as

qualities in the sun, but effects produced by powers in it. Whereas, if rightly considered, these qualities of light and warmth, which are perceptions in me when I am warmed or enlightened by the sun, are no otherwise in the sun, than the changes made in the wax, when it is blanched or melted, are in the sun. They are all of them equally *powers in the sun, depending on its primary qualities;* whereby it is able, in the one case, so to alter the bulk, figure, texture, or motion of some of the insensible parts of my eyes or hands, as thereby to produce in me the idea of light or heat; and in the other, it is able so to alter the bulk, figure, texture, or motion of the insensible parts of the wax, as to make them fit to produce in me the distinct ideas of white and fluid.

25. The reason why the one are ordinarily taken for real qualities, and the other only for bare powers, seems to be, because the ideas we have of distinct colours, sounds, &c., containing nothing at all in them of bulk, figure, or motion, we are not apt to think them the effects of these primary qualities; which appear not, to our senses, to operate in their production, and with which they have not any apparent congruity of conceivable connexion. Hence it is that we are so forward to imagine, that those ideas are the resemblances of something really existing in the objects themselves: since sensation discovers nothing of bulk, figure, or motion of parts in their production; nor can reason show how bodies, *by their bulk, figure, and motion,* should produce in the mind the ideas of blue or yellow, &c. But, in the other case, in the operations of bodies changing the qualities one of another, we plainly discover that the quality produced hath commonly no resemblance with anything in the thing producing it; wherefore we look on it as a bare effect of power. For, through receiving the idea of heat or light from the sun, we are apt to think *it* is a perception and resemblance of such a quality in the sun; yet when we see wax, or a fair face, receive change of colour from the sun, we cannot imagine *that* to be the reception or resemblance of anything in the sun, because we find not those different colours in the sun itself. For, our senses being able to observe a likeness or unlikeness of sensible qualities in two different external objects, we forwardly enough conclude the production of any sensible quality in any subject to be an effect of bare power, and not the communication of any quality which was really in the efficient, when we find no such sensible quality in the thing that produced it. But our senses, not being able to discover any unlikeness between the idea produced in us, and the quality of the object producing it, we are apt to imagine that our ideas are resemblances of something in the objects, and not the effects of certain powers placed in the modification of their primary qualities, with which primary qualities the ideas produced in us have no resemblance.

26. To conclude. Beside those before-mentioned primary qualities in bodies, viz. bulk, figure, extension, number, and motion of their solid parts; all the rest, whereby we take notice of bodies, and distinguish them one from another, are nothing else but several powers in them, depending on those primary qualities; whereby they are fitted, either by immediately operating on our bodies to produce several different ideas in us; or else, by operating on other

bodies, so to change their primary qualities as to render them capable of producing ideas in us different from what before they did. The former of these, I think, may be called secondary qualities *immediately perceivable:* the latter, secondary qualities, *mediately perceivable.*

27 GEORGE BERKELEY
The Source of Ideas Perceived by Sense*

[*Cf.* Selection 18, pp. 201–3.]

8. But, say you, though the ideas themselves do not exist without the mind, yet there may be things like them, whereof they are copies or resemblances, which things exist without the mind in an unthinking substance. I answer, an idea can be like nothing but an idea; a color or figure can be like nothing but another color or figure. If we look but ever so little into our thoughts, we shall find it impossible for us to conceive a likeness except only between our ideas. Again, I ask whether those supposed originals or external things, of which our ideas are the pictures or representation, be themselves perceivable or no? If they are, then they are ideas and we have gained our point; but if you say they are not, I appeal to anyone whether it be sense to assert a color is like something which is invisible; hard or soft, like something which is intangible; and so of the rest.

9. Some there are who make a distinction betwixt *primary* and *secondary* qualities. By the former they mean extension, figure, motion, rest, solidity or impenetrability, and number; by the latter they denote all other sensible qualities, as colors, sounds, tastes, and so forth. The ideas we have of these they acknowledge not to be the resemblances of anything existing without the mind, or unperceived, but they will have our ideas of the primary qualities to be patterns or images of things which exist without the mind, in an unthinking substance which they call "matter." By "matter," therefore, we are to understand an inert, senseless substance, in which extension, figure, and motion do actually subsist. But it is evident from what we have already shown that extension, figure, and motion are only ideas existing in the mind, and that an idea can be like nothing but another idea, and that consequently neither they nor their archetypes can exist in an unperceiving substance. Hence it is plain that the very notion of what is called *matter* or *corporeal substance* involves a contradiction in it.

10. They who assert that figure, motion, and the rest of the primary or

---

* From *A Treatise Concerning the Principles of Human Knowledge.*

original qualities do exist without the mind in unthinking substances do at the same time acknowledge that colors, sounds, heat, cold, and suchlike secondary qualities do not—which they tell us are sensations existing in the mind alone, that depend on and are occasioned by the different size, texture, and motion of the minute particles of matter. This they take for an undoubted truth which they can demonstrate beyond all exception. Now, if it be certain that those original qualities are inseparably united with the other sensible qualities, and not, even in thought, capable of being abstracted from them, it plainly follows that they exist only in the mind. But I desire anyone to reflect and try whether he can, by any abstraction of thought, conceive the extension and motion of a body without all other sensible qualities. For my own part, I see evidently that it is not in my power to frame an idea of a body extended and moved, but I must withal give it some color or other sensible quality which is acknowledged to exist only in the mind. In short, extension, figure, and motion, abstracted from all other qualities, are inconceivable. Where therefore the other sensible qualities are, there must these be also, to wit, in the mind and nowhere else.

11. Again, *great* and *small*, *swift* and *slow* are allowed to exist nowhere without the mind, being entirely relative, and changing as the frame or position of the organs of sense varies. The extension, therefore, which exists without the mind is neither great nor small, the motion neither swift nor slow; that is, they are nothing at all. But, say you, they are extension in general, and motion in general: thus we see how much the tenet of extended movable substances existing without the mind depends on that strange doctrine of *abstract ideas*. And here I cannot but remark how nearly the vague and indeterminate description of matter or corporeal substance, which the modern philosophers are run into by their own principles, resembles that antiquated and so much ridiculed notion of *materia prima*, to be met with in Aristotle and his followers. Without extension, solidity cannot be conceived; since, therefore, it has been shown that extension exists not in an unthinking substance, the same must also be true of solidity.

12. That number is entirely the creature of the mind, even though the other qualities be allowed to exist without, will be evident to whoever considers that the same thing bears a different denomination of number as the mind views it with different respects. Thus the same extension is one, or three, or thirty-six, according as the mind considers it with reference to a yard, a foot, or an inch. Number is so visibly relative and dependent on men's understanding that it is strange to think how anyone should give it an absolute existence without the mind. We say one book, one page, one line; all these are equally units, though some contain several of the others. And in each instance it is plain the unit relates to some particular combination of ideas arbitrarily put together by the mind.

13. Unity I know some will have to be a simple or uncompounded idea accompanying all other ideas into the mind. That I have any such idea answering the word *unity* I do not find; and if I had, methinks I could not miss

finding it; on the contrary, it should be the most familiar to my understanding, since it is said to accompany all other ideas and to be perceived by all the ways of sensation and reflection. To say no more, it is an *abstract idea.*

14. I shall further add that, after the same manner as modern philosophers prove certain sensible qualities to have no existence in matter, or without the mind, the same thing may be likewise proved of all other sensible qualities whatsoever. Thus, for instance, it is said that heat and cold are affections only of the mind, and not at all patterns of real beings existing in the corporeal substances which excite them, for that the same body which appears cold to one hand seems warm to another. Now, why may we not as well argue that figure and extension are not patterns or resemblances of qualities existing in matter, because to the same eye at different stations, or eyes of a different texture at the same station, they appear various and cannot, therefore, be the images of anything settled and determinate without the mind? Again, it is proved that sweetness is not really in the sapid thing, because, the thing remaining unaltered, the sweetness is changed into bitter, as in case of a fever or otherwise vitiated palate. Is it not as reasonable to say that motion is not without the mind, since if the succession of ideas in the mind become swifter, the motion, it is acknowledged, shall appear slower without any alteration in any external object? . . .

29. But, whatever power I may have over my own thoughts, I find the ideas actually perceived by sense have not a like dependence on my will. When in broad daylight I open my eyes, it is not in my power to choose whether I shall see or no, or to determine what particular objects shall present themselves to my view; and so likewise as to the hearing and other senses; the ideas imprinted on them are not creatures of my will. There is therefore some *other* will or spirit that produced them.

30. The ideas of sense are more strong, lively, and distinct than those of the imagination; they have likewise a steadiness, order, and coherence, and are not excited at random, as those which are the effects of human wills often are, but in a regular train or series, the admirable connection whereof sufficiently testifies the wisdom and benevolence of its Author. Now the set rules or established methods wherein the mind we depend on excites in us the ideas of sense are called the *laws* of *nature;* and these we learn by experience, which teaches us that such and such ideas are attended with such and such other ideas in the ordinary course of things.

31. This gives us a sort of foresight which enables us to regulate our actions for the benefit of life. And without this we should be eternally at a loss; we could not know how to act anything that might procure us the least pleasure or remove the least pain of sense. That food nourishes, sleep refreshes, and fire warms us; that to sow in the seedtime is the way to reap in the harvest; and in general that to obtain such or such ends, such or such means are conducive—all this we know, not by discovering any necessary connection between our ideas, but only by the observation of the settled laws of nature, without which we should be all in uncertainty and confusion, and a grown

man no more know how to manage himself in the affairs of life than an infant just born.

32. And yet this consistent, uniform working which so evidently displays the goodness and wisdom of that Governing Spirit whose Will constitutes the laws of nature, is so far from leading our thoughts to Him that it rather sends them awandering after second causes. For when we perceive certain ideas of sense constantly followed by other ideas, and we know this is not of our own doing, we forthwith attribute power and agency to the ideas themselves and make one the cause of another, than which nothing can be more absurd and unintelligible. Thus, for example, having observed that when we perceive by sight a certain round, luminous figure, we at the same time perceive by touch the idea or sensation called heat, we do from thence conclude the sun to be the cause of heat. And in like manner perceiving the motion and collision of bodies to be attended with sound, we are inclined to think the latter an effect of the former.

33. The ideas imprinted on the senses by the Author of Nature are called *real things;* and those excited in the imagination, being less regular, vivid, and constant, are more properly termed *ideas* or *images of things* which they copy and represent. But then our sensations, be they never so vivid and distinct, are nevertheless ideas, that is, they exist in the mind, or are perceived by it, as truly as the ideas of its own framing. The ideas of sense are allowed to have more reality in them, that is, to be more strong, orderly, and coherent than the creatures of the mind; but this is no argument that they exist without the mind. They are also less dependent on the spirit; yet still they are *ideas;* and certainly no idea, whether faint or strong, can exist otherwise than in a mind perceiving it. . . .

28 DAVID HUME
Perceptions of the Mind*

[*Cf.* Selection 19, pp. 204–17.]

Bk. I, Pt. I, Sec. I.—Of the Origin of Our Ideas.

All the perceptions of the human mind resolve themselves into two distinct kinds, which I shall call IMPRESSIONS and IDEAS. The difference betwixt these consists in the degrees of force and liveliness with which they strike upon the mind, and make their way into our thought or consciousness. Those perceptions, which enter with most force and violence, we may name *impressions;* and under this name I comprehend all our sensations, passions and emotions,

* From *A Treatise of Human Nature.*

as they make their first appearance in the soul. By *ideas* I mean the faint images of these in thinking and reasoning; such as, for instance, are all the perceptions excited by the present discourse, excepting only, those which arise from the sight and touch, and excepting the immediate pleasure or uneasiness it may occasion. I believe it will not be very necessary to employ many words in explaining this distinction. Every one of himself will readily perceive the difference betwixt feeling and thinking. The common degrees of these are easily distinguished; tho' it is not impossible but in particular instances they may very nearly approach to each other. Thus in sleep, in a fever, in madness, or in any very violent emotions of soul, our ideas may approach to our impressions: As on the other hand it sometimes happens, that our impressions are so faint and low, that we cannot distinguish them from our ideas. But notwithstanding this near resemblance in a few instances, they are in general so very different, that no-one can make a scruple to rank them under distinct heads, and assign to each a peculiar name to mark the difference.[1]

---

[1] I here make use of these terms, *impression and idea,* in a sense different from what is usual, and I hope this liberty will be allowed me. Perhaps I rather restore the word, idea, to its original sense, from which Mr. *Locke* had perverted it, in making it stand for all our perceptions. By the term of impression I would not be understood to express the manner, in which our lively perceptions are produced in the soul, but merely the perceptions themselves; for which there is no particular name either in the *English* or any other language, that I know of.

There is another division of our perceptions, which it will be convenient to observe, and which extends itself both to our impressions and ideas. This division is into SIMPLE and COMPLEX. Simple perceptions or impressions and ideas are such as admit of no distinction or separation. The complex are the contrary to these, and may be distinguished into parts. Tho' a particular colour, taste, and smell are qualities all united together in this apple, 'tis easy to perceive they are not the same, but are at least distinguishable from each other.

Having by these divisions given an order and arrangement to our objects, we may now apply ourselves to consider with the more accuracy their qualities and relations. The first circumstance, that strikes my eye, is the great resemblance betwixt our impressions and ideas in every other particular, except their degree of force and vivacity. The one seem to be in a manner the reflexion of the other; so that all the perceptions of the mind are double, and appear both as impressions and ideas. When I shut my eyes and think of my chamber, the ideas I form are exact representations of the impressions I felt; nor is there any circumstance of the one, which is not to be found in the other. In running over my other perceptions, I find still the same resemblance and representation. Ideas and impressions appear always to correspond to each other. This circumstance seems to me remarkable, and engages my attention for a moment.

Upon a more accurate survey I find I have been carried away too far by the first appearance, and that I must make use of the distinction of perceptions into *simple and complex,* to limit this general decision, *that all our ideas and impressions are resembling.* I observe, that many of our complex ideas never had impressions, that corresponded to them, and that many of our complex impressions never are exactly copied in ideas. I can imagine to myself such a city as the *New Jerusalem,* whose pavement is gold and walls are rubies, tho' I never saw any such. I have seen *Paris;* but shall I affirm I can form such an idea of that city, as will perfectly represent all its streets and houses in their real and just proportions?

I perceive, therefore, that tho' there is in general a great resemblance betwixt our *complex* impressions and ideas, yet the rule is not universally true, that they are exact copies of each other. We may next consider how the case stands with our *simple* perceptions. After the most accurate examination, of which I am capable, I venture to affirm, that the rule here holds without any exception, and that every simple idea has a simple impression, which resembles it; and every simple impression a correspondent idea. That idea of red, which we form in the dark, and that impression, which strikes our eyes in sunshine, differ only in degree, not in nature. That the case is the same with all our simple impressions and ideas, 'tis impossible to prove by a particular enumeration of them. Every one may satisfy himself in this point by running over as many as he pleases. But if any one should deny this universal resemblance, I know no way of convincing him, but by desiring him to shew a simple impression, that has not a correspondent idea, or a simple idea, that has not a correspondent impression. If he does not answer this challenge, as 'tis certain he cannot, we may from his silence and our own observation establish our conclusion.

Thus we find, that all simple ideas and impressions resemble each other; and as the complex are formed from them, we may affirm in general, that these two species of perception are exactly correspondent. Having discover'd this relation, which requires no further examination, I am curious to find some other of their qualities. Let us consider how they stand with regard to their existence, and which of the impressions and ideas are causes, and which effects.

The *full* examination of this question is the subject of the present treatise; and therefore we shall here content ourselves with establishing one general proposition, *That all our simple ideas in their first appearance are deriv'd from simple impressions, which are correspondent to them, and which they exactly represent.*

In seeking for phaenomena to prove this proposition, I find only those of two kinds; but in each kind the phaenomena are obvious, numerous, and conclusive. I first make myself certain, by a new review, of what I have already asserted, that every simple impression is attended with a correspondent idea, and every simple idea with a correspondent impression. From this constant conjunction of resembling perceptions I immediately conclude, that there is a great connexion betwixt our correspondent impressions and ideas, and that the existence of the one has a considerable influence upon that of the other. Such a constant conjunction, in such an infinite number of instances, can never arise from chance; but clearly proves a dependence of the impressions on the ideas, or of the ideas on the impressions. That I may know on which side this dependence lies, I consider the order of their *first appearance;* and find by constant experience, that the simple impressions always take the precedence of their correspondent ideas, but never appear in the contrary order. To give a child an idea of scarlet or orange, of sweet or bitter, I present the objects, or in other words, convey to him these impressions; but proceed not so absurdly, as to endeavour to produce the impressions by exciting the ideas. Our ideas upon their appearance produce not their correspondent impressions, nor do we perceive any colour, or feel any sensation merely upon thinking of them. On the other hand we find, that any impressions either of the mind or body is constantly followed by an idea, which resembles it, and is only different in the degrees of force and liveliness. The constant conjunction of our resembling perceptions, is a convincing proof, that the one are the causes of the other; and this priority of the impressions is an equal proof, that our impressions are the causes of our ideas, not our ideas of our impressions.

To confirm this I consider another plain and convincing phaenomenon; which is, that where-ever by any accident the faculties, which give rise to any impressions, are obstructed in their operations, as when one is born blind or deaf; not only the impressions are lost, but also their correspondent ideas; so that there never appear in the mind the least traces of either of them. Nor is this only true, where the organs of sensation are entirely destroy'd, but likewise where they have never been put in action to produce a particular impression. We cannot form to ourselves a just idea of the taste of a pineapple, without having actually tasted it.

There is however one contradictory phaenomenon, which may prove, that 'tis not absolutely impossible for ideas to go before their correspondent impressions. I believe it will readily be allow'd, that the several distinct ideas of colours, which enter by the eyes, or those of sounds, which are convey'd by the hearing, are really different from each other, tho' at the same time resembling. Now if this be true of different colours, it must be no less so of the different shades of the same colour, that each of them produces a distinct idea, independent of the rest. For if this shou'd be deny'd, 'tis possible, by the continual gradation of shades, to run a colour insensibly into what is most remote from it; and if you will not allow any of the means to be different, you cannot without absurdity deny the extremes to be the same. Suppose therefore a person to have enjoyed his sight for thirty years, and to have become perfectly well acquainted with colours of all kinds, excepting one particular shade of blue, for instance, which it never has been his fortune to meet with. Let all the different shades of that colour, except that single one, be plac'd before him, descending gradually from the deepest to the lightest, 'tis plain, that he will perceive a blank, where that shade is wanting, and will be sensible, that there is a greater distance in that place betwixt the contiguous colours, than in any other. Now I ask, whether 'tis possible for him, from his own imagination, to supply this deficiency, and raise up to himself the idea of that particular shade, tho' it had never been conveyed to him by his senses? I believe there are few but will be of opinion that he can; and this may serve as proof, that the simple ideas are not always derived from the correspondent impressions; tho' the instance is so particular and singular, that 'tis scarce worth our observing, and does not merit that for it alone we should alter our general maxim.

But besides this exception, it may not be amiss to remark on this head, that the principle of the priority of impressions to ideas must be understood with another limitation, *viz.* that as our ideas are images of our impressions, so we can form secondary ideas, which are images of the primary; as appears from this very reasoning concerning them. This is not, properly speaking, an exception to the rule so much as an explanation of it. Ideas produce the images of themselves in new ideas; but as the first ideas are supposed to be derived from impressions, it still remains true, that all our simple ideas proceed either mediately or immediately from their correspondent impressions.

This then is the first principle I establish in the science of human nature; nor ought we to despise it because of the simplicity of its appearance. For 'tis remarkable, that the present question concerning the precedency of our impressions or ideas, is the same with what had made so much noise in other terms, when it has been disputed whether there be any *innate ideas,* or whether all ideas be derived from sensation and reflexion. We may observe, that in order to prove the ideas of extension and colour not to be innate, philosophers do nothing but shew, that they are conveyed by our senses. To prove the ideas of passion and desire not to be innate, they observe that we have a preceding experience of these emotions in ourselves. Now if we carefully examine these arguments, we shall find that they prove nothing but that ideas are preceded by other more lively perceptions, from which they are derived, and which they represent. I hope this clear stating of the question will remove all disputes concerning it, and will render this principle of more use in our reasonings, than it seems hitherto to have been.

Bk. I, Pt. III, Sec. V.–Of the impressions of the senses and memory.
. . . As to those *impressions,* which arise from the *senses,* their ultimate cause is, in my opinion, perfectly inexplicable by human reason, and 'twill always be impossible to decide with certainty, whether they arise immediately from the object, or are produc'd by the creative power of the mind, or are deriv'd from the author of our being. Nor is such a question any way material to our present purpose. We may draw inferences from the coherence of our perceptions, whether they be true or false; whether they represent nature justly, or be mere illusions of the senses. . . .

THOMAS REID
Sensations as Natural Signs*

[For further discussion of sensation and the objects of perception see Reid's *Essays on the Intellectual Powers of Man*, Essay II, Chapters XVI–XVIII.]

Ch. VI. Section VI. That None of Our Sensations are Resemblances of Any of the Qualities of Bodies

There is no phaenomenon in nature more unaccountable than the intercourse that is carried on between the mind and the external world—there is no phaenomenon which philosophical spirits have shewn greater avidity to pry into, and to resolve. It is agreed by all, that this intercourse is carried on by means of the senses; and this satisfies the vulgar curiosity, but not the philosophic. Philosophers must have some system, some hypothesis, that shews the manner in which our senses make us acquainted with external things. All the fertility of human invention seems to have produced only one hypothesis for this purpose, which, therefore, hath been universally received; and that is, that the mind, like a mirror, receives the images of things from without, by means of the senses; so that their use must be to convey these images into the mind.

Whether to these images of external things in the mind, we give the name of *sensible forms,* or *sensible species,* with the Peripatetics, or the name *of ideas of sensation,* with Locke; or whether, with later philosophers, we distinguish *sensations,* which are immediately conveyed by the senses, from *ideas of sensation,* which are faint copies of our sensations retained in the memory and imagination; these are only differences about words. The hypothesis I have mentioned is common to all these different systems.

The necessary and allowed consequence of this hypothesis is, *that no material thing, nor any quality of material things, can be conceived by us, or made an object of thought, until its image is conveyed to the mind by means of the senses.* . . .

Now, we have considered, in this and the preceding chapter, Extension, Figure, Solidity, Motion, Hardness, Roughness, as well as Colour, Heat, and Cold, Sound, Taste, and Smell. We have endeavoured to shew that our nature and constitution lead us to conceive these as qualities of body, as all mankind have always conceived them to be. We have likewise examined with great attention the various sensations we have by means of the five senses, and are not able to find among them all one single image of body, or of any of its qualities. From whence, then, come those images of body and of its qualities into the mind? Let philosophers resolve this question. All I can say is, that they come not by the senses. I am sure that, by proper attention and care, I may know my sensations, and be able to affirm with certainty what they resemble, and what they do not resemble. I have examined them one by one, and compared

---

* From *An Inquiry into the Human Mind on the Principles of Common Sense.*

them with matter and its qualities; and I cannot find one of them that confesses a resembling feature.

A truth so evident as this—that our sensations are not images of matter, or of any of its qualities—ought not to yield to a hypothesis such as that above-mentioned, however ancient, or however universally received by philosophers; nor can there be any amicable union between the two. . . .

Ch. VI. Section XX. Of Perception in General

Sensation, and the perception of external objects by the senses, though very different in their nature, have commonly been considered as one and the same thing. The purposes of common life do not make it necessary to distinguish them, and the received opinions of philosophers tend rather to confound them; but, without attending carefully to this distinction, it is impossible to have any just conception of the operations of our senses. The most simple operations of the mind, admit not of a logical definition: all we can do is to describe them, so as to lead those who are conscious of them in themselves, to attend to them, and reflect upon them; and it is often very difficult to describe them so as to answer this intention.

The same mode of expression is used to denote sensation and perception; and, therefore, we are apt to look upon them as things of the same nature. Thus, *I feel a pain; I see a tree:* the first denoteth a sensation, the last a perception. The grammatical analysis of both expressions is the same: for both consist of an active verb and an object. But, if we attend to the things signified by these expressions, we shall find that, in the first, the distinction between the act and the object is not real but grammatical; in the second, the distinction is not only grammatical but real.

The form of the expression, *I feel pain,* might seem to imply that the feeling is something distinct from the pain felt; yet, in reality, there is no distinction. As *thinking a thought* is an expression which could signify no more than *thinking,* so *feeling a pain* signifies no more than *being pained.* What we have said of pain is applicable to every other mere sensation. It is difficult to give instances, very few of our sensations have names; and, where they have, the name being common to the sensation, and to something else which is associated with it. But, when we attend to the sensation by itself, and separate it from other things which are conjoined with it in the imagination, it appears to be something which can have no existence but in a sentient mind, no distinction from the act of the mind by which it is felt.

Perception, as we here understand it, hath always an object distinct from the act by which it is perceived; an object which may exist whether it be perceived or not. I perceive a tree that grows before my window; there is here an object which is perceived, and an act of the mind by which it is perceived; and these two are not only distinguishable, but they are extremely unlike in their natures. The object is made up of a trunk, branches, and leaves; but the act of the mind by which it is perceived hath neither trunk, branches, nor leaves. I am conscious of this act of my mind, and I can reflect upon it; but it is too simple to admit of an analysis, and I cannot find proper words to describe it. I find nothing that resembles it so much as the remembrance of the tree, or the imagination of it. Yet both these differ essentially from perception; they differ likewise one from another. It is in vain that a philosopher assures me, that the imagination of the tree, the remembrance of it, and the perception of it, are all one, and differ only in degree of vivacity. I know the contrary; for I am as well acquainted with all the three as I am with the apartments of my own house. I know this also, that the perception of an object implies both a conception of its form, and a belief of its present existence. I know, moreover, that this belief is not the effect of argumentation and reasoning; it is the immediate effect of my constitution.

I am aware that this belief which I have in perception stands exposed to the strongest batteries of scepticism. But they make no great impression upon it. The sceptic asks me, Why do you believe the existence of the external object which you perceive? This belief, sir, is none of my manufacture; it came from the mint of Nature; it bears her image and superscription; and, if it is not right, the fault is not mine: I even took it upon trust, and without suspicion. Reason, says the sceptic, is the only judge of truth, and you ought to throw off every opinion and every belief that is not grounded on reason. Why, sir, should I believe the faculty of reason more than that of perception?—they came both out of the same shop, and were made by the same artist; and if he puts one piece of false ware into my hands, what should hinder him for putting another?

Perhaps the sceptic will agree to distrust reason, rather than give any credit to perception. For, says he, since, by your own concession, the object which you perceive, and that act of your mind by which you perceive it, are quite different things, the one may exist without the other; and, as the object may exist without being perceived, so the perception may exist without an object. There is nothing so shameful in a philosopher as to be deceived and deluded; and, therefore, you ought to resolve firmly to withhold assent, and to throw off this belief of external objects, which may be all delusion. For my part, I will never attempt to throw it off; and, although the sober part of mankind will not be very anxious to know my reasons, yet, if they can be of use to any sceptic, they are these:—

First, because it is not in my power: why, then, should I make a vain attempt? It would be agreeable to fly to the moon, and to make a visit to Jupiter and Saturn; but, when I know that Nature has bound me down by the law of gravitation to this planet which I inhabit, I rest contented, and quietly suffer myself to be carried along in its orbit. My belief is carried along by perception, as irresistibly as my body by the earth. And the greatest sceptic will find himself to be in the same condition. He may struggle hard to disbelieve the informations of his senses, as a man does to swim against a torrent; but, ah! it is in vain. It is in vain that he strains every nerve, and wrestles with nature, and with every object that strikes upon his senses. For, after all, when his strength is spent in the fruitless attempt, he will be carried down the torrent with the common herd of believers.

Secondly, I think it would not be prudent to throw off this belief, if it were in my power. If Nature intended to deceive me, and impose upon me by false appearances, and I, by my great cunning and profound logic, have discovered the imposture, prudence would dictate to me, in this case, even to put up [with] this indignity done me, as quietly as I could, and not to call her an imposter to her face, lest she would be even with me in another way. For what do I gain by resenting this injury? You ought at least not to believe what she says. This indeed seems reasonable, if she intends to impose upon me. But what is the consequence? I resolve not to believe my senses. I break my nose against a post that comes in my way; I step into a dirty kennel; and, after twenty such wise and rational actions, I am taken up and clapped into a madhouse. Now, I confess I would rather make one of the credulous fools whom Nature imposes upon, than of those wise and rational philosophers who resolve to withhold assent at all this expense. If a man pretend to be a sceptic with regard to the informations of sense, and yet prudently keeps out of harm's way as other men do, he must excuse my suspicion, that he either acts the hypocrite, or imposes upon himself. For, if the scale of his belief were so evenly poised as to lean no more to one side than to the contrary, it is impossible that his actions could be directed by any rules of common prudence.

Thirdly, Although the two reasons already mentioned are perhaps two more than enough, I shall offer a third. I gave implicit belief to the informations of Nature by my senses, for a considerable part of my life, before I had learned so much logic as to be able to start a doubt concerning them. And now, when I reflect upon what is past, I do not find that I have been imposed upon by this belief. I find that without it I must have perished by a thousand accidents. I find that without it I should have been no wiser now than when I was born. I should not even have been able to acquire that logic which suggests these sceptical doubts with regard to my senses. Therefore, I consider this instinctive belief as one of the best gifts of Nature. I thank the Author of my being, who bestowed it upon me before the eyes of my reason were opened, and still bestows it upon me, to be my guide where reason leaves me in the dark. And now I yield to the direction of my senses, not from instinct only, but from confidence and trust in a faithful and beneficent Monitor, grounded upon the experience of his paternal care and goodness.

In all this, I deal with the Author of my being, no otherwise than I thought it reasonable to deal with my parents and tutors. I believed by instinct whatever they told me, long before I had the idea of a lie, or thought of the possibility of their deceiving me. Afterwards, upon reflection, I found they had acted like fair and honest people, who wished me well. I found that, if I had not believed what they told me, before I could give a reason of my belief, I had to this day been little better than a changeling. And although this natural credulity hath sometimes occasioned my being imposed upon by deceivers, yet it hath been of infinite advantage to me upon the whole; therefore, I consider it as another good gift of Nature. And I continue to give that credit, from reflection, to those of whose integrity and veracity I have had experience, which before I gave from instinct.

There is a much greater similitude than is commonly imagined, between the testimony of nature given by our senses, and the testimony of men given by language. The credit we give to both is at first the effect of instinct only. When we grow up, and begin to reason about them, the credit given to human testimony is restrained and weakened, by the experience we have of deceit. But the credit given to the testimony of our senses, is established and confirmed by the uniformity and constancy of the laws of nature.

Our perceptions are of two kinds: some are natural and original; others acquired, and the fruit of experience. When I perceive that this is the taste of cyder, that of brandy; that this is the smell of an apple, that of an orange; that this is the noise of thunder, that the ringing of bells; this the sound of a coach passing, that the voice of such a friend: these perceptions, and others of the same kind, are not original—they are acquired. But the perceptions which I have, by touch, of the hardness and softness of bodies, of their extension, figure, and motion, is not acquired—it is original.

In all our senses, the acquired perceptions are many more than the original, especially in sight. By this sense we perceive originally the visible figure and colour of bodies only, and their visible place: but we learn to perceive by the eye, almost everything which we can perceive by touch. The original perceptions of this sense serve only as signs to introduce the acquired.

The signs by which objects are presented to us in perception, are the language of Nature to man; and as, in many respects, it hath great affinity with the language of man to man, so particularly in this, that both are partly natural and original, partly acquired by custom. Our original or natural perceptions are analogous to the natural language of man to man, of which we took notice in the fourth chapter; and our acquired perceptions are analogous to artificial language, which, in our mother-tongue, is got very much in the same manner with our acquired perceptions—as we shall afterwards more fully explain.

Not only men, but children, idiots, and brutes, acquire by habit many perceptions which they had not originally. Almost every employment in life hath perceptions of this kind that are peculiar to it. The shepherd knows every sheep of his flock, as we do our acquaintance, and can pick them out of another flock one by one. The butcher knows by sight the weight and quality of his beeves and sheep before they are killed. The farmer perceives by his eye, very nearly, the quantity of hay in a rick, or of corn in a heap. The sailor sees the burthen, the built, and the distance of a ship at sea, while she is a great way off. Every man accustomed to writing, distinguishes his acquaintance by their handwriting, as he does by their faces. And the painter distinguishes, in the works of his art, the style of all the great masters. In a word, acquired perception is very different in different persons, according to the diversity of objects about which they are employed, and the application they bestow in observing them.

Perception ought not only to be distinguished from sensation, but likewise from that knowledge of the objects of sense which is got by reasoning. There is no reasoning in perception, as hath been observed. The belief which is implied in it, is the effect of instinct. But there are many things, with regard to sensible objects, which we can infer from what we perceive; and such conclusions of reason ought to be distinguished from what is merely perceived. When I look at the moon, I perceive her to be sometimes circular, sometimes horned, and sometimes gibbous. This is simple perception, and is the same in the philosopher and in the clown: but from these various appearances of her enlightened part, I infer that she is really of a spherical figure. The conclusion is not obtained by simple perception, but by reasoning. Simple perception has the same relation to the conclusions of reason drawn from our perceptions, as the axioms in mathematics have to the propositions. I cannot demonstrate that two quantities which are equal to the same quantity, are equal to each other; neither can I demonstrate that the tree which I perceive, exists. But, by the constitution of my nature, my belief is irresistibly carried along by my apprehension of the axiom; and, by the constitution of my nature, my belief is no less irresistibly carried along by my perception of the tree. All reasoning is from principles. The first principles of mathematical reasoning are mathematical axioms and definitions; and the first principles of every kind of reasoning are given us by Nature, and are of equal authority with the faculty of reason itself, which is also the gift of Nature. The conclusions of reason are all built upon first principles, and can have no other foundation. Most justly, therefore, do such principles disdain to be tried by reason, and laugh at all the artillery of the logician, when it is directed against them.

When a long train of reasoning is necessary in demonstrating a mathematical proposition, it is easily distinguished from an axiom; and they seem to be things of a very different nature. But there are some propositions which lie so near to axioms, that it is difficult to say whether they ought to be held as axioms, or demonstrated as propositions. The same thing holds with regard to perception, and the conclusions drawn from it. Some of these conclusions follow our perceptions so easily, and are so immediately connected with them, that it is difficult to fix the limit which divides the one from the other.

Perception, whether original or acquired, implies no exercise of reason; and is common to men, children, idiots, and brutes. The more obvious conclusions drawn from our perceptions by reason, make what we call *common understanding;* by which men conduct themselves in the common affairs of life, and by which they are distinguished from idiots. The more remote conclusions which are drawn from our perceptions, by reason, make what we commonly call *science* in the various parts of nature, whether in agriculture, medicine, mechanics, or in any part of natural philosophy. When I see a garden in good order, containing a great variety of things of the best kinds, and in the most flourishing condition, I immediately conclude from these signs the skill and industry of the gardener. A farmer, when he rises in the morning, and perceives that the neighbouring brook overflows his field, concludes that a great deal of rain hath fallen in the night. Perceiving his fence broken, and his corn trodden down, he concludes that some of his own or his neighbours' cattle have broke loose. Perceiving that his stable-door is broke open, and some of his horses gone, he concludes that a thief has carried them off. He traces the prints of his horses' feet in the soft ground, and by them discovers which road the thief hath taken. These are instances of common understanding, which dwells so near to perception that it is difficult to trace the line which divides the one from the other. In like manner the science of nature dwells so near to common understanding that we cannot discern where the latter ends and the former begins. I perceive that bodies lighter than water swim in water, and that those which are heavier sink. Hence I conclude, that if a body remains wherever it is put under water, whether at the top or bottom, it is precisely of the same weight with water. If it will rest only when part of it is above water, it is lighter than water. And the greater the part above water, compared with the whole, the lighter is the body. If it had no gravity at all, it would make no impression upon the water, but stand wholly above it. Thus, every man, by common understanding, has a rule by which he judges of the specific gravity of bodies which swim in water: and a step or two more leads him into the science of hydrostatics.

All that we know of nature, or of existence, may be compared to a tree, which hath its root, trunk, and branches. In this tree of knowledge, perception is the root, common understanding is the trunk, and the sciences are the branches.

Ch. VI. Section XXI. Of the Process of Nature in Perception

Although there is no reasoning in perception, yet there are certain means and instruments which, by the appointment of nature, must intervene between the object and our perception of it; and, by these, our perceptions are limited and regulated. First, If the object is not in contact with the organ of sense, there must be some medium which passes between them. Thus, in vision, the rays of light; in hearing, the vibrations of elastic air; in smelling, the effluvia of the body smelled—must pass from the object to the organ; otherwise we have no perception. Secondly, There must be some action or impression upon the organ of sense, either by the immediate application of the object, or by the medium that goes between them. Thirdly, The nerves which go from the brain to the organ must receive some impression by means of that which was made upon the organ; and, probably, by means of the nerves, some impression must be made upon the brain. Fourthly, The impression made upon the organ, nerves, and brain, is followed by a sensation. And, last of all, This sensation is followed by the perception of the object.

Thus, our perception of objects is the result of a train of operations; some of which affect the body only, others affect the mind. We know very little of the nature of some of these operations; we know not at all how they are connected together, or in what way they contribute to that perception which is the result of the whole; but, by the laws of our constitution, we perceive objects in this, and in no other way.

There may be other beings who can perceive external objects without rays of light, or vibrations of air, or effluvia of bodies—without impressions on bodily organs, or even without sensations; but we are so framed by the Author of Nature, that, even when we are surrounded by external objects, we may perceive none of them. Our faculty of perceiving an object lies dormant, until it is roused and stimulated by a certain corresponding sensation. Nor is this sensation always at hand to perform its office; for it enters into the mind only in consequence of a certain corresponding impression made on the organ of sense by the object.

Let us trace this correspondence of impressions, sensations, and perceptions, as far as we can—beginning with that which is first in order, the impression made upon the bodily organ. But, alas! we know not of what nature these impressions are, far less how they excite sensations in the mind.

We know that one body may act upon another by pressure, by percussion, by attraction, by repulsion, and probably, in many other ways which we neither know nor have names to express. But in which of these ways objects, when perceived by us, act upon the organs of sense, these organs upon the nerves, and the nerves upon the brain, we know not. Can any man tell me how, in vision, the rays of light act upon the *retina,* how the *retina* acts upon the optic nerve, and how the optic nerve acts upon the brain? No man can. When I feel the pain of the gout in my toe, I know that there is some unusual impression made upon that part of my body. But of what kind is it? Are the small vessels distended with some redundant elastic, or unelastic fluid? Are the fibres unusually stretched? Are they torn asunder by force, or gnawed and corroded by some acrid humour? I can answer none of these questions. All that I feel is pain, which is not an impression upon the body, but upon the mind; and all that I perceive by this sensation is, that some distemper in my toe occasions this pain. But, as I know not the natural temper and texture of my toe when it is at ease, I know as little what change or disorder of its parts occasions this uneasy sensation. In like manner, in every other sensation, there is, without doubt, some impression made upon the organ of sense; but an impression of which we know not the nature. It is too subtile to be discovered by our senses, and we may make a thousand conjectures without coming near the truth. If we understood the structure of our organs of sense so minutely as to discover what effects are produced upon them by external objects, this knowledge would contribute nothing to our perception of the object; for they perceive as distinctly who know least about the manner of perception as the greatest adepts. It is necessary that the impression be made upon our organs, but not that it be known. Nature carries on this part of the process of perception, without our consciousness or concurrence.

But we cannot be unconscious of the next step in this process—the sensation of the mind, which always immediately follows the impression made upon the body. It is essential to a sensation to be felt, and it can be nothing more than we feel it to be. If we can only acquire the habit of attending to our sensations, we may know them perfectly. But how are the sensations of the mind produced by impressions upon the body? Of this we are absolutely ignorant, having no means of knowing how the body acts upon the mind, or the mind upon the body. When we consider the nature and attributes of both, they seem to be so different, and so unlike, that we can find no handle by which the one may lay hold of the other. There is a deep and a dark gulf between them, which our understanding cannot pass; and the manner of their correspondence and intercourse is absolutely unknown.

Experience teaches us, that certain impressions upon the body are constantly followed by certain sensations of the mind; and that, on the other hand, certain determinations of the mind are constantly followed by certain motions in the body; but we see not the chain that ties these things together. Who knows but their connection may be arbitrary, and owing to the will of our Maker? Perhaps the same sensations might have been connected with other impressions, or other bodily organs. Perhaps we might have been so made as to taste with our fingers, to smell with our ears, and to hear by the nose. Perhaps we might have been so made as to have all the sensations and perceptions which we have, without any impression made upon our bodily organs at all.

However these things may be, if Nature had given us nothing more than impressions made upon the body, and sensations in our minds corresponding to them, we should, in that case, have been merely sentient, but not percipient beings. We should never have been able to form a conception of any external object, far less a belief of its existence. Our sensations have no resemblance to external objects; nor can we discover, by our reason, any necessary connection between the existence of the former, and that of the latter.

We might, perhaps, have been made of such a constitution as to have our present perceptions connected with other sensations. We might, perhaps, have had the perception of external objects, without either impressions upon the organs of sense, or sensations. Or lastly, The perceptions we have, might have been immediately connected with the impressions upon our organs, without any intervention of sensations. This last seems really to be the case in one instance—to wit, in our perception of the visible figure of bodies, as was observed in the eighth section of this chapter.

The process of Nature, in perception by the senses, may, therefore, be conceived as a kind of drama, wherein some things are performed behind the scenes, others are represented to the mind in different scenes, one succeeding another. The impression made by the object upon the organ, either by immediate contact or by some intervening medium, as well as the impression made upon the nerves and brain, is performed behind the scenes, and the mind sees nothing of it. But every such impression, by the laws of the drama, is followed by a sensation, which is the first scene exhibited to the mind; and this scene is quickly succeeded by another, which is the perception of the object.

In this drama, Nature is the actor, we are the spectators. We know nothing of the machinery by means of which every different impression upon the organ, nerves, and brain, exhibits its corresponding sensation; or of the machinery by means of which each sensation exhibits its corresponding perception. We are inspired with the sensation, and we are inspired with the corresponding perception, by means unknown. And, because the mind passes immediately from the sensation to that conception and belief of the object which we have in perception, in the same manner as it passes from signs to the things signified by them, we have, therefore, called our sensations *signs of external objects;* finding no word more proper to express the function which Nature hath assigned them in perception, and the relation which they bear to their corresponding objects.

There is no necessity of a resemblance between the sign and the thing signified; and indeed no sensation can resemble any external object. But there are two things necessary to our knowing things by means of signs. First, that a real connection between the sign and thing signified be established, either by the course of nature, or by the will and appointment of men. When they are connected by the course of nature, it is a natural sign; when by human appointment, it is an artificial sign. Thus smoke is a natural sign of fire; certain features are natural signs of anger: but our words, whether expressed by articulate sounds or by writing, are artificial signs of our thoughts and purposes.

Another requisite to our knowing things by signs is, that the appearance of the sign to the mind, be followed by the conception and belief of the thing signified. Without this, the sign is not understood or interpreted; and, therefore, is no sign to us, however fit in its own nature for that purpose.

Now, there are three ways in which the mind passes from the appearance of a natural sign to the conception and belief of the thing signified—by *original principles of our constitution,* by *custom,* and by *reasoning.*

Our original perceptions are got in the first of these ways, our acquired perceptions in the second, and all that reason discovers of the course of nature, in the third. In the first of these ways, Nature, by means of the sensations of touch, informs us of the hardness and softness of bodies; of their extension, figure, and motion; and of that space in which they move and are placed—as hath been already explained in the fifth chapter of this inquiry. And, in the second of these ways, she informs us, by means of our eyes, of almost all the same things which originally we could perceive only by touch. . . .

30

Immanuel Kant
Conditions and Limits of Sensible Cognition

[*Cf.* part of Selection 21, pp. 236–40.]

I.*

General Observations on Transcendental Aesthetic

I. In order to avoid all misapprehensions it will be necessary, first of all, to declare, as clearly as possible, what is our view with regard to the fundamental nature of sensuous knowledge.

What we meant to say was this, that all our intuition is nothing but the representation of phenomena; that things which we see are not by themselves what we see, nor their relations by themselves such as they appear to us, so that, if we drop our subject or the subjective form of our senses, all qualities, all relations of objects in space and time, nay space and time themselves, would vanish. They cannot, as phenomena, exist by themselves, but in us only. It remains completely unknown to us what objects may be by themselves and apart from the receptivity of our senses. We know nothing but our manner of perceiving them, that manner being peculiar to us, and not necessarily shared in by every being, though, no doubt, by every human being. This is what alone concerns us. Space and time are pure forms of our intuition, while sensation forms its matter. What we can know *a priori*—before all real intuition, are the forms of space and time, which are therefore called pure intuition, while sensation is that which causes our knowledge to be called *a posteriori* knowledge, i.e. empirical intuition. Whatever our sensation may be, these forms are necessarily inherent in it, while sensations themselves may be of the most different character. Even if we could impart the highest degree of clearness to our intuition, we should not come one step nearer to the nature of objects by themselves. We should know our mode of intuition, i.e. our sensibility, more completely, but always under the indefeasible conditions of space and time. What the objects are by themselves would never become known to us, even through the clearest knowledge of that which alone is given us, the phenomenon.

It would vitiate the concept of sensibility and phenomena, and render our whole doctrine useless and empty, if we were to accept the view (of Leibniz and Wolf), that our whole sensibility is really but a confused representation of things, simply containing what belongs to them by themselves, though smothered under an accumulation of signs (Merkmal) and partial concepts, which we do not consciously disentangle. The distinction between confused and well-ordered representation is logical only, and does not touch the contents of our

---

* From *Critique of Pure Reason*, A 41–49, B 59–66; B 69–71.

knowledge. Thus the concept of Right, as employed by people of common sense, contains neither more nor less than the subtlest speculation can draw out of it, only that in the ordinary practical use of the word we are not always conscious of the manifold ideas contained in that thought. But no one would say therefore that the ordinary concept of Right was sensuous, containing a mere phenomenon; for Right can never become a phenomenon, being a concept of the understanding, and representing a moral quality belonging to actions by themselves. The representation of a Body, on the contrary, contains nothing in intuition that could belong to an object by itself, but is merely the phenomenal appearance of something, and the manner in which we are affected by it. This receptivity of our knowledge is called sensibility. Even if we could see to the very bottom of a phenomenon, it would remain for ever altogether different from the knowledge of the thing itself.

This shows that the philosophy of Leibniz and Wolf has given a totally wrong direction to all investigations into the nature and origin of our knowledge, by representing the difference between the sensible and the intelligible as logical only. That difference is in truth transcendental. It affects not the form only, as being more or less confused, but the origin and contents of our knowledge; so that by our sensibility we know the nature of things by themselves not confusedly only, but not at all. If we drop our subjective condition, the object, as represented with its qualities bestowed on it by sensuous intuition, is nowhere to be found, and cannot possibly be found; because its form, as phenomenal appearance, is determined by those very subjective conditions.

It has been the custom to distinguish in phenomena that which is essentially inherent in their intuition and is recognised by every human being, from that which belongs to their intuition accidentally only, being valid not for sensibility in general, but only for a particular position and organisation of this or that sense. In that case the former kind of knowledge is said to represent the object by itself, the latter its appearance only. But that distinction is merely empirical. If, as generally happens, people are satisfied with that distinction, without again, as they ought, treating the first empirical intuition as purely phenomenal also, in which nothing can be found belonging to the thing by itself, our transcendental distinction is lost, and we believe that we know things by themselves, though in the world of sense, however far we may carry our investigation, we can never have anything before us but mere phenomena. To give an illustration. People might call the rainbow a mere phenomenal appearance during a sunny shower, but the rain itself the thing by itself. This would be quite right, physically speaking, and taking rain as something which, in our ordinary experience and under all possible relations to our senses, can be determined thus and thus only in our intuition. But if we take the empirical in general, and ask, without caring whether it is the same with every particular observer, whether it represents a thing by itself (not the drops of rain, for these are already, as phenomena, empirical objects), then the question as to the relation between the representation and the object becomes transcendental, and not only the drops are mere phenomena, but even their round shape, nay even the space in which they fall, are nothing by themselves, but only modifications or fundamental dispositions of our sensuous intuition, the transcendental object remaining unknown to us.

The second important point in our transcendental aesthetic is, that it should not only gain favour as a plausible hypothesis, but assume as certain and undoubted a character as can be demanded of any theory which is to serve as an organum. In order to make this certainty self-evident we shall select a case which will make its validity palpable.

Let us suppose that space and time are in themselves objective, and conditions of the possibility of things by themselves. Now there is with regard to both a large number *a priori* apodictic and synthetical propositions, and particularly with regard to space, which for this reason we shall chiefly investigate here as an illustration. As the propositions of geometry are known synthetically *a priori*, and with apodictic certainty, I ask, whence do you take such propositions? and what does the understanding rely on in order to arrive at such absolutely necessary and universally valid truths? There is no other way but by concepts and intuitions, and both as given either *a priori* or *a posteriori*. The latter, namely empirical concepts, as well as the empirical intuition on which they are founded, cannot yield any synthetical propositions except such as are themselves also empirical only, that is, empirical propositions, which can never possess that necessity and absolute universality which are characteristic of all geometrical propositions. As to the other and only means of arriving at such knowledge through mere concepts or intuitions *a priori*, it must be clear that only analytical, but no synthetical knowledge can ever be derived from mere concepts. Take the proposition that two straight lines cannot enclose a space and cannot therefore form a figure, and try to deduce it from the concept of straight lines and the number two; or take the proposition that with three straight lines it is possible to form a figure, and try to deduce that from those concepts. All your labour will be lost, and in the end you will be obliged to have recourse to intuition, as is always done in geometry. You then give yourselves an object in intuition. But of what kind is it? Is it a pure intuition *a priori* or an empirical one? In the latter case, you would never arrive at a universally valid, still less at an apodictic proposition, because experience can never yield such. You must therefore take the object as given *a priori* in intuition, and found your synthetical proposition on that. If you did not possess in yourselves the power of *a priori* intuition, if that subjective condition were not at the same time, as to the form, the general condition *a priori* under which alone the object of that (external) intuition becomes possible, if, in fact, the object (the triangle) were something by itself without any reference to you as the subject, how could you say that what exists necessarily in your subjective conditions of constructing a triangle, belongs of necessity to the triangle itself? For you could not add something entirely new (the figure) to your concepts of three lines, something which should of necessity belong to the object, as that object is given before your knowledge of it, and not by it. If therefore space, and time also, were not pure forms of your intuition, which contains the *a priori* conditions under which alone things can become external objects to you, while, without that subjective condition, they are nothing, you could not predicate anything of external objects *a priori* and synthetically. It is therefore beyond the reach of doubt, and not possible only or probable, that space and time, as the necessary conditions of all experience, external and internal, are purely subjective conditions of our intuition, and that, with reference to them, all things are phenomena only, and not things thus existing by themselves in such or such wise. Hence, so far as their form is concerned, much may be predicated of them *a priori*, but nothing whatever of the things by themselves on which these phenomena may be grounded.

III.[1] If I say that the intuition of external objects and the self-intuition of the mind, represent both (viz. the objects and the mind) in space and time, as they affect our senses, that is, as they appear, I do not mean, that these objects are mere *illusion*. For the objects, as phenomena, nay, even the properties which we ascribe to them, are always looked upon as something really given: and all we do is, that, as their quality depends only on the manner of intuition on the part of the subject in relation to a given object, we distinguish the object, as *phenomenon*, from itself, as an object by itself. Thus, if I assert that the quality of space and time, according to which, as a condition of their existence, I accept both external objects and my own soul, lies in my manner of intuition and not in these objects by themselves, I do not mean to say that bodies *seem* only to exist outside me, or that my soul *seems* only to be given in my self-consciousness. It would be my own fault, if I changed that, which I ought to count as phenomenal, into mere illusion.

This cannot happen, however, according to our principle of the ideality of all sensuous intuitions; on the contrary, it is only when we attribute *objective reality* to those forms of intuition that everything is changed inevitably into mere *illusion*. For if we take space and time as properties that ought to exist as possible in things by themselves, and then survey the absurdities in which we should be involved in having to admit that two infinite things, which are not substances, nor something inherent in substances, but nevertheless must be something existing, nay, the necessary condition of the existence of all things, would remain, even if all existing things were removed, we really cannot blame the good Bishop Berkeley for degrading bodies to mere illusion. Nay, it would follow that even our own existence, which would thus be made dependent on the independent reality of such a non-entity as time, must become a mere illusion, an absurdity which hitherto no one has been guilty of. . . .

---

[1]   [Added in the Second Edition.—*Ed.*]

II.*

*On the Ground of the Distinction of All Subjects
into Phenomena and Noumena*

We have now not only traversed the whole domain of the pure understanding, and carefully examined each part of it, but we have also measured
its extent, and assigned to everything in it its proper place. This domain, however, is an island and enclosed by nature itself within limits that can never be
changed. It is the country of truth (a very attractive name), but surrounded by
a wide and stormy ocean, the true home of illusion, where many a fog bank
and ice that soon melts away tempt us to believe in new lands, while constantly deceiving the adventurous mariner with vain hopes, and involving him
in adventures which he can never leave, and yet can never bring to an end.
Before we venture ourselves on this sea, in order to explore it on every side,
and to find out whether anything is to be hoped for there, it will be useful to
glance once more at the map of that country which we are about to leave, and
to ask ourselves, first, whether we might not be content with what it contains,
nay, whether we must not be content with it, supposing that there is no solid
ground anywhere else on which we could settle; secondly, by what title we
possess even that domain, and may consider ourselves safe against all hostile
claims. Although we have sufficiently answered these questions in the course of
the analytic, a summary recapitulation of their solutions may help to
strengthen our conviction, by uniting all arguments in one point.

We have seen that the understanding possesses everything which it draws
from itself, without borrowing from experience, for no other purpose but for
experience. The principles of the pure understanding, whether constitutive *a
priori* (as the mathematical) or simply relative (as the dynamical), contain
nothing but, as it were, the pure schema of possible experience; for that experience derives its unity from that synthetical unity alone which the understanding originally and spontaneously imparts to the synthesis of imagination,
with reference to apperception, and to which all phenomena, as data of a possible knowledge, must conform *a priori*. . . .

That the understanding cannot make any but an empirical, and never a
transcendental, use of all its principles *a priori*, nay, of all its concepts, is a
proposition which, if thoroughly understood, leads indeed to most important
consequences. What we call the transcendental use of a concept in any proposition is its being referred to things in general and to things by themselves,
while its empirical use refers to phenomena only, that is, to objects of a possible experience. That the latter use alone is admissible will be clear from the
following considerations. What is required for every concept is, first, the logical form of a concept (of thought) in general; and, secondly, the possibility of

---

* From *Critique of Pure Reason*, A 235–260, B 294–315 (with several paragraphs
  or portions thereof omitted).

an object to which it refers. Without the latter, it has no sense, and is entirely empty, though it may still contain the logical function by which a concept can be formed out of any data. The only way in which an object can be given to a concept is in intuition, and though a pure intuition is possible *a priori* and before the object, yet even that pure intuition can receive its object, and with it its objective validity, by an empirical intuition only, of which it is itself nothing but the form. All concepts, therefore, and with them all principles, though they may be possible *a priori*, refer nevertheless to empirical intuitions, that is, to data of a possible experience. Without this, they can claim no objective validity, but are a mere play, whether of the imagination or of the understanding with their respective representations. . . .

That this is the case with all categories and with all the principles drawn from them, becomes evident from the fact that we could not define any one of them (really, that is, make conceivable the possibility of their object),[1] without at once having recourse to the conditions of sensibility or the form of phenomena, to which, as their only possible objects, these categories must necessarily be restricted, it being impossible, if we take away these conditions, to assign to them any meaning, that is, any relation to an object, or to make it intelligible to ourselves by an example what kind of thing could be intended by such concepts. . . .

From this it follows incontestably, that the pure concepts of the understanding never admit of a transcendental, but only of an empirical use, and that the principles of the pure understanding can only be referred, as general conditions of a possible experience, to objects of the senses, never to things by themselves (without regard to the manner in which we have to look at them).

Transcendental Analytic has therefore yielded us this important result, that the understanding *a priori* can never do more than anticipate the form of a possible experience; and as nothing can be an object of experience except the phenomenon, it follows that the understanding can never go beyond the limits of sensibility, within which alone objects are given to us. Its principles are principles for the exhibition of phenomena only; and the proud name of Ontology, which presumes to supply in a systematic form different kinds of synthetical knowledge *a priori* of things by themselves (for instance the principle of causality), must be replaced by the more modest name of a mere Analytic of the pure understanding. . . .

We[2] are met here by an illusion which is difficult to avoid. The categories do not depend in their origin on sensibility, like the forms of *intuition*, space, and time, and seem, therefore, to admit of an application extending beyond the objects of the senses. But, on the other side, they are nothing but *forms of thought*, containing the logical faculty only of comprehending *a priori* in one

---

[1] Additions of the Second Edition.—*Tr.*

[2] [Next five paragraphs, "We are met here . . ." to ". . . as such in a *negative sense* only" were added in the Second Edition.—*Ed.*]

consciousness the manifold that is given in intuition, and they would therefore, if we take away the only intuition which is possible to us, have still less significance than those pure sensuous forms by which at least an object is given, while a peculiar mode of our understanding of connecting the manifold (unless that intuition, in which the manifold alone can be given, is added), signifies nothing at all.

Nevertheless, it seems to follow from our very concept, if we call certain objects, as phenomena, beings of the senses, by distinguishing between the mode of our intuition and the nature of those objects by themselves, that we may take either the same objects in the latter capacity, though they cannot as such come before our intuition, or other possible things, which are not objects of our senses at all, and place them, as objects thought only by the understanding, in opposition to the former, calling them beings of the understanding (*noumena*). The question then arises, whether our pure concepts of the understanding do not possess some significance with regard to these so-called beings of the understanding, and constitute a mode of knowing them?

At the very outset, however, we meet with an ambiguity which may cause great misapprehension. The understanding, by calling an object in one aspect a phenomenon only, makes to itself, apart from that aspect, another representation of *an object by itself*, and imagines itself able to form *concepts* of such an object. As, then, the understanding yields no other concepts but the categories, it supposes that the object in the latter aspect can be thought at least by those pure concepts of the understanding, and is thus induced to take the entirely indefinite concept of a being of the understanding, as of a something in general outside our sensibility, as a *definite* concept of a being which we might know to a certain extent through the understanding.

If by noumenon we mean a thing so far as it is *not an object of our sensuous intuition*, and make abstraction of our mode of intuition, it may be called a noumenon in a *negative* sense. If, however, we mean it by an *object* of a *non-sensuous intuition*, we admit thereby a peculiar mode of intuition, namely, the intellectual, which, however, is not our own, nor one of which we can understand even the possibility. This would be the noumenon in a *positive* sense.

The doctrine of sensibility is at the same time the doctrine of noumena in their negative sense; that is, of things which the understanding must think without reference to our mode of intuition, and therefore, not as phenomena only, but as things by themselves, but to which, after it has thus separated them, the understanding knows that it must not, in this new aspect, apply its categories; because these categories have significance only with reference to the unity of intuitions in space and time, and can therefore *a priori* determine that unity, on account of the mere ideality of space and time only, by means of general connecting concepts. Where that unity in time cannot be found, i.e. in the noumenon, the whole use, nay, the whole significance of categories comes to an end: because even the possibility of things that should correspond to the categories, would be unintelligible. On this point I may refer the reader to what I have said at the very beginning of the general note to the previous chapter. The possibility of a thing can never be proved from the fact that its concept is not self-contradictory, but only by being authenticated by an intuition corresponding to it. If, therefore, we attempted to apply the categories to objects which are not considered as phenomena, we should have to admit an intuition other than the sensuous, and thus the object would become a noumenon in a *positive sense*. As, however, such an intuition, namely, an intellectual one, is entirely beyond our faculty of knowledge, the use of the categories also can never reach beyond the limits of the objects of experience. Beings of the understanding correspond no doubt to beings of the senses, and there may be beings of the understanding to which our faculty of sensuous intuition has no relation at all; but our concepts of the understanding, being forms of thought for our sensuous intuition only, do not reach so far, and what is called by us a noumenon must be understood as such in a *negative sense* only.

. . . If all thought (by means of categories) is taken away from empirical knowledge, no knowledge of any object remains, because nothing can be thought by mere intuition, and the mere fact that there is within me an affection of my sensibility, establishes in no way any relation of such a representation to any object. If, on the contrary, all intuition is taken away, there always remains the form of thought, that is, the mode of determining an object for the manifold of a possible intuition. In this sense the categories may be said to extend further than sensuous intuition, because they can think objects in general without any regard to the special mode of sensibility in which they may be given; but they do not thus prove a larger sphere of objects, because we cannot admit that such objects can be given, without admitting the possibility of some other but sensuous intuition, for which we have no right whatever.

I call a concept problematic, if it is not self-contradictory, and if, as limiting other concepts, it is connected with other kinds of knowledge, while its objective reality cannot be known in any way. Now the concept of a noumenon, that is of a thing which can never be thought as an object of the senses, but only as a thing by itself (by the pure understanding), is not self-contradictory, because we cannot maintain that sensibility is the only form of intuition. That concept is also necessary, to prevent sensuous intuition from extending to things by themselves; that is, in order to limit the objective validity of sensuous knowledge (for all the rest to which sensuous intuition does not extend is called noumenon, for the very purpose of showing that sensuous knowledge cannot extend its domain over everything that can be thought by the understanding). But, after all, we cannot understand the possibility of such noumena, and whatever lies beyond the sphere of phenomena is (to us) empty; that is, we have an understanding which *problematically* extends beyond that sphere, but no intuition, nay not even the conception of a possible intuition, by which, outside the field of sensibility, objects could be given to us, and our understanding could extend beyond that sensibility in its assertory use. The concept of a noumenon is therefore merely *limitative*, and intended to keep the claims of sensibility within proper bounds, therefore of negative use only. But it is not a mere arbitrary fiction, but closely connected with the limitation of sensibility, though incapable of adding anything positive to the sphere of the senses.

A real division of objects into phenomena and noumena, and of the world into a sensible and intelligible world in a positive sense, is therefore quite inadmissible, although concepts may very well be divided into sensuous and intellectual. For no objects can be assigned to these intellectual concepts, nor can they be represented as objectively valid. If we drop the senses, how are we to make it conceivable that our categories (which would be the only remaining concepts for noumena) have any meaning at all, considering that, in order to refer them to any object, something more must be given than the mere unity of thought, namely, a possible intuition, to which the categories could be applied? With all this the concept of a noumenon, if taken as problematical only, remains not only admissible, but, as a concept to limit the sphere of sensibility, indispensable. In this case, however, it is not a particular *intelligible object* for *our* understanding, but an understanding to which it could belong is itself a problem, if we ask how it could know an object, not discursively by means of categories, but intuitively, and yet in a non-sensuous intuition,—a process of which we could not understand even the bare possibility. Our understanding thus acquires a kind of negative extension, that is, it does not become itself limited by sensibility, but, on the contrary, limits it, by calling things by themselves (not considered as phenomena) noumena. In doing this, it immediately proceeds to prescribe limits to itself, by admitting that it cannot know these noumena by means of the categories, but can only think of them under the name of something unknown.

In the writings of modern philosophers, however, I meet with a totally different use of the terms of *mundus sensibilis* and *intelligibilis*, totally different from the meaning assigned to these terms by the ancients. Here all difficulty seems to disappear. But the fact is, that there remains nothing but mere word-mongery. In accordance with this, some people have been pleased to call the whole of phenomena, so far as they are seen, the world of sense; but so far as their connection, according to general laws of the understanding, is taken into account, the world of the understanding. Theoretical astronomy, which only teaches the actual observation of the starry heavens, would represent the former; contemplative astronomy, on the contrary (taught according to the Copernican system, or, it may be, according to Newton's laws of gravitation), the latter, namely, a purely intelligible world. But this twisting of words is a mere sophistical excuse, in order to avoid a troublesome question, by changing its meaning according to one's own convenience. Understanding and reason may be applied to phenomena, but it is very questionable whether they can be applied at all to an object which is not a phenomenon, but a noumenon; and it is this, when the object is represented as purely intelligible, that is, as given to the understanding only, and not to the senses. The question therefore is whether, besides the empirical use of the understanding (even in the Newtonian view of the world), a transcendental use is possible, referring to the noumenon, as its object; and that question we have answered decidedly in the negative.

When *we* therefore say that the senses represent objects to us as they *appear*, and the understanding as they *are*, the latter is not to be taken in a transcendental, but in a purely empirical meaning, namely, as to how they, as objects of experience, must be represented, according to the regular connection of phenomena, and not according to what they may be, as objects of the pure understanding, apart from their relation to possible experience, and therefore to our senses. This will always remain unknown to us; nay, we shall never know whether such a transcendental and exceptional knowledge is possible at all, at least as comprehended under our ordinary categories. With us understanding and sensibility cannot determine objects, unless they are joined together. If we separate them, we have intuitions without concepts, or concepts without intuitions, in both cases representations which we cannot refer to any definite object.

If, after all these arguments, anybody should still hesitate to abandon the purely transcendental use of the categories, let him try an experiment with them for framing any synthetical proposition. An analytical proposition does not in the least advance the understanding, which, as in such a proposition it is only concerned with what is already thought in the concept, does not ask whether the concept in itself has any reference to objects, or expresses only the unity of thought in general (this completely ignoring the manner in which an object may be given). The understanding in fact is satisfied if it knows what it contained in the concept of an object; it is indifferent as to the object to which the concept may refer. But let him try the experiment with any synthetical and so-called transcendental proposition, as for instance, 'Everything that exists, exists as a substance, or as a determination inherent in it,' or 'Everything contingent exists as an effect of some other thing, namely, its cause,' etc. Now I ask, whence can the understanding take these synthetical propositions, as the concepts are to apply, not to some possible experience, but to things by themselves (noumena)? Where is that third term to be found which is always required for a synthetical proposition, in order thus to join concepts which have no logical (analytical) relation with each other? It will be impossible to prove such a proposition, nay even to justify the possibility of any such pure assertion, without appealing to the empirical use of the understanding, and thus renouncing entirely the so-called pure and non-sensuous judgment. There are no principles therefore according to which the concepts of pure and merely intelligible objects could ever be applied, because we cannot imagine any way in which they could be given, and the problematic thought, which leaves a place open to them, serves only, like empty space, to limit the sphere of empirical principles, without containing or indicating any other object of knowledge, lying beyond that sphere.

Introductory Remarks: Antimetaphysical *

1.

The great results achieved by physical science in modern times—results not restricted to its own sphere but embracing that of other sciences which employ its help—have brought it about that physical ways of thinking and physical modes of procedure enjoy on all hands unwonted prominence, and that the greatest expectations are associated with their application. In keeping with this drift of modern inquiry, the physiology of the senses, gradually abandoning the method of investigating sensations in themselves followed by men like Goethe, Schopenhauer, and others, but with greatest success by Johannes Müller, has also assumed an almost exclusively physical character. This tendency must appear to us as not altogether appropriate, when we reflect that physics, despite its considerable development, nevertheless constitutes but a portion of a *larger* collective body of knowledge, and that it is unable, with its limited intellectual implements, created for limited and special purposes, to exhaust all the subject-matter in question. Without renouncing the support of physics, it is possible for the physiology of the senses, not only to pursue its own course of development, but also to afford to physical science itself powerful assistance. The following simple considerations will serve to illustrate this relation between the two.

2.

Colors, sounds, temperatures, pressures, spaces, times, and so forth, are connected with one another in manifold ways; and with them are associated dispositions of mind, feelings, and volitions. Out of this fabric, that which is

---

* From *The Analysis of Sensations*, Chapter I, revised and supplemented English edition, based on a translation by C. M. Williams, published in 1897, from the first German edition (1886).

Ernst Mach (1838–1916), an Austrian, taught mathematics at Graz and, later, physics at both Prague and Vienna. In reaction to the Kantianism of his day, he developed a wholly sensationalistic theory of knowledge and claimed that the various sciences, whose common base lay in sensations, did not differ significantly.

relatively more fixed and permanent stands prominently forth, engraves itself on the memory, and expresses itself in language. Relatively greater permanency is exhibited, first, by certain complexes of colors, sounds, pressures, and so forth, functionally connected in time and space, which therefore receive special names, and are called bodies. Absolutely permanent such complexes are not.

My table is now brightly, now dimly lighted. Its temperature varies. It may receive an ink stain. One of its legs may be broken. It may be repaired, polished, and replaced part by part. But, for me, it remains the table at which I daily write.

My friend may put on a different coat. His countenance may assume a serious or a cheerful expression. His complexion, under the effects of light or emotion, may change. His shape may be altered by motion, or be definitely changed. Yet the number of the permanent features presented, compared with the number of the gradual alterations, is always so great, that the latter may be overlooked. It is the same friend with whom I take my daily walk.

My coat may receive a stain, a tear. My very manner of expressing this shows that we are concerned here with a sum-total of permanency, to which the new element is added and from which that which is lacking is subsequently taken away.

Our greater intimacy with this sum-total of permanency, and the preponderance of its importance for me as contrasted with the changeable element, impel us to the partly instinctive, partly voluntary and conscious economy of mental presentation and designation, as expressed in ordinary thought and speech. That which is presented in a single image receives a single designation, a single name.

Further, that complex of memories, moods, and feelings, joined to a particular body (the human body), which is called the "I" or "Ego," manifests itself as relatively permanent. I may be engaged upon this or that subject, I may be quiet and cheerful, excited and ill-humored. Yet, pathological cases apart, enough durable features remain to identify the ego. Of course, the ego also is only of relative permanency.

The apparent permanency of the ego consists chiefly in the single fact of its continuity, in the slowness of its changes. The many thoughts and plans of yesterday that are continued today, and of which our environment in waking hours incessantly reminds us (whence in dreams the ego can be very indistinct, doubled, or entirely wanting), and the little habits that are unconsciously and involuntarily kept up for long periods of time, constitute the groundwork of the ego. There can hardly be greater differences in the egos of different people, than occur in the course of years in one person. When I recall today my early youth, I should take the boy that I then was, with the exception of a few individual features, for a different person, were it not for the existence of the chain of memories. Many an article that I myself penned twenty years ago impresses me now as something quite foreign to myself. The very gradual character of the changes of the body also contributes to the stability of the ego, but in a much less degree than people imagine. Such things are much less analysed and noticed than the intellectual and the moral ego. Personally, people know themselves very poorly. When I wrote these lines in 1886, Ribot's admirable little book, *The Diseases of Personality* (second edition, Paris, 1888, Chicago, 1895), was unknown to me. Ribot ascribes the principal role in preserving the continuity of the ego to the general sensibility. Generally, I am in perfect accord with his views.

The ego is as little absolutely permanent as are bodies. That which we so much dread in death, the annihilation of our permanency, actually occurs in life in abundant measure. That which is most valued by us, remains preserved in countless copies, or, in cases of exceptional excellence, is even preserved of itself. In the best human being, however, there are individual traits, the loss of which neither he himself nor others need regret. Indeed, at times, death, viewed as a liberation from individuality, may even become a pleasant thought. Such reflections of course do not make physiological death any the easier to bear.

After a first survey has been obtained, by the formation of the substance-concepts "body" and "ego" (matter and soul), the will is impelled to a more exact examination of the changes that take place in these relatively permanent existences. The element of change in bodies and the ego, is in fact, exactly what moves the will[1] to this examination. Here the component parts of the complex are first exhibited as its properties. A fruit is sweet; but it can also be bitter. Also, other fruits may be sweet. The red color we are seeking is found in many bodies. The neighborhood of some bodies is pleasant; that of others, unpleasant. Thus, gradually, different complexes are found to be made up of common elements. The visible, the audible, the tangible, are separated from bodies. The visible is analysed into colors and into form. In the manifoldness of the colors, again, though here fewer in number, other component parts are discerned—such as the primary colors, and so forth. The complexes are disintegrated into elements, that is to say, into their ultimate component parts, which hitherto we have been unable to subdivide any further. The nature of these elements need not be discussed at present; it is possible that future investigations may throw light on it. We need not here be disturbed by the fact that it is easier for the scientist to study relations of relations of these elements than the direct relations between them.

---

[1] Not to be taken in the metaphysical sense.

3.

The useful habit of designating such relatively permanent compounds by single names, and of apprehending them by single thoughts, without going to the trouble each time of an analysis of their component parts, is apt to come into strange conflict with the tendency to isolate the component parts. The vague image which we have of a given permanent complex, being an image which does not perceptibly change when one or another of the component parts is taken away, seems to be something which exists in itself. Inasmuch as it is possible to take away singly every constituent part without destroying the capacity of the image to stand for the totality and to be recognized again, it is imagined that it is possible to subtract *all* the parts and to have something still remaining. Thus naturally arises the philosophical notion, at first impressive, but subsequently recognized as monstrous, of a "thing-in-itself," different from its "appearance," and unknowable.

Thing, body, matter, are nothing apart from the combinations of the elements,—the colors, sounds, and so forth—nothing apart from their so-called attributes. That protean pseudo-philosophical problem of the single thing with its many attributes, arises wholly from a misinterpretation of the fact, that summary comprehension and precise analysis, although both are provisionally justifiable and for many purposes profitable, cannot be carried on simultaneously. A body is one and unchangeable only so long as it is unnecessary to consider its details. Thus both the earth and a billiard-ball are spheres, if we are willing to neglect all deviations from the spherical form, and if greater precision is not necessary. But when we are obliged to carry on investigations in orography or microscopy, both bodies cease to be spheres.

4.

Man is pre-eminently endowed with the power of voluntarily and consciously determining his own point of view. He can at one time disregard the most salient features of an object, and immediately thereafter give attention to its smallest details; now consider a stationary current, without a thought of its contents (whether heat, electricity or fluidity), and then measure the width of a Fraunhofer line in the spectrum; he can rise at will to the most general abstractions or bury himself in the minutest particulars. Animals possess this capacity in a far less degree. They do not assume a point of view, but are usually forced to it by their sense-impressions. The baby that does not know its father with his hat on, the dog that is perplexed at the new coat of its master, have both succumbed in this conflict of points of view. Who has not been worsted in similar plights? Even the man of philosophy at times succumbs, as the grotesque problem, above referred to, shows.

In this last case, the circumstances appear to furnish a real ground of justification. Colors, sounds, and the odors of bodies are evanescent. But their tangibility, as a sort of constant nucleus, not readily susceptible of annihilation, remains behind; appearing as the vehicle of the more fugitive properties attached to it. Habit, thus, keeps our thought firmly attached to this central nucleus, even when we have begun to recognize that seeing, hearing, smelling, and touching are intimately akin in character. A further consideration is, that owing to the singularly extensive development of mechanical physics a kind of higher reality is ascribed to the spatial and to the temporal than to colors, sounds, and odors; agreeably to which, the temporal and spatial links of colors, sounds, and odors appear to be more real than the colors, sounds and odors themselves. The physiology of the senses, however, demonstrates that spaces and times may just as appropriately be called sensations as colors and sounds. But of this later.

5.

Not only the relation of bodies to the ego, but the ego itself also, gives rise to similar pseudo-problems, the character of which may be briefly indicated as follows:

Let us denote the above-mentioned elements by the letters A B C . . . , K L M . . . , $\alpha\beta\gamma$ . . . Let those complexes of colors, sounds, and so forth, commonly called bodies, be denoted, for the sake of clearness, by A B C . . . ; the complex, known as our own body, which is a part of the former complexes distinguished by certain peculiarities, may be called K L M . . . ; the complex composed of volitions, memory-images, and the rest, we shall represent by $\alpha\beta\gamma$ . . . Usually, now, the complex . . . K L M . . . , as making up the ego, is opposed to the complex A B C . . . , as making up the world of physical objects; sometimes also, $\alpha\beta\gamma$ . . . is viewed as ego, and K L M . . . A B C . . . as world of physical objects. Now, at first blush, A B C . . . appears independent of the ego, and opposed to it as a separate existence. But this independence is only relative, and gives way upon closer inspection. Much, it is true, *may* change in the complex $\alpha\beta\gamma$ . . . without much perceptible change being induced in A B C . . . ; and *vice versa*. But many changes in $\alpha\beta\gamma$ . . . do pass, by way of changes in K L M . . . , to A B C . . . ; and *vice versa*. (As, for example, when powerful ideas burst forth into acts, or when our environment induces noticeable changes in our body.) At the same time the group K L M . . . appears to be more intimately connected with $\alpha\beta\gamma$ . . . and with A B C . . . , than the latter with one another; and their relations find their expression in common thought and speech.

Precisely viewed, however, it appears that the group A B C . . . is always codetermined by K L M. A cube when seen close at hand, looks large; when seen at a distance, small; its appearance to the right eye differs from its appearance to the left; sometimes it appears double; with closed eyes it is invisible. The properties of one and the same body, therefore, appear modified by our own body; they appear conditioned by it. But where, now, is that *same* body, which appears so *different?* All that can be said is, that with different K L M different A B C . . . are associated.

A common and popular way of thinking and speaking is to contrast "appearance" with "reality." A pencil held in front of us in the air is seen by us as straight; dip it into the water, and we see it crooked. In the latter case we say that the pencil *appears* crooked, but is in *reality* straight. But what justifies us in declaring one fact rather than another to be the reality, and degrading the other to the level of appearance? In both cases we have to do with facts which present us with different combinations of the elements, combinations which in the two cases are differently conditioned. Precisely because of its environment the pencil dipped in water is optically crooked; but it is tactually and metrically straight. An image in a concave or flat mirror is *only* visible, whereas under other and ordinary circumstances a tangible body as well corresponds to the visible image. A bright surface is brighter beside a dark surface than beside one brighter than itself. To be sure, our expectation is deceived when, not paying sufficient attention to the conditions, and substituting for one another different cases of the combination, we fall into the natural error of expecting what we are accustomed to, although the case may be an unusual one. The facts are not to blame for that. In these cases, to speak of "appearance" may have a practical meaning, but cannot have a scientific meaning. Similarly, the question which is often asked, whether the world is real or whether we merely dream it, is devoid of all scientific meaning. Even the wildest dream is a fact as much as any other. If our dreams were more regular, more connected, more stable, they would also have more practical importance for us. In our waking hours the relations of the elements to one another are immensely amplified in comparison with what they were in our dreams. We recognize the dream for what it is. When the process is reversed, the field of psychic vision is narrowed; the contrast is almost entirely lacking. Where there is no contrast, the distinction between dream and waking, between appearance and reality, is quite otiose and worthless.

The popular notion of an antithesis between appearance and reality has exercised a very powerful influence on scientific and philosophical thought. We see this, for example, in Plato's pregnant and poetical fiction of the Cave, in which, with our backs turned towards the fire, we observe merely the shadows of what passes (*Republic*, vii. I). But this conception was not thought out to its final consequences, with the result that it has had an unfortunate influence on our ideas about the universe. The universe, of which nevertheless we are a part, became completely separated from us, and was removed an infinite distance away. Similarly, many a young man, hearing for the first time of the refraction of stellar light, has thought that doubt was cast on the whole of astronomy, whereas nothing is required but an easily effected and unimportant correction to put everything right again.

6.

We see an object having a point S. If we touch S, that is, bring it into connexion with our body, we receive a prick. We can see S, without feeling the prick. But as soon as we feel the prick we find S on the skin. The visible point, therefore, is a permanent nucleus, to which the prick is annexed, according to circumstances, as something accidental. From the frequency of analogous occurrences we ultimately accustom ourselves to regard all properties of bodies as "effects" proceeding from permanent nuclei and conveyed to the ego through the medium of the body; which effects we call sensations. By this operation, however, these nuclei are deprived of their entire sensory content, and converted into mere mental symbols. The assertion, then, is correct that the world consists only of our sensations. In which case we have knowledge *only* of sensations, and the assumption of the nuclei referred to, or of a reciprocal action between them, from which sensations proceed, turns out to be quite idle and superfluous. Such a view can only suit with a half-hearted realism or a half-hearted philosophical criticism.

7.

Ordinarily the complex $\alpha\beta\gamma$ . . . K L M . . . is contrasted as ego with the complex A B C . . . At first only those elements of A B C . . . that more strongly alter $\alpha\beta\gamma$ . . . , as a prick, a pain, are wont to be thought of as comprised in the ego. Afterwards, however, through observations of the kind just referred to, it appears that the right to annex A B C . . . to the ego nowhere ceases. In conformity with this view the ego can be so extended as ultimately to embrace the entire world. The ego is not sharply marked off, its limits are very indefinite and arbitrarily displaceable. Only by failing to observe this fact, and by unconsciously narrowing those limits, while at the same time we enlarge them, arise, in the conflict of points of view, the metaphysical difficulties met with in this connexion.

As soon as we have perceived that the supposed unities "body" and "ego" are only makeshifts, designed for provisional orientation and for definite practical ends (so that we may take hold of bodies, protect ourselves against pain, and so forth), we find ourselves obliged, in many more advanced scientific investigations, to abandon them as insufficient and inappropriate. The antithesis between ego and world, between sensation (appearance) and thing, then vanishes, and we have simply to deal with the connexion of the elements $\alpha\beta\gamma$ . . . A B C . . . K L M . . . , of which this antithesis was only a partially appropriate and imperfect expression. This connexion is nothing more or less than the combination of the above-mentioned elements with other similar elements (time and space). Science has simply to accept this connexion, and to get its bearings in it, without at once wanting to explain its existence.

On a superficial examination the complex $\alpha\beta\gamma$ . . . appears to be made up of much more evanescent elements than A B C . . . and K L M . . . , in which last the elements seem to be connected with greater stability and in a more permanent manner (being joined to solid nuclei as it were). Although on closer inspection the elements of all complexes prove to be homogeneous, yet even when this has been recognized, the earlier notion of an antithesis of body and spirit easily slips in again. The philosophical spiritualist is often sensible of the difficulty of imparting the needed solidity to his mind-created world of bodies; the materialist is at a loss when required to endow the world of matter with sensation. The monistic point of view, which reflexion has evolved, is easily clouded by our older and more powerful instinctive notions. . . .

13.

Bodies do not produce sensations, but complexes of elements (complexes of sensations) make up bodies. If, to the physicist, bodies appear the real, abiding existences, whilst the "elements" are regarded merely as their evanescent, transitory appearance, the physicist forgets, in his assumption of such a view, that all bodies are but thought-symbols for complexes of elements (complexes of sensations). Here, too, the elements in question form the real, immediate, and ultimate foundation, which it is the task of physiologico-physical research to investigate. By the recognition of this fact, many points of physiology and physics assume more distinct and more economical forms, and many spurious problems are disposed of.

For us, therefore, the world does not consist of mysterious entities, which by their interaction with another, equally mysterious entity, the ego, produce sensations, which alone are accessible. For us, colors, sounds, spaces, times, . . . are provisionally the ultimate elements, whose given connexion it is our business to investigate. It is precisely in this that the exploration of reality consists. In this investigation we must not allow ourselves to be impeded by such abridgments and delimitations as body, ego, matter, spirit, etc., which have been formed for special, practical purposes and with wholly provisional and limited ends in view. On the contrary, the fittest forms of thought must be created in and by that research itself, just as is done in every special science. In place of the traditional, instinctive ways of thought, a freer, fresher view, conforming to developed experience, and reaching out beyond the requirements of practical life, must be substituted throughout. . . .

FOR FURTHER READING

Armstrong, D. M., *Perception and the Physical World.* Routledge & Kegan Paul, London, 1961.

Austin, J. L., *Sense and Sensibilia.* Clarendon Press, Oxford, 1962.

Ayer, A. J., *The Foundation of Empirical Knowledge.* Chaps. 1, 2, & 4. Macmillan, London, 1940.

Ayer, A. J., *The Problem of Knowledge.* Chap. 3. Macmillan, London, 1956.

Barnes, W. H. F., "The Myth of Sense-Data," *Proceedings of the Aristotelian Society*, 45 (1944–45).

Broad, C. D., *The Mind and Its Place in Nature.* Chap. 4. Routledge & Kegan Paul, London, 1925.

Broad, C. D., *Scientific Thought.* Chaps. 7 & 8. Routledge & Kegan Paul, London, 1923.

Campbell, C. A., "Sense Data and Judgment in Sensory Cognition," *Mind*, 56 (1947).

Chisholm, R. M., *Perceiving: A Philosophical Study.* Cornell University Press, Ithaca, N.Y., 1957.

Garnett, A. C., *The Perceptual Process.* Allen & Unwin, London, and University of Wisconsin Press, Madison, 1965.

Goodman, N., C. I. Lewis, and H. Reichenbach, "The Experiential Element in Knowledge," (Symposium), *Philosophical Review*, 61 (1952).

Grice, H. P., "The Causal Theory of Perception," *Proceedings of the Aristotelian Society*, Supplementary Volume 35 (1961).

Hamlyn, D. W., *The Psychology of Perception*. Routledge & Kegan Paul, London, 1957.

Hamlyn, D. W., *Sensation and Perception*. Routledge & Kegan Paul, London, 1961.

Hirst, R. J. (ed.), *Perception and the External World*. The Macmillan Company, New York, 1965.

Hirst, R. J., *The Problems of Perception*. Allen & Unwin, London, and The Macmillan Company, New York, 1959.

Lewis, C. I., *An Analysis of Knowledge and Valuation*. Chaps. 7–9. Open Court, LaSalle, Illinois, 1946.

Lovejoy, A. O., *The Revolt Against Dualism*. Open Court, LaSalle, Illinois, 1929.

Mach, E., *The Analysis of Sensations*. Reprint Edition. Dover Publications, New York, 1959.

Mandelbaum, M., *Philosophy, Science, and Sense Perception*. Chaps. 1 & 4. The Johns Hopkins University Press, Baltimore, 1964.

Merleau-Ponty, M., *Phenomenology of Perception*. Routledge & Kegan Paul, 1962.

Mill, J. S., *An Examination of Sir William Hamilton's Philosophy*. Longman's, London, 1872.

Moore, G. E., *Some Main Problems of Philosophy*. Chap. 2. Allen & Unwin, London, 1953.

Paul, G. A., "Is There a Problem About Sense-Data?," *Proceedings of the Aristotelian Society*, Supplementary Volume 15 (1936).

Plato, *Theaetetus* (translation and commentary by F. M. Cornford). Bobbs-Merrill, New York and Indianapolis, n. d.

Price, H. H., *Perception*. Methuen, London, 1933.

Quinton, A. M., "The Problem of Perception," *Mind*, 64 (1955).

Russell, B., *An Inquiry into Meaning and Truth*. Chaps. 8–11. Allen & Unwin, London, 1940.

Ryle, G., *The Concept of Mind*. Pp. 213–20. Hutchinson, London, 1949.

Ryle, G., *Dilemmas*. Chap. 7. Cambridge University Press, Cambridge, 1954.

Schlick, M., "The Foundations of Knowledge," in *Logical Positivism* (ed. by A. J. Ayer). Free Press, New York, 1959.

Sellars, W., *Science, Perception and Reality*. Routledge & Kegan Paul, London, 1963.

Stace, W. T., *The Theory of Knowledge and Existence*. Chaps. 3 & 4. Clarendon Press, Oxford, 1932.

Swartz, R. J. (ed.), *Perceiving, Sensing, and Knowing*. Doubleday, Garden City, N.Y., 1965.

Warnock, G. J. (ed.), *The Philosophy of Perception*. Oxford University Press, London, 1967.

Whitehead, A. N., *The Concept of Nature*. Chap. 2. Cambridge University Press, London, 1920.

Whitely, C. H., "Physical Objects," *Philosophy*, 34 (1959).

Wittgenstein, L., *Philosophical Investigations*. I. 242–316 & II. xi. Blackwell, Oxford, 1953.

PART FOUR

THE TRANSCENDENCE
OF EXPERIENCE:
MATERIAL THINGS AND MINDS

31 RENÉ DESCARTES
Natural Beliefs and Knowledge of the Independently Real

*Meditations on the First Philosophy**

MEDITATION II

Of the Nature of the Human Mind; and that it is more easily known than the Body.

. . . Let us begin by considering the commonest matters, those which we believe to be the most distinctly comprehended, to wit, the bodies which we touch and see; not indeed bodies in general, for these general ideas are usually a little more confused, but let us consider one body in particular. Let us take, for example, this piece of wax: it has been taken quite freshly from the hive, and it has not yet lost the sweetness of the honey which it contains; it still retains somewhat of the odour of the flowers from which it has been culled; its colour, its figure, its size are apparent; it is hard, cold, easily handled, and if you strike it with the finger, it will emit a sound. Finally all the things which are requisite to cause us distinctly to recognise a body, are met with in it. But notice that while I speak and approach the fire what remained of the taste is exhaled, the smell evaporates, the colour alters, the figure is destroyed, the size increases, it becomes liquid, it heats, scarcely can one handle it, and when one strikes it, no sound is emitted. Does the same wax remain after this change? We must confess that it remains; none would judge otherwise. What then did I know so distinctly in this piece of wax? It could certainly be nothing of all that the senses brought to my notice, since all these things which fall under taste, smell, sight, touch, and hearing, are found to be changed, and yet the same wax remains.

Perhaps it was what I now think, viz. that this wax was not that sweetness of honey, nor that agreeable scent of flowers, nor that particular whiteness, nor that figure, nor that sound, but simply a body which a little while before appeared to me as perceptible under these forms, and which is now perceptible under others. But what, precisely, is it that I imagine when I form such conceptions? Let us attentively consider this, and, abstracting from all that does not belong to the wax, let us see what remains. Certainly nothing remains excepting a certain extended thing which is flexible and movable. But what is

* From *The Philosophical Works of Descartes*, Vol. I, translated by E. S. Haldane and G. R. T. Ross, Cambridge University Press, London, 1931. Reprinted by permission of Cambridge University Press.

the meaning of flexible and movable? Is it not that I imagine that this piece of wax being round is capable of becoming square and of passing from a square to a triangular figure? No, certainly it is not that, since I imagine it admits of an infinitude of similar changes, and I nevertheless do not know how to compass the infinitude by my imagination, and consequently this conception which I have of the wax is not brought about by the faculty of imagination. What now is this extension? Is it not also unknown? For it becomes greater when the wax is melted, greater when it is boiled, and greater still when the heat increases; and I should not conceive [clearly] according to truth what wax is, if I did not think that even this piece that we are considering is capable of receiving more variations in extension than I have ever imagined. We must then grant that I could not even understand through the imagination what this piece of wax is, and that it is my mind (L. *mens,* F. *entendement*) alone which perceives it. I say this piece of wax in particular, for as to wax in general it is yet clearer. But what is this piece of wax which cannot be understood excepting by the [understanding or] mind? It is certainly the same that I see, touch, imagine, and finally it is the same which I have always believed it to be from the beginning. But what must particularly be observed is that its perception is neither an act of vision, nor touch, nor of imagination, and has never been such although it may have appeared formerly to be so, but only an intuition *(inspectio)* of the mind, which may be imperfect and confused as it was formerly, or clear and distinct as it is at present, according as my attention is more or less directed to the elements which are found in it, and of which it is composed.

Yet in the meantime I am greatly astonished when I consider [the great feebleness of mind] and its proneness to fall [insensibly] into error; for although without giving expression to my thoughts I consider all this in my own mind, words often impede me and I am almost deceived by the terms of ordinary language. For we say that we see the same wax, if it is present, and not that we simply judge that it is the same from its having the same colour and figure. From this I should conclude that I knew the wax by means of vision and not simply by the intuition of the mind; unless by chance I remember that, when looking from a window and saying I see men who pass in the street, I really do not see them, but infer that what I see is men, just as I say that I see wax. And yet what do I see from the window but hats and coats which may cover automatic machines? Yet I judge these to be men. And similarly solely by the faculty of judgment which rests in my mind, I comprehend that which I believed I saw with my eyes.

A man who makes it his aim to raise his knowledge above the common should be ashamed to derive the occasion for doubting from the forms of speech invented by the vulgar; I prefer to pass on and consider whether I had a more evident and perfect conception of what the wax was when I first perceived it, and when I believed I knew it by means of the external senses or at least by the common sense (*sensus communis*) as it is called, that is to say by the imaginative faculty, or whether my present conception is clearer now that I have most carefully examined what it is, and in what way it can be known. It would certainly be absurd to doubt as to this. For what was there in this first perception which was distinct? What was there which might not as well have been perceived by any of the animals? But when I distinguish the wax from its external forms, and when, just as if I had taken from it its vestments, I consider it quite naked, it is certain that although some error may still be found in my judgment, I can nevertheless not perceive it thus without a human mind.

But finally what shall I say of this mind, that is, of myself, for up to this point I do not admit in myself anything but mind? What then, I who seem to perceive this piece of wax so distinctly, do I not know myself, not only with much more truth and certainty, but also with much more distinctness and clearness? For if I judge that the wax is or exists from the fact that I see it, it certainly follows much more clearly that I am or that I exist myself from the fact that I see it. For it may be that what I see is not really wax, it may also be that when I see, or (for I no longer take account of the distinction) when I think I see, that I myself who think am nought. So if I judge that the wax exists from the fact that I touch it, the same thing will follow, to wit, that I am; and if I judge that my imagination, or some other cause, whatever it is, persuades me that the wax exists, I shall still conclude the same. And what I have here remarked of wax may be applied to all other things which are external to me [and which are met with outside of me]. And further, if the [notion or] perception of wax has seemed to me clearer and more distinct, not only after the sight or the touch, but also after many other causes have rendered it quite manifest to me, with how much more [evidence] and distinctness must it be said that I now know myself, since all the reasons which contribute to the knowledge of wax, or any other body whatever, are yet better proofs of the nature of my mind! And there are so many other things in the mind itself which may contribute to the elucidation of its nature, that those which depend on body such as these just mentioned, hardly merit being taken into account.

But finally here I am, having insensibly reverted to the point I desired, for, since it is now manifest to me that even bodies are not properly speaking known by the senses or by the faculty of imagination, but by the understanding only, and since they are not known from the fact that they are seen or touched, but only because they are understood, I see clearly that there is nothing which is easier for me to know than my mind. But because it is difficult to rid oneself so promptly of an opinion to which one was accustomed for so long, it will be well that I should halt a little at this point, so that by the length of my meditation I may more deeply imprint on my memory this new knowledge.

MEDITATION VI

Of the Existence of Material Things, and of the real distinction between the Soul and Body of Man.

Nothing further now remains but to inquire whether material things exist. And certainly I at least know that these may exist in so far as they are considered as the objects of pure mathematics, since in this aspect I perceive them clearly and distinctly. For there is no doubt that God possesses the power to produce everything that I am capable of perceiving with distinctness, and I have never deemed that anything was impossible for Him, unless I found a contradiction in attempting to conceive it clearly. Further, the faculty of imagination which I possess, and of which, experience tells me, I make use when I apply myself to the consideration of material things, is capable of persuading me of their existence; for when I attentively consider what imagination is, I find that it is nothing but a certain application of the faculty of knowledge to the body which is immediately present to it, and which therefore exists.

And to render this quite clear, I remark in the first place the difference that exists between the imagination and pure intellection [or conception (L. *intellectionem*, F. *conception*)]. For example, when I imagine a triangle, I do not conceive it only as a figure comprehended by three lines, but I also apprehend (*intueor*) these three lines as present by the power and inward vision of my mind (*acie mentis*), and this is what I call imagining. But if I desire to think of a chiliagon, I certainly conceive truly that it is a figure composed of a thousand sides, just as easily as I conceive of a triangle that it is a figure of three sides only; but I cannot in any way imagine the thousand sides of a chiliagon [as I do the three sides of a triangle], nor do I, so to speak, regard them as present [with the eyes of my mind]. And although in accordance with the habit I have found of always employing the aid of my imagination when I think of corporeal things, it may happen that in imagining a chiliagon I confusedly represent to myself some figure, yet it is very evident that this figure is not a chiliagon, since it in no way differs from that which I represent to myself when I think of a myriagon or any other many-sided figure; nor does it serve my purpose in discovering the properties which go to form the distinction between a chiliagon and other polygons. But if the question turns upon a pentagon, it is quite true that I can conceive its figure as well as that of a chiliagon without the help of my imagination; but I can also imagine it by applying the attention of my mind to each of its five sides, and at the same time to the space which they enclose. And thus I clearly recognise that I have need of a particular effort of mind in order to effect the act of imagination, such as I do not require in order to understand, and this particular effort of mind clearly manifests the difference which exists between imagination and pure intellection (*intellectionem*).

I remark besides that this power of imagination which is in one, inasmuch as it differs from the power of understanding, is in no wise a necessary element in my nature, or in [my essence, that is to say, in] the essence of my mind; for although I did not possess it I should doubtless ever remain the same as I now am, from which it appears that we might conclude that it depends on something which differs from me. And I easily conceive that if some body exists with which my mind is conjoined and united in such a way that it can apply itself to consider it when it pleases, it may be that by this means it can imagine corporeal objects so that this mode of thinking differs from pure intellection only inasmuch as mind in its intellectual activity in some manner turns on itself, and considers some of the ideas which it possesses in itself; while in imagining it turns towards the body, and there beholds in it something conformable to the idea which it has either conceived of itself or perceived by the senses. I easily understand, I say, that the imagination could be thus constituted if it is true that body exists; and because I can discover no other convenient mode of explaining it, I conjecture with probability that body does exist; but this is only with probability, and although I examine all things with care, I nevertheless do not find that from this distinct idea of corporeal nature, which I have in my imagination, I can derive any argument from which there will necessarily be deduced the existence of body.

But I am in the habit of imagining many other things besides this corporeal nature which is the object of pure mathematics, to wit, the colours, sounds, scents, pain, and other such things, although less distinctly. And inasmuch as I perceive these things much better through the senses, by the medium of which, and by the memory, they seem to have reached my imagination, I believe that, in order to examine them more conveniently, it is right that I should at the same time investigate the nature of sense perception, and that I should see if from the ideas which I apprehend by this mode of thought, which I call feeling, I cannot derive some certain proof of the existence of corporeal objects.

And first of all I shall recall to my memory those matters which I hitherto held to be true, as having perceived them through the senses, and the foundations on which my belief has rested; in the next place I shall examine the reasons which have since obliged me to place them in doubt; in the last place I shall consider which of them I must now believe.

First of all, then, I perceived that I had a head, hands, feet, and all other members of which this body—which I considered as a part, or possibly even as the whole, of myself—is composed. Further I was sensible that this body was placed amidst many others, from which it was capable of being affected in many different ways, beneficial and hurtful, and I remarked that a certain feeling of pleasure accompanied those that were beneficial, and pain those which were harmful. And in addition to this pleasure and pain, I also experienced hunger, thirst, and other similar appetites, as also certain corporeal inclinations towards joy, sadness, anger, and other similar passions. And outside myself, in addition to extension, figure, and motions of bodies, I remarked in them hardness, heat, and all other tactile qualities, and, further, light and colour, and scents and sounds, the variety of which gave me the means of distinguishing the sky, the earth, the sea, and generally all the other bodies, one from the other. And certainly, considering the ideas of all these qualities which presented themselves to my mind, and which alone I perceived properly or immediately, it was not without reason that I believed myself to perceive objects quite different from my thought, to wit, bodies from which those

ideas proceeded; for I found by experience that these ideas presented themselves to me without my consent being requisite, so that I could not perceive
any object, however desirous I might be, unless it were present to the organs of
sense; and it was not in my power not to perceive it, when it was present. And
because the ideas which I received through the senses were much more lively,
more clear, and even, in their own way, more distinct than any of those which
I could of myself frame in meditation, or than those I found impressed on my
memory, it appeared as though they could not have proceeded from my mind,
so that they must necessarily have been produced in me by some other things.
And having no knowledge of those objects excepting the knowledge which the
ideas themselves gave me, nothing was more likely to occur to my mind than
that the objects were similar to the ideas which were caused. And because I
likewise remembered that I had formerly made use of my senses rather than
my reason, and recognised that the ideas which I formed of myself were not so
distinct as those which I perceived through the senses, and that they were most
frequently even composed of portions of these last, I persuaded myself easily
that I had no idea in my mind which had not formerly come to me through
the senses. Nor was it without some reason that I believed that this body
(which by a certain special right I call my own) belonged to me more properly
and more strictly than any other; for in fact I could never be separated from it
as from other bodies; I experienced in it and on account of it all my appetites
and affections, and finally I was touched by the feeling of pain and the titillation of pleasure in its parts, and not in the parts of other bodies which were
separated from it. But when I inquired, why, from some, I know not what,
painful sensation, there follows sadness of mind, and from the pleasurable sensation there arises joy, or why this mysterious pinching of the stomach which I
call hunger causes me to desire to eat, and dryness of throat causes a desire to
drink, and so on, I could give no reason excepting that nature taught me so;
for there is certainly no affinity (that I at least can understand) between the
craving of the stomach and the desire to eat, any more than between the perception of whatever causes pain and the thought of sadness which arises from
this perception. And in the same way it appeared to me that I had learned
from nature all the other judgments which I formed regarding the objects of
my senses, since I remarked that these judgments were formed in me before I
had the leisure to weigh and consider any reasons which might oblige me to
make them.

But afterwards many experiences little by little destroyed all the faith
which I had rested in my senses; for I from time to time observed that those
towers which from afar appeared to me to be round, more closely observed
seemed square, and that colossal statues raised on the summit of these towers,
appeared as quite tiny statues when viewed from the bottom; and so in an infinitude of other cases I found error in judgments founded on the external
senses. And not only in those founded on the external senses, but even in those
founded on the internal as well; for is there anything more intimate or more
internal than pain? And yet I have learned from some persons whose arms or

legs have been cut off, that they sometimes seemed to feel pain in the part which had been amputated, which made me think that I could not be quite certain that it was a certain member which pained me, even although I felt pain in it. And to those grounds of doubt I have lately added two others, which are very general; the first is that I never have believed myself to feel anything in waking moments which I cannot also sometimes believe myself to feel when I sleep, and as I do not think that these things which I seem to feel in sleep, proceed from objects outside of me, I do not see any reason why I should have this belief regarding objects which I seem to perceive while awake. The other was that being still ignorant, or rather supposing myself to be ignorant, of the author of my being, I saw nothing to prevent me from having been so constituted by nature that I might be deceived even in matters which seemed to me to be most certain. And as to the grounds on which I was formerly persuaded of the truth of sensible objects, I had not much trouble in replying to them. For since nature seemed to cause me to lean towards many things from which reason repelled me, I did not believe that I should trust much to the teachings of nature. And although the ideas which I received by the senses do not depend on my will, I did not think that one should for that reason conclude that they proceeded from things different from myself, since possibly some faculty might be discovered in me—though hitherto unknown to me—which produced them.

But now that I begin to know myself better, and to discover more clearly the author of my being, I do not in truth think that I should rashly admit all the matters which the senses seem to teach us, but, on the other hand, I do not think that I should doubt them all universally.

And first of all, because I know that all things which I apprehend clearly and distinctly can be created by God as I apprehend them, it suffices that I am able to apprehend one thing apart from another clearly and distinctly in order to be certain that the one is different from the other, since they may be made to exist in separation at least by the omnipotence of God; and it does not signify by what power this separation is made in order to compel me to judge them to be different: and, therefore, just because I know certainly that I exist, and that meanwhile I do not remark that any other thing necessarily pertains to my nature or essence, excepting that I am a thinking thing, I rightly conclude that my essence consists solely in the fact that I am a thinking thing [or a substance whose whole essence or nature is to think]. And although possibly (or rather certainly, as I shall say in a moment) I possess a body with which I am very intimately conjoined, yet because, on the one side, I have a clear and distinct idea of myself inasmuch as I am only a thinking and unextended thing, and as, on the other, I possess a distinct idea of body, inasmuch as it is only an extended and unthinking thing, it is certain that this I [that is to say, my soul by which I am what I am], is entirely and absolutely distinct from my body, and can exist without it.

I further find in myself faculties employing modes of thinking peculiar to themselves, to wit, the faculties of imagination and feeling, without which I can easily conceive myself clearly and distinctly as a complete being; while, on the other hand, they cannot be so conceived apart from me, that is without an intelligent substance in which they reside, for [in the notion we have of these faculties, or, to use the language of the Schools] in their formal concept, some kind of intellection is comprised, from which I infer that they are distinct from me as its modes are from a thing. I observe also in me some other faculties such as that of change of position, the assumption of different figures and such like, which cannot be conceived, any more than can the preceding, apart from some substance to which they are attached, and consequently cannot exist without it; but it is very clear that these faculties, if it be true that they exist, must be attached to some corporeal or extended substance, and not to an intelligent substance, since in the clear and distinct conception of these there is some sort of extension found to be present, but no intellection at all. There is certainly further in me a certain passive faculty of perception, that is, of receiving and recognising the ideas of sensible things, but this would be useless to me [and I could in no way avail myself of it], if there were not either in me or in some other thing another active faculty capable of forming and producing these ideas. But this active faculty cannot exist in me [inasmuch as I am a thing that thinks] seeing that it does not presuppose thought, and also that those ideas are often produced in me without my contributing in any way to the same, and often even against my will; it is thus necessarily the case that the faculty resides in some substance different from me in which all the reality which is objectively in the ideas that are produced by this faculty is formally or eminently contained, as I remarked before. And this substance is either a body, that is, a corporeal nature in which there is contained formally [and really] all that which is objectively [and by representation] in those ideas, or it is God Himself, or some other creature more noble than body in which that same is contained eminently. But, since God is no deceiver, it is very manifest that He does not communicate to me these ideas immediately and by Himself, nor yet by the intervention of some creature in which their reality is not formally, but only eminently, contained. For since He has given me no faculty to recognise that this is the case, but, on the other hand, a very great inclination to believe [that they are sent to me or] that they are conveyed to me by corporeal objects, I do not see how He could be defended from the accusation of deceit if these ideas were produced by causes other than corporeal objects. Hence we must allow that corporeal things exist. However, they are perhaps not exactly what we perceive by the senses, since this comprehension by the senses is in many instances very obscure and confused; but we must at least admit that all things which I conceive in them clearly and distinctly, that is to say, all things which, speaking generally, are comprehended in the object of pure mathematics, are truly to be recognised as external objects.

As to other things, however, which are either particular only, as, for example, that the sun is of such and such a figure, etc., or which are less clearly and distinctly conceived, such as light, sound, pain and the like, it is certain that although they are very dubious and uncertain, yet on the sole ground that God is not a deceiver, and that consequently He has not likewise given me the faculty of correcting, I may assuredly hope to conclude that I have within me the means of arriving at the truth even here. And first of all there is no doubt that in all things which nature teaches me there is some truth contained; for by nature, considered in general, I now understand no other thing than either God Himself or else the order and disposition which God has established in created things; and by my nature in particular I understand no other thing than the complexus of all the things which God has given me.

But there is nothing which this nature teaches me more expressly [nor more sensibly] than that I have a body which is adversely affected when I feel pain, which has need of food or drink when I experience the feelings of hunger and thirst, and so on; nor can I doubt there being some truth in all this.

Nature also teaches me by these sensations of pain, hunger, thirst, etc., that I am not only lodged in my body as a pilot in a vessel, but that I am very closely united to it, and so to speak so intermingled with it that I seem to compose with it one whole. For if that were not the case, when my body is hurt, I, who am merely a thinking thing, should not feel pain, for I should perceive this wound by the understanding only, just as the sailor perceives by sight when something is damaged in his vessel; and when my body has need of drink or food, I should clearly understand the fact without being warned of it by confused feelings of hunger and thirst. For all these sensations of hunger, thirst, pain, etc. are in truth none other than certain confused modes of thought which are produced by the union and apparent intermingling of mind and body.

Moreover, nature teaches me that many other bodies exist around mine, of which some are to be avoided, and others sought after. And certainly from the fact that I am sensible of different sorts of colours, sounds, scents, tastes, heat, hardness, etc., I very easily conclude that there are in the bodies from which all these diverse sense-perceptions proceed certain variations which answer to them, although possibly these are not really at all similar to them. And also from the fact that amongst these different sense-perceptions some are very agreeable to me and others disagreeable, it is quite certain that my body (or rather myself in my entirety, inasmuch as I am formed of body and soul) may receive different impressions agreeable and disagreeable from the other bodies which surround it.

But there are many other things which nature seems to have taught me, but which at the same time I have never really received from her, but which have been brought about in my mind by a certain habit which I have of forming inconsiderate judgments on things; and thus it may easily happen that these judgments contain some error. Take, for example, the opinion which I hold that all space in which there is nothing that affects [or makes an impression on] my senses is void; that in a body which is warm there is something entirely similar to the idea of heat which is in me; that in a white or green body there is the same whiteness or greenness that I perceive; that in a bitter or sweet body there is the same taste, and so on in other instances; that the stars, the towers, and all other distant bodies are of the same figure and size as they appear from far off to our eyes, etc. But in order that in this there should be nothing which I do not conceive distinctly, I should define exactly what I really understand when I say that I am taught somewhat by nature. For here I take nature in a more limited signification than when I term it the sum of all the things given me by God, since in this sum many things are comprehended which only pertain to mind (and to these I do not refer in speaking of nature) such as the notion which I have of the fact that what has once been done cannot ever be undone and an infinitude of such things which I know by the light of nature [without the help of the body]; and seeing that it comprehends many other matters besides which only pertain to body, and are no longer here contained under the name of nature, such as the quality of weight which it possesses and the like, with which I also do not deal; for in talking of nature I only treat of those things given by God to me as a being composed of mind and body. But the nature here described truly teaches me to flee from things which cause the sensation of pain, and seek after the things which communicate to me the sentiment of pleasure and so forth; but I do not see that beyond this it teaches me that from those diverse sense-perceptions we should ever form any conclusion regarding things outside of us, without having [carefully and maturely] mentally examined them beforehand. For it seems to me that it is mind alone, and not mind and body in conjunction, that is requisite to a knowledge of the truth in regard to such things. Thus, although a star makes no larger an impression on my eye than the flame of a little candle there is yet in me no real or positive propensity impelling me to believe that it is not greater than that flame; but I have judged it to be so from my earliest years, without any rational foundation. And although in approaching fire I feel heat, and in approaching it a little too near I even feel pain, there is at the same time no reason in this which could persuade me that there is in the fire something resembling this heat any more than there is in it something resembling the pain; all that I have any reason to believe from this is, that there is something in it, whatever it may be, which excites in me these sensations of heat or of pain. So also, although there are spaces in which I find nothing which excites my senses, I must not from that conclude that these spaces contain no body; for I see in this, as in other similar things, that I have been in the habit of perverting the order of nature, because these perceptions of sense having been placed within me by nature merely for the purpose of signifying to my mind what things are beneficial or hurtful to the composite whole of which it forms a part, and being up to that point sufficiently clear and distinct, I yet avail myself of them as though they were absolute rules by which I might immediately determine the essence of the bodies which are outside me, as to which, in fact, they can teach me nothing, but what is more obscure and confused.

But I have already sufficiently considered how, notwithstanding the supreme goodness of God, falsity enters into the judgments I make. Only here a new difficulty is presented—one respecting those things the pursuit or avoid-

ance of which is taught me by nature, and also respecting the internal sensations which I possess, and in which I seem to have sometimes detected error
[and thus to be directly deceived by my own nature]. To take an example, the
agreeable taste of some food in which poison has been intermingled may induce me to partake of the poison, and thus deceive me. It is true, at the same
time, that in this case nature may be excused, for it only induces me to desire
food in which I find a pleasant taste, and not to desire the poison which is unknown to it; and thus I can infer nothing from this fact, except that my nature
is not omniscient, at which there is certainly no reason to be astonished, since
man, being finite in nature, can only have knowledge the perfectness of which
is limited.

But we not unfrequently deceive ourselves even in those things to which
we are directly impelled by nature, as happens with those who when they are
sick desire to drink or eat things hurtful to them. It will perhaps be said here
that the cause of their deceptiveness is that their nature is corrupt, but that
does not remove the difficulty, because a sick man is none the less truly God's
creature than he who is in health; and it is therefore as repugnant to God's
goodness for the one to have a deceitful nature as it is for the other. And as a
clock composed of wheels and counter-weights no less exactly observes the
laws of nature when it is badly made, and does not show the time properly,
than when it entirely satisfies the wishes of its maker, and as, if I consider the
body of a man as being a sort of machine so built up and composed of nerves,
muscles, veins, blood and skin, that though there were no mind in it at all, it
would not cease to have the same motions as at present, exception being made
of those movements which are due to the direction of the will, and in consequence depend upon the mind [as opposed to those which operate by the disposition of its organs], I easily recognise that it would be as natural to this
body, supposing it to be, for example, dropsical, to suffer the parchedness of
the throat, which usually signifies to the mind the feeling of thirst, and to be
disposed by this parched feeling to move the nerves and other parts in the way
requisite for drinking, and thus to augment its malady and do harm to itself,
as it is natural to it, when it has no indisposition, to be impelled to drink for its
good by a similar cause. And although, considering the use to which the clock
has been destined by its maker, I may say that it deflects from the order of its
nature when it does not indicate the hours correctly; and as, in the same way,
considering the machine of the human body as having been formed by God in
order to have in itself all the movements usually manifested there, I have reason for thinking that it does not follow the order of nature when, if the throat
is dry, drinking does harm to the conservation of health, nevertheless I recognise at the same time that this last mode of explaining nature is very different
from the other. For this is but a purely verbal characterisation depending entirely on my thought, which compares a sick man and a badly constructed
clock with the idea which I have of a healthy man and a well made clock, and
it is hence extrinsic to the things to which it is applied; but according to the

other interpretation of the term nature I understand something which is truly found in things and which is therefore not without some truth.

But certainly although in regard to the dropsical body it is only so to speak to apply an extrinsic term when we say that its nature is corrupted, inasmuch as apart from the need to drink, the throat is parched; yet in regard to the composite whole, that is to say, to the mind or soul united to this body, it is not a purely verbal predicate, but a real error of nature, for it to have thirst when drinking would be hurtful to it. And thus it still remains to inquire how the goodness of God does not prevent the nature of man so regarded from being fallacious.

In order to begin this examination, then, I here say, in the first place, that there is a great difference between mind and body, inasmuch as body is by nature always divisible, and the mind is entirely indivisible. For, as a matter of fact, when I consider the mind, that is to say, myself inasmuch as I am only a thinking thing, I cannot distinguish in myself any parts, but apprehend myself to be clearly one and entire; and although the whole mind seems to be united to the whole body, yet if a foot, or an arm, or some other part, is separated from my body, I am aware that nothing has been taken away from my mind. And the faculties of willing, feeling, conceiving, etc. cannot be properly speaking said to be its parts, for it is one and the same mind which employs itself in willing and in feeling and understanding. But it is quite otherwise with corporeal or extended objects, for there is not one of these imaginable by me which my mind cannot easily divide into parts, and which consequently I do not recognise as being divisible; this would be sufficient to teach me that the mind or soul of man is entirely different from the body, if I had not already learned it from other sources.

I further notice that the mind does not receive the impressions from all parts of the body immediately, but only from the brain, or perhaps even from one of its smallest parts, to wit, from that in which the common sense (*sensus communis*) is said to reside, which, whenever it is disposed in the same particular way, conveys the same thing to the mind, although meanwhile the other portions of the body may be differently disposed, as is testified by innumerable experiments which it is unnecessary here to recount.

I notice, also, that the nature of body is such that none of its parts can be moved by another part a little way off which cannot also be moved in the same way by each one of the parts which are between the two, although this more remote part does not act at all. As, for example, in the cord ABCD [which is in tension] if we pull the last part D, the first part A will not be moved in any way differently from what would be the case if one of the intervening parts B or C were pulled, and the last part D were to remain unmoved. And in the same way, when I feel pain in my foot, my knowledge of physics teaches me that this sensation is communicated by means of nerves dispersed through the foot, which, being extended like cords from there to the brain, when they are contracted in the foot, at the same time contract the inmost portions of the brain which is their extremity and place of origin, and then excite a certain movement which nature has established in order to cause the mind to be affected by a sensation of pain represented as existing in the foot. But because these nerves must pass through the tibia, the thigh, the loins, the back and the neck, in order to reach from the leg to the brain, it may happen that although their extremities which are in the foot are not affected, but only certain ones of their intervening parts [which pass by the loins or the neck], this action will excite the same movement in the brain that might have been excited there by a hurt received in the foot, in consequence of which the mind will necessarily feel in the foot the same pain as if it had received a hurt. And the same holds good of all the other perceptions of our senses.

I notice finally that since each of the movements which are in the portion of the brain by which the mind is immediately affected brings about one particular sensation only, we cannot under the circumstances imagine anything more likely than that this movement, amongst all the sensations which it is capable of impressing on it, causes mind to be affected by that one which is best fitted and most generally useful for the conservation of the human body when it is in health. But experience makes us aware that all the feelings with which nature inspires us are such as I have just spoken of; and there is therefore nothing in them which does not give testimony to the power and goodness of the God [who has produced them[1]]. Thus, for example, when the nerves which are in the feet are violently or more than usually moved, their movement, passing through the medulla of the spine (*spini dorsae medullam*) to the inmost parts of the brain, gives a sign to the mind which makes it feel somewhat, to wit, pain, as though in the foot, by which the mind is excited to do its utmost to remove the cause of the evil as dangerous and hurtful to the foot. It is true that God could have constituted the nature of man in such a way that this same movement in the brain would have conveyed something quite different to the mind; for example, it might have produced consciousness of itself either in so far as it is in the brain, or as it is in the foot, or as it is in some other place between the foot and the brain, or it might finally have produced consciousness of anything else whatsoever; but none of all this would have contributed so well to the conservation of the body. Similarly, when we desire to drink, a certain dryness of the throat is produced which moves its nerves, and by their means the internal portions of the brain; and this movement causes in the mind the sensation of thirst, because in this case there is nothing more useful to us than to become aware that we have need to drink for the conservation of our health; and the same holds good in other instances.

From this it is quite clear that, notwithstanding the supreme goodness of God, the nature of man, inasmuch as it is composed of mind and body, cannot be otherwise than sometimes a source of deception. For if there is any cause which excites, not in the foot but in some part of the nerves which are extended between the foot and the brain, or even in the brain itself, the same movement which usually is produced when the foot is detrimentally affected,

---

[1] Latin version only.—*Tr.*

pain will be experienced as though it were in the foot, and the sense will thus naturally be deceived; for since the same movement in the brain is capable of causing but one sensation in the mind, and this sensation is much more frequently excited by a cause which hurts the foot than by another existing in some other quarter, it is reasonable that it should convey to the mind pain in the foot rather than in any other part of the body. And although the parchedness of the throat does not always proceed, as it usually does, from the fact that drinking is necessary for the health of the body, but sometimes comes from quite a different cause, as is the case with dropsical patients, it is yet much better that it should mislead on this occasion than if, on the other hand, it were always to deceive us when the body is in good health; and so on in similar cases.

And certainly this consideration is of great service to me, not only in enabling me to recognise all the errors to which my nature is subject, but also in enabling me to avoid them or to correct them more easily. For knowing that all my senses more frequently indicate to me truth than falsehood respecting the things which concern that which is beneficial to the body, and being able almost always to avail myself of many of them in order to examine one particular thing, and, besides that, being able to make use of my memory in order to connect the present with the past, and of my understanding which already has discovered all the causes of my errors, I ought no longer to fear that falsity may be found in matters every day presented to me by my senses. And I ought to set aside all the doubts of these past days as hyperbolical and ridiculous, particularly that very common uncertainty respecting sleep, which I could not distinguish from the waking state; for at present I find a very notable difference between the two, inasmuch as our memory can never connect our dreams one with the other, or with the whole course of our lives, as it unites events which happen to us while we are awake. And, as a matter of fact, if someone, while I was awake, quite suddenly appeared to me and disappeared as fast as do the images which I see in sleep, so that I could not know from whence the form came nor whither it went, it would not be without reason that I should deem it a spectre or a phantom formed by my brain [and similar to those which I form in sleep], rather than a real man. But when I perceive things, as to which I know distinctly both the place from which they proceed, and that in which they are, and the time at which they appeared to me; and when, without any interruption, I can connect the perceptions which I have of them with the whole course of my life, I am perfectly assured that these perceptions occur while I am waking and not during sleep. And I ought in no wise to doubt the truth of such matters, if, after having called up all my senses, my memory, and my understanding, to examine them, nothing is brought to evidence by any one of them which is repugnant to what is set forth by others. For because God is in no wise a deceiver, it follows that I am not deceived in this. But because the exigencies of action often oblige us to make up our minds before having leisure to examine matters carefully, we must confess that the life of man is very frequently subject to error in respect to individual objects, and we must in the end acknowledge the infirmity of our nature.

Locke, Bk. II, Ch. XXIII, of the *Essay:*

1. The mind being, as I have declared, furnished with a great number of the simple ideas, conveyed in by the senses as they are found in exterior things, or by reflection on its own operations, takes notice also that a certain number of these simple ideas go constantly together; which being presumed to belong to one thing, and words being suited to common apprehensions, and made use of for quick dispatch, are called, so united in one subject, by one name; which, by inadvertency, we are apt afterward to talk of and consider as one simple idea, which indeed is a complication of many ideas together: because, as I have said, not imagining how these simple ideas *can* subsist by themselves, we accustom ourselves to suppose some *substratum* wherein they do subsist, and from which they do result, which therefore we call *substance.*

Leibniz:

. . . On the contrary, it is rather the *concretum,* as wise, warm, shining, which arises in our mind, than the *abstractions* or qualities (for these and not the ideas are in the substantial object), as knowledge, heat, light, etc., which are much more difficult to comprehend. We may even doubt whether these accidents are veritable existences, as in fact they are very often only relations. We know also that it is these abstractions which cause the greatest difficulties to spring up when we wish to examine them minutely, as those know who are familiar with the subtilties of the scholastics, the most intricate of which falls at once if we will banish abstract existence and resolve to speak ordinarily only by concretes and admit no other terms in scientific demonstrations but those which represent substantial subjects. Thus it is *nodum quaerere in scirpo,*[1] if I may so speak, and reversing things to take the qualities or other abstract terms as the easier and the concrete as something very difficult.

2. So that if any one will examine himself concerning his notion of pure substance in general, he will find he has no other idea of it at all, but only a supposition of he knows not what *support* of such qualities which are capable of producing simple ideas in us; which qualities are commonly called accidents. If any one should be asked, what is the subject wherein colour or weight in-

* From Locke, *An Essay Concerning Human Understanding* and Leibniz, *New Essays Concerning Human Understanding,* translated by A. G. Langley, The Open Court Publishing Company, LaSalle, Ill., 3rd Edition, 1949. All passages from the latter work are reprinted by permission of The Open Court Publishing Company.

[1] To seek a knot in a bulrush, to find a difficulty when there is none.—*Tr.*

heres, he would have nothing to say, but the solid extended parts; and if he were demanded, what is it that solidity and extension adhere in, he would not be in a much better case than the Indian before mentioned who, saying that the world was supported by a great elephant, was asked what the elephant rested on; to which his answer was—a great tortoise; but being again pressed to know what gave support to the broad-backed tortoise, replied—*something, he knew not what.* And thus here, as in all other cases where we use words without having clear and distinct ideas, we talk like children: who, being questioned what such a thing is, which they know not, readily give this satisfactory answer, that it is *something:* which in truth signifies no more, when so used, either by children or men, but that they know not what; and that the thing they pretend to know, and talk of, is what they have no distinct idea of at all, and so are perfectly ignorant of it, and in the dark. The idea then we have, to which we give the *general* name substance, being nothing but the supposed, but unknown, support of those qualities we find existing, which we imagine cannot subsist *sine re substante,* without something to support them, we call that support *substantia;* which, according to the true import of the word, is, in plain English, standing under or upholding.

Leibniz:

In distinguishing two things in substance, the attributes or predicates, and the common subject of these predicates, it is no wonder that we can conceive nothing particular in this subject. It must be so, indeed, since we have already separated from it all the attributes in which we could conceive any detail. Thus to demand something more in this pure *subject in general* than what is necessary in order to conceive that it is the same thing (for example, which understands and wills, which imagines and reasons), is to demand the impossible, and to act contrary to our own supposition, which has been made in making abstraction and conceiving separately the subject and its qualities or accidents. We could apply the same pretended difficulty to the notion of *being* and to all that is clearer and more primitive; for we could demand of the philosophers what they conceive when conceiving *pure being in general;* for all detail being excluded by that means there will also be little to say, when we are asked what is *pure substance in general.* Thus I believe that the philosophers do not deserve to be laughed at, as is here done, in comparing them with an Indian philosopher, who, being asked upon what the earth rested, replied, upon a great elephant; and then when asked what sustained the elephant, replied, a great tortoise; and, at last, when pressed to say upon what the tortoise rested, was compelled to say *something, I know not what.* But this consideration of substance, entirely slender as it appears, is not so empty and sterile as you think. It gives rise to many consequences of greatest importance in philosophy, and which are capable of giving it a new aspect.

3. An obscure and relative idea of *substance in general* being thus made we come to have the ideas of *particular sorts of substances,* by collecting such combi-

nations of simple ideas as are, by experience and observation of man's senses, taken notice of to exist together; and are therefore supposed to flow from the particular internal constitution, or unknown essence of that substance. Thus we come to have the ideas of a man, horse, gold, water, &c.; of which substances, whether any one has any other *clear* idea, further than of certain simple ideas co-existent together, I appeal to every one's own experience. It is the ordinary qualities observable in iron, or a diamond, put together, that make the true complex idea of those substances, which a smith or a jeweller commonly knows better than a philosopher; who, whatever *substantial forms* he may talk of, has no other idea of those substances, than what is framed by a collection of those simple ideas which are to be found in them: only we must take notice, that our complex ideas of substances, besides all those simple ideas they are made up of, have always the confused idea of something to which they belong, and in which they subsist: and therefore when we speak of any sort of substance, we say it is a thing having such or such qualities; as body is a thing that is extended, figured, and capable of motion; spirit, a thing capable of thinking; and so hardness, friability, and power to draw iron, we say, are qualities to be found in a loadstone. These, and the like fashions of speaking, intimate that the substance is supposed always *something besides* the extension, figure, solidity, motion, thinking, or other observable ideas, though we know not what it is.

4. Hence, when we talk or think of any particular sort of corporeal substances, as horse, stone, &c., though the idea we have of either of them be but the complication or collection of those several simple ideas of sensible qualities, which we used to find united in the thing called horse or stone; yet, *because we cannot conceive how they should subsist alone, nor one in another,* we suppose them existing in and supported by some common subject; which support we denote by the name substance, though it be certain we have no clear or distinct idea of that thing we suppose a support.

Leibniz:

As for myself, I believe that this opinion of our ignorance arises from that which demands a kind of knowledge of which the object does not admit. The true mark of a clear and distinct notion of an object is the means we have of knowing therein many truths by *a priori* proofs, as I have shown in a discourse on truths and ideas, published in the "Actes de Leipzig" of the year 1684.

5. The same thing happens concerning the operations of the mind, viz. thinking, reasoning, fearing, &c., which we concluding not to subsist of themselves, nor apprehending how they can belong to body, or be produced by it, we are apt to think these the actions of some other *substance,* which we call *spirit;* whereby yet it is evident that, having no other idea or notion of matter, but something wherein those many sensible qualities which affect our senses do subsist; by supposing a substance wherein thinking, knowing, doubting,

and a power of moving, &c., do subsist, we have as clear a notion of the substance of spirit, as we have of body; the one being supposed to be (without
knowing what it is) the *substratum* to those simple ideas we have from without;
and the other supposed to be (with a like ignorance of what it is) the *substratum*
to those operations we experiment in ourselves within. It is plain then, that the
idea of *corporeal substance* in matter is as remote from our conceptions and apprehensions, as that of *spiritual substance,* or spirit: and therefore, from our not
having any notion of the substance of spirit, we can no more conclude its non-
existence, than we can, for the same reason, deny the existence of body; it
being as rational to affirm there is no body, because we have no clear and distinct idea of the substance of matter, as to say there is no spirit, because we
have no clear and distinct idea of the substance of a spirit. . . .

15. Besides the complex ideas we have of material sensible substances, of
which I have last spoken,—by the simple ideas we have taken from those operations of our own minds, which we experiment daily in ourselves, as thinking,
understanding, willing, knowing, and power of beginning motion, &c., co-ex-
isting in some substance, we are able to frame the *complex idea of an immaterial
spirit.* And thus, by putting together the ideas of thinking, perceiving, liberty,
and power of moving or quieting corporeal motion, joined to substance, of
which we have no distinct idea, we have the idea of an immaterial spirit; and
by putting together the ideas of coherent solid parts, and a power of being
moved, joined with substance, of which likewise we have no positive idea, we
have the idea of matter. The one is as clear and distinct an idea as the other:
the idea of thinking, and moving a body, being as clear and distinct ideas as
the ideas of extension, solidity, and being moved. For our idea of substance is
equally obscure, or none at all, in both: it is but a supposed I know not what,
to support those ideas we call accidents. [It is for want of reflection that we are
apt to think that our senses show us nothing but material things. Every act of
sensation, when duly considered, gives us an equal view of both parts of nature, the corporeal and spiritual. For whilst I know, by seeing or hearing, &c.,
that there is some corporeal being without me, the object of that sensation, I
do more certainly know, that there is some spiritual being within me that sees
and hears. This, I must be convinced, cannot be the action of bare insensible
matter; nor ever could be, without an immaterial thinking being.] . . .

Leibniz:

   It is very well said and very true that the existence of the spirit is *more
 certain* than that of sensible objects.[1]

22. Let us compare, then, our complex idea of an immaterial spirit with
our complex idea of body, and see whether there be any more obscurity in one
than in the other, and in which most. Our idea of *body,* as I think, is *an extended
solid substance, capable of communicating motion by impulse:* and our idea of *soul,* as an

---

[1] [See above, pp. 128–9.—*Ed.*]

immaterial spirit, is of *a substance that thinks, and has a power of exciting motion in body, by willing, or thought.* These, I think, are our complex ideas of soul and body, as contradistinguished; and now let us examine which has most obscurity in it, and difficulty to be apprehended. I know that people whose thoughts are immersed in matter, and have so subjected their minds to their senses that they seldom reflect on anything beyond them, are apt to say, they cannot comprehend a *thinking* thing, which perhaps is true: but I affirm, when they consider it well, they can no more comprehend an *extended* thing. . . .

29. To conclude. Sensation convinces us that there are solid extended substances; and reflection, that there are thinking ones: experience assures us of the existence of such beings, and that the one hath a power to move body by impulse, the other by thought; this we cannot doubt of. Experience, I say, every moment furnishes us with the clear ideas both of the one and the other. But beyond these ideas, as received from their proper sources, our faculties will not reach. If we would inquire further into their nature, causes, and manner, we perceive not the nature of extension clearer than we do of thinking. If we would explain them any further, one is as easy as the other; and there is no more difficulty to conceive how *a substance we know not* should, by thought, set body into motion. So that we are no more able to discover wherein the ideas belonging to body consist, than those belonging to spirit. From whence it seems probable to me, that the simple ideas we receive from sensation and reflection are the boundaries of our thoughts; beyond which the mind, whatever efforts it would make, is not able to advance one jot; nor can it make any discoveries, when it would pry into the nature and hidden causes of those ideas.

Locke, Bk. IV, Ch. IV of the *Essay*:

1. I doubt not but my reader, by this time, may be apt to think that I have been all this while only building a castle in the air; and be ready to say to me:—

'To what purpose all this stir? Knowledge, say you, is only the perception of the agreement or disagreement of our own ideas: but who knows what those ideas may be? Is there anything so extravagant as the imaginations of men's brains? Where is the head that has no chimeras in it? Or if there be a sober and a wise man, what difference will there be, by your rules, between his knowledge and that of the most extravagant fancy in the world? They both have their ideas, and perceive their agreement and disagreement one with another. If there be any difference between them, the advantage will be on the warm-headed man's side, as having the more ideas, and the more lively. And so, by your rules, he will be the more knowing. If it be true, that all knowledge lies only in the perception of the agreement or disagreement of our own ideas, the visions of an enthusiast and the reasonings of a sober man will be equally certain. It is no matter how things are: so a man observe but the agreement of his own imaginations, and talk conformably, it is all truth, all certainty. Such castles in the air will be as strongholds of truth, as the demonstrations of Euclid. That an harpy is not a centaur is by this way as certain knowledge, and as much a truth, as that a square is not a circle.

'But of what use is all this fine knowledge of *men's own imaginations,* to a man that inquires after the reality of things? It matters not what men's fancies are, it is the knowledge of things that is only to be prized: it is this alone gives a value to our reasonings, and preference to one man's knowledge over another's, that it is of things as they really are, and not of dreams and fancies.'

2. To which I answer, That if our knowledge of our ideas terminate in them, and reach no further, where there is something further intended, our most serious thoughts will be of little more use than the reveries of a crazy brain; and the truths built thereon of no more weight than the discourses of a man who sees things clearly in a dream, and with great assurance utters them. But I hope, before I have done, to make it evident, that this way of certainty, by the knowledge of our own ideas, goes a little further than bare imagination: and I believe it will appear that all the certainty of general truths a man has lies in nothing else.

3. It is evident the mind knows not things immediately, but only by the intervention of the ideas it has of them. Our knowledge, therefore, is real only so far as there is a *conformity* between our ideas and the reality of things. But what shall be here the criterion? How shall the mind, when it perceives nothing but its own ideas, know that they agree with things themselves? This, though it seems not to want difficulty, yet, I think, there be two sorts of ideas that we may be assured agree with things.

4. *First,* The first are simple ideas, which since the mind, as has been showed, can by no means make to itself, must necessarily be the produce of things operating on the mind, in a natural way, and producing therein those perceptions which by the Wisdom and Will of our Maker they are ordained and adapted to. From whence it follows, that simple ideas are not fictions of our fancies, but the natural and regular productions of things without us, really operating upon us; and so carry with them all the conformity which is intended; or which our state requires: for they represent to us things under those appearances which they are fitted to produce in us: whereby we are enabled to distinguish the sorts of particular substances, to discern the states they are in, and so to take them for our necessities, and apply them to our uses. Thus the idea of whiteness, or bitterness, as it is in the mind, exactly answering that power which is in any body to produce it there, has all the real conformity it can or ought to have, with things without us. And this conformity between our simple ideas and the existence of things, is sufficient for real knowledge.

5. *Secondly,* All our complex ideas, *except those of substances,* being archetypes of the mind's own making, not intended to be the copies of anything, nor referred to the existence of anything, as to their originals, cannot want any conformity necessary to real knowledge. For that which is not designed to represent anything but itself, can never be capable of a wrong representation, nor mislead us from the true apprehension of anything, by its dislikeness to it: and such, excepting those of substances, are all our complex ideas. Which, as I

have showed in another place, are combinations of ideas, which the mind, by its free choice, puts together without considering any connexion they have in nature. And hence it is, that in all these sorts the ideas themselves are considered as the archetypes, and things no otherwise regarded, but as they are conformable to them. So that we cannot but be infallibly certain, that all the knowledge we attain concerning these ideas is real, and reaches things themselves. Because in all our thoughts, reasonings, and discourses of this kind, we intend things no further than as they are conformable to our ideas. So that in these we cannot miss of a certain and undoubted reality. . . .

Leibniz:

Our certitude would be small, or rather nothing, if it had no other basis of simple ideas than that which comes from the senses. Have you forgotten, sir, how I have shown that ideas are originally in our mind, and that indeed our thoughts come to us from the depths of our own nature, other creatures being unable to have an immediate influence upon the soul. Besides the ground of our certitude in regard to universal and eternal truths is in the ideas themselves, independently of the senses, just as ideas pure and intelligible do not depend on the senses, for example, that of being, unity, identity, etc. But the ideas of sensible qualities, as color, savor, etc. (which in reality are only phantoms), come to us from the senses, i.e. from our confused perceptions. And the basis of the truth of contingent and singular things is in the succession which causes these phenomena of the senses to be rightly united as the intelligible truths demand. That is the difference which should be made, while that which you here make between simple and complex ideas, and ideas complex belonging to substances and to accidents, does not appear to me well founded, since all intelligible ideas have their archetypes in the eternal possibility of things.

Locke, Bk. IV, Ch. IX of the *Essay*:

1. Hitherto we have only considered the essences of things; which being only abstract ideas, and thereby removed in our thoughts from particular existence, (that being the proper operation of the mind, in abstraction, to consider an idea under no other existence but what it has in the understanding,) gives us no knowledge of real existence at all. Where, by the way, we may take notice, that universal propositions of whose truth or falsehood we can have certain knowledge concern not existence: and further, that all particular affirmations or negations that would not be certain if they were made general, are only concerning existence; they declaring only the accidental union or separation of ideas in things existing, which, in their abstract natures, have no known necessary union or repugnancy.

2. But, leaving the nature of propositions, and different ways of predication to be considered more at large in another place, let us proceed now to inquire concerning our knowledge of the *existence of things,* and how we come by

it. I say, then, that we have the knowledge of *our own* existence by intuition; of the existence of *God* by demonstration; and of *other things* by sensation.

3. As for *our own existence,* we perceive it so plainly and so certainly, that it neither needs nor is capable of any proof. For nothing can be more evident to us than our own existence. I think, I reason, I feel pleasure and pain: can any of these be more evident to me than my own existence? If I doubt of all other things, that very doubt makes me perceive my own existence, and will not suffer me to doubt of that. For if I know I feel pain, it is evident I have as certain perception of my own existence, as of the existence of the pain I feel: or if I know I doubt, I have as certain perception of the existence of the thing doubting, as of that thought which I *call doubt.* Experience then convinces us, that we have an *intuitive knowledge* of our own existence, and an internal infallible perception that we are. In every act of sensation, reasoning, or thinking, we are conscious to ourselves of our own being; and, in this matter, come not short of the highest degree of certainty.

Leibniz:

I am entirely agreed as to all this. And I add that the immediate apperception of our existence and of our thoughts furnishes us the first truths *a posteriori,* or of fact, *i.e.* the *first experiences,* as the identical propositions contain the first truths *a priori,* or of reason, *i.e. the first lights (les premières lumières).* Both are incapable of proof, and may be called *immediate;* the former, because they are immediate between the understanding and its object; the latter, because they are immediate between the subject and the predicate.

Locke, Bk. IV, Ch. XI of the *Essay:*

1. The knowledge of our own being we have by intuition. The existence of a God, reason clearly makes known to us, as has been shown.[1]

The knowledge of the existence of *any other thing* we can have only by *sensation:* for there being no necessary connexion of real existence with any *idea* a man hath in his memory; nor of any other existence but that of God with the existence of any particular man: no particular man can know the existence of any other being, but only when, by actual operating upon him, it makes itself perceived by him. For, the having the idea of anything in our mind, no more proves the existence of that thing, than the picture of a man evidences his being in the world, or the visions of a dream make thereby a true history.

2. It is therefore the *actual receiving* of ideas from without that gives us notice of the existence of other things, and makes us know, that something doth exist at that time without us, which causes that idea in us; though perhaps we neither know nor consider how it does it. For it takes not from the certainty of our senses, and the ideas we receive by them, that we know not the manner wherein they are produced: v.g. whilst I write this, I have, by the paper affect-

---

[1] [Book IV, Chap. X.—not included in this collection.—*Ed.*]

ing my eyes, that idea produced in my mind, which, whatever object causes, I call white; by which I know that that quality or accident (i.e. whose appearance before my eyes always causes that idea) doth really exist, and hath a being without me. And of this, the greatest assurance I can possibly have, and to which my faculties can attain, is the testimony of my eyes, which are the proper and sole judges of this thing; whose testimony I have reason to rely on as so certain, that I can no more doubt, whilst I write this, that I see white and black, and that something really exists that causes that sensation in me, than that I write or move my hand; which is a certainty as great as human nature is capable of, concerning the existence of anything, but a man's self alone, and of God.

3. The notice we have by our senses of the existing of things without us, though it be not altogether so certain as our intuitive knowledge, or the deductions of our reason employed about the clear abstract ideas of our own minds; yet it is an assurance that deserves the name of knowledge. If we persuade ourselves that our faculties act and inform us right concerning the existence of those objects that affect them, it cannot pass for an ill-grounded confidence: for I think nobody can, in earnest, be so sceptical as to be uncertain of the existence of those things which he sees and feels. At least, he that can doubt so far, (whatever he may have with his own thoughts,) will never have any controversy with me; since he can never be sure I say anything contrary to his own opinion. As to myself, I think God has given me assurance enough of the existence of things without me: since, by their different application, I can produce in myself both pleasure and pain, which is one great concernment of my present state. This is certain: the confidence that our faculties do not herein deceive us, is the greatest assurance we are capable of concerning the existence of material beings. For we cannot act anything but by our faculties; nor talk of knowledge itself, but by the help of those faculties which are fitted to apprehend even what knowledge is.

But besides the assurance we have from our senses themselves, that they do not err in the information they give us of the existence of things without us, when they are affected by them, we are further confirmed in this assurance by other concurrent reasons:—

4. I. It is plain those perceptions are produced in us by exterior causes affecting our senses: because those that want the *organs* of any sense, never can have the ideas belonging to that sense produced in their minds. This is too evident to be doubted: and therefore we cannot but be assured that they come in by the organs of that sense, and no other way. The organs themselves, it is plain, do not produce them: for then the eyes of a man in the dark would produce colours, and his nose smell roses in the winter: but we see nobody gets the relish of a pineapple, till he goes to the Indies, where it is, and tastes it.

5. II. Because sometimes I find that *I cannot avoid the having those ideas produced in my mind.* For though, when my eyes are shut, or windows fast, I can at pleasure recall to my mind the ideas of light, or the sun, which former sensations had lodged in my memory; so I can at pleasure lay by *that* idea, and take

into my view that of the smell of a rose, or taste of sugar. But, if I turn my eyes at noon towards the sun, I cannot avoid the ideas which the light or sun then produces in me. So that there is a manifest difference between the ideas laid up in my memory, (over which, if they were there only, I should have constantly the same power to dispose of them, and lay them by at pleasure,) and those which force themselves upon me, and I cannot avoid having. And therefore it must needs be some exterior cause, and the brisk acting of some objects without me, whose efficacy I cannot resist, that produces those ideas in my mind, whether I will or no. Besides, there is nobody who doth not perceive the difference in himself between contemplating the sun, as he hath the idea of it in his memory, and actually looking upon it: of which two, his perception is so distinct, that few of his ideas are more distinguishable one from another. And therefore he hath certain knowledge that they are not *both* memory, or the actions of his mind, and fancies only within him; but that actual seeing hath a cause without.

6. III. Add to this, that many of those ideas are *produced in us with pain,* which afterwards we remember without the least offence. Thus, the pain of heat or cold, when the idea of it is revived in our minds, gives us no disturbance; which, when felt, was very troublesome; and is again, when actually repeated: which is occasioned by the disorder the external object causes in our bodies when applied to them: and we remember the pains of hunger, thirst, or the headache, without any pain at all; which would either never disturb us, or else constantly do it, as often as we thought of it, were there nothing more but ideas floating in our minds, and appearances entertaining our fancies, without the real existence of things affecting us from abroad. The same may be said of *pleasure,* accompanying several actual sensations. And though mathematical demonstration depends not upon sense, yet the examining them by diagrams gives great credit to the evidence of our sight, and seems to give it a certainty approaching to that of demonstration itself. For, it would be very strange, that a man should allow it for an undeniable truth, that two angles of a figure, which he measures by lines and angles of a diagram, should be bigger one than the other, and yet doubt of the existence of those lines and angles, which by looking on he makes use of to measure that by.

7. IV. Our *senses* in many cases *bear witness to the truth of each other's report,* concerning the existence of sensible things without us. He that *sees* a fire, may, if he doubt whether it be anything more than a bare fancy, *feel* it too; and be convinced, by putting his hand in it. Which certainly could never be put into such exquisite pain by a bare idea or phantom, unless that the pain be a fancy too: which yet he cannot, when the burn is well, by raising the idea of it, bring upon himself again.

Thus I see, whilst I write this, I can change the appearance of the paper; and by designing the letters, tell *beforehand* what new idea it shall exhibit the very next moment, by barely drawing my pen over it: which will neither appear (let me fancy as much as I will) if my hands stand still; or though I move my pen, if my eyes be shut: nor, when those characters are once made on the paper, can I choose afterwards but see them as they are; that is, have the ideas of such letters as I have made. Whence it is manifest, that they are not barely the sport and play of my own imagination, when I find that the characters that were made at the pleasure of my own thoughts, do not obey them; nor yet cease to be, whenever I shall fancy it, but continue to affect my senses constantly and regularly, according to the figures I made them. To which if we will add, that the sight of those shall, from another man, draw such sounds as I beforehand design they shall stand for, there will be little reason left to doubt that those words I write do really exist without me, when they cause a long series of regular sounds to affect my ears, which could not be the effect of my imagination, nor could my memory retain them in that order.

8. But yet, if after all this any one will be so sceptical as to distrust his senses, and to affirm that all we see and hear, feel and taste, think and do, during our whole being, is but the series and deluding appearances of a long dream, whereof there is no reality; and therefore will question the existence of all things, or our knowledge of anything: I must desire him to consider, that, if all be a dream, then he doth but dream that he makes the question, and so it is not much matter that a waking man should answer him. But yet, if he pleases, he may dream that I make him this answer, That the certainty of things existing in *rerum natura* when we have the testimony of our senses for it is not only as great as our frame can attain to, but as our condition needs. For our faculties being suited not to the full extent of being, nor to a perfect, clear, comprehensive knowledge of things free from all doubt and scruple; but to the preservation of us, in whom they are; and accommodated to the use of life: they serve to our purpose well enough, if they will but give us certain notice of those things, which are convenient or inconvenient to us. For he that sees a candle burning, and hath experimented the force of its flame by putting his finger in it, will little doubt that this is something existing without him, which does him harm, and puts him to great pain: which is assurance enough, when no man requires greater certainty to govern his actions by than what is as certain as his actions themselves. And if our dreamer pleases to try whether the glowing heat of a glass furnace be barely a wandering imagination in a drowsy man's fancy, by putting his hand into it, he may perhaps be wakened into a certainty greater than he could wish, that it is something more than bare imagination. So that this evidence is as great as we can desire, being as certain to us as our pleasure or pain, i.e. happiness or misery; beyond which we have no concernment, either of knowing or being. Such an assurance of the existence of things without us is sufficient to direct us in the attaining the good and avoiding the evil which is caused by them, which is the important concernment we have of being made acquainted with them.

9. In fine, then, when our senses do actually convey into our understandings any idea, we cannot but be satisfied that there doth something *at that time* really exist without us, which doth affect our senses, and by them give notice of itself to our apprehensive faculties, and actually produce that idea which we then perceive: and we cannot so far distrust their testimony, as to doubt that

such *collections* of simple ideas as we have observed by our senses to be united together, do really exist together. But this knowledge extends as far as the present testimony of our senses, employed about particular objects that do then affect them, and no further. For if I saw such a collection of simple ideas as is wont to be called *man,* existing together one minute since, and am now alone, I cannot be certain that the same man exists now, since there is no *necessary connexion* of his existence a minute since with his existence now: by a thousand ways he may cease to be, since I had the testimony of my senses for his existence. And if I cannot be certain that the man I saw last to-day is now in being, I can less be certain that he is so who hath been longer removed from my senses, and I have not seen since yesterday, or since the last year: and much less can I be certain of the existence of men that I never saw. And, therefore, though it be highly probable that millions of men do now exist, yet, whilst I am alone, writing this, I have not that certainty of it which we strictly call knowledge; though the great likelihood of it puts me past doubt, and it be reasonable for me to do several things upon the confidence that there are men (and men also of my acquaintance, with whom I have to do) now in the world: but this is but probability, not knowledge.

10. Whereby yet we may observe how foolish and vain a thing it is for a man of a narrow knowledge, who having reason given him to judge of the different evidence and probability of things, and to be swayed accordingly; how vain, I say, it is to expect demonstration and certainty in things not capable of it; and refuse assent to very rational propositions, and act contrary to very plain and clear truths, because they cannot be made out so evident, as to surmount every the least (I will not say reason, but) pretence of doubting. He that, in the ordinary affairs of life, would admit of nothing but direct plain demonstration, would be sure of nothing in this world, but of perishing quickly. The wholesomeness of his meat or drink would not give him reason to venture on it: and I would fain know what it is he could do upon such grounds as are capable of no doubt, no objection.

Leibniz:

The truth of sensible things is justified by their connection, which depends upon the intellectual truths grounded in reason and upon constant observations in the sensible things themselves even when the reasons do not appear. And as these reasons and observations give us the means of judging the future as related to our interest, and as success corresponds with our rational judgment, we could not demand, nor have indeed, a greater certainty regarding these objects. We can also give a reason for dreams themselves, and for their slight connection with other phenomena. Nevertheless, I believe that we might extend the appellation of knowledge and of certainty beyond actual sensations, since clearness and manifestness go beyond, which I consider as a species of certainty; and it would undoubtedly be folly seriously to doubt whether there are men in the world when we do not see any. *To doubt seriously* is to doubt in relation to the practical, and we might take *certainty* as a knowledge of truth which we cannot doubt in relation to the practical without madness; and sometimes we take it still more generally, and apply it to cases where we could not doubt without deserving to be severely blamed. But *evidence* would be a luminous certainty, *i.e.* where we do not doubt because of the connection we see between ideas. According to this definition of certainty, we are certain that Constantinople is in the world, that Constantine, Alexander the Great, and Julius Caesar lived. It is true that some peasant of Ardennes might justly doubt about these, for lack of information; but a man of letters and of the world could not do so without great derangement of mind.

11. As *when our senses are actually employed about any object,* we do know that it does exist; so by *our memory* we may be assured, that heretofore things that affected our senses have existed. And thus we have knowledge of the past existence of several things, whereof our senses having informed us, our memories still retain the ideas; and of this we are past all doubt, so long as we remember well. But this knowledge also reaches no further than our senses have formerly assured us. Thus, seeing water at this instant, it is an unquestionable truth to me that water doth exist: and remembering that I saw it yesterday, it will also be always true, and as long as my memory retains it always an undoubted proposition to me, that water did exist the 10th of July, 1688; as it will also be equally true that a certain number of very fine colours did exist, which at the same time I saw upon a bubble of that water: but, being now quite out of sight both of the water and bubbles too, it is no more certainly known to me that the water doth now exist, than that the bubbles or colours therein do so: it being no more necessary that water should exist to-day, because it existed yesterday, than that the colours or bubbles exist to-day, because they existed yesterday, though it be exceedingly much more probable; because water hath been observed to continue long in existence, but bubbles, and the colours on them, quickly cease to be. . . .

Leibniz:

It has already been remarked that our memory sometimes deceives us. And we put confidence in it or not, according as it is more or less vivid, and more or less connected with the things we know. And even when we are assured of the principal fact we may often question the circumstances. . . .

13. By which it appears that there are two sorts of propositions:—(1) There is one sort of propositions concerning the existence of anything answerable to such an idea: as having the idea of an elephant, phoenix, motion, or an angel, in my mind, the first and natural inquiry is, Whether such a thing does anywhere exist? And this knowledge is only of particulars. No existence of anything without us, but only of God, can certainly be known further than our

senses inform us. (2) There is another sort of propositions, wherein is expressed the agreement or disagreement of *our abstract* ideas, and their dependence on one another. Such propositions may be universal and certain. So, having the idea of God and myself, of fear and obedience, I cannot but be sure that God is to be feared and obeyed by me: and this proposition will be certain, concerning man in general, if I have made an abstract idea of such a species, whereof I am one particular. But yet this proposition, how certain soever, that 'men ought to fear and obey God' proves not to me the *existence of men* in the world; but will be true of all such creatures, whenever they do exist: which certainty of such general propositions depends on the agreement or disagreement to be discovered in those abstract ideas.

14. In the former case, our knowledge is the consequence of the existence of things, producing ideas in our minds by our senses: in the latter, knowledge is the consequence of the ideas (be they what they will) that are in our minds, producing there general certain propositions. Many of these are called *aeternae veritates,* and all of them indeed are so; not from being written, all or any of them, in the minds of all men; or that they were any of them propositions in any one's mind, till he, having got the abstract ideas, joined or separated them by affirmation or negation. But wheresoever we can suppose such a creature as man is, endowed with such faculties, and thereby furnished with such ideas as we have, we must conclude, he must needs, when he applies his thoughts to the consideration of his ideas, know the truth of certain propositions that will arise from the agreement or disagreement which he will perceive in his own ideas. Such propositions are therefore called *eternal truths,* not because they are eternal propositions actually formed, and antecedent to the understanding that at any time makes them; nor because they are imprinted on the mind from any patterns that are anywhere out of the mind, and existed before: but because, being once made about abstract ideas, so as to be true, they will, whenever they can be supposed to be made again at any time, past or to come, by a mind having those ideas, always actually be true. For names being supposed to stand perpetually for the same ideas, and the same ideas having immutably the same habitudes one to another, propositions concerning any abstract ideas that are once true must needs be *eternal verities.*

Leibniz:

Your division appears to return to mine of *propositions of fact* and *propositions of reason.* Propositions of fact also may become general in a way, but it is by induction or observation, so that it is only a multitude of similar facts, as when it is observed that all quicksilver is evaporated by the force of fire; and this is not a perfect generality, because we do not see its necessity. General propositions of reason are necessary, although the reason also furnishes some which are not absolutely general, and are only probable, as, for example, when we presume an idea to be possible until its contrary is discovered by a more exact research. There are finally *mixed propositions,* drawn from premises, some of which come from facts and observations, and others are necessary propositions; and such are a number of geographical and astronomical conclusions regarding the globe of the earth and the course of the stars, which spring from the combination of the observations of travellers and astronomers with the theorems of geometry and arithmetic. But as, according to the usage of logicians, *the conclusion follows the weakest of the premises* and cannot have more certainty than they, these mixed propositions have only the certainty and generality which belong to the observations. As for the *eternal truths,* it must be observed that at bottom they are all conditional and say in effect: such a thing posited, such another thing is. For example, in saying: *every figure which has three sides will also have three angles,* I say nothing else than that, supposing there is a figure with three sides, *this same* figure will have three angles. . . .

The Scholastics have hotly disputed *de constantia subjecti,* as they called it, *i.e.* how the proposition made upon a subject can have a real truth, if this subject does not exist. The fact is that the truth is only conditional, and says, that in case the subject ever exists, it will be found such. But it will be further demanded, in what is this connection founded, since there is in it some reality which does not deceive. The reply will be, that it is in the connection of ideas. But it will be asked in reply, where would these ideas be if no mind existed, and what then would become of the real ground of this certainty of the eternal truths? This leads us finally to the ultimate ground of truths, viz.: to that Supreme and Universal Mind, which cannot fail to exist, whose understanding, to speak truly, is the region of eternal truths, as St. Augustine has recognized and expresses in a sufficiently vivid way. And in order not to think that it is unnecessary to recur to this, we must consider that these necessary truths contain the determining reason and the regulating principle of existences themselves, and, in a word, the laws of the universe. Thus these necessary truths being anterior to the existence of contingent beings, must be grounded in the existence of a necessary substance. Here it is that I find the original of the ideas and truths which are graven in our souls, not in the form of propositions, but as the sources out of which application and occasion will cause actual judgments to arise.

16. It is said extension is a mode or accident of matter, and that matter is the *substratum* that supports it. Now I desire that you would explain what is meant by matter's *supporting* extension. Say you, I have no idea of matter and, therefore, cannot explain it. I answer, though you have no positive, yet, if you have any meaning at all, you must at least have a relative idea of matter; though you know not what it is, yet you must be supposed to know what relation it bears to accidents, and what is meant by its supporting them. It is evident "support" cannot here be taken in its usual or literal sense—as when we say that pillars support a building; in what sense therefore must it be taken?

17. If we inquire into what the most accurate philosophers declare themselves to mean by *material substance,* we shall find them acknowledge they have no other meaning annexed to those sounds but the idea of being in general together with the relative notion of its supporting accidents. The general idea of being appears to me the most abstract and incomprehensible of all other; and as for its supporting accidents, this, as we have just now observed, cannot be understood in the common sense of those words; it must, therefore, be taken in some other sense, but what that is they do not explain. So that when I consider the two parts or branches which make the signification of the words *material substance,* I am convinced there is no distinct meaning annexed to them. But why should we trouble ourselves any further in discussing this material *substratum* or support of figure and motion and other sensible qualities? Does it not suppose they have an existence without the mind? And is not this a direct repugnance and altogether inconceivable?

18. But, though it were possible that solid, figured, movable substances may exist without the mind, corresponding to the ideas we have of bodies, yet how is it possible for us to know this? Either we must know it by sense or by reason. As for our senses, by them we have the knowledge only of our sensations, ideas, or those things that are immediately perceived by sense, call them what you will; but they do not inform us that things exist without the mind, or unperceived, like to those which are perceived. This the materialists themselves acknowledge. It remains therefore that if we have any knowledge at all of external things, it must be by reason, inferring their existence from what is immediately perceived by sense. But what reason can induce us to believe the existence of bodies without the mind, from what we perceive, since the very patrons of matter themselves do not pretend there is any necessary connection betwixt them and our ideas? I say it is granted on all hands (and what happens in dreams, frenzies, and the like, puts it beyond dispute) that it is possible we might be affected with all the ideas we have now, though no bodies existed without resembling them. Hence it is evident the supposition of external bod-

---

* From *A Treatise Concerning the Principles of Human Knowledge.*

ies is not necessary for the producing our ideas; since it is granted they are produced sometimes, and might possibly be produced always in the same order we see them in at present, without their concurrence.

19. But though we might possibly have all our sensations without them, yet perhaps it may be thought easier to conceive and explain the manner of their production by supposing external bodies in their likeness rather than otherwise; and so it might be at least probable there are such things as bodies that excite their ideas in our minds. But neither can this be said, for, though we give the materialists their external bodies, they by their own confession are never the nearer knowing how our ideas are produced, since they own themselves unable to comprehend in what manner body can act upon spirit, or how it is possible it should imprint any idea in the mind. Hence it is evident the production of ideas or sensations in our minds can be no reason why we should suppose matter or corporeal substances, since that is acknowledged to remain equally inexplicable with or without this supposition. If therefore it were possible for bodies to exist without the mind, yet to hold they do so must needs be a very precarious opinion, since it is to suppose, without any reason at all, that God has created innumerable beings that are entirely useless and serve to no manner of purpose.

20. In short, if there were external bodies, it is impossible we should ever come to know it; and if there were not, we might have the very same reasons to think there were that we have now. Suppose—what no one can deny possible—an intelligence without the help of external bodies, to be affected with the same train of sensations or ideas that you are, imprinted in the same order and with like vividness in his mind. I ask whether that intelligence has not all the reason to believe the existence of corporeal substances, represented by his ideas and exciting them in his mind, that you can possibly have for believing the same thing? Of this there can be no question—which one consideration is enough to make any reasonable person suspect the strength of whatever arguments he may think himself to have for the existence of bodies without the mind.

21. Were it necessary to add any further proof against the existence of matter after what has been said, I could instance several of those errors and difficulties (not to mention impieties) which have sprung from that tenet. It has occasioned numberless controversies and disputes in philosophy, and not a few of far greater moment in religion. But I shall not enter into the detail of them in this place as well because I think arguments *a posteriori* are unnecessary for confirming what has been, if I mistake not, sufficiently demonstrated *a priori*, as because I shall hereafter find occasion to speak somewhat of them.

22. I am afraid I have given cause to think me needlessly prolix in handling this subject. For to what purpose is it to dilate on that which may be demonstrated with the utmost evidence in a line or two to anyone that is capable of the least reflection? It is but looking into your own thoughts, and so trying whether you can conceive it possible for a sound, or figure, or motion, or color to exist without the mind or unperceived. This easy trial may make

you see that what you contend for is a downright contradiction. Insomuch that I am content to put the whole upon this issue: if you can but conceive it possible for one extended movable substance, or, in general, for any one idea, or anything like an idea, to exist otherwise than in a mind perceiving it, I shall readily give up the cause. And, as for all that compages of external bodies which you contend for, I shall grant you its existence, though you cannot either give me any reason why you believe it exists, or assign any use to it when it is supposed to exist. I say the bare possibility of your opinion's being true shall pass for an argument that it is so.

23. But, say you, surely there is nothing easier than to imagine trees, for instance, in a park, or books existing in a closet, and nobody by to perceive them. I answer you may so, there is no difficulty in it; but what is all this, I beseech you, more than framing in your mind certain ideas which you call books and trees, and at the same time omitting to frame the ideas of anyone that may perceive them? But do not you yourself perceive or think of them all the while? This therefore is nothing to the purpose; it only shows you have the power of imagining or forming ideas in your mind; but it does not show that you can conceive it possible the objects of your thought may exist without the mind. To make out this, it is necessary that you conceive them existing unconceived or unthought of, which is a manifest repugnancy. When we do our utmost to conceive the existence of external bodies, we are all the while only contemplating our own ideas. But the mind, taking no notice of itself, is deluded to think it can and does conceive bodies existing unthought of or without the mind, though at the same time they are apprehended by or exist in itself. A little attention will discover to anyone the truth and evidence of what is here said, and make it unnecessary to insist on any other proofs against the existence of *material substance.*

24. It is very obvious, upon the least inquiry into our own thoughts, to know whether it be possible for us to understand what is meant by the *absolute existence of sensible objects in themselves, or without the mind.* To me it is evident those words mark out either a direct contradiction or else nothing at all. And to convince others of this, I know no readier or fairer way than to entreat they would calmly attend to their own thoughts; and if by this attention the emptiness or repugnance of those expressions does appear, surely nothing more is requisite for their conviction. It is on this, therefore, that I insist, to wit, that "the absolute existence of unthinking things" are words without a meaning, or which include a contradiction. This is what I repeat and inculcate, and earnestly recommend to the attentive thoughts of the reader. . . .

73. It is worth while to reflect a little on the motives which induced men to suppose the existence of *material substance;* that so having observed the gradual ceasing and expiration of those motives or reasons, we may proportionably withdraw the assent that was grounded on them. First, therefore, it was thought that color, figure, motion, and the rest of the sensible qualities or accidents did really exist without the mind; and for this reason it seemed needful

to suppose some unthinking *substratum* or substance wherein they did exist, since they could not be conceived to exist by themselves. Afterwards, in process of time, men being convinced that colors, sounds, and the rest of the sensible, secondary qualities had no existence without the mind, they stripped this *substratum* or material substance of those qualities, leaving only the primary ones, figure, motion, and suchlike, which they still conceived to exist without the mind, and consequently to stand in need of a material support. But it having been shown that none even of these can possibly exist otherwise than in a spirit or mind which perceives them, it follows that we have no longer any reason to suppose the being of matter; nay, that it is utterly impossible there should be any such thing so long as that word is taken to denote an *unthinking substratum* of qualities or accidents wherein they exist without the mind.

74. But though it be allowed by the materialists themselves that matter was thought of only for the sake of supporting accidents, and, the reason entirely ceasing, one might expect the mind should naturally, and without any reluctance at all, quit the belief of what was solely grounded thereon, yet the prejudice is riveted so deeply in our thoughts that we can scarce tell how to part with it, and are therefore inclined, since the *thing* itself is indefensible, at least to retain the *name,* which we apply to I know not what abstracted and indefinite notions of being, or occasion, though without any show of reason, at least so far as I can see. For what is there on our part, or what do we perceive among all the ideas, sensations, notions which are imprinted on our minds, either by sense or reflection, from whence may be inferred the existence of an inert, thoughtless, unperceived occasion? And, on the other hand, on the part of an All-sufficient Spirit, what can there be that should make us believe or even suspect He is directed by an inert occasion to excite ideas in our minds?

75. It is a very extraordinary instance of the force of prejudice, and much to be lamented, that the mind of man retains so great a fondness, against all the evidence of reason, for a stupid, thoughtless *somewhat,* by the interposition whereof it would as it were screen itself from the Providence of God and remove him farther off from the affairs of the world. But though we do the utmost we can to secure the belief of matter, though, when reason forsakes us, we endeavor to support our opinion on the bare possibility of the thing, and though we indulge ourselves in the full scope of an imagination not regulated by reason to make out that poor possibility, yet the upshot of all is that there are certain *unknown ideas* in the mind of God; for this, if anything, is all that I conceive to be meant by *occasion* with regard to God. And this at the bottom is no longer contending for the thing, but for the name.

76. Whether, therefore, there are such ideas in the mind of God, and whether they may be called by the name *matter,* I shall not dispute. But if you stick to the notion of an unthinking substance or support of extension, motion, and other sensible qualities, then to me it is most evidently impossible there should be any such thing, since it is a plain repugnance that those qualities should exist in or be supported by an unperceiving substance.

77. But, say you, though it be granted that there is no thoughtless support

of extension and the other qualities or accidents which we perceive, yet there may, perhaps, be some inert, unperceiving substance or *substratum* of some other qualities, as incomprehensible to us as colors are to a man born blind, because we have not a sense adapted to them. But if we had a new sense, we should possibly no more doubt of their existence than a blind man made to see does of the existence of light and colors. I answer, first, if what you mean by the word *matter* be only the unknown support of unknown qualities, it is no matter whether there is such a thing or no, since it no way concerns us; and I do not see the advantage there is in disputing about we know not *what*, and we know not *why*.

78. But, secondly, if we had a new sense, it could only furnish us with new ideas or sensations; and then we should have the same reason against their existing in an unperceiving substance that has been already offered with relation to figure, motion, color, and the like. Qualities, as has been shown, are nothing else but *sensations* or *ideas*, which exist only in a *mind* perceiving them; and this is true not only of the ideas we are acquainted with at present, but likewise of all possible ideas whatsoever.

79. But, you will insist, what if I have no reason to believe the existence of matter? What if I cannot assign any use to it or explain anything by it, or even conceive what is meant by that word? Yet still it is no contradiction to say that matter exists, and that this matter is in general a *substance, or occasion of ideas*, though, indeed, to go about to unfold the meaning or adhere to any particular explication of those words may be attended with great difficulties. I answer, when words are used without a meaning, you may put them together as you please without danger of running into a contradiction. You may say, for example, that twice two is equal to seven, so long as you declare you do not take the words of that proposition in their usual acceptation but for marks of you know not what. And, by the same reason, you may say there is an inert, thoughtless substance without accidents which is the occasion of our ideas. And we shall understand just as much by one proposition as the other.

80. In the *last* place, you will say, What if we give up the cause of material substance and assert that matter is an unknown *somewhat*—neither substance nor accident, spirit nor idea, inert, thoughtless, indivisible, immovable, unextended, existing in no place? For, say you, whatever may be urged against *substance* or *occasion*, or any other positive or relative notion of matter, has no place at all so long as this *negative* definition of matter is adhered to. I answer, You may, if so it shall seem good, use the word *matter* in the same sense as other men use *nothing*, and so make those terms convertible in your style. For, after all, this is what appears to me to be the result of that definition the parts whereof, when I consider with attention, either collectively or separate from each other, I do not find that there is any kind of effect or impression made on my mind different from what is excited by the term *nothing*.

81. You will reply, perhaps, that in the foresaid definition is included what does sufficiently distinguish it from nothing—the positive, abstract idea of *quiddity, entity*, or *existence*. I own, indeed, that those who pretend to the fac-

ulty of framing abstract general ideas do talk as if they had such an idea, which is, say they, the most abstract and general notion of all; that is, to me, the most incomprehensible of all others. That there are a great variety of spirits of different orders and capacities whose faculties both in number and extent are far exceeding those the Author of my being has bestowed on me, I see no reason to deny. And for me to pretend to determine by my own few, stinted, narrow inlets of perception what ideas the inexhaustible power of the Supreme Spirit may imprint upon them were certainly the utmost folly and presumption—since there may be, for aught that I know, innumerable sorts of ideas or sensations, as different from one another, and from all that I have perceived, as colors are from sounds. But how ready soever I may be to acknowledge the scantiness of my comprehension with regard to the endless variety of spirits and ideas that might possibly exist, yet for anyone to pretend to a notion of entity or existence, *abstracted* from *spirit* and idea, from perceiving and being perceived, is, I suspect, a downright repugnance and trifling with words. . . .

135. Having dispatched what we intended to say concerning the knowledge of *ideas,* the method we proposed leads us in the next place to treat of *spirits*—with regard to which, perhaps, human knowledge is not so deficient as is vulgarly imagined. The great reason that is assigned for our being thought ignorant of the nature of spirits is our not having an *idea* of it. But surely it ought not to be looked on as a defect in a human understanding that it does not perceive the idea of spirit if it is manifestly impossible there should be any such idea. And this, if I mistake not, has been demonstrated in section 27;[1] to which I shall here add that a spirit has been shown to be the only substance or support wherein the unthinking beings or ideas can exist; but that this *substance* which supports or perceives ideas should itself be an idea or like an idea is evidently absurd.

136. It will perhaps be said that we want a sense (as some have imagined) proper to know substances withal, which, if we had, we might know our own soul as we do a triangle. To this I answer, that, in case we had a new sense bestowed upon us, we could only receive thereby some new sensations or ideas of sense. But I believe nobody will say that what he means by the terms *soul* and *substance* is only some particular sort of idea or sensation. We may, therefore, infer that, all things duly considered, it is not more reasonable to think our faculties defective in that they do not furnish us with an idea of spirit or active thinking substance than it would be if we should blame them for not being able to comprehend a *round square.*

137. From the opinion that spirits are to be known after the manner of an idea or sensation have risen many absurd and heterodox tenets, and much skepticism about the nature of the soul. It is even probable that this opinion may have produced a doubt in some whether they had any soul at all distinct from their body, since upon inquiry they could not find they had an idea of it.

---

[1] [See above, pp. 202–3.—*Ed.*]

That an *idea* which is inactive, and the existence whereof consists in being perceived, should be the image or likeness of an agent subsisting by itself seems to need no other refutation than barely attending to what is meant by those words. But perhaps you will say that though an idea cannot resemble a spirit in its thinking, acting, or subsisting by itself, yet it may in some other respects; and it is not necessary that an idea or image be in all respects like the original.

138. I answer, if it does not in those mentioned, it is impossible it should represent it in any other thing. Do but leave out the power of willing, thinking, and perceiving ideas, and there remains nothing else wherein the idea can be like a spirit. For by the word *spirit* we mean only that which thinks, wills, and perceives; this, and this alone, constitutes the signification of that term. If therefore it is impossible that any degree of those powers should be represented in an idea, it is evident there can be no idea of a spirit.

139. But it will be objected that, if there is no idea signified by the terms *soul, spirit,* and *substance,* they are wholly insignificant or have no meaning in them. I answer, those words do mean or signify a real thing, which is neither an idea nor like an idea, but that which perceives ideas, and wills, and reasons about them. What I am myself, that which I denote by the term *I,* is the same with what is meant by *soul* or *spiritual substance.* If it be said that this is only quarreling at a word, and that, since the immediate significations of other names are by common consent called *ideas,* no reason can be assigned why that which is signified by the name *spirit* or *soul* may not partake in the same appellation. I answer, all the unthinking objects of the mind agree in that they are entirely passive, and their existence consists only in being perceived; whereas a soul or spirit is an active being whose existence consists, not in being perceived, but in perceiving ideas and thinking. It is therefore necessary, in order to prevent equivocation and confounding natures perfectly disagreeing and unlike, that we distinguish between *spirit* and *idea.* See sect. 27.

140. In a large sense, indeed, we may be said to have an idea or rather a notion of *spirit;* that is, we understand the meaning of the word, otherwise we could not affirm or deny anything of it. Moreover, as we conceive the ideas that are in the minds of other spirits by means of our own, which we suppose to be resemblances of them, so we know other spirits by means of our own soul—which in that sense is the image or idea of them; it having a like respect to other spirits that blueness or heat by me perceived has to those ideas perceived by another.

141. It must not be supposed that they who assert the natural immortality of the soul are of opinion that it is absolutely incapable of annihilation even by the infinite power of the Creator who first gave it being, but only that it is not liable to be broken or dissolved by the ordinary laws of nature or motion. They indeed who hold the soul of man to be only a thin vital flame, or system of animal spirits, make it perishing and corruptible as the body; since there is nothing more easily dissipated than such a being, which it is naturally impossible should survive the ruin of the tabernacle wherein it is enclosed. And this notion has been greedily embraced and cherished by the worst part of man-

kind, as the most effectual antidote against all impressions of virtue and religion. But it has been made evident that bodies, of what frame or texture soever, are barely passive ideas in the mind, which is more distant and heterogeneous from them than light is from darkness. We have shown that the soul is indivisible, incorporeal, unextended, and it is consequently incorruptible. Nothing can be plainer than that the motions, changes, decays, and dissolutions which we hourly see befall natural bodies (and which is what we mean by the *course of nature*) cannot possibly affect an active, simple, uncompounded substance; such a being therefore is indissoluble by the force of nature; that is to say, the soul of man is naturally immortal.

142. After what has been said, it is, I suppose, plain that our souls are not to be known in the same manner as senseless, inactive objects, or by way of *idea*. *Spirits* and *ideas* are things so wholly different that when we say "they exist," "they are known," or the like, these words must not be thought to signify anything common to both natures. There is nothing alike or common in them: and to expect that by any multiplication or enlargement of our faculties we may be enabled to know a spirit as we do a triangle seems as absurd as if we should hope to see a sound. This is inculcated because I imagine it may be of moment toward clearing several important questions and preventing some very dangerous errors concerning the nature of the soul. We may not, I think, strictly be said to have an *idea* of an active being, or of an action, although we may be said to have a *notion* of them. I have some knowledge or notion of my mind, and its acts about ideas, inasmuch as I know or understand what is meant by those words. What I know, that I have some notion of. I will not say that the terms *idea* and *notion* may not be used convertibly, if the world will have it so; but yet it conduces to clearness and propriety that we distinguish things very different by different names. It is also to be remarked that, all relations including an act of the mind, we cannot so properly be said to have an idea, but rather a notion of the relations or habitudes between things. But if, in the modern way, the word *idea* is extended to spirits, and relations, and acts, this is, after all, an affair of verbal concern.

143. It will not be amiss to add that the doctrine of *abstract ideas* has had no small share in rendering those sciences intricate and obscure which are particularly conversant about spiritual things. Men have imagined they could frame abstract notions of the powers and acts of the mind and consider them prescinded as well from the mind or spirit itself as from their respective objects and effects. Hence a great number of dark and ambiguous terms, presumed to stand for abstract notions, have been introduced into metaphysics and morality, and from these have grown infinite distractions and disputes amongst the learned.

144. But nothing seems more to have contributed toward engaging men in controversies and mistakes with regard to the nature and operations of the mind than the being used to speak of those things in terms borrowed from sensible ideas. For example, the will is termed the *motion* of the soul: this infuses a belief that the mind of man is as a ball in motion, impelled and determined by

the objects of sense, as necessarily as that is by the stroke of a racket. Hence arises endless scruples and errors of dangerous consequence in morality. All which, I doubt not, may be cleared, and truth appear plain, uniform, and consistent, could but philosophers be prevailed on to retire into themselves, and attentively consider their own meaning.

145. From what has been said it is plain that we cannot know the existence of other spirits otherwise than by their operations, or the ideas by them excited in us. I perceive several motions, changes, and combinations of ideas that inform me there are certain particular agents, like myself, which accompany them and concur in their production. Hence, the knowledge I have of other spirits is not immediate, as is the knowledge of my ideas, but depending on the intervention of ideas, by me referred to agents or spirits distinct from myself, as effects or concomitant signs.

146. But though there be some things which convince us human agents are concerned in producing them, yet it is evident to everyone that those things which are called "the works of nature," that, the far greater part of the ideas or sensations perceived by us, are not produced by, or dependent on, the wills of men. There is therefore some other spirit that causes them; since it is repugnant that they should subsist by themselves. See sect. 29.[1] But, if we attentively consider the constant regularity, order, and concatenation of natural things, the surprising magnificence, beauty, and perfection of the larger, and the exquisite contrivance of the smaller parts of the creation, together with the exact harmony and correspondence of the whole, but above all the never-enough-admired laws of pain and pleasure, and the instincts or natural inclinations, appetites, and passions of animals; I say if we consider all these things, and at the same time attend to the meaning and import of the attributes: one, eternal, infinitely wise, good, and perfect, we shall clearly perceive that they belong to the aforesaid spirit, "who works all in all," and "by whom all things consist."

147. Hence it is evident that God is known as certainly and immediately as any other mind or spirit whatsoever distinct from ourselves. We may even assert that the existence of God is far more evidently perceived than the existence of men; because the effects of nature are infinitely more numerous and considerable than those ascribed to human agents. There is not any one mark that denotes a man, or effect produced by him, which does not more strongly evince the being of that spirit who is the Author of Nature. For it is evident that in affecting other persons the will of man has no other object than barely the motion of the limbs of his body; but that such a motion should be attended by, or excite any idea in the mind of another, depends wholly on the will of the Creator. He alone it is who, "upholding all things by the word of his power," maintains that intercourse between spirits whereby they are able to perceive the existence of each other. And yet this pure and clear light which enlightens everyone is itself invisible.

---

[1] [See above, p. 296.—*Ed.*]

148. It seems to be a general pretense of the unthinking herd that they cannot *see* God. Could we but see him, say they, as we see a man, we should believe that he is, and, believing, obey his commands. But alas, we need only open our eyes to see the sovereign Lord of all things, with a more full and clear view than we do any one of our fellow creatures. Not that I imagine we see God (as some will have it) by a direct and immediate view; or see corporeal things, not by themselves, but by seeing that which represents them in the essence of God, which doctrine is, I must confess, to me incomprehensible. But I shall explain my meaning: a human spirit or person is not perceived by sense, as not being an idea; when therefore we see the color, size, figure, and motions of a man, we perceive only certain sensations or ideas excited in our own minds; and these being exhibited to our view in sundry distinct collections, serve to mark out unto us the existence of finite and created spirits like ourselves. Hence it is plain we do not see a man—if by *man* is meant that which lives, moves, perceives, and thinks as we do—but only such a certain collection of ideas as directs us to think there is a distinct principle of thought and motion, like to ourselves, accompanying and represented by it. And after the same manner we see God; all the difference is that, whereas some one finite and narrow assemblage of ideas denotes a particular human mind, whithersoever we direct our view, we do at all times and in all places perceive manifest tokens of the divinity: everything we see, hear, feel, or anywise perceive by sense, being a sign or effect of the power of God; as is our perception of those very motions which are produced by men.

149. It is therefore plain that nothing can be more evident to anyone that is capable of the least reflection than the existence of God, or a spirit who is intimately present to our minds, producing in them all that variety of ideas or sensations which continually affect us, on whom we have an absolute and entire dependence, in short "in whom we live, and move, and have our being." That the discovery of this great truth, which lies so near and obvious to the mind, should be attained to by the reason of so very few, is a sad instance of the stupidity and inattention of men who, though they are surrounded with such clear manifestations of the Deity, are yet so little affected by them that they seem, as it were, blinded with excess of light. . . .

34 DAVID HUME
Ideas of Substance and of External Existence*

Bk. I. Pt. I, Sec. VI.—Of modes and substances.

I wou'd fain ask those philosophers, who found so much of their reasonings on the distinction of substance and accident, and imagine we have clear ideas of each, whether the idea of *substance* be deriv'd from the impressions of sensation or reflexion? If it be convey'd to us by our senses, I ask, which of them; and after what manner? If it be perceiv'd by the eyes, it must be a colour; if by the ears, a sound; if by the palate, a taste; and so of the other senses. But I believe none will assert, that substance is either a colour, or sound, or a taste. The idea of substance must therefore be deriv'd from an impression of reflexion, if it really exist. But the impressions of reflexion resolve themselves into our passions and emotions; none of which can possibly represent a substance. We have therefore no idea of substance, distinct from that of a collection of particular qualities, nor have we any other meaning when we either talk or reason concerning it.

The idea of a substance as well as that of a mode, is nothing but a collection of simple ideas, that are united by the imagination, and have a particular name assigned them, by which we are able to recall, either to ourselves or others, that collection. But the difference betwixt these ideas consists in this, that the particular qualities, which form a substance, are commonly refer'd to an unknown *something,* in which they are supposed to inhere; or granting this fiction should not take place, are at least supposed to be closely and inseparably connected by the relations of contiguity and causation. The effect of this is, that whatever new simple quality we discover to have the same connexion with the rest, we immediately comprehend it among them, even tho' it did not enter into the first conception of the substance. Thus our idea of gold may at first be a yellow colour, weight, malleableness, fusibility; but upon the discovery of its dissolubility in *aqua regia,* we join that to the other qualities, and suppose it to belong to the substance as much as if its idea had from the beginning made a part of the compound one. The principle of union being regarded as the chief part of the complex idea, gives entrance to whatever quality afterwards occurs, and is equally comprehended by it, as are the others, which first presented themselves.

That this cannot take place in modes, is evident from considering their nature. The simple ideas of which modes are formed, either represent qualities, which are not united by contiguity and causation, but are dispers'd in different subjects; or if they be all united together, the uniting principle is not regarded as the foundation of the complex idea. The idea of a dance is an instance of the first kind of modes; that of beauty of the second. The reason is

---

* From *A Treatise of Human Nature.*

obvious, why such complex ideas cannot receive any new idea, without changing the name, which distinguishes the mode. . . .

Bk. I. Pt. II, Sec. VI.—Of the idea of existence, and of external existence.

It may not be amiss, before we leave this subject, to explain the ideas of
existence and of *external existence;* which have their difficulties, as well as the ideas
of space and time. By this means we shall be the better prepar'd for the examination of knowledge and probability, when we understand perfectly all those
particular ideas, which may enter into our reasoning.

There is no impression nor idea of any kind, of which we have any consciousness or memory, that is not conceiv'd as existent; and 'tis evident, that
from this consciousness the most perfect idea and assurance of *being* is deriv'd.
From hence we may form a dilemma, the most clear and conclusive that can
be imagin'd, *viz.* that since we never remember any idea or impression without
attributing existence to it, the idea of existence must either be deriv'd from a
distinct impression, conjoin'd with every perception or object of our thought,
or must be the very same with the idea of the perception or object.

As this dilemma is an evident consequence of the principle, that every
idea arises from a similar impression, so our decision betwixt the propositions
of the dilemma is no more doubtful. So far from there being any distinct impression, attending every impression and every idea, that I do not think there
are any two distinct impressions, which are inseparably conjoin'd. Tho' certain sensations may at one time be united, we quickly find they admit of a separation, and may be presented apart. And thus, tho' every impression and
idea we remember be consider'd as existent, the idea of existence is not deriv'd
from any particular impression.

The idea of existence, then, is the very same with the idea of what we
conceive to be existent. To reflect on any thing simply, and to reflect on it as
existent, are nothing different from each other. That idea, when conjoin'd
with the idea of any object, makes no addition to it. Whatever we conceive, we
conceive to be existent. Any idea we please to form is the idea of a being; and
the idea of a being is any idea we please to form.

Whoever opposes this, must necessarily point out that distinct impression,
from which the idea of entity is deriv'd, and must prove, that this impression is
inseparable from every perception we believe to be existent. This we may
without hesitation conclude to be impossible.

Our foregoing (Part I. sect. 7) reasoning concerning the *distinction* of ideas
without any real *difference* will not here serve us in any stead. That kind of distinction is founded on the different resemblances, which the same simple idea
may have to several different ideas. But no object can be presented resembling
some object with respect to its existence, and different from others in the same
particular; since every object, that is presented, must necessarily be existent.

A like reasoning will account for the idea of *external existence.* We may observe, that 'tis universally allow'd by philosophers, and is besides pretty obvious of itself, that nothing is ever really present with the mind but its percep-

tions or impressions and ideas, and that external objects become known to us only by those perceptions they occasion. To hate, to love, to think, to feel, to see; all this is nothing but to perceive.

Now since nothing is ever present to the mind but perceptions, and since all ideas are deriv'd from something antecedently present to the mind; it follows, that 'tis impossible for us so much as to conceive or form an idea of any thing specifically different from ideas and impressions. Let us fix our attention out of ourselves as much as possible: Let us chace our imagination to the heavens, or to the utmost limits of the universe; we never really advance a step beyond ourselves, nor can conceive any kind of existence, but those perceptions, which have appear'd in that narrow compass. This is the universe of the imagination, nor have we any idea but what is there produc'd.

The farthest we can go towards a conception of external objects, when suppos'd *specifically* different from our perceptions, is to form a relative idea of them, without pretending to comprehend the related objects. Generally speaking we do not suppose them specifically different; but only attribute to them different relations, connexions and durations. But of this more fully hereafter (Part IV. sect. 2). . . .

Bk. I. Pt. IV. Sec. II.—Of scepticism with regard to the senses.

Thus the sceptic still continues to reason and believe, even tho' he asserts, that he cannot defend his reason by reason; and by the same rule he must assent to the principle concerning the existence of body, tho' he cannot pretend by any arguments of philosophy to maintain its veracity. Nature has not left this to his choice, and has doubtless esteem'd it an affair of too great importance to be trusted to our uncertain reasonings and speculations. We may well ask, *What causes induce us to believe in the existence of body?* but 'tis in vain to ask, *Whether there be body or not?* That is a point, which we must take for granted in all our reasonings.

The subject, then, of our present enquiry is concerning the *causes* which induce us to believe in the existence of body: And my reasonings on this head I shall begin with a distinction, which at first sight may seem superfluous, but which will contribute very much to the perfect understanding of what follows. We ought to examine apart those two questions, which are commonly confounded together, *viz.* Why we attribute a CONTINU'D existence to objects, even when they are not present to the senses; and why we suppose them to have an existence DISTINCT from the mind and perception. Under this last head I comprehend their situation as well as relations, their *external* position as well as the *independence* of their existence and operation. These two questions concerning the continu'd and distinct existence of body are intimately connected together. For if the objects of our senses continue to exist, even when they are not perceiv'd, their existence is of course independent of and distinct from the perception; and *vice versa*, if their existence be independent of the perception and distinct from it, they must continue to exist, even tho' they be not perceiv'd. But tho' the decision of the one question decides the other; yet that we may the more easily discover the principles of human nature, from whence the decision arises, we shall carry along with us this distinction, and shall consider, whether it be the *senses, reason,* or the *imagination,* that produces the opinion of a *continu'd* or of a *distinct* existence. These are the only questions, that are intelligible on the present subject. For as to the notion of external existence, when taken for something specifically different from our perceptions (Part II. sect. 6), we have already shewn its absurdity.

To begin with the SENSES, 'tis evident these faculties are incapable of giving rise to the notion of the *continu'd* existence of their objects, after they no longer appear to the senses. For that is a contradiction in terms, and supposes that the senses continue to operate, even after they have ceas'd all manner of operation. These faculties, therefore, if they have any influence in the present case, must produce the opinion of a distinct, not of a continu'd existence; and in order to that, must present their impressions either as images and representations, or as these very distinct and external existences.

That our senses offer not their impressions as the images of something *distinct,* or *independent,* and *external,* is evident; because they convey to us nothing but a single perception, and never give us the least intimation of any thing beyond. A single perception can never produce the idea of a double existence, but by some inference either of the reason or imagination. When the mind looks farther than what immediately appears to it, its conclusions can never be put to the account of the senses; and it certainly looks farther, when from a single perception it infers a double existence, and supposes the relations of resemblances and causation betwixt them.

If our senses, therefore, suggest any idea of distinct existences, they must convey the impressions as those very existences, by a kind of fallacy and illusion. Upon this head we may observe, that all sensations are felt by the mind, such as they really are, and that when we doubt, whether they present themselves as distinct objects, or as mere impressions, the difficulty is not concerning their nature, but concerning their relations and situation. Now if the senses presented our impressions as external to, and independent of ourselves, both the objects and ourselves must be obvious to our senses, otherwise they cou'd not be compar'd by these faculties. The difficulty, then, is how far we are *ourselves* the objects of our senses.

'Tis certain there is no question in philosophy more abstruse than that concerning identity, and the nature of the uniting principle, which constitutes a person. So far from being able by our senses merely to determine this question, we must have recourse to the most profound metaphysics to give a satisfactory answer to it; and in common life 'tis evident these ideas of self and person are never very fix'd nor determinate. 'Tis absurd, therefore, to imagine the senses can ever distinguish betwixt ourselves and external objects.

Add to this, that every impression, external and internal, passions, affections, sensations, pains and pleasures, are originally on the same footing; and that whatever other differences we may observe among them, they appear, all of them, in their true colours, as impressions or perceptions. And indeed, if we consider the matter aright, 'tis scarce possible it shou'd be otherwise, nor is it conceivable that our senses shou'd be more capable of deceiving us in the situation and relations, than in the nature of our impressions. For since all actions and sensations of the mind are known to us by consciousness, they must necessarily appear in every particular what they are, and be what they appear. Every thing that enters the mind, being in *reality* as the perception, 'tis impossible any thing shou'd to *feeling* appear different. This were to suppose, that even where we are most intimately conscious, we might be mistaken.

But not to lose time in examining, whether 'tis possible for our senses to deceive us, and represent our perceptions as distinct from ourselves, that is as *external* to and *independent* of us; let us consider whether they really do so, and whether this error proceeds from an immediate sensation, or from some other causes.

To begin with the question concerning *external* existence, it may perhaps be said, that setting aside the metaphysical question of the identity of a thinking substance, our own body evidently belongs to us; and as several impressions appear exterior to the body, we suppose them also exterior to ourselves. The paper, on which I write at present, is beyond my hand. The table is beyond the paper. The walls of the chamber beyond the table. And in casting my eye towards the window, I perceive a great extent of fields and buildings beyond my chamber. From all this it may be infer'd, that no other faculty is requir'd, beside the senses, to convince us of the external existence of body. But to prevent this inference, we need only weigh the three following considerations. *First,* That, properly speaking, 'tis not our body we perceive, when we regard our limbs and members, but certain impressions, which enter by the senses; so that the ascribing a real and corporeal existence to these impressions, or to their objects, is an act of the mind as difficult to explain, as that which we examine at present. *Secondly,* Sounds, and tastes, and smells, tho' commonly regarded by the mind as continu'd independent qualities, appear not to have any existence in extension, and consequently cannot appear to the senses as situated externally to the body. The reason, why we ascribe a place to them, shall be consider'd (Sect. 5) afterwards. *Thirdly,* Even our sight informs us not of distance or outness (so to speak) immediately and without a certain reasoning and experience, as is acknowledg'd by the most rational philosophers.

As to the *independency* of our perceptions on ourselves, this can never be an object of the senses; but any opinion we form concerning it, must be deriv'd from experience and observation: And we shall see afterwards, that our conclusions from experience are far from being favourable to the doctrine of the independency of our perceptions. Mean while we may observe that when we talk of real distinct existences, we have commonly more in our eye their independency than external situation in place, and think an object has a sufficient reality, when its Being is uninterrupted, and independent of the incessant revolutions, which we are conscious of in ourselves.

Thus to resume what I have said concerning the senses; they give us no notion of continu'd existence, because they cannot operate beyond the extent, in which they really operate. They as little produce the opinion of a distinct existence, because they neither can offer it to the mind as represented, nor as original. To offer it as represented, they must present both an object and an image. To make it appear as original, they must convey a falsehood; and this falsehood must lie in the relations and situation: In order to which they must be able to compare the object with ourselves; and even in that case they do not, nor is it possible they shou'd, deceive us. We may, therefore, conclude with certainty, that the opinion of a continu'd and of a distinct existence never arises from the senses. . . .

But tho' we are led after this manner, by the natural propensity of the imagination, to ascribe a continu'd existence to those sensible objects or perceptions, which we find to resemble each other in their interrupted appearance; yet a very little reflection and philosophy is sufficient to make us perceive the fallacy of that opinion. I have already observ'd, that there is an intimate connexion betwixt those two principles, of a *continu'd* and of a *distinct* or *independent* existence, and that we no sooner establish the one than the other follows, as a necessary consequence. 'Tis the opinion of a continu'd existence, which first takes place, and without much study or reflection draws the other along with it, wherever the mind follows its first and most natural tendency. But when we compare experiments, and reason a little upon them, we quickly perceive, that the doctrine of the independent existence of our sensible perceptions is contrary to the plainest experience. This leads us backward upon our footsteps to perceive our error in attributing a continu'd existence to our perceptions, and is the origin of many very curious opinions, which we shall here endeavour to account for.

'Twill first be proper to observe a few of those experiments, which convince us, that our perceptions are not possest of any independent existence. When we press one eye with a finger, we immediately perceive all the objects to become double, and one half of them to be remov'd from their common and natural position. But as we do not attribute a continu'd existence to both these perceptions, and as they are both of the same nature, we clearly perceive, that all our perceptions are dependent on our organs, and the disposition of our nerves and animal spirits. This opinion is confirm'd by the seeming encrease and diminution of objects, according to their distance; by the apparent alterations in their figure; by the changes in their colour and other qualities from our sickness and distempers; and by an infinite number of other experiments of the same kind; from all which we learn, that our sensible perceptions are not possest of any distinct or independent existence.

The natural consequence of this reasoning shou'd be, that our perceptions have no more a continu'd than an independent existence; and indeed philosophers have so far run into this opinion, that they change their system, and distinguish, (as we shall do for the future) betwixt perceptions and objects, of which the former are suppos'd to be interrupted, and perishing, and different

at every different return; the latter to be uninterrupted, and to preserve a continu'd existence and identity. But however philosophical this new system may
be esteem'd, I assert that 'tis only a palliative remedy, and that it contains all
the difficulties of the vulgar system, with some others, that are peculiar to itself. There are no principles either of the understanding or fancy, which lead
us directly to embrace this opinion of the double existence of perceptions and
objects, nor can we arrive at it but by passing thro' the common hypothesis of
the identity and continuance of our interrupted perceptions. Were we not first
persuaded, that our perceptions are our only objects, and continue to exist
even when they no longer make their appearance to the senses, we shou'd
never be led to think, that our perceptions and objects are different, and that
our objects alone preserve a continu'd existence. 'The latter hypothesis has no
primary recommendation either to reason or the imagination, but acquires all
its influence on the imagination from the former.' This proposition contains
two parts, which we shall endeavour to prove as distinctly and clearly, as such
abstruse subjects will permit.

As to the first part of the proposition, *that this philosophical hypothesis has no
primary recommendation, either to reason or the imagination,* we may soon satisfy ourselves with regard to *reason* by the following reflections. The only existences, of
which we are certain are perceptions, which being immediately present to us
by consciousness, command our strongest assent, and are the first foundation
of all our conclusions. The only conclusion we can draw from the existence of
one thing to that of another, is by means of the relation of cause and effect,
which shews, that there is a connexion betwixt them, and that the existence of
one is dependent on that of the other. The idea of this relation is deriv'd from
past experience, by which we find, that two beings are constantly conjoin'd together, and are always present at once to the mind. But as no beings are ever
present to the mind but perceptions; it follows that we may observe a conjunction or a relation of cause and effect between different perceptions, but can
never observe it between perceptions and objects. 'Tis impossible, therefore,
that from the existence of any of the qualities of the former, we can ever form
any conclusion concerning the existence of the latter, or ever satisfy our reason
in this particular.

'Tis no less certain, that this philosophical system has no primary recommendation to the *imagination,* and that that faculty wou'd never, of itself, and
by its original tendency, have fallen upon such a principle. I confess it will be
somewhat difficult to prove this to the full satisfaction of the reader; because it
implies a negative, which in many cases will not admit of any positive proof. If
any one wou'd take the pains to examine this question, and wou'd invent a
system, to account for the direct origin of this opinion from the imagination,
we shou'd be able, by the examination of that system, to pronounce a certain
judgment in the present subject. Let it be taken for granted, that our perceptions are broken, and interrupted, and however like, are still different from
each other; and let any one upon this supposition shew why the fancy, directly
and immediately, proceeds to the belief of another existence, resembling these

perceptions in their nature, but yet continu'd, and uninterrupted, and identical; and after he has done this to my satisfaction, I promise to renounce my present opinion. Mean while I cannot forbear concluding, from the very abstractedness and difficulty of the first supposition, that 'tis an improper subject for the fancy to work upon. Whoever wou'd explain the origin of the *common* opinion concerning the continu'd and distinct existence of body, must take the mind in its *common* situation, and must proceed upon the supposition, that our perceptions are our only objects, and continue to exist even when they are not perceiv'd. Tho' this opinion be false, 'tis the most natural of any, and has alone any primary recommendation to the fancy.

As to the second part of the proposition, *that the philosophical system acquires all its influence on the imagination from the vulgar one;* we may observe, that this is a natural and unavoidable consequence of the foregoing conclusion, *that it has no primary recommendation to reason or the imagination.* For as the philosophical system is found by experience to take hold of many minds, and in particular of all those, who reflect ever so little on this subject, it must derive all its authority from the vulgar system; since it has no original authority of its own. The manner, in which these two systems, tho' directly contrary, are connected together, may be explain'd as follows.

The imagination naturally runs on in this train of thinking. Our perceptions are our only objects: Resembling perceptions are the same, however broken or uninterrupted in their appearance: This appearing interruption is contrary to the identity: The interruption consequently extends not beyond the appearance, and the perception or object really continues to exist, even when absent from us: Our sensible perceptions have, therefore, a continu'd and uninterrupted existence. But as a little reflection destroys this conclusion, that our perceptions have a continu'd existence, by shewing that they have a dependent one, 'twou'd naturally be expected, that we must altogether reject the opinion, that there is such a thing in nature as a continu'd existence, which is preserv'd even when it no longer appears to the senses. The case, however, is otherwise. Philosophers are so far from rejecting the opinion of a continu'd existence upon rejecting that of the independence and continuance of our sensible perceptions, that tho' all sects agree in the latter sentiment, the former, which is, in a manner, its necessary consequence, has been peculiar to a few extravagant sceptics; who after all maintain'd that opinion in words only, and were never able to bring themselves sincerely to believe it.

There is a great difference betwixt such opinions as we form after a calm and profound reflection, and such as we embrace by a kind of instinct or natural impulse, on account of their suitableness and conformity to the mind. If these opinions become contrary, 'tis not difficult to foresee which of them will have the advantage. As long as our attention is bent upon the subject, the philosophical and study'd principle may prevail; but the moment we relax our thoughts, nature will display herself, and draw us back to our former opinion. Nay she has sometimes such an influence, that she can stop our progress, even in the midst of our most profound reflections, and keep us from running on with all the consequences of any philosophical opinion. Thus tho' we clearly perceive the dependence and interruption of our perceptions, we stop short in our career, and never upon that account reject the notion of an independent and continu'd existence. That opinion has taken such deep root in the imagination, that 'tis impossible ever to eradicate it, nor will any strain'd metaphysical conviction of the dependence of our perceptions be sufficient for that purpose.

But tho' our natural and obvious principles here prevail above our study'd reflections, 'tis certain there must be some struggle and opposition in the case; at least so long as these reflections retain any force or vivacity. In order to set ourselves at ease in this particular, we contrive a new hypothesis, which seems to comprehend both these principles of reason and imagination. This hypothesis is the philosophical one of the double existence of perceptions and objects; which pleases our reason, in allowing, that our dependent perceptions are interrupted and different; and at the same time is agreeable to the imagination, in attributing a continu'd existence to something else, which we call *objects*. This philosophical system, therefore, is the monstrous offspring of two principles, which are contrary to each other, which are both at once embrac'd by the mind, and which are unable mutually to destroy each other. The imagination tells us, that our resembling perceptions have a continu'd and uninterrupted existence, and are not annihilated by their absence. Reflection tells us, that even our resembling perceptions are interrupted in their existence, and different from each other. The contradiction betwixt these opinions we elude by a new fiction, which is conformable to the hypotheses both of reflection and fancy, by ascribing these contrary qualities to different existences; the *interruption* to perceptions, and the *continuance* to objects. Nature is obstinate, and will not quit the field, however strongly attack'd by reason; and at the same time reason is so clear in the point, that there is no possibility of disguising her. Not being able to reconcile these two enemies, we endeavour to set ourselves at ease as much as possible, by successively granting to each whatever it demands, and by feigning a double existence, where each may find something, that has all the conditions it desires. Were we fully convinc'd, that our resembling perceptions are continu'd, and identical, and independent, we shou'd never run into this opinion of a double existence; since we shou'd find satisfaction in our first supposition, and wou'd not look beyond. Again, were we fully convinc'd, that our perceptions are dependent, and interrupted, and different, we shou'd be as little inclin'd to embrace the opinion of a double existence; since in that case we shou'd clearly perceive the error of our first supposition of a continu'd existence, and wou'd never regard it any farther. 'Tis therefore from the intermediate situation of the mind, that this opinion arises, and from such an adherence to these two contrary principles, as makes us seek some pretext to justify our receiving both; which happily at last is found in the system of a double existence.

Another advantage of this philosophical system is its similarity to the vulgar one; by which means we can humour our reason for a moment, when it becomes troublesome and solicitous; and yet upon its least negligence or inattention, can easily return to our vulgar and natural notions. Accordingly we find, that philosophers neglect not this advantage; but immediately upon leaving their closets, mingle with the rest of mankind in those exploded opinions, that our perceptions are our only objects, and continue identically and uninterruptedly the same in all their interrupted appearances.

There are other particulars of this system, wherein we may remark its dependence on the fancy, in a very conspicuous manner. Of these, I shall observe the two following. *First,* We suppose external objects to resemble internal perceptions. I have already shewn that the relation of cause and effect can never afford us any just conclusion from the existence or qualities of our perceptions to the existence of external continu'd objects: And I shall farther add, that even tho' they cou'd afford such a conclusion, we shou'd never have any reason to infer, that our objects resemble our perceptions. That opinion, therefore, is deriv'd from nothing but the quality of the fancy above-explain'd, *that it borrows all its ideas from some precedent perception.* We never can conceive any thing but perceptions, and therefore must make every thing resemble them.

Secondly, As we suppose our objects in general to resemble our perceptions, so we take it for granted, that every particular object resembles that perception, which it causes. The relation of cause and effect determines us to join the other of resemblance; and the ideas of these existences being already united together in the fancy by the former relation, we naturally add the latter to compleat the union. We have a strong propensity to compleat every union by joining new relations to those which we have before observ'd betwixt any ideas, as we shall have occasion to observe presently (Sect. 5).

Having thus given an account of all the systems both popular and philosophical, with regard to external existences, I cannot forbear giving vent to a certain sentiment, which arises upon reviewing those systems. I begun this subject with premising, that we ought to have an implicit faith in our senses, and that this wou'd be the conclusion, I shou'd draw from the whole of my reasoning. But to be ingenuous, I feel myself *at present* of a quite contrary sentiment, and am more inclin'd to repose no faith at all in my senses, or rather imagination, than to place in it such an implicit confidence. I cannot conceive how such trivial qualities of the fancy, conducted by such false suppositions, can ever lead to any solid and rational system. They are the coherence and constancy of our perceptions, which produce the opinion of their continu'd existence; tho' these qualities of perceptions have no perceivable connexion with such an existence. The constancy of our perceptions has the most considerable effect, and yet is attended with the greatest difficulties. 'Tis a gross illusion to suppose, that our resembling perceptions are numerically the same; and 'tis this illusion, which leads us into the opinion, that these perceptions are uninterrupted, and are still existent, even when they are not present to the senses. This is the case with our popular system. And as to our philosophical one, 'tis liable to the same difficulties; and is over-and-above loaded with this absurdity, that it at once denies and establishes the vulgar supposition. Philosophers

deny our resembling perceptions to be identically the same, and uninterrupted; and yet have so great a propensity to believe them such, that they arbitrarily invent a new set of perceptions, to which they attribute these qualities. I say, a new set of perceptions: For we may well suppose in general, but
'tis impossible for us distinctly to conceive, objects to be in their nature any
thing but exactly the same with perceptions. What then can we look for from
this confusion of groundless and extraordinary opinions but error and fals-
hood? And how can we justify to ourselves any belief we repose in them?

This sceptical doubt, both with respect to reason and the senses, is a malady, which can never be radically cur'd, but must return upon us every moment, however we may chace it away, and sometimes may seem entirely free
from it. 'Tis impossible upon any system to defend either our understanding or
senses; and we but expose them farther when we endeavour to justify them in
that manner. As the sceptical doubt arises naturally from a profound and intense reflection on those subjects, it always encreases, the farther we carry our
reflections, whether in opposition or conformity to it. Carelessness and inattention alone can afford us any remedy. For this reason I rely entirely upon them;
and take it for granted, whatever may be the reader's opinion at this present
moment, that an hour hence he will be persuaded there is both an external
and internal world; and going upon that supposition, I entend to examine
some general systems both ancient and modern, which have been propos'd of
both, before I proceed to a more particular enquiry concerning our impressions. This will not, perhaps, in the end be found foreign to our present purpose.

Bk. I, Pt. IV. Sec. V.—Of the immateriality of the soul.
Having found such contradictions and difficulties in every system concerning external objects, and in the idea of matter, which we fancy so clear
and determinate, we shall naturally expect still greater difficulties and contradictions in every hypothesis concerning our internal perceptions, and the nature of the mind, which we are apt to imagine so much more obscure, and uncertain. But in this we shou'd deceive ourselves. The intellectual world, tho'
involv'd in infinite obscurities, is not perplex'd with any such contradictions,
as those we have discover'd in the natural. What is known concerning it,
agrees with itself; and what is unknown, we must be contented to leave so.

'Tis true, wou'd we hearken to certain philosophers, they promise to diminish our ignorance; but I am afraid 'tis at the hazard of running us into
contradictions, from which the subject is of itself exempted. These philosophers are the curious reasoners concerning the material or immaterial substances, in which they suppose our perceptions to inhere. In order to put a stop
to these endless cavils on both sides, I know no better method, than to ask
these philosophers in a few words, *What they mean by substance and inhesion?* And
after they have answer'd this question, 'twill then be reasonable, and not till
then, to enter seriously into the dispute.

This question we have found impossible to be answer'd with regard to matter and body: But besides that in the case of the mind, it labours under all the same difficulties, 'tis burthen'd with some additional ones, which are peculiar to that subject. As every idea is deriv'd from a precedent impression, had we any idea of the substance of our minds, we must also have an impression of it; which is very difficult, if not impossible, to be conceiv'd. For how can an impression represent a substance, otherwise than by resembling it? And how can an impression resemble a substance, since, according to this philosophy, it is not a substance, and has none of the peculiar qualities or characteristics of a substance?

But leaving the question *of what may or may not be,* for that other *what actually is,* I desire those philosophers, who pretend that we have an idea of the substance of our minds, to point out the impression that produces it, and tell distinctly after what manner that impression operates, and from what object it is deriv'd. Is it an impression of sensation or of reflection? Is it pleasant, or painful, or indifferent? Does it attend us at all times, or does it only return at intervals? If at intervals, at what times principally does it return, and by what causes is it produc'd?

If instead of answering these questions, any one shou'd evade the difficulty, by saying, that the definition of a substance is *something which may exist by itself;* and that this definition ought to satisfy us: Shou'd this be said, I shou'd observe, that this definition agrees to every thing, that can possibly be conceiv'd; and never will serve to distinguish substance from accident, or the soul from its perceptions. For thus I reason. Whatever is clearly conceiv'd may exist; and whatever is clearly conceiv'd, after any manner, may exist; and whatever is clearly conceiv'd, after any manner, may exist after the same manner. This is one principle, which has been already acknowledg'd. Again, every thing, which is different, is distinguishable, and every thing which is distinguishable, is separable by the imagination. This is another principle. My conclusion from both is, that since all our perceptions are different from each other, and from every thing else in the universe, they are also distinct and separable, and may be consider'd as separately existent, and may exist separately, and have no need of any thing else to support their existence. They are, therefore, substances, as far as this definition explains a substance.

Thus neither by considering the first origin of ideas, nor by means of a definition are we able to arrive at any satisfactory notion of substance; which seems to me a sufficient reason for abandoning utterly that dispute concerning the materiality and immateriality of the soul, and makes me absolutely condemn even the question itself. We have no perfect idea of any thing but of a perception. We have, therefore, no idea of a substance. Inhesion in something is suppos'd to be requisite to support the existence of our perceptions. Nothing appears requisite to support the existence of a perception. We have, therefore, no idea of inhesion. What possibility then of answering that question, *Whether perceptions inhere in a material or immaterial substance,* when we do not so much as understand the meaning of the question? . . .

35

THOMAS REID
Existence and Common Sense*

Ch. V. Section VII.—Of the Existence of a Material World

. . . I beg leave to offer to the consideration of philosophers these two observations. First, That, in all this debate about the existence of a material world, it hath been taken for granted on both sides, that this same material world, if any such there be, must be the express image of our sensation; that we can have no conception of any material thing which is not like some sensation in our minds; and particularly that the sensations of touch are images of extension, hardness, figure, and motion. Every argument brought against the existence of a material world, either by the Bishop of Cloyne, or by the author of the "Treatise of Human Nature," supposeth this. If this is true, their arguments are conclusive and unanswerable; but, on the other hand, if it is not true, there is no shadow of argument left. Have those philosophers, then, given any solid proof of this hypothesis, upon which the whole weight of so strange a system rests. No. They have not so much as attempted to do it. But, because ancient and modern philosophers have agreed in this opinion, they have taken it for granted. But let us, as become philosophers, lay aside authority; we need not, surely, consult Aristotle or Locke, to know whether pain be like the point of a sword. I have as clear a conception of extension, hardness, and motion, as I have of the point of a sword; and, with some pains and practice, I can form as clear a notion of the other sensations of touch as I have of pain. When I do so, and compare them together, it appears to me clear as daylight, that the former are not of kin to the latter, nor resemble them in any one feature. They are as unlike, yea as certainly and manifestly unlike, as pain is to the point of a sword. It may be true, that those sensations first introduced the material world to our acquaintance; it may be true, that it seldom or never appears without their company; but, for all that, they are as unlike as the passion of anger is to those features of the countenance which attend it.

So that, in the sentence those philosophers have passed against the material world, there is an *error personae*. Their proof touches not matter, or any of its qualities; but strikes directly against an idol of their own imagination, a material world made of ideas and sensations, which never had, nor can have an existence.

Secondly, The very existence of our conceptions of extension, figure, and motion, since they are neither ideas of sensation nor reflection, overturns the whole ideal system, by which the material world hath been tried and condemned; so that there hath been likewise in this sentence an *error juris*.

It is a very fine and a just observation of Locke, that, as no human art can create a single particle of matter, and the whole extent of our power over the material world consists in compounding, combining, and disjoining the matter

---

* From *An Inquiry into the Human Mind on the Principles of Common Sense.*

made to our hands; so, in the world of thought, the materials are all made by nature, and can only be variously combined and disjoined by us. So that it is impossible for reason or prejudice, true or false philosophy, to produce one simple notion or conception, which is not the work of nature, and the result of our constitution. The conception of extension, motion, and the other attributes of matter, cannot be the effect of error or prejudice; it must be the work of nature. And the power or faculty by which we acquire those conceptions, must be something different from any power of the human mind that hath been explained, since it is neither sensation nor reflection.

This I would, therefore, humbly propose, as an *experimentum crucis,* by which the ideal system must stand or fall; and it bring the matter to a short issue: Extension, figure, motion, may, any one, or all of them, be taken for the subject of this experiment. Either they are ideas of sensation, or they are not. If any one of them can be shewn to be an idea of sensation, or to have the least resemblance to any sensation, I lay my hand upon my mouth, and give up all pretence to reconcile reason to common sense in this matter, and must suffer the ideal scepticism to triumph. But if, on the other hand, they are not ideas of sensation, nor like to any sensation, then the ideal system is a rope of sand, and all the laboured arguments of the sceptical philosophy against a material world, and against the existence of every thing but impressions and ideas, proceed upon a false hypothesis.

If our philosophy concerning the mind be so lame with regard to the origin of our notions of the clearest, most simple, and most familiar objects of thought, and the powers from which they are derived, can we expect that it should be more perfect in the account it gives of the origin of our opinions and belief? We have seen already some instances of its imperfection in this respect: and, perhaps, that same nature which hath given us the power to conceive things altogether unlike to any of our sensations, or to any operation of our minds, hath likewise provided for our belief of them, by some part of our constitution hitherto not explained.

Bishop Berkeley hath proved, beyond the possibility of reply, that we cannot by reasoning infer the existence of matter from our sensations; and the author of the "Treatise of Human Nature" hath proved no less clearly, that we cannot by reasoning infer the existence of our own or other minds from our sensations. But are we to admit nothing but what can be proved by reasoning? Then we must be sceptics indeed, and believe nothing at all. The author of the "Treatise of Human Nature" appears to me to be but a half-sceptic. He hath not followed his principles so far as they lead him; but, after having, with unparalleled intrepidity and success, combated vulgar prejudices, when he had but one blow to strike, his courage fails him, he fairly lays down his arms, and yields himself a captive to the most common of all vulgar prejudices—I mean the belief of the existence of his own impressions and ideas.

I beg, therefore, to have the honour of making an addition to the sceptical system, without which I conceive it cannot hang together. I affirm, that the belief of the existence of impressions and ideas, is as little supported by reason, as that of the existence of minds and bodies. No man ever did or could offer any reason for this belief. Des Cartes took it for granted, that he thought, and had sensations and ideas; so have all his followers done. Even the hero of scepticism hath yielded this point, I crave leave to say, weakly and imprudently. I say so, because I am persuaded that there is no principle of his philosophy that obliged him to make this concession. And what is there in impressions and ideas so formidable, that this all-conquering philosophy, after triumphing over every other existence, should pay homage to them? Besides, the concession is dangerous: for belief is of such a nature, that, if you leave any root, it will spread; and you may more easily pull it up altogether, than say, Hitherto shalt thou go and no further: the existence of impressions and ideas I give up to thee; but see thou pretend to nothing more. A thorough and consistent sceptic will never, therefore, yield this point; and while he holds it, you can never oblige him to yield anything else.

To such a sceptic I have nothing to say; but of the semi-sceptics, I should beg to know, why they believe the existence of their impressions and ideas. The true reason I take to be, because they cannot help it; and the same reason will lead them to believe many other things.

All reasoning must be from first principles; and for first principles no other reason can be given but this, that, by the constitution of our nature, we are under a necessity of assenting to them. Such principles are parts of our constitution, no less than the power of thinking: reason can neither make nor destroy them; nor can it do anything without them: it is like a telescope, which may help a man to see farther, who hath eyes; but, without eyes, a telescope shews nothing at all. A mathematician cannot prove the truth of his axioms, nor can he prove anything, unless he takes them for granted. We cannot prove the existence of our minds, nor even of our thoughts and sensations. A historian, or a witness, can prove nothing, unless it is taken for granted that the memory and senses may be trusted. A natural philosopher can prove nothing, unless it is taken for granted that the course of nature is steady and uniform.

How or when I got such first principles, upon which I build all my reasoning, I know not; for I had them before I can remember: but I am sure they are parts of my constitution, and that I cannot throw them off. That our thoughts and sensations must have a subject, which we call *ourself,* is not therefore an opinion got by reasoning, but a natural principle. That our sensations of touch indicate something external, extended, figured, hard or soft, is not a deduction of reason, but a natural principle. The belief of it, and the very conception of it, are equally parts of our constitution. If we are deceived in it, we are deceived by Him that made us, and there is no remedy.

I do not mean to affirm, that the sensations of touch do, from the very first, suggest the same notions of body and its qualities which they do when we are grown up. Perhaps Nature is frugal in this, as in her other operations. The passion of love, with all its concomitant sentiments and desires, is naturally suggested by the perception of beauty in the other sex; yet the same perception does not suggest the tender passion till a certain period of life. A blow given to an infant, raises grief and lamentation; but when he grows up, it as naturally stirs resentment, and prompts him to resistance. Perhaps a child in the womb, or for some short period of its existence, is merely a sentient being; the faculties by which it perceives an external world, by which it reflects on its own thoughts, and existence, and relation to other things, as well as its reasoning and moral faculties, unfold themselves by degrees; so that it is inspired with the various principles of common sense, as with the passions of love and resentment, when it has occasion for them.

Ch. V. Section VIII.—Of the Systems of Philosophers Concerning the Senses

All the systems of philosophers about our senses and their objects have split upon this rock, of not distinguishing properly sensations which can have no existence but when they are felt, from the things suggested by them. . . .

. . . How a sensation should instantly make us conceive and believe the existence of an external thing altogether unlike to it, I do not pretend to know; and when I say that the one suggests the other, I mean not to explain the manner of their connection, but to express a fact, which every one may be conscious of—namely, that, by a law of our nature, such a conception and belief constantly and immediately follow the sensation. . . .

. . . That we can have no conception of anything, unless there is some impression, sensation, or idea, in our minds which resembles it, is indeed an opinion which hath been very generally received among philosophers; but it is neither self-evident, nor hath it been clearly proved; and therefore it hath been more reasonable to call in question this doctrine of philosophers, than to discard the material world, and by that means expose philosophy to the ridicule of all men who will not offer up common sense as a sacrifice to metaphysics.

We ought, however, to do this justice both to the Bishop of Cloyne and to the author of the "Treatise of Human Nature," to acknowledge, that their conclusions are justly drawn from the doctrine of ideas, which has been so universally received. On the other hand, from the character of Bishop Berkeley, and of his predecessors, Des Cartes, Locke, and Malebranche, we may venture to say, that, if they had seen all the consequences of this doctrine, as clearly as the author before mentioned did, they would have suspected it vehemently, and examined it more carefully than they appear to have done.

The theory of ideas, like the Trojan horse, had a specious appearance both of innocence and beauty; but if those philosophers had known that it carried in its belly death and destruction to all science and common sense, they would not have broken down their walls to give it admittance.

That we have clear and distinct conceptions of extension, figure, motion, and other attributes of body, which are neither sensations, nor like any sensation, is a fact of which we may be as certain as that we have sensations. And that all mankind have a fixed belief of an external material world—a belief which is neither got by reasoning nor education, and a belief which we cannot shake off, even when we seem to have strong arguments against it and no shadow of argument for it—is likewise a fact, for which we have all the evidence that the nature of the thing admits. These facts are phaenomena of human nature, from which we may justly argue against any hypothesis, however generally received. But to argue from a hypothesis against facts, is contrary to the rules of true philosophy.

Ch. II. Section VI.—Apology for Metaphysical Absurdities—Sensation without a Sentient, a Consequence of the Theory of Ideas—Consequences of This Strange Opinion

. . . It is certain, no man can conceive or believe smelling to exist of itself, without a mind, or something that has the power of smelling, of which it is called a sensation, an operation, or feeling. Yet, if any man should demand a proof, that sensation cannot be without a mind or sentient being, I confess that I can give none; and that to pretend to prove it, seems to me almost as absurd as to deny it.

This might have been said without any apology before the "Treatise of Human Nature" appeared in the world. For till that time, no man, as far as I know, ever thought either of calling in question that principle, or of giving a reason for his belief of it. Whether thinking beings were of an ethereal or igneous nature, whether material or immaterial, was variously disputed; but that thinking is an operation of some kind of being or other, was always taken for granted, as a principle that could not possibly admit of doubt.

If there are certain principles, as I think there are, which the constitution of our nature leads us to believe, and which we are under a necessity to take for granted in the common concerns of life, without being able to give a reason for them—these are what we call the principles of common sense; and what is manifestly contrary to them, is what we call absurd.

Indeed, if it is true, and to be received as a principle of philosophy, that sensation and thought may be without a thinking being, it must be acknowledged to be the most wonderful discovery that this or any other age hath produced. The received doctrine of ideas is the principle from which it is deduced, and of which indeed it seems to be a just and natural consequence. And it is probable, that it would not have been so late a discovery, but that it is so shocking and repugnant to the common apprehensions of mankind, that it required an uncommon degree of philosophical intrepidity to usher it into the world. It is a fundamental principle of the ideal system, that every object of thought must be an impression or an idea—that is, a faint copy of some preceding impression. This is a principle so commonly received, that the author above mentioned, although his whole system is built upon it, never offers the least proof of it. It is upon this principle, as a fixed point, that he erects his metaphysical engines, to overturn heaven and earth, body and spirit. And, indeed, in my apprehension, it is altogether sufficient for the purpose. For, if impressions and ideas are the only objects of thought, then heaven and earth, and body and spirit, and everything you please, must signify only impressions and ideas, or they must be words without any meaning. It seems, therefore, that this notion, however strange, is closely connected with the received doctrine of ideas, and we must either admit the conclusion, or call in question the premises. . . .

. . . We were always apt to imagine, that thought supposed a thinker, and love a lover, and treason a traitor: but this, it seems, was all a mistake; and it is found out, that there may be treason without a traitor, and love without a lover, laws without a legislator, and punishment without a sufferer, succession without time, and motion without anything moved, or space in which it may move: or if, in these cases, ideas are the lover, the sufferer, the traitor, it were to be wished that the author of this discovery had farther condescended to acquaint us whether ideas can converse together, and be under obligations of duty or gratitude to each other; whether they can make promises and enter into leagues and covenants, and fulfil or break them, and be punished for the breach. If one set of ideas makes a covenant, another breaks it, and a third is punished for it, there is reason to think that justice is no natural virtue in this system.

It seemed very natural to think, that the "Treatise of Human Nature" required an author, and a very ingenious one too; but now we learn that it is only a set of ideas which came together and arranged themselves by certain associations and attractions.

After all, this curious system appears not to be fitted to the present state of human nature. How far it may suit some choice spirits, who are refined from the dregs of common sense, I cannot say. It is acknowledged, I think, that even these can enter into this system only in their most speculative hours, when they soar so high in pursuit of those self-existent ideas as to lose sight of all other things. But when they condescend to mingle again with the human race, and to converse with a friend, a companion, or a fellow-citizen, the ideal system vanishes; common sense, like an irresistible torrent, carries them along; and, in spite of all their reasoning and philosophy, they believe their own existence, and the existence of other things.

Indeed, it is happy they do so; for, if they should carry their closet belief into the world, the rest of mankind would consider them as diseased, and send them to an infirmary. Therefore, as Plato required certain previous qualifications of those who entered his school, I think it would be prudent for the doctors of this ideal philosophy to do the same, and to refuse admittance to every man who is so weak as to imagine that he ought to have the same belief in solitude and in company, or that his principles ought to have any influence upon his practice; for this philosophy is like a hobby-horse, which a man in bad health may ride in his closet, without hurting his reputation; but, if he should take him abroad with him to church, or to the exchange, or to the play-house, his heir would immediately call a jury, and seize his estate.

Ch. II. Section VII.—The Conception and Belief of a Sentient Being or Mind Is Suggested by Our Constitution

Leaving this philosophy, therefore, to those who have occasion for it, and can use it discreetly as a chamber exercise, we may still inquire how the rest of mankind, and even the adepts themselves, except in some solitary moments, have got so strong and irresistible a belief, that thought must have a subject, and be the act of some thinking being; how every man believes himself to be something distinct from his ideas and impressions—something which continues the same identical self when all his ideas and impressions are changed. It is impossible to trace the origin of this opinion in history; for all languages have it interwoven in their original construction. All nations have always believed it. The constitution of all laws and governments, as well as the common transactions of life, suppose it.

It is no less impossible for any man to recollect when he himself came by this notion; for, as far back as we can remember, we were already in possession of it, and as fully persuaded of our own existence, and the existence of other things, as that one and one make two. It seems, therefore, that this opinion preceded all reasoning, and experience, and instruction; and this is the more probable, because we could not get it by any of these means. It appears, then, to be an undeniable fact, that, from thought or sensation, all mankind, constantly and invariably, from the first dawning of reflection, do infer a power or faculty of thinking, and a permanent being or mind to which that faculty belongs; and that we as invariably ascribe all the various kinds of sensation and thought we are conscious of, to one individual mind or self.

But by what rules of logic we make these inferences, it is impossible to shew; nay, it is impossible to shew how our sensations and thoughts can give us the very notion and conception either of a mind or of a faculty. The faculty of smelling is something very different from the actual sensation of smelling; for the faculty may remain when we have no sensation. And the mind is no less different from the faculty; for it continues the same individual being when that faculty is lost. Yet this sensation suggests to us both a faculty and a mind; and not only suggests the notion of them, but creates a belief of their existence; although it is impossible to discover, by reason, any tie or connection between one and the other.

What shall we say, then? Either those inferences which we draw from our sensations—namely, the existence of a mind, and of powers or faculties belonging to it—are prejudices of philosophy or education, mere fictions of the mind, which a wise man should throw off as he does the belief of fairies; or they are judgments of nature—judgments not got by comparing ideas, and perceiving agreements and disagreements, but immediately inspired by our constitution.

If this last is the case, as I apprehend it is, it will be impossible to shake off those opinions, and we must yield to them at last, though we struggle hard to get rid of them. And if we could, by a determined obstinacy, shake off the principles of our nature, this is not to act the philosopher, but the fool or the madman. It is incumbent upon those who think that these are not natural principles, to shew, in the first place, how we can otherwise get the notion of a mind and its faculties; and then to shew how we come to deceive ourselves into the opinion that sensation cannot be without a sentient being. . . .

36

IMMANUEL KANT
The Category of Substance and the Transcendental Idea of Self

TRANSCENDENTAL DIALECTIC*

Of Reason in General

All our knowledge begins with the senses, proceeds thence to the understanding, and ends with reason. There is nothing higher than reason, for working up the material of intuition, and comprehending it under the highest unity of thought. As it here becomes necessary to give a definition of that highest faculty of knowledge, I begin to feel considerable misgivings. There is of reason, as there is of the understanding, a purely formal, that is logical use, in which no account is taken of the contents of knowledge; but there is also a real use, in so far as reason itself contains the origin of certain concepts and principles, which it has not borrowed either from the senses or from the understanding. The former faculty has been long defined by logicians as the faculty of mediate conclusions, in contradistinction to immediate ones *(consequentiae immediatae);* but this does not help us to understand the latter, which itself produces concepts. As this brings us face to face with the division of reason into a logical and a transcendental faculty, we must look for a higher concept for this source of knowledge, to comprehend both concepts: though, according to the analogy of the concepts of the understanding, we may expect that the logical concept will give us the key to the transcendental, and that the table of the functions of the former will give us the genealogical outline of the concepts of reason.

In the first part of our transcendental logic we defined the understanding as the *faculty of rules,* and we now distinguish reason from it, by calling it the *faculty of principles.*

The term *principle* is ambiguous, and signifies commonly some kind of knowledge only that may be used as a principle, though in itself, and according to its origin, it is no principle at all. Every general proposition, even though it may have been derived from experience (by induction), may serve as a major in a syllogism of reason; but it is not on that account a principle. Mathematical axioms, as, for instance, that between two points there can be only one straight line, constitute even general knowledge *a priori,* and may therefore, with reference to the cases which can be brought under them, rightly be called principles. Nevertheless it would be wrong to say, that this property of a straight line, in general and by itself, is known to us from principles, for it is known from pure intuition only.

---

* From *Critique of Pure Reason*, A 298–302, B 355–359; A 327–329, B 383–386; A 334–336, B 391–393; A 341–345, B 399–403; B 410–413; B 421–422 (with omissions).

I shall therefore call it knowledge from principles, whenever we know the particular in the general, by means of concepts. Thus every syllogism of reason is a form of deducing some kind of knowledge from a principle, because the major always contains a concept which enables us to know, according to a principle, everything that can be comprehended under the conditions of that concept. As every general knowledge may serve as a major in such a syllogism, and as the understanding supplies such general propositions *a priori,* these no doubt may, with reference to their possible use, be called principles.

But, if we consider these principles of the pure understanding in themselves, and according to their origin, we find that they are anything rather than knowledge from concepts. They would not even be possible *a priori,* unless we relied on pure intuition (in mathematics) or on conditions of a possible experience in general. That everything which happens has a cause, can by no means be concluded from the concept of that which happens; on the contrary, that very principle shows in what manner alone we can form a definite empirical concept of that which happens.

It is impossible therefore for the understanding to supply us with synthetical knowledge from concepts, and it is really that kind of knowledge which I call principles absolutely; while all general propositions may be called principles relatively.

It is an old desideratum, which at some time, however distant, may be realised, that, instead of the endless variety of civil laws, their principles might be discovered, for thus alone the secret might be found of what is called simplifying legislation. Such laws, however, are only limitations of our freedom under conditions by which it always agrees with itself; they refer to something which is entirely our own work, and of which we ourselves can be the cause, by means of these concepts. But that objects in themselves, as for instance material nature, should be subject to principles, and be determined according to mere concepts, is something, if not impossible, at all events extremely contradictory. But be that as it may (for on this point we have still all investigations before us), so much at least is clear, that knowledge from principles (by itself) is something totally different from mere knowledge of the understanding, which, in the form of a principle, may no doubt precede other knowledge, but which by itself (in so far as it is synthetical) is not based on mere thought, nor contains anything general, according to concepts.

If the understanding is a faculty for producing unity among phenomena, according to rules, reason is the faculty for producing unity among the rules of the understanding, according to principles. Reason therefore never looks directly to experience, or to any object, but to the understanding, in order to impart *a priori* through concepts to its manifold kinds of knowledge a unity that may be called the unity of reason, and is very different from the unity which can be produced by the understanding.

This is a general definition of the faculty of reason, so far as it was possible to make it intelligible without the help of illustrations, which are to be given hereafter.

Of Transcendental Ideas

By idea I understand the necessary concept of reason, to which the senses can supply no corresponding object. The concepts of reason, therefore, of which we have been speaking, are *transcendental ideas*. They are concepts of pure reason, so far as they regard all empirical knowledge as determined by an absolute totality of conditions. They are not mere fancies, but supplied to us by the very nature of reason, and referring by necessity to the whole use of the understanding. They are, lastly, transcendent, as overstepping the limits of all experience which can never supply an object adequate to the transcendental idea. . . .

Although we must say that all transcendental concepts of reason are ideas only, they are not therefore to be considered as superfluous and useless. For although we cannot by them determine any object, they may nevertheless, even unobserved, supply the understanding with a canon or rule of its extended and consistent use, by which, though no object can be better known than it is according to its concepts, yet the understanding may be better guided onwards in its knowledge, not to mention that they may possibly render practicable a transition from physical to practical concepts, and thus impart to moral ideas a certain strength and connection with the speculative knowledge of reason. . . .

System of Transcendental Ideas

The relations which all our representations share in common are, 1st, relation to the subject; 2ndly, the relation to objects, either as phenomena, or as objects of thought in general. If we connect this subdivision with the former division, we see that the relation of the representations of which we can form a concept or an idea can only be threefold: 1st, the relation to the subject; 2ndly, the relation to the manifold of the phenomenal object; 3rdly, the relation to all things in general.

All pure concepts in general aim at a synthetical unity of representations, while concepts of pure reason (transcendental ideas) aim at unconditioned synthetical unity of all conditions. All transcendental ideas therefore can be arranged in three classes: the *first* containing the absolute (unconditioned) *unity of the thinking subject;* the *second* the absolute *unity of the series of conditions* of *phenomena;* the *third* the absolute *unity of the condition of all objects of thought in general.*

The thinking subject is the object-matter of *psychology,* the system of all phenomena (the world) the object-matter of *cosmology,* and the being which contains the highest condition of the possibility of all that can be thought (the Being of all beings), the object-matter of *theology.* Thus it is pure reason which supplies the idea of a transcendental science of the soul *(psychologia rationalis),* of a transcendental science of the world *(cosmologia rationalis),* and lastly, of a transcendental science of God *(theologia transcendentalis).* . . .

What kinds of pure concepts of reason are comprehended under these three titles of all transcendental ideas will be fully explained in the following chapter. They follow the thread of the categories, for pure reason never refers direct to objects, but to the concepts of objects framed by the understanding. Nor can it be rendered clear, except hereafter in a detailed explanation, how first, reason simply by the synthetical use of the same function which it employs for categorical syllogisms is necessarily led on to the concept of the absolute unity of the thinking subject; secondly, how the logical procedure in hypothetical syllogisms leads to the idea of something absolutely unconditioned, in a series of given conditions, and how, thirdly, the mere form of the disjunctive syllogism produces necessarily the highest concept of reason, that of a Being of all beings; a thought which, at first sight, seems extremely paradoxical. . . .

Of the Paralogisms of Pure Reason

The logical paralogism consists in the formal faultiness of a conclusion, without any reference to its contents. But a transcendental paralogism arises from a transcendental cause, which drives us to a formally false conclusion. Such a paralogism, therefore, depends most likely on the very nature of human reason, and produces an illusion which is inevitable, though not insoluble.

We now come to a concept which was not inserted in our general list of transcendental concepts, and yet must be reckoned with them, without however changing that table in the least, or proving it to be deficient. This is the concept, or, if the term is preferred, the judgment, *I think*. It is easily seen, however, that this concept is the vehicle of all concepts in general, therefore of transcendental concepts also, being always comprehended among them, and being itself transcendental also, though without any claim to a special title, inasmuch as it serves only to introduce all thought, as belonging to consciousness. However free that concept may be from all that is empirical (impressions of the senses), it serves nevertheless to distinguish two objects within the nature of our faculty of representation. *I,* as thinking, am an object of the internal sense, and am called soul. That which is an object of the external senses is called body. The term *I,* as a thinking being, signifies the object of psychology, which may be called the rational science of the soul, supposing that we want to know nothing about the soul except what, independent of all experience (which determines the I more especially and *in concreto*), can be deduced from the concept of I, so far as it is present in every act of thought.

Now the rational science of the soul is really such an undertaking; for if the smallest empirical element of my thought or any particular perception of my internal state were mixed up with the sources from which that science derives its materials, it would be an empirical, and no longer a purely rational science of the soul. There is therefore a pretended science, founded on the sin-

gle proposition of *I think,* and the soundness or unsoundness of which may well
be examined in this place, according to the principles of transcendental philosophy. It should not be objected that even in that proposition, which expresses the perception of oneself, I have an internal experience, and that
therefore the rational science of the soul, which is founded on it, can never be
quite pure, but rests, to a certain extent, on an empirical principle. For this
inner perception is nothing more than the mere apperception, *I think,* without
which even all transcendental concepts would be impossible, in which we really say, I think the substance, I think the cause, etc. This internal experience
in general and its possibility, or perception in general and its relation to other
perceptions, there being no special distinction or empirical determination of it,
cannot be regarded as empirical knowledge, but must be regarded as knowledge of the empirical in general, and falls therefore under the investigation of
the possibility of all experience, which investigation is certainly transcendental. The smallest object of perception (even pleasure and pain), if added to the
general representation of self-consciousness, would at once change rational
into empirical psychology.

I think is, therefore, the only text of rational psychology, out of which it
must evolve all its wisdom. It is easily seen that this thought, if it is to be applied to any object (my self), cannot contain any but transcendental predicates, because the smallest empirical predicate would spoil the rational purity
of the science, and its independence of all experience.

We shall therefore follow the thread of the categories, with this difference,
however, that as here the first thing which is given is a thing, the I, a thinking
being, we must begin with the category of substance, by which a thing in itself
is represented, and then proceed backwards, though without changing the respective order of the categories, as given before in our table. The topic of the
rational science of the soul, from which has to be derived whatever else that
science may contain, is therefore the following.

I

The Soul is *substance.*

II

As regards its quality, *simple.*

III

As regards the different
times in which it exists,
numerically identical, that
is *unity* (not plurality).

IV

It is in relation to *possible* objects in space.

All concepts of pure psychology arise from these elements, simply by way of combination, and without the admixture of any other principle. This substance, taken simply as the object of the internal sense, gives us the concept of *immateriality;* and as simple substance, that of *incorruptibility;* its identity, as that of an intellectual substance, gives us *personality;* and all these three together, *spirituality;* its relation to objects in space gives us the concept of *commercium* (intercourse) with *bodies;* the pure psychology thus representing the thinking substance as the principle of life in matter, that is, as soul *(anima),* and as the ground of *animality;* which again, as restricted by spirituality, gives us the concept of *immortality.*

In[1] this process of rational psychology, there lurks a paralogism, which may be represented by the following syllogism.

That which cannot be conceived otherwise than as a subject, does not exist otherwise than as a subject, and is therefore a substance.

A thinking being, considered as such, cannot be conceived otherwise than as a subject.

Therefore it exists also as such only, that is, as a substance.

In the major they speak of a being that can be thought in every respect, and therefore also as it may be given in intuition. In the minor, however, they speak of it only so far as it considers itself, as subject, with respect to the thinking and the unity of consciousness only, but not at the same time in respect to the intuition whereby this unity is given as an object of thinking. The conclusion, therefore, has been drawn by a sophism, and more especially by *sophisma figurae dictionis.*[2]

---

[2] The thinking is taken in each of the two premises in a totally different meaning:—in the major, as it refers to an object in general (and therefore also as it may be given in intuition), but in the minor, only as it exists in its relation to self-consciousness, where no object is thought of, but where we only represent the relation to the self as the subject (as the form of thought). In the former, things are spoken of that cannot be conceived otherwise than as subjects; while in the second we do not speak of *things,* but of the *thinking* (abstraction being made of all objects), wherein the *Ego* always serves as the subject of consciousness. The conclusion, therefore, ought not to be that I cannot exist otherwise than as a subject, but only, that in thinking my existence I can use myself as the subject of a judgment only. This is an identical proposition, and teaches us nothing whatever as to the mode of our existence.

---

[1] [All that follows from "In this process . . . ." to ". . . the subject cannot be known" was added to Second Edition.—*Ed.*]

That we are perfectly right in thus resolving that famous argument into a paralogism, will be clearly seen by referring to the general note on the systematical representation of the principles, and to the section on the noumena, for it has been proved there that the concept of a thing, which can exist by itself as a subject, and not as a mere predicate, carries as yet no objective reality, that is, that we cannot know whether any object at all belongs to it, it being impossible for us to understand the possibility of such a mode of existence. It yields us therefore no knowledge at all. If such a concept is to indicate, under the name of a substance, an object that can be given, and thus become knowledge, it must be made to rest on a permanent intuition, as the indispensable condition of the objective reality of a concept, that is, as that by which alone the object can be given. In internal intuition, however, we have nothing permanent, for the *Ego* is only the consciousness of my thinking; and if we do not go beyond this thinking, we are without the necessary condition for applying the concept of substance, that is, of an independent subject, to the self, as a thinking being. Thus the simplicity of the substance entirely disappears with the objective reality of the concept: and is changed into a purely logical qualitative unity of self-consciousness in thinking in general, whether the subject be composite or not.

There is, therefore, no rational psychology, as a *doctrine,* furnishing any addition to our self-knowledge, but only as a *discipline,* fixing unpassable limits to speculative reason in this field, partly to keep us from throwing ourselves into the arms of a soulless materialism, partly to warn us against losing ourselves in a vague, and, with regard to practical life, baseless spiritualism. It reminds us at the same time to look upon this refusal of our reason to give a satisfactory answer to such curious questions, which reach beyond the limits of this life, as a hint to turn our self-knowledge away from fruitless speculations to a fruitful practical use—a use which, though directed always to objects of experience only, derives its principle from a higher source, and so regulates our conduct, as if our destination reached far beyond experience, and therefore far beyond this life.

We see from all this, that rational psychology owes its origin to a mere misunderstanding. The unity of consciousness, on which the categories are founded, is mistaken for an intuition of the subject as object, and the category of substance applied to it. But that unity is only the unity in *thought,* by which alone no object is given, and to which, therefore, the category of substance, which always presupposes a given *intuition,* cannot be applied, and therefore the subject cannot be known. . . .

DISCUSSION · HERMANN WEYL
Subject and Object (The Scientific Implications of Epistemology) *

The doctrine of the subjectivity of sense qualities has been intimately connected with the progress of science ever since Democritus laid down the principle, "Sweet and bitter, cold and warm, as well as the colors, all these things exist but in opinion and not in reality ($νόμω$, $οὐ$ $φύσει$)"; what really exists are unchangeable particles, atoms, which move in empty space. Also Plato (*Theaetetus*, 156e) holds that "properties such as hard, warm, and whatever their names may be, are nothing in themselves," but arise in the encounter of "motions" originating in the subject and in the object. Reality is pure activity; only in the "image," in the consciousness suspended between the motions in suffering. Galileo may be mentioned as another witness, "White or red, bitter or sweet, noisy or silent, fragrant or malodorous, are names for certain effects upon the sense organs." He holds that they can no more be ascribed to the external objects than the titillation or the pain which might be felt when things are touched. A detailed discussion of this is given in the final sections of Descartes' *Principia* and in his *Traité de la Lumière* (the theory of optical perception is indebted to him for important advances), likewise in Locke's *Enquiry Concerning Human Understanding* (Book II, Chap. 8, §§15–22). The subjectivity of sense qualities must be maintained in two regards, one philosophical, the other scientific. In the first place, such a quality by its very nature can only be given in our consciousness through sensation. One sees in it either an inherent attribute of sensation itself or, upon deeper analysis, an entity belonging to the intentional object which the act of consciousness puts before me. But it re-

* Selections from Hermann Weyl, *Philosophy of Mathematics and Natural Science*, revised and augmented English edition, based on a translation by Olaf Helmer (copyright 1949 by Princeton University Press), pp. 110–113, 116–118, 120/122, and 125. Reprinted by permission of Princeton University Press.

Hermann Weyl (1885–1955) taught mathematics and mathematical physics at Zurich, Göttingen, and Princeton University. From 1933 until his death he was Professor of Mathematics at the Institute for Advanced Study, Princeton, N. J. His wide interests led to research work in various branches of mathematics, the philosophy of mathematics, and relativity theory.

mains manifestly incomprehensible how quality disjoint from consciousness can be attributed as a property as such to a thing as such. This is the fundamental tenet of epistemological idealism. In the second place, the qualities in which the objects of the outer world garb themselves for me do not depend on the objects alone. They also depend quite essentially upon the concomitant physical circumstances, for instance, in the case of color, on illumination and on the nature of the medium between the object and my eye, and furthermore upon myself, on my own psycho-physical organization. My sense of vision does not grasp the objects where they are; rather, what I see is determined by the condition of the optical field in its zone of contact with my sensuous body (the retina). These are scientific facts which even the realist cannot deny. How differently the world would appear to our vision if the human eye were sensitive to other wave lengths or if the physiological processes on the retina were to transform the infinite-dimensional realm of composite physically different colors not merely into a two-dimensional but into a three- or four-dimensional manifold!

[To Locke we are indebted for the classical distinction of 'secondary' and 'primary' qualities; the primary ones are the spatio-temporal properties of bodies—extension, shape, and motion. Democritus, Descartes, and Locke held them to be objective. Locke expresses himself as follows: "The ideas of primary qualities of bodies are resemblances of them, and their patterns do really exist in the bodies themselves; but the ideas produced in us by the secondary qualities have no resemblance of them at all" (*op. cit.*, Book II, Chap. 8, beginning of §15). Although Descartes teaches that between an actual occurrence and its perception (sound wave and tone, for instance) there is no more resemblance than between a thing and its name, he yet maintains that the ideas concerning space have objective validity because in contrast to the qualities we recognize them clearly and distinctly. And a fundamental principle of his epistemology claims that whatever we comprehend in such a way is true. In support of this principle, however, he has to appeal to the veracity of God, who does not want to deceive us. Obviously one cannot do without the idea of such a God who guarantees truth, once one has grasped the principle of idealism and yet insists on building up the real world out of certain elements of consciousness that for one reason or another seem particularly trustworthy. "He is the bridge . . . between the lonely, wayward and isolated thinking, which is certain only to its own self-awareness, and the external world. The attempt turned out somewhat naive, but still one sees how keenly Cartesius measured out the grave of philosophy. It is strange, though, how he uses the dear God as the ladder to climb out of it. Yet even his contemporaries did not let him get over the edge" (quotation from Georg Büchner's philosophical notes, G. Büchner, *Werke*, Inselverlag Leipzig, 1922, pp. 268–269). Hobbes in his treatise *De Corpore* starts with a fictitious annihilation of the universe (similar to Husserl's "epoché") in order to let it rise again by a step-by-step construction from reason. But even he uses as building material the general notions which form the residue of experience, in particular those of space and time. This viewpoint has its counterpart in the physics of Galileo, Newton, and Huyghens; for here all occurrences in the world are constructed as intuitively conceived motions of particles in intuitive space. Hence an absolute Euclidean space is needed as a standing medium into which the orbits of motion are traced. Well-known is Galileo's pronouncement in the "Saggiatore" (*Opere*, VI, p. 232), "The true philosophy is written in that great book of nature *(questo grandissimo libro, io dico l'universo)* which lies ever open before our eyes but which no one can read unless he has first learned to understand the language and to know the characters in which it is written. It is written in mathematical language, and the characters are triangles, circles, and other geometric figures."]

Leibniz seems to have been the first to push forward to a more radical conception: "Concerning the bodies I am able to prove that not only light, color, heat, and the like, but motion, shape, and extension too are only apparent qualities" (*Philos. Schriften*, VII, p. 322). Also Berkeley and Hume are to be named here. For d'Alembert, the justification for using the "residue of experience" in the construction of the objective world no longer lies in the clarity and distinctness of the ideas involved as it did for Descartes, but exclusively in the practical success of this method. According to Kant, space and time are merely forms of our intuition. Stumpf (*Über den psychologischen Ursprung der Raumvorstellung*, 1873, p. 22) finds it impossible to imagine the atoms as spatial bodies without color, whose play of motion only engenders those oscillations of the ether which are the carriers of color by virtue of their wave lengths; for no more than color without spatial extension could space (according to Berkeley's and Hume's doctrine) be imagined without the raiment of some quality of color. Intuitive space and intuitive time are thus hardly the adequate medium in which physics is to construct the external world. No less than the sense qualities must the intuitions of space and time be relinquished as its building material; they must be replaced by a four-dimensional continuum in the abstract arithmetical sense. Whereas for Huyghens colors were 'in reality' oscillations of the ether, they now appear merely as mathematical functions of periodic character depending on four variables that as coordinates represent the medium of space-time. What remains is ultimately a *symbolic construction* of exactly the same kind as that which Hilbert carries through in mathematics.

The distillation of this objective world, capable only of representation by symbols, from what is immediately given to my intuition, takes place in different steps, the progression from level to level being enforced by the fact that what exists on one level will reveal itself as the mere apparition of a higher reality, the reality of the next level. A typical example of this is furnished by a body whose solid shape constitutes itself as the common source of its various perspective views. This would not happen unless the point from which it is viewed could be varied and unless the different viewpoints actually taken present themselves as instances of an infinite continuum of possibilities laid out with us. We shall return to this in the next section. A systematic scientific explanation, however, will reverse the order; it will erect the world of symbols as a realm by itself and then, skipping all intermediate levels, attempt to describe the relation that holds between the symbols representing objective conditions on the one hand and the corresponding data of consciousness on the other. . . .

Within the natural sciences the conflicting philosophies of idealism and realism signify principles of method which do not contradict each other. We construct through science an objective world which, in order to explain the sense data, must satisfy the following fundamental principle that was already mentioned on p. 26: *A difference in the perceptions offering themselves to us is always founded on a difference in the real conditions* (Helmholtz). Lambert, in his *Photometria* (1760), enunciates as an axiom the following special case: "An appearance is the same whenever the same eye is affected in the same way." Here the natural sciences proceed realistically. . . .

On the other hand science concedes to idealism that its objective reality is not given but to be constructed (nicht gegeben, sondern aufgegeben), and that it cannot be constructed absolutely but only in relation to an arbitrarily assumed coordinate system and in mere symbols. Above all the central thought of idealism comes into its own in the converse of the above fundamental principle: *the objective image of the world may not admit of any diversities which cannot manifest themslves in some diversity of perceptions;* an existence which as a matter of principle is entirely inaccessible to perception is not admitted. Leibniz says concerning the fiction of absolute motion (Leibniz's fifth letter to Clarke, §52): "I reply that motion is indeed independent of actual observation, but not of the possibility of observation altogether. Motion exists only where a change accessible to observation takes place. If this change is not ascertainable by any observation then it does not exist." To be sure, many physically different colors will produce the same sensation of red; but if one sends all these various reds through the same prism, then the physical differences will manifest themselves in the perceptible differences between the streaks of colored light emerging from the prism. The prism, so to speak, unfolds the hidden differences to our senses. A difference which can in no way be broken down for our perception is non-existent. This is of great importance as a methodical principle of theoretical construction. . . .

And what significance does this objective world, representable only in symbols, have for the everyday life of man, taking place as it does in the sphere of integrated data of perceptions? Helmholtz answers (*op. cit.*, p. 18), "Once we have learned to read those symbols correctly we shall be able with their help to design our actions so that they yield the desired result, namely, that the expected new sensations will arise. A different comparison between conceptions and things not only does not exist in reality—all schools agree on this point—but a different manner of comparison is inconceivable and would be devoid of meaning. . . . Thus such a presentation *(Vorstellung)* of a single individual body is indeed already a concept *(Begriff)* which comprises an infinite number of intuitions in temporal sequence all of which can be derived from it.[1] The presentation of a single individual table that I carry within me is correct and accurate if I am able to derive from it correctly and accurately the sensations I shall experience when I bring my eyes or my hands into this or that definite position with respect to the table. What other kind of similarity there can subsist between such a presentation and the object represented by it I cannot comprehend" *(op. cit.,* p. 26). In the same sense, Leibniz remarks concerning the Cartesian principles *(Philosophische Schriften,* IV, p. 356), "Of the sense data we cannot know more, nor do we have to require more, than that they are in agreement with each other as well as with the indisputable dictates of reason and that thus to a certain extent the future may be predicted from the past. To search for a truth or reality other than thus vouched for would be futile—the sceptic may not demand, the dogmatist not promise more." Or Husserl *(Ideen,* p. 311), "To the essence of a thing-noema there belong ideal possibilities of unlimited development of concordant intuitions that follow, moreover, prescribed directions of determinate type." But in the erection of empirical reality discrepancies will occur which will force us to make "corrections." Owing to its empirical character cognition of reality must of necessity pass through errors. "What is given never implies material existence as certain and necessary but merely as presumptive reality. This means that it can always happen that the further course of experience will force one to abandon what with good empirical justification had earlier been posited." (Husserl, *Ideen,* p. 86.) It might well be within the range of possibility that in the moving picture of perceptions every beginning of concordance would irreparably "explode." In that case the attempt to harmonize them according to principles of reason would fail, and no real world would be constituted.

The requirements which emerge from our discussion for a correct theory of the course of the world may be formulated as follows:

1. *Concordance.* The definite value which a quantity occurring in the theory assumes in a certain individual case will be determined from the empirical data on the basis of the theoretically posited connections. *Every such determination has to yield the same result.* Thus all determinations of the electronic charge e, that follow from observations in combination with the laws established by physical theory, lead to the same value of e (within the accuracy of the observations). Not infrequently a (relatively) direct observation of the quantity in question (for instance, of the location of a comet among the stars at a certain moment) is compared with a computation on the basis of other observations (for instance, the location at the desired moment computed according to Newton's theory from the locations on previous days). The demand

---

[1] In agreement with a number of philosophers writing in English the term *presentation* has been chosen here as the equivalent of Kant's and Helmholtz's *Vorstellung* and Locke's *idea.*—Tr.

of concordance implies consistency,[1] yet transcends the latter in that it brings the theory in contact with experience.

---

[1] Indeed in an inconsistent theory the formula $e = 2e$ would be deducible, and hence the actual value e as well as $2e$ for the electronic charge could be derived from such a theory in combination with the observational data.

---

2. It must in principle always be possible to determine on the basis of observational data the definite value which a quantity occurring in the theory will have in a given individual case. This expresses the postulate that the theory, in its explanation of the phenomena, must not contain redundant parts.

Hume attempted to uphold with inexorable consistency the viewpoint that the given is the whole of reality. Since it became apparent through him that this viewpoint fails completely in the explanation of those cognitive positions which play a basic role in everyday life and in science, he was indeed the first to reveal the problem of reality in its full difficulty. Reason in its function of constituting reality is described by him as the faculty of imagination. With complete sincerity he confesses the irreconcilable conflict between thought and life, into which he finds himself thrown. To carry his approach through is as impossible as to found arithmetic on nothing but the concretely existing numerals. The positivism of a Mach or Avenarius appears to me merely as a less consistent renewal of Hume's attempt; for in their systems theoretical hypostases, strictly avoided by Hume, play once more a considerable role. But then we are back in the midst of theoretical construction, which supplements the given in the interest of totality, and we are no longer forced to use sense data as our building material. Kant's transcendental idealism reestablished the insights already gained by Leibniz. The content of this Section may be considered as an elucidation of Kant's concept of reality as "that which is connected with perception according to laws." He advances beyond Leibniz in transmuting the old metaphysical ontological concepts of substance and causality into methodical principles for the construction of empirical reality. . . .

Postulation of the external world does not guarantee that it will constitute itself out of the phenomena through the cognitive work of reason as it attempts to create concordance. For this to take place it is necessary that the world be governed throughout by simple elementary laws. Thus the mere positing of the external world does not really explain what it was meant to explain, the question of the reality of the world mingles inseparably with the question of the reason for its lawful mathematical harmony. The latter clearly points in another direction of transcendency than that of a transcendental world; towards the origin rather than the product. Thus the ultimate answer lies beyond all knowledge, in God alone; emanating from him, the light of consciousness, its own origin hidden from it, grasps itself in self-penetration, divided and suspended between subject and object, between meaning and being.

Ayer, A. J., *The Foundations of Empirical Knowledge*. Chap. 5. Macmillan, London, 1940.

Bradley, F. H., *Appearance and Reality*. Second Edition, Chaps. 9 & 10. Clarendon Press, Oxford, 1897.

Buford, T. O., ed., *Essays on Other Minds*. University of Illinois Press, Urbana, 1971.

Chisholm, R. M. (ed.), *Realism and the Background of Phenomenology*. Free Press, New York, 1960.

Ducasse, C. J., "Moore's Refutation of Idealism," in *The Philosophy of G. E. Moore* (ed. by P. A. Schilpp). Northwestern University Press, Evanston, Illinois, 1942.

Ewing, A. C., *Idealism*. Methuen, London, 1934.

Ewing, A. C. (ed.), *The Idealist Tradition from Berkeley to Blanshard*. Free Press, New York, 1957.

James, W., *Essays in Radical Empiricism*. Essay 1. Longman's, Green & Co., New York, 1938.

Lean, M. E., *Sense-Perception and Matter*. Routledge & Kegan Paul, London, 1953.

Lovejoy, A. O., *The Revolt Against Dualism*. Open Court, LaSalle, Illinois, 1930.

Malcolm, N., "Knowledge of Other Minds," *The Journal of Philosophy*, 56 (1959)

Mill, J. S., *An Examination of Sir William Hamilton's Philosophy*. Chap. 11. Longman's, London, 1872.

Moore, G. E., "A Defence of Common Sense" and "Proof of an External World," in *Philosophical Papers*. The Macmillan Company, New York, 1959.

Moore, G. E., "The Refutation of Idealism," in *Philosophical Studies*. Routledge & Kegan Paul, London, 1922.

Moore, G. E., *Some Main Problems of Philosophy*. Allen & Unwin, London, 1953.

O'Connor, J., ed., *Modern Materialism: Readings on Mind-Body Identity*. New York, 1969.

Perry, R. B., *et al.*, *The New Realism*. The Macmillan Company, New York, 1912.

Price, H. H., "Our Evidence for the Existence of Other Minds," *Philosophy*, 13 (1938).

Russell, B., *Our Knowledge of the External World*. Second Edition. Norton, New York, 1929.

Santayana, G., *Scepticism and Animal Faith*. Scribner's, New York, 1923.

Smythies, J. R., *Analysis of Perception*. Routledge & Kegan Paul, London, 1956.

Stace, W. T., "The Refutation of Realism," *Mind*, 43 (1934).

Stout, G. F., *Mind and Matter*. Macmillan, London, 1931.

Strawson, P. F., *Individuals*. Chap. 3. Methuen, London, 1959.

Thomson, J. F., "The Argument from Analogy and our Knowledge of Other Minds," *Mind*, 60 (1951).

Wisdom, J., J. L. Austin, and A. J. Ayer, "Other Minds," (Symposium), *Proceedings of the Aristotelian Society*, Supplementary Volume 20, (1946).

Note. This bibliography consists entirely of books and bound monographs inasmuch as journal articles, addresses, etc., are too numerous to list.

(A) = Collected Editions, Separate Works, and Correspondence.
(B) = General Commentaries, Special Studies, and Works of Reference.
(C) = Works Chiefly Biographical.

Hobbes

(A)

The English Works of Thomas Hobbes. Ed. by W. Molesworth. 11 vols., London, 1839–45; repr. Aalen, 1962.
Opera philosophica quae latine scripsit omnia. Ed. by W. Molesworth. 5 vols., London, 1839–45; repr. Aalen, 1961.

Calkins, M. W., ed., *The Metaphysical System of Hobbes.* (selections) LaSalle, Ill., 1905; 2nd ed., 1948.
Cropsey, J., ed., *A Dialogue between a Philosopher and a Student of the Common Laws of England.* Chicago, 1971.
Lamprecht, S. P., ed., *De Cive or The Citizen.* Revised ed., New York, 1949.
Molesworth, W., ed., *Behemoth: The History of the Causes of the Civil Wars of England.* repr. New York, 1963.
Oakeshott, M., ed., *Leviathan.* Oxford and New York, 1947.
Peters, R. S., ed., *Body, Man, and Citizen: Selections from Thomas Hobbes.* New York, 1962.
Plamenatz, J., ed., *Leviathan.* London, 1962.
Schneider, H. W., ed. with introd., *Leviathan, Pts. I and II.* New York, 1958.
Tönnies, F., ed., *The Elements of Law, Natural and Politic.* Cambridge, 1889, 1928; 2nd ed., 1969.
Woodbridge, F. J. E., ed., *Hobbes: Selections.* New York, 1930.

(B)

Baumrin, B. H., ed., *Hobbes' Leviathan: Interpretation and Criticism*. Belmont, Calif., 1969.

Bowle, J., *Hobbes and His Critics*. New York, 1952.

Brandt, F., *Thomas Hobbes' Mechanical Conception of Nature*. London, 1928.

Brown, K. C., ed., *Hobbes Studies*. Oxford, 1965.

Gauthier, D. P., *The Logic of Leviathan*. Oxford, 1969.

Goldsmith, M., *Hobbes's Science of Politics*. New York, 1966.

Gough, J. W., *The Social Contract*. Oxford, 1957.

Hood, F. C., *The Divine Politics of Thomas Hobbes*. Oxford, 1964.

Kemp, J., *Ethical Naturalism: Hobbes and Hume*. London, 1970.

Krook, D., *Three Traditions of Moral Thought*. Cambridge, 1959.

Laird, J., *Hobbes*. London, 1934.

Macdonald, H., and M. Hargreaves, comps., *Thomas Hobbes: A Bibliography*. London, 1952.

Macpherson, C. B., *The Political Theory of Possessive Individualism: Hobbes to Locke*. Oxford, 1962.

McNeilly, F. S., *The Anatomy of Leviathan*. London and New York, 1968.

Mintz, S. L., *The Hunting of Leviathan*. Cambridge, 1962.

Peters, R. S., *Hobbes*. Baltimore, 1956.

Plamenatz, J., *Consent, Freedom, and Political Obligation*. Oxford, 1938.

Polin, R., *Politique et Philosophie chez Thomas Hobbes*. Paris, 1953.

Robertson, G. C., *Hobbes*. Edinburgh and London, 1886; repr. 1910.

Stephen, L., *Hobbes*. London, 1904; repr. 1928.

Strauss, L., *The Political Philosophy of Hobbes*. (translated by E. M. Sinclair) Oxford, 1936; Chicago, 1952.

Tönnies, F., *Hobbes, Leben und Lehre*. Stuttgart, 1896; 3rd Ed., 1925.

Warrender, H., *The Political Philosophy of Hobbes: His Theory of Obligation*. Oxford, 1957.

Watkins, J. W. N., *Hobbes's System of Ideas*. London, 1965.

Woodbridge, F. J. E., ed., *The Philosophy of Hobbes*. Minneapolis, 1903.

(C)

James, D. G., *The Life of Reason; Hobbes, Locke, Bolingbroke*. London and New York, 1949.

DESCARTES

(A)

Oeuvres de Descartes. Ed. by C. Adam and P. Tannery. 12 vols., Paris, 1897–1910; et Supplément: Index général, Paris, 1913.

Correspondance de Descartes. Ed. by C. Adam and G. Milhaud, 8 vols., Paris, 1936.

Anscombe, E., and P. T. Geach, trans. and eds., *Philosophical Writings.* London, 1954.

Bridoux, A., ed., *Oeuvres et Lettres.* Paris, 1937; enlarged ed., 1953.

Chevalier, J., ed., *Lettres sur la morale.* Paris, 1935.

Gilson, É., *Discours de la Méthode, Texte et commentaire.* Paris, 1925; 3rd ed., 1962.

Godoffre, G., ed., *Discours de la méthode.* Manchester, 1941; 2nd ed., Paris, 1961.

Güttler, G., ed., *Meditations.* Munich, 1901.

Haldane, E. S., and G. R. T. Ross, trans., *The Philosophical Works of Descartes.* 2 vols., Cambridge, 1911–12; repr. 1931; New York, 1955, 1967.

Joachim, H. H., trans., and E. E. Harris, ed., *Descartes's Rules for the Direction of the Mind.* Oxford, 1957.

LeRoy, G., trans. and ed., *Regulae ad directionem ingenii: Règles pour la direction de l'esprit.* (Latin text with French translation.) Paris, 1933.

Mesnard, P., ed., *Les passions de l'âme.* Paris, 1937.

Rodis-Lewis, G., trans. and ed., *Meditationes de prima philosophia: méditations métaphysiques.* (Latin text with French translation.) Paris, 1949.

Roth, L., ed., *Correspondence of Descartes and Constantyn Huygens, 1635–47.* Oxford, 1926.

Smith, N. K., trans., *Descartes' Philosophical Writings.* (selections), New York, 1958.

Thouverez, É., ed., *Les méditations métaphysiques.* Paris, 1932.

Veitch, J., trans., *A Discourse on Method.* London and New York, 1912; repr. 1934.

Veitch, J., trans., *The Method, Meditations, and Selections from the Principles of Descartes.* 15th ed., Edinburgh and London, 1913.

(B)

Alquié, F., *La découverte métaphysique de l'homme chez Descartes.* Paris, 1950.

Balz, A. G. A., *Descartes and the Modern Mind.* London and New Haven, 1952

Beck, L. W., *The Method of Descartes: A Study of the 'Regulae'.* Oxford, 1952.

Beck, L. W., *The Metaphysics of Descartes, A Study of the Meditations.* Oxford, 1965.

Blanchet, L., *Les antécédents historiques du 'Je pense, donc je suis'.* Paris, 1920.

Boutroux, E., *Des vérités éternelles chez Descartes.* (Translation from Latin thesis of 1874 by Canguilhem.) Paris, 1927.

Brunschvigg, L., *René Descartes.* Paris, 1937.

Cassirer, E., *Descartes.* New York, 1951.

Chevalier, J., *Descartes.* Paris, 1921; revised ed., Paris, 1957.

Collins, J., *Descartes' Philosophy of Nature.* Oxford, 1971.

Doney, W., ed., *Descartes: A Collection of Critical Essays.* New York, 1967.

Frankfurt, H. G., *Demons, Dreamers, and Madmen: The Defense of Reason in Descartes' Meditations*. Indianapolis, 1970.

Gibson, A. B., *The Philosophy of Descartes*. London, 1932.

Gilson, É., *La liberté chez Descartes et la théologie*. Paris, 1913.

Gilson, É., *Index scolastico-cartésien*. Paris, 1913; 2nd ed., Paris, 1964.

Gilson, É., *Études sur le rôle de la pensée médiévale dans la formation du système cartésien*. Paris, 1930.

Gouhier, H., *La pensée religieuse de Descartes*. Paris, 1924.

Gouhier, H., *Essais sur Descartes*. Paris, 1937.

Gouhier, H., *La pensée métaphysique de Descartes*. Paris, 1962.

Guéroult, M., *Descartes selon l'ordre des raisons*. 2 vols. Paris, 1953.

Guéroult, M., *Études sur Descartes, Spinoza, Malebranche et Leibniz*. Hildesheim, 1970.

Hamelin, O., *Le Système de Descartes*. Paris, 1911; 2nd ed., Paris, 1921.

Jaspers, K., *Descartes und die Philosophie*. Berlin, 1937; 3rd ed., Berlin, 1956.

Keeling, S. V., *Descartes*. London, 1934; 2nd ed., London, 1968.

Kenny, A., *Descartes: A Study of His Philosophy*. New York, 1968.

Koyré, A., *Descartes und die Scholastik*. Bonn, 1923.

Koyré, A., *Entretiens sur Descartes*. New York and Paris, 1944.

Laberthonnière, L., *Études sur Descartes*. 2 vols. Paris, 1935.

Laporte, J., *Le rationalisme de Descartes*. Paris, 1945; 2nd ed., Paris, 1950.

Liard, L., *Descartes*. Paris, 1882; 2nd ed., Paris, 1903.

Milhaud, G., *Descartes savant*. Paris, 1921.

Ogliati, F., *La filosofia di Descartes*. Milan, 1937.

Roth, L., *Spinoza, Descartes and Maimonides*. Oxford, 1924.

Roth, L., *Descartes' Discourse on Method*. Oxford, 1937.

Sebba, G., *Bibliographia Cartesiana: Critical Guide to Descartes Literature, 1800–1960*. The Hague, 1964.

Serrus, C., *La Méthode de Descartes et son application à la métaphysique*. Paris, 1933.

Sesonske, A., and N. Fleming, eds., *Meta-Meditations: Studies in Descartes*. Belmont, Calif., 1965.

Smith, N. K., *Studies in the Cartesian Philosophy*. London and New York, 1902; repr. London, 1962.

Smith, N. K., *New Studies in the Philosophy of Descartes*. London, 1953; repr. London, 1963.

Versfeld, M., *An Essay on the Metaphysics of Descartes*. London, 1940.

Wahl, J., *Du rôle de l'idée de l'instant dans la philosophie de Descartes*. Paris, 1920; 2nd ed., Paris, 1953.

(C)

Adam, C., *Descartes. Sa vie et son oeuvre*. Paris, 1937.

Baillet, A., *La Vie de Monsieur Des-Cartes*. 2 vols. Paris, 1691.

Bouillier, F., *Histoire de la Philosophie cartésienne*. 2 vols. Paris, 1854; 3rd ed., Paris, 1868.

Cohen, G., *Écrivains français en Hollande dans la première moitié du XVIIᵉ siècle.* Paris, 1920.

Espinas, A., *Descartes et la morale.* 2 vols. Paris, 1925.

Gouhier, H., *La Vocation de Descartes.* Paris, 1956.

Haldane, E. S., *Descartes, His Life and Times.* London, 1905.

Leroy, M., *Descartes, le Philosophe au Masque.* Paris, 1929.

Mahaffy, J. P., *Descartes.* London, 1902.

Maritain, J., *The Dream of Descartes.* (translated by L. M. Andison) New York, 1944.

Millet, J., *Histoire de Descartes avant 1637.* Paris, 1867.

Millet, J., *Descartes, son histoire depuis 1637.* Paris, 1870.

Sirven, J., *Les années d'apprentissage de Descartes (1596–1628).* Paris, 1928.

SPINOZA

Spinoza Opera. Ed. by C. Gebhardt. 4 vols., Heidelberg, 1925.

Opera. Ed. by J. Van Vloten and J. P. N. Land. 2 vols., The Hague, 1882; 3rd ed., The Hague, 1914.

Balz, A. G. A., ed., *Writings on Political Philosophy.* New York and London, 1937.

Boyle, A., trans., *Spinoza's Ethics and On the Correction of the Understanding.* London, 1910; revised ed., London and New York, 1959.

Britan, H. H., trans., *The Principles of Descartes' Philosophy* (including *Cogitata Metaphysica*). Chicago, 1905; repr. La Salle, Ill., 1943.

Elwes, R. H. M., trans., *Tractatus politicus.* London, 1883.

Elwes, R. H. M., trans., *Tractatus theologico-politicus.* London, 1883.

Elwes, R. H. M., trans., *The Ethics.* London, 1884.

Gutmann, J., ed., *Ethics, preceded by On the Improvement of the Understanding.* (White-Stirling translation of the *Ethics* and Elwes translation of *De Intellectus Emendatione*) New York and London, 1949.

Hayes, F. A., trans., *Earlier Philosophical Writings: The Cartesian Principles and Thoughts on Metaphysics.* Indianapolis, 1963.

Jessop, T. E., trans. and ed., *Spinoza on Freedom of Thought: Selections from Tractatus theologico-politicus and Tractatus politicus.* Montreal, 1962.

Katz, J., trans., *On the Improvement of the Understanding.* Indianapolis, 1958.

Ratner, J., ed., *The Philosophy of Spinoza.* (selections) New York, 1927.

Sigwart, C., trans. and ed., *Kurzer tractat von Gott, dem menschen und dessen glückseligkeit.* Freiburg and Tübingen, 1881.

Wernam, A. G., trans., *The Political Works of Spinoza.* Oxford, 1958.

White, W. H., and A. H. Stirling, trans., *Ethics.* London, 1899; 4th ed., London, 1929.

White, W. H., and A. H. Stirling, trans., *Tractatus de intellectus emendatione.* New York, 1895.

Wolf, A., trans. and ed., *The Correspondence of Spinoza.* London, 1928; repr. London, 1966.

Wolf, A., trans. and ed., *Spinoza's Short Treatise on God, Man and His Well-Being.* London, 1910; repr. New York, 1963.

(B)

Alexander, S., *Spinoza and Time.* London, 1921.

Bidney, D., *The Psychology and Ethics of Spinoza.* New Haven, 1940; New York, 1962.

Boscherini, E. G., comp., *Lexicon Spinozanum.* 2 vols. The Hague, 1970.

Caird, J., *Spinoza.* Edinburgh, 1899; London, 1910.

Curley, E. M., *Spinoza's Metaphysics: An Essay in Interpretation.* Cambridge, Mass., 1969.

de Deugd, C., *The Significance of Spinoza's First Kind of Knowledge.* Assen, 1966.

Deleuze, G., *Spinoza et le problème de l'expression.* Paris, 1968.

Duff, R. A., *Spinoza's Political and Ethical Philosophy.* Glasgow, 1903.

Feuer, L. S., *Spinoza and the Rise of Liberalism.* Boston, 1958.

Fischer, K., *Spinozas Leben, Werke und Lehre.* Heidelberg, 5th ed., 1909.

Guéroult, M., *Spinoza. Tome I. Dieu (Ethique, I).* Paris, 1968.

Gunn, J. A., *Benedict Spinoza.* Melbourne, 1925.

Guzzo, A., *Il pensiero di Spinoza.* Firenze, 1924.

Hallett, H. F., *Aeternitas, A Spinozistic Study.* Oxford, 1930.

Hallett, H. F., *Benedict De Spinoza, The Elements of His Philosophy.* London, 1957.

Hallett, H. F., *Creation, Emanation, and Salvation: a Spinozistic Study.* The Hague, 1962.

Hampshire, S., *Spinoza.* Harmondsworth, 1951; Baltimore, 1962.

Hubbeling, H. G., *Spinoza's Methodology.* Assen, 1967.

Joachim, H. H., *A Study in Spinoza's Ethics.* Oxford, 1901; repr. New York, 1964.

Joachim, H. H., *Spinoza's Tractatus de Intellectus Emendatione: A Commentary.* Oxford, 1940.

Kline, G. L., *Spinoza in Soviet Philosophy.* London, 1952.

Lachièze-Rey, P., *Les Origines cartésiennes du Dieu de Spinoza.* Paris, 1932; repr. 1950.

Lacroix, J., *Spinoza et le problème de salut.* Paris, 1970.

Léon, A., *Les éléments cartésiens de la doctrine spinoziste.* Paris, 1907.

Martineau, J., *A Study of Spinoza.* London, 1882; 3rd ed., London, 1895.

Matheron, A., *Individu et communauté chez Spinoza.* Paris, 1969.

McKeon, R., *The Philosophy of Spinoza.* New York, 1928.

McShea, R. J., *The Political Philosophy of Spinoza.* New York and London, 1968.

Melamed, S. M., *Spinoza and Buddha: Visions of a Dead God.* Chicago, 1933.

Moreau, J., *Spinoza et le spinozisme.* Paris, 1971.

Oko, A. S., comp., *The Spinoza Bibliography.* Boston, 1964.

Parkinson, G. H. R., *Spinoza's Theory of Knowledge.* Oxford, 1954.

Pollock, F., *Spinoza, His Life and Philosophy.* London, 1880; 2nd ed., 1899; repr. New York, 1966.

Pollock, F., *Spinoza.* London, 2nd ed., 1895.

Powell, E. E., *Spinoza and Religion.* Chicago, 1906.

Préposiet, J., *Spinoza et la liberté des hommes.* Paris, 1967.

Richter, G. T., *Spinozas philosophische Terminologie.* Leipzig, 1913.

Rivaud, A., *Les notions d'essence et d'existence dans la philosophie de Spinoza.* Paris, 1906.

Robinson, L., *Kommentar zu Spinozas Ethik.* Leipzig, 1928.

Roth, L., *Spinoza, Descartes and Maimonides.* Oxford, 1924; repr. New York, 1963.

Roth, L., *Spinoza.* London, 1929; 2nd ed., London, 1935.

Rousset, B., *La perspective finale de "l'Éthique" et le problème de la cohérence du Spino-zisme.* Paris, 1968.

Saw, R. L., *The Vindication of Metaphysics: A Study in the Philosophy of Spinoza.* London, 1951.

Shanks, A., *An Introduction to Spinoza's Ethics.* London, 1938.

Societatis Spinozanae, eds., *Septimana Spinozana.* The Hague, 1933.

Strauss, L., *Spinoza's Critique of Religion.* New York, 1965.

Wolfson, H. A., *The Philosophy of Spinoza.* 2 vols. Cambridge, Mass., 1934; repr. in one vol., Cleveland and New York, 1958.

Zac, S., *L'Idée de Vie dans la Philosophie de Spinoza.* Paris, 1963.

(C)

Browne, L., *Blesséd Spinoza.* New York, 1932.

Brunschwicg, L., *Spinoza et ses contemporains.* Paris, 1923.

Colerus, J., *The Life of Benedict de Spinoza.* London, 1706.

Freudenthal, J., *Die Lebensgeschichte Spinozas in Quellenschriften.* Leipzig, 1899.

Freudenthal, J., *Das Leben Spinozas.* Stuttgart, 1904; repr. 1927.

Friedländer, M. H., *Spinoza, His Life and Philosophy.* London, 1887.

Willis, R., *Benedict de Spinoza: His Life, Correspondence, and Ethics.* London, 1870.

Wolf, A., ed., *The Oldest Biography of Spinoza.* New York, 1927.

Locke

(A)

Works. 10 vols. (Printed for Tegg, Bookseller) London, 1823.

Philosophical Works. Ed. by J. A. St. John. London, 1843; 1862.

Aaron, R. I., and J. Gibb, eds., *An Early Draft of Locke's Essay, Together with Excerpts from his Journals.* Oxford, 1936.

Abrams, P., ed., *Two Tracts on Government.* London, 1967.

Axtell, J. L., ed., *The Educational Writings of John Locke.* London, 1968.

Cranston, M., ed., *An Essay Concerning Human Understanding (abridged).* New York, 1964.

Cranston, M., ed., *Government, Liberty, and Reason.* (selections) New York, 1964.

Fraser, A. C., ed., *An Essay Concerning Human Understanding.* 2 vols. Oxford, 1894; repr. New York, 1959.

Garforth, F. W., ed., *Some Thoughts Concerning Education (abridged).* London and New York, 1964.

Gough, J. W., ed., *The Second Treatise of Civil Government* and *A Letter concerning Toleration.* Oxford, 1946; 3rd ed., New York, 1966.

Klibansky, R., ed., *Epistola de tolerantia.* (English translation from Latin text by J. W. Gough.) Oxford, 1968.

Laslett, P., ed., *Two Treatises of Government.* Cambridge, 1960; New York, 1965.

Pringle-Pattison, A. S., ed., *An Essay Concerning Human Understanding (abridged).* Cambridge, 1915.

Yolton, J. W., ed., *An Essay Concerning Human Understanding (abridged).* 2 vols. London, 1961.

(B)

Aaron, R. I., *John Locke.* London, 1937; 2nd ed., Oxford, 1955.

Alexander, S., *Locke.* New York, 1908.

Bennett, J. F., *Locke, Berkeley, Hume: Central Themes.* Oxford, 1971.

Cousin, V., *Philosophie de Locke.* 4th ed., Paris, 1861.

Dunn, J. M., *The Political Thought of John Locke.* London, 1969.

Fowler, T., *Locke.* New York, 1888; 1902.

Fraser, A. C., *Locke.* Edinburgh and London, 1890; 1913.

Gibson, J., *Locke's Theory of Knowledge and Its Historical Connections.* Cambridge, 1917; 2nd ed., 1931; repr. 1960.

Gough, J. W., *John Locke's Political Philosophy, Eight Studies.* Oxford, 1950.

Hefelbower, S. G., *The Relation of John Locke to English Deism.* Chicago, 1918.

Hofstadter, A., *Locke and Scepticism.* New York, 1935.

Jeffreys, M. V. C., *John Locke: Prophet of Common Sense.* London, 1967.

Klemnt, A., *John Locke: Theoretische Philosophie.* Meisenheim, 1952.

Lamprecht, S. P., *The Moral and Political Philosophy of John Locke.* New York, 1918; repr. 1962.

Maclean, K., *John Locke and English Latitudinarians of the Eighteenth Century.* New Haven, 1936.

MacLachlan, H., *The Religious Opinions of Milton, Locke, and Newton.* London, 1941.

Martin, C. B., and D. M. Armstrong, eds., *Locke and Berkeley: A Collection of Critical Essays.* New York, 1968.

Morris, C. R., *Locke, Berkeley, Hume.* Oxford, 1931.

O'Connor, D. J., *John Locke.* London, 1952.

Polin, R., *La Politique Morale de John Locke.* Paris, 1960.

Seliger, M., *The Liberal Politics of John Locke.* New York, 1969.

Schochet, G. J., comp., *Life, Liberty, and Property: Essays on Locke's Political Ideas.* Belmont, Calif., 1971.

Tucker, J., *A Treatise concerning Civil Government.* London, 1781; repr. New York, 1967.

Woolhouse, R. S., *Locke's Philosophy of Science and Knowledge.* Oxford, 1971.

Yolton, J. W., *John Locke and the Way of Ideas.* Oxford, 1956.

Yolton, J. W., *John Locke: Problems and Perspectives.* Cambridge and New York, 1969.

Yolton, J. W., *Locke and the Compass of Human Understanding.* Cambridge, 1970.

(C)

Cranston, M. W., *John Locke, a Biography.* London and New York, 1957.

Fox Bourne, H. R., *The Life of John Locke.* 2 vols. London, 1876; repr. 1969.

James, D. G., *The Life of Reason; Hobbes, Locke, Bolingbroke.* London and New York, 1949.

King, P. K., ed., *The Life and Letters of John Locke.* London, 1829; repr. 1858.

Leroy, A. L., *Locke: sa vie, son oeuvre.* Paris, 1964.

LEIBNIZ

(A)

Sämtliche Schriften und Briefe. Darmstadt and Leipzig, 1923–71. Published by the Deutschen Akademie der Wissenschaften zu Berlin under the current direction of K. Müller. (This comprehensive and critical edition is incomplete, but several volumes of four series of works are available.)

Die philosophischen Schriften. Ed. by C. I. Gerhardt. 7 vols., Berlin, 1875–90; repr. Hildesheim, 1960–61.

Mathematische Schriften. Ed. by C. I. Gerhardt. 7 vols., Berlin and Halle, 1849–63; repr. Hildesheim, 1962.

Opuscules et fragments inédits de Leibniz. Ed. by L. Couturat. Paris, 1903; repr. Hildesheim, 1961.

Opera Omnia. Ed. by L. Dutens. 6 vols., Geneva, 1768; revised and repr. Hildesheim, 1970.

Opera philosophica quae exstant latina, gallica, germanica omnia. Ed. by J. E. Erdmann. 2 vols., Berlin, 1840.

Nouvelles lettres et opuscules inédits de Leibniz. Ed. by L. A. Foucher de Careil. Paris, 1857; repr. Hildesheim, 1971.

Oeuvres. Ed. by L. A. Foucher de Careil. 7 vols., Paris, 1859–75; repr. Hildesheim, 1969.

Deutsche Schriften. Ed. by G. E. Guhrauer. 2 vols., Berlin, 1838–40; repr. Hildesheim, 1966.

Die Werke von Leibniz, Erste Reihe: *Historisch-politische und staatswissenschaftliche Schriften.* Ed. by O. Klopp. 11 vols., Hanover, 1864–84.

Alexander, H. G., ed., *The Leibniz-Clarke Correspondence, together with extracts from Newton's Principia and Opticks.* Manchester, 1956.

Buchenau, A., and E. Cassirer, eds., *Philosophische Werke.* 4 vols., Leipzig, 1924–26.

Child, J. M., trans. and ed., *Leibniz's Early Mathematical Manuscripts.* Chicago, 1920.

Duncan, G. M., trans. and ed., *The Philosophical Works of Leibnitz.* New Haven, 1890; 2nd ed., 1908.

Gerhardt, C. I., ed., *Briefwechsel zwischen Leibniz und Christian Wolff.* Halle, 1860; repr. Hildesheim, 1963.

Habs, R., trans., *Kleinere philosophische schriften von G. W. Leibniz.* Leipzig, 1883.

Huggard, E. M., trans. *Theodicy.* London, 1952. (Abridgement by D. Allen, Indianapolis, 1966.)

Langley, A. G., trans. and ed., *New Essays Concerning Human Understanding.* New York and London, 1896; 3rd ed., Chicago, 1949.

Latta, R., ed., *Leibniz: The Monadology and Other Philosophical Writings.* Oxford, 1898.

Loemker, L. E., trans. and ed., *Philosophical Papers and Letters.* Chicago, 1956; 2nd ed., Dordrecht, 1970.

Lucas, P. G., and L. Grint, trans., *Discourse on Metaphysics.* Manchester, 1953; repr. 1961.

Mason, H. T., trans. and ed., *The Leibniz-Arnauld Correspondence.* Manchester and New York, 1967.

Montgomery, G. R., trans., *Leibniz: Discourse on Metaphysics, Correspondence with Arnauld, and Monadology.* Chicago, 1902; repr. La Salle, Ill., 1962.

Morris, M., trans. and ed., *The Philosophical Writings of Leibniz.* New York, 1934; repr. London and New York, 1968.

Parkinson, G. H. R., trans. and ed., *Logical Papers.* Oxford, 1966.

Schrecker, P., ed., *G. W. Leibniz: Lettres et fragments inédits.* Paris, 1934.

Schrecker, P., ed., *Opuscula philosophica selecta.* Paris, 1939; French ed., Paris, 1962.

Schrecker, P. and A. M. Schrecker, trans., *Leibniz: Monadology and Other Philosophical Essays.* New York, 1965.

Wiener, P., ed., *Leibniz Selections.* New York, 1951.

(B)

Belaval, Y., *Leibniz, critique de Descartes.* Paris, 1960.

Belaval, Y., *Leibniz: Initiation à sa philosophie.* Paris, 1962.

Bodemann, E., *Der Briefwechsel des Gottfried Wilhelm Leibniz in der Königlichen öffentlichen Bibliothek zu Hannover.* Hanover, 1889; repr. Hildesheim, 1966.

Bodemann, E., *Die Leibniz-Handschriften der Königlichen öffentlichen Bibliothek zu Hannover*. Hanover, 1895; repr. Hildesheim, 1966.

Boutroux, É., *La philosophie allemande au XVIIᵉ siècle*. Paris, 1929; 1948.

Brunner, F., *Études sur la signification historique de la philosophie de Leibniz*. Paris, 1950.

Carr, W. C., *Leibniz*. London, 1929; repr. New York, 1960.

Cassirer, E., *Leibniz's System in seinen wissenschaftlichen Grundlagen*. Marburg, 1902; repr. Hildesheim, 1962.

Chevallier, L., *La Morale de Leibniz*. Paris. 1933.

Couturat, L., *La logique de Leibniz d'après documents inédits*. Paris, 1901; repr. Hildesheim, 1961.

Dewey, J., *Leibniz's New Essays Concerning Human Understanding: A Critical Exposition*. Chicago, 1888; repr. New York, 1961.

Friedmann, G., *Leibniz et Spinoza*. Revised ed., Paris, 1962.

Heinekamp, A., *Das Problem des Guten bei Leibniz*. Bonn, 1969.

Hönigswald, R., *G. W. Leibniz*. Tübingen, 1929.

Jalabert, J., *La théorie leibnizienne de la substance*. Paris, 1947.

Joseph, H. W. B., *Lectures on the Philosophy of Leibniz*. Oxford, 1949.

Kabitz, W., *Die Philosophie des jungen Leibniz*. Heidelberg, 1909.

Kaulbach, F., *Die Metaphysik des Raumes bei Leibniz und Kant*. Köln, 1960.

Mahnke, D., *Leibnizens Synthese von Individualmetaphysik und Universalmathematik*. Halle, 1925.

Martin, G., *Leibniz: Logic and Metaphysics*. (translated by K. J. Northcott and P. G. Lucas) Manchester and New York, 1964.

Merz, J. T., *Leibniz*. Edinburgh, 1884; Revised ed., New York, 1948.

Meyer, R. W., *Leibnitz and the Seventeenth-Century Revolution*. (translated by J. P. Stern) Cambridge, 1952.

Müller, K., *Leibniz-Bibliographie: Verzeichnis der Literatur über Leibniz*. Frankfurt, 1967.

Parkinson, G. H. R., *Logic and Reality in Leibniz's Metaphysics*. Oxford, 1965.

Peursen, C. A. van, *Leibniz*. (translated by H. Hoskins) London, 1969.

Piat, C., *Leibniz*. Paris, 1915.

Pichler, H., *Leibniz: Ein harmonisches Gespräch*. Graz, 1919.

Ravier, É., *Bibliographie des oeuvres de Leibniz*. Paris, 1937; repr. Hildesheim, 1966.

Rescher, N., *The Philosophy of Leibniz*. Englewood Cliffs, N.J., 1967.

Russell, B., *A Critical Exposition of the Philosophy of Leibniz*. London, 1900; 2nd ed., 1958.

Saw, R. L., *Leibniz*. Baltimore, 1954.

Schmalenbach, H., *Leibniz*. Munich, 1921.

Stammler, G., *Leibniz*. Munich, 1930.

Tymiencka, A. T., *Leibniz's Cosmological Synthesis*. Assen, 1964.

Yost, R. M., *Leibniz and Philosophical Analysis*. Berkeley, 1954.

(C)

Fischer, K., *G. W. Leibniz: Leben, Werke, und Lehre.* 5th ed., Heidelberg, 1902; repr. 1920.

Guhrauer, G. E., *Gottfried Wilhelm Freiherr von Leibniz: Eine Biographie.* 2 vols. Breslau, 1842; repr. Hildesheim, 1966. (English translation by J. N. Mackie, *Life of G. W. von Leibnitz,* Boston, 1845.)

Huber, K., *Leibniz.* Munich, 1951.

BERKELEY

(A)

The Works of George Berkeley. Ed. by A. A. Luce and T. E. Jessop. 9 vols., Edinburgh and London, 1948–57.

The Works of George Berkeley. Ed. by A. C. Fraser. 4 vols., Oxford, 1871; repr. Oxford, 1901.

Works. Ed. by G. Sampson. 3 vols., London, 1898.

Armstrong, D. M., ed., *Selected Writings.* New York, 1965.

Fraser, A. C., ed., *Selections from Berkeley, Annotated.* 6th ed., Oxford, 1910.

Jessop, T. E., ed., *Philosophical Writings.* (selections) Edinburgh, 1952.

Lindsay, A. D., ed., *A New Theory of Vision and Other Writings.* London, 1963.

Luce, A. A., ed., *Philosophical Commentaries, generally called the Commonplace Book.* London and New York, 1944.

Turbayne, C. M., ed., *Berkeley: A Treatise Concerning the Principles of Human Knowledge.* Indianapolis, 1970.

(B)

Armstrong, D. M., *Berkeley's Theory of Vision.* Melbourne, 1960.

Bennett, J. F., *Locke, Berkeley, Hume: Central Themes.* Oxford, 1971.

Bracken, H. M., *The Early Reception of Berkeley's Immaterialism, 1710–33.* Revised ed., The Hague, 1965.

Engle, G. W., and G. Taylor, eds., *Berkeley's Principles of Human Knowledge: Critical Studies.* Belmont, Calif., 1968.

Erdmann, B., *Berkeley's philosophie im lichte seines wissenschaftlichen tagebuchs.* Berlin, 1919.

Fraser, A. C., *Berkeley and Spiritual Realism.* London, 1908.

Hedenius, I., *Sensationalism and Theology in Berkeley's Philosophy.* Uppsala, 1936.

Hicks, G. D., *Berkeley.* London, 1932.

Jessop, T. E., *A Bibliography of George Berkeley.* New York, 1968.

Johnston, G. A., *The Development of Berkeley's Philosophy.* London, 1923.

Johnston, G. A., ed., *Berkeley's Commonplace Book.* London, 1930.

Leroy, A. L., *George Berkeley*. Paris, 1959.

Levi, A., *La filosofia di Giorgio Berkeley*. Turin, 1922.

Luce, A. A., *Berkeley and Malebranche: A Study in the Origins of Berkeley's Thought*. Oxford, 1934; repr. 1967.

Luce, A. A., *The Dialectics of Immaterialism: an account of the making of Berkeley's Principles*. London, 1963.

Luce, A. A., *Berkeley's Immaterialism*. Edinburgh and London, 1945.

Martin, C. B., and D. M. Armstrong, eds., *Locke and Berkeley: A Collection of Critical Essays*. New York, 1968.

Morris, C. R., *Locke, Berkeley, Hume*. Oxford, 1931.

Olscamp, P. J., *The Moral Philosophy of George Berkeley*. The Hague, 1970.

Ritchie, A. D., *George Berkeley, A Reappraisal*. Manchester and New York, 1967.

Sillem, E. A., *George Berkeley and the Proofs of the Existence of God*. London and New York, 1957.

Stack, G. J., *Berkeley's Analysis of Perception*. The Hague, 1970.

Steinkraus, W. E., ed., *New Studies in Berkeley's Philosophy*. New York, 1966.

Turbayne, C. M., *The Myth of Metaphor*. New Haven, 1962.

Warnock, G. J., *Berkeley*. London, 1953.

Wild, J., *George Berkeley*. Cambridge, Mass., 1936; repr. 1962.

Wisdom, J. O., *The Unconscious Origin of Berkeley's Philosophy*. London, 1953.

(C)

Fraser, A. C., ed., *Life and Letters of George Berkeley*. Oxford, 1871.

Hone, J. M., and M. M. Rossi, *Bishop Berkeley: His Life, Writings and Philosophy*. London and New York, 1931.

Luce, A. A., *The Life of George Berkeley*. London and New York, 1949.

Rand, B., *Berkeley and Percival*. (correspondence with their lives presented in form of 'a biographical commentary') Cambridge, 1914.

HUME

(A)

Works of David Hume. Ed. by T. H. Green and T. H. Grose. 4 vols., London, 1874–75.

Essays Moral, Political, and Literary. Ed. by T. H. Green and T. H. Grose. 2 vols., London, 1862; repr. 1912.

Aiken, H. D., ed., *Hume's Moral and Political Philosophy*. New York, 1948.

Flew, A., ed., *On Human Nature and the Understanding*. New York, 1962.

Greig, J. Y. T., ed., *The Letters of David Hume*. 2 vols., Oxford, 1932.

Hendel, C. W., ed., *An Inquiry concerning Human Understanding*. New York, 1955.

Hendel, C. W., ed., *An Inquiry concerning the Principles of Morals*. New York, 1957.

Hendel, C. W., ed., *Political Essays*. New York, 1953.

Klibansky, R., and E. C. Mossner, eds., *New Letters of David Hume*. Oxford, 1954; repr. 1970.

MacIntyre, A., ed., *Ethical Writings*. New York, 1965.

Selby-Bigge, L. A., ed., *Enquiries concerning Human Understanding*. Oxford, 1888; repr. 1962.

Selby-Bigge, L. A., ed., *A Treatise of Human Nature*. Oxford, 1888; 2nd ed., 1897.

Smith, N. K., ed., *Hume's Dialogues Concerning Natural Religion*. Oxford, 1935; 2nd ed., London, 1947; repr. 1962.

Wollheim, R., ed., *Hume on Religion*. (selections) London, 1963.

(B)

Árdal, P. S., *Passion and Value in Hume's Treatise*. Edinburgh, 1966.

Basson, A. H., *David Hume*. Baltimore, 1958.

Bennett, J. F., *Locke, Berkeley, Hume: Central Themes*. Oxford, 1971.

Broiles, D., *The Moral Philosophy of David Hume*. The Hague, 1964; 2nd ed., 1969.

Chappell, V. C., ed., *Hume: A Collection of Critical Essays*. New York, 1966.

Church, R. W., *Hume's Theory of the Understanding*. Ithaca, N.Y., 1935.

Della Volpe, G., *La filosofia dell'esperienza di David Hume*. 2 vols. Florence, 1933–35; 2nd ed., 1939.

Flew, A., *Hume's Philosophy of Belief: A Study of his First 'Inquiry'*. London and New York, 1961.

Glathe, A. B., *Hume's Theory of the Passions and of Morals*. Berkeley, 1950.

Hall, R., *A Hume Bibliography from 1930*. York, 1971.

Heinemann, F. H., *David Hume: The Man and His Science of Man*. Paris, 1940.

Hendel, C. W., *Studies in the Philosophy of David Hume*. Princeton, 1925; repr. New York, 1962.

Huxley, T. H., *Hume*. London, 1879; 1902.

Jessop, T. E., *A Bibliography of David Hume and of Scottish Philosophy from Francis Hutcheson to Lord Balfour*. London, 1938; repr. New York, 1966.

Knight, W., *Hume*. Edinburgh, 1914.

Kruse, V., *Hume's Philosophy in his Principal Work, 'A Treatise of Human Nature' and in his Essays*. (translated by P. E. Federspiel) London, 1939.

Kuyper, M. S., *Studies in the Eighteenth-Century Background of Hume's Empiricism*. Minneapolis, 1930.

Kydd, R. M., *Reason and Conduct in Hume's Treatise*. London, 1946; repr. New York, 1964.

Laing, B. M. *David Hume*. London, 1932.

Laird, J., *Hume's Philosophy of Human Nature*. New York, 1931; repr. 1967.

Leroy, A. L., *David Hume*. Paris, 1953.

MacNabb, D. G. C., *David Hume, His Theory of Knowledge and Morality*. London, 1951; 2nd ed., Oxford, 1966.

Maund, C., *Hume's Theory of Knowledge: A Critical Examination*. London, 1937.

Mercer, P., *Sympathy and Ethics*. Oxford, 1972.

Morris, C. R., *Locke, Berkeley, Hume*. Oxford, 1931.

Norton, D. F., and R. H. Popkin, *David Hume: Philosophical Historian*. Indianapolis, 1965.

Passmore, J. A., *Hume's Intentions*. Cambridge, 1952.

Pears, D. F., ed., *David Hume: A Symposium*. London and New York, 1963.

Price, H. H., *Hume's Theory of the External World*. Oxford, 1940.

Santucci, A., *Sistema e ricerca in David Hume*. Turin, 1969.

Sesonske, A., and N. Fleming, eds., *Human Understanding: Studies in the Philosophy of David Hume*. Belmont, Calif., 1965.

Shearer, E. A., *Hume's Place in Ethics*. Bryn Mawr, 1915.

Salmon, C. V., *The Central Problem of David Hume's Philosophy*. Halle, 1929.

Smith, N. K., *The Philosophy of David Hume*. London, 1941.

Zabeeh, F., *Hume, Precursor of Modern Empiricism*. The Hague, 1960.

(C)

Braham, E. G., *The Life of David Hume*. London, 1931.

Burton, J. H., *Life and Correspondence of David Hume*. 2 vols. Edinburgh, 1846.

Greig, J. Y. T., *David Hume*. New York, 1931.

Mossner, E. C., *The Forgotten Hume: Le bon David*. New York, 1943.

Mossner, E. C., *The Life of David Hume*. Edinburgh and Austin, 1954.

REID

(A)

The Collected Works of Thomas Reid. Ed. by Sir W. H. Hamilton. 2 vols., Edinburgh, 1804; 10th ed., 1895.

An Inquiry into the Human Mind on the Principles of Common Sense. Edinburgh, 1764; 5th ed., 1801.

Essays on the Intellectual Powers of Man. Edinburgh, 1785; repr. Cambridge, Mass., 1969.

Essays on the Active Powers of Man. Edinburgh, 1788.

Philosophical Orations of Thomas Reid. Aberdeen, 1937.

Duggan, T., ed., *An Inquiry into the Human Mind*. Chicago and London, 1970.

Woozley, A. D., ed., *Reid's Essay on the Intellectual Powers of Man*. (abridgement) London, 1941.

(B)

Bryson, G., *Man and Society: The Scottish Inquiry of the Eighteenth-Century*. Princeton, 1945.

Grave, S. A., *The Scottish Philosophy of Common Sense*. Oxford, 1960.

Johnston, G. A., ed., *Selections from the Scottish Philosophy of Common Sense*. Chicago and London, 1915.

Pringle-Pattison, A. S., *Scottish Philosophy: A Comparison of the Scottish and German Answers to Hume*. London and Edinburgh, 1885.

Robinson, D. S., *The Story of Scottish Philosophy*. New York, 1961.

(C)

Stewart, D., *Account of the Life and Writings of Thomas Reid*. (Vol. 7 of *The Works of Dugald Stewart*) Cambridge, Mass., 1829.

KANT

(A)

Kant's Gesammelte Schriften. Published by the Deutschen Akademie der Wissenschaften. 28 vols. Berlin, 1902–

Sämmtliche Werke. Ed. by E. Cassirer. 10 vols., Berlin, 1914–23.

Sämmtliche Werke. Ed. by G. Hartenstein. 8 vols., Leipzig, 1867–68.

Sämmtliche Werke. Ed. by J. H. von Kirchmann. 20 vols., Heidelberg, 1870–91.

Abbott, T. K., trans., *Critique of Practical Reason and Other Works on the Theory of Ethics*. London, 1873; repr. of 6th ed., London, 1963.

Abbott, T. K., trans., *Fundamental Principles of the Metaphysics of Morals*. New York, 1949.

Abbott, T. K., trans., *Kant's Introduction to Logic*. London, 1885.

Adickes, E., ed., *Kritik der Reinen Vernunft*. Berlin, 1889.

Bax, E. B., trans., *Kant's Prolegomena*, and *Metaphysical Foundations of Natural Science*. London, 1883.

Beck, L. W., trans. and ed., *Critique of Practical Reason and Other Writings in Moral Philosophy*. Chicago, 1949; New York, 1956.

Beck, L. W., trans., *Foundation of the Metaphysics of Morals* and *What is Enlightenment?* New York, 1959.

Beck, L. W., ed., *Kant: On History*. New York, 1963.

Beck, L. W., trans., *Perpetual Peace*. New York, 1957.

Beck, L. W., ed., *Prolegomena to Any Future Metaphysics*. (revised Mahaffy-Carus translation) New York, 1951.

Bernard, J. H., trans. and ed., *Kant's Kritik of Judgment*. London and New York, 1892; New York, 1951.

Carus, P., trans. and ed., *Kant's Prolegomena to Any Future Metaphysics*. Chicago, 1902; repr. La Salle, Ill., 1947.

Churton, A., trans., *Lectures on Education*. Ann Arbor, Mich., 1960.

Ellington, J., trans., *Immanuel Kant: Metaphysical Foundations of Natural Science.* Indianapolis, 1970.

Ellington, J., trans., *Metaphysical Principles of Virtue.* New York, 1964.

Erdmann, B., ed., *Reflexionen Kants zur kritischen Philosophie.* 2 vols. Leipzig, 1882–84.

Friedrich, C. J., trans., *Inevitable Peace.* Cambridge, Mass., 1948.

Friedrich, C. J., ed., *The Philosophy of Kant: Immanuel Kant's Moral and Political Writings.* New York, 1949.

Gablentz, O. H., ed., *Politische Schriften.* Köln, 1965.

Goerwitz, E. F., trans., *Dreams of a Spirit-Seer, illustrated by Dreams of Metaphysics.* New York, 1900.

Goldthwait, J. T., trans., *Observations on the Feeling of the Beautiful and Sublime.* Berkeley, 1960; repr. 1972.

Greene, T. M., ed., *Kant Selections.* London and New York, 1929.

Greene, T. M., and H. H. Hudson, trans., *Religion within the Limits of Reason Alone.* Chicago and London, 1934; New York, 1960.

Gregor, M. J., trans. and ed., *The Doctrine of Virtue. Part II of the Metaphysic of Morals.* New York, 1964.

Haden, J., trans., *First Introduction to the Critique of Judgment.* Indianapolis, 1965.

Handyside, J., trans., *Kant's Inaugural Dissertation* and *Early Writings on Space.* Chicago and London, 1929.

Hastie, W., trans., *The Philosophy of Law.* Edinburgh, 1887.

Hastie, W., trans. and ed., *Kant's Theory of Politics.* Edinburgh, 1891.

Hastie, W., trans. and ed., *Kant's Cosmogony.* Glasgow, 1900. (New edition, with introduction by M. K. Munitz, published as *Universal Natural History* and *Theory of the Heavens,* Ann Arbor, Mich., 1969.)

Infield, L., trans., *Lectures on Ethics.* London, 1930; New York, 1963.

Kehrbach, K., ed., *Kritik der Reinen Vernunft.* Leipzig, 1877.

Kerferd, G. B., and D. E. Walford, trans., *Selected Pre-Critical Writings and Correspondence with Beck.* Manchester and New York, 1968.

Kirchmann, J. H., ed., *Kritik der Reinen Vernunft.* Leipzig, 1901.

Le Bruch, J., trans. and ed., *Lettres sur la morale et la religion.* Paris, 1969.

Lindell, B. E. A., trans. and comm., *Kant on the Foundation of Morality: A Modern Version of the Grundlegung.* Bloomington, Ill., 1970.

Lucas, P. G., trans., *Prolegomena to Any Future Metaphysics.* Manchester, 1953.

Mahaffy, J. P., ed., *Kant's Critical Philosophy for English Readers.* 3 vols. London, 1872; revised ed., London, 1889.

Manthey-Zorn, O., trans., *The Fundamental Principles of the Metaphysic of Ethics.* New York and London, 1938.

Meiklejohn, J. M. D., trans., *Critique of Pure Reason.* London, 1860; revised ed., New York, 1900.

Menzer, P., ed., *Kants populäre Schriften.* Berlin, 1911.

Menzer, P., ed., *Eine vorlesung Kants über Ethik im Aufträge der Kantsgesellschaft.* Berlin, 1924.

Meredith, J. C., trans. and ed., *Kant's Critique of Aesthetic Judgment*. Oxford, 1911; repr. 1952.

Meredith, J. C., trans. and ed., *Kant's Critique of Teleological Judgement*. Oxford, 1928.

Müller, F. M., trans., *Critique of Pure Reason*. New York and London, 1881; repr. 1896.

Rabel, G., trans. and ed., *Kant*. Oxford, 1963.

Reiss, H., ed., *Kant's Political Writings*. (translated by H. B. Nisbet) Cambridge, 1970.

Schmid, E., *Kritik der reinen Vernunft im Grundrisse*. Jena, 1786.

Semple, J. W., trans., *The Metaphysics of Ethics*. Edinburgh, 1871.

Smith, M. C., trans. and ed., *Perpetual Peace, A Philosophical Essay*. London, 1903.

Smith, N. K., trans., *Critique of Pure Reason*. London, 1929; 1958.

Stirling, J. H., trans. and ed., *Text-book to Kant*. Edinburgh and London, 1881.

Watson, J., trans. and ed., *The Philosophy of Kant as Contained in Extracts from his own Writings*. Glasgow, London and New York, 1901.

Wolff, R. P., ed., *Kant: Foundation of the Metaphysics of Morals: Text and Critical Essays*. (translation of the text by L. W. Beck) Indianapolis, 1969.

Zweig, A., trans. and ed., *Philosophical Correspondence, 1759–99*. Chicago, 1967.

(B)

Acton, H. B., *Kant's Moral Philosophy*. New York, 1970.

Adickes, E., *Bibliography of Writings by and on Kant*. (published as supplements to 'The Philosophical Review') Ithaca, N.Y., 1893 ff.

Adickes, E., *Kant und das Ding an sich*. Berlin, 1924.

Aebi, M., *Kants Begründung der 'Deutschen Philosophie'*. Basel, 1947.

Alexandre, M., *Lecture de Kant*. Paris, 1961.

Ardley, G., *Aquinas and Kant: The Foundations of Modern Science*. London and New York, 1950.

Arnoldt, E., *Kant's Idee vom höchsten Gut*. Köningsberg, 1874.

Beck, L. W., *A Commentary on Kant's Critique of Practical Reason*. Chicago, 1960.

Beck, L. W., ed., *Kant Studies Today*. LaSalle, Ill., 1969.

Beck, L. W., *Studies in the Philosophy of Kant*. Indianapolis, 1965.

Bennett, J. F., *Kant's Analytic*. Cambridge, 1966.

Bird, G., *Kant's Theory of Knowledge; An Outline of One Central Argument in the Critique of Pure Reason*. London and New York, 1962.

Bruch, J. L., *La Philosophie religieuse de Kant*. Paris, 1968.

Caird, E., *The Philosophy of Kant*. London, 1876.

Caird, E., *The Critical Philosophy of Immanuel Kant*. 2 vols. Glasgow, London and New York, 1889.

Cantoni, C., *Emmanuel Kant*. 3 vols. Milan, 1879–84.

Cassirer, E., *Kants Leben und Lehre*. Berlin, 1918.

Cassirer, H. W., *Kant's First Critique*. London, 1954.

Chamberlain, H. S., *Immanuel Kant: A Study and a Comparison with Goethe, Leonardo da Vinci, Bruno, Plato and Descartes.* 2 vols. (translated from German by Lord Redesdale) London and New York, 1914.

Cohen, H., *Kants Begründung der Aesthetik.* Berlin, 1889.

Cohen, H., *Kants Begründung der Ethik.* Berlin, 1877.

Cohen, H., *Kants Theorie der Erfahrung.* Berlin, 1871.

Cousin, V., *The Philosophy of Kant.* (translated from French by A. G. Henderson) London, 1854.

Daval, R., *La métaphysique de Kant.* Paris, 1951.

Delekat, F., *Immanuel Kant: historisch-kritische Interpretation der Hauptschriften.* Heidelberg, 1963.

Destutt de Tracy, A. L. C., *La métaphysique de Kant.* Brussells, 1968.

Dryer, D. P., *Kant's Solution for Verification in Metaphysics.* Toronto, 1966.

Dufrenne, M., *La notion d'a priori.* Paris, 1959.

Duncan, A. R. C., *Practical Reason and Morality: A Study of Immanuel Kant's Foundations for the Metaphysics of Morals.* London, 1957.

Eisler, R., comp., *Kant-Lexikon.* Berlin, 1930.

England, F. E., *Kant's Conception of God.* (contains translation of the *Nova dilucidatio*) London, 1929.

Erdmann, B., *Beiträge zur Geschichte und Revision des Textes von Kants Kritik der reinen Vernunft.* Berlin, 1900.

Ewing, A. C., *Kant's Treatment of Causality.* London, 1924.

Ewing, A. C., *A Short Commentary on Kant's Critique of Pure Reason.* London, 1938.

Fischer, K., *A Critique of Kant.* (translated from German by W. S. Hough) London, 1888.

Garnett, C. B., *The Kantian Philosophy of Space.* New York, 1939.

Gram, M. S., *Kant, Ontology and the a priori.* Evanston, Ill., 1968.

Gregor, M. J., *Laws of Freedom, A Study of Kant's Method of Applying the Categorical Imperative in the Metaphysik der Sitten.* Oxford, 1963.

Hartnack, J., *Kant's Theory of Knowledge.* (translated by M. H. Hartshorne) New York, 1967.

Havet, J., *Kant et le problème du temps.* Paris, 1946.

Heidegger, M., *Kant und das Problem der Metaphysik.* Bonn, 1929. (translated by J. S. Churchill as *Kant and The Problem of Metaphysics,* Bloomington, Ind., 1962.)

Heidegger, M., *What is a Thing?* (translated by W. B. Barton, Jr., and V. Deutsch) Chicago, 1968.

Heidemann, I., *Spontaneität und Zeitlichkeit; ein Problem der Kritik der Reinen Vernunft.* Köln, 1958.

Heimsoeth, H., *Studien zur Philosophie Immanuel Kant.* 2 vols. I., Köln, 1956; II., Bonn, 1970.

Heimsoeth, H., *Transcendentale Dialektik.* 2 vols. Berlin, 1966.

Heinrichs, J., *Das Problem der Zeit in der praktischen Philosophie Kants.* Bonn, 1968.

Hendel, C. W., ed., *The Philosophy of Kant and Our Modern World.* New York, 1957.

Herring, H., *Das Problem der Affektion bei Kant.* Köln, 1953.

Hölder, A., *Darstellung der kantischen Erkenntnisstheorie.* Tübingen, 1873.

Jones, W. T., *Morality and Freedom in the Philosophy of Immanuel Kant.* London, 1940.

Jouffroy, H., *Philosophie critique de Kant.* Leipzig, 1842.

Kaulbach, F., *Die Metaphysik des Raumes bei Leibniz und Kant.* Köln, 1960.

Körner, S., *Kant.* Harmondsworth, 1955.

Kroner, R., *Kant's Weltanschauung.* (English translation by J. E. Smith) Chicago, 1956.

Lamacchia, A., *La filosofia della religione in Kant.* Bari, 1969.

Lindsay, A. D., *Kant.* London, 1934.

Lotz, J. B., ed., *Kant und die Scholastik heute.* Munich, 1955.

Macmillan, R. A. C., *The Crowning Phase of the Critical Philosophy: A Study in Kant's Critique of Judgment.* London, 1912.

Martin, G., ed., *Gesammelte Abhandlungen.* Köln, 1961.

Martin, G., *Immanuel Kant: Ontologie und Wissenschaftstheorie.* Köln, 1951. (translated by P. G. Lucas as *Kant's Metaphysics and Theory of Science,* Manchester, 1955.)

Menzer, P., *Kants Lehre von der Entwicklung in Natur und Geschichte.* Berlin, 1911.

Meyer, J. B., *Kant's Psychologie.* Berlin, 1870.

Milmed, B. K., *Kant and Current Philosophical Issues.* New York, 1961.

Morris, G. S., *Kant's Critique of Pure Reason.* Chicago, 1882.

Muralt, A., *La conscience transcendentale dans le criticisme kantien.* Paris, 1958.

Murphy, J. G., *Kant: The Philosophy of Right.* New York, 1970.

Nolen, D., *La critique de Kant et la métaphysique de Leibniz.* Paris, 1875.

Paton, H. J., *The Categorical Imperative, A Study in Kant's Moral Philosophy.* London, 1946.

Paton, H. J., *Kant's Metaphysic of Experience.* London, 1936.

Paulsen, F., *Immanuel Kant, His Life and Doctrine.* (translated from revised German edition of 1899 by J. E. Creighton and A. Lefevre) New York, 1902.

Penelhum, T., and J. J. MacIntosh, eds., *The First Critique: Reflections on Kant's Critique of Pure Reason.* Belmont, Calif., 1969.

Plaass, P., *Kants Theorie der Naturwissenschaft.* Göttingen, 1965.

Porter, N., *Kant's Ethics, A Critical Exposition.* Chicago, 1886.

Pritchard, H. A., *Kant's Theory of Knowledge.* Oxford, 1909.

Ratke, H., *Systematisches Handlexikon zu Kants Kritik der reinen Vernunft.* Leipzig, 1929.

Renouvier, C. B., *Critique de la doctrine de Kant.* Paris, 1906.

Ross, W. D., *Kant's Ethical Theory: A Commentary on the Grundlegung zur Metaphysik der Sitten.* Oxford, 1954.

Rotenstreich, N., *Experience and its Systematization: Studies in Kant.* The Hague, 1965.

Scheler, M. F., *Der Formalismus in der Ethik und die materiale Wertethik.* (Vol. 2 of Scheler's *Gesammelte Werke*) Bern, 1966.

Schlipp, P. A., *Kant's Pre-Critical Ethics.* Chicago, 1938.

Schurmann, J. G., *Kantian Ethics and the Ethics of Revolution.* London, 1881.

Sellars, W., *Science and Metaphysics: Variations on Kantian Themes*. London, 1968.

Sidgwick, H., *Lectures on the Philosophy of Kant and Other Philosophical Lectures and Essays*. London and New York, 1905.

Smith, A. H., *Kantian Studies*. Oxford, 1947.

Smith, N. K., *A Commentary to Kant's Critique of Pure Reason*. London, 1918.

Stadler, A., *Kant's Teleologie*. Berlin, 1874.

Stadler, A., *Die Grundsätze der reinen Erkenntnisstheorie in der kantischen Philosophie*. Leipzig, 1876.

Stadler, A., *Kant's Theorie der Materie*. Leipzig, 1883.

Staudinger, F., *Noumena*. Darmstadt, 1884.

Strawson, P. F., *The Bounds of Sense: An Essay on Kant's 'Critique of Pure Reason'*. London, 1966.

Swing, T. K., *Kant's Transcendental Logic*. New Haven and London, 1969.

Takeda, S., *Kant und das Problem der Analogie*. The Hague, 1969.

Teale, A. E., *Kantian Ethics*. London, 1951.

Tufts, J. H., *The Sources and Development of Kant's Teleology*. Chicago, 1892.

Vaihinger, H., *Commentar zu Kants Kritik der Reinen Vernunft*. 2 vols. Stuttgart, 1881; 2nd ed., 1892.

Vlachos, G., *La pensée politique de Kant; métaphysique de l'ordre et dialectique du progrès*. Paris, 1962.

Vleeschauwer, H. J., *The Development of Kantian Thought: The History of a Doctrine*. (translated from German by A. R. C. Duncan) London and New York, 1962.

Volkelt, J., *I. Kant's Erkenntnisstheorie nach ihren Grundprincipien analysirt*. Leipzig, 1879.

Vuillemin, J., *Physique et métaphysique kantiennes*. Paris, 1955.

Wallace, W., *Kant*. Edinburgh and London, 1882; repr. 1899.

Ward, J., *A Study of Kant*. Cambridge, 1922.

Watson, J., *Kant and His English Critics*. New York, 1881; London, 1886.

Watson, J., *The Philosophy of Kant Explained*. Glasgow, 1908.

Webb, C. C. J., *Kant's Philosophy of Religion*. Oxford, 1926.

Weldon, T. D., *Introduction to Kant's Critique of Pure Reason*. Oxford, 1945.

Wellek, R., *Immanuel Kant in England, 1793–1838*. Princeton, 1931.

Weygand, K., *Kants Geschichtsphilosophie*. Köln, 1963.

Whitney, G. T., *An Introduction to Kant's Critical Philosophy*. New York, 1914.

Williams, T. C., *The Concept of the Categorical Imperative*. Oxford, 1968.

Wolff, R. P., *Kant's Theory of Mental Activity*. Cambridge, Mass., 1963.

Wood, A. W., *Kant's Moral Religion*. Ithaca, N.Y., 1970.

Wundt, M., *Kant als Metaphysiker*. Stuttgart, 1924.

(C)

Stavenhagen, K., *Kant und Köningsberg*. Göttingen, 1949.

Stuckenberg, J. H. W., *The Life of Immanuel Kant*. London, 1882.

Vorländer, K., *Immanuel Kant, der Mann und das Werk*. 2 vols. Leipzig, 1924.